Lecture Notes in Computer Science   5996

Commenced Publication in 1973
Founding and Former Series Editors:
Gerhard Goos, Juris Hartmanis, and Jan van Leeuwen

Hongbin Zha   Rin-ichiro Taniguchi
Stephen Maybank (Eds.)

Computer Vision – ACCV 2009

9th Asian Conference on Computer Vision
Xi'an, September 23-27, 2009
Revised Selected Papers, Part III

 Springer

Volume Editors

Hongbin Zha
Peking University
Department of Machine Intelligence
Beijing, 100871, China
E-mail: zha@cis.pku.edu.cn

Rin-ichiro Taniguchi
Kyushu University
Department of Advanced Information Technology
Fukuoka, 819-0395, Japan
E-mail: rin@ait.kyushu-u.ac.jp

Stephen Maybank
University of London
Birkbeck College, Department of Computer Science
London, WC1E 7HX, UK
E-mail: sjmaybank@dcs.bbk.ac.uk

Library of Congress Control Number: 2010923506

CR Subject Classification (1998): I.4, I.5, I.2.10, I.2.6, I.3.5, F.2.2

LNCS Sublibrary: SL 6 – Image Processing, Computer Vision, Pattern Recognition,
and Graphics

ISSN   0302-9743
ISBN-10   3-642-12296-5 Springer Berlin Heidelberg New York
ISBN-13   978-3-642-12296-5 Springer Berlin Heidelberg New York

springer.com

© Springer-Verlag Berlin Heidelberg 2010
Printed in Germany

Typesetting: Camera-ready by author, data conversion by Scientific Publishing Services, Chennai, India
Printed on acid-free paper   06/3180

Preface

It gives us great pleasure to present the proceedings of the 9th Asian Conference on Computer Vision (ACCV 2009), held in Xi'an, China, in September 2009. This was the first ACCV conference to take place in mainland China.

We received a total of 670 full submissions, which is a new record in the ACCV series. Overall, 35 papers were selected for oral presentation and 131 as posters, yielding acceptance rates of 5.2% for oral, 19.6% for poster, and 24.8% in total. In the paper reviewing, we continued the tradition of previous ACCVs by conducting the process in a double-blind manner. Each of the 33 Area Chairs received a pool of about 20 papers and nominated a number of potential reviewers for each paper. Then, Program Committee Chairs allocated at least three reviewers to each paper, taking into consideration any conflicts of interest and the balance of loads. Once the reviews were finished, the Area Chairs made summary reports for the papers in their pools, based on the reviewers' comments and on their own assessments of the papers.

The Area Chair meeting was held at Peking University, Beijing during July 6–7, 2009. Thirty-one Area Chairs attended the meeting. They were divided into eight groups. The reviews and summary reports for the papers were discussed within the groups, in order to establish the scientific contribution of each paper. Area Chairs were permitted to confer with pre-approved "consulting" Area Chairs outside their groups if needed. The final acceptance decisions were made at a meeting of all the Area Chairs. Finally, the Program Chairs drew up a single-track technical program which consisted of 12 oral sessions and three poster sessions for the three-day conference. We are glad to see that all of the oral speakers presented their papers at the conference.

The program included three plenary sessions in which world-leading researchers, Roberto Cipolla (University of Cambridge), Larry S. Davis (University of Maryland), and Long Quan (Hong Kong University of Science and Technology), gave their talks. We would like to thank them for their respective presentations on 3D shape acquisition, human tracking and image-based modeling, which were both inspiring and entertaining.

A conference like ACCV 2009 would not be possible without the concerted effort of many people and the support of various institutions. We would like to thank the ACCV 2009 Area Chairs and members of the Technical Program Committee for their time and effort spent in reviewing the submissions. The local arrangement team, led by Yanning Zhang, did a terrific job in organizing the conference. We also thank Katsushi Ikeuchi, Tieniu Tan, and Yasushi Yagi, whose help was critical at many stages of the conference organization. Last but not least, we would like to thank all of the attendees of the conference. Due to their active participation, this was one of the most successful conferences in the history of the ACCV series.

December 2009   Hongbin Zha
                                                  Rin-ichiro Taniguchi
                                                  Stephen Maybank

Organization

icity Chairs

Bin Luo (Anhui University, China)
Chil-Woo Lee (Chonnam National University, Korea)
Hichem Sahli (Vrije University Brussel, Belgium)

ea Chairs

Noboru Babaguchi (Osaka University)
Horst Bischof (Technical University Graz)
Chu-Song Chen (Institute of Information Science, Academia Sinica)
Jan-Michael Frahm (University of North Carolina at Chapel Hill)
Pascal Fua (EPFL: Ecole Polytechnique Fédérale de Lausanne)
Dewen Hu (National University of Defense Technology)
Zhanyi Hu (Institute of Automation, Chinese Academy of Science)
Yi-ping Hung (National Taiwan University)
Ron Kimmel (Technion - Israel Institute of Technology)
Reinhard Klette (University of Auckland)
Takio Kurita (National Institute of Advanced Industrial Science and Technology)
Chil-Woo Lee (Chonnam National University)
Kyoung Mu Lee (Seoul National University)
Fei-Fei Li (Stanford University)
Zhouchen Lin (Microsoft Research Asia)
Kai-Kuang Ma (Nanyang Technological University)
P.J. Narayanan (International Institute of Information Technology, Hyderabad)
Nassir Navab (Technische Universität München)
Tomas Pajdla (Czech Technical University in Prague)
Robert Pless (Washington University)
Long Quan (The Hong Kong University of Science and Technology)
Jim Rehg (Georgia Institute of Technology)
Ian Reid (Oxford University)
Wildes Richard (York University)
Hideo Saito (Keio University)
Nicu Sebe (University of Amsterdam)
Peter Sturm (INRIA)

Organization

Honorary Chairs	Yunhe Pan (Chinese Academy of Engineer China)
	Songde Ma (Institute of Automation, Chinese Academy of Science, China)
	Katsushi Ikeuchi (University of Tokyo, Japan)
General Chairs	Tieniu Tan (Institute of Automation, Chinese Academy of Science, China)
	Nanning Zheng (Xi'an Jiaotong University, China)
	Yasushi Yagi (Osaka University, Japan)
Program Chairs	Hongbin Zha (Peking University, China)
	Rin-ichiro Taniguchi (Kyushu University, Japan)
	Stephen Maybank (University of London, UK)
Organization Chairs	Yanning Zhang (Northwestern Polytechnical University, China)
	Jianru Xue (Xi'an Jiaotong University, China)
Workshop Chairs	Octavia Camps (Northeastern University, USA)
	Yasuyuki Matsushita (Microsoft Research Asia, China)
Tutorial Chairs	Yunde Jia (Beijing Institute of Technology, China)
Demo Chairs	Dacheng Tao (Nanyang Technological University, Singapore)
Publication Chairs	Ying Li (Northwestern Polytechnical University, China)
	Kaiqi Huang (Institute of Automation, Chinese Academy of Science, China)

Akihiro Sugimoto (National Institute of
  Informatics)
David Suter (University of Adelaide)
Guangyou Xu (Tsinghua University)
Yaser Yacoob (University of Maryland)
Ming-Hsuan Yang (University of California at
  Merced)
Hong Zhang (University of Alberta)

Committee Members   Zhonghua Fu (Northwestern Polytechnical
  University, China)
Dongmei Jiang (Northwestern Polytechnical
  University, China)
Kuizhi Mei (Xi'an Jiaotong University, China)
Yuru Pei (Peking University, China)
Jinqiu Sun (Northwestern Polytechnical
  University, China)
Fei Wang (Xi'an Jiaotong University, China)
Huai-Yu Wu (Peking University, China)
Runping Xi (Northwestern Polytechnical
  University, China)
Lei Xie (Northwestern Polytechnical
  University, China)
Xianghua Ying (Peking University, China)
Gang Zeng (Peking University, China)
Xinbo Zhao (Northwestern Polytechnical
  University, China)
Jiangbin Zheng (Northwestern Polytechnical
  University, China)

Reviewers

Abou Moustafa Karim	Azevedo-Marques Paulo	Beng-Jin Andrew Teoh
Achard Catherine	Bagdanov Andrew	Benhimane Selim
Ai Haizhou	Bai Xiang	Benosman Ryad
Alahari Karteek	Bajcsy Peter	Bibby Charles
Allili Mohand Said	Baltes Jacky	Bicego Manuele
Andreas Koschan	Banerjee Subhashis	Blekas Konstantinos
Aoki Yoshmitsu	Barbu Adrian	Bo Liefeng
Argyros Antonis	Barnes Nick	Bors Adrian
Arica Nafiz	Barreto Joao	Boshra Michael
Ariki Yasuo	Bartoli Adrien	Bouaziz Sofien
Arslan Abdullah	Baudrier Etienne	Bouguila Nizar
August Jonas	Baust Maximilian	Boutemedjet Sabri
Awate Suyash	Beichel Reinhard	Branzan Albu Alexandra

Bremond Francois
Bronstein Alex
Bronstein Michal
Brown Matthew
Brown Michael
Brun Luc
Buckley Michael
Caballero Rodrigo
Caglioti Vincenzo
Cagniart Cedric
Camastra Francesco
Cao Liangliang
Cao Liangliang
Carneiro Gustavo
Carr Peter
Castellani Umberto
Cattin Philippe
Celik Turgay
Chan Kap Luk
Chandran Sharat
Chellappa Rama
Chen Haifeng
Chen Hwann-Tzong
Chen Jiun-Hung
Chen Jun-Cheng
Chen Ling
Chen Pei
Chen Robin Bing-Yu
Chen Wei-Chao
Chen Xilin
Chen Yixin
Cheng Jian
Cheng Jian
Cheng Shyi-Chyi
Chetverikov Dmitry
Chia Liang-Tien
Chien Shao-Yi
Chin Tat-jun
Chu Wei-Ta
Chuang Yung-Yu
Chung Albert
Civera Javier
Clipp Brian
Coleman Sonya
Costeira Joao Paulo

Cousty Jean
Csaba Beleznai
Dang Xin
Daras Petros
De La Torre Fernando
Deguchi Koichiro
Demirci Fatih
Demirdjian David
Deng Hongli
Deniz Oscar
Denzler Joachim
Derpanis Konstantinos
Derrode Stephane
Destefanis Eduardo
Dick Anthony
Didas Stephan
Dong qiulei
Donoser Michael
Doretto Gianfranco
Drbohlav Ondrej
Drost Bertram
Duan Fuqing
Dueck Delbert
Duric Zoran
Dutagaci Helin
Dutta Roy Sumantra
   Dutta Roy
Dvornychenko Vladimir
Dyer Charles
Eckhardt Ulrich
Eigensatz Michael
Einhauser Wolfgang
Eroglu Erdem Cigdem
Escolano Francisco
Fan Quanfu
Fang Wen-Pinn
Farenzena MIchela
Fasel Beat
Feng Jianjiang
Feris Rogerio
Ferri Francesc
Fidler Sanja
Fihl Preben
Filliat David
Flitti Farid

Floery Simon
Forstner Wolfgang
Franco Jean-Sebastien
Fraundorfer Friedrich
Fritz Mario
Frucci Maria
Fu Chi-Wing
Fuh Chiou-Shann
Fujiyoshi Hironobu
Fukui Kazuhiro
Fumera Giorgio
Furst Jacob
Furukawa Yasutaka
Fusiello Andrea
Gall Juergen
Gallagher Andrew
Gang Li
Garg Kshitiz
Georgel Pierre
Gertych Arkadiusz
Gevers Theo
Gherardi Riccardo
Godil Afzal
Goecke Roland
Goshtasby A.
Gou Gangpeng
Grabner Helmut
Grana Costantino
Guerrero Josechu
Guest Richard
Guliato Denise
Guo Feng
Guo Guodong
Gupta Abhinav
Gupta Mohit
Hadjileontiadis Leontios
Hamsici Onur
Han Bohyung
Han Chin-Chuan
Han Joon Hee
Hanbury Allan
Hao Wei
Hassab Elgawi Osman
Hautiere Nicolas
He Junfeng

Heitz Fabrice
Hinterstoisser Stefan
Ho Jeffrey
Holzer Stefan
Hong Hyun Ki
Hotta Kazuhiro
Hotta Seiji
Hou Zujun
Hsiao JenHao
Hsu Pai-Hui
Hsu Winston
Hu Qinghua
Hu Weimin
Hu Xuelei
Hu Yiqun
Hu Yu-Chen
Hua Xian-Sheng
Huang Fay
Huang Kaiqi
Huang Peter
Huang Tz-Huan
Huang Xiangsheng
Huband Jacalyn
Huele Ruben
Hung Hayley
Hung-Kuo Chu James
Huynh Cong
Iakovidis Dimitris
Ieng Sio Hoi
Ilic Slobodan
Imiya Atsushi
Inoue Kohei
Irschara Arnold
Ishikawa Hiroshi
Iwashita Yumi
Jaeger Stefan
Jafari Khouzani Kourosh
Jannin Pierre
Jawahar C. V.
Jean Frederic
Jia Jiaya
Jia Yunde
Jia Zhen
Jiang Shuqiang
Jiang Xiaoyi

Jin Lianwen
Juneho Yi
Jurie Frederic
Kagami Shingo
Kale Amit
Kamberov George
Kankanhalli Mohan
Kato Takekazu
Kato Zoltan
Kawasaki Hiroshi
Ke Qifa
Keil Andreas
Keysers Daniel
Khan Saad-Masood
Kim Hansung
Kim Kyungnam
Kim Tae Hoon
Kim Tae-Kyun
Kimia Benjamin
Kitahara Itaru
Koepfler Georges
Koeser Kevin
Kokkinos Iasonas
Kolesnikov Alexander
Kong Adams
Konolige Kurt
Koppal Sanjeev
Kotsiantis Sotiris
Kr Er Norbert
Kristan Matej
Kuijper Arjan
Kukelova Zuzana
Kulic Dana
Kulkarni Kaustubh
Kumar Ram
Kuno Yoshinori
Kwolek Bogdan
Kybic Jan
Ladikos Alexander
Lai Shang-Hong
Lao Shihong
Lao Zhiqiang
Lazebnik Svetlana
Le Duy-Dinh
Le Khoa

Lecue Guillaume
Lee Hyoung-Joo
Lee Ken-Yi
Lee Kyong Joon
Lee Sang-Chul
Leonardo Bocchi
Lepetit Vincent
Lerasle Frederic
Li Baihua
Li Bo
Li Hongdong
Li Teng
Li Xi
Li Yongmin
Liao T.Warren
Lie Wen-Nung
Lien Jenn-Jier James
Lim Jongwoo
Lim Joo-Hwee
Lin Dahua
Lin Huei-Yung
Lin Ruei-Sung
Lin Wei-Yang
Lin Wen Chieh (Steve)
Ling Haibin
Liu Jianzhuang
Liu Ming-Yu
Liu Qingshan
Liu Qingzhong
Liu Tianming
Liu Tyng-Luh
Liu Xiaoming
Liu Xiuwen
Liu Yuncai
Lopez-Nicolas Gonzalo
Lu Juwei
Lu Le
Luo Jiebo
Ma Yong
Macaire Ludovic
Maccormick John
Madabhushi Anant
Manabe Yoshitsugu
Manniesing Rashindra
Marchand Eric

Marcialis Gian-Luca
Martinet Jean
Martinez Aleix
Masuda Takeshi
Mauthner Thomas
McCarthy Chris
McHenry Kenton
Mei Christopher
Mei Tao
Mery Domingo
Mirmehdi Majid
Mitra Niloy
Mittal Anurag
Miyazaki Daisuke
Moeslund Thomas
Monaco Francisco
Montiel Jose
Mordohai Philippos
Moreno Francesc
Mori Kensaku
Moshe Ben-Ezra
Mudigonda Pawan
Mueller Henning
Murillo Ana Cris
Naegel Benoit
Nakajima Shin-ichi
Namboodiri Anoop
Nan Xiaofei
Nanni Loris
Narasimhan Srinivasa
Nevatia Ram
Ng Wai-Seng
Nguyen Minh Hoai
Nozick Vincent
Odone Francesca
Ohnishi Naoya
Okatani Takayuki
Okuma Kenji
Omachi Shinichiro
Pack Gary
Palagyi Kalman
Pan ChunHong
Pankanti Sharath
Paquet Thierry
Park In Kyu

Park Jong-Il
Park Rae-Hong
Passat Nicolas
Patras Yiannis
Patwardhan Kedar
Peers Pieter
Peleg Shmuel
Pernici Federico
Pilet Julien
Pless Robert
Pock Thomas
Prati Andrea
Prevost Lionel
Puig Luis
Qi Guojun
Qian Zhen
Radeva Petia
Rajashekar Umesh
Ramalingam Srikumar
Ren Xiaofeng
Reyes Edel Garcia
Reyes Aldasoro
    Constantino
Ribeiro Eraldo
Robles-Kelly Antonio
Rosenhahn Bodo
Rosman Guy
Ross Arun
Roth Peter
Rugis John
Ruvolo Paul
Sadri Javad
Saffari Amir
Sagawa Ryusuke
Salzmann Mathieu
Sang Nong
Santner Jakob
Sappa Angel
Sara Radim
Sarkis Michel
Sato Jun
Schmid Natalia
Schroff Florian
Shahrokni Ali
Shan Shiguang

Shen Chunhua
Shi Guangchuan
Shih Sheng-Wen
Shimizu Ikuko
Shimshoni Ilan
Sigal Leonid
Singhal Nitin
Sinha Sudipta
Snavely Noah
Sommerlade Eric
Steenstrup Pedersen Kim
Sugaya Yasuyuki
Sukno Federico
Sumi Yasushi
Sun Feng-Mei
Sun Weidong
Svoboda Tomas
Swaminathan Rahul
Takamatsu Jun
Tan Ping
Tan Robby
Tang Chi-Keung
Tang Ming
Teng Fei
Tian Jing
Tian Yingli
Tieu Kinh
Tobias Reichl
Toews Matt
Toldo Roberto
Tominaga Shoji
Torii Akihiko
Tosato Diego
Trobin Werner
Tsin Yanghai
Tu Jilin
Tuzel Oncel
Uchida Seiichi
Urahama K
Urschler Martin
Van den Hengel Anton
Vasseur Pascal
Veeraraghavan Ashok
Veksler Olga
Vitria Jordi

Wagan Asim
Wang Hanzi
Wang Hongcheng
Wang Jingdong
Wang Jue
Wang Meng
Wang Sen
Wang Yunhong
Wang Zhi-Heng
Wei Hong
Whitehill Jacob
Wilburn Bennett
Woehler Christian
Wolf Christian
Woo Young Woon
Wu Fuchao
Wu Hao
Wu Huai-Yu
Wu Jianxin
Wu Yihong

Xiong Ziyou
Xu Ning
Xue Jianru
Xue Jianxia
Yan Shuicheng
Yanai Keiji
Yang Herbert
Yang Ming-Hsuan
Yao Yi
Yaron Caspi
Yeh Che-Hua
Yilmaz Alper
Yin Pei
Yu Tianli
Yu Ting
Yuan Baozong
Yuan Lu
Zach Christopher
Zha Zheng-Jun
Zhang Changshui

Zhang Guangpeng
Zhang Hongbin
Zhang Li
Zhang Liqing
Zhang Xiaoqin
Zhang Zengyin
Zhao Deli
Zhao Yao
Zheng Wenming
Zhong Baojiang
Zhou Cathy
Zhou Howard
Zhou Jun
Zhou Rong
Zhou S.
Zhu Feng
Zhu Wenjun
Zitnick Lawrence

Sponsors

Key Laboratory of Machine Perception (MOE), Peking University.
National Laboratory of Pattern Recognition, Institute of Automation, Chinese
    Academy of Sciences.
National Natural Science Foundation of China.
Microsoft Research.
Fujitsu Inc.
Microview Inc.
Luster Inc.

Table of Contents – Part III

Poster Session 3: Machine Learning, Recognition, Biometrics and Surveillance

Exploiting Intensity Inhomogeneity to Extract Textured Objects from Natural Scenes

Jundi Ding[1,2,*], Jialie Shen[2], HweeHwa Pang[2],
Songcan Chen[3], and Jingyu Yang[1]

[1] Nanjing University of Science and Technology, China
[2] Singapore Management University, School of Information Systems
[3] Nanjing University of Aeronautics and Astronautics, China
dingjundi@nuaa.edu.cn, {jlshen,hhpang}@smu.edu.sg,
s.chen@nuaa.edu.cn, yangjy@mail.njust.edu.cn

Abstract. Extracting textured objects from natural scenes is a challenging task in computer vision. The main difficulties arise from the intrinsic randomness of natural textures and the high-semblance between the objects and the background. In this paper, we approach the extraction problem with a seeded region-growing framework that purely exploits the statistical properties of intensity inhomogeneity. The pixels in the interior of potential textured regions are first found as texture seeds in an unsupervised manner. The labels of the texture seeds are then propagated through their respective inhomogeneous neighborhoods, to eventually cover the different texture regions in the image. Extensive experiments on a large variety of natural images confirm that our framework is able to extract accurately the salient regions occupied by textured objects, without any complicated cue integration and specific priors about objects of interest.

1 Introduction

Extracting salient textured objects in natural scenes has long been a central but tantalizing problem in computer vision. Unlike mosaic texture, natural textures tend to be more random. The texture appearance of an object of interest, e.g. the stripes/blocky-fur of a zebra/wild cat (see the top two rows in Fig.1), may even vary greatly in scale, shape, size and orientation. Textural properties like roughness, linearity, density, directionality, frequency and phase all seem to be far too rudimentary to characterize the plausible regularities behind complex natural textures [1,2,3]. Moreover, the background tends to show a high degree of resemblance in appearance to the contained objects in many situations. The two images in the bottom rows of Fig.1 illustrate such examples. In the square patch marked on each image, the pixels come from both the ground/riffle background and the lizard/otter object (zoomed in second panel). The local differences among them are however very hard to detect in the respective original image. The two factors jointly explain why existing methods based solely

---

* Supported by National Natural Science Foundation of China of Grant No. 60632050.

H. Zha, R.-i. Taniguchi, and S. Maybank (Eds.): ACCV 2009, Part III, LNCS 5996, pp. 1–10, 2010.

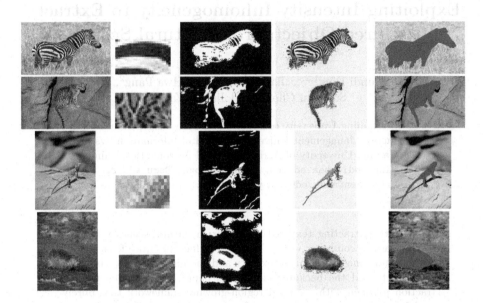

Fig. 1. The success of our INP on a set of challenging images. Our work is to aggregate the inhomogeneous pixels around the textured seeds shown in the third panel (in white). Beginning with an arbitrary object-seed (marked by '+'), our INP accurately extracts each desired object (fourth panel) in one piece which is consistent with human segmentation (fifth panel).

on texture homogeneity seldom achieve satisfactory results in natural texture segmentation.

   To this end, recent years have seen a surge of interests in this field in two directions: cue integration [4,5,6,7] and interactive or semi-supervised segmentation [8,9,10,11]. In the former algorithms, multiple cues including texture are utilized to reach a combined similarity measure for image segmentation. Each cue handled by a separate module is to assess the coherence of nearby pixels or regions with respect to that cue. Note that each module typically comes with its own set of parameters. Careful assignment of these parameter values is a non-trivial job, which critically influences the segmentation results in many cases [5,11]. The ultimate goal of the latter methodology is to extract the desired objects with some useful prior knowledge about the textures, edges, contours, shapes, curvatures or motions of objects. Different priors have a preference towards different types of task-driven segmentations. Such image prior is usually incorporated into the segmentation process in three ways: (i) being "seeds" specified by users in an initialization step [8]; (ii) being a regularization term formulated into a meaningful energy function [9]; (iii) serving as top-down cues globally blended with a bottom-up segmentation process [10,11,5]. Appropriate prior knowledge is beneficial to a good segmentation, but the challenge of automatically obtaining the prior knowledge for a variety of natural images still lies ahead.

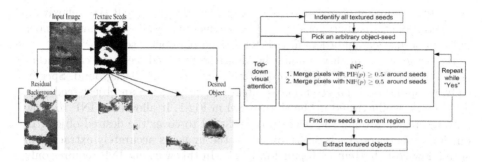

Fig. 2. A general schematic framework (left) and flowchart (right) of INP

In this paper, we focus on a different strategy which exploits solely the statistical inhomogeneity in intensity within the image to segment. In practice, almost all textures involve spatially significant fluctuations or variations in pixel intensity in a low-level perspective [2,12]. That is, the pixels in a textured region do not simply adhere to a piecewise-constant or piecewise-smooth homogeneity in intensity. For example, zebras are easily recognizable by their very black and white striped body. As such, we here address the problem of textured object extraction head on via the intensity inhomogeneity. We believe it to be an intrinsic property of just about any texture in the natural world [2].

Our approach, called *Inhomogeneous Neighborhood Propagation* (INP), is designed to work with a seeded region growing strategy. It is to aggregate the nearby inhomogeneous pixels all together in a bottom-up merge manner. Figure 2 (left) depicts a general schematic framework of our INP. The framework consists of three primary steps: (i) identifying all the inhomogeneous pixels which with high probability are in the interior of potential textured regions, and thereby perform the important role of textured seeds; (ii) propagating the labels of the texture seeds through their respective inhomogeneous neighborhoods by a sensible principle that specifies an equivalence relation over the set of textured seeds; (iii) extracting the desired objects according to human vision from the formed saliently textured regions that are covered by adjacent inhomogeneous pixels in the image. Here it is worthwhile to highlight two aspects:

– INP often identifies many background pixels as textured seeds (see the white areas in the third panel of Fig.1, especially the bottom three cases). The reason is that intensity discontinuities may also be caused by grassy or foliaged clutter, surface markings, occlusions, shadows and reflections. All of them are common in the background of natural images. We have made no effort to simplify the image to segment, so the unbiased statistics of the image are well preserved (including disturbances in the background). In such situations, the background is usually fragmented into pieces by INP, see an example in Fig.2 (left).

– INP is robust to the order of the initial seed selection as it virtually yields a *partition* of the set of textured seeds in mathematics. This means, with respect to its two parameters, INP maps every identified seed pixel into one and only one equivalence class. Namely, INP defines an equivalence relation (ER) over a non-empty, finite set of textured seeds. The properties of an ER (i.e. reflexivity, symmetry and transitivity) ensure that the segmented results are invariant under different seed selection orders in INP for a fixed parameter setting.

By virtue of this quality, among the identified textured seeds, we can concentrate on only the object seeds irrespective of those in the background. Specifically, a top-down visual attention is integrated to position an object-seed with a '+' mark as illustrated in the third panel in Fig.1. It allows our INP to grow only the region around the selected object-seed to cover the desired object. In our implementation, each target object in the image is accurately extracted in such a low-cost shortcut (4th panel in Fig.1). In this way, our INP requires only two stages: textured seeds identification and object-seed labels propagation. Section 2 details the two stages as well as the related key concepts. The algorithmic analysis about parameter sensitivity and computational efficiency is discussed in Section 3. Experiment results and evaluations reported in Section 4 confirm the effectiveness of INP in a variety of natural images. Finally, a conclusion is given in Section 5.

2   Our Method: INP

In general, an image $\mathbf{I}$ is a pair$(\mathcal{I}, I)$, consisting of a finite set of pixels $\mathcal{I}$ in a grid space Z^2 and a mapping I that assigns each pixel $p = (p_x, p_y) \in \mathcal{I}$ with an intensity value $I(p)$ in some arbitrary value space. A textured region here is just described as a function of spatial variations in pixel intensities. In what follows, the work is thus all related to the local intensity contrasts between pixels.

2.1   Textured Seeds Identification

Consider the square neighborhood $N(p)$ of each pixel p, for a given threshold $\varepsilon \geq 0$, there should be pixels in the sets

$$\Omega(p) = \{q \in N(p) : |I(p) - I(q)| > \varepsilon\} \tag{1}$$

$$\Omega'(p) = \{q \in N(p) : |I(p) - I(q)| \leq \varepsilon\} \tag{2}$$

where $N(p) = \{q \in \mathcal{I} : |p_x - q_x| \leq k, |p_y - q_y| \leq k\}$, $k \geq 1$ and $k \in Z$. Since $\Omega_p \bigcup \Omega'_p = N(p)$, it is straightforward for us to define a *pixel inhomogeneity factor* (PIF) as follows:

$$\text{PIF}(p) = \frac{|\Omega(p)|}{|N(p)|} \tag{3}$$

where $|\cdot|$ denotes the cardinality of a set, i.e. the number of elements in the set. This value within $[0,1]$ will be quite discrepant for different pixels. It is obvious that PIF$(p) < 0.5$ when $|\Omega(p)| < |\Omega'(p)|$. In such a situation, the intensity variations between p and most of its adjacent pixels are low. With high probability, they belong to a smooth region [13]. In contrast, PIF$(p) \geq 0.5$ when $|\Omega(p)| \geq |\Omega'(p)|$. It implies that the majority of pixels around p have intensity values much larger or smaller than that of p. In that case, p usually lies in some inhomogeneous image region, such as object contour or boundary [13]. It is thus reasonable to score the intensity inhomogeneity of pixels by $PIF(p) \geq 0.5$.

To ensure that the pixels indeed originated from textured objects, we further highlight the other important aspect of a potential textured pixel p, i.e, most of its neighboring pixels should also have inhomogeneous intensities. In this respect, a *neighborhood inhomogeneity factor* (NIF) is put forward in the following:

$$NIF(p) = \frac{|InNeb(p)|}{|N(p)|} \tag{4}$$

where $InNeb(p) = \{q \in N(p): PIF(q) \geq 0.5, p \in \mathcal{I}\}$. It represents the set of inhomogeneous neighbors of an arbitrary pixel p in the image. Putting the two terms together, the set of seed pixels for growing the desired textured regions is defined as below:

$$SEED = \{p : PIF(p) \geq 0.5, NIF(p) \geq 0.5, p \in \mathcal{I}\} \tag{5}$$

2.2 Inhomogeneous Neighborhood Propagation

Algorithmically, our INP belongs to the family of region growing and merging techniques. This old but popular technique has been revived in the last few years due to its native hierarchy configuration and ease of implementation [10,7,11,5,13]. In region growing, pixels being elementary regions are gradually merged to produce larger and larger regions in a sequence of iterative steps. From a probabilistic viewpoint, a demanding statistical test has to be done to give a merging predicate and an order in merging [10,11,5].

A recent work in [13] turns around to first find the most representative "seed" pixels and then define an equivalence relation on the seed set. Each region of interest in the image is hence associated with an equivalence class. In set theory, it ensures the separability of an arbitrary image, as well as the robustness to the selection order of initial seed pixels. To achieve that, the authors in [13] have come up with the segmentation criterion of ε-neighbor coherence. Based on this idea, we specify a principle of neighbor inhomogeneity for texture segmentation.

For an arbitrary seed $p \in SEED$ in a texture region, its neighbor q satisfying $PIF(q) \geq 0.5$ or $NIF(q) \geq 0.5$ should belong to the same textured region as p.

It is obvious that this principle depicts a "transitive relationship" among the seed pixels. That is, assume the pixels $p, q, t \in SEED$, if $t \in N(q)$ and $q \in N(p)$, t is grouped into the same region as q while q is grouped into the same region as p. In such a way, t is also grouped into the same region as p. Further, like the ε-neighbor coherence criterion in [13], our principle also specifies an equivalence relation on the set of texture seeds.

Equivalence Relation. For any two seed pixels '$p \sim q$' if p, q satisfy either of the two conditions: 1) $p \in N(q)$; 2) there exists a finite number of seed pixels $p_1, p_2, \cdots, p_n$ such that $p \in N(p_1)$, $p_k \in N(p_{k+1})$, $k=1, \cdots, n\text{-}1$, $p_n \in N(q)$.

It is easy to prove the three properties: reflexive ('$p \sim p$'), symmetric ('$p \sim q$' implies '$q \sim p$') and transitive. This principle implies that our INP can start from an arbitrary textured seed to propagate the label through all its inhomogeneous neighbors. Moreover, according to the analysis detailed above, the inhomogeneous pixels involved in the same propagating chain would, with high probability, delineate a single textured object.

Propagation Termination. Such an equivalence relation can partition the set of texture seeds into several equivalence classes. The number of equivalence classes just determines the number of interesting regions. Note that each ultimate textured region contains the texture seeds in an equivalence class and some non-seed texture pixels besides. The presence of these non-seed texture pixels is responsible for the termination of the label propagation. In other words, the growth of a region will stop when there is no new textured seed in this region. Figure 2 (right) summarizes the flowchart of INP for object extraction with an arbitrarily picked object-seed.

3   Algorithm Analysis of INP

Parameter Sensitivity. INP involves two parameters k and ε. On one hand, k determines the size of the local neighborhood of each pixel. In the common case, an optimal k could be chosen in a range of 5-12. However, a "huge" close-shot object usually needs a larger k (≥ 12); while a "little" long-shot object requires a smaller k (≤ 5). On the other hand, with respect to a given neighborhood size k, one can figure out some meaningful statistics in intensity such as $\text{Mean}(k)_p$ and $\text{Ave}(k)$. They are respectively formulated in Eq.6:

$$\text{Mean}(k)_p = \frac{\sum_{q \in N(p)} | I(p) - I(q) |}{| N(p) |}, \text{Ave}(k) = \frac{\sum_{p \in \mathbf{I}}(\text{Mean}(k)_p)}{| \mathbf{I} |} \tag{6}$$

By definition, $\text{Mean}(k)_p$ exposes the mean difference in intensity within the neighborhood of each pixel p; and $\text{Ave}(k)$ is the average value of all $\text{Mean}(k)_p$, which reflects the global variation in intensity in the image.

In addition, the threshold of intensity contrast (see Eq.1 or Eq.2) ε characterizes the degree of inhomogeneity or homogeneity in intensity between pairwise neighboring pixels. For a central pixel p, if ε is larger than the mean intensity difference in its neighborhood $\text{Mean}(k)_p$, most of its neighbors will be in the set $\Omega'(p)$ instead of $\Omega(p)$. From the discussion detailed above, p will be not an inhomogeneous pixel. Otherwise, if ε is smaller than $\text{Mean}(k)_p$, most of its neighbors will appear in the set $\Omega(p)$ and thereby p becomes an inhomogeneous pixel.

However, it is impossible to select a proper ε with regard to $\text{Mean}(k)_p$ which varies with different pixels. A good candidate for ε is $\text{Ave}(k)$, which is invariant for a given k. In practice, the value of ε in our experiments fluctuates around $\text{Ave}(k)$. When intensities of the foreground pixels (e.g. a zebra roaming the grassland) vary sharply, ε is selected to be a little smaller than $\text{Ave}(k)$. If the intensities of the background pixels (e.g. a clutter background with a flying bird)

Fig. 3. Experimental results on Corel images

vary significantly, ε is set to be a little larger than Ave(k). An adaptive ε has been observed in the range [Ave(k)–10, Ave(k)+10] in our experiments.

Computational Efficiency. Recall that INP performs object extraction following the general flowchart shown in Fig.2 (right). It is easy to see that the most time-consuming work is the identification of textured seeds. It requires the calculation of Ω_p for each pixel. Because of the properties of ER, it is not necessary to compute N_p and Ω_p of the pixels which are in the first and last k rows/columns of the image $\mathbf{I}(w, h)$, where w and h are the width and height of the image respectively. Let $N = (w - 2k) * (h - 2k), M = (2k + 1)^2 - 1, k \in Z$, the running time of calculating all Ω_p is O(MN). When k is not very large (≤ 12), it takes nearly O(N) in proportion to the size of the image $\mathbf{N}$. In addition, the recursive propagation procedure for covering all object pixels takes less than O($\mathbf{N}$) as only those pixels around the selected object-seed are scanned once. Besides, the automatic selection of ε requires computing Mean(k)$_p$ and Ave(k). It takes O(MN) like the calculation of Ω_p. Overall, our INP is efficient with a computational complexity of O(MN) that is nearly linear in the size of the image.

4 Experiments and Evaluation Results

We have conducted extensive experiments and comparisons to evaluate the performance of our INP. We first test the qualitative effectiveness of INP on a large number of natural images that contain a variety of challenging textures. All of the sample images are readily available from the Corel image library [13]. For a further quantitative evaluation, we apply our INP to all the 100 gray level images in an open database compiled by Alpert et al. recently in [5]. The F-measure is used to assess the consistency of our results with the ground-truth segmentations in the database.

Qualitative Results on The Corel Dataset. The Corel dataset is commonly used in computer vision. It contains 30,000 images covering a wide range of subject matters. For our extraction task, we are interested in those images that include distinct physical objects in the natural world, particularly the ones that are of animals in natural scenes. The animal furs by nature exhibit a variety of challenging textures. Figure 1 shows several representative samples, where our extraction results (fourth panel) are in marked agreement with human segmentations (red, fifth panel). The salient objects of interest together with the long but thin bodies, legs or tails are all segmented in one piece, even if the animals are camouflaged against their backgrounds due to the shadows, illuminations and reflections. Figure 3 further illustrates our results on a set of challenging images. The leopards in the first panel are in different poses (crouching, sitting, eating, standing, walking, running, etc.) in different cluttered backgrounds. A few "Leopard" images among them occur quite often in the texture segmentation literature [11]. These methods have had to integrate many cues of intensities, contours, shapes and motions in order to produce satisfactory results. It is unclear whether they are robust to the variations in poses, shadows, shapes and motions in our experiments. Exploiting the naive intensity inhomogeneity, our INP succeeds in these difficult "Leopard" images. The integrity of each leopard object is well preserved. Moreover, the "Leopard" objects extracted by INP are consistent with the human semantic perception. Other results are also presented on the images with the animal tiger, butterfly, birds, zebra or giraffe. They exhibit a rich diversity of texture appearances in randomness and irregularity. Despite these difficulties, our INP still yields good figure-ground separation. These extracted salient regions can be useful for content-based or object-based image retrieval, indexing and classification in multimedia analysis.

Quantitative Evaluation of Consistency. A quantitative evaluation of the results produced by segmentation algorithms is challenging, since it is difficult to come up with canonical test sets providing ground truth segmentations. Recently, Alpert et al. has compiled a new database containing 100 gray images along with ground truth segmentations [5]. To avoid potential ambiguities, the selected images clearly depict one object in the background. Each image is segmented manually by three different people. A pixel is declared as foreground only when it was marked as foreground by at least two people. For an objective evaluation, we have applied our INP to all the 100 images. Some results are shown in Fig.4. Note that the salient regions here represent more generic textures in the natural scenes. Visually, our results are very consistent with the human-driven segmentations (in red color) on the same image. To clarify this point, we use the F-measure to assess its consistency quantitatively [5]. The amount of fragmentation is determined simply by the number of segments needed to cover the foreground object. Table 1 presents the F-measure scores of our results on

Fig. 4. Experimental comparisons on a new image database from [5]

Table 1. Our F-measure Score on Test Images from The Dataset in [5]

Image	F-measure Score	Image	F-measure Score
IMG_2577	0.83878	nitpix_P1280114	0.9671
0677845-R1-067-32_a	0.94971	110016671724	0.8092
aaa	0.8092	boy-float-lake	0.9534
Bream_In_Basin	0.96807	caterpiller	0.91923
DSC04575	0.93302	DSC_0959	0.9815
tendrils	0.80518	DSCF0034	0.93466
DSCF0459	0.85897	osaka060102_DYJSN071	0.84795
PIC1092515922117	0.92676	PIC7227	0.96282
PIC1080629574	0.94435	windowCN_0078	0.96394

the test images in Fig.4. The large F-measures (some even approximate to the maximum 1) achieved by INP is another evidence of its effectiveness[1].

---

[1] The averaged F-measure score of our INP is 0.82±0.027 that is competitive with the highest one 0.86±0.012 reported in Table 1 in [5].

5   Summary

In this paper, we present a novel approach called INP to extract textured objects in natural images by exploiting intensity inhomogeneity. Along with a top-down visual attention, INP works by aggregating neighboring inhomogeneous pixels together within a seeded region growing framework. It requires no complicated computations on multi-cue integration or specific priors about the objects of interest. Both theoretical analysis and experiment results confirm that our INP is **easy** to interpret and implement, **efficient** in computational cost and **effective** for textured object extraction in a variety of natural images.

References

1. Julesz, B.: Textons, the elements of texture perception and their interactions. Nature 290, 91–97 (1981)
2. Chen, C., Pau, L.: Texture analysis. In: Wang, P.S.P. (ed.) The Handbook of Pattern Recognition and Computer Vision, 2nd edn., ch. 2.1, pp. 207–248. World Scientific Publishing Co., Singapore (1998)
3. Varma, M., Zisserman, A.: A statistical approach to texture classification from single images. International Journal of Computer Vision 62(1-2), 61–81 (2005)
4. Deng, Y., Manjunath, B.S.: Unsupervised segmentation of color-texture regions in images and video. IEEE Transactions on Pattern Analysis and Machine Intelligence 23(8), 800–810 (2001)
5. Alpert, S., Basri, M., Brandt, A.: Image segmentation by probabilistic bottom-up aggregation and cue integration. In: International Conference on Computer Vision and Pattern Recognition, pp. 1–8 (2007)
6. Liang, K., Tjahjadi, T.: Adaptive scale fixing for multiscale texture segmentation. IEEE Transactions on Image Processing 15(1), 249–256 (2006)
7. Xia, Y., Feng, D., Zhao, R.: Morphology-based multifractal estimation for texture segmentation. IEEE Transactions on Image Processing 15(3), 614–623 (2006)
8. Xiang, S., Nie, F., Zhang, C.: Texture segmentation: An interactive framework based on adaptive features and transductive learning. In: Narayanan, P.J., Nayar, S.K., Shum, H.-Y. (eds.) ACCV 2006. LNCS, vol. 3851, pp. 216–225. Springer, Heidelberg (2006)
9. Paragios, N., Deriche, R.: Geodesic active regions and level set methods for supervised texture segmentation. International Journal of Computer Vision 46(3), 223–247 (2002)
10. Nock, R., Nielsen, F.: Statistical region merging. IEEE Transactions on Pattern Analysis and Machine Intelligence 26(11), 1452–1458 (2004)
11. Sharon, E., Galun, M., Sharon, D., Basri, R., Brandt, A.: Hierarchy and adaptivity in segmenting visual scenes. Nature 442(7104), 810–813 (2006)
12. Suyash, P., Awate, T.T., Whitaker, R.T.: Unsupervised texture segmentation with nonparametric neighborhood statistics. In: Leonardis, A., Bischof, H., Pinz, A. (eds.) ECCV 2006. LNCS, vol. 3952, pp. 494–507. Springer, Heidelberg (2006)
13. Ding, J., Ma, R., Chen, S.: A scale-based coherence connected tree algorithm for image segmentation. IEEE Transactions on Image Processing 17(2), 204–216 (2008)

Convolutional Virtual Electric Field External Force for Active Contours

Yuanquan Wang[1,2] and Yunde Jia[2]

[1] Tianjin Key Lab of Intelligent Computing and Novel Software Technology,
School of Computer Science, Tianjin University of Technology, Tianjin 300191, P.R. China
[2] Beijing Laboratory of Intelligent Information Technology, School of Computer Science,
Beijing Institute of Technology, Beijing 100081, P.R.China
{yqwang,jiayunde}@bit.edu.cn

Abstract. A novel external force called CONvolutional Virtual Electric Field (CONVEF) for active contours is proposed by taking the Virtual Electric Field (VEF) just as a convolution operation and by using modified distance metrics in the convolution kernel. The proposed CONVEF method possesses some desirable properties of VEF such as large capture range and being implemented in real-time by using fast Fourier transform. Meanwhile, the CONVEF snake provides much better segmentation than VEF snake in terms of noise suppression, C-shape concavity convergence, weak edge preserving, and neighbored objects separation. These advantages has been demonstrated and verified on synthetic and real images.

1 Introduction

Shape recovery and object tracking from visual data is of paramount importance in the community of computer vision and the active contour models, or snakes, dominate this field during the last two decades [1]. The philosophy of the snake models involves minimizing a certain energy functional which integrates an initial estimate, geometrical properties of the contour, image data and knowledge-based constraints into a compact expression. They have been one of the most influential ideas in computer vision and steer our attention toward top-down, prior knowledge-driven manner for image understanding [2].

In general, there are two types of active contours according to their representation, i.e., parametric snake [1][2] which adopts an explicit representation and geometric snake [3][4] which resorts to an implicit manner. It usually comes down to solve certain PDEs to minimize the energy functional of snakes. In [5], the associate PDE is treated as a force balance equation, and the internal force is resulted from geometric properties while the external force is from image data. Since the external force drives the snake contour to approach objects, it plays leading role in the evolution of snake and is widely studied in literatures. For example, Xu and Prince [5] proposed the GVF external force which shows high performance in capture range enlarging and concavities convergence and becomes the focus of many research [6][7][8]. Sum and Cheung [9] proposed the boundary vector field external force. Park and Chung [10] and Yuan and Lu [11] simultaneously proposed the virtual electric field (VEF) based

H. Zha, R.-i. Taniguchi, and S. Maybank (Eds.): ACCV 2009, Part III, LNCS 5996, pp. 11–20, 2010.

external force, in which each pixel is considered as a static charge. Jalba *et al* [12] recently proposed the charged particle model, where each pixel is also considered as static charge. The VEF possesses the advantage of being implemented in real time over the GVF while maintaining other desirable properties such as large capture range and concavity convergence.

This paper aims at designing a more effective external force for active contours. The proposed external force takes the VEF just as a convolution operation and utilizes modified distance metrics in the convolution kernel. We refer to this proposed method as CONvolutional Virtual Electric Field(CONVEF). The CONVEF outperforms the VEF in terms of noise suppression, neighbored objects separation and C-shape concavity convergence while remaining other desirable properties.

The remainder of this paper is organized as follows: the VEF snake is briefly reviewed in Section 2; in Section 3, we detail the proposed CONVEF method, experimental results and demonstrations are given in Section 4 and we concludes this paper in Section 5.

2 Brief Review of the VEF Snake

A snake contour is an elastic curve that moves and changes its shape to minimize the following energy [1],

$$E_{snake} = \int \frac{1}{2} \left(\alpha |\mathbf{c}_s|^2 + \beta |\mathbf{c}_{ss}|^2 \right) + E_{ext} (\mathbf{c}(s)) ds \ . \tag{1}$$

where $c(s)=[x(s),y(s)]$, $s \in [0,1]$ is the snake contour parameterized by arc length, $c_s(s)$ and $c_{ss}(s)$ are the first and second derivative of $c(s)$ with respect to s and positively weighted by α and β respectively. $E_{ext}(c(s))$ is the image potential which may result from various events, e.g., lines and edges. By calculus of variation, the Euler equation to minimize E_{snake} is

$$\alpha \mathbf{c}_{ss}(s) - \beta \mathbf{c}_{ssss}(s) - \nabla E_{ext} = 0 \ . \tag{2}$$

This can be considered as a force balance equation

$$\mathbf{F}_{int} + \mathbf{F}_{ext} = 0 \ , \tag{3}$$

where $\mathbf{F}_{int} = \alpha c_{ss}(s) - \beta c_{ssss}(s)$ and $\mathbf{F}_{ext} = -\nabla E_{ext}$. The internal force $\mathbf{F}_{int}$ makes the snake contour to be smooth while the external force $\mathbf{F}_{ext}$ attracts the snake to the desired image features.

Typically, the external energy for gray value image **I** is defined as

$$E_{ext} (\mathbf{c}(s)) = -|\nabla G_\sigma \otimes \mathbf{I}|^2 \ , \tag{4}$$

where G_σ is the Gaussian kernel of standard deviation σ, and the associated external force is

$$\mathbf{F}_{ext} = -\nabla E_{ext} = \nabla |\nabla G_\sigma \otimes \mathbf{I}|^2 \ , \tag{5}$$

i.e., the gradient vector of the edge-map of an image. But this gradient vector is 'my-opic' and the snake contour always can't converge to deep concavities, and the initial contour has to be laid nearby object boundaries. In order to overcome these draw-backs, Xu and Prince [5] proposed the GVF external force by diffusing the gradient vector further away from the edges so as to enlarge the capture range and simultane-ously suppress the noise. Park and Chung [10] pointed out this diffusion based method is computationally expensive, therefore, they proposed the virtual electric field (VEF) method in which each pixel in the image is considered as a virtual electric charge and the virtual electric field at (x_0,y_0) that is created by all other electric charges in region D enveloping (x_0,y_0) is given by

$$\mathbf{E}_{VEF} = \sum_{\substack{(x,y)\in D \\ (x,y)\neq(x_0,y_0)}} \left(\frac{q\cdot(x_0-x)}{d^3}, \frac{q\cdot(y_0-y)}{d^3} \right),$$ (6)

where $d = \sqrt{(x-x_0)^2 + (y-y_0)^2}$, D={(x,y)||x-x_0|≤t, |y-y_0|≤t}, and q is defined as the magnitude of the edge map of an image. The VEF has been shown to be an effective external force for active contours in terms of not only capture range enlarging and concavity convergence, but also the computational burden.

3   CONVEF Snakes

Although the VEF model overcomes the shortcoming of GVF while maintaining other advantages such as large capture range and concavity convergence, but there is still room for improvement, for example, there is no noise suppression mechanism for cluttered background and if two objects are very close to each other, especially when one edge is weak and the other is strong, VEF snakes could fail to tell them apart. Additionally, if the concavity is C-shape, the VEF snakes become ineffective. Moti-vated by these observations, we propose a novel external force by taking the VEF just as a convolution operation and by utilizing modified convolution kernel.

We depart from the concept of electric potential. Following the definitions for (6), the virtual electric potential at (x_0,y_0) is given by

$$P_{VEF} = \sum_{\substack{(x,y)\in D \\ (x,y)\neq(x_0,y_0)}} \frac{q(x,y)}{\sqrt{(x-x_0)^2 + (y-y_0)^2}},$$ (7)

This is a weighted sum and can be rewritten via convolution due to the fact that the weight $1/\sqrt{(x-x_0)^2 + (y-y_0)^2}$ is not correlated with the signal q(x,y). Therefore, the potential takes the following form:

$$P_{VEF} = K_{VEF} \otimes q ,$$ (8)

where $K_{VEF} = 1/r, r = \sqrt{x^2 + y^2}$ and the associated electric field can also be rewritten via convolution, which is the gradient of the electric potential, and reads

$$\mathbf{E}_{VEF} = \nabla P_{VEF} = \nabla\big(K_{VEF} \otimes q\big) = \big(\nabla K_{VEF}\big) \otimes q = \left(-\frac{x}{r^3} \otimes q, -\frac{y}{r^3} \otimes q\right). \qquad (9)$$

If one neglect the physical nature of (7) and take (8) just as a convolution operation, one can utilize some other convolution kernels in (8). These new kernels may not necessarily possess any physical meanings, but they would make VEF more powerful and flexible than the original version. We refer to this convolution based version as CONvolutional Virtual Electric Field(CONVEF) and to the snake models with CON-VEF external force as CONVEF snakes.

We present here one practically effective kernel by modifying the distance metric in K_{VEF}. One nonnegative factor h is introduced into r so that $r_h = \sqrt{x^2 + y^2 + h}$, and the power of r is relaxed from '1' to a certain positive real number n, therefore, the proposed kernel is formulated as follows:

$$K_{CONVEF} = \frac{1}{r_h^n}. \qquad (10)$$

As a result, the corresponding virtual electric potential is

$$P_{CONVEF} = K_{CONVEF} \otimes q, \qquad (11)$$

and the convolutional virtual electric field is given by

$$\mathbf{E}_{CONVEF} = \left(-\frac{x}{r_h^{n+2}} \otimes q, -\frac{y}{r_h^{n+2}} \otimes q\right). \qquad (12)$$

This modification of r makes CONVEF more powerful than VEF, on one hand, the factor h plays a role analogous to scale space filtering, the larger the value of h, the greater the smoothing effect on the results; on the other hand, the larger the value of n, the faster the potential decays with distance and vice versa, this property allows the CONVEF snakes to preserve edges and to tell apart two closely-neighbored objects with large n and to dive into C-shape concavities with small n. To note, we neglect a constant n outside the bracket in (12).

Remarks. Very recently, Li and Acton [13] proposed the vector field convolution (VFC) external force by convolving the image edge map with a vector field kernel which is formulated as

$$K_{VFC} = \left(-\frac{x}{r^{1+\gamma}}, -\frac{y}{r^{1+\gamma}}\right), \qquad (13)$$

where $r = \sqrt{x^2 + y^2}$ and γ is a positive real number. Comparing (13) with (9), it is clear that VFC is essentially an extension of VEF by relaxing the power of r from 3 to $1+\gamma$, so, the VEF is a special case of VFC with $\gamma = 2.0$. Although the proposed CONVEF is derived from the VEF, it can also be considered as an extension of VFC, in fact, the VFC is a special case of the CONVEF with $h=0.0$ in (12). However, the CONVEF is not a naive extension of VFC by introducing the factor h, novelties that one can't find in

[13] include three aspects: *(1)* noise suppression by using a positive factor h; *(2)* fascinating effect of increasing the power of r_h for edge preserving and neighbored objects separating; *(3)* In VFC, the power of r is decreased for noise resistance; we point out this strategy is not a good choice for noise suppression but shows fascinating power for C-shape convergence. We will demonstrate the properties of CONVEF snake with particular emphasis on these three novelties and make a comparison with VFC snake in Section 4. To note, the power of r_h in CONVEF is larger than 2 whereas that of r in VFC is just larger than 1 according to their different derivations.

4   Experimental Results and Analysis

In this section, we demonstrate some desirable properties of CONVEF snakes, and the performances of the VEF, VFC, and CONVEF snakes are compared. The differences of VEF, VFC and CONVEF reside in the distance metrics in the convolution kernels; therefore, their computational costs just depend mainly on the size of the convolution kernels. Thus, the CONVEF can also be implemented in real time using fast Fourier transform as done to VEF and VFC, which has been investigated respectively in [10] and [13], and we will not ply with this issue here. The parameters for all snakes in our experiments are $\alpha = 0.1$, $\beta = 0.1$, time step $\tau = 0.5$ and the size of convolution kernel is the same as that of the image unless otherwise stated.

4.1   Capture Range, Concavity Convergence, and Initialization Insensitivity

We use the U-shape and room images, which are also employed in [5][10][13], to verify some general properties CONVEF snakes. Fig.1 shows the results with different parameter settings for CONVEF; it can be seen from this experiment, although the initial contours are placed inside, or outside, or across the boundaries, the CONVEF snakes can locate objects correctly, even stay on the gaps on the boundaries, and converge to the concavity. This experiment manifests the performance of CONVEF snake on capture range enlarging, insensitivity to initialization, and convergence to U-shape concavity.

4.2   Effect of Factor h: Noise Robustness

To evaluate the noise suppression ability of CONVEF snakes, we first utilize a synthetic circle image contaminated with noise, shown in Fig.2 (a). The edge map shown in Fig.2 (b) is derived by preprocessing the image with a 2D Gaussian kernel of standard deviation 3.0. The results of CONVEF snake are presented in Fig.2(c); one can see from this result the ability for noise suppression of CONVEF snake. In [13], the VFC snake is endowed with the ability of noise resistance by decreasing the value of γ in (13). We also apply the VFC snake to this noisy circle image, and find that, when the value of γ is smaller and smaller, the VFC field is more and more regular, and the VFC snake evolves more and more steadily. When γ is small enough, say 1.2 in this example, the VFC snake can correctly locate the objects, see Fig.2 (d). This observation has been demonstrated in [13].

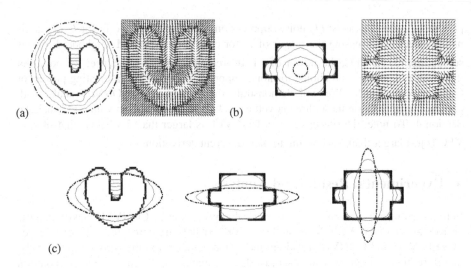

Fig. 1. Convergence of CONVEF Snakes with different initializations and different parameter settings on different images. Parameters are (a) $n=1.5$, $h=2.0$, (b) $n=2.0$, $h=2.0$, (c) From left to right, $n=1.5, h=2.0$; $n=1.5, h=1.0$; $n=2.0, h=2.0$. The dash-dotted lines are initial contours.

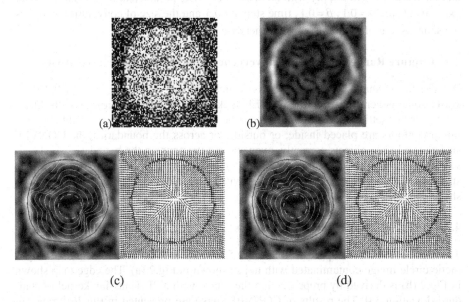

Fig. 2. Comparison of VFC and CONVEF snakes on noise robustness. (a) Noisy synthetic image, (b) Edge map, Convergence of (c) CONVEF snake with $n=1.0, h=16.0$; (d) VFC snake with $\gamma = 1.2$. In (c) and (d), the left is the evolution of snakes; the right is the vector field. The dash-dotted lines are initial contours.

But further studies show that this strategy of decreasing the value of γ is not a good choice for noise suppression. There is an example in Fig.3. The noisy U-shape image is created from that in Fig.1 using the MATLAB function *imnoise(U,'salt &*

pepper',0.1), and this example resembles that in Fig.8 in [13], but there is at least one difference: the noise within the concavity in Fig.3 is heavier than that in [13]; this means it is more difficult for the snakes to converge correctly to the concavity. We also let the noisy image intact as in [13]. The VFC snake with $\gamma = 1.5$ in Fig.3 (a) fails to dive into the concavity even there is serious leakage on other parts of the boundary. As for the CONVEF snake, the result is satisfactory by using a large h to suppress noise and by increasing the value of n to preserve weak edges, see Fig.3 (b). Other parameter settings can also lead to satisfactory results, such as n=2.0, h=6, which are not presented here due to page limitation. This example manifests the drawback of VFC snake and the effectiveness of the CONVEF snake when confronting noise.

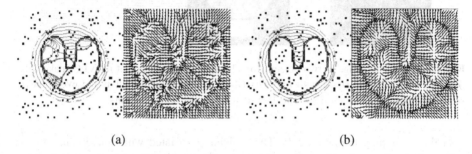

(a)   (b)

Fig. 3. Comparison of VFC and CONVEF snakes on noise robustness. Convergence of (a) VFC snake with $\gamma = 1.5$ (b) CONVEF snake with n=3.0, h=10.0. In each panel, the left is the evolution of snakes; the right is the vector field. The dash-dotted lines are initial contours.

4.3 Effect of Increasing n: Neighbored Objects Separation

Fig.3 demonstrates the use of large *n* for edge preserving when the CONVEF snake is employed to locate objects. One can also make use of large *n* to separate two closely neighbored objects, especially when one edge is weak and the other is strong. In fact, to separate objects is essentially to preserve the edge of each object. We demonstrate this particular application using a synthetic image. Fig.4 (a) shows the original image, where there are one gray disk and one white rectangle on the black background and there are just three pixels between two objects. The edge of the disk is weak and that of the rectangle is strong, see Fig.4 (b). Fig.4(c) is the result of VFC snake, which shows the VFC vectors located on the weak edge of the disk are influenced to point to the neighboring strong ones, leading to the VFC snake moving across the weak edge and sticking to the strong edges. Fig.4 (d) shows the result of CONVEF snake with n=3.0, h=0.0. It is clear the CONVEF vectors on the neighboring edges point in opposite directions; the weak edge is well characterized by the CONVEF field and the snake correctly tells these two closely neighbored objects apart.

4.4 Effect of Decreasing n: C-Shape Convergence

Although the strategy of decreasing the value of *n* is not an ideal choice for noise suppression, there may be some other applications in which the CONVEF snake with

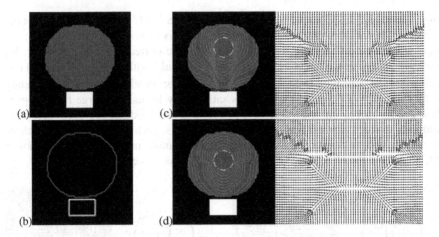

Fig. 4. (a) Synthetic image of two objects, (b) edge map, Convergence of (c) VFC snake with $\gamma = 2.0$, (d) CONVEF snake with $n=3.0, h=0.0$. In (c) and (d), the left is the evolution of snakes; the right is the vector field. The dash-dotted lines are initial contours.

a small n may play important role. The problem associated with convergence to C-shape concavity is one of such applications. The problem associated with convergence to U-shape has been intensively studied using GVF [5], VEF [10] and VFC [13], but regarding C-shape, even S-shape and G-shape, it is seldom reported and will be the focus of this subsection. The difference between C-shape concavity and U-shape concavity is that the C-shape is semi-close, while the U-shape is open. It is very easy for the VEF to form *source* within concave regions and the VEF vectors around the neck of the concave regions are outward; but for CONVEF with a smaller n, the faraway points will be weighed more and the force field will be affected by more points around, as a result, the CONVEF field around the neck of the concavity will point inward the concavity. Fig.5 shows the result of VEF snake on C-shape and the results of CONVEF snake on C-shape, S-shape, and even G-shape. The S-shape and G-shape are a little more complex than the C-shape, since there is orientation rotation especially in the case of G-shape, but CONVEF snake succeeds in all cases.

4.5   Real Images

We apply the CONVEF snakes to real noisy medical images. Fig.6 shows the segmentation results of the VFC, VEF and CONVEF snakes on a human lung CT image. We aim at extracting the parenchyma in the left part and the cancer in the right part, and the difficulties reside in the weak and closely-neighbored boundaries. The results of VFC snake and VEF snake are shown in Fig.6 (a) and (b), respectively, the convergent contours of both snakes leak out although the VEF snake behaves much better than the VFC snake. Fig.6 (c) shows the results of the CONVEF snakes. The experiment exemplifies the abilities of the CONVEF snake for weak edge preserving and neighbored objects separation. The CONVEF snake is also applied to some other real images, such as the ultrasound heart image, and promising results are obtained, but the results are not presented due to limited pages.

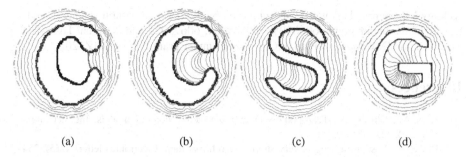

<table>
<tr><td>(a)</td><td>(b)</td><td>(c)</td><td>(d)</td></tr>
</table>

Fig. 5. Convergence of (a) VEF Snake, (b),(c),(d) CONVEF snake with n=0.5,h=0.0. The dash-dotted lines are initial contours.

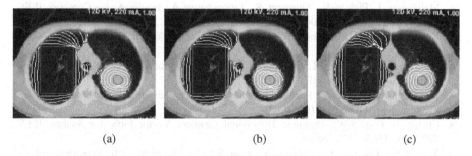

<table>
<tr><td>(a)</td><td>(b)</td><td>(c)</td></tr>
</table>

Fig. 6. Segmentation of the human lung CT image using (a) VFC snake with $\gamma = 1.7$, (b) VEF snake, (c) CONVEF snake with n=1.5, h=0.0. The gray lines are initial contours.

5 Conclusion

In this paper, we have introduced a novel external force for active contours, namely, convolutional virtual electric field (CONVEF). This CONVEF is derived from the VEF by taking the VEF just as a convolution operation and by using modified distance in the convolution kernel. It can also be considered as an extension of the VFC method. The CONVEF snake possesses some desirable properties of the VEF and VFC snakes, such as large capture range, insensitivity to initialization, convergence to U-shape concavity and low computational requirement. In addition, the CONVEF snake also behaves much better than the VEF and VFC snakes in noise suppression, weak edge preserving and C-shape concavity convergence. We have tested the CON-VEF with different objects and images, and the CONVEF snake has been verified as a superior alternative to the VEF snake, even to the VFC snake.

Additionally, the CONVEF can also be extended to 3D space to form the CONVEF active surface and be tailored to specific applications in a straightforward manner similar to that of the VFC method. One can also integrate this CONVEF method into the geometric active contour as done in [3] and there may be potential applications of the CONVEF to extract the curve skeleton [14] and to find axes of symmetry [15].

Acknowledgments. This work was supported by the national natural science foundation of China under grants 60602050, 60805004, 60675021 and National High-Tech Research and Development Plan of China (863) under grant 2006AA01Z120.

References

1. Kass, M., Witkin, A., Terzopoulos, D.: Snakes: active contour models. Int. J. Comput. Vis. 1(4), 321–331 (1988)
2. Blake, A.: Visual tracking: a very short research roadmap. Electronics letters 42(5), 254–256 (2006)
3. Paragios, N., Mellina-Gottardo, O., Ramesh, V.: Gradient Vector Flow Fast Geometric Active Contours. IEEE TPAMI 26, 402–407 (2004)
4. Melonakos, J., Pichon, E., Angenent, S., Tannenbaum, A.: Finsler Active Contours. IEEE TPAMI 30(3), 412–423 (2008)
5. Xu, C., Prince, J.L.: Snakes, Shapes and gradient vector flow. IEEE TIP 17(3), 359–369 (1998)
6. Han, X., Xu, C., Prince, J.L.: Fast numerical scheme for gradient vector flow computation using a multigrid method. IET IP 1(1), 48–55 (2007)
7. Wang, Y., Jia, Y., Liu, L.: Harmonic gradient vector flow external force for snake model. Electron. Lett. 44(2), 105–107 (2008)
8. Cheng, J., Foo, S.W.: Dynamic Directional Gradient Vector Flow for Snakes. IEEE TIP 15(6), 1563–1571 (2006)
9. Sum, K.W., Cheung, Y.S.: Boundary vector field for parametric active contours. PR 40, 1635–1645 (2007)
10. Park, H.K., Chung, M.J.: External force of snake: virtual electric field. Electron. Lett. 38(24), 1500–1502 (2002)
11. Yuan, D., Lu, S.: Simulated static electric field (SSEF) snake for deformable models. In: ICIP, pp. 83–86 (2002)
12. Jalba, A., Wilkinson, M., Roerdink, J.: CPM: A deformable model for shape recovery and segmentation based on charged particles. IEEE TPAMI 26(10), 1320–1335 (2004)
13. Bing, L., Acton, S.T.: Active Contour External Force Using Vector Field Convolution for Image Segmentation. IEEE TIP 16(8), 2096–2106 (2007)
14. Hassouna, M.S., Farag, A.A.: Variational Curve Skeletons Using Gradient Vector Flow. IEEE TPAMI (2009), doi:10.1109/TPAMI.2008.271 0162-8828
15. Shiv Naga Prasad, V., Yegnanarayana, B.: Finding Axes of symmetry from potential fields. IEEE TIP 13(12), 1559–1566 (2004)

An Effective Segmentation for Noise-Based Image Verification Using Gamma Mixture Models

Ling Cai[1], Yiren Xu[1], Lei He[2], Yuming Zhao[1], and Xin Yang[1]

[1] The Department of Automation, Shanghai Jiao Tong University,
Shanghai, 200340 China
{cailing.cs,xuyiren}@gmail.com, {arola_zym,yangxin}@sjtu.edu.cn
http://sites.google.com/site/lingcai2006sjtu/
[2] The National Library of Medicine, National Institutes of Health,
Bethesda, MD 20894, USA
lei.he@nih.gov

Abstract. Image verification has been widely used in numerous websites to prevent them from batch registration or automated posting. One category of the image verification is generated by adding noise into character or digit images to make them hard to be recognized by Optical Character Recognition (OCR). In this paper, we propose a novel probability gradient function for active contour models to efficiently segment this type of images for easier recognition. Experiments on a set of images with different intensities and types of noise show the superiority of the proposed probability gradient to traditional method. The purpose of our paper is to warn some websites who are still using such kind of verification: they should improve their defense method to prevent them from the potential risk.

1 Introduction

Websites often attempt to be interactive. In order to attract more users and present them an enhanced user experience, some websites provide login interface or allow readers to post their comments. However, such interactive applications can cause potential vulnerability if not well protected. At an early time, some automated software can execute batch registration or even hack users' information by brute force. As websites have paid increasingly attention to such security issue, many measures have been taken; and the image verification can be considered as the most active method applied in numerous situations.

Image verification in most cases is an image with noise corrupted or distorted characters, see Fig.1 (from ACCV2009 registration page). After adding different noise or even distorting its contents, such image is difficult to be recognized by common Optical Character Recognition (OCR). However, there still exist loopholes in image verification, and reports show that famous websites such as Yahoo!, Windows Live Hotmail and Gmail all have been broken by some hackers

H. Zha, R.-i. Taniguchi, and S. Maybank (Eds.): ACCV 2009, Part III, LNCS 5996, pp. 21–32, 2010.
© Springer-Verlag Berlin Heidelberg 2010

Fig. 1. Image verification on ACCV2009 registration page

in the recent years. The approach breaking verifications contains two steps: segmentation and recognition. The proposed algorithms [1,2] lay more attentions on the latter but ignore the importance of segmentation. Recently, Chellapilla et al. [3] point out that there are no effective general algorithm to segment image verifications. For this purpose, we propose an segmentation algorithm to achieve the more robust performance in defeating the image verification.

Nowadays, geometric active contour, introduced by Caselles et al [4] and Malladi et al [5], is a widely used image segmentation method. This model, compared to parametric active contour developed by Kass et al. [6], has a better performance to noisy images, mainly because it is capable to automatically handle topological changes. In [7], Chan and Vese present a new level set formulation based on Mumford-Shan model. It concerns the region information instead of the image gradient so that even discontinuous edges can be detected successfully.

Although these contour models show a good performance against the light noise, experiments show that the contour evolution may be corrupted in some strong noise conditions. Thus, in order to improve the robustness of the active contour model in noisy situation, researchers propose different energy terms in two components of the model, internal and external energy (called as E_{int} or E_{ext}). Luo et al. [8] reformulate a new internal energy E_{int} to serve the contour smoothness and a scheme to switch between the region pressure force and the edge force in different phrases. Unlike the internal energy associated with the general contour properties, the external energy tightly corresponds to the image being segmented. In [9], the external energy term E_{ext} is determined by a statistical approach based on the optimal estimation theory. In segmenting images, the algorithm estimates not only the most likely shape of the object but also the optimal parameters for probability distribution function. Regarding its deficiency in handling polygonal-shape objects with arbitrary topology or a group of disconnected objects, the level set version of this probabilistic framework is presented in [10]. However, such algorithm still requires manual selection of the appropriate probability model for the noise distribution. In addition, it cannot handle the non-exponential family noise, such as salt and pepper noise.

Besides on-line estimating the probability function, the off-line analysis on the set of sample shapes generates a shape constraint to drive the level set function to the most likely object shape [11,12]. In order to overcome the limitation in the shape similarity, Cremers et al. [13] design a labeling function to recognize the object shape and introduce a particular shape prior and a set of pose parameters.

Although these approaches based on shape prior model can efficiently extract the object shape from different clutter and enjoy the robustness to noise, they can only work when the variation of object shape is small. As to the case with large changes, like image verification, whose contents are often generated randomly and contain different types of noise, the off-line analysis can hardly get enough samples and is no longer suitable. Therefore, on-line statistical strategy is still more popular than off-line methods.

The above-mentioned contour models mainly focus on the intensity or shape, but the statistical properties of gradient can provide richer information to improve the contour model's robustness. In gradient-considered models, such as snake and geometric active contour, a gradient function is employed to take the image gradient as the parameter and compute the contour external energy, When the evolving curve is close to the object boundary, the large gradient along the boundary makes the function close to 0, which decelerates its movement until it reaches the real object boundary. However, it is not an optimal choice to generalize this function from clear images to noisy images, because they have different gradient distributions. In noisy images, the strong noise with large gradient will be mistakenly considered as the boundary and prohibits the contour from propelling, which leads to a wrong convergence result.

An ideal way for the contour evolution should be propelling quickly in the region within small gradient, while stopping immediately when it encounters the object boundary. However, the current gradient function is deficient and problems lie in: First, the function descents quickly in the 0 neighborhood, which makes the contour unable to evolve fast enough in the region with small gradient. Second, noise pixels usually have a larger gradient than non-boundary pixels, but smaller than boundary ones. The function decreases slowly on the median region, so it only enhances the noise interference in the procedure of evolution. Finally, because the gradient magnitude is finite and its reciprocal can never reach 0, the active contour will never stop evolving even if it reaches the object boundary. To solve such problems, a rational and comprehensive way to construct the gradient function is worth researching.

In this paper, a new statistical method is proposed to generate the gradient function which can truly describe the relationship between the gradient magnitude of pixel and the boundary of object. At first, the image gradient distribution is modeled as gamma mixed models (GaMM) with three components to approximate the distribution of non-edge, edge and noise respectively. Then, we employ Expectation Maximization (EM) scheme to estimate all unknown parameters of the model and calculate the posterior probability belonging to the edge. Based on this probability function, a new gradient function is defined; and after integrating this new function, the active contour model can greatly improve the algorithm's robustness. Compared to statistical framework that can be applied only in the case of the exponential family, our function is effective in non-exponential noise conditions without the prior knowledge of noise distributions. Unlike shape prior framework, the new method does not need the procedure of pre-training, and such on-line method can save considerable resources as well.

2   Gradient Distribution Model and Its Solution

In many literatures, researchers consider images as discrete random variables and propose different probability models over image spaces. In earlier time, the gray image was modeled as Gaussian mixture models for its veracity [14]. As for the gradient histogram, the peak shape is more similar to the gamma model than the Gaussian model. Therefore, Henstock and Chelberg [15] assumed the gradient histogram as the weighted sum of two gamma densities.

Although GaMM with two components can distinctly describe the gradient distribution in certain degrees, it cannot precisely approximate the image properties, especially for noisy images. When the images are modeled as non-edge and edge parts, the noise is not taken into account, so such assumption will greatly impair its efficiency in the case of image verification based on noise, which is the main research object in this paper. In addition, the traditional maximum likelihood (ML) method is used to estimate parameters in GaMM[12]. In fact, ML is suitable for the single distribution rather than mixed distributions.

2.1   Probability Model for Gradient Distribution

To overcome limitations of the GaMM with two parts, we extend it to three components:

$$G(x) = w_1 \frac{x^{\alpha_1-1}e^{-x/\beta_1}}{\Gamma(\alpha_1)\beta_1^{\alpha_1}} + w_2 \frac{x^{\alpha_2-1}e^{-x/\beta_2}}{\Gamma(\alpha_2)\beta_2^{\alpha_2}} + w_3 \frac{x^{\alpha_3-1}e^{-x/\beta_3}}{\Gamma(\alpha_3)\beta_3^{\alpha_3}} \tag{1}$$

where x is the gradient magnitude, $\Gamma(\alpha) = \int_0^\infty t^{\alpha-1}e^{-t}dt, \alpha > 0$ and $w_1 + w_2 + w_3 = 1$. Since GaMM are multi-distribution mixture models, EM algorithm, which estimates values of parameters set $\{w_l, \alpha_l, \beta_l; l = 1, 2, 3\}$ in Eq.(1) to approximate the image gradient distribution, is more rational and reliable than ML algorithm.

2.2   Likelihood Function in EM

In 1977, Dempster et al [16] proposed EM method to iteratively estimate model's parameters by maximizing the likelihood function. The whole process follows two steps: the E-step that computes the distribution of the hidden variable and the M-step that maximizes the object function. The hidden variable is calculated by the assumption that model parameters are correct in E-step; and then the M-step re-estimates those parameters. The convergence of iterative process has been proved in [17].

The object function in M-step to be maximized is defined as

$$Q(\Theta, \Theta^g) = E[log(G(x|\Theta))|x, \Theta^g] \tag{2}$$

where Θ denotes the unknown parameter set $\{w_l, \alpha_l, \beta_l; l = 1, 2, 3\}$ and Θ^g is the current parameter set. The new parameter set Θ in the next iteration should maximize the function Q, i.e., $\Theta = \underset{\Theta}{\operatorname{argmax}} Q(\Theta, \Theta^g)$.

Considering the discrete case and the probability model defined in Eq.(1), the object function can be rewritten as:

$$Q(\Theta, \Theta^g) = \sum_{l=1}^{3} \sum_{i=1}^{N} log(w_l) p(l|x_i, \Theta^g) + \sum_{l=1}^{3} \sum_{i=1}^{N} log(p_l(x_i|\theta_l)) p(l|x_i, \Theta^g) \quad (3)$$

where N represents the number of samples or the total number of pixels in the image specifically. θ_l is the gamma parameters set $\{\alpha_l, \beta_l\}$ of the l-th distribution. $p(l|x_i, \Theta^g)$ is the posterior probability that the i-th sample x_i belongs to part l.

The first term and the second term in Eq.(3) are functions of weight parameters w_l and gamma parameters θ_l respectively. Because of their independence, the object function will reach its maximum whenever the two parts reach their maximum at the same time.

2.3   Estimation of Weighted Parameters

Under the constraint of $\sum_{l=1}^{3} w_l = 1$, Lagrange multiplier λ is introduced to construct a function:

$$L(w_1, w_2, w_3) = \sum_{l=1}^{3} \sum_{i=1}^{N} log(w_l) p(l|x_i, \Theta^g) + \lambda(\sum_{l=1}^{3} w_l - 1) \quad (4)$$

The partial derivative for each w_l is

$$\frac{\partial L}{\partial w_l} = \sum_{i=1}^{N} \frac{1}{w_l} p(l|x_i, \Theta^g) + \lambda \quad (5)$$

Notice, λ should be $-N$ under the constraint of w_l, so $Q(\Theta, \Theta^g)$ can get its maximum when $w_l = (\sum_{i=1}^{N} p(l|x_i, \Theta^g))/N$.

2.4   Estimation of Gamma Parameters

In the second term of Eq.(3), $p_l(x_i|\theta_l)$ represents the l-th gamma component in GaMM, i.e., $p_l(x_i|\theta_l) = \frac{x^{\alpha_l-1} e^{-x/\beta_l}}{\Gamma(\alpha_l)\beta_l^{\alpha_l}}$. This term can be simplified as a function of α_l and β_l:

$$f(\alpha_l, \beta_l) = \sum_{i=1}^{N} p(l|x_i, \Theta^g)[X_1(\alpha_l - 1) - X_2/\beta_l - (log\Gamma(\alpha_l) + \Gamma log\beta_l)] \quad (6)$$

where $\sum_{i=1}^{N} p(l|x_i, \Theta^g)$ is a scale factor, and remains constant to the variables α_l and β_l. X_1 and X_2 are expressed as:

$$X_1 = (\sum_{i=1}^{N} log(x_i) p(l|x_i, \Theta^g)) / \sum_{i=1}^{N} p(l|x_i, \Theta^g)$$

$$X_2 = (\sum_{i=1}^{N} x_i p(l|x_i, \Theta^g)) / \sum_{i=1}^{N} p(l|x_i, \Theta^g)$$

It is only necessary to compute the maximum value of the term in square bracket by taking partial derivative:

$$\frac{\partial f}{\partial \alpha_l} = (X_1 - \frac{\partial(log\Gamma(\alpha_l))}{\partial \alpha_l} - log\beta_l) \tag{7}$$

$$\frac{\partial f}{\partial \beta_l} = \frac{1}{\beta_l^2}(X_2 - \alpha_l \beta_l) \tag{8}$$

Letting Eq(7) and Eq.(8) be 0, we can get $\beta_l = X_2/\alpha_l$, so Eq.(7) can be rewritten as

$$g(\alpha_l) = logX_2 - X_1 \tag{9}$$

where $g(\alpha_l) = log\alpha_l - \frac{\partial(log\Gamma(\alpha_l))}{\partial \alpha_l}$.

It has been proved that g decreases monotonically from ∞ to 0 between the interval of $(0, \infty)$. That is to say, Eq.(4) has a unique solution in $(0, \infty)$. Since $g(\alpha_l)$ is a transcendental equation about α_l and solving $\Gamma(\alpha_l)$ is relatively difficult, we have to use its approximate solution instead.

In 1982, Lawless proposed an empirical formula to solve this transcendental equation, by which the error can be less than 0.0001. It is expressed as:

$$\tilde{\alpha} = \begin{cases} \frac{(0.5000876+0.1648852Y-0.0544274Y^2)}{Y} & 0 < Y \le C \\ \frac{8.898919+9.059950Y+0.9775373Y^2}{17.79728Y+11.968477Y^2+Y^3} & C < Y \le 17 \end{cases} \tag{10}$$

where $Y = logX_2 - X_1$. By this approximation formula, the solution of Eq.(9) can be obtained quickly. Afterwards, we plug $\tilde{\alpha}$ into Eq.(8) to solve the other gamma parameter $\tilde{\beta}$.

3   Constructing the New Gradient Function

After the gradient distribution is divided into three independent parts: non-edge, edge and noise, we can obtain the posterior probability of the pixel belonging to any parts. Among three posterior probabilities, the one belonging to the edge is especially important for segmenting image verifications.

3.1   Gradient Function Based on Posterior Probability

It is assumed that the gradient magnitude of edge is larger than that of non-edge and noise. Therefore, the gamma distribution of edge has the largest mean value among three components, and we select $k = \underset{l}{\operatorname{argmax}}(\alpha_l \beta_l)$ to represent the edge distribution and calculate the posterior probability belonging to the edge.

$$p(edge|x) = \frac{p(x|edge)}{p(x)}p(edge) = \frac{w_k x^{\alpha_k-1} e^{-x/\beta_k}}{\Gamma(\alpha_k)\beta_k^{\alpha_k} G(x)}p(edge) \tag{11}$$

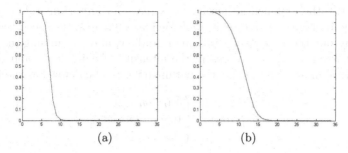

Fig. 2. (a) and (b) Illustrate the new gradient function under light noise and strong noise respectively

Usually, the relatively large and small gradient can be considered as edge and non-edge respectively, but it is still hard to quantify the relationship between the gradient and the edge. The posterior probability $p(edge|x)$, however, can exactly interpret such uncertain phenomenon from the view of statistics theory and expresses the likelihood that the pixel with the gradient magnitude x would be an edge pixel.

The range of probability function $p(edge|x)$ is $[0, 1]$, same as the range of the traditional gradient function. Because of the monotone increasing property with x, it does not meet what active models require for the gradient function. For this reason, we define a new gradient function based on the posterior probability as

$$\bar{g}(x) = 1 - p(edge|x)^s \qquad (12)$$

The shape of $\bar{g}(x)$ shown in Fig.2 is similar to the step function mirrors to the Y-axis; and 1 and 0 in vertical direction correspond to the small and large gradient respectively. Furthermore, it is an adaptive function, whose decreasing interval can vary according to the noise intensity. When the image noise strengthens, the decreasing interval shifts to the right along the axis, and the interval width increases as well.

Compared to the traditional function, the new function has three advantages: Firstly, its value remains 1 around the gradient of 0, which enables the active contour to propagate at highest rate even in small gradient area; Secondly, our function falls down quickly in the median area so that it can reduce the effect of noise to minimum; Finally, when gradient is large, $p(edge|x)$ equals to $G(x)$ and $\bar{g}(x)$ will reach 0, so the contour evolution can stop thoroughly.

3.2   Self Adapting Parameter s

Although we have assumed in the section 3.1 that the gradient magnitude of noise is weaker than that of edge, the stronger noise can still conceal the blur boundary and lead to a wrong segmentation result. As the noise in image verification becomes stronger, such problem can be more serious. In this case, the evolution speed should slow down for the whole contour.

In Eq.(12), the exponential parameter s plays an important role in controlling the speed of curve evolution as well. When s increases, the speed accelerates accordingly but the boundary with small gradient may be missing in the final result. Let $ion = \mathrm{mid}(\alpha_l \beta_l)$ represent the intensity of noise (ion), and by intensive testing in many experiments the parameter s can be defined as the function of ion:

$$s = f(ion) = \begin{cases} 1.0 & ion < 3 \\ 0.5 & 3 \le ion < 4 \\ 0.2 & ion \ge 4 \end{cases} \tag{13}$$

4 Experiments

As analyzed before, our algorithm will consume extra time to construct the new function; however, the proper analysis for the image gradient will lead a robust performance in the evolving process. Since the computing process is based on the gradient histogram, the construction of gradient function will be unrelated to the image size. Furthermore, our function is just a new gradient function; and it does not need to change the energy terms in active contour model. That is to say, most models can integrate this new gradient function to improve the robustness. Currently, the relative new Li model [18] extends on the basis of the Chan-Vese model [7] without necessity to re-initialize repeatedly, and can be realized by highly efficient narrow band scheme method, so it will be applied as the active contour model in our experiments. Some simple image verifications are produced by common noises, such as Gaussian noise. Under strong noise, it is a tough task to extract the region of characters and digits for most segmentation algorithm, even for the active contour model. Fig. 3 depicts the curve evolution for the image verifications based on different noise (the noise types, from top to bottom, are Gaussian, Poisson and salt-pepper respectively). The traditional

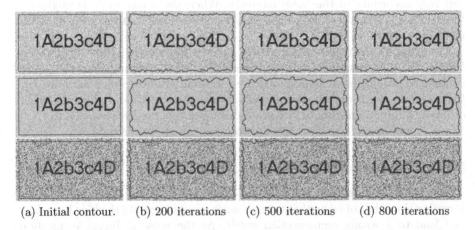

(a) Initial contour.   (b) 200 iterations   (c) 500 iterations   (d) 800 iterations

Fig. 3. Results of the traditional gradient function for image verifications based on Gaussian, gamma and salt-pepper noise (from top to bottom)

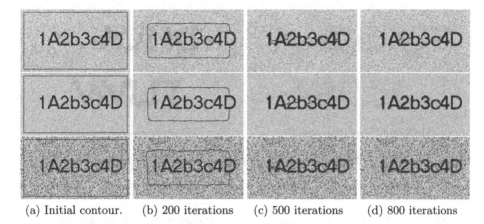

(a) Initial contour.   (b) 200 iterations   (c) 500 iterations   (d) 800 iterations

Fig. 4. Results of our gradient function for image verifications based on Gaussian, gamma and salt-pepper noise (from top to bottom)

gradation function gives the pixel with strong noise a rather small value due to its large gradient magnitude, which stalls the contour evolution.

Our gradient function, however, is constructed by fitting the gradient histogram and calculating the posterior probability of the edge. By this means, it can discriminate the true boundary from noise and define the appropriate function value to reduce the negative effect of noise. After integrating the new gradient function, active contour model is able to handel the strong noise in image verification and march fast in the noise region. As shown in Fig. 4, the contour with the help of our gradient function can quickly converge to the

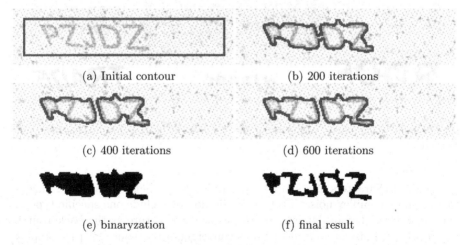

(a) Initial contour   (b) 200 iterations

(c) 400 iterations   (d) 600 iterations

(e) binaryzation   (f) final result

Fig. 5. (a) Is the original image verification with initial contour. (b), (c) and (d) are contour evolution based on our method after 200, 400 and 600 iterations. (e) is the result after binaryzation, (f) is the result after threshold segmentation and morphological.

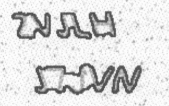

(a) Contour evolution results   (b) Post-processing results

Fig. 6. (a) and (b) Show the results after contour evolution and post-processing respectively

Fig. 7. Some other image verifications and their segmentation results based on our method

boundary of characters in a short time. In high-level image verification, images contain more complex noise. They generally do not include one specific type of noise mentioned before, but mixture types or even texture as the background. Fig. 5 (a) -(d) illustrate our algorithm's convergence procedure for the complex image verification, which is obtained from ACCV2009 registration page. After the curve reaches the character's boundary, we apply binaryzation for the region outside the boundary and the region inside, which is shown in (e). However, some of characters contain loops, such as "D"; and further processes are needed to handle such problem. Here we use threshold segmentation and morphological operator to generate the final result, shown in (f). In addition, the results of other two image verifications from the same web page are illustrated in Fig.6.

We collect more image verifications from different Internet websites. For these image verification based on noise, the proposed algorithm can effectively extract the character regions in these images. The experimental results, illustrated in Fig. 7 (the upper and the lower rows are the boundary result and the final result), indicate again that such kind of image verification simply based on noise can be segmented efficiently, which makes the secure method rather vulnerable and should be applied with caution.

Till now, the above experiments have shown the effectiveness of our algorithm towards noise-based image verification. On the other hand, the processing time is crucial for the segmenting algorithm. The experiments are carried out on a PC with Core 2 processor, 1.86 GHz, 1GB RAM, with Matlab 6, on Windows XP. For a 200×50 image, the average time spent in constructing our gradient function is about 78ms, and the whole processing time is about 1.93s.

5 Conclusion

In this work, a new gradient function for active contour models is proposed to improve the segmentation robustness. Firstly, we employ the GaMM to approximate the image gradient distribution, in which contains three components that represent edge, noise and non-edge, respectively. Secondly, after the GaMM parameters are estimated by EM algorithm, the posterior probability belonging to the edge can be obtained by Bayesian theory. Finally, a new gradient function is proposed to replace the traditional gradient function. Experiments have shown that this new function can be successively applied to segment noise-based image verification in websites. We expect our research can provide web designers some inspiration so that they can further improve their secure methods used in websites.

References

1. Mori, G., Malik, J.: Recognizing Objects in Adversarial Clutter: Breaking a Visual CAPTCHA. In: Conf. Computer Vision and Pattern Recognition, vol. 1, pp. 134–141 (2003)
2. Moy, G., Jones, N., Harkless, C.: Distortion Estimation Techniques in Solving Visual CAPTCHAs. In: Conf. Computer Vision and Pattern Recognition, vol. 2, pp. 23–28 (2004)
3. Chellapilla, K., Larson, K., Simard, P., Czerwinski, M.: Computers Beat Humans at Single Character Recognition in Reading Based Human Interaction Proofs (HIPs). In: Proceeding. E-Mail and Anti-Spam (2005)
4. Caselles, V., Kimmel, R., Sapiro, G.: Geodesic active contours. Int. Journal Computer Vision 22(1), 61–79 (1997)

5. Malladi, R., Sethian, J.A., Vemuri, B.C.: Shape modeling with front propagation: a level set approach. IEEE Trans. Pattern Analysis and Machine Intelligence 17(2), 158–175 (1995)
6. Kass, M., Witkin, A., Terzopoulos, D.: Snakes: active contour models. Int. Journal Computer Vision 1, 321–331 (1987)
7. Chan, T., Vese, L.: Active contours without edges. IEEE Trans. Image Processing 10(2), 266–277 (2001)
8. Luo, H., Lu, Q., Acharya, R., Gaborski, R.: Robust Snake Model. In: Conf. Computer Vision and Pattern Recognition, vol. 1, pp. 1–6 (2002)
9. Chesnaud, C., Refregier, P., Boulet, V.: Statistical Region Snake-Based Segmentation Adapted to Different Physical Noise Models. IEEE Trans. Pattern Analysis and Machine Intelligence 21(11), 1145–1157 (1999)
10. Martin, P., Refregier, P., Goudail, F., Guerault, F.: Influence of the Noise Model on Level Set Active Contour Segmentation. IEEE Trans. Pattern Analysis and Machine Intelligence 26(6), 799–803 (2004)
11. Leventon, M., Grimson, W., Faugeras, O.: Statistical shape influence in geodesic active contours. In: Conf. Computer Vision and Pattern Recognition, vol. 1, pp. 316–323 (2000)
12. Tsai, A., Yezzi, A., Wells, W., Tempany, C., Tucker, D., Fan, A., Grimson, E., Willsky, A.: Model-based curve evolution technique for image segmentation. In: Conf. Computer Vision and Pattern Recognition, vol. 1, pp. 463–468 (2001)
13. Cremers, D., Sochen, N., Schnorr, C.: A multiphase dynamic labeling model for variational recognition-driven image segmentation. Int. Journal Computer Vision 66(1), 67–81 (2006)
14. Lalit, G., Thotsapon, S.: A Gaussian mixture based image segmentation algorithm. Pattern Recognition 31(3), 315–325 (1998)
15. Henstock, P.V., Chelberg, D.M.: Automatic gradient threshold determination for edge detection. IEEE Trans. Image Processing 5(5), 784–787 (1996)
16. Dempster, A.P., Laird, N.M., Rubin, D.B.: Maximum-likelihood from incomplete data via the EM algorithm. Journal of Royal Statistical Society Series B 39(1), 1–38 (1977)
17. Wu, C.F.: On the convergence properties of the EM algorithm. The Annals of Statistics 11(1), 95–103 (1983)
18. Li, C.M., Xu, C.Y., Gui, C.F., Fox, M.D.: Level Set Evolution Without Re-initialization: A New Variational Formulation. In: Conf. Computer Vision and Pattern Recognition, vol. 1, pp. 430–436 (2005)

Refined Exponential Filter with Applications to Image Restoration and Interpolation

Yanlin Geng[1], Tong Lin[1], Zhouchen Lin[2], and Pengwei Hao[1,3]

[1] Center for Information Science, Peking Univ., Beijing 100871, China
{gengyanlin,lintong,phao}@cis.pku.edu.cn
[2] Microsoft Research Asia, Zhichun Road #49, Haidian, Beijing 100190, China
zhoulin@microsoft.com
[3] Dept. of Computer Science, Queen Mary, Univ. of London, London E1 4NS, UK
phao@dcs.qmul.ac.uk

Abstract. Ill-posed linear equations are pervasive in computer vision. A popular way to solve an ill-posed problem is regularization. In this paper, we propose a new criterion for designing the regularizing filter. This criterion reveals the implicit assumption made by regularizing filters. Then with the help of the discrete Picard condition, we refine the exponential filter using our criterion. The effectiveness of our method is demonstrated on image restoration and interpolation.

1 Introduction

Computer vision involves many ill-posed problems [1], such as image restoration, edge detection, optical flow, motion estimation, and surface reconstruction. According to [2], a well-posed problem has three properties: existence, uniqueness and stability of the solution; if any one of these properties does not hold, the problem is ill-posed.

Regularization is a prevailing method to solve ill-posed problems. Based on the methods used, there are mainly three approaches to regularization: optimization, filtering and iterative methods. The first method is actually Tikhonov method [3] and has a Bayesian interpretation; the second one utilizes the spectrum of the problem and devotes to tailoring a suitable filter; the third method settles the problem using an iterative process, and in fact the number of iterations plays the role of regularization. These three methods are closely related, especially under L_2 norm. In this paper we mainly focus on the filtering approach. Before that we would like to introduce Tikhonov regularization.

Many ill-posed problems come from a first kind Fredholm integral equation [4]

$$\int K(x,t)f(t)dt = g(x) . \tag{1}$$

And they can be discretized as linear equations of the form

$$Ax = b . \tag{2}$$

H. Zha, R.-i. Taniguchi, and S. Maybank (Eds.): ACCV 2009, Part III, LNCS 5996, pp. 33–42, 2010.

Based on the idea of balancing the residual and some apriori constraint on the solution, Tikhonov regularization [3] finds the solution by minimizing

$$J(x) := \|b - Ax\|^2 + \alpha[\Omega(x)]^2 . \tag{3}$$

The constraint $\Omega(x)$ ensures the stability of the solution, while the regularization parameter α controls the closeness between the original and the new equation. Thus two important issues in regularization are choosing proper constraints and finding the optimal parameters.

Basically speaking, a proper constraint should penalize what we do not want the solution to exhibit. And there has already been a lot of work on choosing the constraint $\Omega(x)$. For example, ordinary Tikhonov regularization (oTik) takes the constraint as $\|x\|_2$, which restricts the size of the solution. For image restoration, Phillips [5] proposed to use $\|Lx\|_2$, where L is the Laplace operator. This assumes small differences in luminance between neighboring pixels. As a variance, it was shown in [6] that using the total variation can preserve edges better than $\|Lx\|_2$. For sparse solution, lasso [7] suggests using $\|x\|_1$. Although each kind of term has a meaningful interpretation, an interesting question is that, how can we refine the constraint that is being used?

To facilitate the analysis, we consider the filtering approach, which makes use of the spectrum of A. Some exemplar filters include the exponential filter (Exp) [8], modified Tikhonov regularization (MTR) [9], spatial regularization [10], and so on. These methods usually design a filter heuristically: they just modify the filter to satisfy certain subjective request.

In this work, using backward error analysis, we propose a criterion for designing the regularizing filter. This criterion shows that there is a relationship between the constraint and the problem itself (*e.g.*, A and b). We further study the characteristic of a solvable problem, namely the Picard condition [11]; then we show how the Picard condition helps refine the filter for a specific constraint.

2   Designing the Regularizing Filter

In this section, we first introduce the regularizing filter, then we propose our criterion. To make use of the criterion, we consider the Picard condition and show how to refine the exponential filter. For the notation, throughout the paper, we use A_i as the i-th column of a matrix A and b_i as the i-th element of a vector b. Without special clarification, the norm used is the L_2 norm.

2.1   The Regularizing Filter

To solve $Ax = b$, the least squares method minimizes the residual $R(x) = \|b - Ax\|^2$ and the solution is $x = (A^T A)^\dagger A^T b$, where $\dagger$ is the Moore-Penrose pseudo inverse. Suppose the singular value decomposition (SVD) is $A = USV^T$, where U and V are unitary matrices, S is a diagonal matrix with its diagonal elements $s_i \geq 0$ called the singular values; then the solution can be expressed as

$$x = VS^\dagger U^T b =: VS^\dagger \beta = \sum_i \beta_i s_i^{-1} V_i . \tag{4}$$

where $\beta := U^T b$ is called the *Fourier coefficients*.

However, when the small nonzero singular values of A decay gradually to zero, this solution can bias greatly from an acceptable one. This is because in practice, b is often contaminated by noise, thus a very small s_i tends to amplify the noise enormously. In this sense, the problem is ill-posed. To solve this ill-posedness, oTik minimizes $J(x) = \|b - Ax\|^2 + \lambda^2 \|x\|^2$, and the solution is

$$x = \sum s_i^2 (s_i^2 + \lambda^2)^{-1} \beta_i s_i^{-1} V_i =: \sum q_{\text{otik}}(\lambda, s_i) \beta_i s_i^{-1} V_i . \tag{5}$$

Compared to the least squares solution, this solution involves a low pass filter

$$q_{\text{otik}}(\lambda, s) = s^2 (s^2 + \lambda^2)^{-1} , \tag{6}$$

thus noises in high frequencies are restrained. That is why $q(\lambda, s)$ is called the *regularizing filter* [4]; and these $q_i = q(\lambda, s_i)$ are called the *filter factors*.

For a general constraint $\|Lx\|$, let $y = Lx$, we can transform the problem of minimizing $J(x) = \|b - Ax\|^2 + \lambda^2 \|Lx\|^2$ into oTik

$$\min \tilde{J}(y) = \|b - AL^\dagger y\|^2 + \lambda^2 \|y\|^2 . \tag{7}$$

To obtain the filter in this case, we need the generalized SVD of (A, L)

$$A = U \Xi X^{-1} , \quad L = V M X^{-1} , \tag{8}$$

where X is invertible, U and V are orthonormal, Ξ and M are diagonal matrices with the diagonals being ξ and μ, respectively. So $AL^\dagger = U \Xi M^{-1} V^T =: USV^T$, where $S := \Xi M^{-1}$ is a diagonal matrix with its diagonal elements $s_i := \xi_i \mu_i^{-1}$ called the generalized singular values. According to Eqn.(5), we have the solution as $y = \sum q_{\text{otik}}(\lambda, s_i) \beta_i s_i^{-1} V_i$; and substitute this into $x = L^\dagger y$, we obtain

$$x = \sum q_{\text{otik}}(\lambda, s_i) \beta_i \xi_i^{-1} X_i . \tag{9}$$

In the solution above[1], $q_{\text{otik}}(\lambda, s)$ is also called the regularizing filter, where s_i are the generalized singular values.

2.2   Criterion for Designing the Filter

In practice b is often corrupted by noise η, thus we should not solve $Ax = b$ directly. To eliminate the noise, we introduce a perturbation term E and solve $(A + E)x = b + \eta$ instead. This is motivated by the method of backward error analysis in numerical analysis. As the true solution satisfies $Ax = b$, our goal is to find a proper E that is expected to satisfy $Ex = \eta$.

From Eqn.(4), the solution to the exact equation $Ax = b$ is $x = VS^\dagger \beta$, so we get $\eta = EVS^\dagger \beta$. Suppose the variance matrices of η and β are $\sigma^2 I$ and CC^T respectively, we have

$$\sigma^2 I = var(\eta) = var(EVS^\dagger \beta) = (EVS^\dagger C)(EVS^\dagger C)^T . \tag{10}$$

---

[1] If L is rank deficient, an extra $x_0 = \sum_{i>\text{rank}(L)} \beta_i X_i$ should be added to Eqn.(9).

Table 1. Comparison of several filters

Methods	Filter q	Coefficients $|\beta| \propto$
oTik [3]	$s^2(s^2 + \lambda^2)^{-1}$	$s^2\lambda^{-2}$
Exp [8]	$1 - \exp\{-s^2\lambda^{-2}\}$	$\exp\{s^2\lambda^{-2}\} - 1$
MTR [9]	$s^2(s^{2\sigma} + \lambda^{2\sigma})^{-\frac{1}{\sigma}}$	$s^2\{(s^{2\sigma} + \lambda^{2\sigma})^{\frac{1}{\sigma}} - s^2\}^{-1}$

This leads to $E = \sigma W C^\dagger S V^T$, where W is an arbitrary orthonormal matrix. Due to the arbitrariness, we may set $W = U$ and obtain

$$E = \sigma U C^\dagger S V^T . \tag{11}$$

With this estimate of E, we are going to solve $U(I + \sigma C^\dagger)SV^Tx = b$. For a general β, suppose its elements are independent (thus C is diagonal), then the solution is

$$x = \sum \frac{1}{1 + \sigma c_i^{-1}} \frac{\beta_i}{s_i} V_i , \tag{12}$$

where c is the diagonal of C. This solution suggests taking the filter as $q_i = (1 + \sigma c_i^{-1})^{-1}$, which results in $c_i = \sigma q_i(1 - q_i)^{-1}$. Notice that $var(\beta) = CC^T$, we arrive at *our criterion for designing regularizing filter*

$$|\beta_i| \approx \sigma q_i(1 - q_i)^{-1} \propto q_i(1 - q_i)^{-1} . \tag{13}$$

Our criterion suggests that the filter should be designed closely related to the Fourier coefficients $\beta = U^T b$. With this criterion, we can also analyze what a filter models β.

2.3   Using the Picard Condition

According to our criterion $|\beta_i| \approx \sigma q_i(1 - q_i)^{-1}$, a filter q can be designed by modeling β. However, it is difficult to model a general β. Here we consider this problem in the viewpoint of the Picard condition, which is essential for solving an ill-posed problem [11].

The Picard Condition. Suppose the kernel K in Eqn.(1) has a singular value expansion $K(x,t) = \sum s_i u_i(x) v_i(t)$, and $\beta_i := \langle u_i, g \rangle$ are the coefficients. In order that the problem is solvable, the Picard condition requires that [11] $\sum_{i=1}^{\infty}(\beta_i s_i^{-1})^2 < \infty$. While discretized, the Picard condition desires that *the elements of β decay faster than the corresponding singular values on the average*.

In Table 1, we compare some existing filters, most of which assume that $|\beta_i| \propto s_i^2$. This ad hoc setting requires that β_i decays as fast as s_i^2; while the Picard condition desires that β_i decays faster than s_i.

Our Filter 'rExp'. Inspired by the exponential filter, we propose to model

$$|\beta_i| \approx \sigma(\exp\{s_i^\rho\lambda^{-\rho}\} - 1) \quad \text{with} \quad \rho > 1 , \tag{14}$$

$$q_{\text{rexp}}(\lambda, s) = 1 - \exp\{-s^\rho\lambda^{-\rho}\} , \tag{15}$$

Algorithm 1. Choosing Parameters for rExp

---

1 Initialize $\rho = 2$ and estimate σ
2 Loop:
3   Find the optimal λ for $x = \sum (1 - \exp\{-s_i^\rho \lambda^{-\rho}\})\beta_i s_i^{-1} V_i$
4   Update $\rho \leftarrow \text{mean} \left| \ln\{\ln(|\beta_i|\sigma^{-1} + 1)\}/(\ln s_i - \ln \lambda) \right|$
5 End of Loop
6 Find the optimal λ for $x = \sum (1 - \exp\{-s_i^\rho \lambda^{-\rho}\})\beta_i s_i^{-1} V_i$

---

and denote it as the refined exponential filter (rExp). Here a free parameter ρ is incorporated so that we can better model β; and rather than setting it as 2 for convenience, we just require $\rho > 1$ so that the Picard condition is satisfied. In the following paragraph, we also provide an algorithm for determining ρ.

Choosing the Parameters. It is a crucial problem to choose a suitable parameter λ for all regularization schemes. Fortunately there have been several robust and popular ways. For example, L-curve [12] and generalized cross-validation (GCV) [13]. If the noise level is predictable, Morozov discrepancy principle [14] can also be used. Here we also provide an iterative method to choose ρ. With an initial $\rho = 2$, we obtain λ from one of the methods mentioned above. Then from $|\beta_i| \approx \sigma(\exp\{s_i^\rho \lambda^{-\rho}\} - 1)$, we arrive at

$$\rho \approx \text{mean} \left| \frac{\ln\{\ln(|\beta_i|\sigma^{-1} + 1)\}}{\ln s_i - \ln \lambda} \right| . \tag{16}$$

This procedure can be performed repeatedly until we get a proper ρ. The algorithm is summarized in Algorithm 1.

3   Experiments

In the experiments, we apply our method to image restoration and image interpolation. The test images shown in Figure 1 are the 24 Kodak Images[2].

3.1   Image Restoration

A blurred and noisy image can be modeled as $g = h * f + \eta$, where f is the original image, g is the observed image, h is the blurring kernel, $*$ denotes convolution and η is the additive noise. Image restoration is to recover the original image by solving $Hf = g$. In [5], Phillips proposed to minimize

$$\|g - Hf\|^2 + \lambda^2 \|Lf\|^2 , \tag{17}$$

where L is the Laplacian operator. In [6], the authors suggested to minimize $\|g - Hf\|^2 + \lambda^2 \|f\|_{TV}$, where $\|\cdot\|_{TV}$ denotes the total variation. With this kind

---

[2] http://r0k.us/graphics/kodak/

Fig. 1. The 24 Kodak Images used in our experiments

of constraint, edges can be preserved. This method was developed as 'scalar TV' and further as 'adaptive TV' methods [15].

In practice, we often deal with the Toeplitz matrices. A *block-circulant-circulant-block* (BCCB) matrix can be diagonalized very efficiently using *fast Fourier transform* (FFT). Suppose H and L are BCCB matrices, then we have $H = F\Xi F^*, L = FMF^*$, where F is the unitary discrete Fourier transform matrix. Similar to Eqn.(9), the solution is

$$x = \sum q(\lambda, s_i)\beta_i \xi_i^{-1} F_i \,, \tag{18}$$

where $\beta = F^*b$, namely applying the inverse Fourier transform to b.

In the experiment, the images are first degraded by a 3×3 average filter, and then corrupted by white Gaussian noise with a standard deviation $\sigma = 10$. During the restoration, the blurring kernel h is estimated using the method in [16]; H and L are constructed as BCCB matrices so that FFT can be used. We apply rExp to restore the images, followed by a Wiener filter to further reduce the noise. We compare our method with oTik, Exp [8], Wiener filter, and total variation methods (Scalar TV and Adaptive TV) [15]. The results are reported using the *peak signal-to-noise ratio* (PSNR)

$$PSNR = 10 \cdot \log_{10}\{MAX_I^2/MSE\} \,, \tag{19}$$

where MAX_I is the maximum possible pixel value for the image (255 for 8-bits images), and MSE is the mean square error for the original and restored images.

We show the PSNR on the restored images in Figure 2 and detail the average PSNR of each method in Table 2. Our method provides the highest average PSNR on the 24 images; and significant improvement is achieved compared with the exponential filter. We also plot the parameter ρ of our method in Figure 2, which illustrates the necessity of allowing ρ other than 2. For visual comparison,

Table 2. Average PSNR of the 24 restored Kodak images

Methods	oTik	Exp	Wiener	Scalar TV	Adaptive TV	rExp
PSNR	25.29	26.51	26.83	26.87	27.28	27.75

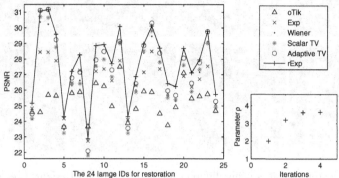

Fig. 2. (Left) PSNR of the 24 restored Kodak images. (Right bottom) The parameter ρ of rExp with respect to iterations on the 5-th Kodak image.

we show blowups of the restored images in Figure 3. It is clear that our method provides restored images visually comparable with Adaptive TV and better than other methods.

3.2 Image Interpolation

Image interpolation is used to render high-resolution images from low-resolution images. A low-resolution image can be modeled as $g = DHf + \eta$, where f and g are the lexicographic order of high-resolution images F and low-resolution images G, respectively. D and H are the matrices that model the decimation and the blurring processes, respectively.

An interesting interpolation algorithm is proposed in [17]. The main idea is to solve the problem using the Tikhonov regularization. Considering the huge sizes of H and D, the authors assume that these matrices are separable:

$$H = H_1 \otimes H_2 , \quad D = D_1 \otimes D_2 , \tag{20}$$

where $\otimes$ represents the Kronecker product. Thus the model is equivalent to

$$G = (D_2 H_2) F (D_1 H_1)^T + \eta . \tag{21}$$

Then with the aid of the Kronecker product and SVD, the computation cost can be reduced greatly. For example, if the decimation factor is 2, then we have

$$D_1 = \begin{bmatrix} 1\,0\,0\,0\,0\ldots \\ 0\,0\,1\,0\,0\ldots \\ 0\,0\,0\,0\,1\ldots \\ \vdots\,\vdots\,\vdots\,\vdots\,\vdots\,\ddots \end{bmatrix} , \quad H_1 = \begin{bmatrix} v_0 & v_1 & \ldots & v_{-1} \\ v_{-1} & v_0 & \ldots & v_{-2} \\ \vdots & \vdots & \ddots & \vdots \\ v_1 & v_2 & \ldots & v_0 \end{bmatrix} , \tag{22}$$

Fig. 3. The restored images using different methods. From left to right: (Top) Original image, Degraded image, oTik, Exp; (Bottom) Wiener, Scalar TV, Adaptive TV, rExp.

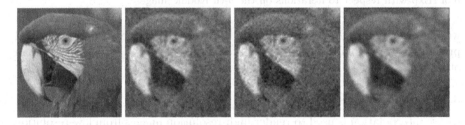

Fig. 4. The interpolated images using different methods. From left to right: Original image, Bicubic, oTik, rExp.

where $v = (v_{-k}, ..., v_{-1}, v_0, v_1, ..., v_k)^T$, and $h = uv^T$ is the blurring kernel. For a 3×3 mask, it is often assumed that $u = v = (a, 1 - 2a, a)^T$. Without any apriori information, we may set $a = 0.25$.

However, it is important to notice that, under the assumption of separability and with the selection of u and v above, the singular values of $D_1 H_1$ range from $|1 - 2a|$ to $\sqrt{(1 - 2a)^2 + 4a^2}$ (see Appendix A). Thus if a is not near 0.5, we can use iterative methods such as the steepest descent or the conjugate gradient to solve Eqn.(21). So we propose our method as follows. First we restore the noisy low-resolution image g using the method we have introduced in Section 3.1, then we employ the separability and solve the normal equation of Eqn.(21) to obtain the high-resolution image F.

In the experiment, we first blur F with a 3×3 average filter. Then we sub-sample the blurred image and add Gaussian noise with $\sigma = 10$ to construct G. We use our method and the method in [17] to compute image F, respectively. For more comparison, we also resize the image G using bicubic interpolation.

Table 3. Average PSNR of the 24 interpolated Kodak images

Methods	Bicubic	oTik	rExp
PSNR	25.04	24.82	25.85

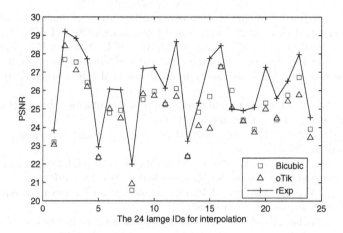

Fig. 5. PSNR of the 24 interpolated Kodak images

It is clear that our method outperforms other methods in both PSNR (Table 3 and Figure 5) and visual aspect (Figure 4).We believe that this benefits from the flexibility of ρ in our method.

4   Conclusions

In this paper, we suggest a criterion for designing the regularizing filter. By incorporating the Picard condition, we propose to refine the exponential filter. Our scheme works effectively for ill-posed problems, which has been demonstrated on image restoration and image interpolation.

References

1. Bertero, M., Poggio, T.A., Torre, V.: Ill-posed problems in early vision. Proc. of the IEEE 76(8), 869–889 (1988)
2. Hadamard, J.: Lectures on Cauchy's problem in linear partial differential equations. Courier Dover Publications (2003)
3. Tikhonov, A.N., Arsenin, V.Y.: Solutions of ill-posed problems. Wiley, New York (1977)
4. Kirsch, A.: An introduction to the mathematical theory of inverse problems. Springer, Heidelberg (1996)
5. Phillips, D.L.: A technique for the numerical solution of certain integral equations of the first kind. Journal of the ACM 9(1), 84–97 (1962)

6. Rudin, L., Osher, S., Fatemi, E.: Nonlinear total variation based noise removal algorithms. Physica D 60, 259–268 (1992)
7. Tibshirani, R.: Regression shrinkage and selection via the lasso. Journal of the Royal Statistical Society, Series B 58(1), 267–288 (1996)
8. Calvetti, D., Lewis, B., Reichel, L.: Smooth or abrupt: a comparison of regularization methods. In: Proc. SPIE, vol. 3461, pp. 286–295 (1998)
9. Li, G., Nashed, Z.: A modified Tikhonov regularization for linear operator equations. Numerical Functional Analysis and Optimization 26, 543–563 (2005)
10. Velipasaoglu, E.O., Sun, H., Zhang, F., Berrier, K.L., Khoury, D.S.: Spatial regularization of the electrocardiographic inverse problem and its application to endocardial mapping. IEEE Transactions on Biomedical Engineering 47(3), 327–337 (2000)
11. Hansen, P.C.: Rank-deficient and discrete ill-posed problems: numerical aspects of linear inversion. SIAM, Philadelphia (1999)
12. Hanke, M., Hansen, P.C.: Regularized methods for large scale problems. Surv. Math. Ind. 3, 253–315 (1993)
13. Golub, G.H., Heath, M., Wahba, G.: Generalized cross-validation as a method for choosing a good ridge parameter. Technometrics, 215–223 (1979)
14. Groetsch, C.W.: The theory of Tikhonov regularization for Fredholm equations of the first kind. Pitman, Boston (1984)
15. Gilboa, G., Sochen, N., Zeevi, Y.Y.: Texture preserving variational denoising using an adaptive fidelity term. In: Proc. VLSM, pp. 137–144 (2003)
16. Biggs, D.S.C., Andrews, M.: Acceleration of iterative image restoration algorithms. Appl. Opt. 36(8), 1766–1775 (1997)
17. Chen, L., Yap, K.H.: Regularized interpolation using Kronecker product for still images. In: Proc. ICIP, vol. 2, pp. 1014–1017 (2005)

Appendix

A   Spectrum of Decimated Toeplitz Matrices

Property. If A is the odd rows of a circulant Toeplitz matrix H

$$H = \begin{bmatrix} b & a & 0 & \dots & 0 & a \\ a & b & a & \dots & 0 & 0 \\ \vdots & \vdots & \vdots & \ddots & \vdots & \vdots \\ a & 0 & 0 & \dots & a & b \end{bmatrix} =: \mathrm{Toep}[b, a, 0, ..., 0, a] , \qquad (23)$$

then the singular values $\sigma(A) \subseteq [|b|, \sqrt{b^2 + 4a^2}]$.

Proof. With a proper permutation matrix P, we have $B := AP = [A_0\ A_1]$, where $A_0 = bI$, $A_1 = aJ$ with $J = \mathrm{Toep}[1, 0, ..., 0, 1]$. Then $BB^T = b^2I + a^2 JJ^T$. Notice $\|JJ^T\|_1 \le \|J\|_1 \|J^T\|_1 = 4$ and the maximum eigen-value $\lambda_{\max}(M) \le \|M\|_p$ for any $p \ge 1$, we get $\lambda(JJ^T) \subseteq [0, 4]$, which leads to $\lambda(BB^T) \subseteq [b^2, b^2 + 4a^2]$. Immediately we obtain that the singular values of B (also of A) range between $|b|$ and $\sqrt{b^2 + 4a^2}$.

Color Correction and Compression for Multi-view Video Using H.264 Features

Boxin Shi, Yangxi Li, Lin Liu, and Chao Xu

Key Laboratory of Machine Perception (Ministry of Education),
Peking University, Beijing, 100871, China
{shiboxin,liyangxi,liulin,xuchao}@cis.pku.edu.cn

Abstract. Multi-view video is a new video application requiring efficient coding algorithm to compress the huge data, while the color variations among different viewpoints deteriorate the visual quality of multi-view video. This paper deals with these two problems simultaneously focusing on color. With the spatial block-matching information from multi-view video coding, color annotated images can be produced given gray input in one view and color input in another view. Then the color images are rendered from colorization process. By discarding most of the chrominance information before encoding and restoring them when decoding, this novel scheme can greatly improve the compression rate without much loss in visual quality, while at the same time produce color images with similar appearance to reference without correction.

1 Introduction

With the improvement of technologies in image processing and computer vision, the "Second-generation image coding" [1] has raised great interest because of its higher potential in coding efficiency and closer relationship with perceptual quality. Different from traditional "transform + entropy coding" compression schemes relying on statistical redundancy, the "Second-generation image coding" focuses on visual redundancy by utilizing features within images and videos. One good example of this kind of system can be found in [2]. The coding efficiency was exploited by removing some parts of an image intentionally then transferred them in a compressed manner, and finally the whole image could be restored in the decoder side. This idea can be concluded as "encoder removes whereas decoder restores" [3], which motivates us in incorporating this next generation compression idea into the next generation video application—*Multi-view Video Coding* (MVC).

The multi-view video captured by a combination of synchronous cameras from different positions can provide people with more realistic experience. Some research groups have proposed several multi-view video systems such as free viewpoint television (FTV) [4] and 3DTV [5]. Although the multi-view video systems own many advantages over the current mono-view video systems, some problems have restricted the widely-use of this technology. First, since the multi-view video sequences are captured by many cameras at the same time, there are

H. Zha, R.-i. Taniguchi, and S. Maybank (Eds.): ACCV 2009, Part III, LNCS 5996, pp. 43–52, 2010.
© Springer-Verlag Berlin Heidelberg 2010

huge amount of data required to capture, process and transfer efficiently. Second, although the set of cameras has been adjusted to the same configuration as precisely as possible, it is still difficult to avoid the chrominance discrepancies among different viewpoints due to the scene illumination, camera calibration and jitter speed. In many cases, color correction has to be used as pre-processing to deal with this problem [6].

Before we introduce the improvement to the aforementioned two problems, we need to define the *reference view* and the *target view* according to their different functions in our scheme. The reference view is one designated camera view seen as having correct color and used as reference by other views when coding; while the target views are all the other views which are encoded referring to reference view. A special point in our scheme is that the reference view is color sequence and the target views are all gray sequences. Given these basic definitions, next we will summarize the solutions. The first problem can be improved because we combine the "encoder removes whereas decoder restores" idea with existed MVC scheme and exploit color redundancy by discarding all the chrominance information in target views before encoding. Then the color is left to be restored through our proposed *color annotation* and *colorization* strategy when decoding. Thus, the coding efficiency is further improved because of the discarded chrominance. Since color is restored as similar to reference as possible, the color similarity between different views are also guaranteed without color correction, which improves the second problem.

In order to implement such a scheme, two critical questions have to be answered in this paper: 1) How to produce the side information using codec to provide enough cues for colorization? 2) How to design the colorization method using the side information from codec to reconstruct the color image without deteriorating the visual quality? In the following we will give a description to our complete framework in Section 2, and the first question will be explained in detail in Section 3 while the second in Section 4. Section 5 is about the implementation issues and experiment results. Finally Section 6 comes as conclusion.

2   Framework of Proposed Scheme

The complete framework of our scheme is shown in Fig. 1. As it is illustrated in the legend in upper-left corner, blocks in different gray-scales are depicted to distinguish different views.

The state-of-the-art MVC scheme is based on H.264/AVC (using H.264 for short in the following statement), and coding efficiency is improved by exploiting not only the temporal motion redundancy between subsequent frames but also spatial motion redundancy between neighboring viewpoints. This solution can be seen as an extension of the traditional motion compensation to different viewpoints. Implementation of MVC schemes considering spatial prediction are introduced in [7] and [8]. In order to emphasize the color redundancy, we use a simplified prediction structure similar to [7] and [8], as it is shown in upper-right corner in Fig. 1. The reference view in our system not only serves as

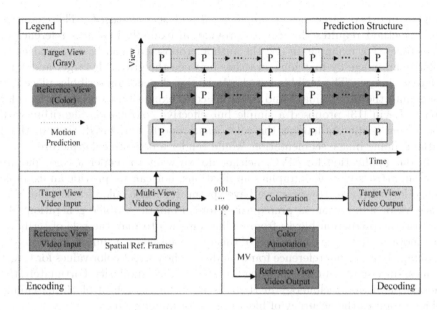

Fig. 1. The framework of our color correction and compression scheme

temporal/spatial reference for motion prediction, but also the spatial reference for color restoration. Mean while, in our scheme, *Motion Vectors* (MVs) not only take the responsibility of motion compensation for coding purposes, but also as side information for colorization. The corresponding blocks from reference views are utilized to indicate the chrominance values for target views according to their MVs from reference views, and this process is called color annotation. Finally the colorization technique will render the color annotated frame covered by partial color to one with complete color appearance.

3   Color Annotation Using H.264 Features

The emerging technology focusing on adding color to gray image provides the possibility of using color redundancy in video coding. In [9] the author succeeded in integrating color transfer [10] into coding pipeline, and improved the coding efficiency, but it was for mono-view video coding and until recently few researches have been done for MVC. On the other hand, current research did not consider utilizing the latest color restoration techniques as well as the advanced features in codec such as H.264. By exploring these current achievements, we find that H.264 codec can provide lot's of useful information to enhance color annotation process, which brings benefits to restoring better color quality.

3.1   Scribble-Based Colorization

The concept of colorization is often used in computer graphics referring to adding color to gray image. According to [11], the existed colorization method is roughly divided into two categories: *example-based* and *scribble-based* . The example-based method requires the user to provide an example image as reference of color tones. For example, in [12] the author proposed a pixel-based approach to colorize an image by matching swatches between the grayscale target and color reference images. The scribble-based colorization depends on scribbles placed by users onto the target image and performs color expansion to produce the color image. Levin [13] proposed a simple but effective colorization algorithm with convincing result. As long as the color was properly annotated, their method, without doing image segmentation, would render a delicate color picture.

In our application for MVC, neither do we want to render a color picture from an artist's view like graphics applications, nor can we provide an example image for reference. However, we have spatial reference color frames and MV-based color annotation as prerequisites for automatic scribble generation. We can use the prediction blocks from coding pipeline to play the role of scribbles to annotate color. The correctness of this idea is based on a simple intuition: the matching blocks from reference frames indicate the correct color values for target frames, since space-time neighboring frames own close similarity. Fortunately, the motion prediction technology in H.264 is powerful enough in block matchinig, which promises the accuracy of blocks for color annotation.

3.2   Color Annotation from H.264 Based MVC

Being the lasted video coding standard, H.264 owns many highlighted features, as described by Wiegand [14]. It is our task to combine these features with our colorization scheme, because we do not want to introduce extra operations to automatic color scribble annotation. The color annotation mainly occurs during the prediction procedure, and among various highlighted features in H.264, two of them contributes significantly to color annotation.

1) Directional spatial prediction for intra coding: This new technique means coding by extrapolating in current picture without reference to other frames. We do not intend to use this technique, however, in our scheme we just want to prevent it in chrominance channels, because we only have gray target sequences and only want to search corresponding blocks in reference views according to luminance similarity. It is the codec who decides how many blocks will be inter/intra coded considering rate-distortion optimization. The intra coding result on gray blocks is still gray, so we can only get chrominance values indicated from inter coding between reference and target views, i.e. in chrominance channels we need to assign each matching block with MVs pointing to chrominance values from reference. Then after the annotation for chrominance, some intra blocks are left without color, and these blocks are just the target for the following colorization tasks. One example of color annotation output from inter coding blocks can be seen in Fig. 2(a), and all the gray areas are left by intra blocks.

2) Variable block-size motion compensation with small block sizes: H.264 supports more flexibility in block sizes including 7 types from 4×4 to 16×16. The larger blocks can save bits and computations in consistent textures while the smaller ones can describe the details in an accurate way. Thus, the color scribbles

(a)   (b)

Fig. 2. Color annotation result: (a)variable-size block; (b) fixed-size block. (Please refer to electronic version for color figures.)

can also be flexible according to luminance consistency, which provides more precise color annotation than using fixed-size blocks. Fig. 2 shows an comparison of color scribbles depicted using 7 types variable-size block and 16×16 fixed-size block only. We can see that in (b) the yellow skirt can not be depicted accurately using fixed-size blocks only.

4   Optimization Based Colorization

The scribble-based colorization method in [13] using optimization is a very simple method with excellent performance. Although in some new researches [15], more surprising result is provided considering edge detection or texture consistency, these methods introduce too many complicated operations beyond our needs. As it is shown in Fig. 2, our scribbles are square blocks covering the majority part of the image, which makes our colorization task much easier than modern graphics problems. In our annotated image, we have matching color blocks assigned by MVs as known color areas and in uncolored areas we have luminance intensity to guide the color expansion. This makes our application situation satisfies the assumption in [13]: neighboring pixels in space-time that have similar intensities should have similar color. Therefore, we colorize our annotated images using the optimization method according to their luminance similarity to their neighbors.

The colorization is controlled by minimizing the difference of a pixel and its neighbors around in the U and V channels of the YUV color space. During our color annotation process, we assign color values according to MVs only in U and V channels, so in U and V channels of target images where the values are zero are the pixels required to be colorized according to their Y values. Take U channel for example, we minimize the difference cost of a pixel $U(x, y)$ with its weighted average of color around neighboring area N (e.g. a 3×3 window), and m, n is the width and height of the picture:

$$\text{cost}(U) = \sum_{x=1}^{m} \sum_{y=1}^{n} (U(x, y) - \sum_{N} w_N U(x + \Delta x, y + \Delta y))^2 \qquad (1)$$

The weight factor w_N is calculated from the square difference between different luminance in Y channel, σ_N is the standard deviation of pixel $U(x,y)$ around the neighboring area N:

$$w_N = \exp\left(\frac{-(Y(x,y) - Y(x + \Delta x, y + \Delta y))^2}{2\sigma_N^2}\right) \tag{2}$$

The optimization problem above can be solved using a common method such as the least squares, because the constraints are linear and the optimization function owns a quadratic form. After the colorization for both U and V channels, we obtain a complete color picture.

5   Experiment Results

5.1   Implementation Issues

Both the MVC prediction structure and color annotation of our scheme are constructed under the framework of H.264, but we introduce many new features according to our application. We design our new codec by revising the H.264 reference software JM v10.2 [16]: 1) In H.264, Decoded Picture Buffer (DPB) stores all the reference frames required to encode the current frame for motion estimation in the temporal direction. However the spatial reference frame must be taken into consideration when designing the DPB for MVC. Thus, we modify original JM's DPB for spatial prediction as it is shown in Fig. 1. 2) In order to produce the color annotated frames, the MVs of inter frame coding between reference and target views have to be utilized. This requires a modification to decoder in generating the color annotated frames. When the decoder performs spatial motion compensation using luminance MVs, we need to attach every MV with the corresponding chrominance blocks from reference frames.

We use two different MVC sequences to test our scheme. The first sequence is called *flamenco2* published by KDDI [17]. It is captured using 5 cross cameras with 20cm spacing, and it is a non-rectified sequence which has severe color variation among different viewpoints. The second sequence is called *rena* published by Nagoya University [18]. This is also a sequence required color correction, and it is capture using 100 cameras with 5cm spacing in 1D-parallel distribution. Both the sequences have a frame rate of 30Hz, and resolution of 640×480.

In our experiment, the flamenco2 is cropped to 320×240 and we extract the first 100 frames from each sequence. In order to show the results in a simple way without losing generality, we choose two neighboring views in each sequence, one as reference and the other as target view. For flamenco2 we use viewpoint 0 as reference while viewpoint 1 as target; for rena the reference and target views are designated from viewpoint 51 and 52 respectively. We test the visual quality and coding bit rate under 4 different *Quantization Parameter* (QP) values: 22, 27, 32, and 37.

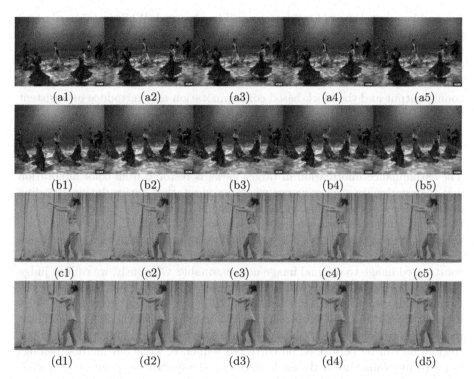

Fig. 3. Visual quality comparison: (a1)-(a5): The first frame from flamenco2, (a1) original reference viewpoint, (a2) original target viewpoint, (a3) color correction result from histogram matching, (a4) color annotation result from proposed method, (a5) colorization result from proposed method; (b1)-(b5) are the corresponding results from the 40th frame of flamenco2; (c1)-(c5) from the first frame of rena; (d1)-(d5) from 40th frame of rena. (Please refer to electronic version for color figures.)

5.2   Experiment Results for Color Correction

Since our color sequence is generated from color annotated frames referring to reference, and we assume that the matching blocks from reference indicating the correct color values, so the colorized results should also be seen as color corrected results. In the comparison of visual quality, we show the first and 40th frames of each sequence with original picture, color corrected result and our colorized output. We use the histogram matching method in [6] as the control group of color correction comparison. For fair comparison, the time-constant mapping function in [6] is not considered, because we do not introduce any time constraint in our method. The result of visual quality comparison can be found in Fig. 3.

The goal of color correction is to make the color appearance of target view similar to reference view as closely as possible. Take (a1) and (a2) in Fig. 3 as an example, there exists severe red color cast phenomenon in (a2) and we want to make it as blue as (a1). The histogram matching output in (a3) solves majority of the problem, but some red residua can still be observed. While in (a5), colorized from the color annotation in (a4), we restore the reference color appearance on target views with a better similarity. The same benefits of proposed method can also be told from the other three groups' results. Some blocking artifacts can be found in our colorized result. This is because our method is based on the decoding output and the block-based color annotation may introduce inconsistent boundaries.

5.3   Experiment Results for Color Compression

The chrominance information in target views is restored from color annotation and colorization on gray sequence when decoding, that means during encoding and transfer stage only luminance sequence is processed in target views, and the reference view is processed with common MVC method. Because the color sequence used in our test owns severe color variations and the final output aims at correcting it towards reference, this makes the calculation of PSNR on reconstructed image to original image not reasonable. Obviously, we cannot judge that a reconstructed image with more precisely corrected color has a lower objective quality due to its corrected color difference to the original one. This is different from the PSNR evaluation in color correction methods like [6]. These methods using color correction as pre-processing before encoding and the PSNR calculation can be performed on corrected sequence, while our method belongs to post-processing and we do not have colorized sequence before finishing decoding. Therefore, we only give the bit rate comparison under different QP values in Table 1.

The bit rate saving of proposed method steps to a higher stair comparing to color correction based pre-processing. In the test of flamenco2, we lower the bit rate by about 20% on average comparing to others. All the saving bits are derived from the chrominance coefficients. The detailed inter frame bits distribution can be read from Table 2 including the bit costs on mode, motion, luminance coefficients (Coeffs. Y) and chrominance coefficients (Coeffs. C). As to the results of rena, the bit rate saving seems too much to be reasonable. But this is the case. The first reason is rena's small camera spacing benefits our spatial prediction based color annotation. The second reason is our scheme does not rely on motion redundancy. The inter frame motion in rena is not so violent, which means the traditional motion-based coding is not able to exert its power. The third reason is this sequence is noisy in chrominance. The poor-quality image brings difficulties to transform based coding. However, color compression does not have these limitations. On the contrary, we can further improve the coding efficiency through saving more bits on chrominance coefficients. From Table 2 we can conclude that the capability of color correction in reducing chrominance coefficients is very limited, while compression through color redundancy can maximum this ability since the bits cost on chrominance coefficients is tending to zero.

However, our scheme also has several limitations: 1) The tradeoff between lower bit rate and better visual quality should be considered according to application, because sometimes the colorized result may not perform well in visual

Table 1. Bit rate comparison (kbps). Method 1 = No correction; Method 2 = Histogram matching; Method 3 = Proposed method

Sequence	Method	QP=22	QP=27	QP=32	QP=37
flamenco2	1	1530.76	822.59	433.46	229.66
	2	1513.69	803.67	410.19	209.97
	3	1229.50	703.51	375.39	193.68
rena	1	1427.09	549.55	268.81	153.71
	2	1840.32	611.96	262.55	140.30
	3	673.62	306.99	158.41	94.44

Table 2. Inter frame bit rate distribution (bits/frame, QP=32). Method 1 = No correction; Method 2 = Histogram matching; Method 3 = Proposed method

Sequence	Method	Mode	Motion	Coeffs. Y	Coeffs. C
flamenco2	1	1122.80	5173.13	5522.36	1693.86
	2	1131.83	5168.40	5221.51	1224.24
	3	1114.83	5156.43	5542.56	6.89
rena	1	1744.13	2776.73	539.22	3004.55
	2	1808.17	2661.33	522.14	2760.91
	3	1684.58	2557.30	616.69	22.16

quality; 2) Our color annotation is based on spatial prediction and the spatial matching will be greatly deteriorated if severe occlusions or great variations exist in the neighboring viewpoints. But when compressing multi-view sequences with small camera spacing like rena, our scheme may bring significant improvement in coding efficiency.

6   Conclusion

This paper introduces a new coding plus color correction scheme for multi-view video by exploring the color redundancy. Some advanced features in H.264 codec are utilized as automatic color annotation, and then an optimization based colorization is performed to render the color picture. Different from motion based coding, we focus on color, and the final output of our method brings benefits to both color correction and color compression problems, to perform more consistent color appearance and save more bits for MVC.

In future works, we will try to incorporate colorization and MVC pipeline more closely with complicated MVC prediction structure. Furthermore, better colorization method should be studied to prevent the blocking artifacts and improve colorized visual quality.

Acknowledgement

This work was supported in part by China 973 Research Program under Grant 2009CB320900.

52   B. Shi et al.

References

1. Reid, M., Millar, R., Black, N.: Second-generation image coding: An overview. ACM Computer Surveys 29, 3–29 (1997)
2. Liu, D., et al.: Image compression with edge-based inpainting. IEEE Transactions on Circuit and Systems for Video Technology 17, 1273–1287 (2007)
3. Rane, S., Sapiro, G., Bertalmio, M.: Structure and texture filling-in of missing image blocks in wireless transmission and compression applications. IEEE Transactions on Image Process. 12, 296–303 (2003)
4. Tanimoto, M.: Free viewpoint television—FTV. In: Picture Coding Symposium, PCS (2004)
5. Matusik, W., Pfister, H.: 3DTV: A scalable system for real-time acquisition, transmission, and autostereoscopic display of dynamic scenes. ACM SIGGRAPH, 814–824 (2004)
6. Fecker, U., Barkowsky, M., Kaup, A.: Histogram-based prefiltering for luminance and chrominance compensation of multiview video. IEEE Transactions on Circuits and Systems for Video Technology 18, 1258–1267 (2008)
7. Kimata, H., et al.: Multi-view video coding using reference picture selection for free-viewpoint video communication. In: Picture Coding Symposium, PCS (2004)
8. Mueller, K., et al.: Multi-view video coding based on H.264/MPEG4-AVC using hierarchical b pictures. In: Proc. Picture Coding Symposium, PCS (2006)
9. Kumar, R., Mitra, S.: Motion estimation based color transfer and its application to color video compression. Pattern Analysis Application 11, 131–139 (2008)
10. Reinhard, E., et al.: Color transfer between images. IEEE Computer Graphics Applications 21, 34–41 (2001)
11. Liu, X., et al.: Intrinsic colorization. ACM SIGGRAPH Asia, 151:1–152:9 (2008)
12. Welsh, T., et al.: Transferring color to grayscale images. ACM SIGGRAPH, 277–280 (2002)
13. Levin, A., Lischinski, D., Weiss, Y.: Colorization using optimization. ACM SIGGRAPH, 689–694 (2004)
14. Wiegand, T., et al.: Overview of the H.264/AVC video coding standard. IEEE Transactions on Circuits and Systems for Video Technology 13, 560–576 (2003)
15. Qu, Y., Wong, T., Heng, P.: Manga colorization. ACM SIGGRAPH, 1214–1220 (2004)
16. H.264/AVC JM reference software, http://iphome.hhi.de/suehring/tml
17. Flamenco2 sequence download, ftp://ftp.ne.jp/kddi/multiview
18. Rena sequence download, http://www.tanimoto.nuee.nagoya-u.ac.jp

A Subjective Method for Image Segmentation Evaluation

Qi Wang and Zengfu Wang[*]

Dept. of Automation, University of Science and Technology of China
crabwq@mail.ustc.edu.cn, zfwang@ustc.edu.cn

Abstract. Image segmentation is an important processing step in many image understanding algorithms and practical vision systems. Various image segmentation algorithms have been proposed and most of them claim their superiority over others. But in fact, no general acceptance has been gained of the goodness of these algorithms. In this paper, we present a subjective method to assess the quality of image segmentation algorithms. Our method involves the collection of a set of images belonging to different categories, optimizing the input parameters for each algorithm, conducting visual evaluation experiments and analyzing the final results. We outline the framework through an evaluation of four state-of-the-art image segmentation algorithms—mean-shift segmentation, JSEG, efficient graph based segmentation and statistical region merging, and give a detailed comparison of their different aspects.

Keywords: Image segmentation, subjective evaluation.

1 Introduction

Image segmentation is an important processing step in many image, video and computer vision applications. Extensive research has been done in creating many different approaches and algorithms for image segmentation [1-10]. However, no single segmentation technique is universally useful for all applications and different techniques are not equally suited for a particular task. Hence there needs a way of comparing them so that the better ones can be selected. To properly position the state of the art of image segmentation algorithms, many efforts have been spent on the development of performance evaluation methods.

Typically, researchers show their segmentation results on a few images and point out why their results look better than others. In fact, we never know from such studies if their results are good or typical examples, whether they are for a particular image or set of images, or more generally, for a whole class of images. Other evaluation methods include analytical and empirical goodness methods [11]. For analytical methods [12, 13], performance is judged not on the output of the segmentation method but on

---

[*] Corresponding author: Zengfu Wang. Address: Dept. of Automation, University of Science and Technology of China, Hefei, Anhui 230027, P.R.China. This work was supported by the National Natural Science Foundation of China (No.60875026).

H. Zha, R.-i. Taniguchi, and S. Maybank (Eds.): ACCV 2009, Part III, LNCS 5996, pp. 53–64, 2010.
© Springer-Verlag Berlin Heidelberg 2010

the basis of their properties, principles, complexity, requirements and so forth, without reference to a concrete implementation of the algorithm or test data. But until now, this kind of methods may only be useful for simple algorithms or straightforward segmentation problems. The difficulty is the lack of general theory for image segmentation [14]. As for empirical goodness methods, some goodness metrics such as uniformity within regions [15], contrast between regions [16] and shape of segmented regions [17] are calculated to measure the quality of an algorithm. The great disadvantage is that the goodness metrics are at best heuristics, and may exhibit strong bias towards a particular algorithm [18]. To address these problems, it has been widely agreed that a benchmark, which includes a large set of test images and some objective performance measures, is necessary for image segmentation evaluation. Several important works [19-23] emerged and among these, one widely influential prior work is Berkeley benchmark presented by Martin et al. [19]. Unfortunately, both Martin's and other researchers' work suffer from a series of shortcomings, which are discussed in [20].

This paper presents a segmentation evaluation method that was motivated by the following two proposals.

(1) The first one is that an evaluation method should produce results that correlate with the perceived quality of segmentation images. This was noted by Cinque et al. [24]:"Although it would be nice to have a quantitative evaluation of performance given by an analytical expression, or more visually by means of a table or graph, we must remember that the final evaluator is man and that his subjective criteria depend on his practical requirements." Though those methods mentioned above can be very useful in some applications, their results do not necessarily coincide with the human perception of the goodness of segmentation.

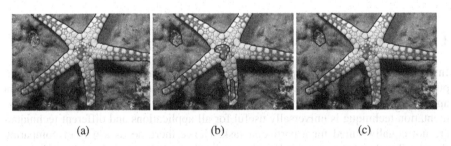

(a)   (b)   (c)

Fig. 1. Illustration of segmentation comparison where the blue boundaries in the images indicate the segmentation results. The left image (a) is the ground-truth segmentation. The middle (b) and right (c) are respectively the results produced by two segmentation algorithms.

(2) The second one is that existing benchmark based evaluation methods, usually objective methods, cannot properly reflect the goodness of different segmentation algorithms, so human subjects are needed to directly evaluate the output of segmentation algorithms. Generally, these methods define different functions, which measure the discrepancy between an algorithm's results and the ground-truth segmentations, to produce a quantitative value as a representation of the algorithm's quality. But actually, the human labeled ground-truth segmentations are another kind of expression of the pictures' semantic meaning and it is not convincing to measure it by a quantitative

value, especially when there are several ground-truth segmentations for one picture just as Martin's benchmark. Indeed, it is still a known difficult task to exactly quantify the semantic meaning. "In the absence of explicit semantics, the only alternative is to turn to human subjects, who will introduce implicit semantics through their understanding of the images [23]." Take the segmentations in Fig. 1 as an example. Suppose the left image (a) is a ground-truth segmentation, the middle (b) and right (c) are two segmentation results by different algorithms. If we evaluate the algorithms through hit rate by comparing the segmented boundaries with the ground-truth ones, the two algorithms will be considered as the same in performance. Nevertheless, most of us will think the algorithm producing the right segmentation result (c) is better than the one producing the middle one (b).

The approach taken to evaluate segmentation algorithms in this work is to measure their performance by human subjects, to use real images of different types in the evaluation and to select the parameters for each algorithm in a meaningful way that is not biased towards any algorithm. Aspects that distinguish our work with the previous are the following:

(1) Firstly, we test segmentation algorithms on images of different types and analyze their performance separately. This is often overlooked by other evaluation methods, which usually draw a thorough conclusion on a bunch of mixed test images. As a matter of fact, it can be a distinguished property that different algorithms may perform differently on each categorized images.

(2) Secondly, our selected input parameters of each algorithm for the final evaluation process are more reasonable. Most exiting evaluation methods merely gave a mathematic metric without considering the parameter selection problem or challenged this crucial step with ambiguity. In this work, we use a coarse-to-fine method to select 10 "best" parameter sets for each algorithm from a large parameter space. The final evaluation is made on the basis of each algorithm's 10 parameter sets. Therefore, our conclusion is more robust and can reflect the algorithms' real performance.

(3) In our analysis of the experimental data, we use the statistical technique and psychological model Intraclass Correlation Coefficient. This makes our experimental conclusion more reasonable and acceptable.

The remainder of this paper is organized as follows. In Section 2, we introduce the images used in our experiments and four algorithms to be evaluated. In Section 3, we describe our parameter selection procedure for each algorithm and in Section 4, experiments are conducted to assess the performance of the four segmentation algorithms. Finally, discussion and conclusion are made in Section 5.

2 Images and Segmentation Algorithms

Any scheme for evaluating segmentation algorithms must choose a test-bed of images with which to work. In this paper we employ the publicly available Berkeley image segmentation database [25], to which existing evaluation method frequently refer. 50 natural images of different types are carefully selected from the database. They are categorized as textured and nontextured, each of which compose half of the dataset. To ensure wide variety, we intentionally collect images with various contents, such as human, animal, vehicle, building, landscape, etc. All images are colored RGB format of 481×321 or 321×481 in size.

We also select four segmentation algorithms in our evaluation, which are mean-shift segmentation (MS) [4], JSEG [1], efficient graph-based method (EGB) [3] and statistical region merging (SRM) [2], based on the following three considerations.

(1) They well represent different categories of image segmentation methods.

(2) All of them are relatively new methods and published in well-known publications.

(3) The implementations of these methods are publicly available.

3   Parameter Selection

Selecting the input parameters of each algorithm is a critical step in performance evaluation because the resulting quality varies greatly with the choice of parameters. Most existing evaluation methods treat this complex problem with ambiguity or do not mention it at all. In this paper, we select parameters in a prudent manner. For each algorithm, the plausible meaningful range of each parameter is determined by consulting the original paper and doing a preliminary experiment, through which we can get a general idea of the parameters' effects on the algorithm's results. We try our best to make sure each parameter of a specific algorithm samples the entire reason-able parameter space, with no bias toward any parameter or algorithm. After this initial parameter selection, we then choose ten parameter settings for each algorithm through five persons' evaluation. Our final results are based on the ten parameter settings of each algorithm. This is called the final parameter selection.

3.1   Initial Parameter Selection

According to the principles mentioned above, we choose the initial combinations of parameter settings for each algorithm as follows.

(1) Mean-shift segmentation (MS). The mean-shift based segmentation technique is one of many techniques under the heading of "feature space analysis." There are three parameters for the user to specify. The first parameter h_s, and second parameter h_r, are respectively the radius of the spatial dimensions and color dimensions for gradient estimation. The third one, M (minimum region), controls the number of regions in the segmented image. Our preliminary experiment on dozens of images tells us that the reasonable maximum of the three parameters are respectively about 49, 30.5 and 7000. Therefore, we give 7×7×7 combinations of mean-shift parameters, where $h_s \in \{7, 14, 21, 28, 35, 42, 49\}$, $h_r \in \{6.5, 10.5, 14.5, 18.5, 22.5, 26.5, 30.5\}$ and $M \in \{50, 200, 700, 1000, 3000, 5000, 7000\}$.

(2) JSEG segmentation (JSEG). JSEG is a much more different method based on region growing using multiscale "J-images." The algorithm has three parameters that need to be determined by the user. The first one is a threshold q for the quantization process. The second one is the region merging threshold m and the last one l is the number of scales desired for the image. The ranges of the three parameters are bounded by the author in the implementation as $q \in [0, 600]$, $m \in [0, 1]$ and $l \in \{1, 2, 3\}$. Consequently, the initial 7×7×3 JSEG parameter settings are combinations of

the just referred three, where $q \in \{85, 170, 255, 340, 425, 510, 595\}$, $m \in \{0.15, 0.30, 0.45, 0.60, 0.75, 0.90, 1.00\}$ and $l \in \{1, 2, 3\}$.

(3) Efficient graph-based segmentation (EGB). This is typically a graph-based segmentation method by comparing and merging pairwise regions. The algorithm required three parameters to be set: σ, k and Min. σ is used to smooth the input image before segmenting it. k is the value for the threshold function and Min represents the minimum component size enforced by post-processing. On the basis of a preliminary experiment, the initial $7 \times 7 \times 7$ parameter settings are determined as $\sigma \in \{0.15, 0.30, 0.45, 0.60, 0.75, 0.90, 1.00\}$, $k \in \{200, 500, 800, 1000, 2000, 3000, 4000\}$ and $Min \in \{50, 200, 700, 1000, 3000, 5000, 7000\}$.

(4) Statistical region merging based segmentation (SRM). The key idea of this method is to formulate image segmentation as an inference problem and then process it with region merging and statistical means. There is only one parameter Q, which control the coarseness of the segmentation, to be decided by the user. Q is an integer number confined in the range of $[1, 256]$ according to the original paper but our preliminary experiment shows a shrunken range of $[1, 80]$ is more appropriate.

We can easily find that all the first three algorithms (MS, JSEG and EGB) have three parameters and we ensure each parameter equally samples the reasonable parameter space. Some of the parameters have the same meaning (e.g. M and Min). Thus they are given the same numerical value. While this method does not guarantee that the optimal input parameter set is identified — indeed there is currently no accepted method that will guarantee finding the optimal input parameters without ground truth — it does avoid biasing the results toward any of the algorithm. Unfortunately, the fourth SMR algorithm only depends on one parameter. This makes it harder to compare it with the other three. Adding two more parameters by modifying the algorithm is a way of addressing this problem [22, 26]. However, this is not an easy task and furthermore, modifying the algorithm may divert it greatly from the original one. Thereby we handle this demanding problem by shrinking the initial parameter settings to less than one third of the first three parameters' choices.

3.2 Final Parameter Selection

In this stage, the number of every algorithm's initial parameter combinations is reduced to 10. The methodology employed here is by the subjective evaluation of 5 participants, major in computer vision, on 20 images. Half of the images are textured and the other half are nontextured.

In the first place, each algorithm produces results on the 20 training images with all its initial parameter combinations. But the forms of segmentation results differ greatly with each other as showed in Fig. 2. MS produces results with two kinds of forms, white-black boundary map and region map with mean color within the region. JSEG gives its segmentation results in the form of boundary map superimposed on the original map, while EGB with region map filled with random color and SRM with boundary map superimposed on the mean color region map. In order to exempt the influence of different segmentation representations on participants' ratings, we program to transform the three kinds of results of MS, EGB and SRM into one uniform representation, boundary map superimposed on the original map, which is the same as the results of JSEG. Participants are then asked to rate the segmentation results from a scale of one to seven. There is no time limit but the participants are asked to make their standard of "goodness" consistent in the whole procedure and for one image, the scores of four algorithm must be rated at one time. The rating score indicates the easiness of identifying the perceptually different objects from the segmentation results. The higher the score is, the easier the different objects can be identified. After doing this, the results of each algorithm with a rating no less than five are collected in together. We then use a voting process to decide the most representative parameter settings for each algorithm. Parameters with the highest ten voting scores are selected as the algorithm's final parameter settings. The results of final parameter selection are listed in Table 1.

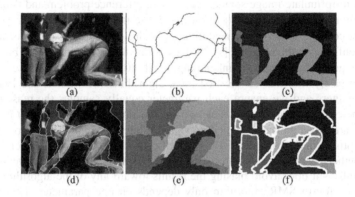

Fig. 2. The different representations of the four algorithms' segmentation results: (a) an original image; (b, c) the segmentation results of MS; (d) the segmentation result of JSEG; (e) the segmentation result of EGB; (f) the segmentation result of SRM

4   Algorithm Evaluation

Getting the ten parameter settings for each algorithm, we then use a subjective way to evaluate the four segmentation algorithms. In this experiment, 30 images are used. Each image is processed by each algorithm with all its 10 parameter combinations. The total 1200 segmentation results are then evaluated by 20 persons major in computer vision in a similar way as described in the final parameter selection step.

4.1   Consistency between Participants' Ratings

Before we start our evaluation, it is important to known whether the ratings are consistent across the participants. This is estimated using one form of the Intraclass Correlation Coefficient psychological model [27, 28]. The ICC (3, k) form is appropriate for the task because it measures the expected consistency of the k participants' mean ratings. The ICC (3, k) model is defined as:

$$ICC(3, k) = \frac{bms - ems}{ems}, \tag{1}$$

Table 1. The final parameter selection results. There are 10 parameter combinations for each algorithm.

Algorithms	Parameters	Parameter Combination Number									
		1	2	3	4	5	6	7	8	9	10
MS	h_s	14	14	14	21	21	21	35	42	49	49
	h_r	14.5	14.5	22.5	18.5	18.5	18.5	10.5	18.5	22.5	22.5
	M	5000	7000	5000	3000	5000	7000	5000	3000	5000	7000
JSEG	q	340	340	425	425	510	510	595	595	595	595
	m	0.60	0.75	0.75	0.60	0.75	0.60	0.60	0.75	1.00	1.00
	l	1	1	1	1	1	1	1	1	2	3
EGB	σ	0.30	0.30	0.45	0.45	0.45	0.45	0.45	0.75	1.00	1.00
	k	1000	2000	500	800	800	1000	1000	800	500	500
	Min	7000	7000	5000	5000	7000	5000	7000	5000	3000	5000
SRM	Q	1	4	8	12	16	20	24	28	32	36

where bms represents mean square of the ratings between targets, ems means total error mean square, and k is the number of participants. The values of ICC can range from zero to one, where zero means no consistency and one means complete consistency. This ICC model is used for every segmentation algorithm to examine the correlation of participants' ratings. Since 20 participants are involved in the procedure, the ICC (3, 20) for each algorithm is 0.9258(MS), 0.9702(JSEG), 0.9692(EGB) and 0.9617 (SRM). These figures give an indication that a consensus about ratings exists. This is a critical result since it establishes the validity of comparing the ratings in our experiments.

4.2 Performance and Parameters

In this part, we examine the algorithms' performance under different parameters. In the first place, the rating scores are used to determine the two parameter settings using two different criteria. The best single overall parameter setting, termed the fixed parameters, is identified by averaging the ratings across the participants, averaging these results across images, and finding the parameter set with the highest average. The best parameter setting for each individual image, termed the adapted parameters, is also found. This is done by averaging the ratings across participants and identifying the parameters that have the highest average rating for each image.

The fixed parameters for each algorithm are: MS (35, 10.5, 5000), JSEG (595, 0.60, 1), EGB (1.00, 500, 3000) and SRM (32). The adapted parameters for each image are show in Table 2. Since all the images are from Berkeley database, their names are labeled with numbers as they were.

We calculate their mean ratings under the two parameter settings by averaging the ratings across images and participants and then compare their relative performance. For fixed parameters, their mean ratings are 4.73(MS), 4.76(JSEG), 4.37(EGB) and 4.13(SRM). For adapted ones, they are 5.12(MS), 5.01(JSEG), 4.73(EGB) and 4.43(SRM).We can see clearly that the performance of the two algorithms — MS and JSEG — are better than that of EGB and SRM in both fixed and adapted parameter settings, while for MS and JSEG, or EGB and SRM, the difference in them is trivial. We can also find that for every algorithm, the adapted parameters outperform the

Table 2. The adapted parameters for each image. Image names are labeled with the numbers in the Berkley database.

Image	Adapted Parameters For Each Image			
	MS	JSEG	EGB	SRM
3096	(14, 14.5, 5000)	(340, 0.60, 1)	(0.30, 1000, 7000)	1
8143	(35, 10.5, 5000)	(395, 1.00, 3)	(0.30, 1000, 7000)	36
12003	(14, 22.5, 5000)	(510, 0.75, 1)	(1.00, 500, 3000)	32
15088	(49, 22.5, 5000)	(510, 0.75, 1)	(1.00, 500, 5000)	1
48055	(42, 18.5, 3000)	(340, 0.60, 1)	(1.00, 500, 5000)	36
58060	(35, 10.5, 5000)	(595, 0.60, 1)	(1.00, 500, 5000)	20
62096	(14, 14.5, 5000)	(340, 0.60, 1)	(0.45, 1000, 5000)	20
95006	(42, 18.5, 3000)	(340, 0.60, 1)	(1.00, 500, 5000)	28
101085	(35, 10.5, 5000)	(595, 1.00, 3)	(1.00, 500, 3000)	36
102061	(14, 22.5, 5000)	(340, 0.60, 1)	(0.75, 800, 5000)	24
108005	(35, 10.5, 5000)	(425, 0.60, 1)	(1.00, 500, 3000)	32
138078	(14, 14.5, 5000)	(595, 1.00, 2)	(0.45, 1000, 5000)	36
153077	(42, 18.5, 3000)	(510, 0.60, 1)	(0.45, 500, 5000)	36
157055	(21, 18.5, 3000)	(425, 0.60, 1)	(1.00, 500, 3000)	36
164074	(21, 18.5, 7000)	(425, 0.60, 1)	(0.45, 1000, 7000)	24
181079	(14, 14.5, 5000)	(595, 0.75, 1)	(0.45, 1000, 5000)	1
197017	(14, 14.5, 5000)	(595, 1.00, 3)	(0.45, 500, 5000)	32
198054	(14, 22.5, 5000)	(340, 0.60, 1)	(0.45, 500, 5000)	4
216081	(14, 14.5, 5000)	(595, 1.00, 3)	(0.45, 500, 5000)	32
219090	(35, 10.5, 5000)	(340, 0.75, 1)	(1.00, 500, 3000)	20
220075	(35, 10.5, 5000)	(340, 0.60, 1)	(0.30, 1000, 7000)	16
249061	(14, 14.5, 5000)	(595, 1.00, 3)	(0.75, 800, 5000)	36
253027	(35, 10.5, 5000)	(510, 0.60, 1)	(1.00, 500, 5000)	28
271031	(35, 10.5, 5000)	(340, 0.60, 1)	(0.45, 500, 5000)	36
277095	(35, 10.5, 5000)	(340, 0.60, 1)	(0.30, 2000, 7000)	36
309004	(35, 10.5, 5000)	(510, 0.60, 1)	(0.45, 500, 5000)	36
314016	(35, 10.5, 5000)	(595, 0.60, 1)	(0.45, 800, 5000)	32
351093	(14, 14.5, 5000)	(595, 0.60, 1)	(0.45, 1000, 5000)	36
370036	(21, 18.5, 3000)	(595, 1.00, 3)	(1.00, 500, 3000)	32
372047	(14, 22.5, 5000)	(340, 0.60, 1)	(1.00, 500, 3000)	16

fixed parameters. This is a significant result because it implies that the amount of effort expected in parameter optimization can influence the measured performance of the algorithm. Therefore, equal effort must be put in optimizing the parameters in a real application.

4.3 Performance and Image Category

In this experiment, we examine the interaction between the algorithms' performance and the image categories. The relative performance of the algorithms is calculated separately by averaging the ratings across images of a specific category and participants. For textured images, their mean ratings are 4.28(MS), 3.78(JSEG), 3.66(EGB) and 3.03(SRM). For nontextured ones, they are 4.56(MS), 4.76(JSEG), 4.21(EGB) and 4.32(SRM). Generally, the four algorithms perform better on nontextured images than on textured images. This suggests that each algorithm leaves something to be improved when confronted with textured images. How to deal with texture is still a problem required to be noticed while developing segmentation algorithms. As for their relative performance, we can find that the MS algorithm performs significantly better than the other three for textured images, while SRM is the poorest and, JSEG and EGB are nearly of the same level. For nontextured images, JSEG and MS produce better results than SRM and EGB. The difference between MS and JSEG is marginal. The same is true for EGB and SRM.

4.4 Stability with Respect to Different Images

Performance variation with respect to different images under one particular parameter combination is an important property. Here we first average ratings of every image under every parameter setting across participants and then calculate the variance of 30 images' ratings under every parameter combination. At last the 10 variances of the algorithm are averaged as a representation of the algorithm's stability under different images. The variances for the four algorithms are respectively 2.85(MS), 2.55(JSEG), 1.38(EGB) and 1.79(SRM). From these figures, we can see that the stability of the four algorithm is EGB>SRM>JSEG>MS. Though MS and JSEG produce better results than EGB and SRM, their stability with respect to images is not as good as EGB and SRM.

4.5 Stability with Respect to Different Parameter Settings

An algorithm's performance may vary greatly under different parameter settings. In this experiment, we look at an algorithm's stability across the 10 best parameter combinations. We average the ratings of a particular image across participants and then compute the variance of an image's 10 ratings. After that, we average the variance results across 30 images. Experimental results are 0.91(MS), 1.45(JSEG), 0.46(EGB) and 1.16(SRM), which show that the relative stability are EGB>MS>SRM>JSEG. When employing a sensitive algorithm such as JSEG, we should pay more attention to the parameter selection because it may affect the results greatly.

4.6 Processing Time Comparison

Processing speed is a critical consideration in many applications. Sometimes it is much more important than other properties discussed above. However, except for MS algorithm, none of the other three algorithms give a running time registration in their original implementation programs. So we make a little change in the original programs to make them capable of registering the processing time while segmenting an image. After that, we calculate the mean processing time of an algorithm by averaging time across all images and parameter settings. All the programs are run on a computer with Pentium 4 CPU 2.93GHz and 1G memory.

The processing time (in seconds) are 44.34(MS), 9.88(JSEG), 0.61(EGB) and 0.39(SRM). Obviously, we can see that MS is the most time-consuming algorithm, so it is not appropriate for real time applications. JSEG runs more quickly than MS, but it still can not satisfy the need of real time situations. Fortunately, EGB and SRM are both quick enough in a real time system and SRM stands out with the quickest speed.

5 Discussion and Conclusion

In this paper, we have presented a subjective method for comparing the quality of image segmentation algorithms. To demonstrate the utility of our proposed method, we performed a detailed comparison between four algorithms: mean-shift segmentation (MS), JSEG, efficient graph-based method (EGB) and statistical region merging (SRM). The algorithms were compared with respect to different parameter settings, image categories and processing time. Also, two kinds of stability were considered: stability with respect to parameters for a given image and stability with respect to different images for a given parameter combination. Our experimental results show that no single algorithm can outperform others in all aspects mentioned above. For example, MS and JSEG perform better than EGB and SRM in terms of parameter settings and different image categories, while their stability and processing time are not as good as the other two properties. Therefore, there should be a trade-off between these characteristics in the selection of a real application.

We can also find that, from the perspective of recognizing the different objects in images, even the state-of-the-art segmentation algorithms are far from perfect. This can be demonstrated from the mean scores in Section 4.2 and Section 4.3. We believe that, only after knowing how to solve this object recognition segmentation, can we make a great progress in image segmentation. Additionally, an effective object recognition segmentation method can facilitate many related applications, such as contend based image retrieval. Our future research involves developing a new segmentation algorithm consistent with human perception and this work is under way.

Our comparison in this experiment is an overall one rarely done in previous evaluation papers. We can get a complete understanding of the algorithms after this evaluation. This is informative when confronting with a problem of segmentation method selection in real applications.

However, this evaluation method has its shortcomings. First, subjective evaluation is a tedious and time-consuming work. In these experiments, the entire 50 images require thousands of ratings for every participant. This severely limits the number of images used in the evaluation, which brings out the second shortcoming that the ability to generalize our experimental results may be limited. In this work, 20 images were used in the parameter selection process and another 30 images are used in the algorithm evaluation process. This is not a large number compared with those objective evaluation methods. In spite of this, we argue that our evaluation conclusion is meaningful and useful. For one reason, the rating scores of different participants are consistent with each other as the psychological model ICC (3, k) demonstrates. For another, though it is not a large number of images, they have diverse image characteristics, and it is larger enough than those which claim their superiority over others on just several images. Besides, some of the properties compared in our experiments vary greatly with different algorithms and we believe it can reflect the actual quality of the algorithm.

References

1. Deng, Y., Manjunath, J.B.S.: Unsupervised Segmentation of Color-texture Regions in Images and Video. IEEE Transactions on Pattern Analysis and Machine Intelligence 23(8), 800–810 (2001)
2. Nock, R., Nielsen, F.: Statistical Region Merging. IEEE Transactions on Pattern Analysis and Machine Intelligence 26(11), 1452–1458 (2004)
3. Felzenszwalb, P.F., Huttenlocher, D.P.: Efficient Graph-based Image Segmentation. International Journal of Computer Vision 59(2), 167–181 (2004)
4. Comaniciu, D., Meer, P.: Mean shift: a Robust Approach toward Feature Space Analysis. IEEE Transactions on Pattern Analysis and Machine Intelligence 24(5), 603–619 (2002)
5. Shi, J., Malik, J.: Normalized Cuts and Image Segmentation. IEEE Transactions on Pattern Analysis and Machine Intelligence 22(8), 888–905 (2000)
6. Cheng, H.D., Jiang, X.H., Wang, J.: Color Image Segmentation Based on Homogram Thresholding and Region Merging. Pattern Recognition 35, 373–393 (2002)
7. Crevier, D.: Image Segmentation Algorithm Development Using Ground Truth Image Data Sets. Computer Vision and Image Understanding 112(2), 143–159 (2008)
8. Benlamri, R., Al-Marzooqi, Y.: Free-form Object Segmentation and Representation from Registered Range and Color Images. Image and Vision Computing 22, 703–717 (2004)
9. Mushrif, M.M., Ray, A.K.: Color Image Segmentation: Rough-set Theoretic Approach. Pattern Recognition Letters 29, 483–493 (2008)
10. Wang, S., Siskind, J.M.: Image Segmentation with Ratio Cut. IEEE Transactions on Pattern Analysis and Machine Intelligence 25(6), 675–690 (2003)
11. Zhang, Y.J.: A Survey on Evaluation Methods for Image Segmentation. Pattern Recognition 29(8), 1335–1346 (1996)
12. Liedtke, C.E., Gahm, T., Kappei, F., Aeikens, B.: Segmentation of Microscopic Cell Scenes. Analytical and Quantitative Cytology and Histology 9(3), 197–211 (1987)
13. Abdou, I.E., Pratt, W.K.: Quantitative Design and Evaluation of Enhancement/thresholding Edge Detectors. Proceedings of the IEEE 67(5), 753–763 (1979)
14. Haralick, R.M., Shapiro, L.G.: Computer and Robot Vision. Addison-Wesley, New York (1992)
15. Huang, Q., Dom, B.: Quantitative Methods of Evaluating Image Segmentation. In: International Conference on Image Processing, vol. 3, pp. 53–56 (1995)
16. Levine, M.D., Nazif, A.M.: Dynamic Measurement of Computer Generated Image Segmentations. IEEE Transactions on Pattern Analysis and Machine Intelligence 7(2), 155–164 (1985)
17. Sahoo, P.K., Soltani, S., Wong, A.K.C., Chen, Y.C.: A Survey of Thresholding Techniques. Computer Vision, Graphics, and Image Processing 41(2), 233–260 (1988)
18. Monteiro, F.C., Campilho, A.C.: Performance Evaluation of Image Segmentation. In: Campilho, A., Kamel, M.S. (eds.) ICIAR 2006. LNCS, vol. 4141, pp. 248–259. Springer, Heidelberg (2006)
19. Martin, D., Fowlkes, C., Tal, D., Malik, J.: A Database of Human Segmented Natural Images and Its Application to Evaluating Segmentation Algorithms and Measuring Ecological Statistics. In: Proc. International Conference on Computer Vision, vol. 2, pp. 416–423 (2001)
20. Ge, F., Wang, S., Liu, T.: Image-segmentation Evaluation from the Perspective of Salient Object Extraction. In: IEEE Computer Society Conference on Computer Vision and Pattern Recognition, vol. 1, pp. 1146–1153 (2006)

21. Zhang, H., Fritts, J.E., Goldman, S.A.: Image Segmentation Evaluation: A Survey of Unsupervised Methods. Computer Vision and Image Understanding 110, 260–280 (2008)
22. Unnikrishnan, R., Pantofaru, C., Hebert, M.: Toward Objective Evaluation of Image Segmentation Algorithms. IEEE Transactions on Pattern Analysis and Machine Intelligence 29(6), 929–944 (2007)
23. Shaffrey, C.W., Jermyn, I.H., Kingsbury, N.G.: Phychovisual Evaluation of Image Segmentation Algorithms. In: Proceedings of Advanced Concepts for Intelligent Vision Systems (2002)
24. Cinque, C., Guerra, C., Levialdi, S.: Reply: On the Paper by R. M. Haralick. CVGIP: Image Understanding 60(2), 250–252 (1994)
25. http://www.eecs.berkeley.edu/Research/Projects/CS/vision/grouping/segbench/
26. Health, M.D., Sarkar, S., Sanocki, T., Bowyer, K.W.: A Robust Visual Method for Assessing the Relative Performance of Edge-detection Algorithms. IEEE Transactions on Pattern Analysis and Machine Intelligence 19(12), 1338–1359 (1997)
27. Shrout, P.E., Fleiss, J.L.: Intraclass Correlation: Uses in Assessing Rater Reliability. Psychology Bulletin 86(2), 420–428 (1979)
28. http://www.nyu.edu/its/statistics/Docs/intracls.html

Real-Time Object Detection with Adaptive Background Model and Margined Sign Correlation

Ayaka Yamamoto and Yoshio Iwai

Graduate School of Engneering Science, Osaka University
1-3 Machikaneyamacho, Toyonaka, Osaka, 560-8531 Japan
yamamoto@yachi-lab.sys.es.osaka-u.ac.jp,
iwai@sys.es.osaka-u.ac.jp

Abstract. In recent years, the detection accuracy has significantly improved under various conditions using sophisticated methods. However, these methods require a great deal of computational cost, and have difficulty in real-time applications. In this paper, we propose a real-time system for object detection in outdoor environments using a graphics processing unit (GPU). We implement two algorithms on a GPU: adaptive background model, and margined sign correlation. These algorithms can robustly detect moving objects and remove shadow regions. Experimental results demonstrate the real-time performance of the proposed system.

Keywords: Object detection, Real-time system, GPU, Adaptive background model, Margined sign correlation.

1   Introduction

Object detection algorithms can be applied to various practical systems, such as person recognition, traffic monitoring and security systems. To realize these applications, many approaches for object detection have been proposed, and brought significant improvements in detection accuracy. The real-time performance, however, is also important for effective detection.

Graphics hardware has recently been used to achieve real-time performance. In [7], [8], field programmable gate arrays or other LSI chips were used to implement algorithms for object detection. However, restrictions of their architectures still hinder effective performance. Recently, object detection algorithms on graphics processing units (GPU) have been proposed [10], [11], [12]. GPUs, which were originally devices for 3D-graphics processing, have been remarkably improved for their programmability in recent years [9]. This programmability and their low price have resulted in a current trend of general purpose computing on a GPU (GPGPU). In [10], a pedestrian detection algorithm using a histogram of oriented gradient features and support vector machine classifiers runs on a GPU. In [11], a background subtraction on the CIELAB color space

H. Zha, R.-i. Taniguchi, and S. Maybank (Eds.): ACCV 2009, Part III, LNCS 5996, pp. 65–74, 2010.

is sped up using a GPU. In [12], a background segmentation algorithm based on the extended colinearity criterion is also sped up using a GPU.

There are many object detection methods, which are based on various types of features [10], inter-frame difference [2] and background subtraction [1], [5], [11]. The background subtraction technique is commonly used for its simplicity. However, to deal with dynamic and local illumination changes, background models should be sophisticated at the pixel [1], region [5] or frame level [11]. In particular, pixel-level background models can be implemented on a GPU by designing a background subtraction process per pixel for programmable pipelines. We have proposed an adaptive background model (ABM) and margined sign correlation (MSC) for object detection in the previous paper [1]. The previously proposed method can detect moving objects robustly, but the method has huge computational cost. In this paper, we propose a real-time system for object detection by implementing the ABM and MSC on a GPU. This paper is organized as follows: Section 2 briefly reviews the algorithms of the ABM and MSC, which are effective algorithms for object detection in outdoor environments. Section 3 explains the proposed system implemented on the GPU. Experimental results are shown and discussed in Section 4. Conclusions are given in Section 5.

2   ABM and MSC[1]

We briefly explain the ABM and MSC in this section. We assume that a camera and lights are relatively static in a background scene; therefore, a complex reflection model including the surface normal, light direction, and camera direction is not needed. In addition to the background subtraction technique, we apply the MSC for texture analysis. The MSC robustly detects spatial difference for illumination changes and can find object regions that are classified as background by chroma difference.

2.1   Adaptive Background Model

The pixel value $E(x, t)$ is given by the following equation:

$$E(x,t) = S_a(x,t)R_a(x)I_a(x,t) + S_d(x,t)R_d(x)I_d(x,t), \qquad (1)$$

where $I_a(x, t)$ and $I_d(x, t)$ are the intensity of the ambient light and the sunlight, respectively. $R_i(x)$ is a diagonal matrix including albedo and specular reflections of an object surface, and $S_i(x, t)$, which varies from 0 to 1, is the degree of brightness of the light at point x at time t. The value of $S_i(x, t) = 0$ indicates that the ray of light source i is obstructed at point x and time t, while $S_i(x, t) = 1$ means that all rays of light source i reach point x at time t. $S_a(x, t)$ is always 1 in outdoor scenes because I_a is an ambient light source (rays from the sky). Finally, by substituting $L_i(x, t) = R_i(x)I_i(x, t)$ in Eq. 1, the following equation can be obtained:

$$E(x,t) = L_a(x,t) + S_d(x,t)L_d(x,t). \qquad (2)$$

Additionally, L_a and L_d are assumed to be Gaussian processes:

$$L_a(\boldsymbol{x}, t) = L_a(\boldsymbol{x}, t-1) + \varepsilon_{S_a}, \tag{3}$$

$$L_d(\boldsymbol{x}, t) = L_d(\boldsymbol{x}, t-1) + \varepsilon_{S_d}, \tag{4}$$

where $\varepsilon_{S_a} \sim N(\boldsymbol{0}, \Sigma_{S_a})$ and $\varepsilon_{S_d} \sim N(\boldsymbol{0}, \Sigma_{S_d})$.

2.2 Margined Sign Correlation

The margined sign correlation (MSC) is an extension of sign cross correlation and is defined as follows:

$$\mathrm{MSC}_m(f(\boldsymbol{x}), g(\boldsymbol{x})) = \frac{\langle \mathrm{sgn}_m(f(\boldsymbol{x})), \mathrm{sgn}_m(g(\boldsymbol{x})) \rangle}{\|\mathrm{sgn}_m(f(\boldsymbol{x}))\| \cdot \|\mathrm{sgn}_m(g(\boldsymbol{x}))\|}, \tag{5}$$

$$\|\mathrm{sgn}_m(f(\boldsymbol{x}))\| = \sqrt{\langle \mathrm{sgn}_m(f(\boldsymbol{x})), \mathrm{sgn}_m(f(\boldsymbol{x})) \rangle}, \tag{6}$$

$$\langle \mathrm{sgn}_m(f(\boldsymbol{x})), \mathrm{sgn}_m(g(\boldsymbol{x})) \rangle = \int_{\boldsymbol{x}^* \in N(\boldsymbol{x})} \mathrm{sgn}_m(f(\boldsymbol{x}^*) - f(\boldsymbol{x})) \mathrm{sgn}_m(g(\boldsymbol{x}^*) - g(\boldsymbol{x})) d\boldsymbol{x}^*, \tag{7}$$

$$\mathrm{sgn}_m(x) = \begin{cases} +1 & |m| \le x \\ 0 & -|m| \le x < |m|, \\ -1 & x < |m| \end{cases} \tag{8}$$

where $N(\boldsymbol{x})$ is a neighborhood of $\boldsymbol{x}$, and m is the margin in consideration of noise. In the case of $m = 0$, $\mathrm{MSC}_0(\mathrm{f}(\boldsymbol{x}), \mathrm{g}(\boldsymbol{x}))$ is equivalent to the peripheral increment sign correlation [6], and when $f(\boldsymbol{x})$, $g(\boldsymbol{x})$ are replaced to median (or mean) of $f(\boldsymbol{x})$, $g(\boldsymbol{x})$, $\mathrm{MSC}_0(\mathrm{f}(\boldsymbol{x}), \mathrm{g}(\boldsymbol{x}))$ is equivalent to the sign cross correlation. $\mathrm{MSC}_m(\mathrm{f}, \mathrm{g})$ is not defined if $\|\mathrm{sgn}_m(f(\boldsymbol{x}))\| = 0$ or $\|\mathrm{sgn}_m(g(\boldsymbol{x}))\| = 0$. This means that the calculation of the cross correlation makes no sense because of noise in image f (or g).

3   GPU-Based Implementation of the Proposed Algorithm

Because of the recent development of the GPU, the GPGPU has been attracting attention in the research field [10], [11], [12]. Programmable pipelines in the current GPUs support vectorized floating-point operations, which bring fast processing. The graphics pipelines have programmable vertex and fragment stages, and typically, GPGPU applications only use the fragment stage (Fig. 1). In spite of this development , there are two limitations for GPU-based implementations. The first is that a branch condition is not supported due to the Single Instruction Multiple Data architecture of the current GPU. This means that a branch condition must be expressed in a suitable way for the fragment shader program. The second is the slow data transfer between the GPU and the CPU, so transfer times need to be reduced.

In our research, the fragment program is designed for the whole process for each pixel, so we need only one data transfer from the GPU to the CPU. This section describes each step of the proposed system.

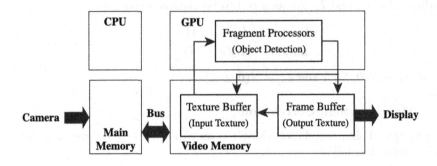

Fig. 1. GPGPU programming model

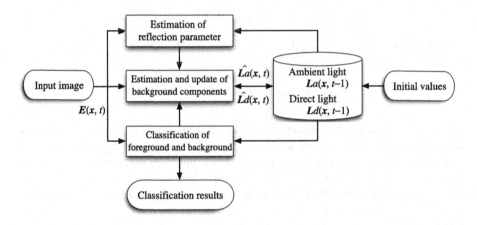

Fig. 2. Overview of the proposed system for object detection

3.1   Overview of the Proposed System

Fig. 2 illustrates the overview of the proposed system. The system consists of three parts: brightness estimation, background components estimation, and classification of foreground and background. We assume that a background pixel is expressed by the ABM [1]. Then, sudden illumination changes like shadows can be expressed by the reflectance parameter S_d of two background components L_a, L_d.

After estimation of the brightness, each pixel is classified as either object or background region based on chroma and texture differences between an input image and the estimated background. The use of not only chroma but also texture difference reduces misclassification caused by the color similarity between objects and background regions. In this paper, we use the MSC [1] for analyzing textures.

During the classification, background components are updated by using a Kalman filter. When a pixel is classified as background, the background components are replaced by estimated values. The above processes are performed on the GPU for all pixels.

3.2 Estimation of Brightness

The reflectance parameter $S_d(\boldsymbol{x}, t)$ is estimated from an input image and background components $\boldsymbol{L}_a(\boldsymbol{x}, t)$ and $\boldsymbol{L}_d(\boldsymbol{x}, t)$. However, the true values of $\boldsymbol{L}_a(\boldsymbol{x}, t)$ and $\boldsymbol{L}_d(\boldsymbol{x}, t)$ are unknown, so we first use $\tilde{\boldsymbol{L}}_a(\boldsymbol{x}, t-1)$ and $\tilde{\boldsymbol{L}}_d(\boldsymbol{x}, t-1)$ as plug-in estimates for $\boldsymbol{L}_a(\boldsymbol{x}, t)$ and $\boldsymbol{L}_d(\boldsymbol{x}, t)$. These estimates are suitable for a very short time, and then the reflection parameter can be calculated from the following equation:

$$\tilde{S}_d(\boldsymbol{x}, t) = \langle \boldsymbol{E}(\boldsymbol{x}, t) - \tilde{\boldsymbol{L}}_a(\boldsymbol{x}, t-1), \frac{\tilde{\boldsymbol{L}}_d(\boldsymbol{x}, t-1)}{\| \tilde{\boldsymbol{L}}_d(\boldsymbol{x}, t-1) \|^2} \rangle, \tag{9}$$

where $\langle , \rangle$ expresses an inner product of vectors. We can deal with sudden changes of direct light, such as shadows and occlusion by clouds, by adjusting the reflection parameter.

3.3 Classification of Foreground and Background

Foreground objects are detected using two different measures of difference: the chroma difference and the texture difference. Object detection and shadow removal are performed using the chroma difference between object color $\boldsymbol{E}(\boldsymbol{x}, t)$ and the estimated background model, $\boldsymbol{L}_a(\boldsymbol{x}, t)$ and $\boldsymbol{L}_d(\boldsymbol{x}, t)$. The chroma difference $D(\boldsymbol{x}, t)$ is defined by the following equation:

$$D(\boldsymbol{x}, t) = \| \boldsymbol{E}(\boldsymbol{x}, t) - (\tilde{\boldsymbol{L}}_a(\boldsymbol{x}, t-1) + \tilde{S}_d(\boldsymbol{x}, t)\tilde{\boldsymbol{L}}_d(\boldsymbol{x}, t-1)) \| . \tag{10}$$

Here we also use $\tilde{\boldsymbol{L}}_a(\boldsymbol{x}, t-1)$ and $\tilde{\boldsymbol{L}}_d(\boldsymbol{x}, t-1)$ as plug-in estimates of $\boldsymbol{L}_a(\boldsymbol{x}, t)$ and $\boldsymbol{L}_d(\boldsymbol{x}, t)$. The decision based on the chroma difference is made from the following criterion:

$$\begin{cases} \text{background} & D(\boldsymbol{x}, t) < D_{th}, \\ \text{object} & otherwise, \end{cases} \tag{11}$$

where D_{th} is a threshold value that determines whether a pixel is an object region or not.

The chroma classifier is effective for removing shadows; however, it cannot detect objects similar to the background color. Therefore, we use another classifier which evaluates spatial relations of luminance contrast, i.e., texture difference. Luminance contrast largely corresponds to the green color component, so we consider the spatial difference of the green component only. This significantly reduces the computational resources compared with the previous work [1]. The texture difference classifier is defined as follows:

$$\begin{cases} \text{background} & \text{MSC}_m(E_G(\boldsymbol{x}, t) - \tilde{L}_{a_G}(\boldsymbol{x}, t-1), \tilde{L}_{d_G}(\boldsymbol{x}, t-1)) \geq E_{th}, \\ \text{object} & otherwise, \end{cases} \tag{12}$$

where we also use $\tilde{\boldsymbol{L}}_a(\boldsymbol{x}, t-1)$ and $\tilde{\boldsymbol{L}}_d(\boldsymbol{x}, t-1)$ as plug-in estimates of $\boldsymbol{L}_a(\boldsymbol{x}, t)$ and $\boldsymbol{L}_d(\boldsymbol{x}, t)$, and E_{th} as a threshold value.

Table 1. Final decision based on two classifier

		chroma difference	
		background	foreground
texture	background	background	foreground
difference	foreground	foreground	foreground

Finally the system determines whether a pixel is in the background regions or not by using the two classifiers' decisions. In the system, the decision is made by logic, as shown in Table 1.

3.4   Estimation and Update of Background Components

Estimation and update of ambient light. During the classification process, the system calculates observation $\hat{L}_a(x, t)$ from Eq. 2 by substituting $S_d(x, t)$ and $L_d(x, t)$ for $\tilde{S}_d(x, t)$ and $\tilde{L}_d(x, t-1)$ as follows:

$$\hat{L}_a(x, t) = E(x, t) - \tilde{S}_d(x, t)\tilde{L}_d(x, t-1). \tag{13}$$

When a pixel is classified as a background pixel, the system estimates $\tilde{L}_a(x, t)$ from observation $\hat{L}_a(x, t)$ using a Kalman filter to avoid the case where a pixel is too bright such that:

$$\tilde{S}_d(x, t) \leq S_{a th}, \tag{14}$$

where $S_{a th}$ is the threshold value of this filtering process, and is proportional to ϵ_{S_a}. The filtering process can reduce outliers where ambient light is not observed adequately and can stabilize the estimates of ambient light.

Estimation and update of direct light. The system calculates the observation $\hat{L}_d(x, t)$ from Eq. 2 by substituting $S_d(x, t)$ and $L_d(x, t)$ for $\tilde{S}_d(x, t)$ and $\tilde{L}_d(x, t-1)$ as follows:

$$\hat{L}_d(x, t) = E(x, t) + (1 - \tilde{S}_d(x, t))\tilde{L}_d(x, t-1). \tag{15}$$

The system estimates $\tilde{L}_d(x, t)$ from observation $\hat{L}_d(x, t)$ using a Kalman filter, when a pixel is classified as a background pixel and satisfies the condition expressed by the following equation:

$$\tilde{S}_d(x, t) \geq S_{d th}. \tag{16}$$

This indicates that the system selectively updates the direct light component by filtering dark pixels where the direct light component would be small, and this filtering process also stabilizes the estimates of direct light.

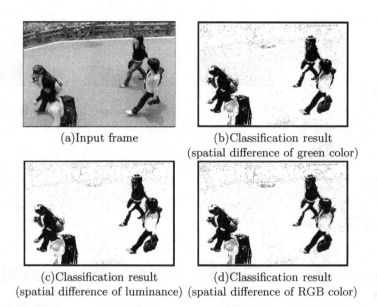

(a)Input frame

(b)Classification result
(spatial difference of green color)

(c)Classification result
(spatial difference of luminance)

(d)Classification result
(spatial difference of RGB color)

Fig. 3. An input frame and classification result based on different spatial difference

4   Experimental Results

We evaluate the performance of the proposed system with respect to both the execution time and the detection rate. Our system works on two 64-bit Quad-Core Intel Xeon Processors (2.8 GHz) with 4 GB memory and on a NVIDIA GeForce 8800 GT graphics card with 512 MB memory. The frame size of a video sequence is 720×486 pixels. For evaluation, we use color images (8 bits color) captured in an outdoor environment at about noon on 8 May 2005 (fair weather, occasionally cloudy). We set the margin m to SD/2 which is half the maximum variance of two Kalman filters. In our experiments, the MSC was calculated on the neighborhood size 7×7 pixels, which is the largest size for real-time processing on our GPU.

Fig. 3 (a) shows an input frame used for the evaluation and Figs. 3 (b), (c), and (d) show results obtained from the GPU system based on different spatial differences; G, luminance, and RGB (RGB is used in the previous work [1]). Fig. 4 shows histograms of MSC values based on the different spatial differences: G, luminance, and RGB. Figs. 4 (1a), (2a), (3a), and (4a) show regions of interest (ROI) while the remaining fighres are histograms of each ROI. In Figs. 3 (b), (c), and (d), white regions represent the background. The number of pixels of object regions manually classified in Fig. 3 (a) is 64533 pixels, while the number of pixels of shadow regions is 11342 pixels. Table 2 shows both the object detection and shadow removal rates for the images shown in Figs. 3 (b), (c), and (d). Table 3 shows speed performance of our GPU system with different texture differences, compared to the CPU-based software system.

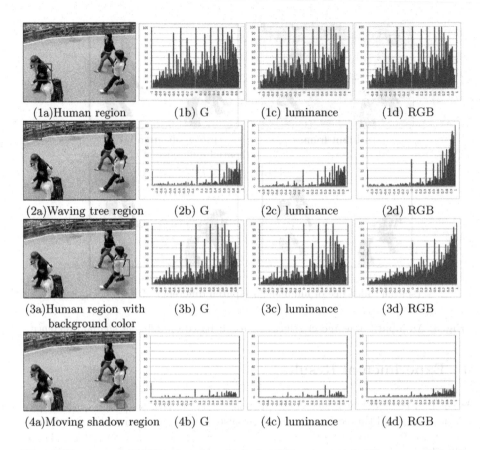

(1a)Human region   (1b) G   (1c) luminance   (1d) RGB

(2a)Waving tree region   (2b) G   (2c) luminance   (2d) RGB

(3a)Human region with   (3b) G   (3c) luminance   (3d) RGB
      background color

(4a)Moving shadow region   (4b) G   (4c) luminance   (4d) RGB

Fig. 4. Histogram of MSC values based on the different spatial differences: G, luminance, and RGB

Table 2. Object detection rates and shadow removal rates

	object region		shadow region	
	pixel	rate(%)	pixel	rate(%)
G	51054	79.11	10683	94.19
luminance	50746	78.64	10731	94.61
RGB	49595	76.85	11014	97.11

From Table 2, when the spatial difference of the green color is used, the detection rate of object regions becomes better than the luminance and RGB color, while the removal rate of shadow regions becomes worse. These can be seen especially in human head regions and a shadow region in Figs. 3 (b), (c), and (d); however the difference amongst three results are small enough to be ignored. Figs. 4 (1b), (1c), (2b), (2c), (3b), (3c), (4b), and (4c) also show quite similar results between the green component and the luminance. In addition, in

Table 3. Speed performance using three different texture classifiers

	G		luminance		RGB	
	processing time (sec)	frame/sec (fps)	processing time (sec)	frame/sec (fps)	processing time (sec)	frame/sec (fps)
CPU	1.40	0.71	1.75	0.57	2.67	0.38
GPU	0.13	7.5	0.17	6.0	0.23	4.3
CPU/GPU	10.8		10.3		11.6	

Figs. 4 (2b), (2d), (4b) and (4d), the histograms of the waving tree and shadow regions are sharpened by using the spatial difference of the luminance (the green component) compared with the RGB difference used in the previous work [1]. In Figs. 4 (3b) and (3d), the histogram of the luminance (the green component) difference becomes gentle-slope in comparison with that of the RGB difference. This means that our texture classifier can detect background regions and remove shadow regions more efficiently.

From Table 3, our GPU system executes more than 10 times faster than the CPU-based system. In addition, our system executes more than 1.7 times faster by using the spatial difference of the green component as compared to that of the RGB color. When the spatial difference of the green color is used, our system processes at a speed of 0.13 seconds per frame. Based on the results, it is clear that the proposed system is suitable for various practical online applications.

5 Conclusion

In this paper, we developed the GPU-based algorithm for object detection in outdoor environments. The adaptive background model, which can deal with global illumination changes and shadows, is suitable for GPU implementation because of its pixel-level modeling and simple form. Our system can detect spatial differences faster on the GPU by only using green color information for the margined sign correlation. Experimental results demonstrated that our system can be used in real time without degradation in performance. As a result, our system works 10 times faster than the software-based implementation system, so our system is suitable for real-time applications in outdoor environments.

In the future, we will improve our system to be stable for long periods under various conditions.

References

1. Yoshimura, H., Iwai, Y., Yachida, M.: Object detection with adaptive background model and margined sign cross correlation. In: 18th International Conference on Pattern Recognition, Hong Kong, vol. 3, pp. 19–23 (2006)
2. Huang, K., Wang, L., Tan, T., Maybank, S.: A real-time object detecting and tracking system for outdoor night surveillance. Pattern Recognition 1, 432–444 (2008)

3. Toyama, K., Krumm, J., Brumitt, B., Meyers, B.: Wallflower: principles and practice of background maintenance. In: 7th IEEE International Conference on Computer Vision, Kerkyra, Greece, vol. 1, pp. 255–261 (1999)
4. Stauffer, C., Grimson, W.E.L.: Adaptive background mixture models for real-time tracking. In: IEEE Computer Society Conference on Computer Vision and Pattern Recognition, Fort Collins, CO, USA, vol. 2, pp. 246–252 (1999)
5. Monnet, A., Mittal, A., Paragios, N., Ramesh, V.: Background modeling and subtraction of dynamic scene. In: 9th IEEE International Conference on Computer Vision, pp. 1305–1312 (2003)
6. Kaneko, S., Satoh, Y., Igarashi, S.: Robust object detection in image sequence using peripheral increment sign correlation. In: 5th Japan-France Congress on Mechatronics, pp. 287–292 (2001)
7. Price, A., Pyke, J., Achiri, D., Cornall, T.: Real time object detection for an unmanned aerial vehicle using an FPGA based vision system. In: Proceedings 2006 IEEE International Conference on Robotics and Automation, pp. 2854–2859 (2006)
8. Hayashi, H., Nakada, K., Morie, T.: Moving object detection algorithm inspired by the sequence detection in the hippocampus and its digital LSI implementation. International Congress Series, vol. 1301, pp. 35–38 (2007)
9. Owens, J.D., Luebke, D., Govindaraju, N., Harris, M., Krüger, J., Lefohn, A.E., Purcell, T.J.: A Survey of General-Purpose Computation on Graphics Hardware. Computer Graphics Forum 26, 80–113 (2007)
10. Zhang, L., Nevatia, R.: Efficient scan-window based object detection using GPGPU. In: IEEE Computer Society Conference on Computer Vision and Pattern Recognition Workshops, Anchorage, AK, pp. 1–7 (2008)
11. Fukui, S., Iwahori, Y., Woodham, R.J.: GPU based extraction of moving objects without shadows under intensity changes. In: IEEE Congress on Evolutionary Computation, pp. 4165–4172 (2008)
12. Griesser, A., Roeck, D.S., Neubeck, A., Gool, L.V.: GPU-based foreground-background segmentation using an extended colinearity criterion. In: Proceedings of Vision, Modeling and Visualization 2005, pp. 319–326 (2005)

A 7-Round Parallel Hardware-Saving Accelerator for Gaussian and DoG Pyramid Construction Part of SIFT

Jingbang Qiu, Tianci Huang, and Takeshi Ikenaga

Graduate School of Information, Product, and System, WASEDA Univ.
808-0135 Japan
megisgem0630@ruri.waseda.jp

Abstract. SIFT, short for Scale Invariant Feature Transform, is regarded as one of the most robust feature detection algorithms. The Gaussian and DoG Pyramid Construction part, functioning as computation basis and searching spaces for other parts, proves fatal to the system. In this paper, we present an FPGA-implementable hardware accelerator for this part. Stratified Gaussian Convolution scheme and 7-Round Parallel Computation scheme are introduced to reduce the hardware cost and improve process speed, meanwhile keeping high accuracy. In our experiment, our proposal successfully realizes a system with max clock frequency of 95.0 MHz, and on-system process speed of up to 21 fps for VGA format images. Hardware cost of Slice LUTs is reduced by 12.1% compared with traditional work. Accuracy is kept as high as 98.27% against original software solution. Our proposed structure proves to be suitable for real-time SIFT systems.

1 Introduction

In recent years, Feature Point Detection has been of great attention. Feature points can be used in various circumstances, such as, Object Recognition, Robot Localization and Mapping, Panorama Stitching, 3D Scene Modeling, Recognition and Track-ing, 3D Descriptor for Human Action Recognition, and so forth. The SIFT algorithm, short for Scale Invariant Feature Transform, is proposed by David Lowe in [1][2]. Regarded as one of the most robust feature point detection algorithms, a significant advantage of SIFT over other algorithms is that, the feature points detected are invariant to image scaling and rotation, while at the same time robust to changes in illumination, noise, occlusion and minor changes in viewpoint. Although SIFT is powerful, time consumption of the algorithm is relatively huge as a result of complex processes to achieve its robustness.Hardly any real-time system exists for VGA image processing.

GPU-based system has been proposed in [3][4][5]. Although accelerated, this method greatly depends on the performance of the GPU chip and the PC environment, and the results vary much from computer to computer. Recently, researches have been focusing on hardware accelerators for the SIFT algorithm.

H. Zha, R.-i. Taniguchi, and S. Maybank (Eds.): ACCV 2009, Part III, LNCS 5996, pp. 75–84, 2010.

Hardware acceleration implementations are proposed in [6][7][8][9][10] introducing some successful SIFT hardware design examples. Although these systems are far from perfect and are not able to reach real-time computation for VGA images, the results showed a promising view of hardware implementation of SIFT.

According to [6], SIFT can be structurally divided into 4 major parts, Gaussian Pyramids and DoG Pyramids Construction (GDPC), Feature Point Detection, Orientation Calculation, Descriptor Creation.

In this paper, we focus on hardware implementation of GDPC part.

1.1 Previous Work on Gaussian and DoG Pyramid Construction

The GDPC part is the very first part of the SIFT algorithm. This part generates the Gaussian Pyramids and DoG Pyramids which are the computation basis and searching spaces for other parts. Although this part takes only 10% of computation complexity of the whole system, it proves to be fatal to the system.

In [7], the author proposed a GDPC hardware accelerator using 5 Gaussian Convolution Units (GCUs) to build up the system. Based on Linear Separable characteristics of Gaussian Convolution, the author breaks down 2D GCU into 2-time 1D-based 2D GCU so that hardware cost increases almost linearly with Gaussian Kernel Width. Although it is reasonable to use 5 GCUs at once as it is, the problem is that these 5 GCUs have various Gaussian Kernel Widths. The GCU with the largest width (27) consumes almost 3 times hardware cost of the GCU with the smallest width (11). As a result, hardware cost is high.

In [9], Gaussian filter is implemented in pipeline architecture. They also use the 1D-based 2D GCU structure. The Max Clock Frequency reaches as high as 149MHz. However, due to relevance between Gaussian Images of adjacent intervals, to update one pixel at the last interval, the system needs to update $(3 \times 4 \times 4 + 1 + 9 \times 6 \times 4) = 265$ pixels at the 2nd interval[1]. The system has to wait before these 265 pixels are fully computed. As a result, the system is unable to make full advantage of the pipeline architecture. As a whole system, only up to 30 frames of QVGA images can be processed per second, that is to say, less than 10 frames of VGA image per second. The speed is far from sufficient.

In [10], a robotic system is implemented with SIFT algorithm with Stratix II FPGA board. It is claimed that the system could process one VGA image in 60ms. However, no structural information and no information on SIFT version is given.

The remainder of this paper is arranged as follows. Our proposal for GDPC hardware accelerator will be given in SECTION 2, including Stratified Gaussian Convolution Scheme, 7-Round Parallel Computation Scheme, as well as respective expected improvement. Afterwards, experimental environment, hardware synthesis details, software simulation, and detailed analysis on accuracy will be given in SECTION 3. SECTION 4 briefly concludes our work.

---

[1] [9] uses 7×7 Gaussian Kernel.

2   A 7-Round Hardware-Saving Architecture for GDPC

Our proposal is to develop a hardware system with lower hardware cost and is common in use, meanwhile, keeping similar accuracy and accelerating process speed. Our proposed hardware architecture is specified, but not confined, for the VGA and QVGA image processing. After modifying some parameter, our proposal could also be utilized in processing of other image sizes.

In our proposal, we use the 1D-based 2D GCU introduced in [7][9] to realize Gaussian Convolutions(GCs). 8 registers are used to represent one pixel in Gaussian Images, while 6 registers in DoG Images.

2.1   Stratified Gaussian Convolution(SGC)

A key feature of GC is that, by multiplication, a single, larger GC to an image can be divided into 2 successive GCs, the square sum of whose Gaussian Kernel Radii is square of the larger Gaussian Kernel Radius that were actually applied, as indicated in Formula 3. Define 2D discrete Gaussian function as in Formula 1.

$$G^{'}(r,c,\sigma,R) : \begin{cases} = \frac{1}{2\pi\sigma^2} \cdot exp^{-\frac{r^2+c^2}{2\sigma^2}}, -R \le r \le R, -R \le c \le R; \\ = 0, otherwise. \end{cases} \quad (1)$$

where R is Gaussian Convolution Radius[2], dependent to σ by the Formula 2. On the other hand, σ can be decided by R.

$$R = \frac{[(int)(\sigma \times 8 + 1.5)]|1 - 1}{2}. \quad (2)$$

So, we have,

$$L(r,c,\sigma_0) = G^{'}(r,c,\sigma_0,R_0) * I(r,c) = G^{'}(r,c,\sigma_1,R_1) * L(r,c,\sigma_2). \quad (3)$$

where $L(r,c,\sigma_2) = G^{'}(r,c,\sigma_2,R_2) * I(r,c)$;
    and $R_0 = \sqrt{R_1^2 + R_2^2}$.

For example, applying successive GCs with Gaussian Kernel Radii of 6 and 8 give the same results as applying a single GC with Gaussian Kernel Radius of 10, since $\sqrt{(6^2 + 8^2)} = 10$. By doing this, we may stratify a larger-width GC into smaller-width GCs.

In our proposal, 5 GCs are stratified based on Formula 3 using stratifying method listed in Table 1.

The system first computes the GC with Stratified Kernel Radius (1st) and then computes the GC with Stratified Kernel Radius (2nd). In this way, a larger GC could be computed by two successive smaller GCs as indicated in Formula 3.

Our proposal only stratifies the 4th and the 5th GCs into 2 parts. Other GCs are remained as they are. There are good reasons for applying such a stratifying method.

---

[2] Gaussian Convolution Width (W) and Gaussian Convolution Radius (R) have the relation by $W = 2 \times R + 1$.

1. **Data Re-Using**
   Stratified Kernel Radii (1st) of the 4th and the 5th GC are the same with Gaussian Kernel Radius of the 3rd GC. When computing the second part of the 4th and the 5th GC, it is possible to re-use the data generated from the 3rd GC as input. As a result, hardware specified for the first part of 4th and the 5th GC is needless.
2. **Hardware Saving**
   The 4th GC and the 5th GC are so large that they consume almost twice and even 3 times the hardware cost of the 1st GC would do. Thus, it is wise to break them down into 2 or more stages and re-use the hardware resources.
3. **Process Convenience**
   Although the 3rd GC also consumes almost twice the hardware cost of the 1st GC, there is strong reason that we keep the 3rd GC in the first part of computation without being stratified. In the VGA (or QVGA) image case, the Scale 3 image generated from the 3rd GC is re-used as original image of the next Octave. As a result, keeping the 3rd GC without stratifying enables the system to compute the 1st to the 3rd GC of the next Octave during the time when system is computing the second part of the 4th and 5th GC of the previous octave. This also underlies the possibility of parallel solution to be mentioned below.

By applying this scheme, it is possible that we may theoretically save about 17.8% hardware cost under the assumption that hardware cost of a GC is proportional to its Gaussian Kernel Width compared with(Formula 4).

$$T_{heoretical}Hardware S_{aving} = 1 - \frac{11 + 12 + 17 + 17 + 19}{11 + 12 + 17 + 23 + 27} \approx 17.8\%. \qquad (4)$$

2.2   7-Round Parallel Computation Scheme

According to the Stratified Gaussian Convolution Scheme, it is possible and reasonable to arrange the hardware into a parallel structure as shown in Fig. 1. For a VGA (or QVGA) image, 6 rounds of GDPC computation are originally needed to generate 6 groups of Gaussian Pyramids and 5 groups of DoG Pyramids. In

Table 1. Stratification of Gaussian Convolution (VGA)

Gaussian Convolution	From	To	Gaussian kernel Radius	Stratified kernel Radius(1st)	Stratified kernel Radius(2nd)
1^{st}GC	Scale0	Scale1	5	5	—
2^{nd}GC	Scale0	Scale2	6	6	—
3^{rd}GC	Scale0	Scale3	8	8	—
4^{th}GC	Scale0	Scale4	11	8	8
5^{th}GC	Scale0	Scale5	13	8	9

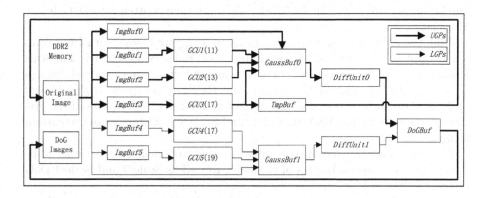

Fig. 1. Hardware architecture of our proposed accelerator. Numbers in the brackets denote Gaussian Convolution Widths of Gaussian Convolutions. UGP denotes Upper Gaussian Path. LGP denotes Lower Gaussian Path.

our proposal, GDPC is computed for 7 rounds. Nevertheless, process speed is still improved.

Process schedule of our proposed system is shown in Table 2. The whole process can be divided into 5 steps, including Loading Image, Gaussian Convolution (UGP GC and LGP GC), Differential Operation (UGP Diff and LGP Diff), Storing, and Down-Sampling.

In the 1st round, only UGP operations are computed. Scale 1, Scale 2 and Scale 3 Gaussian Images of Octave 0 are generated through $GCU1$, $GCU2$, and $GCU3$. Scale 3 Gaussian Image is stored into $TmpBuf$, which is in the next clock stored into Original Image Memory. DoG Images are generated through

Table 2. System process flow. OI denotes original image as system input. PI denotes input image from previous octave.

	1st Round	2nd Round	3rd Round	4th Round	5th Round	6th Round	7th Round
Loading Image	OI	PI	PI	PI	PI	PI	PI
UGP GC	Yes	Yes	Yes	Yes	Yes	Yes	No
LGP GC	No	Yes	Yes	Yes	Yes	Yes	Yes
UGP Diff	Yes	Yes	Yes	Yes	Yes	Yes	No
LGP Diff	No	Yes	Yes	Yes	Yes	Yes	Yes
Storing	Yes	Yes	Yes	Yes	Yes	Yes	Yes
Down Sampling	No	Yes	Yes	Yes	Yes	Yes	Yes

DiffUnit0 and are stored in *DoGBuf*, which are then written into DoG Image Memory.

From the 2nd round on, LGP operations are computed along with UGP computations. Scale 4 and Scale 5 Gaussian Images of the previous Octave, and Scale 1, Scale 2, Scale 3 Gaussian Images of the current Octave are generated through *GCU4* and *GCU5*, and *GCU1*, *GCU2*, and *GCU3* respectively. *DiffUnit0* and *DiffUnit1* are both used to generate Scale 3 and Scale 4 DoG Images of the previous Octave, as well as Scale 0, Scale1, and Scale 2 DoG Images of the current Octave.

The last round (7th round) computes only LGP operations, generating Scale 4 and Scale 5 Gaussian Images of Octave 5, as well as Scale 3 and Scale 4 DoG Images of Octave 5.

Under the assumption that computation time of a GCU is proportional to Gaussian Kernel Width, time consumption of a GC with Gaussian Kernel Radius of 1 may be represented as $O(1)$. Time consumption of conventional work in [6] for one single image would be $63.6 \times O(1)$. In the same way, using the same Clock Frequency, time consumption of our proposal is $47.6 \times O(1)$. Expected Acceleration Ratio (EAR) is about 25.2% over [7]. Moreover, as the Gaussian Convolution is stratified, critical path should be shortened. Therefore, the max clock frequency can be further improved, and actual EAR is expected to be larger.

2.3   Memory Operations Using Dual-Port DDR2 Memory

Dual-port DDR2 memory is embedded on Virtex(R)-V FPGA board. Two independent ports of 36-bit read/wirte width are provided. Read or Write memory operations can be finished in one clock, and the two ports can independently be Read or Write. This provides a variety of memory operation assignment. In our implementation, we assign dual-port DDR2 memory operations as in Table 3.

Table 3. Dual-port DDR2 memory port assignment

	Port A	Port B	Contents	Clocks
Loading Image ($1^{st} round$)	36-bit Read	36-bit Read	17 pixels ×8 bits	2
Loading Image ($2^{nd} round$ to $6^{th} round$)	36-bit Read	36-bit Read	36 pixels ×8 bits	4
Loading Image ($7^{th} round$)	36-bit Read	36-bit Read	19 pixels ×8 bits	3
Storing ($1^{st} round$)	36-bit Write	No Use	3 pixels ×5 bits	1
Storing ($2^{nd} round$ to $6^{th} round$)	36-bit Write	36-bit Write	5 pixels ×5 bits	1
Storing ($1^{st} round$)	36-bit Write	No Use	2 pixels ×5 bits	1

Table 4. Comparisons on hardware synthesis with conventional work in [7][9]

Item	Proposed Architecture	Conventional Work[7]	Conventional Work[9]
Image Size	VGA(QVGA)	VGA	QVGA
Registers/Pixel(G/DoG)	8/6	11/8	8/6
Computation Rounds/Image	409,500(102,375)	409,500	102,375
Max Clock Frequency	95.0 MHz	82.0 MHz	149 MHz
Process Speed	21(81) fps	16 fps	30 fps
Slice Registers	6,120	6,333	7,256
Slice LUTs	5,011	5,825	15,137

In this case, for all 409,500 rounds of computations of one VGA image, altogether 2,252,100 clocks are needed to finish all 6 Gaussian Pyramids and 5 DoG Pyramids.

3 Experimental Results and Analysis

Our experimental results are given in this section and compared with conventional work in [7][9]. Our software experiments are done with Microsoft(R) Visual Studio(R) 2008 Professional Edition on a PC with Intel(R) Core(TM)2 CPU 6700 @ 2.66 GHz 2.67 GHz, 2.00 GB RAM. Hardware Synthesis is done with Xilinx ISE WebPACK 10.1 on FPGA board of Xilinx Virtex(R)-V, XC5VLX330. In this paper, only tested results of VGA processing are shown. Original software solution is given in [11].

3.1 Hardware Synthesis

Hardware proposals in [7] are re-constructed on Virtex(R)-V FPGA board so that results can be comparable[3].

Hardware synthesis detail comparisons are shown in Table 4. As conventional work introduced in [7] did not consider memory operations, its process speed is re-estimated using dual-port DDR2 memory. For all 409,500 rounds of computations, it takes altogether 5,125,000 clocks, resulting in actual process speed at around 16 fps[4].

Compared with conventional work in [7], our system achieves about 15.9% higher max clock frequency, with accelerated Process Speed of 21 VGA images per second, which is 31.3% faster. Acceleration is brought by SGC scheme and 7-Round Parallel Computation scheme. This fits the assumption in SECTION 2.2. Thanks to SGC scheme and data-reuse, hardware consumption is also reduced by 8.4% totally.

Compared with conventional work in [9], although our proposal does not achieve as high max clock frequency, our Process Speed (81 fps for QVGA)

---

[3] [7] is originally implemented on Altera FPGA board.

[4] Clock Frequency is set at 82.0 MHz which is the same as [7].

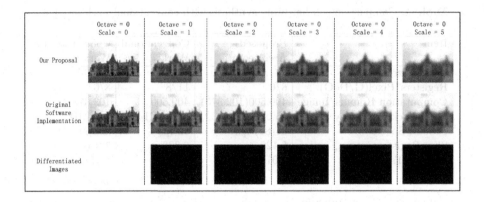

Fig. 2. Comparisons between our proposal and original software implementation

is about 1.8 times faster. As explained in SECTION 1.1, a huge control unit is needed due to relevance of GCs, as a result of which, Slice LUTs are hugely consumed. Hardware consumption is totally reduced by 50.3% by our proposed architecture.

In [10], although detailed design information is not give, it is claimed that process speed could possibly reach 15 fps for a VGA image. The speed is slower than ours.

Compared with systems provided by [7][9][10], our proposed architecture computes in a faster fashion, consuming less hardware.

3.2 Software Simulation

The software simulation of our architecture is based on PC with Microsoft(R) Visual Studio(R) 2008. Our proposal is re-constructed on software environment strictly with integer computation and transfer the results back to corresponding floating point values for easier analysis. Processed VGA images by our proposal and processed VGA images by original software implementation are compared in Fig. 2.

In our experiment, T_{hd} is pre-defined as 0.02, which is half of the Contrast Pre-Elimination Threshold in the original software implementation. According to the definition of DoG images, differences should be less than half of the Contrast Pre-Elimination Threshold so that in DoG Pyramids there will be no mis-eliminations theoretically.

In Fig. 2, differentiated images between original software implementation and our proposal are almost black except for very small number of white points, showing that our proposal generates almost the same Gaussian Images as the original software implementation. In another word, our proposal successfully keeps a high accuracy. Here, we only show Differentiated Images of Octave 0. Limited by page spaces, all Differentiated Images for other Octaves are not displayed.

For all 50 images in our evaluation dataset, the averaged accuracy rate is 98.2%.

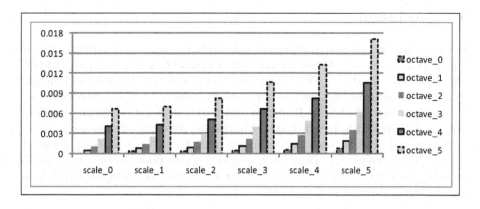

Fig. 3. AAD analysis between our proposal and original software implementation

3.3   Detailed Analysis on Accuracy

Averaged Absolute Difference (AAD) is introduced as the evaluating function in order to further analyze the accuracy of our system by Formula 5.

$$AAD(o, s) = \sqrt{\frac{\sum_{i=1}^{n}[P_{SW}(o, s, i) - P_{HW}(o, s, i)]^2}{n}}. \tag{5}$$

where $AAD(*)$ denotes Averaged Absolute Difference of between two selected images of certain Octave ans Scale; o denotes Octave; s denotes Scale; $P_{SW}(*)$ denotes pixel value in a software-generating image; $P_{HW}(*)$ denotes pixel value in a hardware-generating image; i denotes the ith pixel in a image; n denotes the total number of pixels in one image.

Here, AAD si used to indicate differences between our proposal and original software solution. A smaller AAD would indicate that data generated by our proposal is more similar with original software solution, that is to say, keeping higher accuracy level. AAD analysis is only done for Gaussian Images as differences of DoG Images are proportional to that of Gaussian Images. AAD analysis of 50 tested images is shown in Fig. 3.

Fig. 3 shows, when scale up-grows, AAD also grows larger. This is because when scale grows, Gaussian Kernel Width is getting larger, and consequentially our proposal generates larger AAD with software solution. Also, in the same scale, AAD grows when octave grows. This is due to the structure of SIFT. Because Scale 3 Image of each octave is used as the original image of the next octave, differences will be passed down to the next octave. In this way, the AAD is reasonably getting larger and larger when octave and interval grow.

Contrast Pre-Elimination Threshold of the system is 0.04 in floating point value. If AAD values for Gaussian Images are smaller than half of the Contrast Threshold (0.02), there would be theoretically no error contrast elimination in the DoG Images because the DoG Images would have differences smaller than 0.04. As in Fig. 3, all AAD is smaller than 0.02. Thus, the results are of high accuracy.

4 Conclusion

In this paper, we proposed a 7-round parallel hardware-saving architecture for hardware accelerator of Gaussian and DoG Pyramid Construction part of SIFT algorithm. By introducing Stratified Gaussian Convolution Scheme and 7-Round Parallel Computation Scheme, we successfully achieve to reduce the hardware cost, consuming 6,120 Slice Registers and 5,011 Slice LUTs, which is afford-able by a Vertix(R)-V FPGA board. Meanwhile, max clock frequency achieves 95.0MHz, and process speed is accelerated to 21 fps in VGA processing and 81 fps in QVGA processing. The two proposed schemes prove to be a triumph in reducing both hard ware cost and computation time. Our proposed system is suitable for real-time SIFT systems.

References

1. Lowe, D.G.: Object recognition from local scale-invariant features. In: ICCV 1999 Proceedings, Corgu, Greece, pp. 1150–1157 (1999)
2. Lowe, D.G.: Distinctive image features from scale-invariant keypoints. IJCV 60(2), 91–110 (2004)
3. Dermitzakis, K., McKenzie, E.: A gpu implementation of the sift algorithm: An msc project proposal (2007),
   www.inf.edu.ac.uk/events/jamboree/2007/Posters/k-dermizakis.dpf
4. Sinha, S.N., Frahm, J.-M., Pollefeys, M., Genc, Y.: Gpu-based video feature track-ing and matching. Technical Report TR, Department of Computer Science, UNC Chapel Hill 06(012) (2006)
5. Heymann, S., Muller, K., Smolic, A., Frohlich, B., Wiegand, T.: Sift implemen-tation and optimization for general-purpose gpu. In: WSCG 2007 Proceedings, University of West Bohemia, Plzen, Campus Bory, p. G03 (2007)
6. Qiu, J., Huang, T., Ikenaga, T.: Hardware accelerator for feature point detec-tion part of sift algorithm and corresponding hardware-friendly modification. In: SASIMI 2009 Proceedings, Okinawa, Japan, pp. 213–218 (2009)
7. Qiu, J., Huang, T., Ikenaga, T.: 1d-based 2d gaussian convolution unit based hard-ware accelerator for gaussian dog pyramid construction in sift. In: IEICE 2009 Proceedings, Matsuyama, Japan, pp. 1150–1157 (2009)
8. Qiu, J., Huang, T., Huang, Y., Ikenaga, T.: A hardware accelerator with variable pixel representation and skip mode prediction. In: MVA 2009 Proceedings, Tokyo, Japan, pp. 1150–1157 (2009)
9. Bonato, V., Marques, E., Constantinides, G.A.: A parallel hardware architecture for scale and rotation invariant feature detection. IEEE trans. on CSVT 18(12), 1703–1712 (2008)
10. Se, S., Ng, H.K., Jasiobedzki, P., Moyung, T.J.: Vision based modeling and local-ization for planetary exploration rovers. In: ICA 2004, p. 11 (2004)
11. Rob hess - school of eecs @ oregon state university,
    http://web.engr.oregonstate.edu/hess/
12. Kawasaki, H., Furukawa, R.: Shape reconstruction from cast shadows using copla-narities and metric constraints. In: Yagi, Y., Kang, S.B., Kweon, I.S., Zha, H. (eds.) ACCV 2007, Part II. LNCS, vol. 4844, pp. 847–857. Springer, Heidelberg (2007)

Weighted Map for Reflectance and Shading Separation Using a Single Image

Sung-Hsien Hsieh, Chih-Wei Fang, Te-Hsun Wang,
Chien-Hung Chu, and Jenn-Jier James Lien[*]

Department of Computer Science and Information Engineering,
National Cheng Kung University, Taiwan 70101, R.O.C.
`parvaty,nat,dsw_1216,piggy,jjlien@csie.ncku.edu.tw`

Abstract. In real world, a scene is composed by many characteristics. Intrinsic images represent these characteristics by two components, reflectance (the albedo of each point) and shading (the illumination of each point). Because reflectance images are invariant under different illumination conditions, they are more appropriate for some vision applications, such as recognition, detection. We develop the system to separate them from a single image. Firstly, a presented method, called Weighted-Map Method, is used to separate reflectance and shading. A weighted map is created by first transforming original color domain into new color domain and then extracting some useful property. Secondly, we build Markov Random Fields and use Belief Propagation to propagate local information in order to help us correct misclassifications from neighbors. According to our experimental results, our system can apply to not only real images but also synthesized images.

Keywords: Intrinsic Image, Reflectance, Shading, Weighted Map.

1 Introduction

For the scene in real world, we can find some characteristics on it. Some characteristics contain some useful information about the objects. Barrow and Tenebaum [1] proposed using intrinsic images to represent some of these characteristics. An image is modeled as a product of two major images: one associated with the light source called the shading images and the other remaining constant under different illumination conditions called the reflectance images.

In many vision applications, it is helpful for using shading and reflectance images. Two images have their own advantages. We have mentioned that the reflectance images remains constant under different illumination conditions. For some vision applications, such as pattern recognition [9], scene interpretation [4], and object recognition [2] are preferable to be conducted on reflectance images. Unlike reflectance images, shading images varies with different illumination conditions. These images can be used for objectives as shading analysis [3], color constancy [5], illumination assessment [6], and image segmentation [14]. By [1], the intrinsic image decomposition is to separate shading images and reflectance images like Fig. 1. Let $I(x, y)$ be the

---

[*] Corresponding author.

H. Zha, R.-i. Taniguchi, and S. Maybank (Eds.): ACCV 2009, Part III, LNCS 5996, pp. 85–95, 2010.
© Springer-Verlag Berlin Heidelberg 2010

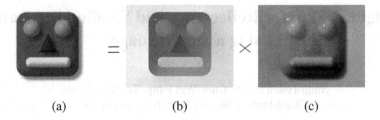

(a)   (b)   (c)

Fig. 1. An input image is equal to the product of a shading image and a reflectance image. (a) Original image. (b) Reflectance image. (c) Shading image.

input image and $S(x, y)$ be the shading image and $R(x, y)$ be the reflectance image. Then, we have under expression:

$$I(x, y) = S(x, y) \times R(x, y) \tag{1}$$

All pixels of the input image satisfy Eq. 1. If a image have n pixels, we have n equations to solve. But we have twice unknowns, $S(x, y)$ and $R(x, y)$, it becomes a difficult problem. Obviously, we need additional information in order to solve the equations.

In this paper, we present an intrinsic image decomposition method for a single color image. We follow the assumption, which was presented by Tappen *et al.* [13] that image derivatives are caused by either shading changes or reflectance changes. We transform this color image into a new color space which called LUM-RG-BY color domain. The transformed color image creates a weighted map. The weighted map is used to classify intrinsic images. After the classification, we use gradient information and loopy belief propagation to correct the misclassifications.

2 Related Work

It is a nontrivial task to decompose an image into its shading and reflectance images because it is ill-posed problem [1]. Additional information should be introduced. Weiss [15] used image sequences to achieve the purpose. This approach could create full frequency images, but required multiple images of a fixed scene. Images under different illumination conditions are also used in shading removal from surveillance images [10].

Tappen *et al.* [13] presented an algorithm for recovering shading and reflectance images from a single image and made the assumption that image derivatives is caused either by shading changes or by reflectance changes, but not both. They used the color information: (1) If the ratio between two adjacent pixels is almost equal in all r, g, b channels, the derivative is classified as shading. (2) Otherwise, the derivative is classified as reflectance. In addition to the color information, they use Adaboost [7] to train the structure of patterns, and then classify gray-scale images. Two methods are combined together with the probability model. They also used belief propagation [16] to process ambiguous areas.

Some algorithms such as Retinex[10] presented the assumption that the derivatives along reflectance changes have much larger magnitudes than those caused by shading. However, this assumption doesn't always hold real images. For example, spot light source easily lead to strong shadow and the derivatives caused by shadow are larger than those caused by reflectance changes.

We have organized the rest of this paper in the following way: Section 3 describes our system flowchart in detail. Our weighted-map method for intrinsic image decomposition will be described in Section 4 and Section 5. In Section 6 will demonstrate some experimental results. Finally, conclusions and the future work are presented in Section 7.

3 Separation of Reflectance and Shading

Fig. 2 shows a flowchart for our approach to the image decomposition from a single image. The approach consists of three major modules: Intrinsic Derivative Component

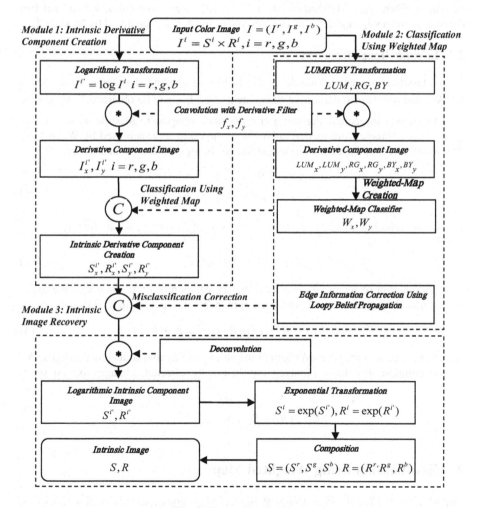

Fig. 2. The system flowchart

Creation, Classification Using Weighted Map, and Intrinsic Image Recovery. We will discuss about Module 1 and Module 3 in this section and then put Module 2 in later section.

3.1 Intrinsic Derivative Component Creation

In Module 1, our goal is to extract image derivatives. Let I^i be color channel images. First of all, I^i is transformed into to the logarithmic domain in Eq. 2:

$$I^{i'} = \log I^i = \log(S^i \times R^i) = S^{i'} + R^{i'}, \quad i = r, g, b \tag{2}$$

This step transforms multiplicative composition into additive composition of shading and reflectance of I^i. Next, the transformed image $I^{i'}$ is next convolved with f_x and f_y. In this paper, the horizontal derivative filter, f_x, is defined as [0, -1, 1] and the vertical derivative filter, f_y, is defined as [0, -1, 1] [t]. After the convolution, we can get two derivative images $I_x^{i'}$ and $I_y^{i'}$. The two derivative images are separated by Module 2.

3.2 Intrinsic Image Recovery

After classification using Module 2, the estimated shading derivative components, $S_x^{i'}, S_y^{i'}$, and reflectance derivative components, $R_x^{i'}, R_y^{i'}$, can be obtained. They can be used to recover the actual shading and reflectance images. In Module 3, we recover each intrinsic image from its derivatives with the same approach used by Weiss [15]. The solution for the intrinsic component images in log domain, $S^{i'}$ and $R^{i'}$ are:

$$\begin{aligned} S^{i'} &= g * [(f_x^r * S_x^{i'}) + (f_y^r * S_y^{i'})] \\ R^{i'} &= g * [(f_x^r * R_x^{i'}) + (f_y^r * R_y^{i'})] \end{aligned} \tag{3}$$

where $*$ is convolution, f_x^r and f_y^r are reverse copy of f_x and f_y. g is satisfied by:

$$g * [(f_x^r * f_x) + (f_y^r * f_y)] = \delta \tag{4}$$

The computation of g can be done by using the efficiently FFT. Then we take exponential transformation on these intrinsic components in log domain as follows:

$$S^i = \exp(S^{i'}), \quad R^i = \exp(R^{i'}), \quad i = r, g, b \tag{5}$$

After this step, we can get each channel image of shading and reflectance images. We have to compose this channel images into shading or reflectance images like Eq. 6.

$$\begin{aligned} S &= (S^r, S^g, S^b) \\ R &= (R^r, R^g, R^b) \end{aligned} \tag{6}$$

4 Classification Using Weighted Map

Our Module 2, Classification Using Weighted Map, comprises two major processes, namely Color Domain Transformation and Weighted Map Creation and Classification.

The respective objectives of these two processes are as follows; (1) to find a new color domain with well-separated property for shading and reflectance. (2) to create weighted maps in the x- and y-directions to classify the derivatives extracted by Module 1 as either shading-induced or reflectance-induced based on a pre-specified threshold value.

4.1 Color Domain Transformation

At first step, the input image was converted to L, M, S digital images, where L, M, S respectively stand for images with the spectral functions of the long-wavelength-sensitive, middle-wavelength-sensitive, and short-wavelength-sensitive cones of human visual system. In Eq. 7, we can see the transformation from RGB channel to LMS channel is linear. So we can obtain the LMS image easily from a single image.

$$
\begin{bmatrix} L \\ M \\ S \end{bmatrix} = \begin{bmatrix} 0.3811 & 0.5783 & 0.0402 \\ 0.1967 & 0.7244 & 0.0782 \\ 0.0241 & 0.1288 & 0.8444 \end{bmatrix} \begin{bmatrix} R \\ G \\ B \end{bmatrix}
\tag{7}
$$

In Fig. 3, it is observed that the shading and reflectance components in the original image are retained in each of the three channel images. However, in this study, this problem is resolved by further transforming the LMS channel images into the LUM-RG-BY color domain [8], in which LUM, RG and BY denotes the luminance, red-green, and blue-yellow channels, respectively. The transformation process is performed in accordance with Eq. 8

$$
\begin{aligned}
LUM &= L + M \\
RG &= \frac{L - M}{LUM} \\
BY &= \frac{S - 0.5 * LUM}{S + 0.5 * LUM}
\end{aligned}
\tag{8}
$$

We can covert RGB color image into LUM-RG-BY color space through LMS color space. The LUM, RG, BY images are shown in Fig. 4. The shading components only appear in the LUM channel image, and reflectance components appear in all three channel images.

After color domain transformation, we convolute LUM, RG, BY channel images with the same horizontal and vertical derivative filter, f_x and f_y in section 3.

4.2 Weighted-Map Creation and Classification

In this section, we create a weighted map to classify intrinsic images. Since the shading components only appear in LUM channel image, we are able to extract the reflectance components from RG and BY channel images.

We build reflectance-related maps, M, to extract the reflectance components from RG, BY images. The value of $M_x(x, y)$ can be computed from $RG_x(x, y)$ and $BY_x(x, y)$. Similarly, $M_y(x, y)$ can be determined from $RG_y(x, y)$ and $BY_x(x, y)$. We choose the max absolute value from RG and BY images as its value, like Eq. 9.

$$
\begin{aligned}
M_x(x, y) &= \max(|RG_x(x, y)|, \ |BY_x(x, y)|) \\
M_y(x, y) &= \max(|RG_y(x, y)|, \ |BY_y(x, y)|)
\end{aligned}
\tag{9}
$$

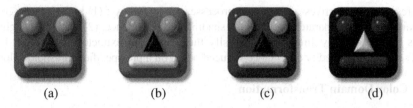

Fig. 3. (a) Original image. (b) L channel image. (c) M channel image. (d) S channel image.

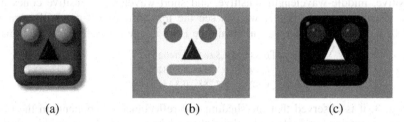

Fig. 4. The LUM, RG, BY channel images. We can see the shading component only has significant changes in LUM channel image. The reflectance component is in all three channel images (a) LUM channel image. (b) RG channel image. (c) BY channel image.

Then we take an operation between LUM images and reflectance-related maps:

$$W_x(x, y) = |LUM_x(x, y)| \cdot * M_x(x, y)$$
$$W_y(x, y) = |LUM_y(x, y)| \cdot * M_y(x, y)$$

(10)

where .* is pixel-by-pixel multiplication. Since the reflectance derivatives are associated with sharp changes and the shading derivatives are associated with smooth changes, in weighted map, the reflectance derivatives are larger than the shading derivatives. Fig. 5 illustrates the weighted map. Because there is significant difference between shading and reflectance derivatives in weighted map, a threshold is used to distinguish between shading derivatives and reflectance derivatives like Eq. 11.

$$\text{if} \begin{cases} W_x > Threshold_x, \text{Reflectance} \\ \text{otherwise, Shading} \end{cases} ; \text{if} \begin{cases} W_y > Threshold_y, \text{Reflectance} \\ \text{otherwise, Shading} \end{cases}$$

(11)

There is a problem for reflectance and shading changes being ambiguous since no definite border exists between them. We choose a threshold based on our experiment. It is a future work for deciding a threshold by using training or other method.

5 Misclassification Correction

After classification, the result is shown in Fig. 6(a). Green around eyes penetrates into the rest region because reflectance derivatives are discontinuous like Fig 6(b).

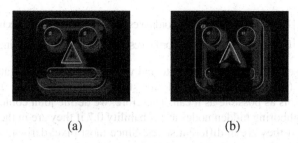

(a)   (b)

Fig. 5. The reflectance derivatives are larger than the shading derivatives in our weighted map. (a) W_x image. (b) W_y image.

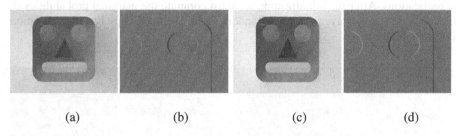

(a)   (b)   (c)   (d)

Fig. 6. (a) The reconstructed reflectance image. (b) The reflectance derivative image. Reflectance derivatives are discontinuous in its eyes. (c) The reconstructed reflectance image after misclassification correction. (d) The reflectance derivative image after misclassification correction. Original discontinuities in eyes are corrected.

Classification using weighted map is pixel-by-pixel, so some pixel derivatives of the same edge are classified as reflectance, and some are classified as shading. In deconvolution, the misclassifications lead to reconstruct intrinsic images badly. Since we know that edges belong to reflectance, our idea is to correct misclassifications by using edge information. In Fig. 6(c)(d), shows the result after correction.

5.1 Neighboring Pixel Modeling Using Markov Random Fields

There are many methods for extracting edges from a single image. We use the sobel operator to find edges. However, edges extracted by the sobel operator may be influenced by noise. For example, edge could be extracted too thick due to shadow, and part of the edge possibly includes shading components. Therefore, we can't directly classify all derivatives on the edge as reflectance derivative components. Our method is to gather classifications of neighboring pixels and is based on these classifications for correcting misclassifications. We create a Markov Random Field [16] for propagating classifications of neighboring pixels.

After applying the sobel operator, pixels of every edge are modeled by a Markov Random Field. We initialize every Markov Random Field by previous classifications using weighted map, like Eq. 12.

$$x_{i,j} \;,\; y_{i,j} = \begin{cases} 1, & \text{if pixel derivative at coordinates}(i,j) \text{ is classified as Reflectance} \\ 0, & \text{if pixel derivative at coordinates}(i,j) \text{ is classified as Shading} \end{cases} \qquad (12)$$

where $x_{i,j}$ represents the hidden node state and $y_{i,j}$ represents the observation node state at coordinates (i,j). We assumed that the state $x_{i,j}$ should be the same with its neighboring pixels as possible as it can. Therefore, we define joint compatibility function of two neighboring hidden nodes as probability 0.7 if they are in the same state or probability 0.3 if they are in different states. Since most pixel derivatives of the edge are classified as reflectance, it is expected that shading derivatives are reclassified as reflectance derivatives. On the other hand, if pixel derivatives classified as reflectance are approximately equal to ones classified as shading, it tends to reserve the original classifications. After the initialization, we must compute the marginal probabilities of hidden node states in every Markov Random Field. We use Loopy belief propagation [16] to compute them.

(a)   (b)   (c)   (d)

Fig. 7. (a)(b)(c)(d) are the same with Fig. 6(a)(b)(c)(d) expect the input image

5.2 Edge Information Correction Using Loopy Belief Propagation

Loopy belief propagation is an algorithm for computing marginals of function. We use it to find an approximate solution on our Markov Random Field. It is difficult to get exact solution due to computational complexity. We run Loopy Belief Propagation until it converges and gets marginal probabilities of hidden node states. These probabilities can be used to correct our misclassifications. The state of node with max probability is selected to become a new state. For example, if state 1 of node $x_{i,j}$ is higher than state 0, then $x_{i,j}$ should be classified as Reflectance. Fig. 7 is the same with Fig. 6 expect the input image.

6 Experimental Results

In this section, we demonstrate our experimental results. In Fig. 8, we show the result of weighted-map method for real scenes. These input images include obvious shadow. Some papers like [10][15] consider shadow as shading components. In our case, the shadow is classified as shading components correctly. However, there are some problems on reflectance images. For example, in Fig. 8(f), though we succeed in separating shadow from its original input image, the reflectance image which was ever covered by shadow in the original image is darker than what we expect. Because shadow affects

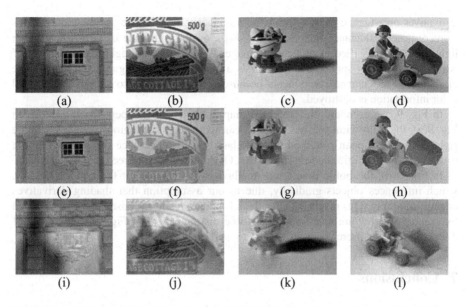

Fig. 8. (a)(b)(c)(d) are original input images. (e)(f)(g)(h) are reflectance images. (i)(j)(k)(l) are shading images.

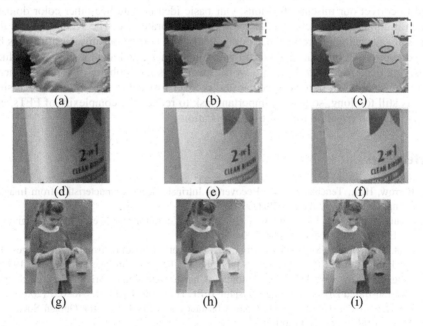

Fig. 9. (a)(d)(g) are original input images. (b)(e)(h) are reflectance images using our method. (c)(f)(i) are reflectance images using Tappen's method.

derivatives on edges, it causes deconvolution inaccurate when we use these derivatives to reconstruct reflectance images. In Fig. 8(g), on the right side of kitty's head, high light region is classified to reflectance image. We call this highlight region "specular" which is caused by spot light. Specular is a challenge to distinguish and tends to be classified as reflectance components because the spot light is so strong that original color information is destroyed.

In Fig. 9, we compare our weighted-map method with Tappen's method [13]. In Fig. 9(a), the pillow image, two methods can work for most regions. However, in the right eyebrow, Tappan's method fails to classify it as reflectance components. In the lower right fold, a little shadow still exists. Our method can succeed in these regions.

In Fig. 9(d), the bottle image, our method is appropriate for the type of shadow, which influences objects gradually, due to our assumption that shading derivatives change smoothly. Our result is better than Tappen's result because derivatives caused by gradual shadow are small and easy to be distinguished. In Fig. 9(g), the color of Tappan's result is more accuracy than out result.

7 Conclusions

In this paper, we present an effective approach to recover intrinsic images from a single image. Based on Tappen's assumption, we use the weighted map to separate intrinsic images by LUM-RG-BY color domain and the edge information is considered to correct our misclassifications. Our basic idea is to utilize other color domain which illumination and chrominance are easily separated by. The second idea is the edges always belong to reflectance components. We correct our misclassifications by the edge information. Our method can work on synthetic and real images and produce satisfying decomposition. In future work, specular is the problem to solve. We need more information to remove specular and recover lost color. Finally, the processing time is still too long, so it is an important task to reduce the complexity of FFTs and loopy belief propagation for real-time applications.

References

1. Barrow, H.G., Tenebaum, J.M.: Recovering Intrinsic Scene Characteristics from Images. Computer Vision Systems, 3–26 (1978)
2. Chang, S.L., Chen, L.S., Chung, Y.C., Chen, S.W.: Automatic license plate recognition. IEEE Trans. on ITS 5(1), 42–54 (2004)
3. Funt, B.V., Drew, M.S., Brokington, M.: Recovering Shading from Color Images. In: Sandini, G. (ed.) ECCV 1992. LNCS, vol. 588, pp. 124–132. Springer, Heidelberg (1992)
4. Fang, C., Chen, S.W., Fuh, C.S.: Automatic Change Detection of Driving Environments in a Vision-Based Driver Assistance System. IEEE Trans. on NN 14(3), 646–657 (2003)
5. Finlayson, G.D., Hordley, S.D.: Color Constancy at a Pixel. J. of the Optical Society of America 18(2), 253–264 (2001)
6. Finlayson, G.D., Hordley, S.D., Cheng, L., Drew, M.S.: On the Removal of Shadows form Images. IEEE Trans. on PAMI 28(1), 59–68 (2006)
7. Freund, Y., Schapire, R.E.: A Decision-Theoretic Generalization of On-Line Learning and an Application to Boosting. J. Computer and System Sciences 55(1), 119–139 (1997)

8. Kingdom, F.A.A., Rangwala, S., Hammmamji: Chromatic Properties of the Color Shading Effect. Vision Research, 1425–1437 (2005)
9. Leung, T., Malik, J.: Recognizing Surfaces Using Three-Dimensional Taxons. In: IEEE ICCV, pp. 1010–1017 (1999)
10. Matsushita, Y., Nishino, K., Ikeuchi, K., Sakauchi, M.: Illumination Normalization with Time-Dependent Intrinsic Images for Video Surveillance. In: Proc. 2003 CVPR, vol. 1, pp. 3–10 (2003)
11. Olshausen, B.A., Field, D.J.: Emergence of Simple Cell Receptive Field Properties by Learning a Sparse Code for Natural Images, 607–608 (1996)
12. Simoncelli, E.P.: Statistical models for images: compression, restoration and synthesis. In: Asilomar Conference on Signals, Systems and Computers, pp. 673–678 (1997)
13. Tappen, M.F., Freeman, W.T., Adelson, E.H.: Recovering Intrinsic Images from a Single Image. IEEE Trans. on PAMI 27(9), 1459–1472 (2005)
14. Tsai, Y.T., Lien, J.J.: Efficient Object Segmentation Using Digital Matting for MPEG Video Sequences. In: Narayanan, P.J., Nayar, S.K., Shum, H.-Y. (eds.) ACCV 2006. LNCS, vol. 3852, pp. 591–601. Springer, Heidelberg (2006)
15. Weiss, Y.: Deriving Intrinsic Images from Image Sequences. In: IEEE ICCV, pp. 68–75 (2001)
16. Yedidia, J., Freeman, W.T., Weiss, Y.: Understanding Belief Propagation and its Generalizations. MITSUBISHI Electric Research Lab. TR-2001-22 (2002)

Polygonal Light Source Estimation

Dirk Schnieders, Kwan-Yee K. Wong, and Zhenwen Dai

Department of Computer Science,
The University of Hong Kong,
Pokfulam Road, Hong Kong
{sdirk,kykwong,zwdai}@cs.hku.hk

Abstract. This paper studies the problem of light estimation using a specular sphere. Most existing work on light estimation assumes distant point light sources, while this work considers an area light source which is estimated in 3D space by reconstructing its edges. An empirical analysis on existing methods for line estimation from a single view is carried out, and it is shown that line estimation for a single view of a sphere is an ill-conditioned configuration.

By considering a second identical sphere, a closed form solution for single view polygonal light estimation is proposed. In addition, this paper also proposes an iterative approach based on two unknown views of just a single sphere. Experimental results on both synthetic and real data are presented.

1 Introduction

The calibration of light sources plays an important role in both computer graphics and computer vision. For instance, combining computer-generated models with the real world, as in augmented reality, requires known light positions for realistic rendering. Many computer vision techniques make the common assumption of distant point light sources, which conveniently reduces the complexity in modeling the image formation and allows a simple light source position estimation. As an example, consider the classic shape from shading (SfS) technique that recovers the 3D shape of an object by relating the intensity values to the normal vectors and light source direction. Motivated by the possibility that SfS could be extended to deal with area light sources, this paper studies the problem of recovering polygonal area light sources from images of a specular sphere.

There exists a relatively large amount of research dealing with distant point illuminant estimation, and many early results were published in the context of SfS [1,2,3]. A survey of those and related methods can be found in [4]. Other related work on light estimation includes a method developed by Yang and Yuille [5] which estimates light directions from a Lambertian sphere by locating the occluding boundary of light sources. Their method was extended by Zhang and Yang [6] who introduced the concept of critical points which have their normal vectors perpendicular to the light direction. Later Wang and Samaras [7] further extended this method and estimated light from a single view of an object with

H. Zha, R.-i. Taniguchi, and S. Maybank (Eds.): ACCV 2009, Part III, LNCS 5996, pp. 96–107, 2010.

known geometry by a robust minimization of a global error. Wong et. al. [8] introduced a method for recovering both the light directions and camera poses from a single sphere of unknown radius. In addition to the estimation of light directions, Takai et. al. [9] proposed a method for estimation of near point light sources and ambient light from a single image. This is achieved by employing a pair of reference spheres as light probes.

Because of the relative high complexity involved in estimating area light sources, the literature in this field is rather sparse. In [10], Debevec estimated global illumination in the context of augmented reality without assuming specific types of light source, but did not estimate parameters such as distance and size of the illuminants.

In this paper an area light source is recovered from an image of the specular highlight it produces on a sphere. Unlike Zhou and Kambhamettu's method [11] which uses an iterative approach for estimating area light sources from specularities observed on two spheres, this paper provides a closed form solution by treating an area light source as a polygon in 3D space composed of a set of lines. Such lines are independently determined as the intersections of the reflection rays. We call this type of light source a polygonal light source.

There exists previous work on estimating a line from a single view. Lanman et. al. [12] formulated the problem and solved it in theory, but practical results remained inaccurate. In [13], the authors solved their inaccurate line estimation by carefully estimating all parameter of their system. In this paper it will be shown that even with ground truth calibration, single view line estimation from a single view of a sphere cannot be accurately solved. A closed form solution of two spheres is therefore proposed. This paper also develops an iterative approach based on two unknown views of just a single sphere. The rotation relating the two unknown views can be estimated by assuming a rectangular light source.

A related paper by Gasparini and Sturm [14] also utilizes 3D lines in non-central images. In their interesting work, a system that deals with the structure from motion problem for general camera models is proposed.

The rest of the paper is organized as follows. Section 2 considers the problem of line estimation from a single view. In the first part of this section, a theoretical description for the estimation is given, while the second part provides empirical results which show that single view line estimation is an ill-conditioned problem. Knowing that a single view of a single sphere is insufficient, Section 3 formulates the problem for (a) a single view of two spheres and (b) two views of a single sphere. Experimental results on both synthetic and real data are shown in Section 4, followed by conclusions in Section 5.

2   Line Estimation from a Single View

Consider a pinhole camera viewing a line $\mathcal{L}$. Together with the camera center the line defines a plane. Any line lying on this plane will project to the same line on the image, which makes line reconstruction from a single view ambiguous.

Instead of considering the image l of the line, let us now consider an image l_s of the line $\mathcal{L}$ formed by its reflection on a sphere. While l is a 2D line, l_s will in general be a curve. The viewing lines defined by the back-projection of the points on l_s will intersect the sphere and reflect according to the law of reflection. The resulting rays, which we call reflection rays will intersect $\mathcal{L}$. In contrast to the case of a pinhole camera viewing a line, the reflection rays will not meet at a single point, and this enables line reconstruction from a single view.

Proposition 1. *The reflection rays constructed from an image of the reflection of a line $\mathcal{L}$ on a sphere will intersect two lines, namely the line $\mathcal{L}$ and a line $\mathcal{A}$ passing through the sphere center and the camera center.*

Proof. Let us denote the back-projection of a point $x \in l_s$ as the viewing line $\mathcal{V}$ and its reflection on the sphere with center S as the reflection line $\mathcal{R}$. The viewing line will leave the camera center C, pass through the point x, and intersect the sphere at a point P. Let V and R be the unit vectors in the directions of the viewing line and the reflection line respectively. The law of reflection states that the incident angle must be equal to the reflection angle, and the reflection direction is therefore given by $R = (2N \cdot V)N - V$, where N is the unit normal vector at point P. The reflection line $\mathcal{R}$ passes through P in the direction R and will, by construction, intersect the line $\mathcal{L}$ at some point L. All the reflection rays constructed in such a way will intersect the line $\mathcal{L}$.

   To show the intersection with the other line, note that the lines $\mathcal{V}$, $\mathcal{R}$ and $\mathcal{N}$ are coplanar, where $\mathcal{N}$ is defined as the line from S in direction N. As the camera center C is on $\mathcal{V}$ and the sphere center S is on $\mathcal{N}$, it follows that the line $\mathcal{A}$ from the camera center C to the sphere center S also lies on the same plane as $\mathcal{V}$, $\mathcal{R}$ and $\mathcal{N}$, and making an angle of $\gamma = 180 - (\alpha + \beta)$ with $\mathcal{R}$, where $\alpha = \angle(\mathcal{N}, \mathcal{R})$ and $\beta = \angle(\mathcal{A}, \mathcal{N})$ (see Fig. 1). This applies to all reflection rays and it follows that any reflection ray $\mathcal{R}$ will intersect $\mathcal{A}$ and $\mathcal{L}$.   □

In 1874, Schubert published his work *Kalkül der Abzählenden Geometrie* in which he showed that the number of lines intersecting four arbitrary lines will be zero, one, two or infinite [15]. Unless the four lines lie on a doubly ruled surface

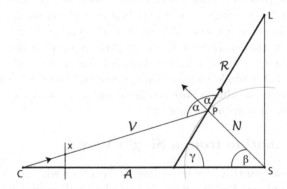

Fig. 1. The image of a line $\mathcal{L}$ on a sphere with center S is determined by reflected viewing rays $\mathcal{R}$ which will intersect two lines, the line $\mathcal{L}$ and a line $\mathcal{A}$ passing through S and camera center C

(single sheet hyperboloid, hyperbolic paraboloid or plane), they will not produce infinite intersecting lines [14,16]. Therefore in the general case the reflection rays in our system will intersect at most two lines, and under a degenerate case the reflection rays lie on a doubly ruled surface and produce infinite intersecting lines. In practice the degenerate case can easily be detected, because the reflection rays will produce a Plücker hyperplane matrix with a nullspace larger than two dimensions.

Corollary 1. *Reconstruction of a line from its reflection on a sphere becomes possible by solving for the two lines intersecting its reflection rays and selecting the one which does not pass through the camera center.*

2.1 Line Intersection in Plücker Space

In order to formulate line intersections algebraically, we adopt the 6-vector Plücker line coordinates representation for directed lines in P^3[17]. Two points $P = (p_x, p_y, p_z, 1)$ and $Q = (q_x, q_y, q_z, 1)$ define a line $\mathcal{L}$ as

$$\mathcal{L} = (l_0, l_1, l_2, l_3, l_4, l_5)$$
$$= (p_x q_y - q_x p_y, p_x q_z - q_x p_z, p_x - q_x, p_y q_z - q_y p_z, p_z - q_z, q_y - p_y). \quad (1)$$

With this notation, lines in P^3 are mapped to homogeneous points $\mathcal{L} = (l_0, l_1, l_2, l_3, l_4, l_5)$ or hyperplanes $\overline{\mathcal{L}} = (l_4, l_5, l_3, l_2, l_0, l_1)$ in 5 dimensional Plücker coordinate space.

A major advantage of this representation is the simplicity of the incidence operation. Given two lines $\mathcal{A}$ and $\mathcal{B}$, the incidence operation is the inner product between the homogeneous Plücker representation of line $\mathcal{A}$ and the hyperplane Plücker representation of line $\mathcal{B}$

$$\mathcal{A} \cdot \overline{\mathcal{B}} = a_0 b_4 + a_1 b_5 + a_2 b_3 + a_3 b_2 + a_4 b_0 + a_5 b_1. \quad (2)$$

Since the inner product will be zero for intersecting lines, solving for n lines $\mathcal{I}_1, \mathcal{I}_2, ..., \mathcal{I}_n$ that intersect m given lines $\mathcal{L}_1, \mathcal{L}_2, ..., \mathcal{L}_m$ is equivalent to finding the n-dimensional nullspace of a matrix formed by the Plücker hyperplane representations of the given lines:

$$Mx = \begin{bmatrix} \overline{\mathcal{L}_1} \\ \overline{\mathcal{L}_2} \\ \vdots \\ \overline{\mathcal{L}_m} \end{bmatrix} x = 0. \quad (3)$$

Finding the set of lines x that map M to a null vector, implies that for each row i the inner product $\overline{\mathcal{L}_i} \cdot x$ equals zero. Given the m reflection lines from the previous section and the task of finding the $n = 2$ intersecting lines, we can simply solve for those lines by finding the nullspace of the matrix M with singular value decomposition

$$M = U\Sigma V^{\mathrm{T}} = \begin{bmatrix} u_{11} & \cdots & u_{1m} \\ \vdots & & \vdots \\ u_{m1} & \cdots & u_{mm} \end{bmatrix} \begin{bmatrix} \sigma_1 & & \\ & \ddots & \\ & & \sigma_6 \\ 0 & \cdots & 0 \\ \vdots & & \vdots \\ 0 & \cdots & 0 \end{bmatrix} \begin{bmatrix} v_{11} & \cdots & v_{16} \\ \vdots & & \vdots \\ v_{61} & \cdots & v_{66} \end{bmatrix}^{\mathrm{T}}. \quad (4)$$

For $n = 2$, M is a rank four matrix and will span a two dimensional subspace that can be parameterized by the two points $a = (v_{15}, \cdots, v_{65})$ and $b = (v_{16}, \cdots, v_{66})$, which correspond to the two smallest singular values σ_5 and σ_6. Fortunately not all points on the 5-dimensional line $\mathcal{L}(t) = at + b$ are 3-dimensional lines, but just those lines $\mathcal{A}$ that satisfy

$$\mathcal{A} \cdot \overline{\mathcal{A}} = 0. \quad (5)$$

Teller and Hohmeyer[18] were the first to formulate and solve this problem by intersecting the line $\mathcal{L}(t)$ with all points that satisfy (5). This produces the quadratic equation

$$(a \cdot \overline{a})t^2 + 2(a \cdot \overline{b}) + (b \cdot \overline{b}) = 0, \quad (6)$$

for which the two real roots correspond to the two intersecting lines. As a result of proposition 1, the nullspace of matrix M will in general be two dimensional. In practice nearly coplanar reflection lines will result in a nullspace with higher dimensions. Due to numerical instabilities, incorrect solutions will likely be selected. An empirical analysis has been performed which considers this problem and is described in the next section.

2.2   Empirical Analysis

In order to study the feasibility of the theoretical formulation above, we analyze synthetically generated images empirically. A specular sphere reflecting a line was rendered using an OpenGL Shading Language program. The reflected line light source was detected by thresholding and subsequent Bezier spline curve fitting, which allowed sub-pixel-accurate sample points for computing the reflection lines. As we are dealing with synthetic data, all camera and sphere parameters are readily available and the reflection lines can be determined. One practical concern about the theoretical formulation in Section 2 is the numerical instability in the case of nearly coplanar reflection lines. Coplanar reflection lines are undesirable because all lines on that plane will intersect the reflection lines and as a result the nullspace selection will be unstable. We use the average angle that lines make with a best fitting plane, as a planarity measurement.

In the first experiment we rendered a synthetic sphere of radius $S_r = 1$ and center $S = (0, 0, 0)^{\mathrm{T}}$ with a synthetic camera. Without loss of generality, let the camera be located at $C = (0, 0, -5)^{\mathrm{T}}$ pointing in the negative z-direction and a line be positioned parallel to the x-axis piercing the y-axis at $L = (0, -5, 0)$. Let A be the vector from S to C and B the shortest vector from S to the line light source. The distance $|A|$ between the camera center and the sphere center as

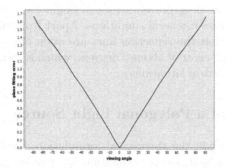

Fig. 2. This plot shows the plane fitting error against the viewing angle. A linear relationship between this angle and the planarity measurement can be identified, with better results for larger angles.

well as the distance $|B|$ between the line and the sphere center is kept constant at 5 units, while the camera is being rotated around the x-axis in 10 degree intervals. Let us define the angle $\angle(A, B)$ as the viewing angle. Fig. 2 plots the plane fitting error against this viewing angle. A linear relationship between the viewing angle and the planarity measurement can be identified, with better results (smaller error) for larger viewing angles.

Fig. 3 plots the plane fitting error while translating the light source along y-axis (left) and translating the camera center along z-axis (right) with constant viewing angle. These plots show a strong relationship between light and camera distances to the plane fitting error. Shorter distances between sphere center and light produce least coplanar reflection rays compared to larger distances. The opposite is true for distances between sphere center and camera center.

The synthetic experiments above show that the coplanarity of the reflection rays depends on the two distances $|\mathcal{A}|$ and $|\mathcal{B}|$ as well as the viewing angle. An increase in the plane fitting error can be observed with large viewing angles, small light distances and relatively large camera distances. This is undesirable

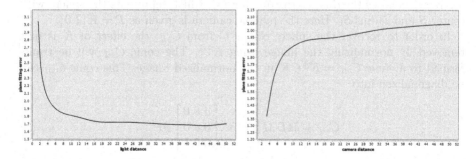

Fig. 3. Plots for plane fitting error while translating the light source along the y-axis (left) and translating the camera center along the z-axis (right) with constant viewing angle

for line reconstruction as it prevents robust single view line estimation from spherical reflections under general conditions. Apart from this, the experiments in this section show that the reflection lines are often close to coplanar, with a maximum plane fitting error of about 3 degrees, which is insufficient for accurate line estimation in practical situations.

3   Estimation of a Polygonal Light Source

In this section, we apply the theoretical formulation developed above for the problem of polygonal light source estimation by treating the light source as a polygon composed of a set of lines. Each line in the set will be independently reconstructed and a polygon will be calculated from the reconstructed lines. It has been shown in the previous section that in practice a line cannot be uniquely reconstructed from a single view of a single sphere, and setups with an additional sphere or an additional view are considered.

In the following, two procedures that estimate polygonal light sources given just the intrinsic camera parameters K are considered. Section 3.2 introduces a closed form solution given a single view of two spheres of the same radius, while Section 3.3 introduces an iterative approach based on two unknown views of a single sphere. Both of the methods require a known translation between the camera center C to the sphere center S. For this reason a solution [8] for estimating the sphere center from its silhouette is described in the following section.

3.1   Where Is the Sphere?

The sphere silhouette, being a conic, can be represented by a 3x3 symmetric matrix C_{sil}, given by

$$\begin{aligned} C_{sil} &= (PQ_s^*P^{\mathrm{T}})^* \\ &= (KK^{\mathrm{T}} - (KS/S_r)(KS/S_r)^{\mathrm{T}})^*, \end{aligned} \tag{7}$$

where Q_s^* denotes the dual to the quadric Q_s, which represents the sphere with center S and radius S_r. Here the pinhole camera is given as $P = K[I\ 0]$.

In order to recover the sphere center C from C_{sil}, the effect of K is first removed by normalizing the image using K^{-1}. The conic C_{sil} will be transformed to a conic $\hat{C}_{sil} = K^{\mathrm{T}}CK$ in the normalized image. This conic $\hat{C}_{sil}$ can be diagonalized into

$$\hat{C}_{sil} = MDM^{\mathrm{T}} = M \begin{bmatrix} a & 0 & 0 \\ 0 & a & 0 \\ 0 & 0 & b \end{bmatrix} M^{\mathrm{T}}, \tag{8}$$

where M is an orthogonal matrix whose columns are the eigenvectors of $\hat{C}_{sil}$, and D is a diagonal matrix consisting of the corresponding eigenvalues. The matrix M^{T} defines a rotation that will transform $\hat{C}_{sil}$ to the circle D with radius

$r = \sqrt{-\frac{b}{a}}$ centered at the origin. This transformation corresponds to rotating the camera about its center until its principle axis passes through the sphere center. The distance d between the camera center and sphere center is given as

$$d = S_r \frac{\sqrt{1+r^2}}{r}. \tag{9}$$

Finally, the sphere center can be recovered as

$$C = M[0\ 0\ d]^{\mathrm{T}}$$
$$= dm_3, \tag{10}$$

where m_3 is the third column of M.

3.2 Two Spheres and a Single View

This section gives a solution for polygonal light estimation by introducing a second, identical sphere into the scene. Two identical spheres for light estimation have been utilized before [19]. In contrast to previous work, this section provides a closed form solution. Note that the iterative method provided by Zhou et. al. [19] gives no guarantee for convergence.

Firstly the relative locations of both identical spheres are estimated by the method given in section 3.1. The reflecting rays $\mathcal{R}_1, ..., \mathcal{R}_m$ for the first sphere and the reflecting rays $\mathcal{R}'_1, ..., \mathcal{R}'_n$ for the second sphere will form the equation

$$Mx = \begin{bmatrix} \overline{\mathcal{R}_1} \\ \vdots \\ \overline{\mathcal{R}_m} \\ \overline{\mathcal{R}'_1} \\ \vdots \\ \overline{\mathcal{R}'_n} \end{bmatrix} x = 0. \tag{11}$$

The reflection lines for a single sphere will be relatively coplanar. However, by including the reflection lines from a second sphere, an intersecting line can be determined, which corresponds to an edge of the light source. Repeating this process for all sides of the polygonal light source results in n lines in space. Correspondence for the n sides of the light source can be achieved easily because the order of the edges will not change in the specular reflection.

3.3 Two Views of a Single Sphere

In the following method two images of a single sphere are taken from two distinct viewpoints. Projection matrices for the two cameras can be written as

$$P_1 = K_1[I\ C_1]$$
$$P_2 = K_2[E\ C_2], \tag{12}$$

where K_1 and K_2 are the two camera calibration matrices (assumed to be known) and C_1 and C_2 are determined from the method described in Section 3.1. The sphere center is the world origin and the first camera is chosen as a reference view. The unknown 3x3 rotation matrix E is independent from the image C_{sil} of the sphere but can be determined from the specular reflection. This follows from the fact that the location of the highlight on the sphere surface depends on the cameras location as well as the light location.

Given the correct rotation matrix E, the reflection lines for both views corresponding to an edge of the light source can be determined. Note that the resulting reflection lines for a single view will be relatively coplanar, but by including the reflection lines from the other view, an intersecting line can be determined which gives an edge of the light source. This process is repeated for all edges of the light source.

To solve for the unknown rotation, an optimization over the 3-dimensional rotation space is performed using the cost

$$E_{cost} = w_1\alpha_r + w_2 d_r + k, \tag{13}$$

where w_1 and w_2 are weight coefficients determined experimentally, α_r is the average angle between the reflection lines and d_r the average distance between them.

To add additional constraint on the rotation E, a rectangular light source is assumed and k is a measurement of how rectangular the given lines $\{\mathcal{W}, \mathcal{X}, \mathcal{Y}, \mathcal{Z}\}$ are, and is defined as

$$\begin{aligned} k = \angle(\mathcal{W}, \mathcal{Y}) + \angle(\mathcal{X}, \mathcal{Z}) \\ + |\angle(\mathcal{W}, \mathcal{X}) - 90| + |\angle(\mathcal{X}, \mathcal{Y}) - 90| \\ + |\angle(\mathcal{Y}, \mathcal{Z}) - 90| + |\angle(\mathcal{Z}, \mathcal{W}) - 90|. \end{aligned} \tag{14}$$

Instead of performing an optimization directly on the parameterized search space, an initial global minimum is found by subdividing the search space. The optimization is subsequently initialized with the global minimum of the subdivision. This procedure avoids an early termination of the optimization in a local minimum.

4   Experimental Results

The closed form solution of Section 3.2 and the iterative method of Section 3.3 for recovering a polygonal light source have been implemented. Experiments on both synthetic and real data were carried out, and the results are presented in the following sections.

4.1   Synthetic Experiments

A synthetic experiment with a rectangular light source and (a) a single view of two spheres and (b) two views of a single sphere has been performed. An

OpenGL Shading Language program has been written to model the specular reflection of the polygonal light sources on the spheres. Both the silhouette of the spheres and the edges of the specular highlight were extracted automatically by thresholding and subsequent fitting of Bezier spline curves.

All ground truth data is available for the edges of the light source and estimation errors can be calculated as the angle between the estimated edges and ground truth edges. Their average was 3.77 degree for experiment (a) and 1.63 degree for experiment (b). The distance between those lines was used as a second error measurement and their average was $0.079S_r$ for experiment (a) and $0.058S_r$ for experiment (b), where S_r is the radius of the sphere.

4.2 Experiments on Real Data

For the first experiment on real data, two identical plastic white cue snooker balls were imaged from a single viewpoint. The spheres were put below a standard rectangular fluorescent office lamp. The light source has a dimension of $270mm$ x $1170mm$ while the snooker balls' diameter is $57mm$. The intrinsic parameters of the camera were obtained using Zhang's camera calibration method [20]. Cubic Bezier-spline snake was applied to extract the contours of the sphere in the images, and conics were then fitted to these contours using a direct least squares method [21]. Edges from the specular reflection of the rectangular light source were picked and matched manually. One of the spheres is shown in a crop of the image in Fig. 4(a), and Fig. 4(b) illustrates a synthetically generated view of the sphere reflecting the estimated light source. We compared the size of

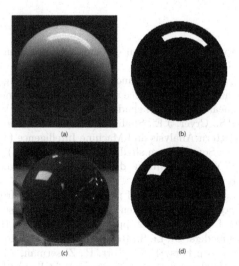

Fig. 4. (a) A standard rectangular fluorescent office lamp is illuminating a plastic white cue snooker ball. (b) A synthetically generated view of the sphere reflecting the estimated light source for the two sphere single view case. (c) A blue snooker ball is enlightened by a smaller rectangular desk light source. (d) The synthetically generated view with estimated light source for the two view single sphere case.

the estimation result with the specification of the light source and found an approximate error of $13mm$ x $52mm$ for the $270mm$ x $1170mm$ light source.

Two views of a single sphere were taken in a second experiment. This time a blue snooker ball was enlightened by a smaller rectangular desk light source with a dimension of $68mm$ x $33mm$. A crop of the image is shown in Fig. 4(c), and Fig. 4(d) illustrates a synthetically generated view of the sphere reflecting the estimated light source. In this case the estimation result had an error of $5mm$ x $3mm$ for the $68mm$ x $33mm$ light source.

5   Conclusion

This paper recovers a polygonal light source from the image of a specular sphere. Its main contributions are

1. an empirical analysis, which shows that line estimation from a single view of a single sphere is not possible in practice;
2. a closed form solution for recovering a polygonal light source from a single view of two spheres; and
3. an iterative approach for rectangular light source estimation based on two views of a single sphere.

Experiments on both synthetic and real images show promising results. In future research, we would like to study the possibility of extending SfS to handle the more complex lighting conditions of a polygonal light source.

References

1. Zheng, Q., Chellappa, R.: Estimation of illuminant direction, albedo, and shape from shading. In: CVPR (1991)
2. Brooks, M.J., Horn, B.K.P.: Shape and source from shading. In: Proceedings of the 9th International Joint Conference on Artificial Intelligence (1985)
3. Pentland, A.P.: Linear shape from shading. Int. J. Comput. Vision (1990)
4. Zhang, R., Tsai, P.S., Cryer, J.E., Shah, M.: Shape from shading: A survey. IEEE Transactions on Pattern Analysis and Machine Intelligence (1999)
5. Yang, Y., Yuille, A.: Sources from shading. In: CVPR (1991)
6. Zhang, Y., Yang, Y.H.: Illuminant direction determination for multiple light sources. In: CVPR (2000)
7. Wang, Y., Samaras, D.: Estimation of multiple illuminants from a single image of arbitrary known geometry. In: Heyden, A., Sparr, G., Nielsen, M., Johansen, P. (eds.) ECCV 2002. LNCS, vol. 2352, pp. 272–288. Springer, Heidelberg (2002)
8. Wong, K.Y.K., Schnieders, D., Li, S.: Recovering light directions and camera poses from a single sphere. In: Forsyth, D., Torr, P., Zisserman, A. (eds.) ECCV 2008, Part I. LNCS, vol. 5302, pp. 631–642. Springer, Heidelberg (2008)
9. Takai, T., Niinuma, K., Maki, A., Matsuyama, T.: Difference sphere: an approach to near light source estimation. In: CVPR (2004)
10. Debevec, P.: Rendering synthetic objects into real scenes: bridging traditional and image-based graphics with global illumination and high dynamic range photography. In: SIGGRAPH (1998)

11. Zhou, W., Kambhamettu, C.: A unified framework for scene illuminant estimation. Image Vision Computing (2008)
12. Lanman, D., Wachs, M., Taubin, G., Cukierman, F.: Reconstructing a 3d line from a single catadioptric image. In: 3DPVT (2006)
13. Lanman, D., Crispell, D., Wachs, M., Taubin, G.: Spherical catadioptric arrays: Construction, multi-view geometry, and calibration. In: 3DPVT (2006)
14. Gasparini, S., Sturm, P.: Multi-view matching tensors from lines for general camera models. In: CVPR Workshops (2008)
15. Schubert, H.: Kalkül der Abzählenden Geometrie. Teubner (1874)
16. Hilbert, D.: Geometry and the Imagination. Chelsea Pub. Co. (1952)
17. Hartley, R.I., Zisserman, A.: Multiple View Geometry in Computer Vision, 2nd edn. Cambridge University Press, Cambridge (2004)
18. Teller, S., Hohmeyer, M.: Determining the lines through four lines. J. Graph. Tools (1999)
19. Zhou, W., Kambhamettu, C.: Estimation of the size and location of multiple area light sources. In: ICPR (2004)
20. Zhang, Z.: Flexible camera calibration by viewing a plane from unknown orientations. In: ICCV (1999)
21. Fitzgibbon, A.W., Fisher, R.B.: A buyer's guide to conic fitting. In: BMVC (1995)

Face Relighting Based on Multi-spectral Quotient Image and Illumination Tensorfaces

Ming Shao, Yunhong Wang, and Peijiang Liu

School of Computer Science and Engineering, Beihang University, Beijing, China
{shaoming,pjliu}@cse.buaa.edu.cn,
yhwang@buaa.edu.cn

Abstract. In this paper, a new approach to face relighting by the product of reflectance image and illumination Tensorfaces is proposed. With a pair of multi-spectral images, a near infrared and a visual image, the intrinsic images decomposition can be implemented and corresponding reflectance image is derived. Besides, the illumination images obtained from last step as well as the input visual images constitute a 3-D tensor, on which super-resolution and maximum a posteriori probability estimation are carried out. And then, illumination Tensorfaces under specific light are derived, by which face under target illumination can be synthesized. In contrast to commonly used shape models or shape dependent models, the proposed method only relies on Lambertian assumption and manages to recover reflectance of the face. Besides, compared with the existing methods, i.e. Tensorfaces and Quotient Image, our methods properly preserve the identity of the subject as well as the texture details. Experiments show that the proposed method is not only simple when deriving intrinsic images, but also practical when performing face relighting.

1 Introduction

Face relighting plays an increasingly essential role in image processing, computer vision and graphic communities owing to its various applications, i.e. face detection and recognition, image retrieval, video conference, virtual reality, movie special effects, and digital face cloning. For realistic face synthesis, the following three properties are critical to hold: retaining facial features, reproducing various skin reflectance and preserving the identity of a subject. Although a great number of face relighting algorithms have been proposed previously aimed at dealing with the problems mentioned above, synthesizing a plausible facial image is still a challenge task. In fact, instead of improving the quality of synthesized images, most of existing face relighting work pays more attention on enhancing the recognition rate.

In face relighting, most algorithms factorize a single or multiple images into lighting and reflectance components firstly and many methods are proposed in recent years aimed at solving this factorization problems: Illumination Cone [1], Quotient Image [2], Spherical Harmonic Subspace [3], [4], Morphable faces [5], [6], Tensorfaces [7], [8], Intrinsic Images [9], [10], and subspace model-based approach using BRDF [11], as depicted in Fig. 1. All these methods can be clearly categorized based

H. Zha, R.-i. Taniguchi, and S. Maybank (Eds.): ACCV 2009, Part III, LNCS 5996, pp. 108–117, 2010.

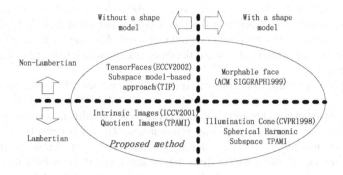

Fig. 1. Recent work concerned with face relighting. Italic: method proposed in this paper.

on whether a 3-D shape model or the Lambertian assumption is used or not. In this paper, under Lambertian assumption, we propose a method to synthesize new facial images by illumination Tensorfaces and intrinsic images without a shape model.

The term "intrinsic images" is first introduced by Barrow and Tenenbaum [9] in 1978 to refer to a midlevel decomposition of the sort depicted in Fig. 2. The observed image is the product of two images: an illumination image and a reflectance image. Because of a shortness of a full 3D description of the scene, we call this a midlevel description. The physical causes of changes in lighting at different points are not made explicit in reflectance image, and we rarely see any highlights or cast shadow. However in the illumination image, not only shadow but also specularity is depicted.

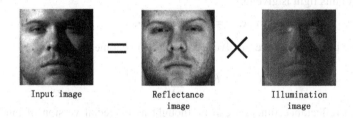

Fig. 2. The intrinsic image decomposition. The input image is decomposed into two parts, a reflectance image and an illumination image.

The major contribution of this paper is to derive intrinsic images from Multi-Spectral Quotient Image and implement face relighting by the product of reflectance images and illumination Tensorfaces to render a more realistic image other than only enhancing recognition rates. Weiss [10] proposed an intrinsic images decomposition method with assumption that illumination images will give rise to sparse filter outputs. However, images sequences are necessary in his method for approaching this problem as a maximum-likelihood estimation, which sometimes is impossible for few inputs. As to our method, only a pair of multi-spectral images, a near infrared (NIR) and a visual image (VIS) are enough to derive the reflectance image. In addition, unlike the Illumination Cone [1], Spherical Harmonic Subspace [3], [4] or Morphable face [5], [6], the proposed method does not need a 3-D shape, leading to a practical but simple solution of face relighting. Besides, the existing method, i.e. Tensorfaces [7], though providing a reasonable illumination simulation on face, fails to preserve the identity properly. The proposed method can cover this drawback since the identity information is largely retained in the reflectance image, which remains still during the relighting process.

The paper is organized as follows. In section 2, we introduce the multi-spectral properties and make an explanation of what we call "Multi-Spectral Quotient Image". Section 3 sets up two 3-D training tensors as the basic multilinear analysis tool, which include factors of identity, pixels and illumination. Then super-resolution is carried out aimed at obtaining the "true" identity of input image in high-resolution tensor space and the target illumination Tensorfaces are derived, by which the relighting procedure can proceed. Section 4 discusses the experimental database and results before conclusions are drawn in section 5.

2   Multi-spectral Quotient Image

In this section, we first take a brief view of intrinsic image decomposition model, and then we will introduce what we call Multi-Spectral Quotient Image and justify its correctness.

2.1   Intrinsic Images Decomposition Models

According to Lambertian reflectance function, if a distant light source l reaches a surface point with albedo R and normal direction n, then intensity I, reflected by the point due to this light is given by:

$$I(x, y) = R(x, y)n(x, y) \cdot l .\tag{1}$$

When more light sources are involved, equation (1) becomes:

$$I(x, y) = R(x, y)\sum_{i=1}^{k} n(x, y) \cdot l_i .\tag{2}$$

Lambertian reflectance function can be thought as a special version of intrinsic images, where R stands for a view independent reflectance (albedo) value, and L is the shading of Lambertian surface:

$$L(x, y) = \sum_{i=1}^{k} \max(n(x, y) \cdot l_i, 0) .\tag{3}$$

Combining equation (2) with (3), we obtain:

$$I(x, y) = R(x, y)L(x, y) .\tag{4}$$

Recovering two intrinsic images R and L from a single input remains a difficult problem for computer vision systems since it is a classic ill-posed problem. In [10], Weiss focus on a slightly easier version of the problem. Given a sequence of T images whose reflectance images are constant over time and illumination images change, the decomposition can be derived. Fig. 2 shows one examples of reflectance and illumination images from Yale B face database gained by Weiss's method.

2.2 Multi-spectral Images Properties

Spectral measurements from human tissue have been used for many years for characterization and monitoring applications. The interaction of light with human tissue has been studied extensively [12], [13], [14] and a model for skin color in multi-spectral has been built [15]. In this paper, we only focus on two typical spectral, point visual light (VIS) source of 520nm and point near infrared (NIR) light source of 850nm in that their appearances are fairly distinct and each of them includes different facial features of the same subject, as depicted in Fig. 3.

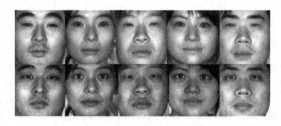

Fig. 3. An example of NIR and VIS image pairs. The first row is a group of five NIR facial images under frontal illumination and the second row is the counterpart of VIS images which are taken simultaneously using a two CCD camera.

There are two reasons for this phenomenon. First, due to different skin, eyes and lips reflectance between NIR and VIS, the intensity (I) of images is quite different, which indicates that the reflectance varies with spectral changes. This sort of changes regarding spectral has been explicitly revealed in [16] and serve as the main reason for the brightness difference between two images. For example, the skin under NIR is brighter than that under VIS, whereas the eyeballs and eyebrows possess the reverse trend. Another reason is that under NIR, skin has a larger penetration depth than for visible wavelengths enabling imaging the subsurface characteristics. We employ tissue thickness that reduces the light intensity to 37 percent of the intensity at the surface to describe this parameter. The optical penetration depth is defined as $1/\sqrt{3\mu_a\mu_s'}$ where μ_a and μ_s' are the absorption coefficient and reduced scattering coefficient of the tissue, respectively. For a typical person, we have μ_a =0.77mm^{-1} and μ_s' =1.89 mm^{-1} in the visual light and μ_a =0.02mm^{-1} and μ_s' =1.31 mm^{-1} in near infrared, which means a 0.479mm and a 3.567mm penetration depth of facial skin respectively. At the latter depth, the tissue is smoother than the surface part and has more unified reflectance, giving rise to a better expression of facial shape and illumination information. These unique properties of multi-spectral images enlighten us to derive a novel but simple method to carry out intrinsic image decomposition in the following parts.

2.3 Multi-spectral Quotient Image

According to Lambertian model, the VIS and NIR images reflectance function can be expressed as:

$$I_{VIS}(x,y) = R_{VIS}(x,y) \cdot \max(n_{VIS}(x,y) \cdot l_{VIS}, 0) , \qquad (5)$$

$$I_{NIR}(x, y) = R_{NIR}(x, y) \cdot \max(n_{NIR}(x, y) \cdot l_{NIR}, 0) , \qquad (6)$$

where all parameters share the same meaning with equation (1) and " $\cdot$ " denotes dot product. Specifically, subscripts of parameters indicate that they pertain to VIS and NIR images respectively. In this paper, a pair of multi-spectral images is captured simultaneously with roughly the same light intensity and direction which guarantees that the parameter l_{VIS} is close to l_{NIR}. Besides, since the images of one subject are taken at the same time, the shape n_{VIS} and n_{NIR} are exactly the same. Combining this with equation (5) and (6), we obtain the following deduction of Multi-Spectral Quotient Image (MQI):

$$\text{MQI} = \frac{I_{VIS}(x, y)}{I_{NIR}(x, y)} = \frac{R_{VIS}(x, y)}{R_{NIR}(x, y)} \cdot \alpha = \frac{R_{VIS}(x, y)}{c} \cdot \alpha = \beta \cdot R_{VIS}(x, y) , \qquad (7)$$

where α is a constant, denoting the ratio of $|l_{VIS}|$ to $|l_{NIR}|$ for they are not identical with each other, though very close and c is the reflectance of NIR image at skin area. Term $\max(n_{VIS}(x, y) \cdot l_{VIS}, 0) / \max((n_{NIR}(x, y) \cdot l_{NIR}), 0)$ is omitted for light source direction and shape vector on face between these two spectral are nearly the same, leaving only the light intensity ratio α between VIS and NIR. Here notice that we use constant c instead of $R_{NIR}(x, y)$ to represent the reflectance of face under NIR environment due to spectral characteristics as we mentioned in section 3.1. Therefore, the skin area of NIR image turns out to be a "pseudo illumination image" and MQI equals to reflectance image of VIS multiplying some constant β. However, areas other than skin on face render slightly different reflectance which cannot be approximately expressed by only one fixed parameter c. The bias of them can be greatly improved by a pre-trained mask which will be explained detailedly in section 3.2. Fig. 4 shows some MQI examples.

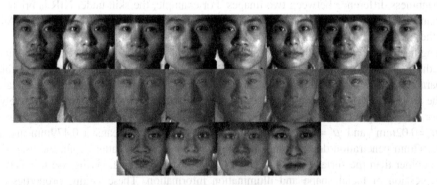

Fig. 4. Some examples of the Multi-Spectral Quotient Image. The first row contains facial images under arbitrary illuminations and images of second row are corresponding illumination images of inputs. The final row is their reflectance images gained with the proposed method.

3   Relighting with Illumination Tensorfaces

In this section, a tensor structure for face images of different modalities involving changes from visual images to illumination images and people identity is set up at first. Then an algorithm for super-resolution in tensor parameter vector space is derived. Finally, with the reflectance image achieved from last section and the illumination Tensorfaces gained in this section, face relighting can be performed. Fig. 5 depicts the whole process of the proposed method, which includes 4 steps, 1) modeling face in tensor space, 2) super-resolution and Bayesian inference, 3) Multi-Spectral Quotient Image, 4) face relighting.

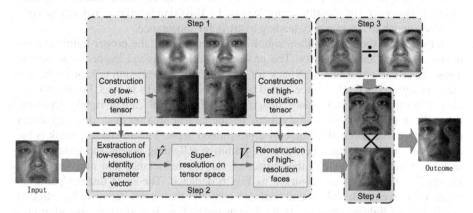

Fig. 5. The whole procedure of the proposed method, including 4 steps, where $\hat{V}$ and V are the identity parameter vectors for the low-resolution input face image and unknown high-resolution image.

3.1 Modeling Face Images in Tensor Space

First a tensor structure is constructed from multi-modal face images and HOSVD is used to decompose them [7]. The decomposed model can be expressed as:

$$D = Z \times_1 \mathbf{U}_{idens} \times_2 \mathbf{U}_{illums} \times_3 \mathbf{U}_{pixels} , \qquad (8)$$

where tensor D groups the multi-modal face images into tensor structure, and core tensor Z governs the interactions between the 3 mode factors. The mode matrix $\mathbf{U}_{idens}, \mathbf{U}_{illums}$ and $\mathbf{U}_{pixels}$ span the parameter space of different people identities, illuminations, and face images respectively. Specifically, the illumination factors in this paper involve changes from a frontal visual image to its corresponding illumination image.

In order to carry out super-resolution in tensor space using Bayesian inference to simulate an illumination image from a given frontal face, a low-resolution and its counterpart high-resolution training tensor space are set up at first. Since the down-sampling image maintains most of its low frequency information, the shape structure, the identity is retained. By projecting a frontal image into the low-resolution training tensor space, we can achieve its identity parameter vector $\hat{V}$. For the purpose of re-lighting, we use Bayesian model to perform multi-modal face image super-resolution and derive input image's "true" identity V in high-resolution tensor space. Then, by implementing multilinear algebraic operations, the illumination image under some lighting is recovered. For more details on super-resolution in tensor space, readers can refer to [17].

3.2 Face Relighting

Face relighting performs by the product of reflectance images and illumination images. In fact, a direct simulation to form an image under some illumination using Tensorfaces without intrinsic factorization process is feasible and Tensorfaces can provide a reasonable lighting simulation in that the first several eigenvectors of a serial of images with varying illuminations are able to represent most of lighting changes. However, the identity vector learned by Bayesian inference may not be right or close enough to the true one, leading to artificial appearance.

In this paper, the learned illumination Tensorfaces retain the proper lighting information, yet the "false" identity. The product of reflectance and learned illumination Tensorfaces can cover this drawback for most identity information is kept in the former. However, since reflectance varied between NIR and VIS in eyes, lip, mouth and skin respectively, the reflectance image gained from MQI cannot rightly represent them all. In this paper, we mainly focus on the largest area on face, skin and adjust other areas to the acceptable range by a pre-trained mask. This re-shading mask is the average of quotient images between the primitive relighting results and ground truth images, which can eliminate the impact of varying reflectance and other uncertain factors, i.e. brightness and contrast, as Fig. 6 depicted. The most distinct parts between primitive result and ground truth are eyes and the former seems to be artificial due to lack of lighting changes. In the last image of Fig. 6, re-shading operation provides a more acceptable simulation around the eye area.

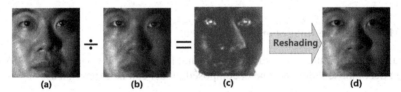

(a)   (b)   (c)   (d)

Fig. 6. The generation and utility of pre-trained re-shading mask. (a) Ground truth, (b) primitive result, (c) re-shading mask, (d) outcome after re-shading.

4   Experiments and Results

The experiments aim at evaluating the proposed method of intrinsic image decomposition and showing the utility of this decomposition in image processing. What's more, with illumination Tensorfaces, face relighting can be employed on the given frontal visual images. All images in our experiments are captured with JAI AD080 digital camera, which can take NIR and VIS images at the same time for it possesses two CCD sensors, sensitive to near infrared and visible light respectively.

The first part of this section reveals how the proposed intrinsic decomposition method is applied in the image synthesis with a simple image addition. Given an image

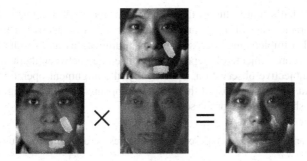

Fig. 7. An example of image synthesis. The bend-aid image is directly added to the facial image under arbitrary illumination, resulting in an artificial synthesized image in the first row. In the second row, the bend-aid is firstly added to the reflectance image, and then multiplied by the illumination image.

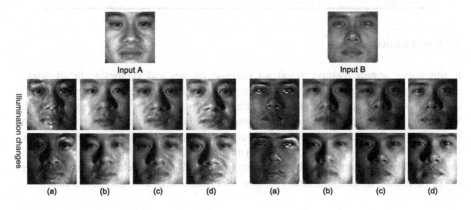

Fig. 8. Qualitative comparison with Quotient Image [2], Tensorfaces [7] and ground truth images. (a) Quotient Image, (b) Tensorfaces, (c) proposed method, (d) ground truth images.

in arbitrary illumination, we find that a direct image addition will lead to an unreal result, for additional parts rarely carry any illumination. However, if the additional part is added to the reflectance image at first, and then multiplied by the illumination image, the result seems fairly true, as Fig. 7 depicted.

The second experiment presents face relighting and images captured are VIS and NIR ones. The VIS database contains 100 subjects under several illuminations with pure green LED (520nm) while the NIR database with frontal illumination (850nm) is taken simultaneously. In this paper, 50 subjects are randomly selected to be probe set, and others for training. Fig. 8 shows some example of the proposed method, from which we can see that Quotient Image leads to some highlight areas around the edge of eyes, nose, brows and mouth due to lack of dense alignment and its result does not appear convincing because the lighting effect is not consistent in different parts of the face. Tensorfaces perform reasonably well in lighting simulation, but fail to preserve the identity, resulting in a unlike face compared with ground truth. Our synthesized images are more realistic and perceptually closer to the ground truth images and handle both specularity and shadow well. What's more, due to the better performance on retaining texture details of face, the characteristics of inputs are fairly preserved. An objective test using correlation score is also implemented across different illuminations and results are shown in Table 1. These scores objectively represent the difference between them and are consistent with the subjective observation. Specifically, the alignment operation benefits the Tensorfaces and eliminates most of their blurring appeared when training images do not share the same shape with the probe set.

Table 1. Comparison of the average correlation scores across different illuminations for 4 algorithms

Algorithm	Quotient Image	Tensor-faces	Proposed method before re-shading	Proposed method after re-shading
Correlation Scores	0.9448	0.9813	0.9773	0.9859

5   Conclusions

In this paper, a new method to extract intrinsic images and synthesize facial images under different lighting conditions has been proposed. Firstly, the reflectance image of a subject is simply recovered through dividing its frontal VIS by NIR image. Then, the VIS image is projected to the low-resolution training tensor space in order to obtain the target illumination images. Finally, the image under some illumination can be synthesized with a product operation. The experimental results of our method are promising and proved to be more realistic than existing methods, i.e. Tensorfaces and Quotient Image on texture details, specularity or shadow simulation and identity preservation.

Acknowledgement

This work was supported by the opening funding of the State Key Laboratory of Virtual Reality Technology and Systems (Beihang University).

References

1. Georghiades, A.S., Belhumeur, P.N., Kriegman, D.J.: From Few to many: Illumination cone models for face recognition under variable lighting and pose. IEEE Trans. Pattern Anal. Mach. Intell. 23(6), 643–660 (2001)
2. Shashua, A., Riklin-Raviv, T.: The quotient image: Class-based re-rendering and recognition with varying illuminations. IEEE Trans. Pattern Anal. Mach. Intell. 23(2), 129–139 (2001)
3. Basri, R., Jacobs, D.: Lambertian reflectance and linear subspaces. IEEE Trans. Pattern Anal. Mach. Intell. 25(2), 218–233 (2003)
4. Ramamoorthi, R., Hanrahan, P.: On the relationship between radiance and irradiance: determining the illumination from images of a convex Lambertian object. JOSA A 18(10), 2448–2459 (2001)

5. Blanz, V., Vetter, T.: A morphable model for the synthesis of 3D faces. In: Proc. ACM SIGGRAPH (1999)
6. Blanz, V., Scherbaum, K., Vetter, T., Seidel, H.: Exchanging faces in images. Presented at the Proc. EuroGraphics (2004)
7. Vasilescu, M.A.O., Terzopoulos, D.: Multilinear analysis of image ensembles: Tensor-Faces. In: Proc. IEEE ECCV (2002)
8. Lee, J., Moghaddam, B., Pfister, H., Machiraju, R.: A bilinear illumination model for robust face recognition. In: Proc. IEEE Int. Conf. Computer Vision (2005)
9. Barrow, H.G., Tenenbaum, J.M.: Recovering Intrinsic scene Characteristics from Images. Computer Vision System (1978)
10. Weiss, Y.: Deriving Intrinsic Images from Image Sequences. In: Proc. of IEEE ICCV (2001)
11. Shim, H., Luo, J., Chen, T.: A Subspace Model-Based Approach to Face Relighting Under Unknown Lighting and Poses. IEEE Trans. Image Process. 17(8), 1331–1341 (2008)
12. Tuchin, V.: Tissue Optics: Light Scattering Methods and Instruments for Medical Diagnosis. SPIE Press, Bellingham (2000)
13. Anderson, R., Parrish, J.: The Optics of Human Skin. J. Investigative Dermatology 77(1), 13–19 (1981)
14. Gemert, M., Jacques, S., Sternborg, H., Star, W.: Skin Optics. IEEE Trans. Biomedical Eng. 36(12), 1146–1154 (1989)
15. Angelopoulou, E., Molana, R., Daniilidis, K.: Multispectral Skin Color for Modeling. In: Proc. of IEEE International Conference on Computer Vision and Pattern Recognition (2001)
16. Pan, Z., Healey, G., Prasad, M., Tromberg, B.: Face Recognition in Hyperspectral Images. IEEE Trans. Pattern Anal. Mach. Intell. 25(12), 1552–1560 (2003)
17. Jia, K., Gong, S.: Multi-modal tensor face for simultaneous super-resolution and recognition. In: Proc. IEEE Int. Conf. Computer Vision (2005)

Perception-Based Lighting Adjustment
of Image Sequences

Xiaoyue Jiang[1,2,3,*], Ping Fan[1,2], Ilse Ravyse[1,2], Hichem Sahli[1,2],
Jianguo Huang[1,3], Rongchun Zhao[1,3], and Yanning Zhang[1,3]

[1] VUB-NPU Joint Research Group on Audio Visual Signal Processing (AVSP)
x.y.jiang@bham.ac.uk
[2] Vrije Universiteit Brussel, Department ETRO, VUB-ETRO,
Pleinlaan 2, 1050 Brussels
{pfan,icravyse,hsahli}@etro.vub.ac.be
[3] Northwestern Polytechnic University, Xi'an 710072, P.R. China
{ynzhang,rczhao}@nwpu.edu.cn

Abstract. In this paper, we propose a 2-step algorithm to reduce the
lighting influences between frames in an image sequence. First, the lighting parameters of a perceptual lighting model are initialized using an
entropy measure. Then the difference between two successive frames is
used as a cost function for further optimization the above lighting parameters. By applying the proposed lighting model optimization on an
image sequence, the neighboring frames become similar in brightness and
contrast while features are enhanced. The effectiveness of the proposed
approach is illustrated on the detection and tracking of facial features.

1   Introduction

Most of the image analysis techniques for video sequences consider tracking of
features or objects. Tracking algorithms intend to find similar regions/points in
successive frames. This correspondence process, is easily influenced by illuminations when real images are captured. Therefore illumination is regarded as a
critical factor for robust feature detection and tracking algorithms [1,2]. For a
specific object, e.g. the human face, these challenges are mainly caused by the
variations of pose, expression, occlusion and illumination. Several algorithms
have been proposed dealing with the pose and motion (expression) changes (e.g.
[3,4,5]) and less investigation has been made to cope with the illumination or
lighting changes as pre-processing step.

Recently, several algorithms have been proposed for the adjustment of the
lighting conditions of images before further analysis. To simulate the function
of low frequency lighting, the 3D geometric information of objects has been
used in [6,7,8]. However, recovering the 3D information from images is still an
open problem in computer vision. In addition, its computation complexity is
too expensive to be afforded by an online tracking problem. Although pose-
illumination methods have demonstrated their effectiveness [9,10,11], they still

---

* Actually at School of Psychology, University of Birmingham, B15 2TT, UK.

H. Zha, R.-i. Taniguchi, and S. Maybank (Eds.): ACCV 2009, Part III, LNCS 5996, pp. 118–129, 2010.
© Springer-Verlag Berlin Heidelberg 2010

required to have the 3D model of objects or the training of basis images for different objects. To alleviate this complexity, other class of algorithms have been proposed for enhancing images and reducing the illumination influences, among them we can cite, the quotient image algorithm [12,13], and perception based lighting balance algorithm [14].

In this paper, the difference between successive frames is used as a cost function for optimizing a lighting model of an image sequence. For each image frame, to ensure convergence, the algorithm works in two steps. First initial values of a lighting model parameters are estimated using as measure the entropy of the current image. These values are then used as initial guesses for a constrained least squares optimization problem, considering two successive frames. It is worth pointing out that the proposed algorithm do not only allow shadow removal [15,16], but also adjust the global lighting conditions to be more uniform and enhance the local features of the image.

The paper is organized as follows. We first introduce the used perception based lighting model in Section 2. In Section 3 we give an overview of the proposed lighting adjustment algorithm for image sequence. Section 4 discusses qualitative and quantitative results of the lighting adjustment in the case of facial features detection and tracking. Finally, some conclusions are drawn in Section 5.

2   Lighting Model

The Human Vision System (HVS) can adapt very well under enormously changed lighting conditions. People can see well at daytime and also at night. That is due to the accurate adaptation ability of the HVS. However, image capturing devices seldom have this adaptation ability. For an image taken under extreme lighting conditions, such as the images shown in first row of Fig 2(b), a proper lighting adjustment algorithm should not only adjust the brightness of the images, but also enhance the features of the image, especially for the dark regions. To reach this goal, we propose to reduce the light variations by an adaptive adjustment of the image. Here, we employ a model of photoreceptor adaptation in Human Vision System   [17] in which three parameters (α, f, m) control the lighting adjustment. The adjusted image Y is modeled as a function of these lighting parameters and the input image X as:

$$Y(\alpha, m, f; X) = \frac{X}{X + \sigma(X_a)} V_{max} \tag{1}$$

where σ, referred to as *semi-saturation constant*, X_a the *adaptation level*, and V_{max} determines the maximum range of the output value (we use $V_{max} = 255$ to have grey image output in the range of $[0, 255]$). The semi-saturation constant σ describes the image intensity and its contrast through the parameters f and m, respectively [17]:

$$\sigma(X_a) = (fX_a)^m \tag{2}$$

The adaptation level, X_a, controls the amount of detail in the adjusted images:

$$X_a(x, y) = \alpha X_a^{local}(x, y) + (1 - \alpha)X_a^{global} \tag{3}$$

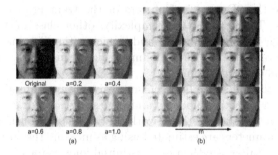

Fig. 1. (a) Adaptation level v.s. α parameter (b) lighting adjustment v.s. m and f parameters

where the global adaption level X_a^{global} is the mean grey level of the image X, and X_a^{local} is the local adaptation level corresponding to the low-frequency information of the images, which can be obtained by convolving the image with a Gauss or Wiener kernel. The parameter α controls the contribution of each term.

The effect of the three parameters on the lighting model (Eq.1) is illustrated in Fig.1. Fig.1(a) depicts, for different values of α, the obtained adjusted images. As one can notice, the details are gradually enhanced with increasing values of α. When $\alpha = 1$, i.e.$X_a = X_a^{local}$, all the details are shown including the noise. Fig.1(b), shows the lighting adjustment results for a fixed value of α, and for different values of f (columns) and m (rows). The image contrast is enhanced when m increases, while the image brightness is enhanced when f is decreasing.

3   Image Sequence Lighting Adjustment

In capturing an image sequence $X_k, k = 1, \cdots N$, the influence of the scene lighting may not be neglected. Often the variations of the lighting conditions cannot be avoided while recording, and therefore lighting adjustment methods must be used before further processing. In this paper, we propose a tow-steps lighting adjustment approach. First, the initial optimal parameters, α_k^0, f_k^0, m_k^0 of each frame X_k are calculated using entropy as objective function. These values are then used as initial guesses for a constrained least squares optimization problem for further refinement of those parameter. In this step, the objective function is the difference between the adjusted previous frame Y_{k-1} and the current frame X_k. The two steps are detailed in the following sections, and experimental results are presented in section 4.

3.1   Single Image Enhancement

It is well known that an image with large entropy value indicates that the distribution of its intensity values is more uniform, i.e. each intensity value has almost the same probability to appear in the image. Hence, the image cannot be locally too bright or too dark. Entropy $H(X)$, defined as:

$$H(X) = -\sum_{i=0}^{255} p(i) log_2(p(i)) \tag{4}$$

where $p(i)$ is the probability of the intensity values i in the whole image, can be employed to evaluate image lighting quality. When all the intensity values have the same probability in the image, the entropy can reach its maximum value 8. However, not all the images can reach the entropy $H(X) = 8$ when they are in their best situation. The optimal entropy value, H_o, is image content dependent. In this paper, we set $H_o = 7$ as the expected optimal entropy for all the images. Therefore the objective function for the lighting adjustment of every single image is

$$J_1(\alpha, m, f) = \underset{\substack{a\in[0,1];m\in[0.3,1) \\ f\in[\exp(-8),\exp(8)]}}{\arg\min} |H(Y(\alpha, m, f; X)) - H_o| \tag{5}$$

The lighting parameter α controls the adaptation level of the images, as in Eq.3. It can adjust the image much more than the other two parameters (f, m). Therefore an alternate optimization strategy is used [14]. First, the parameter α is optimized with fixed m and f. Then the parameter m and f are optimized with fixed α. These two optimizations are repeated until convergence. To initialize, we estimate $\hat{\alpha}$ with fixed m and f which are selected according to the luminance situation of the image. The contrast-control parameter m can be determined by the key k of the image [17], as

$$m = 0.3 + 0.7k^{1.4} \tag{6}$$

The key of the image evaluates the luminance range of the image and is defined as

$$k = \frac{L_{max} - L_{av}}{L_{max} - L_{min}} \tag{7}$$

where L_{av}, L_{min}, L_{max} are the log average, log minimum and log maximum of the luminance respectively. For color images, we use the luminance image computed as $L = 0.2125I_r + 0.7154I_g + 0.0721I_b$, where I_r, I_g, I_b are the red, green, blue channels. The brightness-control parameter f is set to 1. Then the simplex search algorithm [18] is applied for determining the optimal $\hat{\alpha}$. Fixing the value $\hat{\alpha}$ in J_1, the simplex search algorithm is then used to search for optimal $\hat{m}$ and $\hat{f}$. The alternate optimization will stop when the objective function J_1 is smaller than a given threshold.

This approach can adjust an image to have suitable brightness and contrast. Also, it can enhance the local gradient of the image due to the adjustment of the parameter α. However, entropy does not relate to intensity directly. Different images can have the same entropy value while their brightness is different. For example, the images in the second row of Fig. 2(a) and (b), being the lighting adjusted results of the images of the first row, have the same entropy values, but their lighting conditions are not similar. Consequently, for a sequence of images, we still need to adjust the brightness and contrast of successive frames to be similar and therefore enhance their features.

3.2 Lighting Adjustment of Successive Images

In video sequences, the difference between successive frames is due to object and/or camera motions and lighting changes. Whereas the former differences are exploited in object tracking and camera motion estimation, the latter, i.e. lighting differences, are such that the required brightness constancy assumption for tracking gets violated. In this paper, we show that for tracking of slow movement in a sequence captured by a fixed camera, the lighting problem can be reduced by applying a lighting adjustment method. Indeed, the lighting of the overall sequence could be made more uniform (in a sequential manner) by considering the changes between successive frames. We propose to use the difference between successive frames as an objective function to estimate the optimal lighting parameters of the current frame X_j, provided that the previous frame X_{j-1} has been adjusted, i.e. given Y_{j-1}:

$$J_2(\alpha, m, f) = \underset{\substack{\alpha \in [0,1]; m \in [0.3,1) \\ f \in [\exp(-8), \exp(8)]}}{\arg\min} \sum_x \sum_y \left(Y(\alpha, m, f; X_j(x, y)) - Y_{j-1} \right)^2 \quad (8)$$

With Eq.1, the difference $e(\alpha, m, f) = Y(\alpha, m, f; X_j) - Y_{j-1}$ between frames can be written as (for simplicity we drop the pixel index (x, y)):

$$e = \frac{X_j}{X_j - (f_j X_{a_j})^{m_j}} - \frac{X_{j-1}}{X_{j-1} - (f_{j-1} X_{a_{j-1}})^{m_{j-1}}} \quad (9)$$

To simplify the computation of the partial derivatives of the objective function J_2, we consider the following error term:

$$\tilde{e} = \frac{X_j - (f_j X_{a_j})^{m_j}}{X_j} - \frac{X_{j-1} - (f_{j-1} X_{a_{j-1}})^{m_{j-1}}}{X_{j-1}}$$

$$= \frac{(f_j X_{a_j})^{m_j}}{X_j} - \frac{(f_{j-1} X_{a_{j-1}})^{m_{j-1}}}{X_{j-1}} \quad (10)$$

Let $\hat{Y}_{j-1} = (f_{j-1} X_{a_{j-1}})^{m_{j-1}} / X_{j-1}$ and apply log to both side of Eq.10, we can simplify the difference between frames further as

$$\hat{e} = \log \frac{(f_j X_{a_j})^{m_j}}{X_j} - \log \hat{Y}_{j-1}$$

$$= m_j \log f_j + m_j \log X_{a_j} - \log X_j - \log \hat{Y}_{j-1} \quad (11)$$

Then the objective function J_2 can be rewriten as

$$\hat{J}_2(\alpha_j, m_j, f_j) = \underset{\substack{\alpha \in [0,1]; m \in [0.3,1) \\ f \in [\exp(-8), \exp(8)]}}{\arg\min} \sum_x \sum_y \left(m_j \log f_j + m_j \log X_{a_j} - \log X_j - \log \hat{Y}_{j-1} \right)^2$$

$$(12)$$

This formulation allows easily estimating the partial derivatives, and we apply the interior-point algorithm [19] to solve the optimization problem $\hat{J}_2$, with initial values of the lighting parameters α_j^0, f_j^0 and m_j^0 obtained by minimizing Eq.5.

4   Experimental Results

The proposed lighting adjustment algorithms of the previous section have been tested on the PIE facial database [20], from which we selected images under different lighting conditions to compose 3 test sequences, here referred to as L1, L2 and L3. We intend to take these sequences as typical examples to demonstrate the performance of the algorithm in slight lighting variations (L1), overall dark sequences (L2) and suddenly changing light variations (L3). To show the benefits of the proposed image sequence lighting adjustment approach, we compare it to state-of-art lighting adjustment methods for single images , namely, the quotient image (QI) algorithm [12,13], and the well known histogram equalization (HE) approach.

The lighting conditions of the test sequences can be described as follows. Sequence L1 and L2 are composed of 19 frames taken from the same person. The first row of Fig. 2 shows the first 4 frames of L1 and L2. The images in L1 are taken with ambient lighting and 19 different point light sources. The positions of these light points, are 10, 07, 08, 09, 13, 14, 12, 11, 06, 05, 18, 19, 20, 21, and 22, respectively. The images in L2 are taken under the same light point source but without ambient lighting, so they appear to be more dark. Sequence L3 is composed of 39 images which come from L1 and L2 alternately. Thus the lighting condition of the images in L3 is ambient lighting on and off alternately. The first row of Fig. 4 shows the frames 9 to 14 of L3.

To evaluate the lighting quality of the adjusted images, the *key value* (Eq. 7) and entropy are depicted in Figure 3. The *key value* of an image evaluates the luminance range of the image. The entropy, being the mean entropy of the 3 color channels, relates to the distribution of the intensity values in each channel. The key value of all adjusted frames and the original sequence of L3 are shown in Fig. 3(d). The key value zigzags due to the alternate brightness of the original sequence L3. For a sequence with reduced lighting variation the key value should

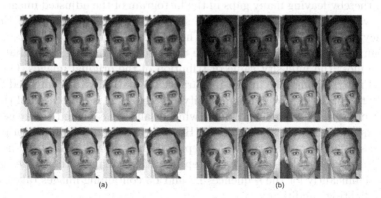

(a)   (b)

Fig. 2. Lighting adjustment results of frame 1 to 4 in L1 and L2. (a) and (b) are results of L1 and L2: from top to bottom are original images, entropy-based optimization, and 2-step optimization results, respectively.

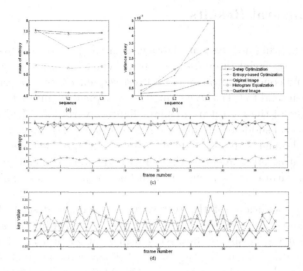

Fig. 3. Entropy and image key curves. (a)and (b) are the mean entropy and the variance of key of all the frames in the original sequences and adjusted results of the sequences, respectively. (c) and (d) are the entropy value and key value of every frame in L3 and different adjusted results of L3, respectively.

stay constant throughout the sequence. Therefore, we show the variance of the key value in Fig. 3(b). For all the 3 test sequences, the variance of the key value of the results of the proposed 2-step optimization algorithm is smaller than that of the other algorithms except HE algorithm. However, HE algorithm costs the entropy value of images, whose results are even worse than the original images (Fig. 3(a)). The reason is that HE algorithm can make the intensity distribution uniform only by skipping values in the intensity range [0,255] of the adjusted images, thereby leaving many gaps in the histogram of the adjusted images. The entropy value of the QI results are the smallest because of the loss of the low frequency information in the images. The proposed algorithm is the largest in the mean of entropy, Fig. 3(a), and we can also see from Fig. 4(a) that these resemble most the intensity value distribution of the original images. Our goal is indeed not to change the image appearance dramatically (as compared to QI) but only to obtain a good lighting quality. Therefore, it is quite normal that we couldn't improve L1 sequence so much, which is already captured at a reasonable lighting quality with the ambient light. However, we were still able to adjust its brightness to be more uniform while keeping its high image quality, as shown in Figure 2(a). On the other hand, our 2-step algorithm enhanced the image lighting quality significantly for the sequences L2 and L3 containing images taken under extreme lighting conditions.

Next, we examine the effect of the lighting adjustment methods on the object's edges of Fig. 4(b) to determine if the methods are appropriate as pre-processing for feature detection methods. Considering the edges in the adjusted images, our

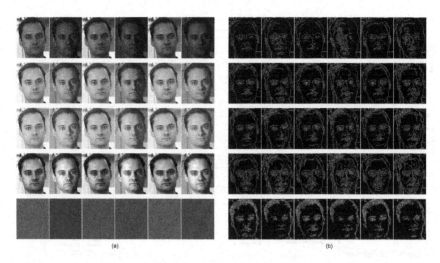

Fig. 4. Lighting adjustment results of frame 9 to 14 in sequence L3.(a) from top to bottom are the original images, entropy-based optimization, 2-step optimization , histogram equalization(HE), and quotient image(QI) results, respectively. (b) the edge of corresponding images in (a).

proposed algorithm enhances the feature of images. This is especially the case for those images taken in a dark environment. Also, highlight are compensated and the influence of shadows on the edges are reduced. The HE algorithm was able to enhance the contrast of the image but at the same time it enhanced noise as well. As we already mentioned, the QI algorithm removed most low frequency information of the image thereby included some important features of the image.

The advantage of the image difference-based optimization step is illustrated for facial feature tracking (on the sequences L1 to L3). We demonstrate that the difficulty of tracking a modified object appearance due to lighting changes can be overcome by employing our proposed algorithm as pre-processing. In this paper, we focus on the results of a template-based eye and mouth corner tracker. That tracker is part of a previously developed approach to automatically locate frontal facial feature points under large scene variations (illumination, pose and facial expressions) [3]. This approach consisted of three steps: (i) we use a kernel-based tracker to detect and track the facial region; (ii) we constrain a detection and tracking of eye and mouth facial features by the estimated face pose of (i) by introducing the parameterized feature point motion model into a Lukas-Kanade tracker; (iii) we detect and track 83 semantic facial points, gathered in a shape model, by constraining the shapes rigid motion and deformation parameters by the estimated face pose of (i) and by the eyes and mouth corner features location of (ii).

The performance of the tracking of the eyes and mouth corners (6 feature points) on the original and adjusted image sequences L1 to L3 is displayed in

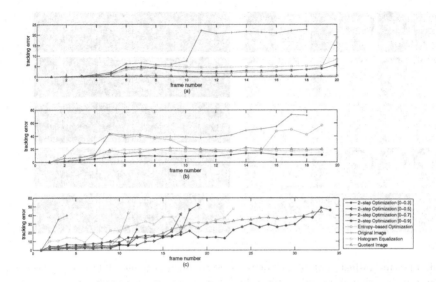

Fig. 5. Feature points tracking error

Figure 5. The tracking error per frame is calculated as the average distance between the real positions (manually identified) and the tracked positions of the 6 feature points in the image. When tracking was lost, the graph is truncated. Figure 5(a) shows that all adjustments of the sequence L1 allow to track until the end of that sequence. The QI shows the smallest tracking error because it enhances the gradient features in the image, but at the cost of obtaining visually unpleasant images (see last row of Fig.4(a)). Compared to the HE results, our two-step optimization does reach a better tracking performance. Because the initial lighting variations in sequence L1 are not that big, the entropy-step alone may already improve the tracking. The benefit of the image difference-based optimization step becomes obvious via the tracking error graphs of the dark sequence L2 in Fig. 5(b). Here, the tracking errors on the 2-step optimization are the smallest. This shows that local features are enhanced very well, but also that taking care of correspondences between images is indeed important. QI and HE adjustments perform worse in tracking. For QI, the reason is that it may enhance the local features (gradients) only when the noise level is not high, i.e. images taken in good lighting conditions such as in L1. On the alternating dark and light sequence L3 the tracking of the original and entropy-optimized sequence is very quickly lost, as shown in Fig. 5(c). It is thus crucial to take into account the sequence aspects in lighting adjustment. It is worth noting that the tracking for our proposed algorithm results was lost only when a part of the image were in deep shadow (such as frame 12, 17 and 19). Although no adjustment method can track until the end of the sequence, we see that a larger enhancement of the local features may allow to track longer (reduced entropy). That was done by enlarging the alpha range from $[0, 0.3]$ to $[0, 0.9]$ in the 2-step optimization

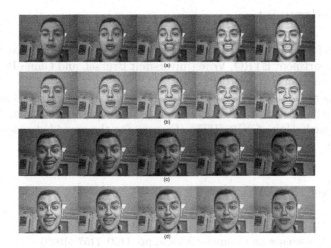

Fig. 6. Shape tracking results. (a) original sequence M1, (b) adjusted sequence M1, (c) original sequence M2, (d) adjusted sequence M2.

(Eq.5 and Eq.8). When comparing the errors before tracking was lost, we see that reducing frame differences, especially with small alpha range, increases the accuracy of the tracking. This shows that enhancing image sequence quality can also help to track.

Finally we tested the constrained shape model tracking (step (iii) of [3]) on an image sequence[1] with high illuminations changes as well as head motion. Before adjustment, shown in Fig. 6(a), (c), some tracked features could not be well delineated due to the illumination changes in the image sequence. The intensity and texture of the face image were improved by our lighting adjustment and therefore all shape points were tracked more efficiently as shown in Fig. 6(b), (d).

5 Conclusion

Most algorithms dealing with the lighting problem only aim at adjusting the lighting conditions of a single image. In this paper we proposed a 2-step lighting adjustment algorithm to reduce the influence of the variation of lighting conditions in an image sequence. First, an entropy-based algorithm is applied to calculate initial lighting parameters of a perceptual lighting model. Then the difference between current and previous frames is employed as an objective function for the further optimization of those lighting parameters. Using this criteria, successive frames are adjusted to have similar brightness and contrast. Image lighting quality, measured by entropy and key value, but also local features are enhanced. We did demonstrate the effectiveness of the proposed algorithm for subsequent image processing, such as detection and tracking.

---

[1] http://www.dia.fi.upm.es/ pcr/downloads.html

Acknowledgement

This work is funded by Joint Research Group on Audio Visual Signal Processing (AVSP), Department ETRO, Vrije Universiteit Brussel, and China Postdoctoral Science Foundation (No.20070421129).

The authors would like to thank Fadi Dornaika from Institut Geographique National, Laboratoire MATIS (France) and Franck Davoine from Heudiasyc Mixed Research Unit, CNRS/UTC (France) for the provided video sequence M1 and M2.

References

1. Lowe, D.G.: Object recognition from local scale-invariant features. In: Proc. International Conference on Computer Vision, pp. 1150–1157 (1999)
2. Schneiderman, H., Kanade, T.: A statistical method for 3d object detection applied to faces and cars. In: IEEE International Conference on Computer Vision, pp. 746–751 (2000)
3. Hou, Y., Sahli, H., Ravyse, I., Zhang, Y., Zhao, R.: Robust shape-based head tracking. In: Blanc-Talon, J., Philips, W., Popescu, D., Scheunders, P. (eds.) ACIVS 2007. LNCS, vol. 4678, pp. 340–351. Springer, Heidelberg (2007)
4. Xiao, R., Li, M., Zhang, H.: Robust multipose face detection in images. IEEE Trans. Circuits and Systems for video technology 12, 31–41 (2004)
5. Zhou, Y., Gu, L., Zhang, H.: Bayesian tangent shape model: estimating shape and pose parameters via bayesian inference. In: Proceedings of IEEE Conference on Computer Vision and Pattern Recognition, vol. 1, pp. 109–116 (2003)
6. Lee, J., Moghaddam, B., Pfister, H., Machiraju, R.: A bilinear illumination model for robust face recognition. In: Proc. IEEE International Conference on Computer Vision (2005)
7. Wang, Y., Liu, Z., Hua, G., Wen, Z., Zhang, Z., Samaras, D.: Face re-lighting from a single image under harsh lighting conditions. In: Proceedings of IEEE International Conference on Computer Vision and Pattern Recognition 2007 (2007)
8. Zhang, L., Wang, S., Samaras, D.: Face synthesis and recognition from a single image under arbitrary unknown lighting using a spherical harmonic basis morphable model. In: Proc. IEEE Conf. Computer Vision and Patter Recognition (2005)
9. Hager, G.D., Belhumeur, P.N.: Efficient region tracking with parametric models of geometry and illumination. IEEE Transactions on Pattern Analysis and Machine Intelligence 20, 1025–1039 (1998)
10. Kale, A., Jaynes, C.: A joint illumination and shape model for visual tracking. In: Proceedings of Computer Vision and Pattern Recognition, pp. 602–609 (2006)
11. Xu, Y., Roy-Chowdhury, A.K.: Integrating motion, illumination, and structure in video sequences with applications in illumination-invariant tracking. IEEE Transactions on Pattern Analysis and Machine Intelligence 29, 793–806 (2007)
12. Gross, R., Brajovic, V.: An image processing algorithm for illumination invariant face recognition. In: Kittler, J., Nixon, M.S. (eds.) AVBPA 2003. LNCS, vol. 2688, pp. 10–18. Springer, Heidelberg (2003)
13. Wang, H., Li, S., Wang, Y.: Generalized quotient image. In: IEEE Conf. Computer Vision and Pattern Recogniton, pp. 498–505 (2004)

14. Jiang, X., Sun, P., Xiao, R., Zhao, R.: Perception based lighting balance for face detection. In: Narayanan, P.J., Nayar, S.K., Shum, H.-Y. (eds.) ACCV 2006. LNCS, vol. 3852, pp. 531–540. Springer, Heidelberg (2006)
15. Liu, F., Gleicher, M.: Texture-consistent shadow removal. In: Forsyth, D., Torr, P., Zisserman, A. (eds.) ECCV 2008, Part IV. LNCS, vol. 5305, pp. 437–450. Springer, Heidelberg (2008)
16. Wang, Y.: Real-time moving vehicle detection with cast shadow removal in video based on conditional random field. IEEE Tran. on Circuits and Systems for Video Technology 19, 437–441 (2009)
17. Reinhard, E., Devlin, K.: Dynamic range reduction inspired by photoreceptor physiology. IEEE Trans. Visualization and Computer Graphics 11, 13–24 (2005)
18. Nelder, J.A., Mead, R.: A simplex method for function minimization. Computer Journal 7, 308–313 (1965)
19. Waltz, R.A., Morales, J.L., Nocedal, J., Orban, D.: An interior algorithm for nonlinear optimization that combines line search and trust region steps. Mathematical Programming 107, 391–408 (2006)
20. Sim, T., Baker, S., Bsat, M.: The cmu pose, illumination, and expression (pie) database. In: Processing of the IEEE International Conference on Automatic Face and Gesture Recognition (2002)

Ultrasound Speckle Reduction via Super Resolution and Nonlinear Diffusion

Bo Wang, Tian Cao, Yuguo Dai, and Dong C. Liu

Computer Science College, Sichuan University, China, 610064
{bowanghawk,ct.radiate,daiyuguo,dongcliu}@gmail.com

Abstract. Recently, some diffusion-based filtering methods have been developed such as anisotropic diffusion (AD) or nonlinear diffusion (ND), which can reduce the speckle noise, at the same time, preserve and enhance the edge/borders in ultrasound image. However, because of the granular pattern of speckle, it is quite difficult to reduce speckle exactly through diffusion-based methods only. In this paper, we propose a super resolution (SR) based ND method. We firstly reduce and compound speckle noise in a sequence of ultrasound images by using a fast SR method for ultrasound image. After this process, ultrasound speckle is much smaller, and the edge and structure are much clearer as complementary information of different images was used. To reduce the noise of the SR improved image, we use a local coherence based ND method. In the end, experimental results of the proposed method are compared with some other AD methods to demonstrate its effectiveness.

1 Introduction

Ultrasound imaging systems are widely used because of its real-time image formation, portability, low cost and noninvasive nature. However, due to the nature of ultrasound imaging, speckle as a dominant noise decreases the resolution of ultrasound image. Moreover, because of the presence of speckle, it is quite difficult to directly use common image processing methods in ultrasound image (such as feature detection, image segmentation and image registration). Therefore, finding appropriate method to reduce speckle noise in ultrasound image is a hot area for researchers in medical image processing. After Perona and Malik's seminal work [1], since 2000, many researchers studied anisotropic diffusion (AD) based ultrasound speckle reduction methods, such as speckle reducing anisotropic diffusion (SRAD) [2], and oriented speckle reducing anisotropic diffusion (OSRAD) [3] and semi-implicit scheme based nonlinear diffusion method in ultrasound speckle reduction (SIND) [4]. These methods have similar results in reducing speckle noise and preserving edge in ultrasound image.

However, all of above AD methods process ultrasound B mode image directly without utilizing an advanced image restoration method. In this way, affecting by the granular speckle, they all cannot reduce ultrasound speckle noise exactly. In order to get better denoising result, we firstly use a new ultrasound image fast super resolution (SR) method [5] to restore ultrasound image. This method can reconstruct an enhanced ultrasound image from a sequence of ultrasound images by using a maximum

H. Zha, R.-i. Taniguchi, and S. Maybank (Eds.): ACCV 2009, Part III, LNCS 5996, pp. 130–139, 2010.
© Springer-Verlag Berlin Heidelberg 2010

a-posteriori framework. Moreover, this method can automatically escape the errors generated by outliers in a sequence of input images. After the image restoration, we will get an improved ultrasound image in which the speckle noise is much smaller and structures are much clearer. To reduce the noise in the restored image, we propose to employ local coherence to control diffusion coefficients in our ND method. In addition, our ND method can be discretized by additive operator splitting (AOS) scheme [6] so that we can use large time step size (TSS) in the process of iteration to do speedup. To our knowledge, this is the first paper to address the speckle reduction of SR restored ultrasound images.

This paper is organized as follows. Section 2 shortly introduces the ultrasound image fast SR method [5]. Section 3 presents our AD method in which we use local coherence to control diffusion coefficients at each point of image. Section 4 demonstrates the experimental results. Section 5 presents the conclusion.

2 Fast Super Resolution for Ultrasound Image Reconstruction

The SR problem is an ill-posed inverse problem. In [5], the authors used a maximum a-posteriori (MAP) approach with transformation information, and they utilized AD [1] for regularization. During this process, a frequency domain approach to registration [7] is used for get better registration result, because incorrect registration may severely affect final result. In addition, the authors proposed a robust and efficient implementation.

2.1 Super-Resolution Model

The goal of SR is to improve the spatial resolution of an image. This type of problem is an inverse problem, wherein the source of information, or high-resolution (HR) image, is estimated from the observed data, or low-resolution (LR) images. Each of the LR images $\{Y_k, k=1,2,...,N\}$ $[M{\times}M]$ can be modeled by a sequence of geometric warping, blurring, and downsampling operations on the high resolution $L{\times}L$ image X, followed by additive noise. We can represent Y_k and X as column vectors with length M^2 and L^2 respectively. The model can be formulated as [8]:

$$Y_k = D_k H_k F_k X + V_k \quad k = 1,2,...,N \tag{1}$$

where D_k is the downsampling matrix of size $[M^2{\times}L^2]$, H_k is the blurring matrix of size $[L^2{\times}L^2]$ representing the ultrasound system's point spread function (PSF), F_k is the geometric warp matrix of size $[L^2{\times}L^2]$, V_k is the additive noise, and N is the number of available input LR images.

In [5], the author introduced that using a maximum a-posteriori (MAP) estimator of X to maximize the probability density function (PDF) $P(X|Y_k)$, taking the log function and Bayes rule to the conditional probability, and assuming the V_k is additive Gaussian noise with mean value of zero and variance of σ_k^2, the conditional probability in (1) can be written as:

$$P(Y_1, Y_2, ..., Y_N \mid X) = \frac{1}{(2\pi\sigma^2)^{\frac{M}{2}}} \exp\left\{-\sum_{k=1}^{N} \frac{1}{2\sigma^2} \|Y_k - D_k H_k F_k X\|^2\right\} \tag{2}$$

The noise is assumed to be identically distributed with variance of σ^2, which is absorbed by the parameter $\lambda = 1/2\sigma^2$. Letting $dE/dX = 0$, the steepest descent (SD) algorithm is an efficient method to reach the solution X by the following iterative process until an iteration convergence criterion is met:

$$X_{i+1} = X_i - \mu \left[\lambda \sum_{k=1}^{N} F_k^T H_k^T D_k^T (D_k H_k F_k X_i - Y_k) - \nabla \bullet [C\nabla X] \right] \tag{3}$$

where μ is the step size, which should be small enough. C is the diffusion coefficient of the anisotropic diffusion method [1]. The second term is the detail recovery term that combines information from different frames to update X, and the last term is a smoothing term, or regularization factor, that suppresses instability. The second term can be implemented by convolution with some appropriate kernels. In this paper, a faster and robust implementation is applied [9].

2.2 The Fast and Robust Implement

Before introducing the implementation, there are several assumptions:

- All the input images are the same size, and all the decimation operations are also the same, i.e., $\forall k$, $D_k = D$.
- The sequence input images are acquired by the same ultrasound system at the same depth so all the blur operations are assumed equal, i.e., $\forall k$, $H_k = H$. Moreover, the region-of-interest (ROI) is sufficiently small so that H is assumed to be linear space invariant (LSI), and the matrix H is block circulant.
- The ROI needed to reconstruct the result is small enough so that translational displacement at all points inside may be considered equal. A rigid registration will be applied for motion estimation [7]. Therefore, the matrices F_k are all block circulant and linear space invariant.

With these assumptions, H and F_k are block circulant matrices which commute ($F_k H = H F_k$ and $F_k^T H_k^T = H_k^T F_k^T$). So, the second term in (3) can be written as [10]:

$$\sum_{k=1}^{N} F_k^T H_k^T D_k^T (D_k H_k F_k X_i - Y_k) = H^T R_0 H X_i - H^T P_0 \tag{4}$$

where

$$R_0 = \sum_{k=1}^{N} F_k^T D^T D F_k^T \quad \text{and} \quad P_0 = (\sum_{k=1}^{N} F_k^T D^T Y_k) \tag{5}$$

To compensate for potential outlier images in the sequence, we propose replacing the summation in (5) with a scaled pixel-wise median to increase robustness [9].

$$R_0 = N \cdot median\{F_k^T D^T DF_k\}_{k=1}^N \text{ and } P_0 = N \cdot median\{F_k^T D^T Y_k\}_{k=1}^N \tag{6}$$

Using (6), manually pre-selecting proper frames from a cine loop is no longer necessary. The improvement in (6) gives a fast and robust method to implement the updates of X corresponding to the second term in (3), but the results will be degraded by speckle noise. So the author adopted a Perona and Malik's AD [1] in their method to achieve an edge-enhancing regularization during the SR process [5].

3 Nonlinear Diffusion Method

After using above SR method to do image restoration, we get an enhanced and compounded ultrasound image from a sequence of ultrasound images. In the restored image, speckle has been compounded so that it is no longer a granular pattern. It turns to be much smaller. To reduce the image noise in the restored ultrasound image, we propose to use a local coherence based ND method. Local coherence is defined from structure matrix, it is as,

$$\begin{pmatrix} I_x^2 & (I_x I_y) \\ (I_x I_y) & I_y^2 \end{pmatrix} \tag{7}$$

where I_x and I_y are partial derivatives at certain point in the image, before compute structure matrix at each point, we convolute the image I with a Gaussian mask. Using eigenvalue decomposition, (7) could be written as

$$J(I) = (w_1 \quad w_2) \begin{pmatrix} u_1 & 0 \\ 0 & u_2 \end{pmatrix} \begin{pmatrix} w_1^T \\ w_x^T \end{pmatrix} \tag{8}$$

where u_1 and u_2 are eigenvalues, w_1 and w_2 are eigenvectors.

Our diffusion equation is as

$$\frac{\partial I}{\partial t} = div[l \cdot \nabla I] \tag{9}$$

Where l is the local coherence function, the independent variable of l is the absolute value of the difference of two eigenvalues, the definition of l is,

$$l(|\mu_1 - \mu_2|) = 1/1 + (|\mu_1 - \mu_2|/K)^2 \tag{10}$$

where μ_1 and μ_2 are the eigenvalues of structure matrix at each point, structure matrix is as $J(\nabla I_\sigma) = (\nabla I_\sigma \cdot \nabla I_\sigma^T)$. Here, ∇I_σ is the gradient of a smoothed version of I which is obtained by convolving I with a Gaussian of standard deviation σ. Converting (9) to a matrix-vector notation and adopting AOS scheme, (9) comes down to the following iteration scheme

$$I^{t+1} = \frac{1}{2} \sum_{l=1}^{2} [U + 2\tau T_l(I^t)]^{-1} I^t \tag{11}$$

where U is a KL by KL identity matrix (the size of image is $K{\times}L$), τ is the time step size (TSS), $T_i(I^t)$ is a tridiagonal matrix, with $T_i(I^t) = [t_{ij}(I^t)]$ and

$$
t_{ij}(I^t) = \begin{cases} l_j^t/h^2 & [j \in \mathrm{N}(i)], \\ -\sum_{n \subset \mathrm{N}(i)} l_n^t/h^2 & (j = i), \\ 0 & (\text{else}). \end{cases} \tag{12}
$$

where l is the diffusion coefficient. $\mathrm{N}(i)$ is the set of the two neighbors of pixel i. From the criteria for discrete nonlinear diffusion scale-spaces proposed by Weickert [6], we find that (9) can by discretized by AOS scheme to do speedup.

4   Experiment and Results

To evaluate the effectiveness of the proposed method, we conducted simulation and *in vivo* experiments. In the experiment of simulated ultrasound image speckle reduction, we analyzed different kinds of AD methods quantitatively. In each experiment, we compared the proposed method with Parona and Malik's method (P&M AD) [1], SRAD [2] and semi-implicit scheme based nonlinear diffusion (SIND) [4].

4.1   Results of Simulation Experiment

In this experiment, we firstly simulated ultrasound B mode image as [2, 11]. In this method, ultrasound radio-frequency (RF) image was generated by convoluting a 2-D point spread function with a 2-D echogeneity image. The parameters used in our simulation are: the pulse width was 1.2, the lateral beam width was 1.5, the center frequency was 5 MHz. The size of echogeneity image was 256×256. The gray values of different objects in the echogeneity image are: the dark circular at top left corner was 2, the rectangular target at top right corner was 25, the bright small circular at middle left area was 18, the dark circular at bottom left corner was 4, the simulated artery interior was 3, the simulated vascular wall was 20, the three small cysts were 2, the five bright point targets were 40, the background was 10. The following are the echogeneity image and simulated ultrasound image (both images are log-compressed and normalized with the same way for better displaying).

Because in the SR method we needed to use a sequence of ultrasound images to generate one restored image, so we used the simulated ultrasound image in figure 1.b as one in the set of simulated ultrasound images needed for restoration. Moreover, we generated another 15 simulated ultrasound images. Nine of them are generated by using the same echogeneity image as figure 1.a. To generate the other six simulated outliers, we used six different echogeneity images as outliers. Two of the simulated outliers are showed as figure 2.a - 2.b. The fast SR method we used was about six times than traditional SR methods. In the SR method, the size of final restored image was as, $M_{new}{\times}N_{new} = k{\cdot}(M_{old}{\times}N_{old})$, where k is the square root of the number of images in the data set. In our experiment, we had 16 simulated images in the data set, so

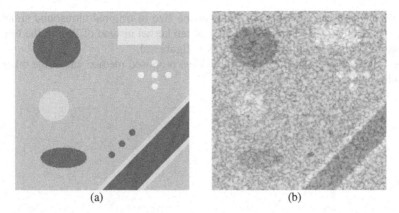

Fig. 1. Ultrasound B mode image simulation result. (a) The echogeneity image. (b) The generated ultrasound simulated image.

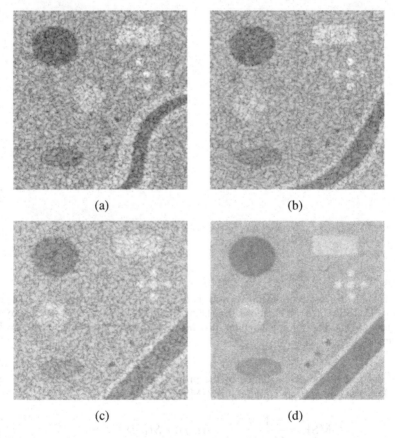

Fig. 2. The result of SR method on a sequence of 16 ultrasound B mode simulated images. (a)-(b) two outliers generated by different echogeneity images. (c) One simulated image generated by the echogeneity image as figure 1.a. (d) The result of the SR method.

the size of the restored image is 4 times of the size of original ultrasound simulated images. In addition, the authors used a Gaussian kernel instead of PSF in the blurring processing [5]. The result of SR method is as figure 2.d.

The following are the filtering results of the proposed method and some other AD methods.

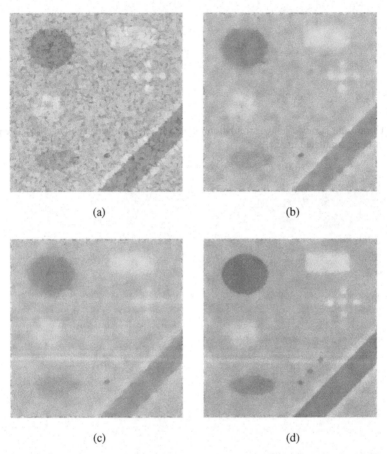

(a)   (b)

(c)   (d)

Fig. 3. The filtering results of the proposed method and some other AD methods. (a) The result of P&M AD, TSS = 0.25, 30 iterations. (b) The result of SRAD, TSS = 0.25, 25 iterations. (c) The result of SIND, TSS = 1.5, 5 iterations. (d) The result of the proposed method, TSS = 1.5, 5 iterations.

In order to test the performance of the proposed method, two metrics were computed. The first one is mean squared error (MSE), it is defined as,

$$\text{MSE} = \frac{1}{M \times N} \sum_{(i,j)=1}^{M \times N} (\hat{S}(i,j)) - S(i,j))^2 \tag{13}$$

where S and $\hat{S}$ are the reference and filtered images respectively.

The second metric is contrast-to-noise-ratio (CNR), which is sometimes referred as lesion signal-to-noise ratio [11], it is,

$$CNR = \frac{|\mu_1 - \mu_2|}{\sqrt{\sigma_1^2 + \sigma_2^2}} \qquad (14)$$

where μ_1 and σ_1^2 are the mean and variance of intensities of pixels in a region of interest (ROI), and μ_2 and σ_2^2 are the mean and variance of intensities of pixels in a background region.

The computed values of MSE are summarized in Table 1. And obtained values of CNR are summarized in Table 2.

Table 1. MSE values on the simulated image

Method	MSE
Noisy	262.56
P&M AD	137.41
SRAD	23.96
SIND	26.55
Proposed method	17.83

Table 2. CNR values on the simulated image

Method	ROI 1	ROI 2	ROI 3	ROI 4
Noisy	3.17	1.90	1.29	1.46
P&M AD	4.19	2.65	1.61	1.92
SRAD	6.21	5.74	3.24	3.16
SIND	5.91	6.34	3.82	3.75
Proposed method	7.61	7.48	4.29	4.87

From the values of MSE and CNR on different diffusion-based filtering methods, we can see that the proposed SR based ND method is much better than some other AD methods.

4.2 Results of In Vivo Experiment

The following filtering results of *in vivo* ultrasound image show that the proposed method can preserve structure details and edges more accurately than other AD methods. The SR method improved original ultrasound B mode image greatly by compounding speckle and enhancing structure and edge through introducing complementary information in data set. In this way, the proposed ND method can get a much better result than other non-image-restored diffusion-based filtering methods.

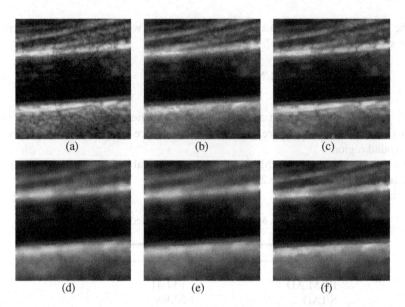

Fig. 4. The results of the proposed method and some other diffusion-based filtering methods on *in vivo* ultrasound image. (a) The original ultrasound image. (b) The result of the SR method. (c) The result of P&M AD, TSS = 0.25, 30 iterations. (d) The result of SRAD, TSS = 0.25, 20 iterations. (e) The result of SIND, TSS = 1.5, 3 iterations. (d) The result of the proposed method, TSS = 1.5, 3 iterations.

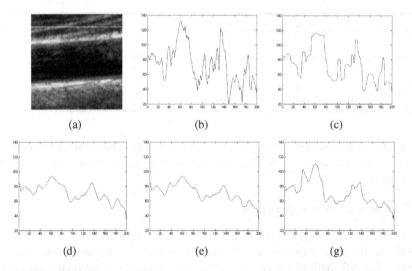

Fig. 5. Profiles along the highlight line in ultrasound image. (a) Original image showing the highlight line. (b) Profiles along the highlight line in the original image (c)-(g) Profiles along the highlight line in the images processed by P&M AD, SRAD, SIND, the proposed method.

5 Conclusion

In this paper we present a new SR based nonlinear ND method for speckle reduction and experimental evaluation. From the experimental results we can see that the proposed method can reduce ultrasound speckle noise more exactly than other AD methods. Our new method can also preserve and enhance edge and structure details much better. The reason is that we combine the SR method and the ND method. We firstly improve the ultrasound image quality by the SR method. On the basis of this process, we propose a local coherence ND method to reduce the image noise of the restored image. In this way, we get a much better filtering result than other diffusion-based filtering methods.

To test the proposed method, in the future, we would like to do more experiments in different *in vivo* ultrasound images. Moreover, because the speed of the SR method we used is still not fast enough for real-time application, we would like to explore the possibility to use parallel processing to do speedup. In addition, registration in the SR method is very important, inaccurate registration will result in a poor image restoration. So, improving the registration method in the SR method is another future work.

References

1. Perona, P., Malik, J.: Scale-space and edge detection using anisotropic diffusion. IEEE Trans. Pattern Anal. and Machine Intell. 12(7), 629–639 (1990)
2. Yu, Y., Acton, S.T.: Speckle reducing anisotropic diffusion. IEEE Trans. Image Process. 11(11), 1260–1270 (2002)
3. Krissian, K., Westin, C.F., Kikinis, R., Vosburgh, K.G.: Oriented speckle reducing anisotropic diffusion. IEEE Trans. Image Processing 16(5), 1412–1424 (2007)
4. Wang, B., Liu, D.C.: Semi-Implicit Scheme based Nonlinear Diffusion Method in Ultrasound Speckle Reduction. In: IEEE International Ultrasonics Symposium, pp. 1390–1393 (2008)
5. Dai, Y., Wang, B., Liu, D.C.: A Fast and Robust Super Resolution Method for Intima Reconstruction in Medical Ultrasound. In: The 3rd IEEE International Conference on Bioinformatics and Biomedical Engineering, pp. 1–4 (2009)
6. Weichert, J., Romeny, B., Viergever, M.A.: Efficient and reliable schemes for nonlinear diffusion filtering. IEEE Trans. Image Processing 7(3), 398–410 (1998)
7. Vandewalle, P., Susstrunk, S., Vetterli, M.: A frequency domain approach to registration of aliased images with application to super-resolution. J. Appl. Signal Processing 2006, 1–14 (2006)
8. Farsiu, S., Robinson, D., Elad, M., Milanfar, P.: Advances and challenges in superresolution. Int. J. Imag. Syst. Technol. 14(2), 47–57 (2004)
9. Zomet, A., Rav-Acha, A., Peleg, S.: Robust super-resolution. In: Proceeding of the Int. Conf. on CVPR, vol. 1, pp. 645–650 (2001)
10. Aharoni, E., Abramorich, G.: Edge preserving super-resolution Image Reconstruction, Technical report, The vision research and image science laboratory (1999)
11. Zhang, F., Yoo, Y.M., Koh, L.M., Kim, Y.: Nonlinear diffusion in Laplacian pyramid domain for ultrasonic speckle reduction. IEEE Trans. Med. Imag. 26(2), 200–211 (2007)

Background Estimation Based on Device Pixel Structures for Silhouette Extraction

Yasutomo Kawanishi[1], Takuya Funatomi[2],
Koh Kakusho[3], and Michihiko Minoh[2]

[1] Graduate School of Informatics, Kyoto University
ykawani@mm.media.kyoto-u.ac.jp
[2] Academic Center for Computing and Media Studies, Kyoto University
{funatomi,minoh}@media.kyoto-u.ac.jp
[3] Department of Human System Interaction, Kwansei University
kakusho@kwansei.ac.jp

Abstract. We propose a novel technique for background estimation on the tabletop systems that have an information display on the tabletop and observe tabletop objects with a camera. In such systems, the background of an image observed with the camera includes the image shown on the tabletop display. The background varies according to the information presented on the tabletop display. Although we can estimate the background image from a displayed image based on traditional geometric registration and photometric correction, the background image is not sufficiently accurate in terms of pixel value blending for background subtraction. We estimate the background image in high accuracy based on the pixel structures of the display and the camera. We experimentally evaluate the methods by comparing the estimated image with the observed image.

1 Introduction

The tabletop systems that have an information display on the tabletop and observe tabletop objects with a camera have recently been applied to human interfaces in tabletop tasks [1] [2]. Showing instructional information on the display in the tabletop can provide deictic instructions to users about the objects on the tabletop.

When showing such instructional information in an easily viewable area for the user, the system has to understand the positions of the objects on the tabletop.

In the tabletop systems, the method often used is one that obtains the position and posture of the target objects using a tag, like ARToolkit, and calculates object regions using an object model. However, such a technique cannot be applied to objects that are too small to append tags. In this paper, we propose a technique for acquiring object regions from an observed image directly without using such tags.

There are two approaches that acquire object regions from an observed image directly. One approach is to build models of the objects and extract the object

H. Zha, R.-i. Taniguchi, and S. Maybank (Eds.): ACCV 2009, Part III, LNCS 5996, pp. 140–151, 2010.

regions that match the model from the image. The other approach is to build a model of the background and extract the object regions that do not match the model from the image. We chose the second approach because the first method requires the preparation of many models for various shapes of objects, whereas the second technique requires the preparation of only one background model, which is not related to the objects.

When the background is varying, we can not use the observed image captured when no objects are on the tabletop as the background model. A number of background models able to deal with dynamic backgrounds have been proposed for use in cases when the background changes.

In the tabletop systems considered in this study, the background changes dynamically according to the displayed instructional information. Therefore, for background subtraction, we attempted to estimate the background image from the displayed image. When the background can be estimated, object regions can be extracted from an observed image by background subtraction.

To estimate the background when an arbitrary image is displayed, the relationships of the position and color between each pixel of the displayed and observed images are required. The relationships are computed by geometric registration and color correction techniques used in projector-camera systems [3]. In related works, by applying geometric and photometric conversions based on relationships of images projected by a projector, compensation of the projected images is achieved. In this study, we estimate the background image when an arbitrary image is displayed using the similar approach.

Geometric conversion based on geometric relationship and photometric conversion based on photometric relationship are applied in this order. Traditional geometric conversion includes homography transformation and interpolation. Homography transformation makes a pixel center on a coordinate system onto another coordinate system. Because the transformed pixel center are not always mapped to a pixel center on the latter coordinate system, to calculate the RGB value of each pixel of converted image, interpolation is needed. In the interpolation, it is assumed that the RGB value of a pixel is at the center of the pixel. Although different pixel structures exists in that each pixel can have three RGB devices (display) or one device of RGB devices (camera), traditional geometric conversion does not take into account such pixel structures.

When we estimate the background of an image with the traditional approach, because of its low accuracy, there are large differences between the observed image and the estimated image, especially in positions that display large differences in pixel values between nearby pixels. In tabletop systems, when we use characters or arrows that have sharp edges for presenting information, the estimated background image will show a large difference. When we extract object regions by background subtraction using the estimated background image, if the pixels that show large differences are clustered, the clustered pixels will be extracted as error regions. If the error regions are large, the system will not be able to find objects in the correct regions.

To avoid this, background estimation with high accuracy is needed. In this paper, we propose a novel technique for background estimation on the tabletop systems by modeling the pixel structures of the display and the camera and using interpolation based on these models in geometric conversion. This interpolation based on pixel structures has the advantage of being robust for various relative resolutions of the display and the camera. Especially when the difference of the relative resolutions of the dispaly and the camera is large, the effect of the pixel structure is large. In such case, although the error of traditional method is large, our method works still better than the traditional method. By estimating the background image to high accuracy with this technique, we can extract object regions by background extraction with fewer errors.

This paper is organized as follows. Section 2 describes the method of estimation using traditional image conversion and discusses the associated problems. Section 3 describes the method of estimation using the proposed image conversion that takes into consideration pixel structures. Section 4 outlines experiments that quantify the performance of the proposed method. Finally, Section 5 provides a conclusion and outlines future work.

2   Background Estimation Using the Traditional Approach

2.1   Overview of Background Estimation

In general, observed images have nonlinear distortion caused by optical properties of the lens. In this study, it is assumed that this distortion has been calibrated.

An image for presenting information on the tabletop systems is displayed on the tabletop display, which is a surface in 3D space, and the observed image is captured from the image plane of the camera. The relationship between the two surfaces is called Homography transformation. This transformation can be described as a homography matrix.

We can calculate the homography matrix using pairs of pixels, one of which is in the displayed image and the other in the observed image. Using a checker pattern board, we can obtain the position of the pixel pairs at the corners of the checker pattern. In this case, by showing the checker pattern image on the display and observing it with the camera, we can calculate the homography matrix between the display surface and the image plane of the camera.

The homography matrix for geometric conversion (denoted by H), the position of a pixel on the displayed image I^s (denoted by (x, y)), and the position of a pixel on the geometrically converted image I^t from I^s (denoted by (i, j)) are described as

$$s \begin{pmatrix} i \\ j \\ 1 \end{pmatrix} = \begin{pmatrix} si \\ sj \\ s \end{pmatrix} = H \begin{pmatrix} x \\ y \\ 1 \end{pmatrix} \quad (s : \text{constant}). \qquad (1)$$

In computer systems, a color image is handled as a set of discrete pixels that have a three-dimensional color vector. When we geometrically convert an image with

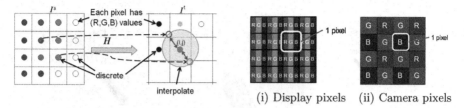

Fig. 1. Traditional geometric conversion

(i) Display pixels   (ii) Camera pixels

Fig. 2. The pixel structures

a matrix (1), the converted pixel position do not always match a pixel position on the converted image. Pixel values of the converted image are calculated by interpolating the converted pixels around the pixel (Fig.1). The pixel value of (i, j) on I^t is calculated by transforming all of the pixels of I^s onto the converted image I^t with the matrix H, and interpolating with its neighbor converted pixels on I^t. In this case, the interpolation is performed assuming that the values of a pixel are at the center of the pixel.

This homography transformation and interpolation is called "geometric conversion". After "geometric conversion", we can obtain the background image by "photometric conversion," which converts the pixel value based on color correspondence using color lookup tables. A method of calculating this color correspondence is proposed by Nayar et al. [4]. We can obtain image I^o, which is a photometrically converted image from the geometrically converted image I^t, by this method using a color lookup table.

2.2   Errors in Geometric Conversion

In the interpolation in the geometric conversion, it is assumed that each pixel is discrete in that its RGB values are at the center of the pixel. However, the display has three independent RGB devices, and the camera observes each RGB color in independent pixels. A magnified view of this is shown in Fig.2. When we estimate the background image, errors caused by the difference in these color expressions appear.

We then calculate the difference between the estimated background image and the observed image to evaluate the conversion errors. We use the image in Fig.3 (i) as an example of information displayed on the tabletop systems.

We use a 20 inch wide LCD (DELL; resolution 1900×1200) and an IEEE-1394 digital camera (Flea; Point-grey Research; resolution 1024×768). In this evaluation, we set the camera to the specified camera resolution, and the resolution of the display is set to be almost the same as the camera resolution. We used a 20 inch wide LCD display made by DELL and Flea which is an IEEE-1394 digital camera made by Pointgrey Research. The camera was calibrated using Zhang's calibration technique [5].

The observed image is shown in Fig.3 (ii); the estimated image and the image resulting after background subtraction are shown in Fig.4.

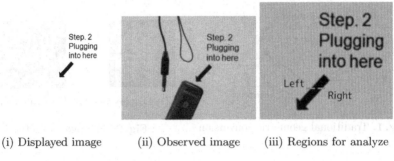

(i) Displayed image   (ii) Observed image   (iii) Regions for analyze

Fig. 3. Images for evaluation

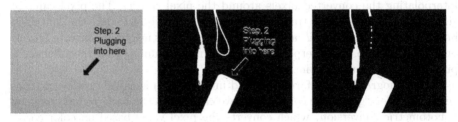

(i) Estimated image   (ii) Result of background subtraction (iii) Error-removed image

Fig. 4. Resultant images

In the characters and arrow region, errors are present that are not in the object region, as can be seen from Fig.4 (ii). This is caused by clustered pixels which have a large variation.

When we use characters or arrows for instructional information on the table-top systems, their sharp edges cause the edges to be extracted as error regions. If an error appears, the system cannot distinguish the error regions from the object regions.

In this case, we can reduce the error regions as noise, but when the error regions are large, small object regions are also removed as noise. We continuously apply erosion to the estimated background image to remove all the error regions and simultaneously apply dilation to the image. The object region resembling a string loop is thus removed as noise (Fig.4 (iii)).

2.3   Analysis

To analyze the errors, we compare the pixel values in the edge regions of the estimated and observed images. Fig.5 and 6 show the pixel values in the edge regions (15 pixels each) of the images shown in Fig.3 (iii) (Left and Right lines respectively).

Looking at the region within the frame shown in Fig.5, values of R and G are smaller than those of B in the observed image. Moreover, looking at the region

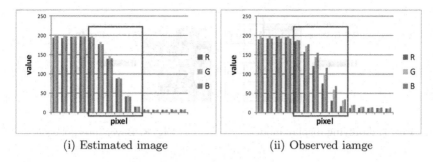

(i) Estimated image   (ii) Observed iamge

Fig. 5. Pixel values of the Left line in Fig.3 (iii)

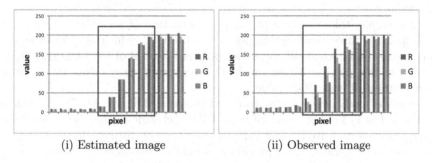

(i) Estimated image   (ii) Observed image

Fig. 6. Pixel values of the Right line in Fig.3 (iii)

within the frame in Fig.6, values of G and B are smaller than those of R in the observed image. However, in the estimated image, values of R, G, and B are almost identical. This suggests that the color of each pixel appears uneven in the observed image, and the color cannot be reconstructed using the traditional geometric conversion method.

This is because that although the display and the camera treat R, G and B devices independently and each device has size, the traditional interpolation in geometric conversion treats a three-dimensional color as a point. Therefore, the traditional method could not simulate the display-camera conversion accurately.

In our proposed method, we resolve this problem and perform interpolation in geometric conversion that models the structures of the display and the camera in order to achieve accurate background image estimation.

3   Geometric Conversion Based on Pixel Structures

3.1   Pixel Structures

Display pixel structure. To express arbitrary colors in each pixel, most displays express colors via a juxtapositional additive color mixture system using the three primary colors red (R), green (G), and blue (B). The juxtapositional

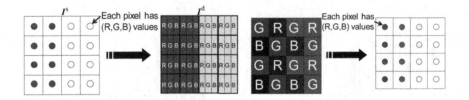

Fig. 7. Applying display model   **Fig. 8.** Bayer interpolation

additive color mixture system is a photometric property that mixes multiple colors into one color by using color regions too small to be distinguishable by the human eye.

For example, take the case of the pixel structure of an LCD. An ordinary LCD arranges three small rectangles of R, G, and B, which are the three primary colors, and each small rectangle comprises a pixel of the LCD (Fig.2 (i)). Because of this pixel structure, an LCD can express many colors by adjusting the brightness of each RGB value.

We model each pixel of the displayed image as follows (Fig.7). A pixel of the image has 1/3 of the width of three RGB rectangle regions. The shape and arrangement of each RGB pixel vary for each type of display. However, we can discuss them by building an appropriate model that covers every type of display. Therefore, in the following sections, we use the LCD model.

Camera pixel structure. The color acquisition methods of a camera also vary according to each type of camera. In this paper, we describe the Bayer format, which is the most popular camera pixel structure. We also discuss all methods by building an appropriate model for each type of structure.

The Bayer pattern is a pixel arrangement pattern, whose system is as follows. There are three types of light-receiving element: One receives only red light waves (R), the second only green light waves (G), and the third only blue light waves (B). These three types of elements are arranged as follows (see also Fig.2 (ii)).

- $i = 2m + 1, j = 2n$, (if $m, n \in \mathbb{N}$):red
- $i = 2m, j = 2n + 1$, (if $m, n \in \mathbb{N}$):blue
- otherwise:green

where $\mathbb{N}$ is a natural number, $0 \leq i \leq$ width of I, and $0 \leq j \leq$ height of I.

Because each element can receive only one color (R, G, or B), we have to interpolate the other colors from neighboring elements. The most common interpolation method is linear interpolation.

An example of Bayer interpolation is shown in Fig.8. It shows that image I^c observed with a camera is converted to image I^t by Bayer interpolation. After this interpolation, the image becomes an ordinary image with RGB values in each pixel.

3.2   Proposed Interpolation in Geometric Conversion

For camera and display pixels that have the structures described below, we can simulate the conversion "display on an LCD and observation using a camera." We apply the display pixel structure model described in 3.1 to the input image I^s and obtain displayed image I^d that reflects the pixel structure.

The pixel values are interpolated based on the size of the pixels. As each RGB subpixel of I^d is rectangle, its four corner points are converted geometrically onto the coordinate system of the image I^c (Fig.9).

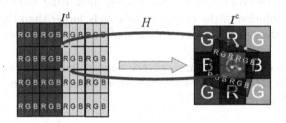

Fig. 9. Interpolation based on pixel structures

The pixel value $I^c(i,j)$ at (i,j) in image I^c is calculated by summing RGB subpixel values of the pixels in I^d in the pixel region $I^c(i,j)$ weighted by each RGB subpixel region size. We denote the number of pixels which lap over $I^c(i,j)$ by the homography transformation as N_{ij}, those pixels as $I^d(x_p, y_p), N(p = 1, \cdots, N)$, their RGB subpixels as $I^d(x_p, y_p)^R, I^d(x_p, y_p)^G$, and $I^d(x_p, y_p)^B$, overlapped regions of transformed those RGB subpixels and $I^c(i,j)$ as $A_{ij}(p)^R, A_{ij}(p)^G$, and $A_{ij}(p)^B$, and pixel size of $I^c(i,j)$ as $A_{i,j}$. Now, we can describe the pixel value $I^c(i,j)$ as

$$
I^c(i,j) = \begin{cases} \sum_{p=1}^{N_{ij}} I^d(x_p, y_p)^R \cdot A_{ij}(p)^R / A_{ij} \\ \quad (i = 2m, j = 2n+1, (m, n \in \mathbb{N})) \\ \sum_{p=1}^{N_{ij}} I^d(x_p, y_p)^B \cdot A_{ij}(p)^B / A_{ij} \\ \quad (i = 2m+1, j = 2n, (m, n \in \mathbb{N})) \\ \sum_{p=1}^{N_{ij}} I^d(x_p, y_p)^G \cdot A_{ij}(p)^G / A_{ij} \\ \quad (otherwise). \end{cases} \tag{2}
$$

Finally, we convert image I^c based on the camera pixel structure described in 3.1 and obtain the geometrically converted image I^t (Fig.8). After photometric conversion to I^c, we can obtain the estimated image based on display and camera pixel structures.

4   Experimental Results

Using our proposed method and the traditional method, we experimentally compared estimated images to an observed image in order to evaluate the accuracy of background estimation.

We used a checker pattern image whose grid measures 100×100 pixels. The pattern has flat regions of brightness and sharp edges.

To show the effectiveness of our method with various resolutions and positions regarding the display and camera, we tested four cases as follows:

case A: The resolution of the camera is relatively larger than the resolution of the display (the camera observes an area of the display measuring 500×450 pixels).

case B: The resolution of the camera is the same as the resolution of the display (the camera observes an area of the display measuring 1000×750 pixels).

case C: The resolution of the display is relatively larger than the resolution of the camera (the camera observes an area of the display measuring 1300×900 pixels).

case D: The resolution of the camera is the same as the resolution of the display; the display is rotated about $45°$ (the camera observes an area of the display measuring 1000×750 pixels).

In each case, we show the evaluation image on the display and observe it using the camera.

To examine the accuracy of estimation, we obtain differences between the input images and estimated images converted using both methods.

We then calculate the integrated histogram of the differences. The calculation is applied to a region measuring 480×360 pixels at the center of the image. Results are shown in a semi-logarithmic graph in Fig.10. It is better that the threshold which used in background subtraction is small. On the other hand, it is necessary for the threshold to be larger than the maximum noise of the observed image. We took two images for the same objects and obtained their difference to evaluate the minimum possible threshold. The results are shown in Fig.10 as "limit".

These graphs show the numbers of error pixels binarizing with thresholds in the horizontal axis. In those graphs, the smallerer the threshold is, the more accurate background subtraction is performed.

In case B, errors in both the methods are relatively small than other cases. This is because the resolution of the display and that of the camera are nearly equal, hence the effect of the pixel structures is small.

In case A and C, because the large divergence between resolution of the camera and that of the display, the effect of the pixel structure is large. In case D, because of the rotation of the camera, the error of the traditional method is larger than case B. In these cases, the traditional method which is not based on the pixel structures can not convert images in high accuracy. On the other hand, our proposed method can convert images as high accuracy as the conversion of case B.

Now look at the threshold 32 as shown in Fig.10. In this threshold, the number of error pixels of the "limit" is 0. In case B, the error pixel of the traditional method is 5003 and that of the proposed method is 573. In this case, we could reduce the error about $1/9$ of the traditional method.

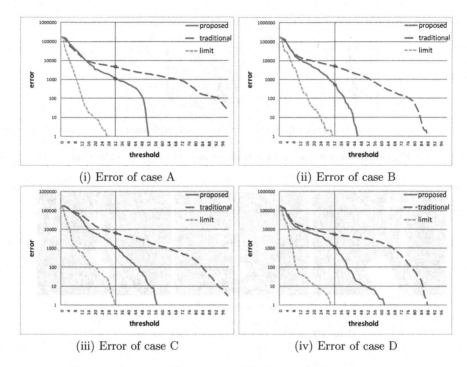

(i) Error of case A

(ii) Error of case B

(iii) Error of case C

(iv) Error of case D

Fig. 10. Integrated histograms of background subtraction error

We applied background subtraction using the threshold 32 to the images shown in Fig.3 (i) and Fig.11 (i) which are the background displayed images. Fig.3 (i) includes only text for instruction of a tabletop task. Fig.11 (ii) includes also text and a picture for instruction of a tabletop task. The results are shown in Fig.4 (ii) and Fig.12. In Fig.4 (ii) and Fig.12 (ii) which are processed by the traditional method, the noise regions are clustered. The largest cluster is as large as the thin cable (diameter:1mm) which we suppose that it is one of the most small objects in tabletop tasks. On the other hand, in Fig.12 (i) and (iii) which are processed by our proposed method, the noise regions are enough smaller than the thin cable in the image. This provides evidence for the effectiveness of the proposed method based on pixel structures for the tabletop system.

We additionaly analyze the reason of the error which still remained in our proposed method. We calculate integrated histograms of the differences in several region of the images and calculate the thresholds which makes the error 0. The result shows that the threshold in a region far from the center of the image is larger than the threshold in a region near the center of the image.

We may say it is caused by insufficient accuracy of the lens distortion correction and lens blur. In this study, we assume there are no lens distortion and the focus of the camera is set on the display surface in evaluation. It seems reasonable to suppose that the residual between the proposed method and "limit"is caused by insufficiency of the assumption.

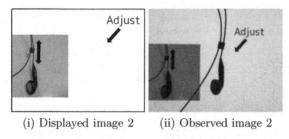

(i) Displayed image 2   (ii) Observed image 2

Fig. 11. Example image 2 for background subtraction evaluation

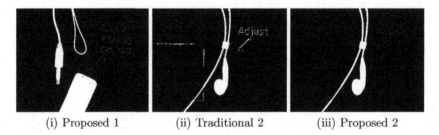

(i) Proposed 1   (ii) Traditional 2   (iii) Proposed 2

Fig. 12. Result of background subtraction

5   Conclusion

We have proposed a technique for background estimation on tabletop systems that have an information display on a tabletop and observe tabletop objects with a camera.

We estimated the background image by geometric and photometric conversion. Although the display and the camera treat R, G and B devices independently and each device has size, the interpolation in traditional geometric conversion treated a three-dimensional color as a point. Therefore, the interpolation in the traditional geometric conversion does not work accurately. We modeled the display and camera pixel structure and improve the interpolation with the model. Through this method, we obtained the background image in high accuracy.

We experimentally evaluated our proposed method and the traditional method by comparing the estimated image with the observed image. We show the effectiveness of our method in various relative resolutions between the camera and the display.

In this paper, we have assumed that the focus of the camera is set at the center of the LCD, but in practice lens blur remains in the observed images. In addition, the focus is sometimes off in fringes because of variations in the distance between the camera and the display surface. Therefore, remaining errors should be considered as a blur of the observed images.

If we can estimate the blur of the observed image and apply the blur to the estimated image, these errors will be reduced. In future work, we would like to estimate the blur of the observed image for reducing remaining errors and build a tabletop system with object recognition.

References

1. Kakehi, Y., Naemura, T., Matsushita, M.: Tablescape plus: Interactive small-sized vertical displays on a horizontal tabletop display. In: Proc. of the 2nd IEEE International Workshop on Horizontal interactive Human-Computer Systems, pp. 155–162 (2007)
2. Patten, J., Ishii, H., Hines, J., Pangaro, G.: Sensetable: A wireless object tracking platform for tangible user interfaces. In: Proc. of Conference on Human Factors in Computing Systems, CHI 2001 (2001)
3. Brown, M., Majumder, A., Yang, R.: Camera-based calibration techniques for seamless multiprojector displays. IEEE Trans. Vis. Comput. Graph. 11, 193–206 (2005)
4. Nayar, S.K., Peri, H., Grossberg, M.D., Belhumeur, P.N.: A projection system with radiometric compensation for screen imperfections. In: Proc. International Workshop on Projector-Camera Systems, PROCAMS 2003 (2003)
5. Zhang, Z.: A flexible new technique for camera calibration. Trans. on Pattern Anal. Machine Intell., 1330–1334 (2000)

Local Spatial Co-occurrence for Background Subtraction via Adaptive Binned Kernel Estimation

Bineng Zhong, Shaohui Liu, and Hongxun Yao

Department of Computer Science and Engineering, Harbin Institute of Technology
{bnzhong,yhx}@vilab.hit.edu.cn, shliu@hit.edu.cn

Abstract. We present a nonparametric background subtraction method that uses the local spatial co-occurrence correlations between neighboring pixels to robustly and efficiently detect moving objects in dynamic scenes. We first represent each pixel as a joint feature vector consisting of its spatial coordinates and appearance properties (e.g., intensities, color, edges, or gradients). This joint feature vector naturally fuses spatial and appearance features to simultaneously consider meaningful correlation between neighboring pixels and pixels' appearance changes, which are very important for dynamic background modeling. Then, each pixel's background model is modeled via an adaptive binned kernel estimation, which is updated by the neighboring pixels' feature vectors in a local rectangle region around the pixel. The adaptive binned kernel estimation is adopted due to it is computationally inexpensive and does not need any assumptions about the underlying distributions. Qualitative and quantitative experimental results on challenging video sequences demonstrate the robustness of the proposed method.

1 Introduction

Background subtraction in video is a basic task in many computer vision and video analysis applications, such as intelligence video surveillance, human machine interfaces, indexing for multimedia, people detection and tracking and robotics. Accurate moving object detection will greatly improve the performance of object tracking, recognition, classification and activity analysis. However, designing robust background subtraction methods is still an open issue, especially considering various complicated variations that may occur in dynamic scenes, e.g., trees waving, water rippling, illumination changes, camera jitters, etc.

Over the years, many methods have been proposed to achieve the goal of robust background subtraction. According to different background subtraction approaches, these methods can be classified as parametric and nonparametric methods.

One popular parametric technique is to model each pixel intensity or color value in a video frame with a Gaussian distribution [1]. This model does not work well in the case of dynamic natural environments. To deal with this problem, the Gaussian Mixture Model (GMM) [2] is used to model each pixel. But it cannot adapt to the case where the background has quick variations [3]. Numerous improvements of the original method developed by Stauffer and Grimson [2] have been proposed over the recent years and a good survey of these improvements is presented in [4]. Some background subtraction methods treat pixel value changes as a time series and consider a predictive model to

H. Zha, R.-i. Taniguchi, and S. Maybank (Eds.): ACCV 2009, Part III, LNCS 5996, pp. 152–161, 2010.

capture the most important variation based on past observations. In [5], an autoregressive model is proposed to capture the properties of dynamic scenes. Monnett et al. [6] model the background as a dynamic texture, where the first few principal components of the variance of a set of background images comprise an autoregressive model. In [7], a Hidden Markov Model approach is adopted.

Rather than using parametric techniques, a number of nonparametric approaches are proposed to model background distribution in complex environments where background statistics cannot be described parametrically. In W4 system [8], the background scene is statically modeled by the minimum and maximum intensity values and maximal temporal derivative for each pixel recorded over some period, and is updated periodically. A non-statistical clustering technique to construct a background model is presented in [9]. The background is encoded on a pixel-by-pixel basis and samples at each pixel are clustered into the set of codewords. Heikkila and Pietikainen [10] propose a novel approach based on the discriminative LBP histogram. However, simple grayscale operations make LBP rather sensitive to noise and it is also not so efficient on uniform regions. In [11], scene is coarsely represented as the union of pixel layers and foreground objects are detected by propagating these layers using a maximum-likelihood assignment. However, the limitations of the method are high-computational complexity and the requirement of an extra offline training step. Elgammal et al. [12] are among the first to utilize the kernel density estimation technique to model the background color distribution, which has been successful applied in background subtraction literature. Another significant contribution of this work is the incorporation of spatial constraints into the formulation of foreground classification. In the second phase of their approach, pixel values that could be explained away by distributions of neighboring pixels are reclassified as background, allowing for greater resilience against dynamic backgrounds. In [13], the background and foreground models are first constructed via kernel density estimation technique separately, which are then used competitively in a MAP-MRF decision framework. Mittal and Paragios [14] propose the use of variable bandwidths for kernel density estimation to enable modeling of arbitrary shapes of the underlying density in a more natural way. Then, density estimation is performed in a higher-dimensional space consisting of intensity and optical flow for the purpose of modeling and subtraction of dynamic scenes. Parag and Elgammal [15] use a boosting method (RealBoost) to choose the best feature to distinguish the foreground for each of the areas in the scene. One key problem with kernel density estimation techniques is their high computational requirement due to the large number of samples needed to model the background. To accelerate the computational speed of kernel density estimation, some innovative works, such as fast Gauss transform (FGT) in [16] and binned kernel estimators in [17, 18], have been presented. A Bayesian framework that incorporates spectral, spatial, and temporal features to characterize the background appearance is proposed in [19]. Under this framework, the background is represented by the most significant and frequent features, i.e., the principal features, at each pixel.

In this paper, we present a nonparametric background subtraction method that uses the local spatial co-occurrence correlations between neighboring pixels to robustly and efficiently detect moving objects in dynamic scenes such as waving trees, ripples in water, illumination changes, camera jitters etc. The key idea is to represent each pixel as a joint feature vector consisting of its spatial coordinates and appearance properties (e.g., intensities, color, edges, or gradients). The intuition is that image variations at neighboring pixels could be similarly affected by environmental effects (e.g. the small movements of the dynamic scenes); it should be possible to represent a pixel using its spatial and appearance features simultaneously to consider both meaningful correlation between neighboring pixels and its appearance changes. Background modeling problem is then formulated as the problem of modeling the joint feature vector distribution in a local neighboring rectangle region for each pixel. Each pixel's background model is modeled via a nonparametric method, i.e. adaptive binned kernel estimation [18], which provides a practical means of dramatically reducing computational burdens while closely approximating the kernel density estimation [17]. Qualitative and quantitative experimental results on challenging video sequences demonstrate the robustness of the proposed method by comparing it with the widely used GMM.

The rest of the paper is organized as follows. Section 2 presents our background subtraction algorithm. Experimental results are given in Section 3. Finally, we conclude this work in Section 4.

2   The Proposed Background Subtraction Method

In this section, we introduce our approach to background subtraction. The goal is to construct and maintain a statistical representation of the scene that the camera sees. In our algorithm, a background model is constructed for each pixel location. A joint feature vector is extracted to represent each pixel on the current video frame and compared to the background model for classification. Each pixel's background model is then updated by the neighboring pixels' feature vectors in a local rectangle region around the pixel.

2.1   Pixel Representation

To achieve the goal of robust background modeling, a good scene or pattern representation is one of the key issues. Representation issues include: what level (e.g. pixel, patch or frame level) representation and feature are desirable for the description of a pattern, and how to effectively extract the feature from the incoming video frame.

In this paper, to instantiate our joint feature vector, we represent each pixel by a three-dimension feature vector consisting of its spatial coordinates and intensity. The advantages of using the joint feature vector for dynamic background modeling are as follows. First, it explicitly considers the meaningful correlation between pixels in the spatial vicinity. For example, a center pixel in current frame would be a neighboring pixel in the next frame due to the small movements of dynamic scenes. The center pixel's intensity will change non-periodically. However, the joint feature vector is more robust to this change due to the spatial coordinates are directly used to model and exploit the spatial co-occurrence correlations between the center pixel and its neighboring pixels. Second, since each kind of feature has its strength and weakness and is particularly applicable for handling a certain type of variation, the joint feature vector can naturally fuse multiple features to make it more robust to different type of variations.

2.2 Binned Kernel Estimation Based Background Modeling

Nonparametric techniques can adapt to arbitrary unknown data distribution due to the advantages that they do not need to specify the underlying model and estimate its parameters explicitly. This characteristic enables the nonparametric techniques to become powerful tools for background modeling application. Since the background modeling problem, especially in dynamic scenes, involves multivariate multimodal densities in which the data are clustered in irregular forms in the feature space and do not follow a standard parametric form. The kernel density estimation technique is one of nonparametric techniques, which has been successful applied in background subtraction literature. But from the point of view of time and space complexity, the kernel density estimation technique is not efficient due to the large number of samples needed to model the background.

In this paper, to improve the time and space complexity of kernel density estimation technique, we adopt adaptive binned kernel estimation to construct each pixel's background model. Adaptive binned kernel estimation provides a practical means of dramatically reducing computational burdens while closely approximating the kernel density estimation.

Let $\{x_i | x_i \in \mathbb{R}^D, i = 1,2, \dots n\}$ be a recent sample set of the joint feature vector values in a local neighboring region around a pixel. Using this sample set, the probability density function that this pixel will have the joint feature vector value x_t at time t can be estimated as

$$Pr(x_t) = \frac{1}{n}\sum_{i=1}^{n} K_H(x_t - x_i) \tag{1}$$

where $K_H(x) = |H|^{-\frac{1}{2}}K(H^{-\frac{1}{2}}x)$. Here, $K(\cdot)$ is a kernel function with a symmetric positive defined bandwidth matrix $H \in \mathbb{R}^{D \times D}$. Some commonly used kernel functions are the Uniform kernel, the Gaussian kernel, the Epanechnikov kernel, the Cosinus Kernel and the Triangular kernel. Employing the profile definition, the general kernel density estimation becomes

$$Pr(x_t) = \frac{c_\kappa}{n|H|^{\frac{1}{2}}}\sum_{i=1}^{n} \kappa(M^2(x_t, x_i, H)) \tag{2}$$

where $\kappa(\cdot)$ is a profile of the kernel $K(\cdot)$, $M^2(x_t, x_i, H) = (x_t - x_i)^T H^{-1}(x_t - x_i)$ is the Mahalanobis distance from x_t to x_i, and c_κ is a normalization constant. Computing this estimation for the given pixel x_t would require n kernel evaluations. It is true that this numbers can be much reduced if one uses a kernel with compact support so that for the given pixel x_t, many of the indices i would be such that $M^2(x_t, x_i, H)$ fall outside the support of K. But then one also needs to perform a test to see if this is the case.

Since computational efficiency is an important property of background modeling for practical applications, we adopt the binned kernel estimation to speed up considerably the computation.

Binning technique, in its simplest form, can be described as follows: consider the feature space is quantized with m levels. Then, we can use the function $b: \mathbb{R}^D \to \{1,2, \dots, m\}$ associates to a given pixel's feature vector x_i the index $b(x_i)$ of its bin in the quantized feature space. Thus, an estimate of m bins histogram, characterizing the underlying distribution for the pixel to be classified, is given by the following standard bin counting procedure:

$$\mathbf{h} = \{h_u | h_u = C \sum_{i=1}^{n} \delta[b(x_i) - u], u = 1, 2, \ldots m\} \tag{3}$$

where δ is the Kronecker delta function and C is a normalization constant ensuring $\sum_{u=1}^{m} h_u = 1$. The binned kernel estimator for the pixel having the joint feature vector value x_t at time t is then

$$\Pr(x_t) = \sum_{u=1}^{m} h_u \delta[b(x_t) - u] \tag{4}$$

The advantage of binning stems essentially from the fact that the $b(x_t)$ need to be computed only once and, assuming that $K(\cdot)$ has compact support, only a small number p among them are nonzero and need to be evaluated.

2.3 Foreground Detection

Foreground detection is done after getting the background model. The incoming pixel having the joint feature vector value x_t is classified as foreground if it does not adhere to the model of the background. Formally, the classifier can be formulized as the following:

$$\text{Label}(x_t) = \begin{cases} \text{foreground}, & \text{if } \Pr(x_t) < Th \\ \text{background}, & \text{otherwise} \end{cases} \tag{5}$$

where Th is a user-settable threshold.

2.4 Updating the Background

Each pixel's background model is adapted over time using the neighboring pixels' feature vectors in a local rectangle region around the pixel. Specifically, for one sample x_i, the background distribution at time t+1 is updated as follows:

$$h_u = \begin{cases} (1 - \alpha)h_u + \alpha, & \text{if } b(x_i) = u \\ h_u, & \text{otherwise} \end{cases} \tag{6}$$

where α is the learning rate of the background model. This updating process is repeated until all neighboring pixels' feature vectors are used.

3 Experiments

The performance of the proposed method for modeling the background and detecting moving objects is evaluated in this section. The algorithm is implemented using C++, on a machine with Intel Pentium Dual 2.0 GHz processor and has achieved the processing speed of 20 fps at the resolution of 160×120 pixels. To the authors' knowledge, there is still a lack of globally accepted baseline algorithms for the extensive evaluation of background subtraction algorithms. Few of background subtraction algorithms are open source. Even that we can implement those methods, the parameters tuning is always a problem to achieve the results reported in original literature. This makes the comparison of the different approaches rather difficult. Since the GMM method [2] is widely applied in practice and the source code is publicly available (e.g., GMM in OpenCV), we compare the performance of our method to it. Both qualitative and quantitative comparisons are used to evaluate our approach.

3.1 Qualitative Evaluation

We have tested our method and GMM using five challenging image sequences from the existing literatures. Identical parameters are used in the five sequences, although better results could be obtained by customizing the values for each sequence. In our implementation, the size of local rectangle region is 10×10, the feature space (i.e. X*Y*Intensity) is quantized with 2*2*26 levels, and the threshold Th is set as 1.0e-8.

Fig.1 shows qualitative comparison results of our method, the ground truth and the GMM on the *Waving_Trees* sequence presented in [5]. The *Waving_Trees* sequence is from an outdoor scene that contains heavily swaying trees. This is a very difficult scene from the background modeling point of view. Since our method is designed to explicitly consider the meaningful correlation between pixels in the spatial vicinity, it manages the situation relatively well. While the GMM generates large number of false foreground pixels under this difficulty condition, due to the quick variations and the non-periodic motions of the waving trees.

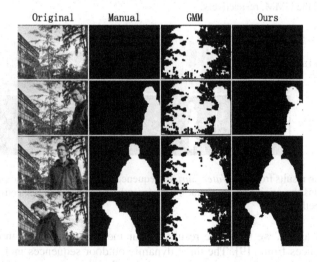

Fig. 1. Qualitative comparison results of our method, the ground truth and the GMM on the *Waving_Trees* sequence. The first column contains the original video frames. The second contains the corresponding ground truth frames. The last two columns contain the detection results of our method and the GMM, respectively.

Fig.2 shows a qualitative illustration of the results as compared to the ground truth and the GMM on the *Camera_Jitter* sequence from [13]. The *Camera_Jitter* sequence contains average camera jitter of about 14.66 pixels. It can be seen that our method has almost no false detections in spite of the camera motion. It also can be seen that the GMM produces a large number of false foreground pixels under this condition.

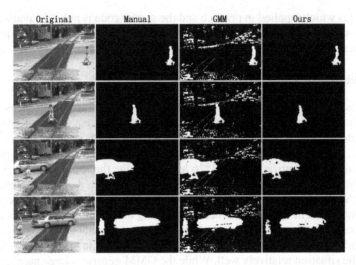

Fig. 2. Qualitative comparison results of our method, the ground truth and the GMM on the *Camera_Jitter* sequence. The first column contains the original video frames. The second contains the corresponding ground truth frames. The last two columns contain the detection results of our method and the GMM, respectively.

Fig. 3. Detection results from the *Water_Surface* sequence, which contains the ocean waves. The first row contains the original video frames. The second row contains the detection results obtained by our method.

In Fig.3, 4 and 5, we show the results of our method using other three dynamic outdoor sequences from [19]. The three dynamic outdoor sequences include the *Water_Surface* sequence with the ocean waves, the *Campus* sequence with large-area waving leaves and the *Fountains* sequence with moving objects in the front of a fountain. The challenges in these three dynamic scenes are that the backgrounds are continuously changing and have quick variations. Our method gives good results because it represents each pixel using its spatial and appearance features simultaneously to consider both meaningful correlation between neighboring pixels and its appearance changes. In the case of the *Fountains* sequence, our method produces some false background pixels. It should be noticed that most of the false background pixels occur on the background areas where the foreground objects are similar to parts of the backgrounds in intensity (see Fig.5). This is because our method exploits intensity to represent the pixels.

Fig. 4. Detection results from the *Campus* sequence, which contains large-area waving leaves. The first row contains the original video frames. The second row contains the detection results obtained by our method.

Fig. 5. Detection results from the *Fountains* sequence, which contains moving objects in the front of a fountain. The first row contains the original video frames. The second row contains the detection results obtained by our method.

3.2 Quantitative Evaluation

In order to provide a quantitative perspective about the quality of foreground detection with our approach, we manually mark the foreground regions in every frame from the *Waving_Trees* and *Camera_Jitter* sequence to generate ground truth data, and make comparison with the GMM. In the most background subtraction work, quantitative evaluation is usually done in terms of the number of false negatives (the number of foreground pixels that were missed) and false positives (the number of background pixels that were marked as foreground). However, it is found that when averaging the measures over various environments, they are not accurate enough. In this paper, a new similarity measure presented by Li et al. [19] is used to evaluate the detection results of foreground objects. Let A be a detected region and B be the corresponding ground truth, the similarity between A and B is defined as

$$S(A, B) = \frac{A \cap B}{A \cup B} \qquad (7)$$

$S(A, B)$ varies between 1 and 0 according to their similarity. If A and B are the same, $S(A, B)$ approaches 1, otherwise 0 if A and B have the least similarity. It integrates the false positive and negative errors in one measure.

The quantitative comparison results on the *Waving_Trees* and *Camera_Jitter* sequence are reported in fig.6. It should be noticed that, for our method, there are a few of the false positives and false negatives that occur on the contour areas of the foreground objects (see Fig.1 and 2). This is because our method uses the spatial co-occurrence correlations in a local neighboring region. According to the overall results, the proposed method outperforms the GMM for the used test sequences with dynamic backgrounds.

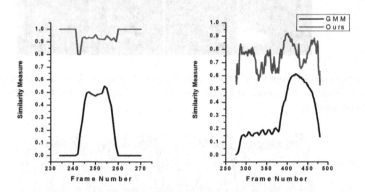

Fig. 6. Quantitative comparison results of our method and the GMM on the *Waving_Trees* and *Camera_Jitter* sequence. The left figure is the comparison results on the *Waving_Trees* sequence. The right figure is the comparison results on the *Camera_Jitter* sequence.

4 Conclusion and Future Work

We explore in this paper the method of exploiting the spatial co-occurrence correlations between neighboring pixels for background subtraction. Our study shows that the spatial co-occurrence correlations are helpful to achieve robust moving objects detection in dynamic scenes such as waving trees, ripples in water, illumination changes, camera jitters etc. We first represent each pixel as a joint feature vector consisting of its spatial coordinates and intensity, which simultaneously consider meaningful correlation between neighboring pixels and pixel's appearance changes. Then, each pixel's background model is constructed via adaptive binned kernel estimation, which is computationally inexpensive and does not need any assumptions about the underlying distributions. Extensive comparison experiments on several challenging video sequences demonstrate the advantage of the proposed method over the GMM. However, a detailed comparison of the proposed method with other background subtraction methods that make a claim of modeling dynamic scenes is the subject of future research. We are in the process of comparing and contrasting these methods with our method in terms of their detection ability and processing speed.

Acknowledgements

This work is supported by National Basic Research Program of China (2009CB320906), National Natural Science Foundation of China (60775024) and Specialized Research Fund for the Doctoral Program of Higher Education of China (20060213052).

References

1. Wren, C.R., Azarbayejani, A., Darrell, T., Pentland, A.P.: Pfinder: Real-Time Tracking of the Human Body. TPAMI 19(7), 780–785 (1997)
2. Stauffer, C., Grimson, W.E.L.: Learning Patterns of Activity Using Real-Time Tracking. TPAMI 22(8), 747–757 (2000)
3. Javed, O., Shafique, K., Shah, M.: A Hierarchical Approach to Robust Background Subtraction using Color and Gradient Information. In: IEEE Workshop on Motion and Video Computing, pp. 22–27 (2002)
4. Bouwmans, T., El Baf, F., Vachon, B.: Background Modeling using Mixture of Gaussians for Foreground Detection - A Survey. Recent Patents on Computer Science 1(3), 219–237 (2008)
5. Toyama, K., Krumm, J., Brumitt, B., Meyers, B.: Wallflower: Principles and Practice of Background Maintenance. In: ICCV, vol. 1, pp. 255–261 (1999)
6. Monnet, A., Mittal, A., Paragios, N., Visvanathan, R.: Background Modeling and Subtraction of Dynamic Scenes. In: ICCV, vol. 2, pp. 1305–1312 (2003)
7. Kato, J., Watanabe, T., Joga, S., Rittscher, J., Blake, A.: An HMM-Based Segmentation Method for Traffic Monitoring Movies. TPAMI 24(9), 1291–1296 (2002)
8. Haritaoglu, I., Harwood, D., Davis, L.S.: W4: Real-time Surveillance of People and Their Activities. TPAMI 22(8), 809–830 (2000)
9. Kim, K., Chalidabhongse, T.H., Harwood, D., Davis, L.: Real-time Foreground-Background Segmentation using Codebook Model. Real-Time Imaging 11(3), 167–256 (2005)
10. Heikkila, M., Pietikainen, M.: A Texture-Based Method for Modeling the Background and Detecting Moving Objects. TPAMI 28(4), 657–662 (2006)
11. Patwardhan, K.A., Sapiro, G., Morellas, V.: Robust Foreground Detection in Video Using Pixel Layers. TPAMI 30(4), 746–751 (2008)
12. Elgammal, A., Harwood, D., Davis, L.: Non-parametric Model for Background Subtraction. In: Vernon, D. (ed.) ECCV 2000. LNCS, vol. 1843, pp. 751–767. Springer, Heidelberg (2000)
13. Sheikh, Y., Shah, M.: Bayesian Modeling of Dynamic Scenes for Object Detection. TPAMI 27(11), 1778–1792 (2005)
14. Mittal, A., Paragios, N.: Motion-based Background Subtraction using Adaptive Kernel Density Estimation. In: CVPR, July 2004, vol. 2, pp. 302–309 (2004)
15. Parag, T., Elgammal, A., Mittal, A.: A Framework for Feature Selection for Background Subtraction. In: CVPR, vol. 2, pp. 1916–1923 (2006)
16. Elgammal, A.M., Duraiswami, R., Davis, L.S.: Efficient Kernel Density Estimation Using the Fast Gauss Transform with Applications to Color Modeling and Tracking. TPAMI 25(11), 1499–1504 (2003)
17. Hall, P., Wand, M.: On the Accuracy of Binned Kernel Estimators. J. Multivariate Analysis (1995)
18. Sain, S.: Multivariate Locally Adaptive Density Estimates. Computational Statistics and Data Analysis (2002)
19. Li, L., Huang, W., Gu, I.Y.H., Tian, Q.: Statistical Modeling of Complex Backgrounds for Foreground Object Detection. TIP 13(11), 1459–1472 (2004)

Gable Roof Description by Self-Avoiding Polygon*

Qiongchen Wang, Zhiguo Jiang, Junli Yang, Danpei Zhao, and Zhenwei Shi

Image Center, Beihang University, Beijing China
qcwang.buaa@gmail.com, jiangzg@buaa.edu.cn,
lqwrl.yjl0406@gmail.com, {zhaodanpei,shizhenwei}@buaa.edu.cn,

Abstract. In this paper, we present a Self-Avoiding Polygon (SAP) model for describing and detecting complex gable rooftops from nadir-view aerial imagery. We demonstrate that a broad range of gable rooftop shapes can be summarized as self-avoiding polygons, whose vertices correspond to roof corners. The SAP model, defined over the joint space of all possible SAPs and images, combines the shape prior embedded in SAP and a set of appearance features (edge, color and texture) learned from training images. Given an observed image, the posterior probability of the SAP model measures how well each SAP fits the observed data. Our inference algorithm follows the MAP framework, i.e. detecting the best gable roof is equivalent to finding the optimal self-avoiding polygon on the image plain. Even though the entire state space of all SAPs is enormous, we find that by using A^* search, commonly our algorithm can find the optimal solution in polynominal time. Experiments on a set of challenging image shows promising performance.

Keywords: Gable Roof, Self-Avoiding Polygon (SAP).

1 Introduction

Automatic building roof delineation from aerial imagery has been an important research topic in computer vision, remote sensing and cartography for the past decades. Extensive work has been done on this task from different perspectives, such as fusing multiple information (DEM) [1], using 3D information [2,1], among others. But little has been reported on automatic roof delineation from single nadir-view aerial imagery. Challenges are twofolds: 1) Shape variety. Building rooftops have big variations in both topology and geometry. Examples in Fig. 1 may help to visualize some of these variety. Such variations cannot be accounted for in fixed shape templates. Even existing compositional models, such as [3,2,4], are still based on manual specified rules and hence limited in generality. 2) Local ambiguity. Because of their distinguishable characteristics, local structures such as straight-lines, corners and parallel lines are favored in man made structures (building, road, etc.) detection literature. But these local elements are also notoriously noisy. On the one hand, occlusions will lead to failure of local edge detector, which will probably cause miss-detection of local structures. On the other hand, background clutters inevitably generates excessive amount of false alarms, which, if is

---

* This research has been supported by the National Natural Science Foundation of China (NSFC) under the grant (60776793).

H. Zha, R.-i. Taniguchi, and S. Maybank (Eds.): ACCV 2009, Part III, LNCS 5996, pp. 162–171, 2010.

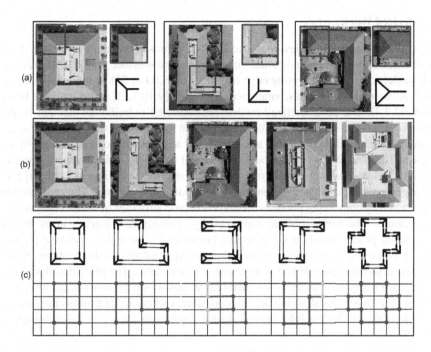

Fig. 1. (a) Appearance based roof corners; (b) examples for gable roof with arbitrary shape; (c) Illustrations of the Self-avoiding polygon representation. First row shows how gable roof can be decomposed into corners and edges, second row shows how those corners and edges generate a Self-avoiding polygon.

not thresholded properly, will bog down the algorithm into endless futile search. It is always a headache to strike a balance between over-kill and under-threshold for methods that make use of local structures.

In this paper, we address the problem of shape variety by proposing the self-avoiding polygon (SAP) model. A SAP is a closed sequence of moves on a lattice which dose not visit the same point more than once except the point the moves start with. It plays a central role in the modeling of crystal growth and polymers [5]. As demonstrated in Fig. 1 that a broad range of gable rooftop shapes can be summarized as SAPs, whose vertices correspond to two types of commonly shared roof corners. We believe the SAP is a compact yet expressive representation for all rectilinear building rooftops. To address the local ambiguity, our efforts are twofolds. Firstly, we adopt learning based local structure detectors, which optimally integrate all appearance features (e.g. edge, texture and color) extracted from a large neighborhood. Such methods have been proved to be extremely effective to address local ambiguities [6,7]. Secondly, our inference algorithm detects the best gable roof by searching the entire state space of all possible SAPs. Since the global information is much more stable than local structures, our method is more robust against local noise. To achieve efficient inference, A^* search algorithm is exploited to search the state space.

1.1 Related Work

In this section, we briefly review roof detection algorithms in literature, especially those model-based approach. For a detailed survey, we refer the reader to [8]. Most previous work model roofs by aggregating edge features under 2D or 3D geometry constrains. There are two major categories, parameterized models [9,10,1,11] and component based models [2,3,4]. The parameterized models are restricted to buildings that can be described by prototype shapes. Therefore, the model in this category can handle few shape variations. It is also difficult to find an optimal way to combine the large number of parameters. The component based model shows great flexibility and expressive power in modeling various building types. For example the approach of Bignone et al. [3] propose a generic roof model based on planar roof patch components. The roof patches are extracted by combining photometric and chromatic attributes of image regions with edge features. The entire roof are composed by grouping roof patches in an overall optimization process under a set of spatial constraints. The major challenge for this category is the local ambiguity. Instead of depending purely on edge features, richer information should be combined in detection of components. The inference algorithms for both two categories are based on hierarchical bottom-up hypothesis and top-down verifications. Due to local ambiguity, it is possible for bottom-up process miss-detect correct hypothesis, thus such framework does not necessary assure global optimality.

2 Model Representation and Probabilistic Distribution

2.1 The SAP Model

The corners of gable roof, some of which are shown in Fig.1(a), are typical features for discriminating gable roofs and also play important roles in our representation. The state space of gable corners C on image lattice Λ with domain D is defined as a dictionary:

$$\Omega_C = \{C_{(x,y,s,\theta,t)}, \forall(x,y,s,\theta,t)\}, \tag{1}$$

where $(x,y) \in D$ is the center position of C, $s \in \{k, k = 1, ..., K\}$ and $\theta \in \{2\pi\frac{w}{16}, w = 0, ..., 15\}$ denotes scale and orientation respectively, $t \in \{1, 2\}$ represents two types of gable roof corners as shown in Fig.1(a).

As shown in Fig.1(c), a complex gable roof is represented with a close sequence of corners composing a self-avoiding polygon denoted by P:

$$P = \langle n, (C_1, ..., C_i, ..., C_n, C_{n+1}) \rangle, \tag{2}$$

$$C_1 \triangleq C_{n+1}, \tag{3}$$

$$C_i \Rightarrow C_j, j = i + 1, i = 1, ..., n.$$

where $n \in [minN, maxN]$ means the number of corners in P, each node $C_i \in \Omega_C$ is a corner. Equation (3) means that the start and end should be same in order to form a closed loop. $C_i \Rightarrow C_j$ denotes a set of constraints that two neighboring nodes must satisfy. To define $C_i \Rightarrow C_j$, we first suppose $C_i = C_{(x_i,y_i,s_i,\theta_i,t_i)}$, then $C_i \Rightarrow C_j$ if and only if there exists (θ_i, θ_j) such that

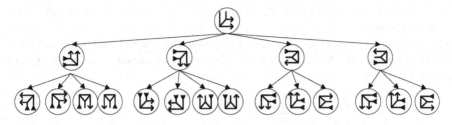

Fig. 2. Constraints for neighboring corners in a SAP. The arrows represent open bounds to be connected with a neighboring corner. Given a roof corner, all valid choices of its neighbor are displayed by its children nodes.

$$s_i = s_j;$$
$$\theta_j = \theta_i + \pi \; or \; \theta_i - \pi/2, \; if \; t_i = 1, t_j = 1,$$
$$\theta_j = \theta_i + \pi \qquad\qquad , \; if \; t_i = 1, t_j = 2,$$
$$\theta_j = \theta_i + \pi \; or \; \theta_i + \pi/2, \; if \; t_i = 2, t_j = 1,$$
$$\theta_j = \theta_i + \pi \qquad\qquad , \; if \; t_i = 2, t_j = 2. \tag{4}$$

A more intuitive way to illustrate these constraints is shown in Fig.2.

The state space of P is determined by the number of node n and each node $C_i = (x_i, y_i, s_i, \theta_i, t_i)$. Given a P, we can generate a shape template of gable roof by connecting all open bonds of each node into a loop, as illustrated in Figure. 1 (c).

2.2 Probabilistic Distribution

The joint distribution on P and an image I can be written in Gibbs form:

$$p(P, I) = \frac{1}{Z} \exp(-E(P) - E(P, I)). \tag{5}$$

where Z is the partition function. The first energy term $E(P)$ represents a set of constraints serving as shape priors. Besides the constraints specified in equation (4), we penalize situation when point (x_{i+1}, y_{i+1}) is not close to the line crossing point (x_i, y_i) toward direction θ_i. We also penalize situation when (x_i, y_i), (x_{i+1}, y_{i+1}) are too close to each other.

The second energy term $E(P, I)$ measures how good a gable rooftop generated from P fits the image I, and is given by generalizing a pseudo-likelihood function:

$$E(P, I) = - \sum_{s \in \Lambda/R} \log p(I(s); y(s) = 0 | I(N(s)/s))$$
$$- \sum_{s \in R} \log p(I(s); y(s) = 1 | I(N(s)/s)). \tag{6}$$

where $x \in \Lambda$ is a pixel, $I(x)$ is the intensity value at the given pixel x, $N(x)$ is a neighborhood on pixel x, $N(x)/x$ includes all the pixels in the neighborhood except x, $R \subset \Lambda$ is the image domain occupied by the rooftop generated from P, Λ/R means on the image lattice Λ except R, $p(I(x); y(x) = 1 | I(N(x)/x))$ is a conditional joint probability,

$y(x) = 1$ indicate that pixel x is on the rooftop, while $y(x) = 0$ indicate that pixel x is on the background.

By adding $\sum_{x \in R} \log p(I(x); y(x) = 0 | I(N(x)/x))$ to the first right-hand-side term and subtracting it from the second right-hand-side term of equation(6), we can re-express the equation(6) as:

$$E(P, I) = - \sum_{x \in \Lambda} \log p(I(x); y(x) = 0 | I(N(x)/x))$$

$$- \sum_{x \in R} \frac{\log p(y(x) = 1 | I(N(x)))}{\log p(y(x) = 0 | I(N(x)))}. \tag{7}$$

where the first right-hand-side term does not depend on P and hence can be ignored. To compute the second right-hand-side term we further divide R into three sets: corners(C), boundaries(B) and interior area (A).

$$- \sum_{x \in R} \frac{\log p(y(x) = 1 | I(N(x)))}{\log p(y(x) = 0 | I(N(x)))} = E_{corner} + E_{bound} + E_{area},$$

$$E_{corner} = - \sum_{x \in C} \log \frac{p(y(x) = 1 | I(N(x)))}{p(y(x) = 0 | I(N(x)))} \approx - \sum_{x \in C} \log \frac{p(l_C(x) = 1 | I(N(x)))}{p(l_C(x) = 0 | I(N(x)))}, \tag{8}$$

$$E_{bound} = - \sum_{x \in B} \log \frac{p(y(x) = 1 | I(N(x)))}{p(y(x) = 0 | I(N(x)))} \approx - \sum_{x \in B} \log \frac{p(l_B(x) = 1 | I(N(x)))}{p(l_B(x) = 0 | I(N(x)))}, \tag{9}$$

$$E_{area} = - \sum_{x \in A} \log \frac{p(y(x) = 1 | I(N(x)))}{p(y(x) = 0 | I(N(x)))} \approx - \sum_{x \in A} \log \frac{p(l_A(x) = 1 | I(N(x)))}{p(l_A(x) = 0 | I(N(x)))}. \tag{10}$$

where $l_C(x) = 1$ or 0 indicate pixel x is "on" or "off" the corner of a gable roof. Similar definition is used for $l_B(x)$ and $l_A(x)$. The approximate equal signs in equation (8,9,10) hold true under the assumption that all three sets are independent to each other, and background distributions $p(l(x) = 0 | I(N(x)))$ equal to $p(y(x) = 0 | I(N(x)))$. The right hand side of equation (8),(9) and (10) represent posterior probability ratios of a pixel x belonging to the corner, boundary and interior area respectively given a image patch centered at x. We will discuss how to obtain them in the next section.

2.3 Learning Local Appearance Model

Boundaries, corners and interior areas are the "local structures" discussed in section 1. As we know, these structures are very noisy in aerial imagery. To overcome this problem, partly, we adopted learning based appearance models that integrates edge, color and texture features from the entire image patch.

For corners, we adopt the active basis model [7] because it has larger context and allows small geometric deformation. The log posterior ratio can be represented by:

$$E_{corner} = - \log \frac{p(l_C(x) = 1 | I(N(x)))}{p(l_C(x) = 0 | I(N(x)))} = - \log \frac{p(I|B)}{q(I)} \frac{p(l_C(x) = 1)}{p(l_C(x) = 0)} = - \sum_{j=1}^{k} \lambda_j r_j + \log z_j.$$

where $B = (B_i, i = 1, \ldots, n)$ is a template composed of a set of Gabor wavelets B_i. r_j is convolution response of the jth Gabor wavelets with image I and λ_j is the jth

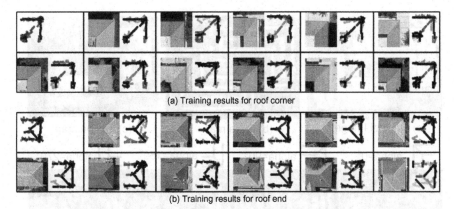

(a) Training results for roof corner

(b) Training results for roof end

Fig. 3. Learning corner templates from aligned image patches. The first plot displays the learned corner templates with each gray bar representing a Gabor wavelet. For the remaining 11 pairs of examples, the left plot shows the training image patch I centered at a roof corner, and the right plot shows the corresponding template.

coefficients. $q(I)$ refers to the background distribution, z_i is normalizing constant. As illustrated by Fig. 3, these parameters can be learned from a set of training image patches centered at the gable roof corner using a shared pursuit algorithm. For more details about this learning process, please refer to [7].

E_{bound} and E_{area} is learned by training discriminative classifiers based on local cues within the neighborhood, which is done in spirit similar to the approach in [6]. The cues include edge color texture and brightness. We use a $\tilde{N}(s) = 30 \times 30$ neighborhood to learn an approximated posterior probability. It is worth mention that the energy functions of all three types are computed at a given scale. For different scales, we resize the image, which equivalent to change the size of image patch.

3   Model Inference Algrorithm

The task of the inference algorithm is to find a P^* that maximize the posteriori probability given I.

$$P^* = \arg\max_{P \in \Omega_P} p(P|I) = \arg\max p(P, I). \tag{11}$$

where Ω_P is the whole space of all possible SAPs. This can be done in a principled way using the A^* search algorithm [12]. As shown in Fig. 5, A^* prioritizes search not only based on the cost of a path traveled so far, but also on an estimate of the cost to get to the goal, called 'heuristics'. This keeps search balancing between local path cost and global path cost, and assures the search to converge to the path with least cost quickly. We first define four basic data structures in the algorithm process (To fix notation, we will use X to denote the current node in the search algorithm, Y as previous node, G denote the goal node):

– *A Saliency Map Array.* It is the fundamental data structure for searching in the SAP space. It stores energy maps for the corners, boundaries and inner areas, computed

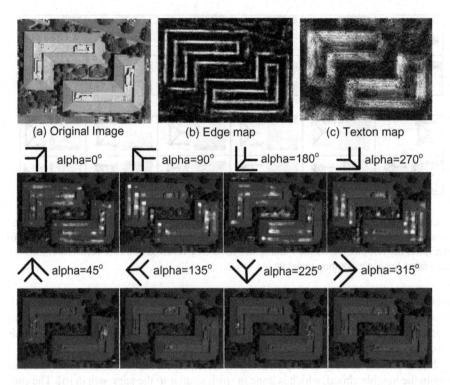

Fig. 4. Saliency maps computed at a given scale, darker the pixel, higher the energy (cost).(a) original image,(b) saliency map for boundary,(c) saliency map for inner area. The rest 8 images are saliency maps of corner at the orientation given above the image.

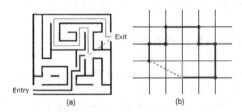

Fig. 5. An illustration for A^* heuristics. (a) Search in maze, A^* search combines $cost\_so\_far$ (solid line) with a heuristic $cost\_to\_goal$ (dashed line) to balance between local and global cost. (b) Search SAP on lattice, solid line and dashed line correspond to $cost\_so\_far$ and $cost\_to\_goal$.

from an input image. In each map, the value in each pixel equals to cetain type of energy at that pixel, as defined by equation (8,9,10). All saliency maps are normalized, according to the largest and smallest value of each type into [0, 1]. The lower the energy (cost) is, the more likely there exists an element on this pixel. For a given scale, we have 16×2 saliency maps for corner, representing for 16 different orientations and 2 types. We have one saliency map for boundaries and one for inner area, because they are orientation independent. Fig. 4 illustrates a gable roof image and its corresponding saliency maps at a given scale. Only 8 orientation of corner are displayed.

- *A Priority Queue.* Also known as *Open Set.* It maintains a queue of corners with different priorities which determine the order in which the search visit corners. Here the priority of a corner is the *total_cost* of it which we will discuss later.
- *A Closed Set.* It stores nodes that already being traversed, it may be used to make the search more efficient.
- *A Neighborhood Tree.* As shown in Fig. 2, it determines which type and orientation of corner can be connected to the current one. Then the neighborhood of current node in the search are limited in a sub-tree. In our algorithm, we define a function *neighborhood_nodes(X)* to get all the possible nodes in its the neighborhood of X.

The algorithm traverses various paths from start node then back to start node. For each node X traversed, it maintains 4 values computed from the following functions (The pseudo code of algorithm is given in Algorithm1):

Algorithm 1. $A^*(InitSet)$

$ClosedSet \Leftarrow empty$
$PriorityQueue \Leftarrow InitSet$
while $PriorityQueue \neq empty$ **do**
    $X \Leftarrow PriorityQueue[0]$ {The node with highest priority in $PriorityQueue$}
    if $X = start\_node(X) \wedge path\_length(X) \geq minN$ **then**
        return $path\_reconstruct(X)$
    end if
    remove X from $PriorityQueue$
    if $path\_length(X) \geq maxM$, **then** *continue* **endif**
    add X to $ClosedSet$
    for all Y such that $Y \in neighbor\_nodes(X)$ **do**
        if $Y \in ClosedSet$, **then** *continue* **endif**
        $Goal \Leftarrow start\_node(X)$
        $UpdataCost \Leftarrow cost\_so\_far(Y, X) + cost\_to\_goal(Y, Goal)$
        if $Y \notin PriorityQueue$ **then**
            add Y with its cost $UpdataCost$ and *came_from* node X to $PriorityQueue$
        else if $TotalCost[Y] > UpdataCost$ **then**
            update the cost and *came_from* node of Y by $UpdateCost$ and X
        end if
    end for
end while

- *came_from(X).* It stores the previous node of X in the path, which will be used in function *start_node(X)* for tracing back to the start node of the path from node X.
- *cost_so_far(X, Y).* The smallest cost from the initial node to current node. It is the sum of two values. The first is the "path cost", which is the sumation of all energies defined by the posterior function. It equals to the sum of all saliency maps covered by the current path. The second is the "path length", which is the length of the current path used to encourage SAPs with shorter perimeter.

- $cost\_to\_goal(X, G)$. The estimated (or 'heuristic') distance from current node to goal. To be sure of the 'heuristic' is admissible, or is not overestimated, we only consider the "path length" and set the "path cost" to be zero. An example is shown in Fig. 5 (b), where the dashed green line indicates the estimated distance, the solid green line indicates the real path. The "path length to go" equal the length of the dashed green line. Since the search must be a walk on the lattice, the length of dashed line must be shorter than the length of the solid green line. Thus it guarantees that the estimate is admissible.
- $total\_cost$.The sum of $cost\_so\_far(X)$ and $cost\_to\_goal(X)$.

4   Experiment

We evaluate our SAP model on a number of challenging gable roofs. The main goals are to show its ability to delineating complex gable roof tops with various topological and geometrical configurations, in presence of boundary occlusions and background clutters. The first experiment is to learn templates of roof corners using the shared pursuit algorithm of [7]. The training set has $M = 35$ of instances for each type of gable roof corner. The algorithm returns $n = 40$ Gabor wavelets as illustrated in Fig. 3. To reduce searc space, we use a preprocess to determine the scale. We compute saliency maps of roof corners at 10 continous scales. The max score of each scale is ploted into a curve as illustrated in Fig. 6 (b). The scale with maximun score is selected as the global scale, which will be used by the search algorithm. We demonstrate some final results by connecting the searched corners using straight lines, as shown in Fig. 7. It is also worth mention that although the whole search space of our algorithm is very

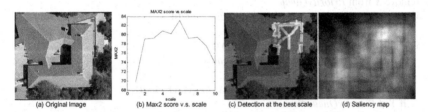

(a) Original Image   (b) Max2 score v.s. scale   (c) Detection at the best scale   (d) Saliency map

Fig. 6. The scale is predetermined by finding the best corner. (a) original image,(b) max2 score at 10 different scales. max2 score is the biggest score for corners at all orientation and location.(c) detected corner at scale 6 with the max score, (d) Saliency map of scale 6.

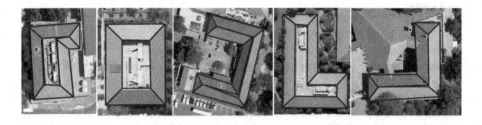

Fig. 7. Detection results for complex gable roofs

huge, we discover in experiments that the A^* algorithm only search a few branches with lowest cost in the *Neighborhood Tree*.. Therefore, the actual computing time grows linearly (not exponentially) with search depth, which agrees with the polynominal time complexity of A^* search in best case.

5 Discussion and Conclusion

We have addressed the problem of detection and description complex gable roofs from nadir-view aerial imagery. We proposed a SAP model and an efficient A^* search algorithm for complex gable roof representation and inference. We formulated the problem under the MAP framework. For our future work, we will focus on developing more efficient addmisible heuristics to guide the search to convergy to the goal faster. And we still need to do much work to generalize the SAP model to more types of roofs. More shape prior should be added to constrain SAP model in a smaller space.

References

1. Kim, Z., Nevatia, R.: Automatic description of complex buildings from multiple images. Computer Vision and Image Understanding 96(1), 60–95 (2004)
2. Fischer, A., Kolbe, T.H., Lang, F., Cremers, A.B., Forstner, W., Pluemer, L., Steinhage, V.: Extracting buildings from aerial images using hierarchical aggregation in 2D and 3D. Computer Vision and Image Understanding 72(2), 185–203 (1998)
3. Bignone, F., Henricsson, O., Fua, P., Stricker, M.: Automatic extraction of generic house roofs from high resolution aerial imagery. In: Buxton, B.F., Cipolla, R. (eds.) ECCV 1996. LNCS, vol. 1064, pp. 83–96. Springer, Heidelberg (1996)
4. Scholze, S., Moons, T., Gool, L.J.V.: A probabilistic approach to roof patch extraction and reconstruction. In: Automatic Extraction of Man-Made Objects from Aerial and Space Image, III, pp. 195–204 (2001)
5. Bousquet-Melou, M.: Convex polyominoes and heaps of segments. Journal of Physics A: Mathematical and General 25, 1925–1934 (1992)
6. Dollar, P., Tu, Z.W., Belongie, S.J.: Supervised learning of edges and object boundaries. In: CVPR (2006)
7. Wu, Y.N., Si, Z.Z., Fleming, C., Zhu, S.C.: Deformable template as active basis. In: ICCV, pp. 1–8 (2007)
8. Mayer, H.: Automatic object extraction from aerial imagery: A survey focusing on buildings. Computer Vision and Image Understanding 74(2), 138–149 (1999)
9. Chellappa, R., Davis, L.S., Lin, C.L., Moore, T., Rodriguez, C., Rosenfeld, A., Zhang, X., Zheng, Q.: Site model supported monitoring of aerial images. In: CVPR, pp. 694–699 (1994)
10. Lin, C., Nevatia, R.: Building detection and description from a single intensity image. Computer Vision and Image Understanding 72(2), 101–121 (1998)
11. Katartzis, A., Sahli, H.: A stochastic framework for the identification of building rooftops using a single remote sensing image. IEEE Trans. Geoscience and Remote Sensing 46(1), 259–271 (2008)
12. Russel, S., Norvig, P.: Artificial Intelligence: a Modern Approach. Prentice-Hall, Englewood Cliffs (1995)

Tracking Endocardial Boundary and Motion via Graph Cut Distribution Matching and Multiple Model Filtering

Kumaradevan Punithakumar[1], Ismail Ben Ayed[1], Ali Islam[2],
Ian Ross[3] and Shuo Li[1,4]

[1] GE Healthcare, London, Ontario, Canada
[2] St. Joseph's Health Care, London, Ontario, Canada
[3] London Health Science Center, London, Ontario, Canada
[4] University of Western Ontario

Abstract. Tracking the left ventricular (LV) endocardial boundary and motion from cardiac magnetic resonance (MR) images is difficult because of low contrast and photometric similarities between the heart wall and papillary muscles within the LV cavity. This study investigates the problem via *Graph Cut Distribution Matching (GCDM)* and *Interacting Multiple Model (IMM) smoothing*. GCDM yields initial frame segmentations by keeping the same photometric/geometric distribution of the cavity over cardiac cycles, whereas IMM constrains the results with prior knowledge of temporal consistency. Incorporation of prior knowledge that characterizes the dynamic behavior of the LV enhances the accuracy of both motion estimation and segmentation. However, accurately characterizing the behavior using a single Markovian model is not sufficient due to substantial variability in heart motion. Moreover, dynamic behaviors of normal and abnormal hearts are very different. This study introduces multiple models, each corresponding to a different phase of the LV dynamics. The IMM, an effective estimation algorithm for Markovian switching systems, yields the state estimate of endocardial points as well as the model probability that indicates the most-likely model. The proposed method is evaluated quantitatively by comparison with independent manual segmentations over 2280 images acquired from 20 subjects, which demonstrated competitive results in comparisons with a recent method.

1 Introduction

Tracking myocardial boundary and motion plays a leading role in the diagnosis of cardiovascular diseases. It allows analyzing and quantifying myocardial motion [1]. Magnetic Resonance (MR) sequences are widely used for analyzing cardiac function, and provide a large number of images[1]. Therefore, tracking based on manual delineation of the Left Ventricular (LV) boundary in all these images is

---

[1] Typically, the number of images per subject is equal to 200.

H. Zha, R.-i. Taniguchi, and S. Maybank (Eds.): ACCV 2009, Part III, LNCS 5996, pp. 172–182, 2010.
© Springer-Verlag Berlin Heidelberg 2010

prohibitively time consuming, and automating the process has been the subject of an intense research effort recently [2,3]. This problem is difficult due to the low contrast and photometric similarities between connected cardiac regions - for instance, the papillary muscles within the cavity and heart wall have approximately the same intensity. Therefore, standard segmentation methods based solely on intensity information cannot yield accurate tracking. To overcome this difficulty, most of existing methods constrain the solution with prior geometric properties, such as the shape of the LV cavity learned *a priori* from a finite training set [4]. Unfortunately, such training information is not sufficiently reliable to recover the substantial variability between subjects [1]. Furthermore, these methods do not account for *temporal consistency* of cardiac motion.

The system proposed in this study consists of two complementary steps. The first step, referred to as Graph Cut Distribution Matching (GCDM), yields initial segmentation of the LV cavity within each frame by keeping the same photometric/geometric distribution of the cavity over cardiac cycles. This is done by minimizing a distribution-matching energy which measures the similarity between a given segmentation of the first frame and the unknown segmentation of the current frame. Based on global distribution information learned from the first frame in the current data, GCDM overcomes some of the difficulties inherent to cardiac images without resorting to *a priori* training.

The second step, referred to as Interacting Multiple Model (IMM) smoothing, constrains the segmentation results with prior knowledge of temporal consistency via *multiple models*. Incorporation of such prior knowledge, which characterizes the dynamic behavior of the LV motion, enhances the accuracy of both segmentation and tracking. Particularly, a cyclic temporal model is well suited for periodic cardiac motion [3,5]. However, due to the substantial variability in the dynamics of the LV of a normal heart, accurate representation of the motion with a single Markovian model is not sufficient. Moreover, the dynamics of normal and abnormal hearts are very different. Therefore, the LV dynamics can be viewed as a *Markovian switching system*, which has both *continuous* (noise) and *discrete* (model) uncertainties. For such systems, the IMM is an effective solution. It yields the state estimate as well as the model probability indicating the most-likely model. Furthermore, in IMM filtering, the state estimates are updated using only the past observations. However, if a delay in estimation can be tolerated, the results could be drastically improved using future measurements. As such, IMM smoothing [6] can be further exploited for our problem.

The proposed method is evaluated quantitatively by comparison with independent manual segmentations over 2280 images acquired from 20 subjects, which demonstrated competitive results in comparisons with a recent method.

2   Graph Cut Distribution Matching

Consider a MR cardiac sequence containing N frames[2] $\mathbf{I}_p^n = \mathbf{I}^n(p) : \mathcal{P} \subset \mathbb{R}^2 \to \mathcal{I}$, $n \in [1..N]$, with $\mathcal{P}$ the positional array and $\mathcal{I}$ the space of photometric variables.

---

[2] The number of frames N is typically equal to 20 or 25.

For each frame $n \in [2..N]$, this first stage consists of dividing $\mathcal{P}$ into two regions–the *heart cavity* and the its complement in $\mathcal{P}$–according to *photometric* and *geometric* criteria. We state the problem as the minimization of a discrete cost function with respect to a binary variable (labeling), $\mathcal{L}^n(p) : \mathcal{P} \rightarrow \{0,1\}$, which defines a variable partition of $\mathcal{P}$: the *heart cavity* $\mathbf{C}^n$ corresponding to region $\{p \in \mathcal{P}/\mathcal{L}^n(p) = 1\}$ and its complement, the *background* $\mathbf{B}^n$ corresponding to region $\{p \in \mathcal{P}/\mathcal{L}^n(p) = 0\}$. The optimal labeling is obtained by minimizing an energy containing two kernel density matching terms, an intensity matching term and a distance matching term. To introduce the energy, we first consider the following definitions for any labeling $\mathcal{L} : \mathcal{P} \rightarrow \{0,1\}$, any image $\mathbf{I} : \mathcal{P} \subset \mathbb{R}^2 \rightarrow \mathcal{I}$, and any space of variables $\mathcal{I}$.

• $\mathbf{P}_{\mathcal{L},\mathbf{I}}^{\mathcal{I}}$ is the Kernel Density Estimate (KDE) of the distribution of image data $\mathbf{I}$ within region $\mathbf{R}_{\mathcal{L}} = \{p \in \mathcal{P}/\mathcal{L}(p) = 1\}$

$$\forall i \in \mathcal{I}, \quad \mathbf{P}_{\mathcal{L},\mathbf{I}}^{\mathcal{I}}(i) = \frac{\sum_{p \in \mathbf{R}_{\mathcal{L}}} K(i - \mathbf{I}_p)}{\mathbf{A}_{\mathcal{L}}}, \quad \text{with} \quad K(y) = \frac{1}{\sqrt{2\pi\sigma^2}} exp^{-\frac{y^2}{2\sigma^2}}, \quad (1)$$

with $\mathbf{A}_{\mathcal{L}}$ is the number of pixels within $\mathbf{R}_{\mathcal{L}}$: $\mathbf{A}_{\mathcal{L}} = \sum_{\mathbf{R}_{\mathcal{L}}} 1$, and σ is the width of the Gaussian kernel. Note that choosing K equal to the Dirac function yields the histogram.

• $\mathcal{B}(f, g)$ is the *Bhattacharyya* coefficient[3] measuring the amount of overlap (similarity) between two distributions f and g: $\mathcal{B}(f, g) = \sum_{i \in \mathcal{I}} \sqrt{f(i)g(i)}$.

We assume that a segmentation of frame $\mathbf{I}^1$, i.e., a labeling $\mathcal{L}^1$ defining a partition $\{\mathbf{C}^1, \mathbf{B}^1\}$, is given. Using prior information from this frame, the photometric and geometric model distributions of the cavity are learned, and used in the following distribution matching constraints to segment subsequent frames.

Photometric constraint. Given the learned model of intensity, which we denote $\mathbf{M}^{\mathcal{I}} = \mathbf{P}_{\mathcal{L}^1,\mathbf{I}^1}^{\mathcal{I}}$, the purpose of this term is to find for each subsequent frame $\mathbf{I}^n$ a region $\mathbf{C}^n$ whose intensity distribution most closely matches $\mathbf{M}^{\mathcal{I}}$. To this end, we minimizes the following intensity matching function with respect to $\mathcal{L}$:

$$\mathcal{B}^{\mathcal{I}}(\mathcal{L}, \mathbf{I}^n) = -\mathcal{B}(\mathbf{P}_{\mathcal{L},\mathbf{I}^n}^{\mathcal{I}}, \mathbf{M}^{\mathcal{I}}) = -\sum_{i \in \mathcal{I}} \sqrt{\mathbf{P}_{\mathcal{L},\mathbf{I}^n}^{\mathcal{I}}(i)\mathbf{M}^{\mathcal{I}}(i)} \qquad (2)$$

Geometric constraint. The purpose of this term is to constrain the segmentation with prior geometric information (shape, scale, and position of the cavity) obtained from the learning frame. Let c be the centroid of cavity $\mathbf{C}^1$ in the learning frame and $\mathbf{D}(p) = \frac{\|p-c\|}{N_{\mathbf{D}}} : \mathcal{P} \rightarrow \mathcal{D}$ a *distance image* measuring at each point $p \in \mathcal{P}$ the normalized distance between p and c, with $\mathcal{D}$ the space of distance variables and $N_{\mathbf{D}}$ a normalization constant. Let $\mathbf{M}^{\mathcal{D}} = \mathbf{P}_{\mathcal{L}^1,\mathbf{D}}^{\mathcal{D}}$ the model distribution of distances within the cavity in the learning frame. We seek a region $\mathbf{C}^n$ whose distance distribution most closely matches $\mathbf{M}^{\mathcal{D}}$ by minimizing:

$$\mathcal{B}^{\mathcal{D}}(\mathcal{L}, \mathbf{D}) = -\mathcal{B}(\mathbf{P}_{\mathcal{L},\mathbf{D}}^{\mathcal{D}}, \mathbf{M}^{\mathcal{D}}) = -\sum_{d \in \mathcal{D}} \sqrt{\mathbf{P}_{\mathcal{L},\mathbf{D}}^{\mathcal{D}}(d)\mathbf{M}^{\mathcal{D}}(d)} \qquad (3)$$

---

[3] Note that the values of $\mathcal{B}$ are always in $[0, 1]$, where 0 indicates that there is no overlap, and 1 indicates a perfect match between the distributions.

Note that this geometric prior is invariant to rotation, and embeds *implicitly* uncertainties with respect to scale via the kernel width σ in (1). The higher σ, the more scale variations allowed. In our experiments, $\sigma = 2$ was sufficient to handle effectively variations in the scale of the cavity. This geometric prior relaxes (1) complex learning/modeling of geometric characteristics and the need of a training set and (2) *explicit* optimization with respect to geometric transformations.

The discrete energy function. The discrete energy function we minimize contains the photometric and geometric matching terms as well as a regularization term for smooth segmentation boundaries. For each $n \in [2..N]$, the first stage of our algorithm computes the optimal labeling $\mathcal{L}_{opt}^n$ minimizing:

$$\mathcal{F}(\mathcal{L}, \mathbf{I}^n) = \mathcal{B}^{\mathcal{I}}(\mathcal{L}, \mathbf{I}^n) + \mathcal{B}^{\mathcal{D}}(\mathcal{L}, \mathbf{D}) + \lambda \mathbf{S}(\mathcal{L}) \tag{4}$$

where $\mathbf{S}(\mathcal{L})$ is related to the length of the partition boundary given by [7]:

$$\mathbf{S}(\mathcal{L}) = \sum_{\{p,q\} \in \mathcal{N}} \frac{1}{\|p-q\|} \delta_{\mathcal{L}_p \neq \mathcal{L}_q}, \quad \text{with } \delta_{x \neq y} = \begin{cases} 1 & \text{if } x \neq y \\ 0 & \text{if } x = y \end{cases}, \tag{5}$$

and $\mathcal{N}$ is a neighborhood system containing all unordered pairs $\{p,q\}$ of neighboring elements of $\mathcal{P}$. λ is a positive constant that balances the relative contribution of $\mathbf{S}$.

Graph cut optimization. The distribution matching terms in $\mathcal{F}(\mathcal{L}, \mathbf{I}^n)$ do not afford an analytical form amenable to graph cut optimization. The ensuing problem is *NP-hard*. Furthermore, gradient-based optimization procedures are computationally very expensive and difficult to apply. To overcome this problem, we compute a first-order approximation of the Bhattacharyya measures in $\mathcal{F}(\mathcal{L}, \mathbf{I}^n)$ by introducing an auxiliary[4] labeling which corresponds to an arbitrary, fixed partition. For any labeling $\mathcal{L}$, the intensity matching term minus a constant reads:

$$\mathcal{B}^{\mathcal{I}}(\mathcal{L}, \mathbf{I}^n) - \underbrace{\mathcal{B}^{\mathcal{I}}(\mathcal{L}^a, \mathbf{I}^n)}_{Constant} \approx \underbrace{\sum_{p \in \mathcal{P}} \delta \mathcal{B}_{p, \mathcal{L}^a, \mathcal{L}}^{\mathcal{I}}}_{Variations\ of\ \mathcal{B}^I} = -\frac{1}{2} \sum_{p \in \mathcal{P}} \sum_{i \in \mathcal{I}} \sqrt{\frac{\mathbf{M}^{\mathcal{I}}(i)}{\mathbf{P}_{\mathcal{L}^a, \mathbf{I}^n}^{\mathcal{I}}(i)}} \delta \mathbf{P}_{p, \mathcal{L}^a, \mathcal{L}}^{\mathcal{I}}(i),$$

$$\tag{6}$$

where $\delta \mathcal{B}_{p, \mathcal{L}^a, \mathcal{L}}^{\mathcal{I}}$ and $\delta \mathbf{P}_{p, \mathcal{L}^a, \mathcal{L}}^{\mathcal{I}}(i))$ are the elementary variations of, respectively, $\mathcal{B}^{\mathcal{I}}(\mathcal{L}^a, \mathbf{I}^n)$ and $\mathbf{P}_{\mathcal{L}^a, \mathbf{I}^n}^{\mathcal{I}}(i)$, each corresponding to changing the label of pixel p from $\mathcal{L}^a(p)$ to $\mathcal{L}(p)$. Elementary variation $\delta \mathcal{B}_{p, \mathcal{L}^a, \mathcal{L}}^{\mathcal{I}}$ is computed in the rightmost equality of (6) with the first-order expansion of the Bhattacharyya measure $\mathcal{B}^{\mathcal{I}}(\mathcal{L}, \mathbf{I}^n)$. Then, we compute elementary variations $\delta \mathbf{P}_{p, \mathcal{L}^a, \mathcal{L}}^{\mathcal{I}}(i)$, $i \in \mathcal{I}$ using the the kernel density estimate in (1), which yields after some manipulations:

$$\delta \mathbf{P}_{p, \mathcal{L}^a, \mathcal{L}}^{\mathcal{I}}(i) = \begin{cases} \delta_{\mathcal{L}^a(p) \neq 1} \dfrac{K(i - \mathbf{I}_p^n) - \mathbf{P}_{\mathcal{L}^a, \mathbf{I}^n}^{\mathcal{I}}(i)}{A_{\mathcal{L}^a} + 1} & \text{if } \mathcal{L}(p) = 1 \\[2mm] \delta_{\mathcal{L}^a(p) \neq 0} \dfrac{\mathbf{P}_{\mathcal{L}^a, \mathbf{I}^n}^{\mathcal{I}}(i) - K(i - \mathbf{I}_p^n)}{A_{\mathcal{L}^a} - 1} & \text{if } \mathcal{L}(p) = 0 \end{cases} \tag{7}$$

---

[4] Note that $\mathcal{L}^a$ is an arbitrary, fixed labeling which can be obtained from a given segmentation of the first frame.

where $\delta_{x\neq y}$ given by (5). Finally, using (7) in (6) and after some manipulations, the intensity matching term reads as the sum of unary penalties plus a constant:

$$\mathcal{B}^{\mathcal{I}}(\mathcal{L}, \mathbf{I}^n) \approx constant + \sum_{p\in\mathcal{P}} \mathbf{b}_{p,\mathbf{I}^n}^{\mathcal{I}}(\mathcal{L}(p)), \qquad (8)$$

with $\mathbf{b}_{p,\mathbf{I}}^{\mathcal{I}}$ given, for any image $\mathbf{I}: \mathcal{P}\subset\mathbb{R}^2\to\mathcal{I}$ and any space of variables $\mathcal{I}$, by

$$\mathbf{b}_{p,\mathbf{I}}^{\mathcal{I}}(1) = \frac{\delta_{\mathcal{L}^a(p)\neq 1}}{2(\mathbf{A}_{\mathcal{L}^a}+1)}(\mathcal{B}^{\mathcal{I}}(\mathcal{L}^a,\mathbf{I}) - \sum_{i\in\mathcal{I}} K(i-\mathbf{I}_p)\sqrt{\frac{\mathbf{M}^{\mathcal{I}}(i)}{\mathbf{P}_{\mathcal{L}^a,\mathbf{I}}^{\mathcal{I}}(i)}})$$

$$\mathbf{b}_{p,\mathbf{I}}^{\mathcal{I}}(0) = \frac{\delta_{\mathcal{L}_p^a\neq 0}}{2(\mathbf{A}_{\mathcal{L}^a}-1)}(\sum_{i\in\mathcal{I}} K(i-\mathbf{I}_p)\sqrt{\frac{\mathbf{M}^{\mathcal{I}}(i)}{\mathbf{P}_{\mathcal{L}^a,\mathbf{I}}^{\mathcal{I}}(i),}} - \mathcal{B}^{\mathcal{I}}(\mathcal{L}^a,\mathbf{I})) \qquad (9)$$

Using a similar computation for the distance matching term, adopting the same notation in (9) for distance image $\mathbf{D}$, and ignoring the constants, the problem reduces to optimizing the following sum of unary and pairwise (submodular) penalties:

$$\mathcal{L}^{opt} = \arg\min_{\mathcal{L}:\mathcal{P}\to\{0,1\}} \sum_{p\in\mathcal{P}}\{\mathbf{b}_{p,\mathbf{I}^n}^{\mathcal{I}}(\mathcal{L}(p)) + \mathbf{b}_{p,\mathbf{D}}^{\mathcal{D}}(\mathcal{L}(p))\} + \lambda\mathbf{S}(\mathcal{L}) \qquad (10)$$

In combinatorial optimization, a global optimum of the sum of unary and pairwise (submodular) penalties can be computed efficiently in low-order polynomial time by solving an equivalent max-flow problem [8]. In our case, it suffices to build a weighted graph $\mathcal{G} = \langle\mathbf{N},\mathbf{E}\rangle$, where $\mathbf{N}$ is the set of nodes and $\mathbf{E}$ the set of edges connecting these nodes. $\mathbf{N}$ contains a node for each pixel $p\in\mathcal{P}$ and two additional terminal nodes, one representing the foreground region (i.e., the cavity), denoted $\mathbf{T_F}$, and the other representing the background, denoted $\mathbf{T_B}$. Let $\mathbf{w}_{p,q}$ be the weight of the edge connecting neighboring pixels $\{p,q\}$ in $\mathcal{N}$, and $\{\mathbf{w}_{p,\mathbf{T_F}},\mathbf{w}_{p,\mathbf{T_B}}\}$ the weights of the edges connecting each pixel p to each of the terminals. By setting the edge weights as follows:

$$\mathbf{w}_{p,\mathbf{T_F}} = \mathbf{b}_{p,\mathbf{I}^n}^{\mathcal{I}}(0) + \mathbf{b}_{p,\mathbf{D}}^{\mathcal{D}}(0); \quad \mathbf{w}_{p,\mathbf{T_B}} = \mathbf{b}_{p,\mathbf{I}^n}^{\mathcal{I}}(1) + \mathbf{b}_{p,\mathbf{D}}^{\mathcal{D}}(1); \quad \mathbf{w}_{p,q} = \frac{\lambda}{\|p-q\|},$$

we compute, using the max-flow algorithm of Boykov and Kolmogorov [8], a minimum cut $\mathcal{C}_{opt}^n$ of $\mathcal{G}$, i.e., a subset of edges in $\mathbf{E}$ whose removal divides the graph into two disconnected subgraphs, each containing a terminal node, and whose sum of edge weights is minimal. This minimum cut, which assigns each node (pixel) p in $\mathcal{P}$ to one of the two terminals, induces an optimal labeling $\mathcal{L}_{opt}^n$ ($\mathcal{L}_{opt}^n(p) = 1$ if p is connected to $\mathbf{T_F}$ and $\mathcal{L}_{opt}^n(p) = 0$ if p is connected to $\mathbf{T_B}$), which minimizes globally the approximation in (10).

3   Dynamic Model for Temporal Periodicity

Let (x,y) be a Cartesian point on the boundary between the segmentation regions obtained with graph cut distribution matching $\mathbf{R}_{\mathcal{L}_{opt}^n} = \{p\in\mathcal{P}/\mathcal{L}_{opt}^n(p) = 1\}$

and $\mathbf{R}_{\mathcal{L}^n_{opt}}^c = \{p \in \mathcal{P}/P\mathcal{L}^n_{opt}(p) = 0\}$. Consider the state vector $\xi = [\bar{x} \, x \, \dot{x}]^T$ that describes the dynamics of the point in x-coordinate direction, where $\dot{x}$ and $\bar{x}$ denote, respectively, velocity and the mean position over cardiac cycle. We assume the heart motion is periodic. A *continuous state-space* model that describes the cyclic motion of the point is given by,

$$\dot{\xi}(t) = \begin{bmatrix} 0 & 0 & 0 \\ 0 & 0 & 1 \\ \omega^2 & -\omega^2 & 0 \end{bmatrix} \xi(t) + \begin{bmatrix} 1 & 0 \\ 0 & 0 \\ 0 & 1 \end{bmatrix} w(t) = A(\omega)\xi(t) + Bw(t) \qquad (11)$$

where ω is the angular frequency, and $w(t)$ the white noise that accounts for approximating the unpredictable modeling errors arising in LV motion. Model (11) is linear for a given ω and can be viewed as an approximation of the temporal periodic model used in [5] where the higher-order terms of the Fourier expansion were neglected. A bank of models can be effectively used in parallel to closely match the changing dynamics of boundary points as discussed in Section 4. The *discrete-time equivalent* of (11) can be derived as

$$\xi_{k+1} = \begin{bmatrix} 1 & 0 & 0 \\ 1 - \cos(\omega T) & \cos(\omega T) & \frac{1}{\omega}\sin(\omega T) \\ \omega \sin(\omega T) & -\omega \sin(\omega T) & \cos(\omega T) \end{bmatrix} \xi_k + w_k = F(\omega)\xi_k + w_k \qquad (12)$$

where w_k is the process noise of the discrete-model. We can consider the state vector $x = [\bar{x} \, x \, \dot{x} \, \bar{y} \, y \, \dot{y}]^T$ that describes the dynamics in x-y plane. The discrete state-space model in x-y plane is given by

$$\mathbf{x}_{k+1} = \begin{bmatrix} F(\omega) & \mathbf{0}_{3\times 3} \\ \mathbf{0}_{3\times 3} & F(\omega) \end{bmatrix} \mathbf{x}_k + v_k = F_k \mathbf{x}_k + v_k \qquad (13)$$

The single Markovian model in (13) is insufficient to describe the LV dynamics due to the following reasons: (1) The angular frequency that characterizes the motion of a LV point for normal subjects changes over time. (2) The dynamics of LV motion differ significantly in systolic and diastolic phases of heart beat. (3) The LV dynamics of abnormal subjects differ significantly from those of normal subjects. Therefore, the LV dynamics is a *hybrid system* – a system which has both *continuous* (noise) and *discrete* (model) uncertainties – and, as such, it requires an interacting multiple model (IMM) approach. In the context of tracking maneuvering targets [9]. IMM estimation is shown to be very effective in the cases of hybrid systems. In the next section, we devise IMM to track the motion of the LV.

4   Interacting Multiple Model Algorithm

Let the system consists of n discrete set of models denoted by $M = \{M^1, \ldots, M^n\}$. Let $\mu_0^j = P\{M_0^j\}$ be the prior probability of model M^j, and $p_{ij} = P\{M_k^j | M_{k-1}^i\}$ be the probability of switching model from i to model j, with M_k^j being the model M^j at time step k. The system equations corresponding to M_k^j is given by: $x_k = F_k^j x_{k-1} + w_{k-1}^j$ and $z_k = H_k^j x_k + v_k^j$. The one cycle recursion of the IMM filter can be summarized as follows.

Interaction. The mixing probabilities $\mu_k^{i|j}$ for each model M^i and M^j are calculated as follows. $\bar{c}_j = \sum_{i=1}^{n} p_{ij} \mu_{k-1}^i$ and $\mu_k^{i|j} = \frac{1}{\bar{c}_j} \sum_{i=1}^{n} p_{ij} \mu_{k-1}^i$ where μ_{k-1}^i is the model probability. The inputs to each filter are calculated by

$$m_{k-1}^{0j} = \sum_{i=1}^{n} \mu_k^{i|j} m_{k-1}^i \ and \ P_{k-1}^{0j} = \sum_{i=1}^{n} \mu_k^{i|j} [P_{k-1}^i + (m_{k-1}^i - m_{k-1}^{0j})(m_{k-1}^i - m_{k-1}^{0j})^T].$$

Filtering. Kalman filter [9] is used for mode-conditioned state estimates:

$$[m_k^{-,i}, P_k^{-,i}] = \text{KF}_p(m_{k-1}^{0j}, P_{k-1}^{0j}, F(\omega^i), Q_k^i) \ and \ [m_k^i, P_k^i] = \text{KF}_u(m_k^{-,i}, P_k^{-,i}, z_k, H_k^i, R_k^i)$$

where KF_p and KF_u denote prediction and update equations of Kalman filter, respectively. The probability of model M_k^j being correct (mode probability) is computed as a function of the likelihoods of the other filters: $\mu_k^i = \frac{\Lambda_k^i \bar{c}_i}{\sum_{i=1}^{n} \Lambda_k^i \bar{c}_i}$ where likelihood of model M^i is given by $\Lambda_k^i = \mathcal{N}(v_k^i; 0, S_k^i)$ where v_k^i is the measurement residual and S_k^i innovation covariance for model M^i in the Kalman filter update step.

Mixing. The estimate of the IMM algorithm is calculated by combining individual mode-conditioned filter estimates using mode probabilities as follows: $m_k = \sum_{i=1}^{n} \mu_k^i m_k^i$ and $P_k = \sum_{i=1}^{n} \mu_k^i [P_k^i + (m_k^i - m_k)(m_k^i - m_k)^T]$.

4.1   Fixed-Interval IMM-Smoother

If an estimation delay can be tolerated, the performance of the filtering algorithm can be improved drastically by smoothing. In cardiac images, the delay in estimation is not significant as the imaging frequency is relatively high. There are several variations of smoothing available [10]. Here, we use a *fixed-interval smoothing*, which is the most common type. The optimal solution for fixed-interval smoothing is to fuse the posterior distributions obtained by two optimal IMM estimators, one running forward and the other backward using an equivalent reverse-time Markov model. However, obtaining the equivalent reverse-time model and the optimal forward/backward IMM estimators are difficult. The approximate fixed-interval smoother [6], which uses simpler fusion technique and an approximation of the required backward IMM algorithm directly from original Markov switching system with white Gaussian noise, is used to resolve the problem.

5   Experiments

The proposed method was applied to 120 short-axis sequences of cardiac cine MR images, with a temporal resolution of 20 frames/cardiac cycle, acquired from 20 subject: the endocardial boundary was tracked in a total of 2280 images including apical, mid-cavity and basal slices, and the results were evaluated quantitatively by comparisons with the manual segmentations performed independently by a medical professional. The results were also compared with the recent LV boundary tracking method in [2], using the same data.

Parameter settings. The regularization and kernel width parameters were unchanged for all the datasets in GCDM: α set equal to 0.15, the kernel width σ to 2 for distance distributions, and to 10 for intensity distributions. Four dynamic models were used in the IMM (the values were measured in squared pixels and $w_0 = 2\pi/(\text{heart period})$): (1) $\omega = \omega_0/2$, $q_1 = 0.02$, $q_2 = 0.1$, $R_k = 0.5$ (2) $\omega = \omega_0/2$, $q_1 = 0.2$, $q_2 = 1$, $R_k = 8$ (3) $\omega = 2\omega_0$, $q_1 = 0.02$, $q_2 = 0.1$, $R_k = 0.5$ (4) $\omega = 2\omega_0$, $q_1 = 0.2$, $q_2 = 1$, $R_k = 8$. The filters were initialized by *two-point differencing* [9].

Quantitative performance evaluation. We used two criteria to evaluate the performances of the algorithms.

- **Root mean squared error:** The *Root Mean Squared Error (RMSE)* is computed using *symmetric nearest neighbor correspondences* between manual and automatic LV boundaries using 24 equally-spaced points along the boundary. The *RMSE* over N number of points is given by: $RMSE = \sqrt{\frac{1}{N}\sum_{i=1}^{N}(\hat{x}_i - \tilde{x}_i)^2 + (\hat{y}_i - \tilde{y}_i)^2}$, where $(\hat{x}_i, \hat{y}_i)$ is a point on the automatic boundary and $(\tilde{x}_i, \tilde{y}_i)$ is the corresponding point on the manual boundary. Table 1 reports the *RMSE* for the proposed method and [2] averaged over all the dataset. The proposed method yielded an *RMSE* of 2.4 pixels, whereas the method in [2] yielded 3.1. The average *RMSE* plotted against the time step is shown in Fig. 2(a). The proposed algorithm yielded a lower *RMSE* compared to [2] and, therefore, a higher conformity to the manual segmentation.

- **Dice metric:** We computed the *Dice Metric (DM)*, a common measure of similarity between manual and automatic segmentation [2]. The *DM* is given by: $DM = \frac{2\mathbf{V_{am}}}{\mathbf{V_a}+\mathbf{V_m}}$, where $\mathbf{V_a}$, $\mathbf{V_m}$ and $\mathbf{V_{am}}$ are the volumes of, respectively, the automatically segmented cavity, the corresponding hand-labeled cavity, and the intersection between them. Note that *DM* is always between 0 and 1, where 1 means a perfect match. The proposed method yielded a *DM* equal to 0.915 ± 0.002, whereas the method in [2] yielded 0.884 ± 0.008, for all the data analyzed (refer to Table 1 where *DM* is expressed as mean $\pm$ standard deviation). We also evaluated the algorithm using the *reliability function* of the obtained Dice metrics, defined for each $d \in [0, 1]$ as the probability of obtaining *DM* higher than d over all volumes: $\mathcal{R}(d) = Pr(DM > d) =$(number of volumes segmented with *DM* higher than d)/(total number of volumes). In

Table 1. The *RMSE* and *DM* statistics for the proposed method (GCDM-IMM) and method in [2]

Performance measure	RMSE (pixels)	DM
GCDM-IMM	2.4	0.915 ± 0.002
Method in [2]	3.1	0.884 ± 0.008

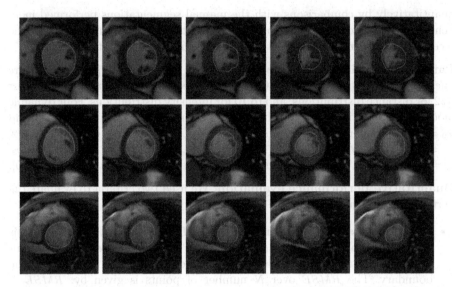

Fig. 1. Representative examples of the LV boundary tracking using the proposed method: mid-cavity (1st row), basal (2nd row) and apical (3rd row) frames. The first row depicts typical examples where the proposed method included accurately the papillary muscles inside the target cavity, although these have an intensity profile similar to the surrounding myocardium.

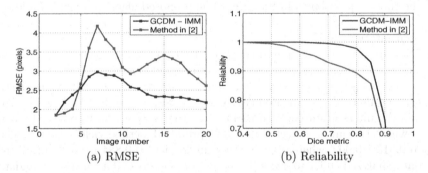

(a) RMSE   (b) Reliability

Fig. 2. Comparison between automatic and manual segmentations of 2280 images, for both the proposed method (GCDM-IMM) and the method in [2]

comparison to method [2], the proposed algorithm led to a higher reliability curve, as depicted in Fig. 2(b).

Visual inspection. In figures 3 and 1, we give a representative sample of the results for 3 subjects. Fig. 3 shows the trajectory of LV points estimated using the proposed GCDM-IMM method. The first row in Fig. 1 depicts typical examples where the proposed method included accurately the papillary muscles inside the target cavity, although these have an intensity profile similar to the surrounding myocardium.

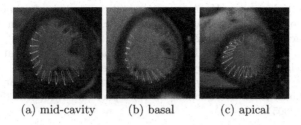

(a) mid-cavity   (b) basal   (c) apical

Fig. 3. Trajectory of LV endocardial boundary points estimated using the proposed method

6   Conclusions

This study investigates the problem of tracking endocardial boundary and motion via Graph Cut Distribution Matching (GCDM) and Interacting Multiple Model (IMM) smoothing. GCDM yields initial frame segmentations by keeping the same photometric/geometric distribution of the cavity over cardiac cycles, whereas IMM constrains the results with prior knowledge of temporal consistency. The proposed method is evaluated quantitatively using root mean squared error and Dice metric, by comparison with independent manual segmentations over 2280 images acquired from 20 subjects, which demonstrated significantly better results as compared to a recent method [2].

References

1. Jolly, M.P.: Automatic recovery of the left ventricular blood pool in cardiac cine MR images. In: Metaxas, D., Axel, L., Fichtinger, G., Székely, G. (eds.) MICCAI 2008, Part I. LNCS, vol. 5241, pp. 110–118. Springer, Heidelberg (2008)
2. Ben Ayed, I., Lu, Y., Li, S., Ross, I.: Left ventricle tracking using overlap priors. In: Metaxas, D., Axel, L., Fichtinger, G., Székely, G. (eds.) MICCAI 2008, Part I. LNCS, vol. 5241, pp. 1025–1033. Springer, Heidelberg (2008)
3. Spottiswoode, B., Zhong, X., Hess, A., Kramer, C., Meintjes, E., Mayosi, B., Epstein, F.: Tracking myocardial motion from cine DENSE images using spatiotemporal phase unwrapping and temporal fitting. IEEE Transactions on Medical Imaging 26(1), 15–30 (2007)
4. Andreopoulos, A., Tsotsos, J.K.: Efficient and generalizable statistical models of shape and appearance for analysis of cardiac MRI. Medical Image Analysis 12(3), 335–357 (2008)
5. McEachen, J., Nehorai, A., Duncan, J.: Multiframe temporal estimation of cardiac nonrigid motion. IEEE Transactions on Image Processing 9(4), 651–665 (2000)
6. Helmick, R., Blair, W., Hoffman, S.: Fixed-interval smoothing for Markovian switching systems. IEEE Transactions on Information Theory 41(6), 1845–1855 (1995)
7. Boykov, Y., Kolmogorov, V.: Computing geodesics and minimal surfaces via graph cuts. In: Proceedings of the Ninth IEEE International Conference on Computer Vision, vol. 1, pp. 26–33 (2003)

8. Boykov, Y., Kolmogorov, V.: An experimental comparison of min-cut/max- flow algorithms for energy minimization in vision. IEEE Transactions on Pattern Analysis and Machine Intelligence 26(9), 1124–1137 (2004)
9. Bar-Shalom, Y., Kirubarajan, T., Li, X.R.: Estimation with Applications to Tracking and Navigation. John Wiley & Sons, Inc., New York (2002)
10. Rong Li, X., Jilkov, V.: Survey of maneuvering target tracking. Part V: Multiple-model methods. IEEE Transactions on Aerospace and Electronic Systems 41(4), 1255–1321 (2005)

Object Detection with Multiple Motion Models

Zhijie Wang and Hong Zhang

Department of Computing Science, University of Alberta, Canada
{zhijie,zhang}@cs.ualberta.ca

Abstract. Existing joint detection and tracking algorithms generally assume one single motion model for objects of interest. However, in real world many objects have more than one motion model. In this paper we present a joint detection and tracking algorithm that is able to detect objects with multiple motion models. For such an object, a discrete variable is added into the object state to estimate its motion model. In this way, the proposed algorithm will not fail to detect objects changing their motion models as the existing algorithms. Experimental results show that our proposed algorithm has a better performance than the existing joint detection and tracking algorithms with different single motion models, in detecting objects with multiple motion models.

1 Introduction

Object detection is an important task in computer vision. One primary objective is to determine how many objects of interest exist in an image and track them. Object detection may be employed in various applications such as intelligent surveillance system, man-machine interface and robotics. This paper specifically deals with detecting objects with multiple motion models.

There has been much research in the object detection problem. Popular detection methods include background subtraction [1,2] and appearance modeling (for example, Harr-like features [3] and Eigenface [4]). These methods however make a decision directly on the basis of a single frame. Therefore, the results are often unsatisfactory when input is noisy. To deal with this problem, a class of joint detection and tracking (JDT) algorithms ([5,6,7,8]) have been proposed. They make decisions based on the integrated information over time. As a result they tend to be more accurate than those single-frame based algorithms above. However, the problem of these JDT algorithms is that they assume that each object has only one single motion model. Consequently, they may fail when objects move unpredictably or experience unexpected motion.

The goal of our research is to propose a new algorithm that detects objects going through irregular motion with the help of multiple motion models. There has been some work, such as [9,10], uses a hybrid state to index motion models in the filter to deal with objects with multiple motion models. However they only focus on tracking, while our work makes use of this idea in detection and finally provides an algorithm suitable for detecting objects with multiple motion models. With a discrete variable to indicate different motion models, our

H. Zha, R.-i. Taniguchi, and S. Maybank (Eds.): ACCV 2009, Part III, LNCS 5996, pp. 183–192, 2010.

proposed algorithm is able to exploit an object's a priori motion information for its detection, and it has the ability to adjust its filter's model according to the object's different motion models. As a result, our proposed algorithm is able to accumulate detection evidence even though the object changes its motion pattern, rather than lose track of the object as the existing JDT algorithms. Finally, the object can be detected when the accumulated evidence is strong.

The rest of this paper is organized as follows. In Section 2, the general *Bayesian sequential estimation* solution for detecting objects with a single motion model is first described, and then our new solution for objects with multiple motion models is proposed. The proposed solution is implemented with a particle filter in Section 3. Section 4 includes the experimental results showing the performance of the proposed algorithm, and finally the conclusion is drawn in Section 5.

2   Bayesian Sequential Estimation

In this section, we first describe how *Bayesian sequential estimation* works in general to detect objects with a singe motion model, and then we discuss how we change the original algorithm and make it suitable for detecting objects with multiple motion models.

2.1   Detect Objects with a Single Motion Model

Bayesian sequential estimation solves the object detection problem by recursively computing the posterior probability density function (pdf) $p(X_t|Z^t)$. Z^t includes all the observations $\{z_1, \ldots, z_t\}$ up to time t. X_t is the joint object state defined as a variable length vector

$$X_t = [x_t \ E_t]. \tag{1}$$

x_t is the state of object at time t, and $E_t \in \{0, 1\}$ is a discrete existence variable indicating whether the object exists at time t. E_t is modeled by a Markov chain whose transitions are specified by a transitional probability matrix (TPM)

$$\Pi = \begin{bmatrix} 1 - P_b & P_b \\ P_d & 1 - P_d \end{bmatrix} \tag{2}$$

where P_b denotes the probability of object birth and P_d denotes the probability of object death.

The posterior pdf $p(x_t, E_t = 1|Z^t)$ can be derived according to

$$p(x_t, E_t = 1|Z^t) = \alpha \, p(z_t|x_t, E_t = 1) \, p(x_t, E_t = 1|Z^{t-1}). \tag{3}$$

$p(z_t|x_t, E_t = 1)$ is the measurement model updating the predicted state according to the current observation, and it can be defined according to different applications. $p(x_t, E_t = 1|Z^{t-1})$ is the predicted state function which can be defined as follows,

$$p(x_t, E_t = 1|Z^{t-1})$$

$$= \int p(x_t, E_t = 1|x_{t-1}, E_{t-1} = 1)p(x_{t-1}, E_{t-1} = 1|Z^{t-1})dx_{t-1}$$

$$+ p(x_t, E_t = 1, E_{t-1} = 0|Z^{t-1})$$

$$= \int p(x_t|x_{t-1}, E_t = 1, E_{t-1} = 1)(1 - P_d)p(x_{t-1}, E_{t-1} = 1|Z^{t-1})dx_{t-1}$$

$$+ p_b(x_t)P_b. \tag{4}$$

On the right hand side (RHS) of the above equation, $p(x_t|x_{t-1}, E_t = 1, E_{t-1} = 1)$ is the state transition probability function specified by the object's motion model. $p(x_{t-1}, E_{t-1} = 1|Z^{t-1})$ is the previous posterior pdf which is already known. $p_b(x_t)$ is the initial object pdf where subscript 'b' stands for "birth". If no apriori knowledge is available, it may be assumed to be uniformly distributed.

Once the posterior pdf $p(x_t, E_t = 1|Z^t)$ is computed, the probability that an object exists may be calculated as

$$P_{E_t=1} = \int p(x_t, E_t = 1|Z^t)dx_t. \tag{5}$$

Additionally, the state of the object can be estimated as the marginal of the pdf $p(x_t, E_t = 1|Z^t)$.

2.2 Objects with Multiple Motion Models

The above algorithm assumes that the state transition probability function $p(x_t|x_{t-1}, E_t = 1, E_{t-1} = 1)$ in (4) is specified by a single motion model $x_t = f(x_{t-1}, w(t-1))$ where $w(t-1)$ is the process noise. However in practical problems, objects may have more than one motion model. For example, an aircraft moving in a constant velocity may accelerate suddenly. In this case if we use a constant velocity model to define the state transition probability function $p(x_t|x_{t-1}, E_t = 1, E_{t-1} = 1)$, then the algorithm will lose the track as well as the detection of the aircraft after it accelerates. Therefore, there is a need to change the above original algorithm so that it is able to detect objects with multiple motion models.

To switch among different motion models, the original joint object state is changed to

$$X_t = [x_t \; \alpha_t \; E_t]. \tag{6}$$

A discrete variable α_t is added to the object state to indicate its motion model. $\alpha_t \in \{1, \ldots, M_m\}$ and M_m is the number of possible motion models. α_t is modeled by a Markov chain whose transitions are specified by an $M_m \times M_m$ TPM $\Pi = [\pi_{ij}]$ where

$$\pi_{ij} = Pr\{\alpha_t = j|\alpha_{t-1} = i\}, \; (i, j \in \{1, \ldots, M_m\}). \tag{7}$$

With variable α_t, the filter can switch among the different motion models and find the one fit the object's actual model best. In this way, the filter will not lose the track of the object when it changes its motion model. In contrast, it can still follow the object and accumulate the detection evidence continuously.

Additionally, the original predicted state function in (4) is changed to

$$p(x_t, \alpha_t, E_t = 1 | Z^{t-1})$$

$$= \sum_{\alpha_{t-1}} \int p(x_t, \alpha_t, E_t = 1 | x_{t-1}, \alpha_{t-1}, E_{t-1} = 1)$$

$$p(x_{t-1}, \alpha_{t-1}, E_{t-1} = 1 | Z^{t-1}) dx_{t-1} + p(x_t, \alpha_t, E_t = 1, E_{t-1} = 0 | Z^{t-1})$$

$$= \sum_{\alpha_{t-1}} \int p(x_t | \alpha_t, x_{t-1}, E_t = 1, E_{t-1} = 1) Pr\{\alpha_t | \alpha_{t-1}\}(1 - P_d)$$

$$p(x_{t-1}, \alpha_{t-1}, E_{t-1} = 1 | Z^{t-1}) dx_{t-1} + p_b(x_t) Pr_b\{\alpha_t\} P_b. \tag{8}$$

$Pr\{\alpha_t | \alpha_{t-1}\}$ is specified by (7). $Pr_b\{\alpha_t\}$ is the probability of the initial object motion model where subscript 'b' stands for "birth", and if no a priori knowledge is available, it may be assumed to be uniformly distributed. The difference between this new predicted state function and the original one in (4) is that the state transition probability function $p(x_t | \alpha_t, x_{t-1}, E_t = 1, E_{t-1} = 1)$ is specified by its $\alpha_t th$ motion model. Here α_t can be one of the object's possible motion models, rather than the same motion model all the time as in the original algorithm.

After the above changes, this new algorithm is able to take advantage of the a priori motion information of objects of interest and achieve a better performance than the original algorithm in detecting objects with multiple motion models.

3   Particle Filter Implementation

The *Bayesian sequential estimation* solution derived in the previous section for detecting objects with multiple motion models will now be implemented with a particle filter described in Fig. 1. Briefly, it is assumed that the posterior pdf at the previous time is approximated by a set of weighted particles $\{(x_{t-1}^i, \alpha_{t-1}^i, E_{t-1}^i, w_{t-1}^i)\}_{i=1}^N$. w_{t-1}^i is the ith particle's weight at time $t-1$. The input to the algorithm is the set of particles at a previous time and the current observed image, and the output is the set of particles at the current time. We will next explain the algorithm in more details.

- The first step predicts the current existence variable according to the previous existence variable and the TPM specified by (2).
- Given the existence variable predicted, the second step predicts the object's current state based on the previous state and the predicted state function defined in (8).
- The third step weights the particles representing the predicted state given the current observed image. To achieve the detection mechanism, the likelihood

---

Input: $\{(x_{t-1}^i, \alpha_{t-1}^i, E_{t-1}^i, w_{t-1}^i)\}_{i=1}^N$, z_t

Output: $\{(x_t^i, \alpha_t^i, E_t^i, w_t^i)\}_{i=1}^N$

1. Given $\{E_{t-1}^i\}_{i=1}^N$, generate $\{E_t^i\}_{i=1}^N$ according to the TPM specified by (2).

2. Based on $\{E_{t-1}^i\}_{i=1}^N$ and $\{E_t^i\}_{i=1}^N$, generate $\{(x_t^i, \alpha_t^i)\}_{i=1}^N$ from $\{(X_{t-1}^i, \alpha_{t-1}^i)\}_{i=1}^N$ according to (8).

3. Given z_t, compute the weights $\{w_t^i\}_{i=1}^N$ for $\{(x_t^i, \alpha_t^i)\}_{i=1}^N$ according to (9).

4. Normalize $\{w_t^i\}_{i=1}^N$ to $\{\tilde{w}_t^i\}_{i=1}^N$.

5. Resample from $\{(x_t^i, \alpha_t^i, E_t^i, \tilde{w}_t^i)\}_{i=1}^N$ for N times to obtain a new set of particles $\{(x_t^i, \alpha_t^i, E_t^i, 1/N)\}_{i=1}^N$.

Fig. 1. The particle filter implementation of the proposed JDT algorithm

ratio is used as the particle weight here rather than the measurement model $p(z^t|X_t)$. The likelihood ratio can be calculated as

$$L(z_t|X_t) = \frac{p(z_t|X_t)}{p_B(z_t|X_t)}. \tag{9}$$

$p_B(z_t|X_t)$ is the probability of that the object specified by X_t belongs to background.

- The fourth step performs normalization.
- The fifth and last step is the standard resampling step, which converts the set of weighted particles back to an equivalent set of unweighted particles approximating the current posterior pdf.

Once the posterior pdf $p(x_t, \alpha_t, E_t = 1|Z^t)$ is approximated by the set of particles. The probability that the object exists is estimated based on (5) as

$$P_{E_k=1} = \frac{1}{N} \cdot \sum_{i=1}^N \delta(E_k^i, 1). \tag{10}$$

δ here is the Kroneker delta function. $\delta(i, j) = 1$, if $i = j$, and zero otherwise.

4 Experimental Results

In this section, we will show the superiority of our proposed algorithm for detecting objects with multiple motion models on both a synthetic experiment and a real experiment involving the detection of an object in a video sequence in a mining application. Experimental results will show that incorporating multiple motion models into JDT algorithms is able to benefit detecting objects that vary their motion pattern. In the following, we will describe the results on both experiments.

4.1 Synthetic Experiment

In this experiment, we create a scenario where one object moves back and forth as shown in Fig. 2a. The object is a square with the pattern as shown in Fig. 2b.

Fig. 2. (a) Experimental scenario. The background is represented by nested rectangles each of a different shape and an object by a small square with the texture shown in the right panel. (b) Object appearance used in the experiment. Note that in this work an object is modeled in general by its intensity histogram in a rectangular region, although with modification, other types of object models can be accommodated by the algorithm.

The object moves from one side to the other in a constant velocity for 10 frames before it changes its direction, and then it repeats the same motion pattern. This motion pattern is assumed known a priori and we use two motion models to describe the object, one at a constant velocity ($v_t = v_{t-1}$) and the other with the same speed with the previous time but in the opposite direction ($v_t = -v_{t-1}$). We incorporate these two models into our detection algorithm. We compare our new algorithm with the original JDT algorithm using only one constant velocity model to show that the latter one is not sufficient to deal with objects with more than one motion model. We also compare our proposed algorithm with another JDT algorithm using a random walk model to show that the naive algorithm does not work well either.

For all three competing algorithms above, the measurement model is defined as

$$p(z_t|X_t) = \Pi_{i=1}^{E_t} p(z_{i,t}|X_{i,t}) = \Pi_{i=1}^{E_t} \frac{1}{\sqrt{2\pi}\delta} exp(\frac{-dist(q_{i,t}, q^*)^2}{2\delta^2}).$$

$q_{i,t}$ is the intensity histogram computed from image $z_{i,t}$, which is extracted from the object region specified by $X_{i,t}$. $dist(q_{i,t}, q^*)$ is the distance between the object's histogram and the reference histogram q^*.

Although this scenario of multiple motion models is simple, it is sufficient to illustrate the problems of interest, and compare the performances of the competing algorithms. Fig. 3a shows the detection results of the one motion model (OMM) algorithm, the two motion model (MMM) algorithm (our algorithm) and the random walk (RW) algorithm. The x-axis is the frame number and the y-axis is the existence probability of having one object ($Pr\{E_t = 1\}$). The horizontal dashed line at existence probability of 0.5 typically indicates the threshold that determines whether the object exists. The results show that our new algorithm can detect the object consistently with the existence probability above 0.5 throughout. However the OMM algorithm may lose the track as expected when the object moves with a motion pattern inconsistent with the single motion model assumed by the particle filter, so that its existence probability drops suddenly every 10 frames and leads to incorrect detection decisions.

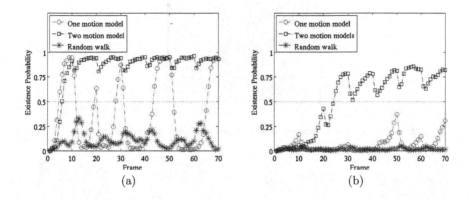

Fig. 3. (a) Existence probability curves of the two motion mode algorithm (our algorithm), one motion model algorithm and random walk algorithm. (b) Existence probability curves of the three algorithms when significant noise exists in the video.

Additionally, we also checked the performance of a naive algorithm using a random walk model, which amounts to assuming no a priori motion information. Therefore to deal with the possible change of motion model, it has to diverge its prediction with a large variance. As a result, when the observation model's variance is not small enough, *i.e.* when significant noise exists, the object cannot be detected. Furthermore, we also test the three algorithms on the same video with a higher level of observation noise than that in Fig. 3a and their results are shown in Fig. 3b. Due to our new algorithm's flexibility to deal with multiple motion models, it is able to accumulate the evidence even though the object changes its model, and finally detect the object after the evidence is accumulated to be strong enough. However the OMM algorithm will lose its accumulated evidence every time the object changes its model, and as a result the object can never be detected. The same can be said of the RW algorithm, when significant noise exists, indicating that conservative prediction is unable to detect the object.

4.2 Large Lump Detection

We have also tested our proposed algorithm in a real experiment involving a video sequence whose purpose is to detect the presence of large lumps in the feed to a crusher in the oilsand mining industry. In the dry feed preparation stage of oil sand mining, detecting large lumps in the feed to a crusher (Fig. 4) is extremely important. In the following, we will show better performance of our proposed algorithm than JDT algorithms with one motion model in this real problem.

With a simple inspection of the large lump video sequence, generally lumps move from top to bottom along a verticle line. Initially lumps move slowly and then gradually faster and faster on a conveyor, and finally they drop suddenly when they reach the end to fall into the crusher. Therefore, lumps may be

Fig. 4. Two large lumps on a chute before they fall into a crusher

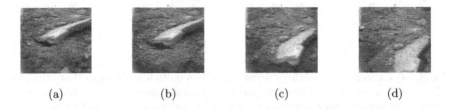

(a)   (b)   (c)   (d)

Fig. 5. Sequence of Lump 1. (a) Frame 1, (b) Frame 2, (c) Frame 7 (d) Frame 8.

considered to have two motion models, a small constant acceleration model on the conveyor and a large constant acceleration model off the conveyor. We incorporate these two motion models into our algorithm to detect lumps and compare the results with JDT algorithms using only one motion model. The observation model used in these algorithms can be found in [11] where an effective feature detector is proposed specifically for this large lump problem.

Fig. 5 shows a few consecutive frames where one lump moves down into the crusher. Initially, it moves really slowly, for example from frame 1 (Fig. 5a) to frame 2 (Fig. 5b), and then gradually faster until frame 7 (Fig. 5c). From frame 7 (Fig. 5c) to frame 8 (Fig. 5d) the lump moves much faster than before. Fig. 6 shows the comparison of four algorithms, our algorithm MMM using two constant acceleration models and three OMM algorithms using a small constant

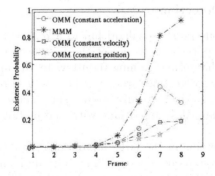

Fig. 6. Comparison of four algorithms detecting the large lump in Fig. 5

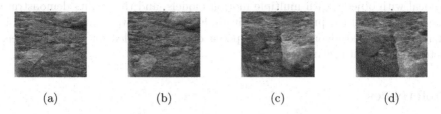

(a)   (b)   (c)   (d)

Fig. 7. Sequence of Lump 2. (a) Frame 1, (b) Frame 2, (c) Frame 17 (d) Frame 18

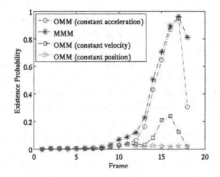

Fig. 8. Comparison of four algorithms detecting the large lump in Fig. 7

acceleration model, a constant velocity model and a constant position model. All the three OMM algorithms do not match the actual lump motion model very well, and especially from frame 7 to frame 8 when the lump changes its acceleration rate the OMM algorithms obviously lose the track as well as the detection of the lump. Our MMM algorithm, in contrast, continues accumulating the evidence and finally detects the lump. Even from frame 7 to frame 8, our algorithm still can adjust itself according to the change of the lump's motion model by finding the filter's model that optimally matches the actual lump model. Fig. 7 shows another lump moving slowly from frame 1 (Fig. 7a) to frame 2 (Fig. 7b) and then gradually faster until frame 17 (Fig. 7c) and finally much faster from frame 17 to frame 18 (Fig. 7d). Fig. 8 shows the comparison of the four algorithms as Fig. 6. Again our algorithm shows the superiority than the OMM algorithms especially at the last frame when the lump moves fast.

5   Conclusion

To summarize, a JDT algorithm that can deal with objects having multiple motion models has been proposed. The novel feature in the proposed algorithm is that it can incorporate multiple motion models into the filter to exploit the a priori information about the objects of interest and reliably detect objects having multiple motion models. Although the experiments are not complicated, they illustrate the original OMM JDT algorithm's intrinsic problem of unable to deal with objects with multiple motion models, and the results demonstrate the superiority of the proposed algorithm. Finally, what we want to point out is that the proposed algorithm in this paper can be extended for multiple object detection straightforwardly.

References

1. Yaser Sheikh, M.S.: Bayesian modeling of dynamic scenes for object detection. IEEE Transactions on Pattern Analysis and Machine Intelligence 27, 1778–1792 (2005)
2. Li, L., Huang, W., Gu, I.Y.H., Tian, Q.: Statistical modeling of complex backgrounds for foreground object detection. IEEE Transactions on Image Processing 13, 1459–1472 (2004)
3. Viola, P., Jones, M.: Robust real-time object detection. International Journal on Computer Vision 57, 137–154 (2004)
4. Tsai, C.C., Cheng, W.C., Taur, J.S., Tao, C.W.: Face detection using eigenface and neural network. In: International Conference on Systems, Man and Cybernetics, vol. 5, pp. 4343–4347. IEEE, Los Alamitos (2006)
5. Ristic, B., Arulampalam, S., Gordon, N.J.: Beyond the kalman filter: Particle filters for tracking applications (2004)
6. Rutten, M.G., Ristic, B., Gordon, N.J.: A comparison of particle filters for recursive trackbeforedetect. In: International Conference on Information Fusion, vol. 1, pp. 169–175 (2005)
7. Isard, M., MacCormick, J.: Bramble: A bayesian multiple-blob tracker. In: Proc. International Conference on Computer Vision, vol. 2, pp. 34–41. IEEE, Los Alamitos (2001)
8. Jacek Czyz, B.R., Macq, B.: A color-based particle filter for joint detection and tracking of multiple objects. In: Proc. of International Conference on Acoustics, Speech and Signal Processing, vol. 2, pp. 217–220. IEEE, Los Alamitos (2005)
9. McGinnity, S., Irwin, G.W.: Multiple model bootstrap filter for maneuvering target tracking. IEEE Transactions on Aerospace and Electronic Systems 36, 1006–1012 (2000)
10. Isard, M., Blake, A.: A mixed-state condensation tracker with automatic model-switching. In: Proc. International Conference on Computer Vision, pp. 107–112 (1998)
11. Wang, Z., Zhang, H.: Large lump detection using a particle filter of hybrid state variable. In: International Conference on Advances in Pattern Recognition, pp. 14–17 (2009)

An Improved Template Matching Method for Object Detection

Duc Thanh Nguyen, Wanqing Li, and Philip Ogunbona

Advanced Multimedia Research Lab, ICT Research Institute
School of Computer Science and Software Engineering
University of Wollongong, Australia

Abstract. This paper presents an improved template matching method that combines both spatial and orientation information in a simple and effective way. The spatial information is obtained through a generalized distance transform (GDT) that weights the distance transform more on the strong edge pixels and the orientation information is represented as an orientation map (OM) which is calculated from local gradient. We applied the proposed method to detect humans, cars, and maple leaves from images. The experimental results have shown that the proposed method outperforms the existing template matching methods and is robust against cluttered background.

1 Introduction

Object detection is an active research topic in Computer Vision. Generally speaking, existing object detection methods can be categorized into learning-based approach and template-based approach. In the learning based approach, object signatures (e.g. the features used to describe the objects) are obtained through training using positive/negative samples [1], [2], [3], [4] and object detection is often formulated as a problem of binary classification. In the template based approach, objects are described explicitly by templates and the task of object detection becomes to find the best matching template given an input image. The templates can be represented as intensity/color images [5], [6] when the appearance of the objects has to be considered. Appearance templates are often specific and lack of generalization because the appearance of an object is usually subject to the lighting condition and surface property the object. Therefore, binary templates representing the contours of the objects are often used in object detection since the shape information can be well captured by the templates [7], [8], [9]. Given a set of binary templates representing the object, the task of detecting whether an image contains the object eventually becomes the calculation of the matching score between each template and the image. The commonly used matching method is known as "Chamfer matching" which calculates the "Chamfer distance" [10] or "Hausdorff distance" [11], [12] between the template and the image through the Distance Transform (DT) image [13] in which each pixel value represents its distance to the nearest binary edge pixel. This paper is about an effective method to match a binary template with an image by using both

H. Zha, R.-i. Taniguchi, and S. Maybank (Eds.): ACCV 2009, Part III, LNCS 5996, pp. 193–202, 2010.
© Springer-Verlag Berlin Heidelberg 2010

194   D.T. Nguyen, W. Li, and P. Ogunbona

the strength and orientation of the image and template edges. For simplicity, we shall use the term "template" to refer to "binary template" hereafter.

As well known, Chamfer matching produces high false positives in images having cluttered background. This is probably due to the interference of the edge pixels in the background on the DT image. For a cluttered image, there are often numerous strong and weak edge pixels from both background and foreground. They contribute indiscriminatively to the DT image in a conventional distance transform regardless of their edge magnitude and orientation. Fig. 1 represents an example where the spatial distances between the image point p and template point q are same in the left and the right image whereas the pair (p, q) in the left image actually presents a better match. Fig. 2 illustrates an example of human detection in cluttered background obtained by applying the Chamfer matching [10]. As shown in the 5th and 6th images, true detections have larger matching distance to the template (1st image) than false detections.

To reduce the false positives, magnitude [14] and orientation of edges [15], [16], [17] can be included in the matching as additional information to the DT image. A number of attempts have been made along this direction in the past. For example, in [14], various salience factors such as edge strength and curvature of connected edges are employed to weight the DT image during matching, but the distance is still computed based only on the spatial information. In terms of orientation, Gavrila [15] quantized the orientation of edge pixels into different bins of angles and then created the DT images for every edge orientation. Olson et al.[16] and Jain et al.[17] combined the orientation with spatial information in

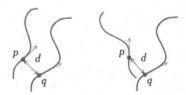

Fig. 1. The red curves and blue curves represent the image edges and template edges respectively while the (red/blue) arrows represent the corresponding edge orientations

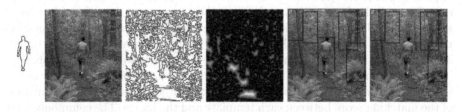

Fig. 2. From left to right: the template, input image, edge image, DT image, and the detection results (blue rectangles). The detection results represent those locations whose Chamfer distances to the template are smaller than 0.36 (the 5th image) and 0.35 (the 6th image).

the definition of the matching score. In [16], Olson et al. considered each image point as a set of 3 elements (xy−coordinates and orientation), the Hausdorff distance was employed to the spatial coordinates and orientations separately. To facilitate the matching, the orientation is discretized and DTs are created for each of the discrete orientations, thus the computational complexity is increased. In [17], the matching score between a template point and an image point is defined as a product of the spatial and orientation distances. The spatial distance is calculated using the conventional DT, e.g. [13], without considering the strength or magnitude of the edges.

In this paper, we introduce a generalized distance transform (GDT) and an orientation map (OM) to encode respectively the spatial and orientation information. The GDT allows us to weight the DT image more on the strong edge points during the DT. A new matching score is defined by linearly combining the distances calculated using GDT and OM and is proved to be Euclidean. The new matching method is used and verified in the experiments of detecting humans, cars and maple leaves from images. The results have shown that the proposed matching method outperforms existing methods and is robust against the interference of cluttered background.

The remainder of this paper is organized as follows. In section 2, we describe the proposed template matching method in which a generalized distance transform and an orientation map are employed. For comparison, we also briefly review Olson's and Jain's methods. Experimental results along with some comparative analysis are presented in section 3. Finally, conclusions and future work are given in section 4.

2   Template Matching with Edge Orientation

Let $p(s_p, o_p)$ and $q(s_q, o_q)$ be two points on an image where $s_p = (x_p, y_p)$ and $s_q = (x_q, y_q)$ are the spatial coordinates of p and q respectively; o_p and o_q are the edge orientations at p and q. Let $d_s(p, q)$ denote a spatial distance between p and q, e.g. Euclidean distance; and $d_o(p, q)$ be a measurement to measure the difference in orientation between p and q. Let T and I be a binary template and a test image respectively, $D(T, I)$ denote the matching score or distance (dissimilarity) between T and I.

2.1   Olson's and Jain's Methods

In [16], Olson et al. defined the matching score $D(T, I)$ in the form of the Hausdorff distance as,

$$D(T, I) = \max_{t \in T} \max\{d_s(t, t^*), d_o(t, t^*)\} \tag{1}$$

where t^* is the closest pixel of t in the image I with respect to the spatial and orientation distances, i.e. $t^* = \arg\min_{q \in I} \max\{d_s(t, q), d_o(t, q)\}$. The orientation component $d_o(\cdot)$ is encoded as,

$$d_o(p, q) = |o_p - o_q| \tag{2}$$

The matching score in (1) is calculated using the DTs created for every discrete orientation. Hence, the computational complexity depends on the number of distinct orientation values. As can be seen in (2), $d_o(p, q)$ cannot guarantee that the difference between o_p and o_q is always an acute angle. In addition, in (1), the spatial component, d_s and orientation component, d_o are of different scales. Thus, both d_s and d_o need to be normalized before being used to compute the matching score.

In the work of Jain et al. [17], the matching score is defined as,

$$D(T, I) = \frac{1}{|T|} \sum_{t \in T} 1 - \exp(-\rho d_s(t, t^*)) d_o(t, t^*) \tag{3}$$

where $|T|$ is the number of pixels in T, ρ is a positive smoothing factor, and $t^* \in I$ is the closest pixel of t in term of spatial distance, i.e. $t^* = \arg\min_{q \in I} d_s(t, q)$. The orientation component $d_o(p, q)$ is defined as,

$$d_o(p, q) = |\cos(o_p - o_q)| \tag{4}$$

2.2   Proposed Method

As shown in the previous section, t^* in both (1) and (3) is determined based on the conventional DT image without considering the quality of edge pixels. In other words, the strong and weak edges contribute equally to spatial distance in the DT image. Our observation has shown that cluttered background often produces dense weak edges at various orientations that can severely interfere with the DT. We, therefore, propose the Generalized Distance Transform (GDT) and orientation map (OM) that are able to take into consideration the strength and orientation of edges for reliable and robust matching.

Generalized Distance Transform (GDT). Let $\mathcal{G}$ be a regular grid and $\Psi : \mathcal{G} \rightarrow \mathbb{R}$ a function on the grid. According to Felzenszwalb and Huttenlocher [18], the GDT of Ψ can be defined as,

$$D_\Psi(p) = \min_{q \in \mathcal{G}} \{d_s(p, q) + \Psi(q)\}, \tag{5}$$

where $d_s(p, q)$ is some measure of the spatial distance between point p and q in the grid. Intuitively, for each point p we find a point q that is close to p, and for which $\Psi(q)$ is small. For conventional DT of an edge image using $L^2 - norm$, $d_s(p, q)$ is the Euclidean distance between p and q, and $\Psi(q)$ is defined as

$$\Psi(q) = \begin{cases} 0, & \text{if } (q) \in e \\ \infty, & \text{otherwise} \end{cases} \tag{6}$$

where e is the edge image obtained using some edge detector.

Notice that the conventional DT does not consider the quality of the edge points in e and a cluttered background often contains many weak edge points.

In order to reduce the impact of these weak edge points, we define the $\Psi(q)$ as follow such that more trust is placed on the strong edge points.

$$\Psi(q) = \begin{cases} \frac{\eta}{\sqrt{I_x^2 + I_y^2}}, & \text{if } (q) \in e \\ \infty, & \text{otherwise} \end{cases} \tag{7}$$

where $I_x = \partial I / \partial x$ and $I_y = \partial I / \partial y$ are the horizontal and vertical gradients of the image I at position q; η is a positive constant controlling the contribution of the gradient's magnitude at q. By using this definition, the GDT is computed not only based on the spatial distance but also on the strength of the edges. If $\eta = 0$, (7) becomes (6) and $D_\Psi(p)$ becomes $d_s(p, p^*)$ where $p^* = \arg\min_{q \in I} d_s(p, q)$.

Using the algorithm proposed in [18], the GDT can be computed in $O(knm)$ time, where $n \times m$ is the image's size, k ($= 2$ in our case) indicates the number of dimensions.

Orientation Map (OM). Let p^* be the closest edge point to the pixel p,

$$p^* = \arg\min_{q \in \mathcal{G}} \{d_s(p, q) + \Psi(q)\}$$

and the orientation value at p is defined as,

$$O_\Psi(p) = \arctan(I_{x^*} / I_{y^*}) \tag{8}$$

where I_{x^*} and I_{y^*} are the gradients at p^*. In other words, the orientation of edge pixels will be propagated to their nearest non-edge pixels.

The orientation map $O_\Psi(p)$ provides additional information to match a template with a test image. We can see that, $O_\Psi(p)$ and $D_\Psi(p)$ can be calculated simultaneously without increasing computational complexity. In addition, compared with the work of Olson et al. [16], the computation of the GDT and OM is independent of the template and the number of edge orientations.

Once the GDT and OM is calculated, the matching score $D(T, I)$ is defined as,

$$D(T, I) = \frac{1}{|T|} \sum_{t \in T} \sqrt{\alpha D_\Psi^2(t) + (1 - \alpha) \sin^2 |O_\Psi(t) - o_t|} \tag{9}$$

Notice that $D_\Psi(t)$ obtained from (5) needs to be normalized to $(0, 1)$ before being used in (9). α is positive weight representing the relative importance of the spatial component against the orientation component, $\sin^2 |O_\Psi(t) - o_t|$. The use of $\sin(\cdot)$ to encode the distance in orientation guarantees that the difference in orientation is always considered only for acute angles. In (9), the value of α is in general application dependent. However, $\alpha = 0.5$ works well for our experiments.

In (9), o_t is the orientation at point $t \in T$. Since T is a binary template, o_t cannot be obtained directly using the gradient image. As illustrated in Fig. 3, in this case, we sample T uniformly along the contours and then trace all points of T clockwise. o_t can be approximated as the angle of the normal vector of the

Fig. 3. Left: The gradient vector of a point in the contour of a binary template. Right: Templates with the approximated gradient vectors (grey lines).

line connecting the two points $(t - 1)$ and $(t + 1)$ which are the previous and next consecutive points of t on T.

Notice that if $\alpha = 1$ and $\eta = 0$, the prosed method becomes the conventional template matching method [10], i.e.,

$$D(T, I) = \frac{1}{|T|} \sum_{t \in T} D_{\Psi}(t) \tag{10}$$

where $\Psi(\cdot)$ is defined as in (6).

3   Experimental Results

The proposed template matching method was evaluated by employing it to detect humans, cars and maple leaves from images. The process of detecting these objects can be summarized as follows. Given a set of templates describing the target object and an input image, we first scan the input image by a detection window W at various scales and positions. Let I_W be the image of a detection window W, the best matching template T^* is obtained as,

$$T^* = \arg\min_{T} D(T, I_W) \tag{11}$$

where $D(T, I_W)$ is defined as in (9). Once the best matching template, T^* is found, a verification is required to ascribe a degree of confidence on whether I_W contains a target object. In this paper, the verification was simply done by comparing $D(T, I_W)$ with a threshold.

Human Detection. We evaluated the performance of human detection task on pedestrian test set USC-A [19]. This set includes 205 images with 313 un-occluded humans in upper right standing poses from frontal/rear viewpoints. Many of them have cluttered backgrounds. The detection was conducted by scanning a 45×90 window on the images at various scales (from 0.6 to 1.4) and each detection window was matched with 5 templates (binary contours of human body shape). The detection results were then compared with the ground truth given at [19] using the criteria proposed in [6]. The criteria include the relative distance between the centres of the detected window and the ground truth box with respect to the size of the ground truth box and the overlapping between the

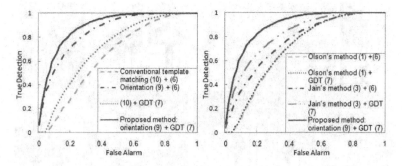

Fig. 4. ROCs of the proposed method and its variants (left), other methods (right) on the USC-A dataset. Notice that we do not merge overlapping detection windows. In the right image, the two ROCs of Olson's method with and without using GDT are not much different from each other.

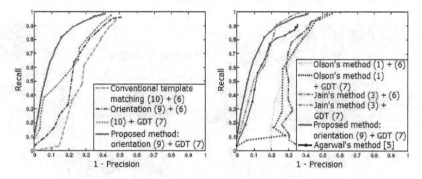

Fig. 5. PR curves of the proposed method and its variants (left), other methods (right) on the UIUC dataset where the result of [5] is copied from the original paper

detection window and the ground truth. The achieved ROC and some detection results are shown in Fig. 4 and Fig. 6(a) respectively.

Car Detection. In the detection of cars, we used the UIUC car dataset [5] and a set of 20 templates. This dataset contains 170 images with 200 cars in the side view and under different resolutions and low contrast with highly textured backgrounds. In this dataset, all cars are approximately the same size and some are partially occluded. The images are scanned with steps of 5 pixels and 2 pixels in the horizontal and vertical directions respectively. We also employed the evaluation scheme proposed by Agarwal and Roth [5]. The precision-recall (PR) curve of the proposed method is presented in Fig. 5 and some detection results are shown in Fig. 6(b).

Leaf Detection. We selected 66 of 186 images (of 896×592 size) containing maple leaves (one leaf per image) on different backgrounds from [20] and one

(a)

(b)

(c)

Fig. 6. Some experimental results of human detection (a), car detection (b), and maple leaf detection (c)

template shown in Fig. 3. On this dataset, the proposed method achieved 100% of true detection with no false positives whereas at the lowest misclassification, computed by $FalsePositive + FalseNegative$, the conventional template matching achieved 62/66 of true detection with 6 false positives. Some results are shown in Fig. 6(c).

Comparison. In addition to the performance evaluation, we compared the proposed method with its variants and other methods. The comparison has been made mainly on the two datasets: USC-A and UIUC since the number of data from these datasets is large enough to achieve a credible comparison. The purpose of this comparison is to show the robustness brought by weighting strong edges using the GDT (7) and the use of orientation in matching separately, as well as in the combination of both of them. For example, the conventional template matching was implemented as the special case of the proposed method by not using orientation and weighting edges, i.e. $\Psi(\cdot)$ is defined as in (6) and the matching score is given as in (10).

For comparison with other works, we implemented the method proposed by Olson et al. [16] and Jain et al. [17]. In our implementation, the spatial distances, d_s, in (1) and (3) are computed by two different ways: using (6) as conventional DT and the proposed GDT (7). For car detection, we compared the proposed method with the work of Agarwal et al. [5] where the appearance of the objects was employed. Fig. 4 and Fig. 5 are the ROCs and PR curves achieved by the proposed method, its variants, and other methods. It can be seen that the proposed method combining both GDT and orientation performs superiorly in comparison with its variants and other existing methods.

4   Conclusion

This paper proposes an improved template matching method which is based on the orientation map (OM) and generalized distance transform (GDT) that uses the edge magnitude to weight the spatial distances. The matching score is then defined as a linear combination of the distances calculated from the GDT image and OM. We compared the performance of the proposed algorithm with existing methods in the cases of detecting humans, cars and maple leaves. The experimental results show that the proposed method improved the detection performance by both increasing the true positive and negative rate. To further speed up the matching process, the combination of the proposed algorithm with a hierarchical template matching framework, such as the one in [7] or [8] will be our future work.

References

1. Viola, P., Jones, M.: Rapid object detection using a boosted cascade of simple features. In: Proc. IEEE Conference on Computer Vision and Pattern Recognition, vol. 1, pp. 511–518 (2001)

2. Dalal, N., Triggs, B.: Histograms of oriented gradients for human detection. In: Proc. IEEE Conference on Computer Vision and Pattern Recognition, vol. 1, pp. 886–893 (2005)
3. Zhang, H., Gao, W., Chen, X., Zhao, D.: Object detection using spatial histogram features. Image and Vision Computing 24, 327–341 (2006)
4. Ferrari, V., Fevrier, L., Jurie, F., Schmid, C.: Groups of adjacent contour segments for object detection. IEEE Trans. Pattern Analysis and Machine Intelligence 30(1), 36–51 (2008)
5. Agarwal, S., Roth, D.: Learning a sparse representation for object detection. In: Heyden, A., Sparr, G., Nielsen, M., Johansen, P. (eds.) ECCV 2002. LNCS, vol. 2353, pp. 113–127. Springer, Heidelberg (2002)
6. Leibe, B., Seemann, E., Schiele, B.: Pedestrian detection in crowded scenes. In: Proc. IEEE Conference on Computer Vision and Pattern Recognition, vol. 1, pp. 878–885 (2005)
7. Gavrila, D.M., Philomin, V.: Real-time object detection for smart vehicles. In: Proc. International Conference on Computer Vision, vol. 1, pp. 87–93 (1999)
8. Gavrila, D.M.: A Bayesian, exemplar-based approach to hierarchical shape matching. IEEE Trans. Pattern Analysis and Machine Intelligence 29(8), 1408–1421 (2007)
9. Thanh, N.D., Ogunbona, P., Li, W.: Human detection based on weighted template matching. In: Proc. IEEE Conference on Multimedia and Expo. (2009)
10. Barrow, H.G., Tenenbaum, J.M., Bolles, R.C., Wolf, H.C.: Parametric correspondence and chamfer matching: Two new techniques for image matching. In: Proc. International Joint Conference on Artificial Intelligence, vol. 2, pp. 659–668 (1977)
11. Huttenlocher, D.P., Klanderman, G.A., Rucklidge, W.J.: Comparing images using the hausdorff distance. IEEE Trans. Pattern Analysis and Machine Intelligence 15(9), 850–863 (1993)
12. Rucklidge, W.J.: Locating objects using the hausdorff distance. In: Proc International Conference on Computer Vision, pp. 457–464 (1995)
13. Borgefors, G.: Hierarchical chamfer matching: A parametric edge matching algorithm. IEEE Trans. Pattern Analysis and Machine Intelligence 10(6), 849–865 (1988)
14. Rosin, P.L., West, G.A.W.: Salience distance transforms. Graphical Models and Image Processing 57(6), 483–521 (1995)
15. Gavrila, D.M.: Multi-feature hierarchical template matching using distance transforms. In: Proc. International Conference on Pattern Recognition, vol. 1, pp. 439–444 (1998)
16. Olson, C.F., Huttenlocher, D.P.: Automatic target recognition by matching oriented edge pixels. IEEE Trans. Image Processing 6(1), 103–113 (1997)
17. Jain, A.K., Zhong, Y., Lakshmanan, S.: Object matching using deformable templates. IEEE Trans. Pattern Analysis and Machine Intelligence 18(3), 267–278 (1996)
18. Felzenszwalb, P.F., Huttenlocher, D.P.: Distance transforms of sampled functions. Technical report, Cornell Computing and Information Science (2004), http://www.cs.cornell.edu/~dph/papers/dt.pdf
19. http://iris.usc.edu/~bowu/DatasetWebpage/dataset.html
20. http://www.vision.caltech.edu/htmlfiles/archive.html

Unfolding a Face: From Singular to Manifold

Ognjen Arandjelović

Trinity College, University of Cambridge
Cambridge CB2 1TQ
United Kingdom
oa214@cam.ac.uk

Abstract. Face recognition from a single image remains an important task in many practical applications and a significant research challenge. Some of the challenges are inherent to the problem, for example due to changing lighting conditions. Others, no less significant, are of a practical nature – face recognition algorithms cannot be assumed to operate on perfect data, but rather often on data that has already been subject to pre-processing errors (e.g. localization and registration errors). This paper introduces a novel method for face recognition that is both trained and queried using only a single image per subject. The key concept, motivated by abundant prior work on face appearance manifolds, is that of *face part manifolds* – it is shown that the appearance seen through a sliding window overlaid over an image of a face, traces a trajectory over a 2D manifold embedded in the image space. We present a theoretical argument for the use of this representation and demonstrate how it can be effectively exploited in the single image based recognition. It is shown that while inheriting the advantages of local feature methods, it also implicitly captures the geometric relationship between discriminative facial features and is naturally robust to face localization errors. Our theoretical arguments are verified in an experimental evaluation on the Yale Face Database.

1 Introduction

Much recent face recognition work has concentrated on recognition using video sequences as input for training and querying the algorithm. This trend has largely been driven by the inherent advantages of acquiring and exploiting for recognition as much data as possible, as well as the increased availability of low-cost cameras and storage devices.

A concept that has gained particular prominence in this body of research, and one that is of interest in this paper, is that of *face manifolds* [1]. The key observation is that images of faces are (approximately) constrained to lie on a non-linear manifold, of a low dimensionality compared to the image space it is embedded in. This is a consequence of textural and geometric smoothness of faces and the manner in which light is reflected off them – a small change in imaging parameters, such as the head pose or illumination direction, thus produces a small change in the observed appearance, as illustrated in Fig. 1.

In this paper, however, we are interested in recognition from individual images – a single, near frontal facial image per person is used both to train the algorithm, as well

H. Zha, R.-i. Taniguchi, and S. Maybank (Eds.): ACCV 2009, Part III, LNCS 5996, pp. 203–213, 2010.
© Springer-Verlag Berlin Heidelberg 2010

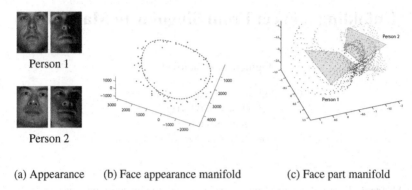

(a) Appearance   (b) Face appearance manifold   (c) Face part manifold

Fig. 1. (a) Textural and geometric smoothness of faces gives rise to appearance manifolds. (b) Motivated by previous research into face appearance manifolds, which as a representation demonstrated impressive results on the task of face recognition from video, in this paper we introduce face part manifolds (c).

as to query it. Although when available, recognition from video has distinct advantages, for practical reasons single image based recognition is preferred in a large number of applications. In some cases video may be unavailable (e.g. when face recognition is used for browsing or organizing photographic collections); in others it may be impractical to obtain (e.g. for passports or national identification cards).

2 Unfolding a Face

An observation frequently used by face recognition algorithms, is that not all parts of a face are equally discriminative with respect to the person's identity. For example, the appearance of the eye or mouth regions is often considered to carry more identifying information than, say, the cheek or forehead regions [2,3]. Furthermore, due to the smoothness of the face surface, local appearance is affected less with small head pose changes than holistic appearance and is more easily photometrically normalized. These are the key advantages of *local-feature based* recognition approaches (see e.g. [4,5,6,7,8]) over those which are holistic in nature. On the other hand, by effectively ignoring much of facial area, these methods do not fully utilize all the available appearance information. The geometrical relationship between fiducial features is also often left unexploited.

In this paper we demonstrate how the principles motivating the use of facial appearance manifolds, largely popularized by video based work, can be adapted to recognition from single images. The resulting representation, a set of samples from a highly non-linear *2D manifold of face parts*, inherits all of the aforementioned strengths of local feature based approaches, without the associated drawbacks.

2.1 Manifold of Face Parts

The modelling of face appearance images as samples from a manifold embedded in image space is founded on the observation that appearance changes slowly with variation in imaging parameters. Depending on which parameters are considered in the modelling process, successful methods have been formulated that use video and person specific appearance manifolds of pose (or, equivalently, motion) [9], person specific manifolds of illumination and pose [10] or indeed the global face manifold of identity, illumination and pose [11,12].

The assumption that face appearance is constrained to a manifold can be expressed as a mapping f from a lower dimensional face space to a high dimensional image space $f : \mathbb{R}^d \rightarrow \mathbb{R}^D$, such that:

$$\forall \Theta_1, \Theta_2 \in \mathbb{R}^D. \ \exists \Theta_3 \in \mathbb{R}^D :$$
$$\left\| f(\Theta_1) - f(\Theta_3) \right\| < \left\| f(\Theta_1) - f(\Theta_2) \right\| \tag{1}$$

Strictly speaking, this condition does not actually hold. While mostly smooth, the face texture does contain discontinuities and its geometry is such that self-occlusions occur. However, as an appropriate practical approximation and a conceptual tool, the idea has proven very successful.

Low-level features. In this paper we define a face part to be any square portion of face image. We then represent the entirety of facial appearance by the set of all face parts of a certain, predefined size. Formally, an image $I \in \mathbb{R}^W \times \mathbb{R}^H$ produces set of samples $p \in \mathbb{R}^s \times \mathbb{R}^s$:

$$P(s) = \Big\{ p \equiv I(x+1 : x+s, y+1 : y+s) \ |$$
$$x = 0 \ldots W - s, \ y = 0 \ldots H - s \Big\} \tag{2}$$

This is illustrated in Fig. 2 and can be thought of as appearance swept by a window overlaid on top of the face image and sliding across it.

The same smoothness properties of faces that gave rise to the concept of face appearance manifolds allow the set of face part appearances $P(s)$ to be treated as being constrained to a *face part manifold*. This manifold is 2-dimensional, with the two dimensions corresponding to the sliding window scanning the image in horizontal and

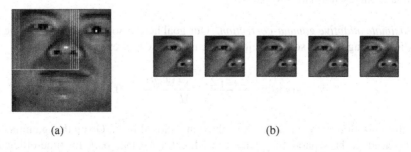

(a)   (b)

Fig. 2. (a) We obtain a set of data point samples from the 2D face part manifold by sliding a square window of a fixed size in horizontal (shown) and vertical directions over the original image of a face. Five consecutive samples are shown in (b). As argued from theory, due to the geometric and textural smoothness of faces, the appearance change between them is very gradual. This is quantified in Fig. 3.

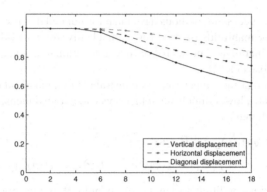

Fig. 3. The value of normalized cross-correlation between a reference face region and regions scanned by the sliding window (see Fig. 2) in the horizontal (red line), vertical (blue line) and diagonal (black line) directions, as a function of its displacement

vertical directions. The required smoothness condition of (1) is qualitatively illustrated in Fig. 2 and quantitatively in Fig. 3

2.2 Photometric Normalization

Local appearance based representations have important advantages for recognition. Specifically, in a more spatially constrained region, the variation in both the surface geometry and the corresponding texture will be smaller than across the entire face. This uniformity allows for simpler correction of lighting. Furthermore, the *distributed* nature of our representation also allows for increased robustness to troublesome face regions, which may not get normalized correctly.

We process each face part in four steps, as follows:

1. approximate adaptive gamma-correction
2. local contrast scaled high-pass filter
3. image energy normalization to unity

Approximate adaptive gamma-correction. Our goal here is to power transform the intensities of image pixels so that their average is as close to grey as possible:

$$\hat{\gamma} = \arg\min_{\gamma} \left| \frac{\sum_{x=1}^{N} \sum_{y=1}^{M} I(x,y)^{\gamma}}{N \cdot M} - 0.5 \right|^2 . \tag{3}$$

This minimization problem cannot be solved in a closed form. Given that gamma correction needs to be separately applied to each extracted face part, for time-efficiency reasons we do not compute the optimal gamma $\hat{\gamma}$ exactly. Instead, we use its approximate value:

$$\gamma^* = \frac{0.5}{\langle I \rangle}, \tag{4}$$

where $\langle I \rangle$ is the mean image patch intensity:

$$\langle I \rangle = \frac{\sum_{x=1}^{N} \sum_{y=1}^{M} I(x,y)}{N \cdot M}. \tag{5}$$

Local contrast scaled high-pass filter. In most cases, the highest inter- to intra- personal information content in images of faces is contained in higher frequency components, low frequencies typically being dominated by ambient and directional illumination effects [13]. We make use of this by applying a high-pass filter to gamma corrected patches.

$$I_l = I * G_{\sigma=2} \tag{6}$$
$$I_h = I - I_l. \tag{7}$$

An undesirable artefact of high-pass filtering is the sensitivity of the result to the overall image contrast: the same facial feature illuminated more strongly will still produce a higher contrast result, then when imaged in darker conditions. We adjust for this by scaling the high-pass filter output by local image intensity, estimated using the low-pass image:

$$\hat{I} = \frac{I_h(x,y)}{I_l(x,y)}. \tag{8}$$

Image energy normalization to unity. The final step of our photometric adjustment involves the normalization of the total image patch energy:

$$\bar{I}(x,y) = \frac{I(x,y)}{\sqrt{E(I)}}, \tag{9}$$

where $E(I)$ is the original energy:

$$E(I) = \sum_{x,y} I(x,y)^2. \tag{10}$$

The results of our photometric normalization cascade are illustrated on examples of face parts in Fig. 4.

2.3 Global Representation

We have already argued that the face parts appearances extracted from a single image can be thought of as set of dense samples from the underlying face part manifold. The analogy between the relationships of face parts and this manifold and that of face images and the corresponding face appearance manifolds, is tempting but there is a number of important differences between the two.

If the entire range of variation in the appearance of a person is considered, regardless of the manner in which the face is illuminated or the camera angle, the appearance should never be the same as that of another person[1]. Although imaging parameters do

---

[1] Exceptions such as in the case of twins are not of relevance to the issue at hand.

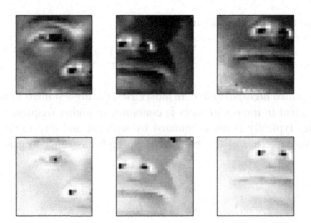

Fig. 4. Examples of appearance of three facial regions before any processing (top row) and after our photometric adjustment (bottom row). The effects of illumination are largely normalized, while the prominence of actual facial features is emphasized.

affect the discriminative power that an image has for recognition, this is far more pronounced in the case of face parts which inherently vary in information content [14]. A uniform region, such as may be observed in the cheek or forehead regions, after photometric normalization described in the previous section, is nearly uniformly grey and virtually void of person-specific information, see Fig. 5. Such parts will be clustered in an apex from which all face part manifolds radiate, as illustrated on an example in Fig. 1. It should be noted that these are non-informative only in isolation. In the context of other parts, they shape the face part manifold and by affecting the geodesic distance between discriminative regions, implicitly capture geometric relationship between them. Both observations highlight the need to represent and use extracted face part manifold samples in a unified, holistic manner.

Manifold structure, modelling and discrimination. The shape that face part manifolds take in image space is greatly dependent on the sliding window size. This is illustrated in Fig. 6. For very small part sizes, of the order of 10% of face image size, the information content of any patch is so small that the corresponding manifold is so highly curved and self-intersecting, that its structure is entirely lost in the sampling process. In contrast, large parts, with dimensions comparable to that of the original image, produce manifolds with a far simpler structure.

Irrespective of the chosen part size, all face part manifolds will have a common origin at the cluster of nearly uniform, non-informative parts. While many parts will fall within or near this region of image space, it can be observed that manifolds corresponding to individuals with different identities can be discriminated between by looking the direction they extend in from it. This is illustrated in Fig. 1(b). An important corollary of this observation is that for recognition, it is not necessary to accurately model the exact shapes of part manifolds. Rather, it is sufficient to discriminate between the minimal hyperplanes they are embedded in.

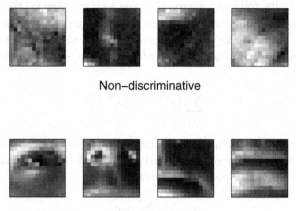

Non–discriminative

Discriminative

Fig. 5. One of the difficulties introduced by employing a dense, local representation of a face is caused by a large number of non-discriminative local appearance patches (top row). Such, similar looking regions can result from images of faces of different individuals, in contrast to information containing, person specific ones (bottom row). The algorithm used to compare two sets of patches (one corresponding to a known, database individual and one to a novel, query image) must take this observation into account.

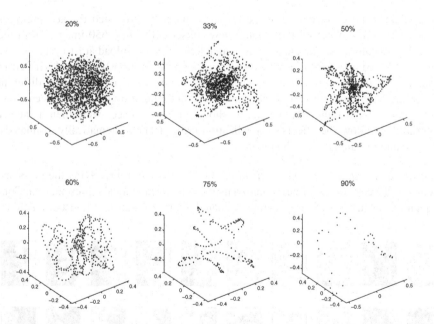

Fig. 6. Distributions of differently sized face parts in the image space, extracted from a single image of a face. The data is shown projected to the first three principal components. The ratio of face part sliding window size to the size of the original face image is shown above each plot.

Thus, we adopt the following approach. Given a set of extracted face parts $P^{(i)} = \{p_1^{(i)}, p_2^{(i)} \ldots\}$, we first shift the image space origin to the non-informative, uniformly grey image. The adjusted face part appearance variation is represented by the hyperplane defined by the eigenvectors associated with the largest eigenvalues of the data covariance matrix:

$$C^{(i)} = \sum_j \left(p_j^{(i)} - \pi\right)\left(p_j^{(i)} - \pi\right)^T, \tag{11}$$

where π is the grey image. Finally, the distance η between two sets of face part samples is estimate by considering the weighted sum of the largest canonical correlations $\rho_1 \ldots \rho_N$ between the corresponding hyperplanes:

$$\eta = 1 - \sum_i \alpha_i \rho_i. \tag{12}$$

If the basis vectors of the two hyperplanes are B_i and B_j, the canonical correlations $\rho_1 \ldots \rho_N$ are computed as the first N singular values of the matrix $B_i^T B_j$.

3   Evaluation

We evaluated the performance of the proposed method and tested the key premises argued for in this paper on the frontal view subset containing 650 images from the Yale Face Database B. The database is available for free download at http://cvc. yale.edu/projects/yalefacesB/yalefacesB.html and is described in detail in [15]. It contains 64 images for each subject and pose, corresponding to different and greatly varying illumination conditions (63 employing a single light source and an additional ambient light only image), as shown in Fig. 7. Faces were then manually registered (to allow the effects of localization errors to be systematically evaluated), cropped and rescaled to 50×50 pixels.

Holistic representation and normalization. One of the ideas underlying the proposed method is the case for face representation using some form of local representation. Consequently, our first set of experiments evaluated the performance of holistic matching,

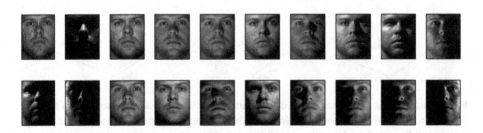

Fig. 7. A cross-section through the range of appearance variation due to illumination changes, present in the Yale Face Database B data set

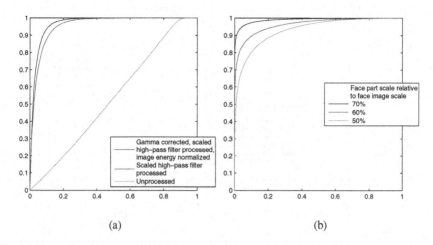

(a)   (b)

Fig. 8. Measured recognition performance, displayed in the form of Receiver-Operator Characteristic (ROC) curves, for (a) holistic appearance matching after different photometric normalization techniques, and for (b) the proposed method for different face part sizes

using the same basic representation for face appearance as we later use for face parts. The results are summarized in Fig. 8(a).

The extreme variability in illumination conditions present in our data set is evident by the no better than random performance of unprocessed appearance (green). As expected, high-pass filtering produces a dramatic improvement (red), which is further increased with gamma correction and image energy normalization (blue), resulting in the equal error rate of 8.5%.

Proposed method and influence of face part size. The second set of experiments we conducted was aimed at evaluating the overall performance of the proposed algorithm and examining how it is affected by the choice of face part scale. This set of results is summarized in Fig. 8(b). For the optimal choice of the sliding window size, which is roughly 70% of the size of the cropped face, our method significantly outperforms all of the holistic matching methods. The observed deterioration in performance with decreased part size is interesting. We believe that this is not a reflection of inherently reduced discriminative power of the representations based on smaller part sizes, but rather of our linear model used to represent appearance variation within a set.

Sensitivity to face localization errors. Our final experiment tested how holistic and the proposed local, dense representation of face appearance perform in the presence of face localization errors. Having manually performed face registration, we were able to systematically introduce small translational errors between faces which are matched, thus obtaining a family of ROC curves for different error magnitudes. These are shown in Fig. 9. The superiority of our method over holistic recognition is very apparent; while the recognition success of the latter starts to rapidly degrade even with an alignment disparity of only one pixel and performing no better than random at six pixels, our method shows impressive robustness and only a very slight dip in performance.

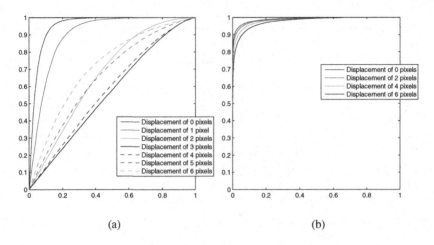

(a)   (b)

Fig. 9. Performance degradation of the (a) best holistic and (b) the proposed method with relative displacement of compared images

4   Conclusion

We introduced a novel method for face recognition from single images. Our algorithm is based on 2D manifold-like structures embedded in the image space and which we call *face part manifolds*. Very much like the face appearance manifolds they were inspired by, these are shown to be representations with significant discriminative power. What makes them particularly attractive is the observation that they naturally reconcile the differences between local feature based and holistic recognition approaches. They inherit the simplicity of the basic element and the distributed nature of the former, while making full use of available appearance and facial geometry information like the latter. A thorough theoretical analysis of the method is followed by its empirical verification on the Yale Face Database.

References

1. Lui, Y.M., Beveridge, J.R.: Grassmann registration manifolds for face recognition, vol. 2, pp. 44–57 (2008)
2. Mita, T., Kaneko, T., Stenger, B., Hori, O.: Discriminative feature co-occurrence selection for object detection. PAMI 30(7), 1257–1269 (2008)
3. Matas, J., Bilek, P., Hamouz, M., Kittler, J.: Discriminative regions for human face detection (2002)
4. Sivic, J., Everingham, M., Zisserman, A.: Person spotting: video shot retrieval for face sets, pp. 226–236 (2005)
5. Arca, S., Campadelli, P., Lanzarotti, R.: A face recognition system based on local feature analysis. In: Kittler, J., Nixon, M.S. (eds.) AVBPA 2003. LNCS, vol. 2688, pp. 182–189. Springer, Heidelberg (2003)
6. Bolme, D.S.: Elastic bunch graph matching. Master's thesis, Colorado State University (2003)

7. Heo, J., Abidi, B., Paik, J., Abidi, M.A.: Face recognition: Evaluation report for FaceIt®. In: Proc. International Conference on Quality Control by Artificial Vision, vol. 5132, pp. 551–558 (2003)

8. Stergiou, A., Pnevmatikakis, A., Polymenakos, L.: EBGM vs. subspace projection for face recognition. In: Proc. International Conference on Computer Vision Theory and Applications (2006)

9. Lee, K., Kriegman, D.: Online learning of probabilistic appearance manifolds for video-based recognition and tracking, vol. 1, pp. 852–859 (2005)

10. Arandjelović, O., Cipolla, R.: A pose-wise linear illumination manifold model for face recognition using video, vol. 113 (2008)

11. Sim, T., Zhang, S.: Exploring face space. In: Proc. IEEE Workshop on Face Processing in Video, p. 84 (2004)

12. Arandjelović, O., Cipolla, R.: Face recognition from video using the generic shape-illumination manifold, vol. 4, pp. 27–40 (2006)

13. Fitzgibbon, A., Zisserman, A.: On affine invariant clustering and automatic cast listing in movies, pp. 304–320 (2002)

14. Gao, Y., Wang, Y., Feng, X., Zhou, X.: Face recognition using most discriminative local and global features, vol. 1, pp. 351–354 (2006)

15. Georghiades, A.S., Belhumeur, P.N., Kriegman, D.J.: From few to many: Illumination cone models for face recognition under variable lighting and pose 23(6), 643–660 (2001)

Fingerspelling Recognition through Classification of Letter-to-Letter Transitions

Susanna Ricco and Carlo Tomasi

Department of Computer Science
Duke University
Durham, NC 27708
{sricco,tomasi}@cs.duke.edu

Abstract. We propose a new principle for recognizing fingerspelling sequences from American Sign Language (ASL). Instead of training a system to recognize the static posture for each letter from an isolated frame, we recognize the dynamic gestures corresponding to transitions between letters. This eliminates the need for an explicit temporal segmentation step, which we show is error-prone at speeds used by native signers. We present results from our system recognizing 82 different words signed by a single signer, using more than an hour of training and test video. We demonstrate that recognizing letter-to-letter transitions without temporal segmentation is feasible and results in improved performance.

1 Introduction

The native language of the Deaf Community in the United States is *American Sign Language* (ASL), which defines a vocabulary of gestures corresponding to frequently used words. When no standard sign exists for a desired word, signers use *fingerspelling*, spelling out the word using gestures that correspond to the letters in the English alphabet. Unlike word-level signs, fingerspelling gestures use a single hand, and most do not require motion. Instead, different letters are primarily distinguished by the positions of the signer's fingers, called the *handshape*.

The naïve approach to fingerspelling recognition is to learn to recognize each letter's handshape in isolation before tackling letters in sequence. We believe a more reliable system recognizes *transitions between letters* rather than the letters themselves. This approach avoids the need to select which frames to classify into letters, a process that is error-prone at conversational speed. In addition, emphasis on transitions leverages information about the shape of a signer's hand *as a letter is being formed* to differentiate between letters that are easily confused in static frames. The naïve solution discards this helpful information.

In this work, we present a system that recognizes transitions between fingerspelled letters. In Sect. 2, we review previous work on fingerspelling recognition. These existing recognition systems rely on an initial time segmentation process to identify a single isolated frame for each letter to be recognized. In Sect. 3, we demonstrate situations where proposed time segmentation techniques fail,

H. Zha, R.-i. Taniguchi, and S. Maybank (Eds.): ACCV 2009, Part III, LNCS 5996, pp. 214–225, 2010.

necessitating the shift to letter-to-letter transitions. In Sect. 4, we describe a system that uses traditional techniques from word-level ASL and speech recognition to model the transitions. Section 5 illustrates the technique on an example vocabulary. The results show that modeling transitions between letters improves recognition performance when prior temporal segmentation is not assumed.

2   Related Work

The automatic translation of ASL into written English has been an active area of research in computer vision for over a decade. Traditionally, researchers have considered recognition of word-level gestures and fingerspelled letters to be isolated problems and have developed separate techniques to address the two. The two independent systems could eventually be combined to translate sequences containing both word-level and fingerspelled signs by segmenting the video into word-level or fingerspelled only segments using a binary classifier [1] and running the appropriate system on the extracted segments.

Most systems designed to recognize word-level gestures use Hidden Markov Models (HMMs) to model each hand's location and velocity over time. Techniques differ mainly in the degree to which handshape information is considered. Some methods [2,3] use only very basic handshape information, if any; others [4] use a complete description of the bending angles at 18 joints in the hand, which are measured using an instrumented glove such as a CyberGlove.

In contrast, existing fingerspelling recognition systems classify static handshapes in isolation. The complexity in the handshapes that must be differentiated led some researchers [5,6] to use joint bending angles from a CyberGlove as the input features. Unfortunately, these gloves are both intrusive and expensive. Hernandez-Rebollar et al. [7] built their own instrumented glove in an attempt to provide a low-cost option. Other researchers [8,9,10,11] focused on improving vision-based methods to create systems that are relatively inexpensive and require only passive sensing. These systems have performed well in restricted environments. Birk et al. [12] report recognition rates as high as 99.7% for a single signer when presented with isolated images of each letter.

A related and active area of research is the recovery of arbitrary 3D hand poses from a single image [13]. In theory, one could construct a fingerspelling recognition system by taking a single image of the signer's hand, inferring the corresponding 3D hand pose, and then matching this pose to the static poses defined for each letter. Like traditional systems, however, a technique relying on pose reconstruction still uses an isolated image of a letter as the input to be recognized.

To find the necessary single frame, researchers apply a threshold to the total motion in the image. Recognition is performed on low-motion frames. Different techniques are used to measure the motion of the signer, ranging from the total energy in the difference between two consecutive frames [10] to the velocity of the hand directly measured using the instrumented gloves [6]. Motion-thresholding techniques work well as long as signers pause as they sign each letter. However, they begin to fail when this assumption breaks down and individual letters become hidden in the smooth flow of high-speed fingerspelling gestures.

To our knowledge, Goh and Holden's fingerspelling recognition system [14] is the only current technique that does not require an explicit segmentation into individual letters prior to recognition. This system is trained to recognize fingerspelling using the Australian Sign Language (Auslan) alphabet, with individual HMMs for each Auslan letter chained together using an explicit grammar to form word-level HMMs. A new sequence is classified as the word whose HMM maximizes the probability of the observations, consisting of coarse descriptions of handshape and the velocities of points along the boundary of the silhouette. They report a best word-level accuracy of 88.61% on a test set of 4 examples of 20 different words.

3   The Case for Transitions

The assumption that signers pause at each letter is consistently violated at conversational speed. Proficient signers commonly fingerspell at 40-45 words per minute (WPM), and it is impossible to pause at every letter at this speed. At 45 WPM, many letters are not formed exactly, but are combined with neighboring letters in fluid motions. Even if a signer does pass through the exact handshape defined for a letter, the aliasing resulting from a comparatively low frame rate can cause this handshape to be missed.

Our experiments show that thresholding methods fail to accurately identify letters at conversational speed. We took clips from interpreter training videos [15] of native signers and identified frames to classify using a method similar to the one described by Lamar et al. [10], which measures motion in each frame by image differencing. In the first version, we select all frames with motion below a set threshold; in the second, we select only frames corresponding to local minima of motion that fall below the threshold. Figure 1(a) shows 30 frames from a man signing *rpreter* (part of *interpreter*), with frames corresponding to local minima below a set threshold surrounded by red boxes. The seven frames that best represent the seven signed letters as determined by a human expert are outlined in blue.

The threshold misses the first three (r, p, and r in frames 4, 8, and 12) and last (r in frame 30) letters completely. Frame 18 is incorrectly identified as a letter frame; it is actually the midpoint of the transitional motion from the letter e to t, where the signer changes the direction of motion of the index finger. Also note that the handshapes selected by the expert for r and e in frames 12 and 15 do not exactly match the handshapes defined in the ASL manual alphabet for these letters.[1] The signer never forms the exact handshapes during his smooth motion from the p in frame 8 to the t in frame 20. This would cause errors in recognition for a system trained on the defined static poses for each letter, even if these frames were selected for classification.

---

[1] An introduction to the ASL manual alphabet can be found at
http://www.lifeprint.com/asl101/fingerspelling/abc.htm

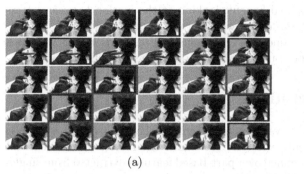 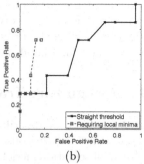

(a)   (b)

Fig. 1. The last 30 frames (left-to-right, top-to-bottom, in (a)) from the word *interpreter* with the closest frame to each of the seven letters outlined in blue. The four frames outlined in red (numbers 15, 18, 20, and 26) are those selected using a fixed threshold on the motion in the frame. ROC curves (b) show the effect of varying the threshold. Selecting all frames below the threshold (solid black) identifies too many incorrect frames; selecting only local minima below the threshold (dashed red) is incapable of finding letters where the signer does not pause. (Figure best viewed in color.)

The receiver operating characteristic (ROC) curves in Fig. 1(b) show the effect of varying the threshold. The dashed line corresponds to an algorithm that selects only local minima. Because some letters actually occur at local maxima, not minima, this algorithm can never identify all the letters, no matter what the threshold. The solid line corresponds to an algorithm that selects every frame with motion below the threshold. This algorithm eventually finds all the letter frames but includes almost all transition frames as well. Clips of different words from a number of different signers show similar poor performance. In fact, we observed that the more common a specific combination of letters was, the less likely it was for those letters to occur at local minima.

Human experts recognize the difficulty in trying to extract individual letters from continuous fingerspelling, often teaching students to look for the "shape of the word" instead of picking out each letter. Research has shown young deaf children also use this method, initially perceiving fingerspelled words as single units rather than as sequences of individual letters [16]. We adopt a similar approach, recognizing motions between letters and eliminating the need for an initial time

Fig. 2. Hand silhouettes from consecutive frames of the fingerspelled words *at* (left) or *an* (right). The final handshapes (letters *t* and *n*) appear similar, but handshapes are clearly different during the transition. In *at*, only the index finger must move to all for correct placement of the thumb. In *an*, the index and middle fingers must both move.

segmentation step. As an added benefit, looking at the motion between letters can help differentiate between letters whose static handshapes appear similar. Figure 2 shows consecutive frames from the fingerspelled words *at* and *an*, which have similar final handshapes but contain distinguishing transitional motions.

4   Recognizing Transitions

In this section, we describe a system that recognizes the gestures corresponding to motions between consecutive letters. We model the motion using an HMM with an observation model defined over part-based features extracted from single-camera video of an unadorned signer. Because we recognize changes in handshape over time using an HMM, our approach is related to the handshape channel model used by Vogler and Mexatas [17] to recognize word-level signs involving changes in handshape. Our method differs in that it is glove-free. The use of similar recognition techniques is intentional because it allows the two systems to be combined into one that would recognize both aspects of ASL.

4.1   Handshape Representation

We use a part-based method to represent handshape. Part-based methods are sparse representations that match regions of the image to codewords in a specified dictionary. Typically, codewords are learned from training data or provided by a human expert. We learn codewords that capture important information about the position of each finger but that can be easily computed from images recorded by a single camera.

Extracting Hand Silhouettes. Before learning parts, we extract the silhouette of the signer's dominant hand from each frame. Our train and test sets are constructed so that skin can be accurately detecting using an intensity threshold. In realistic environments, a more robust skin detection algorithm [18] would be needed. After locating the region corresponding to the dominant hand and arm based on its position in the frame, we discard the portion corresponding to the arm by finding the wrist, a local minimum in the horizontal thickness of the region. Our algorithm deals with slight errors in wrist detection by learning to include small unremoved arm pieces in the dictionary of parts. Finally, extracted silhouettes from each frame (examples shown in Fig. 2) are translated so that their centroids align and are stored as 201×201-pixel binary masks.

Unsupervised Learning of a Dictionary of Parts. These silhouettes can be partitioned into a small number of mostly convex parts. Each part is defined by its shape and location relative to the centroid of the silhouette. The largest part corresponds to the palm and any bent fingers occluding it. The remainder of the silhouette consists of disconnected parts corresponding to extended or partially extended groups of fingers or to sections of the arm that were not properly removed. In Fig. 3(b), the silhouette from Fig. 3(a) has been broken into parts. The outline of each piece is shown.

(a)   (b)   (c)   (d)

Fig. 3. A hand silhouette (a) is broken into parts, indicated by their outlines in (b). The reconstruction of this silhouette using the dictionary of parts in (d) is shown in (c). This dictionary was learned from the training set described in Sect. 5. Each part is displayed using the corresponding binary mask, with multiple non-overlapping non-palm parts drawn in the same image to conserve space. We successfully learn semantically meaningful palms and groups of fingers in an unsupervised fashion.

We extract parts from silhouettes using morphological operations. The palm part is extracted by performing a sequence of erosions and dilations. After a few erosions, the appendages disappear, indicated by the convexity of the shape exceeding a fixed threshold. The dilations return the shape, corresponding to the palm, to its original size but do not regrow the removed appendages. No morphological operations are performed on the non-palm parts, which remain when the extracted palm is subtracted from the original silhouette. All parts are represented by binary masks with dimensions equal to the size of the input silhouette (201×201 pixels). The location of the non-zero region encodes the location of the part relative to the centroid of the hand.

The final dictionary contains parts representing the most frequently occurring pieces. After extracting pieces from a training set, we cluster the palm pieces and the non-palm pieces separately using k-means clustering. To increase clustering speed, we reduce the dimensionality of each piece using PCA. We include the medioids of each returned cluster in our dictionary. Increasing the size of the dictionary improves the expressiveness of the representation but decreases computational efficiency and requires more training data. The dictionary learned from our training set (see Sect. 5) is shown in Fig. 3(d). Each connected component (20 palms and 40 non-palms) is a separate part.

Reconstruction from Parts. Given a learned dictionary, we compute representations of novel hand silhouettes by reconstructing the new shape as closely as possible while simultaneously using as few parts as possible. We first extract the palm part from the novel silhouette using morphological operations and select the part from the palm section of the dictionary that minimizes the total number of incorrect pixels. Next, we greedily add parts from the remaining (non-palm) portion of the dictionary until adding parts no longer improves the reconstruction. At each iteration, we tentatively add each unused part to the reconstruction by increasing the value of all pixels inside its mask by one, selecting the part which most reduces the total number of incorrect pixels in the reconstruction. To improve the invariance of the representation we search over a small set of affine transformations when finding the best fitting part. At termination, we return a bit-vector indicating which parts make up the final reconstruction. Figure 3(c) shows the reconstruction of the silhouette from Fig. 3(a) that uses five parts from the dictionary in Fig. 3(d).

4.2 Hidden Markov Model

We train separate HMMs to recognize the transition between each pair of letters. To recognize fingerspelling sequences without knowing when each transition begins, we chain together the individual HMMs (called *subunits*). In this section, we describe the topology of the resulting HMM, the observation model, and the training and recognition processes. Rabiner's tutorial [19] provides a good review of HMMs and the related algorithms referenced here.

HMM Topology and Observation Model. Each subunit is a five-state Bakis topology HMM [20] (see Fig. 4). Observations in the first and last states usually correspond to the handshapes of the two letters. Observations in the three internal states capture configurations appearing during the transition. Skip transitions accommodate transitional motions performed at varying rate and phase relative to video sampling times. In the complete HMM, we connect subunits together using a bigram language model over letter transitions, introducing transitions between final and initial states of the subunits that form trigrams.

With our representation of handshape, each frame contains one palm and any combination of the non-palms. Thus, with a dictionary containing P palm parts and F non-palm parts, there are $P \cdot 2^F$ possible observations at each frame. It is too costly to try to learn or store the exact distribution over all possible observations. Instead, we approximate with the factored distribution

$$\mathcal{P}(p, f_1, \ldots, f_F) = \mathcal{P}(p) \prod_{i=1}^{F} \mathcal{P}(f_i|p), \qquad (1)$$

which requires only $(P-1)+P \cdot F$ parameters for each state. The $P-1$ parameters define a multinomial distribution over palm parts. The remaining parameters define $P \cdot F$ binomial distributions over the existence or non-existence of each non-palm part conditioned on the palm used.

Training. The subunits are trained independently using isolated sequences corresponding to the desired letter pair. Given a clip of continuous fingerspelling, we hand-label a single frame for each letter signed. (These frames are the ones previous methods use for recognition.) We then use all the frames between the two labeled frames as an example of a given transition. During training, we ensure that each sequence ends in the final state of the subunit by adding a non-emitting state reachable only from the final emitting state. The parameters of each subunit HMM are estimated using the standard Baum-Welch algorithm [19]. Initial observation models are learned by assuming that the true path for each training sequence traverses all five states and remains in each state for $\frac{1}{5}$ of the total number of frames. The state transitions are initialized to be uniform over those allowed by our topology. Figure 4 shows the learned HMM for the $a \rightarrow t$ transition. Each state is represented by its most probable observation.

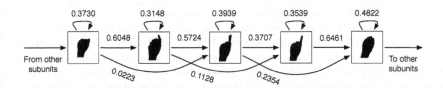

Fig. 4. A letter-to-letter transition HMM trained to recognize the $a \to t$ transition. Edges correspond to transitions with non-zero probability. States model handshapes found at different points during the transitional motion. The most likely observation is displayed to represent each state.

Recognition. To recognize a sequence of letters we compute the Viterbi path [19] through the full HMM. Our recognized sequence of letters follows from the sequence of subunits the path traverses. The path traverses a subunit only if it reaches one of the final two states, which keeps us from recognizing a letter pair when only the first letter of the pair is actually signed.

5 Results

To construct a challenging test vocabulary, we built a third-order letter-level model of English words (from Joyce's *Ulysses*), and included the 50 most common letter pairs. These 50 digrams account for 48% of all letter pairs, and contain 18 different letters. We then listed all trigrams (a total of 186) containing these 50 digrams that occurred with a frequency of at least 10^{-4}. We built an 82-word vocabulary (listed in Fig. 5) containing each trigram at least once. The perplexity, 2^H (where H is entropy [21]), of this vocabulary is 5.53 per digram. By comparison, the perplexity of an equivalent model built from the 1,000 most common English words is 10.31. Our reduced perplexity results from the prevalence of vowels in the top 50 digrams.

Our training set consists of 15 frame-per-second video of 10 examples of each word (29,957 frames total); a separate testing set contains 10 additional examples of each word (28,923 frames). Training and test data amount to about 65 minutes of video. Each frame is originally 640×480 pixels, with the hand occupying a region no larger than 200×200 pixels. We learn the dictionary of parts using unlabeled frames from the training set and train the HMMs using labeled frames. No portion of the training set was used to test the performance of any algorithm.

5.1 Competing Algorithms

To isolate the effect of recognizing letter transitions from choices of handshape representation and probabilistic model, we compare our performance to two alternate systems (`Alt1` and `Alt2`), both of which share our handshape representation and observation model. Both `Alt1` and `Alt2` use an HMM with one state corresponding to each letter, with observation models trained on isolated instances of the corresponding letters. The HMM for `Alt1` contains a single state

alas, andes, aroma, atoned, beating, bed, below, berate, bestowal, chased, cheat, cheng, chinese, chisel, chow, coma, conde, contend, coral, corinth, courant, delores, easter, eden, elitist, eraser, halo, handed, hang, hare, healed, helen, hero, hinder, hither, home, hour, lane, larine, latest, lathered, line, long, male, marathon, master, mate, meander, medea, mentor, merited, near, rarest, realist, releases, rise, roman, ron, row, sealer, sentinel, serene, teal, testing, that, then, these, this, thor, tithed, tome, urease, urine, velour, venerate, vera, vest, wales, wand, war, wasteland, water

Fig. 5. The 82-word vocabulary

Table 1. Performance of Alt2 and L2L with and without a dictionary, averaged over the entire test set (10 examples each of 82 different words). Most recognition errors in L2L without a dictionary are single letter substitutions or missing final letters.

	Alt2	Alt2+dict	L2L	L2L+dict
Digrams correct	53.44%	60.61%	69.64%	72.85%
Words recognized with no incorrect letters	31.83%	86.59%	57.32%	92.68%
Per letter performance on full words	76.97%	90.86%	86.85%	94.75%

modeling all non-letter handshapes. In the Alt2 HMM, we form 18 identical copies of the non-letter state, one for each letter state. The replicated non-letter states permit transitions between only those pairs of letters that occur in our vocabulary. In both systems, recognition is performed by computing the Viterbi path and discarding the frames assigned to the non-letter state(s).

5.2   Performance Comparison

We classified isolated digrams and entire words using our method (L2L) and the comparison methods that recognize letters only (Alt1 and Alt2). Figure 6(a) shows the distribution of recognition performance for the three algorithms over the isolated digrams. To quantify the severity of a recognition error on a word, we compute the letter error rate (LER) for each word by computing the ratio of the number of incorrect letters (insertions, deletions, or substitutions) to the total number of letters recognized. The *per letter performance* for that word is then $1 - \text{LER}$. Figure 6(b) shows the distribution of per letter performance over our test words. L2L outperforms the alternative techniques on both isolated digrams and full words.

Adding an explicit dictionary to both Alt2 and L2L will improve performance by restricting the space of possible words. Table 1 contains a summary of recognition performance of both techniques with and without a dictionary. While adding a dictionary improves the performance of both Alt2 and L2L, modeling transitions results in better recognition accuracy than modeling letters in isolation with or without the help of a dictionary.

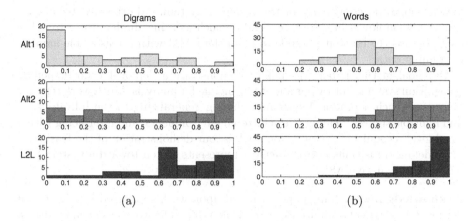

Fig. 6. A comparison of the performance of the proposed method to the two alternatives. All graphs show a count distribution of the fraction of letters recognized correctly. (a) Counts over 50 isolated digrams. (b) Counts over 82 different words. Top row: `Alt1`; middle row: `Alt2`; bottom row: L2L (our method). L2L recognizes a larger percentage of digrams and words with increased accuracy.

6   Discussion

We have introduced a principle for fingerspelling recognition that bypasses the difficult task of identifying an isolated frame for each letter and no longer ignores the dynamic nature of fingerspelling sequences. Our experiments show that modeling transitions between letters instead of isolated static handshapes for each letter improves recognition accuracy. Modeling transitions results in a recognition system that leverages information available while a letter is being formed to disambiguate between letters whose handshapes appear similar in single-camera video. Additionally, because the letter transition model includes multiple HMM states for each letter depending on the surrounding context, it can learn differences in handshape caused by coarticulation [22].

The benefit of modeling transitions is most apparent when no dictionary is used to aid recognition. While dictionaries are commonly used in deployed speech or word-level ASL recognition, we believe a system that does not rely on an explicit dictionary is more suited to fingerspelling recognition. Signers use fingerspelled signs exactly when the word they need is uncommon enough to not have a word-level sign. Thus, a deployed system would be most useful when it could correctly interpret uncommon words such as proper nouns that are likely not to be included in a reasonably-sized dictionary constructed during training.

The largest drawback to modeling and recognizing transitions between letters instead of isolated letters is the increase in the number of classes from 26 to 26^2. Although this increases the need for training data, it does not pose an insurmountable obstacle. For example, a hybrid method that models interesting transitions in detail but uninformative transitions at the level of `Alt2` would help manage the complexity of the resulting system. Additionally, techniques commonly employed in speech recognition such as tying similar states together could be used to make it possible to train the HMM with a reasonable amount of training data.

Our goal in this paper was not to demonstrate a deployable fingerspelling recognition system, but rather a useful principle for analysis. Much work remains before we reach a practical system, including generalizing to the full alphabet and multiple signers, dealing with cluttered environments, and interfacing with a word-level recognition system. Nonetheless, our demonstration of the feasibility of modeling transitions between letters represents a step toward a system that will recognize native ASL.

Acknowledgments. This paper is based upon work supported by a National Science Foundation Graduate Research Fellowship. The work has been funded in part by NSF grant IIS-0534897. We thank Ronald Parr and Svetlana Lazebnik for many useful discussions.

References

1. Tsechpenakis, G., Metaxas, D., Neidle, C.: Learning-based dynamic coupling of discrete and continuous trackers. Computer Vision and Image Understanding 104(2-3), 140–156 (2006)
2. Starner, T., Pentland, A., Weaver, J.: Real-Time American Sign Language Recognition Using Desk and Wearable Computer Based Video. IEEE Transactions on Pattern Analysis and Machine Intelligence 20(12), 1371–1375 (1998)
3. Vogler, C., Metaxas, D.: A Framework for Recognizing the Simultaneous Aspects of American Sign Language. Computer Vision and Image Understanding 81(3), 358–384 (2001)
4. Fang, G., Gao, W., Chen, X., Wang, C., Ma, J.: Signer-independent Continuous Sign Language Recognition Based on SRN/HMM. In: IEEE ICCV Workshop on Recognition, Analysis, and Tracking of Faces and Gestures in Real-Time, pp. 90–95 (2001)
5. Allen, J., Asselin, P., Foulds, R.: American Sign Language Finger Spelling Recognition System. In: IEEE 29th Annual Northeast Bioengineering Conference, pp. 285–286 (2003)
6. Oz, C., Leu, M.: Recognition of Finger Spelling of American Sign Language with Artificial Neural Network Using Position/Orientation Sensors and Data Glove. In: 2nd International Symposium on Neural Networks, pp. 157–164 (2005)
7. Hernandez-Rebollar, J., Lindeman, R., Kyriakopoulos, N.: A Multi-Class Pattern Recognition System for Practical Finger Spelling Translation. In: 4th International Conference on Multimodal Interfaces, pp. 185–190 (2002)
8. Dreuw, P., Keysers, D., Deselaers, T., Ney, H.: Gesture Recognition Using Image Comparison Methods. In: Gibet, S., Courty, N., Kamp, J.-F. (eds.) GW 2005. LNCS (LNAI), vol. 3881, pp. 124–128. Springer, Heidelberg (2006)
9. Feris, R., Turk, M., Raskar, R., Tan, K., Ohashi, G.: Exploiting Depth Discontinuities for Vision-Based Fingerspelling Recognition. In: IEEE Workshop on Real-time Vision for Human-Computer Interaction (2004)

10. Lamar, M., Bhuiyan, M., Iwata, A.: Hand Alphabet Recognition using Morphological PCA and Neural Networks. In: International Joint Conference on Neural Networks, pp. 2839–2844 (1999)
11. Tomasi, C., Petrov, S., Sastry, A.: 3D Tracking = Classification + Interpolation. In: International Conference on Computer Vision, pp. 1441–1448 (2003)
12. Birk, H., Moeslund, T., Madsen, C.: Real-Time Recognition of Hand Alphabet Gestures Using Principal Component Analysis. In: 10th Scandinavian Conference on Image Analysis, pp. 261–268 (1997)
13. Athitsos, V., Sclaroff, S.: Estimating 3D Hand Pose from a Cluttered Image. In: IEEE Conference on Computer Vision and Pattern Recognition, pp. 432–439 (2003)
14. Goh, P., Holden, E.: Dynamic Fingerspelling Recognition using Geometric and Motion Features. In: International Conference on Image Processing, pp. 2741–2744 (2006)
15. Videos used in experiments include clips from the John A. Logan College Interpreter Training Program (www.jalc.edu/ipp) and the DVDs Fast Expressive Fingerspelling Practice, Fingerspelled Stories from 10 to 45 words per minute (both available from www.drsign.com), and Fingerspelling: Expressive and Receptive Fluency (www.dawnsign.com)
16. Padden, C.: Learning to fingerspell twice: Young signing children's acquisition of fingerspelling. In: Marschark, M., Schick, B., Spencer, P. (eds.) Advances in Sign Language Development by Deaf Children, pp. 189–201. Oxford University Press, New York (2006)
17. Vogler, C., Metaxas, D.: Handshapes and Movements: Multiple-Channel American Sign Language Recognition. In: 5th International Workshop on Gesture and Sign Language Based Human-Computer Interaction, pp. 247–258 (2003)
18. Jones, M., Rehg, J.: Statistical Color Models with Application to Skin Detection. International Journal of Computer Vision 46(1), 81–96 (2002)
19. Rabiner, L.: A Tutorial on Hidden Markov Models and Selected Applications in Speech Recognition. Proceedings of the IEEE 77(2), 257–286 (1989)
20. Bakis, R.: Continuous speech recognition via centisecond acoustic states. Journal fo the Acoustical Society of America 59(S1), S97 (1976)
21. Jelinek, F., Mercer, R., Bahl, L., Baker, J.: Perplexity–a measure of the difficulty of speech recognition tasks. Journal of the Acoustical Society of America 62(S1), S63 (1977)
22. Jerde, T., Soechting, J., Flanders, M.: Coarticulation in Fluent Fingerspelling. Journal of Neuroscience 23(6), 2383 (2003)

Human Action Recognition Using Non-separable Oriented 3D Dual-Tree Complex Wavelets

Rashid Minhas[1], Aryaz Baradarani[1], Sepideh Seifzadeh[2],
and Q.M. Jonathan Wu[1]

[1] Department of Electrical and Computer Engineering
minhasr@uwindsor.ca, aryaz@ieee.org
[2] School of Computer Science
University of Windsor, Ontario, N9B3P4, Canada
{seifzad,jwu}@uwindsor.ca
http://www.uwindsor.ca/cvss

Abstract. This paper introduces an efficient technique for simultaneous processing of video frames to extract spatio-temporal features for fine activity detection and localization. Such features, obtained through motion-selectivity attribute of 3D dual-tree complex wavelet transform (3D-DTCWT), are used to train a classifier for categorization of an incoming video. The proposed learning model offers three core advantages: 1) significantly faster training stage than traditional supervised approaches, 2) volumetric processing of video data due to the use of 3D transform, 3) rich representation of human actions in view of directionality and shift-invariance of DTCWT. No assumptions of scene background, location, objects of interest, or point of view information are made for activity learning whereas bidirectional 2D-PCA is employed to preserve structure and correlation amongst neighborhood pixels of a video frame. Experimental results compare favorably to recently published results in literature.

1 Introduction

In recent years, research community has witnessed considerable interest in activity recognition due to its imperative applications in different areas such as human-computer interface, gesture recognition, video indexing and browsing, analysis of sports events and video surveillance. Despite the fact that initially good results were achieved, traditional action recognition approaches have inherent limitations. Different representations have been proposed in action recognition such as optical flow [3], geometrical modeling of local parts space-time templates, and hidden Markov model (HMM) [4]. Geometrical model [1,8,12] of local human parts are used to recognize the action using static stances in a video sequence which match a sought action. In space-time manifestation [21], outline of an object of interest is characterized in space and time using silhouette. The volumetric analysis of video frames has also been proposed [6] where video alignment is usually unnecessary and space-time features contain descriptive information for an action classification. In [6] promising results are achieved

H. Zha, R.-i. Taniguchi, and S. Maybank (Eds.): ACCV 2009, Part III, LNCS 5996, pp. 226–235, 2010.
© Springer-Verlag Berlin Heidelberg 2010

assuming that background is known for preliminary segmentation. For action recognition use of space-time interest points has been proved to be a thriving technique [11] without any requirement for pre-segmentation or tracking of individual dynamic objects in a video. Recently, classifiers that embed temporal information in a recognition process [18] and event recognition in still images [10] have been proposed where distinct scene and object recognition schemes are applied to identify an event.

A novel action learning framework using 3D dual-tree complex wavelet transform (3D-DTCWT) is proposed to process volumetric data of a video sequence instead of searching a specific action through feature detection in individual frames and finding their temporal behavior. Proposed by Kingsbury [9], 2D dual-tree complex wavelet transform has two important properties; the transformation is nearly shift-invariant and has a good directionality in its subbands. The idea of multiresolution transform for motion analysis was proposed in [5] and further developed as 3D wavelet transform in video denoising by Selesnick et al. [15], which is an important step to overcome the drawbacks of previously introduced video denoising techniques.These limitations are due to separable implementation of 1D transforms in a 3D space, and also due to an artifact called *checkerboard* effect which has been extensively explained in an excellent survey on theory, design and application of DTCWT in [17]. Selesnick et al. refined their work in [16] introducing non-separable 3D wavelet transform using Kingsbury's filter banks [9,17] to provide an efficient representation of *motion*-selectivity.

For real time processing, complex wavelet coefficients of different subbands are represented by lower dimension feature vectors obtained using bidirectional 2D-PCA, i.e., a variant of 2D-PCA [20]. Extreme learning machine (ELM) is applied to classify the actions represented by feature vectors. ELM is a supervised learning framework [7], single hidden layer feedforward neural network, that is trained at speed of thousands times faster than traditional learning schemes such as gradient descent approach in traditional neural networks.

2   Dual-Tree Complex Filter Banks

Consider the two-channel dual-tree filter bank implementation of the complex wavelet transform. Shown in Fig. 1, the primal filter bank in each level defines the real part of the wavelet transform. The dual filter bank depicts the imaginary part when both the primal and dual filter banks work in parallel to make a dual-tree structure. Recall that the scaling and wavelet functions associated with the analysis side of the primal are defined by two-scale equations $\phi_h(t) = 2\sum_n h_0[n]\phi_h(2t-n)$ and $\psi_h(t) = 2\sum_n h_1[n]\phi_h(2t-n)$. The scaling function ϕ_f and wavelet function ψ_f in the synthesis side of the primal are similarly defined via f_0 and f_1. The same is true for the scaling functions ($\widetilde{\phi}_h$ and $\widetilde{\phi}_f$) and wavelet functions ($\widetilde{\psi}_h$ and $\widetilde{\psi}_f$) of the dual filter bank $\widetilde{\mathbf{B}}$. The dual-tree filter bank defines analytic complex wavelets $\psi_h + j\widetilde{\psi}_h$ and $\widetilde{\psi}_f + j\psi_f$, if the wavelet functions of the two filter banks form Hilbert transform pairs. Specifically, the analysis wavelet $\widetilde{\psi}_h(t)$ of $\widetilde{\mathbf{B}}$ is the Hilbert transform of the analysis wavelet

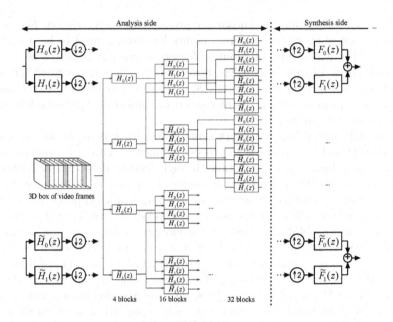

Fig. 1. Typical schematic of a 3D-DTCWT structure with the real and imaginary parts of a complex wavelet transform. Only the analysis side is shown in details in this figure.

$\psi_h(t)$ of $\mathbf{B}$, and the synthesis wavelet $\psi_f(t)$ of $\mathbf{B}$ is the Hilbert transform of $\widetilde{\psi}_f(t)$. That is, $\widetilde{\Psi}_h(\omega) = -j\mathtt{sign}(\omega)\Psi_h(\omega)$ and $\Psi_f(\omega) = -j\mathtt{sign}(\omega)\widetilde{\Psi}_f(\omega)$, where $\Psi_h(\omega)$, $\Psi_f(\omega)$, $\widetilde{\Psi}_h(\omega)$, and $\widetilde{\Psi}_f(\omega)$ are the Fourier transforms of wavelet functions $\psi_h(t)$, $\psi_f(t)$, $\widetilde{\psi}_h(t)$, and $\widetilde{\psi}_f(t)$ respectively, $\mathtt{sign}$ represents the signum function, and j is the square root of -1. This introduces limited redundancy and allows the transform to provide approximate shift-invariance and more directionality selection of filters [9,17] while preserving properties of a perfect reconstruction and computational efficiency with improved frequency responses. It should be noted that these properties are missing in discrete wavelet transform (DWT). The filter bank $\mathbf{B}$ constitutes a biorthogonal filter bank [19] if and only if its filters satisfy the no-distortion condition

$$H_0(\omega)F_0(\omega) + H_1(\omega)F_1(\omega) = 1 \qquad (1)$$

and the no-aliasing condition

$$H_0(\omega + \pi)F_0(\omega) + H_1(\omega + \pi)F_1(\omega) = 0. \qquad (2)$$

The above no-aliasing condition is automatically satisfied if $H_1(z) = F_0(-z)$ and $F_1(z) = -H_0(-z)$. The wavelets of the dual filter bank exhibits similar characteristics, i.e., $\widetilde{H}_1(z) = \widetilde{F}_0(-z)$ and $\widetilde{F}_1(z) = -\widetilde{H}_0(-z)$ where z refers to the z-transform. A complete procedure of DTCWT design and its application for moving object segmentation is presented in [22] and [2] respectively.

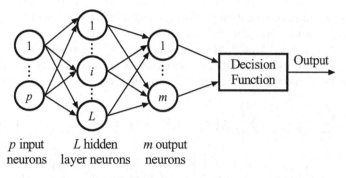

p input   L hidden   m output
neurons   layer neurons   neurons

Fig. 2. Simplified structure of ELM

2.1   Non-separable 3D Dual-Tree Complex Wavelet Transform

Generally, wavelet bases are optimal for the category of one dimensional signals. In case of 2D (two dimensional), however, the scalar 2D discrete wavelet transform (2D-DWT) cannot be an optimal choice [17] because of the weak line (curve)-singularities of DWT although it is still better than the discrete cosine transform (DCT). In video, however, the situation is even worse and the edges of objects move in more spatial directions (motion) yielding a 3D edge effect. The 3D-DTCWT includes a number of wavelets which are expansive than real 3D dual-tree wavelet transform. This is related to the real and imaginary parts of a 3D complex wavelet with two wavelets in each direction. Fig. 1 shows the structure of a typical 3D-DTCWT. Note that the wavelets associated with 3D-DTCWT are free of the checkerboard effect. The effect remains disruptive for both the separable 3D-CWT (complex wavelet transform) and 3D-DWT. Recall that for 3D-DTCWT, in stage three (the third level of the tree), there are 32 subbands from which 28 are counted as wavelets excluding the scaling subbands, compared with the 7 wavelets for separable 3D transforms. Thus, 3D-DTCWT can better localize motion in its several checkerboard-free directional subbands compared with 2D-DWT and separable 3D-DWT with less number of subbands and checkerboard phenomena. It should be noted that there is a slight abuse of using the term subband here. It is more reasonable to use the terms of 'blocks' or 'boxes' instead of 'subbands' in a 3D wavelet structure.

2.2   Extreme Learning Machine

It is a well known fact that the slow learning speed of feedforward neural networks (FNN) has been a major bottleneck in different applications. Huang et al. [7] showed that single-hidden layer feedforward neural network, also termed as extreme learning machine (ELM), can exactly learn N distinct observations for almost any nonlinear activation function with at most N hidden nodes (see Fig. 2). Unlike the popular thinking that network parameters need to be tuned, one may not adjust the input weights and first hidden layer biases but they are randomly assigned. Such an approach has been proven to perform learning at an extremely fast speed, and obtains better generalization performance for activation functions that are infinitely differentiable in hidden layers. For N arbitrary distinct samples (x_i, γ_i) where $x_i = [x_{i1}, x_{i2}, \ldots, x_{ip}]' \in R^p$ and $\gamma_i = [\gamma_{i1}, \gamma_{i2}, \ldots, \gamma_{im}]' \in R^m$ (The superscript " $'$ " represents the transpose) represent input samples and label respectively. A standard ELM with L hidden nodes and an activation function $g(x)$ is modeled as

$$\sum_{i=1}^{L} \beta_i g(x_l) = \sum_{i=1}^{L} \beta_i g(w_i.x_l + b_i) = o_l, \ l \in \{1, 2, 3, \ldots, N\} \tag{3}$$

where $w_i = [w_{i1}, w_{i2}, \ldots, w_{ip}]'$ and $\beta_i = [\beta_{i1}, \beta_{i2}, \ldots, \beta_{im}]'$ represent the weight vectors connecting the input nodes to an ith hidden node and from the ith hidden node to the output nodes respectively. b_i shows a threshold for an ith hidden node, and $w_i.x_l$ represents inner product of w_i and x_l. The above modeled ELM can reliably approximate N samples with zero error as

$$\sum_{l=1}^{L} \|o_l - \gamma_l\| = 0 \tag{4}$$

$$\sum_{i=1}^{L} \beta_i g(w_i.x_l + b_i) = \gamma_l, \ l \in \{1, 2, \ldots, N\} \tag{5}$$

The above N equations can be written as $\varUpsilon\beta = \varGamma$ where $\beta = [\beta_1', \ldots, \beta_L']'_{L \times m}$ and $\varGamma = [\gamma_1', \ldots, \gamma_N']'_{N \times m}$. In this formulation $\varUpsilon$ is called the hidden layer output matrix of ELM where ith column of $\varUpsilon$ is the output of ith hidden node output with respect to inputs $x_1, x_2, \ldots, x_N$. If the activation function g is infinitely differentiable, the number of hidden nodes are such that $L \ll N$. Thus

$$\varUpsilon = (w_1, \ldots, w_L, b_1, \ldots, b_L, x_1, \ldots, x_N) \tag{6}$$

Traditionally, training of ELM requires minimization of an error function ε in terms of the defined parameters as

$$\varepsilon = \sum_{l=1}^{N} (\sum_{i=1}^{L} \beta_i g(w_i x_l + b_i) - \gamma_l)^2 \tag{7}$$

3   Proposed Algorithm

Our proposed framework assigns an action label to an incoming video based upon observed activity. Initial feature vectors are extracted after segmenting moving objects in various frames of an input sequence. Each video frame is converted to gray level and a square dimension matrix. No further pre-processing is applied to input data and we assume no additional information about location, view point, activity, background and data acquisition constraints. We do not require knowledge of background or static objects since a robust moving object detection and segmentation algorithm is applied to extract movements in a video [2]. After segmentation, video frames contain moving object information only. Applying

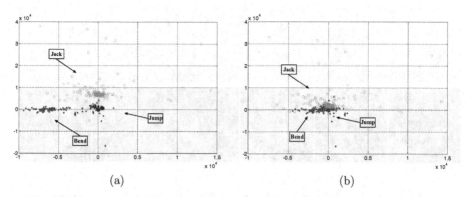

Fig. 3. Spatio-temporal information captured by (a) bidirectional 2D-PCA, (b) PCA

3D-DTCWT on segmented video sequence of size (Q, M, P) results into a box of video frames of size $(Q/2, M/2, P/2)$ where Q, M, and P represent rows, columns and number of frames respectively.

To avoid the curse of dimensionality bidirectional 2D-PCA is employed which requires multiplication between two feature matrices computed in row and column directions using 2D-PCA [20]. As opposed to PCA, 2D-PCA is based on 2D image matrices rather than 1D vectors, therefore the image matrix does not need to be vectorized prior to feature extraction. We propose a modified scheme to extract features using 2D-PCA by computing two image covariance matrices of the square training samples in their original and transposed forms respectively while the training image mean need not be necessarily equal to zero. The vectorization of mutual product of such 2D-PCA matrices results into a considerably smaller sized *subband* feature vectors that retain better structural and correlation information amongst neighboring pixels. Fig. 4 shows better ability of bidirectional 2D-PCA to represent the spatio-temporal information of various actions performed by actor Daria. Fig. 4(a) and (b) are plotted against three different videos that contain activity of Jack, Bend and Jump respectively. The first two components of subband feature vectors obtained using bidirectional 2D-PCA and traditional PCA are plotted. In Fig. 4(a), the separability of different action classes is noticeable whereas components are merged for the feature vectors obtained using PCA (Fig. 4(b)). Procedure of the proposed algorithm is briefly summarized below.

INPUT: A video sequence consisting of frames $a_i, 1 \leq i \leq P$
OUTPUT: Recognized Action
Step 1:   Apply segmentation and extract video frames $b_i, 1 \leq i \leq P$ with moving objects only (see Fig. 4).
Step 2:   Compute coefficients $C_f^d, d \leq 28, f \leq P/2$ (d, f represent filters orientation and number of coefficient matrices) using 3D-DTCWT on volumetric video data $b_i, 1 \leq i \leq P$.

Fig. 4. First row: Randomly selected actions. Bending, Running, Jack, Jump, Side, and Skip (left to right). Second row: Segmented frames using our technique in [2].

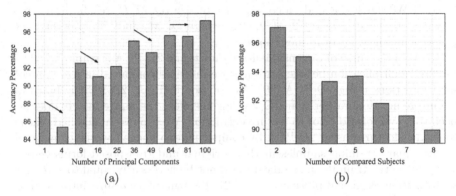

Fig. 5. Accuracy analysis. (a) Video classification for increasing size of feature vectors, (b) Varying number of compared videos.

Step 3: Compute feature vectors using coefficients computed in Step 2. Calculate coefficient covariance matrices G:

$$G_d = \frac{1}{f}\sum_{i=1}^{f}(C_i^d - \overline{C})'(C_i^d - \overline{C}), \overline{C} = \sum_{i=1}^{f} C_d^d, d \in \{1, 2, \ldots, 28\}, i \leq f.$$

Step 4: Evaluate the maximizing criteria $J(X)$ for projection vector X.

$$J(X) = X'G_dX, d \in \{1, 2, \ldots, 28\}.$$

Step 5: 2D-PCA for coefficient matrix C_i^l is represented as $Y_d = C_i^dX, d \in \{1, 2, \ldots, 28\}, i \leq f$.

Step 6: Determine bidirectional 2D-PCA as $Y_d^{bi} = Y_d'.Y_d, d \in \{1, 2, \ldots, 28\}$.

Step 7: Convert matrices $Y_d^{bi}, d \in \{1, 2, \ldots, 28\}$ into vector form.

Step 8: Train ELM using training feature vectors (computed in Steps 1–7).

Step 9: Test the action in an incoming video using feature vectors.

4   Results and Discussion

To test the performance of our proposed method, publicly available datasets [6] are used in experiments. These datasets contain different subjects which perform

Table 1. Confusion table for dataset [6]

	Bend	Jump	Jack	Side	Walk	Run	Skip	Wave1	Wave2
Bend	9								
Jump		8		1					
Jack			9						
Side			1	8					
Walk					9				
Run						8			1
Skip					8	1			
Wave1								9	
Wave2									9

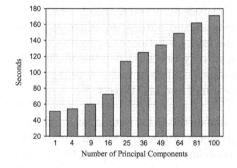

Fig. 6. Computational complexity of our proposed method

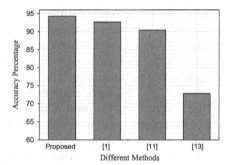

Fig. 7. Performance analysis of different methods

nine distinct actions and therefore we have various videos with varying number of frames. In Fig. 4, first row shows some randomly selected video frames for various subjects along with their segmentation in second row. A leave-one-out cross validation scheme is applied whereas results presented in this section are averaged values for 10 runs of the same experiment through random selection of subjects and/or actions in the dataset.

It is also worth to point out that the dimension of individual feature vectors may also affect the video classification since larger feature vectors retain more information at the expense of higher computational complexity. However, anticipating improved classification by monotonically increasing the size of feature vectors is not a rationale approach. As presented in Fig. 5(a), the accuracy is not constantly increasing by raising the dimensionality of feature vectors; especially classification precision is dwindling or remains constant at arrow locations while the computational complexity of classification is ever-increasing. In our experiments, we achieve reasonable degree of action recognition for the size of feature vectors varying from 36 to 100. In the past, as per the best knowledge of authors, classification accuracy has been reported for a fixed number of training and testing actions/subjects whereas it is an interesting investigation to judge the accuracy of a classifier by analyzing its performance for randomly selected combinations of training and testing videos. As shown in Fig. 5 (b), our proposed method achieves an average classification precision of 94.2% for varying number and combinations of subjects/videos. Insightful investigation reveals the fact that for a larger number of compared videos of the same or different actions/object has higher probability for false alarms [see Fig. 5(b)] due to apparently the same activity observed in small number of adjacent frames such as standing, similar movements in between repetition of an action etc. Fig. 6 represents the computational complexity (combined for training and testing) of our proposed classifier for activity recognition and classification after extraction of feature vectors of all videos of the dataset [6] with respect to the employed processor. Categorization time is another important factor to measure the performance of a classification framework. Our proposed method completes classification of *subband* feature vectors at considerably faster speed. This is an additional improvement on existing methods since proposed technique requires significantly less time for identification and categorization due to enormously simple structure of a classifier comprising of only one hidden layer of neurons yet producing promising results. Table 1 shows confusion table, with achieved accuracy of 95.04%, for a random combination of one and three videos used for testing and training purpose respectively.

Fig. 7 presents accuracy analysis of various methods for human action recognition; it is clear that our proposed scheme outperforms well-known techniques in terms of accuracy and computational complexity. We achieve 94.2% correct action labeling that is an average value for varying number and combinations of randomly selected videos instead of relying on a specific number and/or combination of video sets.

5   Conclusion

A new human action recognition framework is presented based on volumetric video data processing rather than frame by frame analysis. Our method assumes no *a priori* knowledge about activity, background, view points and/or acquisition constraints in an arriving video. Shift-invariance and motion selectivity properties of 3D-DTCWT support reduced artifacts and resourceful processing of a video for better quality and well-localized activity categorization. *Subband* feature vectors, computed using bidirectional 2D-PCA, are input to an ELM that offers classification at considerably higher speed in comparison with other learning approaches such as classical neural networks, SVM and AdaBoost.

Acknowledgment

This work was partially funded by the Natural Science and Engineering Research Council of Canada.

References

1. Ali, S., Basharat, A., Shah, M.: Chaotic invariants for human action recognition. In: Proc. of Int. Conf. on CV (2007)
2. Baradarani, A., Wu, J.: Moving object segmentation using the 9/7-10/8 dual-tree complex filter bank. In: Proc. of the 19th IEEE Int. Conf. on PR, Florida, pp. 7-11 (2008)
3. Black, M.J.: Explaining optical flow events with parameterized spatio-temporal models. In: Proc. of Int. Conf. on CVPR, pp. 1326-1332 (1999)
4. Brand, M., Oliver, N., Pentland, A.: Coupled HMM for Complex Action Recognition. In: Proc. of Int. Conf. on CVPR (1997)
5. Burns, T.J.: A non-homogeneous wavelet multiresolution analysis and its application to the analysis of motion, PhD thesis, Air Force Institute of Tech. (1993)
6. Gorelick, L., Blank, M., Shechtman, E., Irani, M., Basri, R.: Actions as space time shapes. IEEE Trans. on PAMI, 2247-2253 (2007)
7. Huang, G.B., Zhu, Q.Y., Siew, C.K.: Extreme learning machine: theory and applications. Neurocomputing (2005)
8. Jiang, H., Drew, M.S., Li, Z.N.: Successive convex matching for action detection. In: Proc. of Int. Conf. on CVPR (2006)
9. Kingsbury, N.G.: Complex wavelets for shift invariant analysis and filtering of signals. Journal of Applied and Computational Harmonic Analysis 10(3), 234-253 (2001)
10. Li, L.-J., Li, F.-F.: What, where and who? Classifying events by scene and object recognition. In: Proc. of Int. Conf. on CV (2007)
11. Liu, J., Ali, S., Shah, M.: Recognizing human actions using multiple features. In: Proc. of Int. Conf. on CVPR (2008)
12. Mori, G., Ren, X., Efros, A.A., Malik, J.: Recovering human body configurations: combining segmentation and recognition. In: Proc. of Int. Conf. on CVPR (2004)
13. Niebels, J. L.F.-F.: A hierarchical model of shape and appearance for human action classification. In: Proc. of Int. Conf. on CVPR (2007)
14. Selesnick, I.W.: Hilbert transform pairs of wavelet bases. IEEE Signal Processing Letters 8, 170-173 (2001)
15. Selesnick, I.W., Li, K.Y.: Video denoising using 2D and 3D dual-tree complex wavelet transforms, Wavelet Applications in Signal and Image. In: Proc. SPIE 5207, San Diego (August 2003)
16. Selesnick, I.W., Shi, F.: Video denoising using oriented complex wavelet transforms. In: Proc. of the IEEE Int. Conf. on Acoust., Speech, and Signal Proc., May 2004, vol. 2, pp. 949-952 (2004)
17. Selesnick, I.W., Baraniuk, R.G., Kingsbury, N.G.: The dual-tree complex wavelet transform – a coherent framework for multiscale signal and image processing. IEEE Signal Processing Magazine 6, 123-151 (2005)
18. Smith, P., Victoria, N.D., Shah, M.: TemporalBoost for event recognition. In: Proc. of Int. Conf. on CV (2005)
19. Strang, G., Nguyen, T.: Wavelets and Filter Banks. Wellesley, Cambridge (1996)
20. Yang, J., Zhang, D., Frangi, F., Yang, J.-Y.: Two-dimensional PCA: a new approach to appearance based face representation and recognition. IEEE Trans. on PAMI (1), 131-137 (2004)
21. Yilmaz, A., Shah, M.: Actions sketch: a novel action representation. In: Proc. of Int. Conf. on CVPR (2005)
22. Yu, R., Baradarani, A.: Sampled-data design of FIR dual filter banks for dual-tree complex wavelet transforms. IEEE Trans. on Signal Proc. 56(7), 3369-3375 (2008)

Gender from Body: A Biologically-Inspired Approach with Manifold Learning

Guodong Guo[1], Guowang Mu[2], and Yun Fu[3]

[1] Computer Science & Electrical Engineering, West Virginia University, USA
Guodong.Guo@mail.wvu.edu
[2] Computer Science, North Carolina Central University, USA
gmu@nccu.edu
[3] BBN Technologies, Cambridge, MA, USA
yfu@bbn.com

Abstract. In this paper we study the problem of gender recognition from human body. To represent human body images for the purpose of gender recognition, we propose to use the biologically-inspired features in combination with manifold learning techniques. A framework is also proposed to deal with the body pose change or view difference in gender classification. Various manifold learning techniques are applied to the bio-inspired features and evaluated to show their performance in different cases. As a result, different manifold learning methods are used for different tasks, such as the body view classification and gender classification at different views. Based on the new representation and classification framework, a gender recognition accuracy of about 80% can be obtained on a public available pedestrian database.

1   Introduction

Gender recognition has many useful applications. For instance, gender information extracted from images can be used to count the number of men and women entering a shopping mall or movie theater. A "smart building" might use gender for surveillance and control of access to certain areas. Gender recognition is also an important research topic in both psychology [1,2,3] and computer vision [4,5,6].

SEXNET [4] is probably the first work to recognize gender from human faces using a neural network. Later on, other researchers have focused on face-based gender recognition, see some recent works [5,6] and references therein. Almost all previous research on gender recognition uses human faces, either in psychology study or computational recognition. Is it possible to use other cues than faces for gender recognition? Very recently, Cao et al. [7] presented an interesting work where the human body images are used for gender recognition. They describe a patch-based gender recognition (PBGR) approach in [7], and use the histogram of oriented gradient (HOG) operator [8] for feature extraction in each patch, and use a boosting method [9] for classification.

The advantages of using human bodies over faces are that (1) human bodies can still be used for gender recognition even in low resolution images captured by

H. Zha, R.-i. Taniguchi, and S. Maybank (Eds.): ACCV 2009, Part III, LNCS 5996, pp. 236–245, 2010.

Fig. 1. Some examples of human body images used for gender recognition

the security video cameras, while the faces might not be used due to insufficient resolution; (2) faces or important facial features might be occluded by hair, mask, or sun glasses such that the faces cannot be used for gender recognition, while the bodies can still be used; (3) extreme face pose changes such as presenting profile views or even back views make the face no useful for gender recognition; and (4) capturing faces with a close-by camera might be too intrusive for some people or in some situations, while the bodies can usually be captured at a distance.

In this paper we plan to investigate new representations for human body-based gender recognition, which is described in Section 2. Then we propose a framework for automatic gender recognition considering different body views in Section 3. The experiments on gender recognition are presented in Section 4. Finally, the conclusion is given.

2   Human Body Representation

We use the biologically-inspired features (BIF) combined with manifold learning for representing human body images. Some representative methods are evaluated in learning the manifold from the BIF.

2.1   Biologically-Inspired Features

It has been a long-term research goal to understand how objects are recognized in the visual cortex. Theories and algorithms from neuroscience and psychology might have great impact on the design of computational methods. Here we investigate the biologically-inspired features for the problem of gender recognition from human body. To our best knowledge, this is the first time that the BIFs are investigated for this problem.

Riesenhuber and Poggio [10] proposed a set of features derived from a feed-forward model of the primate visual object recognition pathway. The framework of the model contains alternating layers called simple (S) and complex (C) cell units creating increasing complexity as the layers progress from the primary visual cortex (V1) to inferior temporal cortex (IT). Specifically, the first layer of the model, called the S1 layer, is created by convolving an array of Gabor filters

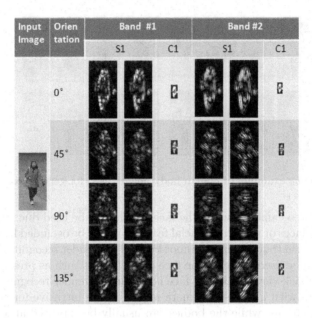

Fig. 2. Visualization of the Bio-inspired features using two bands and four orientations

at four orientations and 16 scales, over the input image. Adjacent two scales of S1 units are then grouped together to form eight 'bands' of units for each orientation. The second layer, called the C1 layer, is then generated by taking the maximum values within a local spatial neighborhood and across the scales within a band. The advantage of taking the "max" operation within a small range of position and scale is to tolerate small shifts and changes in scale.

Serre et al. [11] extended the model of Riesenhuber and Poggio to include two higher level layers, called S2 and C2, for object recognition. In the S2 layer, template matching is performed to match the patches of C1 units with some pre-learned prototype patches that are extracted from natural images. This S2 layer gets intermediate features that are more selective and thus useful for discriminating between classes of objects. These S2 units are then convolved over an entire image and C2 units are assigned the maximum response value on S2. Mutch and Lowe [12] built on Serre et al.'s work for object category recognition and proposed some improvements. Meyers and Wolf [13] used biologically-inspired features for face recognition by concatenating the C1 units to form a so-called S2 facial features (S2FF) and used a relevant component analysis technique for feature dimension reduction.

For human body based gender recognition, we found that using the S2 and C2 features (via pre-learned prototypes [11]) does not work well for our problem. Instead, we only use the C1 features. Based on our experience, the point of view is that the C2 features might be useful for recognizing object categories, e.g., trees, cars, bikes, etc., but not necessarily show high performance for recognition of objects within the same category, such as human faces or bodies. Serre et al. have showed that the C2 features do not outperform the HOG features [8] in pedestrian detection. Meyers and Wolf [13] used the C1 features for face recognition. In our approach, only the C1 features are used for gender recognition from human body images.

2.2 Manifold Learning

Suppose there is a set of human body images $\mathcal{X} = \{\mathbf{x}_i\}_{i=1}^{n} \in \mathbb{R}^D$, in the image space $\mathcal{I}$, with ground truth labels, $\mathcal{L} = \{l_i : l_i \in \mathbb{N}\}_{i=1}^{n}$, e.g., males and females. The goal of manifold learning is to learn a low-dimensional manifold $\mathcal{M}$ in the embedded subspace of $\mathcal{I}$, such that the new representation $\mathcal{Y} = \{\mathbf{y}_i\}_{i=1}^{n} \in \mathbb{R}^d$ satisfies $d \ll D$. In linear embedding, the methods find $D \times d$ matrix $\mathbf{P}$ satisfying $\mathbf{Y} = \mathbf{P}^T\mathbf{X}$, where $\mathbf{Y} = [\mathbf{y}_1 \ \mathbf{y}_2 \ \cdots \ \mathbf{y}_n]$, $\mathbf{X} = [\mathbf{x}_1 \ \mathbf{x}_2 \ \cdots \ \mathbf{x}_n]$, and $\mathbf{P} = [\mathbf{p}_1 \ \mathbf{p}_2 \ \cdots \ \mathbf{p}_d]$.

Principal Component Analysis (PCA) [14]: As a traditional unsupervised dimensionality reduction algorithm, the PCA finds the embedding that maximizes the projected variance, namely,

$$\mathbf{p} = \underset{\mathbf{p}, \ \|\mathbf{p}\|=1}{\operatorname{argmax}} \mathbf{p}^T\mathbf{S}\mathbf{p},$$

where $\mathbf{S} = \sum_{i=1}^{n}(\mathbf{x}_i - \bar{\mathbf{x}})(\mathbf{x}_i - \bar{\mathbf{x}})^T$ is the scatter matrix, and $\bar{\mathbf{x}}$ is the mean vector of $\{\mathbf{x}_i\}_{i=1}^{n}$.

Orthogonal Locality Preserving Projections (OLPP) [15]: The OLPP finds the embedding that preserves essential manifold structure by measuring the local neighborhood distance information. Define the affinity weight $s_{ij} = \exp\left(-\|\mathbf{x}_i - \mathbf{x}_j\|^2/t\right)$ when $\mathbf{x}_i$ and $\mathbf{x}_j$ are k nearest neighbors of each other, otherwise $s_{ij} = 0$. Define symmetric matrix $\mathbf{S}(i, j) = s_{ij}$, diagonal matrix $\mathbf{D}(i, i) = \sum_j s_{ji}$, and Laplacian matrix $\mathbf{L} = \mathbf{D} - \mathbf{S}$. The objective of OLPP is

$$\mathbf{p} = \underset{\mathbf{p}, \ \mathbf{p}^T\mathbf{X}\mathbf{D}\mathbf{X}^T\mathbf{p}=1}{\operatorname{argmin}} \sum_{i=1}^{n}\sum_{j=1}^{n}(\mathbf{p}^T\mathbf{x}_i - \mathbf{p}^T\mathbf{x}_j)^2 s_{ij}$$

Marginal Fisher Analysis (MFA) [16]: The MFA conducts supervised learning with Fisher criterion. It constructs the within-class graph $\mathcal{G}_w$ and between-class graph $\mathcal{G}_b$ considering both discriminant and geometrical structure in the data. In contrast to the OLPP [15], now define two Laplacian matrices, one is for within-class, $\mathbf{L}_w$, and the other is for between-class, $\mathbf{L}_b$. The objective of MFA is

$$\mathbf{p} = \underset{\mathbf{p}}{\operatorname{argmin}} \frac{\mathbf{p}^T\mathbf{X}\mathbf{L}_w\mathbf{X}^T\mathbf{p}}{\mathbf{p}^T\mathbf{X}\mathbf{L}_b\mathbf{X}^T\mathbf{p}}$$

Locality Sensitive Discriminant Analysis (LSDA) [17]: The LSDA is another supervised method that constructs the similar graphs and objective as MFA but solves in a different way. The objective of LSDA is

$$\begin{cases} \operatorname{argmin} \sum_{i,j=1}^{n} (\mathbf{p}^T\mathbf{x}_i - \mathbf{p}^T\mathbf{x}_j)^2 s_{ij}^{(w)} \\ \operatorname{argmax} \sum_{i,j=1}^{n} (\mathbf{p}^T\mathbf{x}_i - \mathbf{p}^T\mathbf{x}_j)^2 s_{ij}^{(b)} \end{cases}$$

and compute $\mathbf{p}_i$ as the eigenvector of

$$\mathbf{X}(\alpha\mathbf{L}_b + (1-\alpha)\mathbf{S}_w)\mathbf{X}^T\mathbf{p} = \lambda\mathbf{X}\mathbf{D}_w\mathbf{X}^T\mathbf{p}$$

associated with the largest eigenvalues, where $\alpha \in [0,1]$ is an empirical constant.

2.3   Our Representations for Human Bodies

We investigate the combination of bio-inspired features and manifold learning as a new representation of human bodies for body-based gender recognition. Both the unsupervised PCA and supervised OLPP, MFA, and LSDA are used for manifold learning. Some interesting results can be observed in our gender recognition experiments. Manifold learning (or subspace analysis) is an active research topic in computer vision recently. Usually, manifold learning methods are applied to raw images directly [15,16,17]. However, the misalignment or no-perfect aligning of human body images might cause problems for subspace analysis methods if they are applied to the images directly. When the bio-inspired features rather than the raw images are used as the input, the manifold leaning methods might not suffer from the alignment problem, since the "MAX" operation in obtaining the $C1$ features from $S1$ can endure small translations, rotations, and scale changes [10,11]. Note that the bio-inspired features that we used here do not have the C2 layer as in [10,11].

3   Gender Recognition

We use the linear support vector machines (SVMs) [18] for classification. The nonlinear SVMs perform no better than the linear SVMs for gender recognition from human bodies, and even worse than the linear SVMs in some cases. For human body images, there is a pose variation problem. The human bodies may have frontal or back view, as shown in Figure 1. So we need to consider the pose problem in gender recognition from body images, not simply take it as a two-class classification problem between the male and female. We propose a framework to classify the views first, and then recognize the gender at each classified view, as shown in Figure 3.

Since the classification of frontal and back views is not perfect, any incorrect classification might decrease the performance of gender recognition that follows the view classification. To deal with this problem, we propose a special processing in view classification.

A confidence measure is used for view classification between the frontal and back views. The signed distance to the linear SVM hyperplane is used to determine the confidence. Let $d(x) = w^T x + b$ be the signed distance from a test sample x to the hyperplane (w, b). If $d(x) > t_1$ with $t_1 > 0$, it is confident to

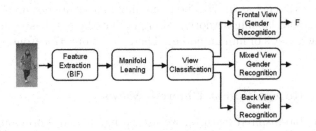

Fig. 3. The framework for automatic gender recognition using human body images

classify sample x as positive; If $d(x) < -t_2$ with $t_2 > 0$, it is then confident to classify x as negative; Otherwise, sample x is classified as "either positive or negative". In our case, we used the mixed view (a mixture of frontal and back views) to represent the situation of "either positive or negative," which looks like a "new" class. In this way, we can reduce the influence of view classification on the following gender recognition. In other words, if a test human body x is a frontal view with high confidence, the system recognizes the gender of x using only the trained classifier for frontal views. Similarly, if x is a back view with high confidence, the system recognizes the gender of x using only the trained classifier for back views. Otherwise, if x has low confidence to be classified as frontal or back view, the system does not really classify x into one of the two views. Instead, the system uses a mixed view that contains both frontal and back views in training to recognize the gender of x.

Experimentally we found that the four representations, i.e., "BIF+PCA," "BIF+OLPP," "BIF+LSDA," and "BIF+MFA," work quite differently in different situations. Thus different representations were chosen for different classification tasks in the whole framework of gender recognition, as shown in Figure 3. See experiments for details.

4   Experiments

The gender recognition experiments are performed on a pedestrian detection database that contains human bodies of both frontal and back views. The ground truth of gender is labeled manually. A standard five-fold cross validation is used to measure the performance.

4.1   The Database

There is no standard database for gender recognition using human body images. In this research, we choose to use the MIT pedestrian database [19] which is a common database for pedestrian detection. Some examples are shown in Figure 1. Each pedestrian image has a size of 64 by 128 pixels. The original database has more than 900 images. The gender was manually labeled for the MIT pedestrian database, and from which 600 males and 288 females were selected for gender recognition experiments as in [7]. The remaining images are not used due to the difficulty in manual labeling. Another thing is that the database contains both frontal and back views of human bodies. There are about 47% frontal views and 53% back views.

4.2 Gender Recognition at Different Views

To extract the bio-inspired features, we used 6 bands and 8 orientations in S1 layer. The filters have 12 sizes, ranging from 7×7 to 29×29. Partial results of the BIFs with 2 bands and 4 orientations are displayed in Figure 2 for illustration. The dimension of the BIF is 10,720 for each input image. Then manifold learning methods are applied to the extracted BIFs rather than to raw images. Given the same BIFs, different methods for manifold learning may result in different number of features, as shown in Figure 4.

First, the gender recognition is performed at different views: frontal, back, and mixed. The mixed view contains both the frontal and back views without separation. For the frontal view gender recognition given the extracted BIF, the PCA method obtains about 300 features from the original 10,720. The highest accuracy for gender recognition is 79.1% using about 200 features, as shown in the top left of Figure 4. The LSDA method obtains about 235 features with the highest accuracy of 79.5% using about 150 features. The MFA and OLPP methods deliver only about 117 features. Similar phenomena about the number of reduced features can be observed in the back view and mixed view gender recognition. There are more images in the mixed view, so more features are derived after manifold learning.

The gender recognition accuracies for each view are shown in Table 1. The best representation for gender recognition at frontal view is the "BIF+LSDA," which gives an accuracy of 79.5%. This accuracy is higher than the 76.0% of the PBGR method [7]. The "BIF+LSDA" representation is also the best for back view gender recognition, with an accuracy of 84.0%. This accuracy is about 10% higher than the PBGR method [7]. For the mixed view, the "BIF+PCA" representation gives the highest accuracy of 79.2%. It is also higher than the accuracy of 75.0% based on the PBGR method [7]. As a result, our new representations have higher accuracies than the PBGR approach [7] for gender recognition in each case.

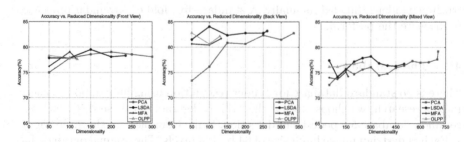

Fig. 4. Gender recognition accuracies versus feature dimensions by using manifold learning on the bio-inspired features

Table 1. Gender recognition accuracies at different views independently

Method	Frontal View	Back View	Mixed View
PBGR [7]	76.0±1.2%	74.6±3.4%	75.0±2.9%
BIO+PCA	79.1±3.0%	82.8±5.1%	**79.2±1.4%**
BIO+OLPP	78.3±3.5%	82.8±4.6%	77.1±1.9%
BIO+LSDA	**79.5±2.6%**	**84.0±3.9%**	78.2±1.1%
BIO+MFA	79.1±2.2%	81.7±5.2%	75.2±2.1%

In terms of the performance at different views, gender recognition at the back view has higher accuracies than the frontal view. This result is interesting. One may design a system using the back view only for body-based gender recognition. For the mixed view, gender recognition performance is usually worse than both the frontal and back views, or close to the lower of the two cases. As a result, using the mixed view is not a good idea for gender recognition.

Another purpose of showing the experimental results at different views is to provide some guidance in designing an automatic gender recognition system that takes all views into consideration.

4.3 Automatic Gender Recognition

First let us look at the view classification performance. Using a standard five-fold cross validation, we measure the view classification accuracies based on the four different body representations. As shown in Table 2, the highest accuracy is 84.3%, given by the "BIF+PCA" representation. This accuracy is not very high. For a test example, if we use the classified view (frontal or back) for gender recognition, the performance might be influenced because of using possibly an incorrect view for the test example. To deal with this problem, we propose a framework to reduce the effect of wrong view classification, as shown in Figure 3.

As stated in Section 3, we use confidence measure in view classification. The threshold values can be chosen by $t_1, t_2 \in (1,2)$. Experimentally, we found $t_1 = 1.7$ and $t_2 = 1.5$ are a good choice. If the distance from a test example to the linear SVM hyperplane satisfies $-t_2 \leq d(x) \leq t_1$, the mixed view will be used for gender recognition for the test example x. Now let us measure the view classification accuracy using three views: frontal, back, and mixed. The "BIF+PCA" is selected as the representation since it works best for the

Table 2. The accuracies of view classification (frontal vs. back). The approximate dimensions are the average over five runs in the five-fold cross validation.

Method	View Classification Accuracy
PCA (dim.≈707)	**84.3±2.1%**
OLPP(dim.≈115)	82.9±2.4%
LSDA(dim.≈300)	83.7±2.6%
MFA(dim.≈173)	82.6±1.8%

Table 3. Automatic gender recognition from human bodies

Representation for Human Body View Classification	Three-View Classification Accuracy (Frontal, Back, and Mixed)	Representations for Gender Recognition in Each View		Gender Recognition Accuracy
BIF+PCA	99.3±0.5%	Frontal View	BIF+LSDA	80.6±1.2%
		Mixed View	BIF+PCA	
		Back View	BIF+LSDA	

two-view classification (see the first row in Table 2). As shown in Table 3, the view classification accuracy is as high as 99.3%.

Then different representations are used for gender recognition at different views, as listed in the third column of Table 3. The best choice for each view is based on the results in Table 1. Now the gender recognition accuracy is 80.6%, which is higher than the 75.0% given by the PBGR approach [7] where only the mixed view was used for gender recognition.

5   Conclusion

We have presented a new representation for gender recognition from human body. Our representation combines the biologically inspired features with manifold learning techniques. A framework is proposed to deal with the human body pose variation (e.g, frontal and back views) in gender recognition. The recognition accuracy can be above 80% based on our new representation and classification framework, which is higher than the 75% accuracy using the PBGR approach. Experimentally, we found that the "BIF+LSDA" representation is better than others for gender recognition at either frontal or back view, while the "BIF+PCA" performs better in both body view classification and gender recognition with the mixed view. In the future, we will further evaluate our approach on a larger database that may also contain side views.

References

1. Bruce, V., Burton, A., Hanna, E., Healey, P., Mason, O.: Sex discrimination: How do we tell the difference between male and female faces? Perception 22, 131–152 (1993)
2. Yamaguchi, M.K., Hirukawa, T., Kanazawa, S.: Judgment of sex through facial parts. Perception 24, 563–575 (1995)
3. Wild, H.A., Barrett, S.E., Spence, M.J., O'Toole, A.J., Cheng, Y.D., Brooke, J.: Recognition and sex categorization of adults' and children's faces: examining performance in the absence of sex-stereotyped cues. J. of Exp. Child Psychology 77, 269–291 (2000)

4. Golomb, B., Lawrence, D., Sejnowski, T.: Sexnet: A neural network identifies sex from human faces. In: Advances in Neural Information Processing Systems, vol. 3, pp. 572–577 (1991)
5. Baluja, S., Rowley, H.A.: Boosting sex identification performance. Int. J. of Comput. Vision 71(1), 111–119 (2007)
6. Yang, Z., Ai, H.: Demographic classification with local binary patterns. In: Int. Conf. on Biometrics, pp. 464–473 (2007)
7. Cao, L., Dikmen, M., Fu, Y., Huang, T.: Gender recognition from body. In: ACM Multimedia (2008)
8. Dalal, N., Triggs, B.: Histograms of oriented gradients for human detection. In: Conf. on Comput. Vision and Pattern Recognit., pp. 886–893 (2005)
9. Freund, Y., Schapire, R.: Experiments with a new boosting algorithm. In: Proc. the Thirteen International Conference on Machine Learning, pp. 148–156 (1996)
10. Riesenhuber, M., Poggio, T.: Hierarchical models of object recognition in cortex. Nature Neuroscience 2(11), 1019–1025 (1999)
11. Serre, T., Wolf, L., Bileschi, S., Riesenhuber, M., Poggio, T.: Robust object recognition with cortex-like mechanisms. IEEE Trans. Pattern Anal. Mach. Intell. 29(3), 411–426 (2007)
12. Mutch, J., Lowe, D.: Object class recognition and localization using sparse features with limited receptive fields. In: Conf. on Comput. Vision and Pattern Recognit., pp. 11–18 (2006)
13. Meyers, E., Wolf, L.: Using biologically inspired features for face processing. Int. J. Comput. Vis. 76, 93–104 (2008)
14. Webb, A.R.: Statistical Pattern Recognition, 2nd edn. John Wiley, Chichester (2002)
15. Cai, D., He, X., Han, J., Zhang, H.: Orthogonal laplacianfaces for face recognition. IEEE Trans. on Image Processing 15, 3608–3614 (2006)
16. Yan, S., Xu, D., Zhang, B., Zhang, H., Yang, Q., Lin, S.: Graph embedding and extensions: A general framework for dimensionality reduction. IEEE Trans. Pattern Anal. Mach. Intell. 29, 40–51 (2007)
17. Cai, D., He, X., Zhou, K., Han, J., Bao, H.: Locality sensitive discriminant analysis. In: Proc. Int. Joint Conf. on Artificial Intell. (2007)
18. Vapnik, V.N.: Statistical Learning Theory. John Wiley, New York (1998)
19. Oren, M., Papageorgiou, C., Sinha, P., Osuna, E., Poggio, T.: Pedestrian detection using wavelet templates. In: Conf. on Comput. Vision and Pattern Recognit., pp. 193–199 (1997)

Fingerprint Orientation Field Estimation: Model of Primary Ridge for Global Structure and Model of Secondary Ridge for Correction

Huanxi Liu, Xiaowei Lv, Xiong Li, and Yuncai Liu

Institute of Image Processing and Pattern Recognition
Shanghai Jiao Tong University, China
{lhxsjtu,lvxwei,lixiong,whomliu}@sjtu.edu.cn

Abstract. Although many algorithms have been proposed for orientation field estimation, the results are not so satisfactory and the computational cost is expensive. In this paper, a novel algorithm based on straight-line model of ridge is proposed for the orientation field estimation. The algorithm comprises four steps, preprocessing original fingerprint image, determining the primary and secondary ridges of fingerprint foreground block using the top semi-neighbor searching algorithm, estimating block direction based on straight-line model of such a primary ridge and correcting the spurious block directions. Experimental results show that it achieves satisfying estimation accuracy with low computational time expense.

Keywords: Fingerprint orientation field; Primary and secondary ridges; Top semi-neighbor searching algorithm; Straight-line model of ridge.

1 Introduction

Among various biometric techniques, the fingerprint recognition is most popular and reliable for automatic personal identification [1]. Generally, the estimation of orientation field is usually a basic processing step for a whole recognition system.

Many approaches have been proposed for orientation field estimation, which can broadly be categorized as filter-based approach [2], gradient-based approach [3, 4], model-based approach [5-7], and approach based on neural networks [8]. Among these approaches, the former three approaches are used popularly. On the whole, these literatures mentioned above can produce good fingerprint orientation fields to some extent, but they bring a high time consumption. So these methods are not quite suitable for an on-line fingerprint identification system. To overcome the weakness, Ji et al. [9] propose an orientation field estimation method only using a primary ridge, which reaches a tradeoff between the time complexity and perfection to some extent. However, they only use four discrete directions to represent a fingerprint orientation field and estimate the block direction using projective variance. It is obvious that their algorithm cannot represent perfect orientation field and the computation time increases monotonically as the predefined direction number or the pixel number of primary ridge increases. To further reduce the computational complexity and improve the quality of orientation field, we propose a novel orientation field estimation method

H. Zha, R.-i. Taniguchi, and S. Maybank (Eds.): ACCV 2009, Part III, LNCS 5996, pp. 246–255, 2010.

based on Ref. [9]. This method can achieve satisfying estimation accuracy with low computational time expense.

The remainder of this paper is organized as follows. The preprocessing algorithm of fingerprint image is introduced in the next section. The details of our proposed orientation field estimation approach are presented in Section 3. Many convincible experimental results are shown in Section 4. Finally, Section 5 contains the conclusion of our work.

2 Preprocessing Algorithm for Original Fingerprint Image

To obtain high-quality binary fingerprint images, unlike Ji's work [9], we take image quality into consideration during the whole preprocessing step. Firstly, let us define some notations. Suppose I is an original fingerprint image of size $r \times c$, and $I(s,t)$ is the intensity of the pixel (s,t), where $0 \le s < r$ and $0 \le t < c$. We divide the image I into a series of non-overlapped blocks of size $w \times w$, and the block size needs to be properly chosen so that not less than two ridges are contained by a fingerprint block. The block (i,j) of the fingerprint image is denoted as $B(i,j)$, where $0 \le i < r/w$ and $0 \le j < c/w$. $B_{i,j}(m,n)$ denotes the intensity of pixel (m,n) within block $B(i,j)$, where $0 \le m < w$ and $0 \le n < w$. All these blocks can be categorized as foreground and background which are to be labeled by $L(B(i,j))$. Furthermore, $L(B(i,j)) = 1$ and $L(B(i,j)) = 0$ indicate that block $B(i,j)$ belongs to foreground and background, respectively. In this paper, the type $L(B(i,j))$ of a fingerprint block is determined as

$$L(B(i,j)) = \begin{cases} 1 & if \quad S(i,j) > T_s(i,j), \\ 0 & else, \end{cases}$$

$$T_s(i,j) = Q_f \phi,$$

(1)

where $T_s(i,j)$ is a given segmentation threshold, ϕ is a constant, which is experientially set to 60, and Q_f denotes the quality factor of fingerprint image. To reduce the computational complexity and save the execution time, the value of parameter Q_f is determined experimentally. For high-quality, median-quality and low-quality fingerprint images, Q_f is set to 1.36, 1 and 0.5, respectively. Herein, the pixel intensity variance $S(i,j)$ of the fingerprint block $B(i,j)$ is defined as

$$S(i,j) = \frac{1}{w \times w} \sum_{m=0}^{w-1} \sum_{n=0}^{w-1} (B_{i,j}(m,n) - \tilde{B}(i,j))^2,$$

(2)

where $\tilde{B}(i,j)$ denotes the mean pixel intensity value of the fingerprint block $B(i,j)$, and it is directly calculated using

$$\tilde{B}(i,j) = \frac{1}{w \times w} \sum_{m=0}^{w-1} \sum_{n=0}^{w-1} B_{i,j}(m,n). \tag{3}$$

Herein, only the foreground block $B(i,j)$ ($L(B(i,j)) = 1$) is binarized, and the binarization threshold $T_b(i,j)$ for which is dynamically calculated using

$$T_b(i,j) = \tilde{B}(i,j) + \eta,$$
$$\eta = Q_f \gamma, \tag{4}$$

where η is a adjustable value and it is the product of the quality factor Q_f and the constant γ. The parameter γ is experientially set to 25. Based on such a rule, the foreground block is binarized via

$$B_{i,j}^b(m,n) = \begin{cases} 1 & if \quad B_{i,j}(m,n) > T_b(i,j), \\ 0 & else, \end{cases} \tag{5}$$

where $B_{i,j}^b(m,n)$ denotes the final binary value of pixel (m,n) within the foreground block $B(i,j)$.

3   Fingerprint Orientation Field Estimation

3.1   Top Semi-neighbor Searching Algorithm

Suppose the neighborhood structure is 3×3 , and then for a given pixel (m,n) , its top semi-neighbor is defined as $(m+a, n+d)$, where $\{a = -1, d \in \{-1,0,1\}\} \cup \{a = 0, d = -1\}$. Similarly, the bottom semi-neighbor can be defined as $(m+e, n+f)$, where $\{e = 0, f = 1\} \cup \{e = 1, f \in \{-1,0,1\}\}$. These notions have been detailedly illustrated in Fig.1 (a). In Fig.1 (a), the squares denote pixels in the binary fingerprint image block $B^b(i,j)$. For pixel P (the blue square), its top and bottom semi-neighbors are red and yellow squares, respectively.

Let $R_{i,j}$ denote the response matrix (see Fig.1 (b)), which has the same size with $B^b(i,j)$, and the response of each pixel within $B^b(i,j)$ is labeled using element $R_{i,j}(m,n)$. $R_{i,j}(m,n) \in \{0,1\}$ denotes pixel (m,n) response type. Furthermore, if pixel (m,n) produces a response, and then $R_{i,j}(m,n) = 1$, otherwise $R_{i,j}(m,n) = 0$. Based on such a rule, the top semi-neighbor searching algorithm means that for a given pixel (m,n) , if there is at least one response in its top semi-neighbor, then pixel (m,n) produces a response, meanwhile, element $R_{i,j}(m,n)$ is set to 1. The proposed algorithm can be illustrated in Fig.1. For pixel P in Fig.1 (a), since there is a response in its top semi-neighbor (see Fig.1 (b), the red circle), it produces a response and the associated element within response matrix $R_{i,j}$ is set to 1 (see Fig.1 (b), the blue circle). Contrastively, the pixel Q doesn't produce a response because of no response in its top semi-neighbor (see Fig.1 (b), the red box).

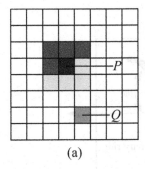 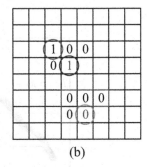

(a)   (b)

Fig. 1. The top semi-neighbor searching algorithm: (a) the top and bottom semi-neighbors of pixel P within block $B^b(i,j)$; (b) $R_{i,j}$, the response matrix for block $B^b(i,j)$

3.2 Determining Primary and Secondary Ridges

The processing steps of determining the primary and secondary ridges using the proposed algorithm can be depicted as follows: First, we scan the binary block to find the first non-zero pixel and force it to produce a response, and as a consequence, the associated element within response matrix is set to 1. Second, we apply the top semi-neighbor searching algorithm on other non-zero pixels within the binary block until no response is produced. Under this status, the non-zero pixel number of response matrix is just the pixel number of ridge, and then we label the ridge using its pixel number. Furthermore, we need to remove the ridge from the binary block so as to process the next ridge. Such steps are repeated, till all ridges have been labeled using pixel numbers. Finally, by comparing these pixel numbers of ridges, the ridge related to the maximal pixel number is determined as the primary ridge, and the ridge related to the secondary pixel number is determined as the secondary one, then all other ridges are removed.

3.3 Block Direction Estimation Based on Straight-Line Model of Ridge

Denote the fingerprint block as a portion of the coordinate plane (also called the Cartesian plane) shown in Fig.2. Suppose the origin of the orthogonal coordinate system is located at pixel $(w/2, w/2)$ within the block $B(i,j)$, where w is the height or width of fingerprint block $B(i,j)$. Thus, the new coordinate of any pixel (m,n) , namely (x,y), can be computed using

$$x = n - w/2,$$
$$y = w/2 - m,$$

(6)

where (m,n) is the original coordinate of pixel within the block $B(i,j)$, and (x,y) is the new coordinate within the orthogonal coordinate system.

Since the local direction of a block is mainly decided by the primary ridge [9], we model the primary ridge using a straight-line equation (see Fig.2). As we known, the

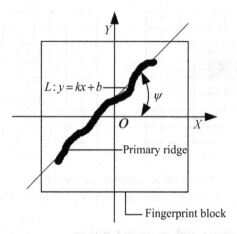

Fig. 2. Block direction estimation using the straight-line model of primary ridge

value of a fingerprint block's orientation, $D_{i,j}$, is defined within $[0,\pi)$, so it can be regarded as the angle ψ of inclination of the straight-line L, i.e.,

$$D_{i,j} = \begin{cases} \tan^{-1}(k) & if \quad 0 \le k < +\infty, \\ \tan^{-1}(k)+\pi & if \quad -\infty < k < 0, \end{cases} \tag{7}$$

where k is the slope of the straight-line L. Without loss of generality, we suppose the pixel number of primary ridge is H (usually $H \gg 2$). For any pixel $(x_h, y_h)\,(1 \le h \le H)$ within the primary ridge, it should meet the straight-line equation L, i.e.,

$$y_h = kx_h + b, \tag{8}$$

where (x_h, y_h) is the new coordinate within the orthogonal coordinate system. Obviously, Eq. (8) is the problem of the first-order polynomial fitting. Solving Eq. (8) using least squares method gives

$$\begin{bmatrix} b \\ k \end{bmatrix} = \begin{bmatrix} H & \sum_{h=1}^{H} x_h \\ \sum_{h=1}^{H} x_h & \sum_{h=1}^{H} x_h^2 \end{bmatrix}^{-1} \begin{bmatrix} \sum_{h=1}^{H} y_h \\ \sum_{h=1}^{H} x_h y_h \end{bmatrix}. \tag{9}$$

After the coefficient k is solved, we can obtain the block direction, $D_{i,j}$, by using Eq. (7). Finally, the directions of all foreground blocks are integrated into an initial orientation field.

3.4 Correcting Spurious Block Direction

To improve the initial orientation field, we propose a correction scheme originating from Refs. [8-10]. As we known, the direction of fingerprint block, $D_{i,j}$, is defined within $[0, \pi)$, but we can partition the fingerprint blocks into distinct directional classes in terms of our requirements [8]. Without loss of generality, let N_c denote the number of directional classes, then the ranges for these classes $C_l\,(0 \le l < N_c)$ can be determined as

$$Ra(C_l) = \begin{cases} [0, \pi/2N_c - \theta) \cup [\pi - (\pi/2N_c) + \theta, \pi) & if \quad l = 0, \\ [(2\pi l - \pi)/2N_c - \theta, (2\pi l + \pi)/2N_c - \theta) & if \quad 1 \le l < N_c/2, \\ [(N_c - 1)\pi/2N_c - \theta, (N_c + 1)\pi/2N_c + \theta) & if \quad l = N_c/2, \\ [(2\pi l - \pi)/2N_c + \theta, (2\pi l + \pi)/2N_c + \theta) & if \quad N_c/2 < l < N_c, \end{cases} \tag{10}$$

where $Ra(C_l)$ denotes the range of class C_l, and θ is the correction angle because the estimated block direction may deviate from the true direction due to the presence of noise and deformations. Let $O^p(I)$ denote the orientation field estimated by primary ridges, and $O^s(I)$ denote the orientation field estimated by secondary ridges, where I denotes the fingerprint image, and $O^p(I), O^s(I) \in [0, \pi)$. $D^p_{i,j}$ and $D^s_{i,j}$ denote these two directions of a same block (i, j) in $O^p(I)$ and $O^s(I)$, respectively. For a block direction within $O^p(I)$, whether the direction is estimated correctly is determined by

$$\bar{M}(i, j) = \begin{cases} 0 & if \quad Jc(D^p_{i,j}) \ne Jc(D^s_{i,j}), \\ 1 & if \quad Jc(D^p_{i,j}) = Jc(D^s_{i,j}), \end{cases} \tag{11}$$

where $Jc(\eta)$ is a function, whose output value is l if $\eta \in Ra(C_l)$. $\bar{M}$ is a matrix of the same size as $O^p(I)$ and element $\bar{M}(i, j) \in \{0, 1\}$ indicates whether the direction of block (i, j) in $O^p(I)$ is estimated correctly. $\bar{M}(i, j) = 1$ means that the direction is estimated correctly, otherwise, it is estimated wrongly and needs a correction.

These detected spurious directions within $O^p(I)$ will be corrected one-by-one by analyzing the statistical number pattern of neighbor directions [9-10]. In this paper, the spurious direction is restored to the center of the range of the class that appears most frequently in the 3×3 neighborhood structure. Let $Sum(C_l)$ denote the number of class C_l appearing in the neighborhood structure, and $\bar{D}^p_{i,j}$ denote the detected spurious direction in $O^p(I)$. Suppose the class C_q satisfies $C_q = \arg\ \max[Sum(C_l)]$, where $0 \le l < N_c$, the spurious direction $\bar{D}^p_{i,j}$ in $O^p(I)$ is corrected as

$$\bar{D}^p_{i,j} = \begin{cases} 0 & if \quad q = 0, \\ \pi q/N_c & else, \end{cases} \tag{12}$$

where notation $\bar{D}^p_{i,j}$ denotes the correction result of spurious direction $\bar{D}^p_{i,j}$.

4 Experimental Results and Discussion

To show the effectiveness of our approach we choose two sets of fingerprint images to estimate the orientation fields for them. Set 1 consists of four distinct databases of *FVC2004*, *DB1_A-DB4_A*. Set 2 contains 3300 fingerprint images captured with a scanner manufactured by Digital Biometrics, whose size is 328×356.

4.1 Estimation Accuracy

To compare conveniently, we use four discrete directions to represent a fingerprint orientation field as well. An example of orientation field estimation is shown in Fig.3. From the figure, we can clearly see that our algorithm can accurately estimate the orientation field in the delta region (see the red triangle) and the core region (see the red circle). Also, we numerically evaluate the orientation field estimation accuracy. Similar to Ji's work [9], the estimation accuracy is computed by S_0/S_1, where S_0 and S_1 denote the correct-direction block number and foreground block number, respectively. Based on such a rule, on *DB1_A*, *DB2_A*, *DB3_A*, *DB4_A* and Set 2, the average estimation accuracies by our algorithm are 98.71%, 97.45%, 99.08%, 98.52% and 97.69%, respectively, and the average estimation accuracies by Ji's algorithm are 98.02%, 94.88%, 98.21%, 97.19% and 95.37%, respectively. These statistical data demonstrate that our proposed algorithm achieves satisfying accuracy and has higher estimation accuracy than Ji's. This is because, on one hand, we take image quality into consideration and introduce the quality factor Q_f during the preprocessing step to obtain high-quality binary fingerprint images; on the other hand, we introduce the correction angle θ to overcome the effect of noise and deformations on fingerprint orientation field estimation.

4.2 Computational Complexity

Firstly, on *DB1_A*, *DB2_A*, *DB3_A*, *DB4_A* and Set 2, the average time expenses by our algorithm are 259ms, 154ms, 207ms, 173ms and 199ms, respectively. The

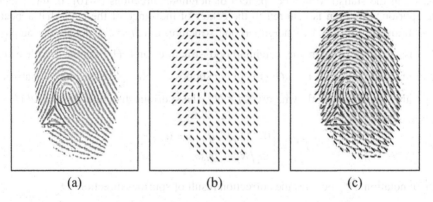

(a)   (b)   (c)

Fig. 3. Computation of orientation field: (a) original Set 2:264_01; (b) orientation field for (a); (c) overlapped image

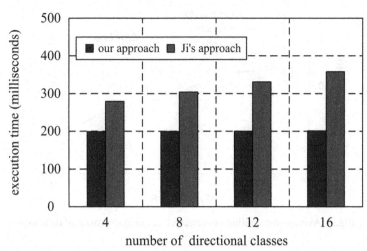

Fig. 4. Average execution time comparisons of our approach and Ji's approach on all fingerprint samples

maximal time expense is about 259ms, which is acceptable for an automatic fingerprint identification system (AFIS).

In addition, the proposed algorithm for fingerprint orientation field estimation is compared with the Ji's work [9] from the computational complexity. Given the two sets of fingerprint images, we change N_c to some extent and the comparison results of average processing times under various parameters are shown in Fig.4. The figure indicates that the average processing time of Ji's method increases monotonically as the predefined direction number increases, whereas, our average processing time remains almost constant. This indicates that our algorithm not only can represent more perfect orientation field, but also has high computational efficiency.

4.3 Recognition Performance Comparison

In this subsection, similar to Ji's work [9], we implement the fingerprint recognition system [11] using different orientation field estimation methods still on the two sets of fingerprint images. These methods include original orientation field estimation method [11], Ji's method [9] and ours. For the three systems (i.e. using original method, Ji's method and ours), only the orientation field estimation step is different and other steps are as the same. So, based on the recognition results for each system, the average results over all databases are shown in Fig.5.

By the receiver operating curves (ROCs), we can see that the proposed orientation field estimation method has better performance than the other two methods. Statistically compared with the original system [11], on *DB1_A*, the FRR can be reduced more than 5.0% on average by our method, and on *DB2_A*, *DB3_A*, *DB4_A* and Set 2, the average decreases caused by our method are about 8.6%, 4.3%, 4.1% and 7.0%,

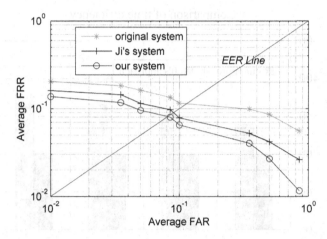

Fig. 5. Average recognition performance comparisons over all databases

respectively. Similarly, compared with the Ji's system [9], on *DB1_A*, *DB2_A*, *DB3_A*, *DB4_A* and Set 2, the average decreases caused by our method are about 1.3%, 2.1%, 1.6%, 1.5% and 2.4%, respectively. In addition, we can see that the performance improvements on relatively low-quality *DB2_A* and Set 2 are more than those on other relatively high-quality databases, i.e., *DB1_A*, *DB3_A* and *DB4_A*. This is because we have taken image quality into consideration, and introduced the quality factor Q_f during the preprocessing step. These performance comparisons further exhibit that our estimation method of orientation field is of great helpfulness to improve the performance of the fingerprint recognition system, even on low-quality fingerprint databases.

5   Conclusions

In this paper, a novel algorithm based on straight-line model of ridge is proposed for the orientation field estimation. The contribution of this paper mainly lies in three points:

1. We have built an orientation field estimation framework by combining the primary ridge and the secondary ridge.
2. The proposed top semi-neighbor search strategy greatly reduces the computational cost for determining the primary and secondary ridges. More importantly, different from previous works, the computation time of block direction estimation is almost invariant with respect to N_c.
3. To obtain high-quality binary fingerprint images, we introduce the quality factor Q_f during the preprocessing step. Furthermore, we introduce the correction angle θ to overcome the effect of noise and deformations on fingerprint orientation field estimation.

References

1. Zhou, J., Gu, J.W.: Modeling orientation fields of fingerprints with rational complex functions. Pattern Recogn. 37(2), 389–391 (2004)
2. O'Gorman, L., Nickerson, J.V.: An approach to fingerprint filter design. Pattern Recogn. 22(1), 362–385 (1987)
3. Ratha, N.K., Chen, S., Jain, A.K.: Adaptive flow orientation-based feature extraction in fingerprint images. Pattern Recogn. 28(11), 1657–1672 (1995)
4. Bazen, A.M., Gerez, S.H.: Systematic methods for the computation of the directional fields and singular points of fingerprints. IEEE Trans. Pattern Anal. Mach. Intell. 24(7), 905–919 (2002)
5. Zhou, J., Gu, J.: A model-based method for the computation of fingerprints' orientation field. IEEE Trans. Image Process. 13(6), 821–835 (2004)
6. Gu, J., Zhou, J., Zhang, D.: A combination model for orientation field of fingerprints. Pattern Recogn. 37(3), 543–553 (2004)
7. Li, J., Yau, W.Y., Wang, H.: Constrained nonlinear models of fingerprint orientations with prediction. Pattern Recogn. 39(1), 102–114 (2006)
8. Nagaty, K.A.: On learning to estimate the block directional image of a fingerprint using a hierarchical neural network. Neural Networks 16(1), 133–144 (2003)
9. Ji, L.P., Yi, Z.: Fingerprint orientation field estimation using ridge projection. Pattern Recogn. 41(5), 1491–1503 (2008)
10. Nagaty, K.A.: Fingerprints classification using artificial neural networks: a combined structural and statistical approach. Neural Networks 14(9), 1293–1305 (2001)
11. Jain, A., Hong, L., Bolle, R.: On-line fingerprint verification. IEEE Trans. Pattern Anal. Mach. Intell. 19(4), 302–313 (1997)

Gait Recognition Using Procrustes Shape Analysis and Shape Context

Yuanyuan Zhang[1], Niqing Yang[1], Wei Li[1], Xiaojuan Wu[1,*], and Qiuqi Ruan[2]

[1] School of Information Science and Engineering, Shandong University,
27 Shanda Nanlu, 250100 Jinan, China
zhangyy1984@gmail.com, ynqing@sdu.edu.cn, liwei1266@gmail.com,
xiaojwu@sdu.edu.cn
[2] Institute of Information Science, Beijing Jiaotong University,
No.3 Shangyuan Residence Haidian District, 100044 Beijing, China
qqruan@center.njtu.edu.cn

Abstract. This paper proposes a novel algorithm for individual recognition by gait. The method of *Procrustes* shape analysis is used to produce *Procrustes* Mean Shape (PMS) as a compressed representation of gait sequence. PMS is adopted as the gait signature in this paper. Instead of using the *Procrustes* mean shape distance as a similarity measure, we introduce shape context descriptor to measure the similarity between two PMSs. Shape context describes a distribution of all boundary points on a shape with respect to any single boundary point by a histogram of log-polar plot, and offers us a global discriminative characterization of the shape. Standard pattern recognition techniques are used to classify different patterns. The experiments on CASIA Gait Database demonstrate that the proposed method outperforms other algorithms in both classification performance and verification performance.

Keywords: Gait recognition, *Procrustes* shape analysis, shape context descriptor, *Procrustes* Mean Shape (PMS).

1 Introduction

Among various biometrics like face, iris and fingerprint, gait is a more attractive biometric feature for human identification. Gait signals can be detected from a long distance and measured at low resolution. Therefore, gait can be used in such situations that face or iris information is not available in high enough resolution for recognition. From the perspective of surveillance, gait is a particularly attractive modality. Recently, the study of gait recognition, which concerns recognizing individuals by the way they walk, has received an increasing interest from researchers in the computer vision community.

Many contributions have been made to this rapidly developing domain. Gait recognition techniques mainly fall into two categories namely model-based and model-free approaches. The model-based approaches usually model the human

---

* Corresponding author.

H. Zha, R.-i. Taniguchi, and S. Maybank (Eds.): ACCV 2009, Part III, LNCS 5996, pp. 256–265, 2010.
© Springer-Verlag Berlin Heidelberg 2010

body structure and extract image features to map them into the structural components of models or to derive motion trajectories of body parts. Bhanu and Han [1] proposed a kinematic-based method to identify individuals. It estimates 3D human walking parameters by performing a least square fit of the 3D kinematic model to the 2D silhouette images. A genetic algorithm is then used for feature selection. The advantage of model-based approaches is that models can handle occlusion and noise better and offer the ability to derive gait features directly from model parameters. They also help to reduce the dimensionality needed to represent the data. However, they suffer from high computational costs. The majority of current approaches are model-free. They typically analyze the image sequence by motion or shape and characterize the whole motion pattern of the human body by a compact representation regardless of the underlying structure. Based on body shape and gait, Lee et al. [2] described a moment-based representation of gait appearance for the purpose of person identification. Sarkar et al. [3] proposed a baseline algorithm for human identification using spatiotemporal correlation of silhouette images. Han and Bhanu [4] proposed a spatiotemporal gait representation called Gait Energy Image to characterize human walking properties. Wang et al. [5] employed a compressed representation of gait sequences and obtained encouraging classification performance.

Inspired by Wang [5]'s work, we made further exploration to it in this paper. We use *Procrustes* shape analysis to produce *Procrustes* Mean Shape (PMS) of each gait sequence in the database. Quite different and novel, instead of using the *Procrustes* Mean Shape Distance (MSD) as Wang did, we introduce Shape Context (SC) descriptor [6] to measure the similarity of two PMSs. The experiments on *dataset-A* and *dataset-B* in CASIA Gait Database [7] show that SC is an efficient and powerful shape descriptor for similarity measure. We gain favorable performance after combing PMS and SC.

2 Related Work

Intuitively, recognizing people through gait depends greatly on how the silhouette shape of an individual changes over time. Shape is an important cue as it captures a prominent element of an object. Therefore, gait may be considered to be composed of a set of static poses and their temporal variations can be analyzed to obtain distinguishable signatures. Based upon the above consideration, Wang et al. [5] depicted the human shape using the method of *Procrustes* shape analysis. Pose changes of segmented silhouettes over time are represented as an associated sequence of complex configurations in a two-dimensional (2D) shape space and are further analyzed by the *Procrustes* shape analysis method to obtain an eigenshape as gait signature.

In the field of shape matching and shape similarity measuring, several shape descriptors have been proposed, ranging from moments and Fourier descriptors to Hausdorff distance and the medial axis transform. For a detailed discussion of shape matching techniques, the reader is referred to paper [8]. Belongie and Malik [6] firstly introduced the idea of shape context descriptor. Shape context describe a distribution of the remaining boundary points with respect to one point on the boundary. Histogram of a log-polar plot of the shape boundary gives the shape context for that particular boundary point, thus offering a globally discriminative characterization. Their work showed remarkable results involving character recognition using gimpy images. It also had an extensive testing for silhouette images from trademarks, handwritten digits and the COIL dataset.

3   *Procrustes* Shape Analysis

Procrustes shape analysis [9] is a popular method in directional statistics. It is intended for coping with 2D shapes and provides a good method to find mean shapes. To reduce redundant information, the shape boundary can be easily obtained and stored using a border following algorithm based on connectivity. As we can see in Fig. 1, (x_i, y_i) is a random pixel on the boundary. Let the centroid (x_c, y_c) of the shape be the origin of the 2D shape space. The two axes Re and Im represent the real and imaginary part of a complex number, respectively.

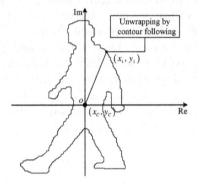

Fig. 1. Illustration of computing PMS

As shown in Fig. 1, we can then unwrap each shape anticlockwise into a set of boundary pixel points sampled along its outer-contour in a common complex coordinate system. Each shape can be described as a vector of ordered complex numbers with M elements, $u = [u_1, u_2, \ldots, u_M]^T$, $u_i = (x_i - x_c) + j \times (y_i - y_c)$. Therefore, each gait sequence will be accordingly converted into an associated sequence of such 2D shape configurations. Given a set of m shapes, we can find their mean shape $\hat{u}$ by computing the following matrix:

$$S_u = \sum_{i=1}^{m} \frac{u_i u_i^*}{u_i^* u_i}, \tag{1}$$

where, the superscript $*$ represents the complex conjugation transposition. $\hat{u}$ is the so-called *Procrustes* Mean Shape (PMS) which is the dominant eigenvector

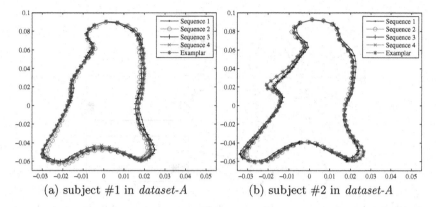

(a) subject #1 in *dataset-A*   (b) subject #2 in *dataset-A*

Fig. 2. Two examples of the PMS in *dataset-A*. Note that the sample points in the PMS depicted here are re-sampled to a visible level for reading convenience.

of S_u, i.e., the eigenvector that corresponds to the greatest eigenvalue of S_u. Two examples of PMSs are shown in Fig. 2.

To compare two different PMSs, the *Procrustes* Mean Shape Distance (MSD) was used by Wang [5] to measure the similarity between them. Instead of using the MSD, this paper treats the similarity measure totally in a different way as described below.

4   Shape Context

The concept of shape context was originally introduced to measure similarities between shapes and recognize objects. Similar to PMS, a shape is represented by a discrete set of N points, $P = \{p_1, p_2, \ldots, p_N\}$, sampled from the internal or external contours on the object. Assuming contours are piecewise smooth, we can obtain as good an approximation to the underlying continuous shapes as desired by picking N to be sufficiently large. Note that, the point number N here can be either equal to the number M in PMS or not.

Consider the set of vectors originating from a random point p_i to all other points on the shape. These vectors actually express the configuration of the entire shape relative to the reference point. For the point p_i, we compute a coarse histogram h_i relative to the coordinates of the remaining $N - 1$ points,

$$h_i(k) = \#\{q \neq p_i : (q - p_i) \in bin(k)\}, \tag{2}$$

where, the symbol $\#$ represents number counting, and the histogram is defined to be the shape context (SC) of p_i. This formula means counting the number of boundary points within each sector or bin to form the SC. We use bins that are uniform in log-polar space, making the descriptor more sensitive to positions of nearby sample points than to those points farther away. Fig. 3 shows the process of generating the SC. As can be seen in Fig. 3, the SCs of two neighboring points,

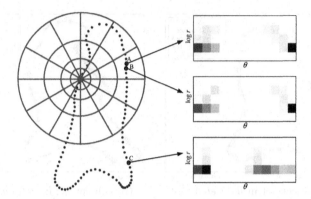

Fig. 3. Illustration of computing SCs for a PMS. The circles and lines attached on the PMS are the diagram of log-polar histogram bins used in computing the SCs. We use 5 bins for log-radius and 12 bins for θ. Examples of SCs for three points A, B, and C are shown in the right column (Dark = large value).

A and B, are more similar than the SC of point C which is far away. This is because A and B have similar structures relative to the whole shape.

Consider a point p_i on the first shape and a point q_j on the second shape. Let C_{ij} denotes the cost of matching these two points. As SCs are distributions represented as histograms, it is natural to use the χ^2 test statistic:

$$C_{ij} = C(p_i, q_j) = \frac{1}{2} \sum_{k=1}^{K} \frac{[h_i(k) - h_j(k)]^2}{[h_i(k) + h_j(k)]}, \tag{3}$$

where $h_i(k)$ and $h_j(k)$ denote the K-bin normalized histogram at p_i and q_j, respectively. Given the cost matrix with elements C_{ij} between all pairs of points p_i on the first shape and q_j on the second shape, we want to minimize the total cost of matching,

$$H(\pi) = \sum_i C(p_i, q_{\pi(i)}). \tag{4}$$

Obviously, $\pi(\cdot)$ is a permutation of p_i and q_j. This is an instance of the square assignment problem, which can be solved in $O(N^3)$ time using the Hungarian method [10]. However, we can use the more efficient algorithm of [11] to reduce the computational cost. The input to the assignment problem is a square cost matrix, and the result is a permutation $\pi(\cdot)$ so that $\sum_i C_{i,\pi(i)}$ is minimized.

We measure the SC distance between two shapes, P and Q, as the symmetric average of the matching costs over best matching pairs, i.e.

$$D(P,Q) = \min(\frac{1}{N_p} \sum_{p \in P} arg \min C(p, \pi(p)), \frac{1}{N_q} \sum_{q \in Q} arg \min C(q, \pi(q))), \tag{5}$$

where, N_p and N_q are point numbers on each shape, respectively. Given such a dissimilarity measure, we can use different classification techniques to recognize objects.

5   Gait Recognition Using PMS and SC

In the scheme of our work, we first use *Procrustes* shape analysis to find the PMS of each gait sequence as gait signature for recognition. Then SC is adopted as a similarity measure between one PMS and the others to provide evidences for classification. The block diagram in Fig. 4 summarizes the major steps in a gait recognition system combining PMS and SC.

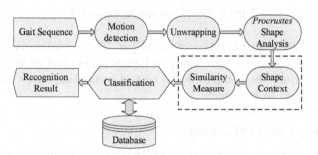

Fig. 4. The diagram of gait recognition algorithm using PMS and SC

In Fig. 4, the two steps in the dotted rectangle are the major differences to Wang's [5] work, and they are also the originality of our work.

Gait recognition is a traditional pattern classification problem which can be solved by measuring similarities or dissimilarities among gait sequences. We try three different simple classification methods, namely the nearest neighbor classifier (NN), the k-nearest-neighbor classifier (kNN, $k=3$), and the nearest neighbor classifier with class exemplar (ENN).

6   Experimental Results

6.1   Gait Data

Here, we use *dataset-A* and *dataset-B* in CASIA Gait Database [7] to verify the effectiveness of the proposed algorithm. *Dataset-A* (used to be NLPR database) is quite familiar to researchers in gait recognition. It has 80 sequences belonging to 20 pedestrians at three different viewing angles. We use the sequences with a lateral viewing angle here. *Dataset-B* is a more large-scale and relatively fresh database, and it has 124 different pedestrians (94 males, 30 females). All the subjects were asked to walk naturally on the concrete ground along a straight line in an indoor environment. Each subject walked along the straight line 10 times (6 for normal walking, 2 for walking with a bag, and 2 for walking with a coat). Some examples of this dataset are shown in Fig. 5. Here, we only use 6 times' normal walk at lateral view that is 744 sequences.

We assume that all silhouettes have been extracted from original human walking sequences. Edge detection and segmentation are then used to the image to

(a) normal walking   (b) walking with a bag   (c) walking with a coat

Fig. 5. Sample images in *dataset-B*

obtain a clear silhouette boundary of the object. The boundary points are sampled to M points. In our experiments, M equals to 360 just as Wang [5] did in his work. To reduce the computational cost of computing shape context, each PMS is re-sampled to 100 points.

6.2   Classification Performance

We use the *leave-one-out* cross-validation rule to obtain the unbiased estimate of the Correct Classification Rate (CCR). Each time we leave one sequence out as a probe sample and train on the remainder. The CCRs of the original PMS method [5] and the proposed method on both datasets are reported in Table 1. From this table we can see the superiority of our method compared with the original PMS using MSD.

Table 1. The classification performance comparison on two datasets

Methods	A-NN	A-kNN	A-ENN	B-NN	B-kNN	B-ENN
Original PMS [5]	71.25%	72.50%	88.75%	88.98%	86.69%	91.13%
PMS + SC	88.75%	81.25%	98.75%	94.49%	93.15%	97.18%

Another useful classification performance measure is the rank order statistic, which was first introduced by the FERET protocol for the evaluation of face recognition algorithms [12]. It is defined as the cumulative match scores (CMS) that the real class of a test measurement is among its top k matches. The CMS curves on two datasets are shown in Fig. 6. It is noted that the CCR is equivalent to the score when $rank = 1$.

6.3   Verification Performance

We also estimate False Acceptance Rate (FAR) and False Reject Rate (FRR) via the *leave-one-out* rule in terms of verification performance. Equal Error Rate (EER) demonstrates the degree of balance between FAR and FRR numerically. The smaller the values of ERRs the better is the performance. The EERs of original PMS using MSD and the proposed method on two datasets are reported in Table 2.

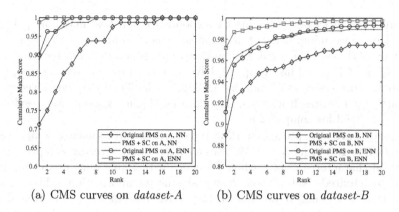

(a) CMS curves on *dataset-A*   (b) CMS curves on *dataset-B*

Fig. 6. CMS comparison on two datasets

Table 2. The verification performance comparison on two datasets

Methods	*A*-EER	*B*-EER
Original PMS [5]	0.1994	0.1282
PMS + SC	0.1324	0.1081

Table 3. Comparison of recent algorithms on *dataset-A*

Methods	Top1	Top5	Top10
BenAbdelkader [13]	82.50%	93.75%	100.0%
Lee [2]	87.50%	98.75%	100.0%
Wang [5]	88.75%	96.25%	100.0%
Chen [14]	91.25%	96.25%	100.0%
Our method	98.75%	100.0%	100.0%

6.4 Comparisons

We also compare the performance of the proposed algorithm with other famous algorithms using the same silhouette data from the *dataset-A* with a lateral viewing angle. Based on the FERET protocol with rank of 1, 5, and 10, the best results of the algorithms are reported in Table 3, from which we can see that our method compares favorably with others.

7 Discussion

Plenty of experimental results have shown that SC is a rich and powerful shape descriptor for shape matching and object recognition. One may wonder why not directly use SC to represent the contour that the pedestrians generate while walking and obtain similarity measure between one pedestrian and another. That is because the processes of finding correspondence and best matching pairs are highly time consuming. It is not an applicable method for a practicable system, especially in the domain of gait recognition which generally needs batch processing. Anyway, Chen and his group [14] have once tried to represent gait sequence by four key stances chosen from one walking cycle. Then they employed SC to generate gait features from those key stances. Their experimental results are listed in Table 3 for comparison.

As many work have proved [5], PMS is a excellent way to make a compact representation to gait sequences. PMS uses a single complex vector to represent the structural characteristics of a whole sequence with frame number varying from dozens to hundreds, yet without losing any useful information. This compact characterization makes it possible to take advantage of the descriptive ability of SC just as we did in this paper. On the other hand, SC is a rich and powerful shape descriptor and offers us a global discriminative features. Moreover, SC leads to a robust score for measuring shape similarity to distinguish different objects. By taking advantage of the active points of those two methods, we obtain favorable performance relative to the existing algorithms.

8   Conclusion

In this paper, a novel gait recognition algorithm is exhibited by combining two kinds of shape descriptors, *Procrustes* shape analysis and shape context descriptor. We take advantage of the compressed representation characteristic of *Procrustes* shape analysis to represent the continuously pose changing of pedestrian gait sequences. The mean shape of a set of complex vectors is adopted as gait signature for recognition. The shape context, which is a rich and effective shape descriptor, is employed to describe PMSs and to offer a similarity measure of different shapes instead of using MSD. The computational cost of the matching process is largely decreased, and the discriminating power of the PMS is also re-exploited to an encouraging level. Experiments on both small size and large scale datasets have demonstrated the effectiveness and superiority of the proposed algorithm.

Acknowledgments. This work is supported by the National Natural Science Foundation of China under grant NO.60675024. Many thanks to *Tingting Guo* from School of Foreign Languages and Literature, Shandong University for linguistic advice. Portions of the research in this paper use the CASIA Gait Database collected by Institute of Automation, Chinese Academy of Sciences.

References

1. Bhanu, B., Han, J.: Individual Recognition by Kinematic-based Gait Analysis. In: 16th International Conference on Pattern Recognition, pp. 343–346. IEEE Computer Society, Quebec (2002)

2. Lee, L., Grimson, W.E.L.: Gait Analysis for Recognition and Classification. In: International Conference on Automatic Face and Gesture Recognition, pp. 148–155. IEEE Computer Society, Washington (2002)
3. Sarkar, S., Phillips, P.J., Liu, Z., Vega, I.R., Grother, P., Bowyer, K.W.: The HumanID Gait Challenge Problem: Data Sets, Performance, and Analysis. IEEE Trans. Pattern Anal. Mach. Intell. 27, 162–177 (2005)
4. Han, J., Bhanu, B.: Individual Recognition Using Gait Energy Image. IEEE Trans. Pattern Anal. Mach. Intell. 28, 316–322 (2006)
5. Wang, L., Tan, T., Hu, W., Ning, H.: Automatic Gait Recognition Based on Statistical Shape Analysis. IEEE Trans. Image Process. 12, 1120–1131 (2003)
6. Belongie, S., Malik, J., Puzicha, J.: Shape matching and object recognition using shape contexts. IEEE Trans. Pattern Anal. Mach. Intell. 24, 509–522 (2002)
7. CASIA Gait Database, http://www.sinobiometrics.com
8. Veltkamp, R.C., Latecki, L.J.: Properties and Performance of Shape Similarity Measures. In: IFCS 2006 Conference: Data Science and Classification, pp. 47–56. Springer, Berlin (2006)
9. Kent, J.T.: New Directions in Shape Analysis. Art of Statistical Science: A Tribute to G. S. Watson, pp. 115–127. Wiley, New York (1992)
10. Papadimitriou, C.H., Steiglitz, K.: Combinatorial optimization: algorithms and complexity. Prentice-Hall, Englewood Cliffs (1982)
11. Jonker, J., Volgenant, A.: A Shortest Augmenting Path Algorithm for Dense and Sparse Linear Assignment Problems. Computing 38, 325–440 (1987)
12. Phillips, P.J., Moon, H., Rizvi, S.A., Rauss, P.J.: The FERET Evaluation Methodology for Face Recognition Algorithms. IEEE Trans. Pattern Anal. Mach. Intell. 22, 1090–1104 (2000)
13. BenAbdelkader, C., Cutler, R., Davis, L.: Motion-based recognition of people in EigenGait space. In: IEEE International Conference on Automatic Face and Gesture Recognition, pp. 267–272. IEEE Computer Society, Washington (2002)
14. Chen, S., Ma, T., Huang, W., Gao, Y.: Gait Recognition Based on Shape Context Descriptor (in Chinese). Chinese journal of Pattern Recognition and Artificial Intelligence 20, 794–799 (2007)

Person De-identification in Videos

Prachi Agrawal and P.J. Narayanan

Center for Visual Information Technology,
IIIT - Hyderabad, India
prachi@research.iiit.ac.in, pjn@iiit.ac.in

Abstract. Advances in cameras and web technology have made it easy to capture and share large amounts of video data over to a large number of people through services like Google Street View, EveryScape, etc. A large number of cameras oversee public and semi-public spaces today. These raise concerns on the unintentional and unwarranted invasion of the privacy of individuals caught in the videos. To address these concerns, automated methods to *de-identify* individuals in these videos are necessary. De-identification does not aim at destroying all information involving the individuals. Its goals are to obscure the identity of the actor without obscuring the action. This paper outlines the scenarios in which de-identification is required and the issues brought out by those. We also present a preliminary approach to de-identify individuals from videos. A bounding box around each individual present in a video is tracked through the video. An outline of the individuals is approximated by carrying out segmentation on a 3-D Graph of space-time voxels. We explore two de-identification transformations: exponential space-time blur and line integral convolution. We show results on a number of public videos and videos collected in a plausible setting. We also present the preliminary results of a user-study to validate the effectiveness of the de-identification schemes.

1   Introduction

Advances in cameras and web technology have made it easy to capture and share large amounts of video data over the internet. This has raised concerns regarding the privacy of individuals. For example, when photographs of a monument are taken to create a panoramic view of the scene, people present are not aware of it and their consent is not taken before making them public. Technologies like Google Street View, EveryScape, etc., have a high chance of invading into one's private life without meaning to do so. Parents have also expressed concern on the possible compromise of the security of their children. The recent furore over Street View in Japan and the UK underscores the need to address the privacy issue directly. An increasing number of video cameras observe public spaces like airports, train stations, shops, and streets. While there may be a possible security need to see the individuals in them, identifying the action suffices in most cases. The actor need be identified only rarely and only to authorized personnel.

There is, thus, a need to *de-identify* individuals from such videos. De-identification aims to remove all identification information of the person from an image or video, while maintaining as much information on the action and its context. Recognition and de-identification are opposites with the former making use of all possible features to

H. Zha, R.-i. Taniguchi, and S. Maybank (Eds.): ACCV 2009, Part III, LNCS 5996, pp. 266–276, 2010.
© Springer-Verlag Berlin Heidelberg 2010

identify an object while the latter trying to obfuscate the features to thwart recognition. De-identification should be resistant to recognition by humans and algorithms. Identifying information captured on video can include face, silhouette, posture, gait, etc. Three types of videos need de-identification to not compromise the privacy of individuals. *Casual videos* that are captured for other purposes and get shared. Examples include images used by projects like Google StreetView, the net-cameras fitted in public spaces that can be viewed over the internet, videos or photos on sharing sites, etc. Individuals appear in these videos purely unintentionally and there is no need to know their identities. All individuals should therefore be de-identified irrevocably and early, perhaps at the camera itself. *Public surveillance videos* come from cameras watching spaces such as airports, streets, stores, etc. There is no intention to capture any specific set of persons, but there is an explicit intention to capture people occupying the space. These videos may be viewed at a monitoring station to look for anomalies but also to judge how users react to situations or products. These may be displayed on public monitors and a recorded version may be accessible to many people. The types of actions performed by individuals in these videos may be important, but not their identities. Hence de-identification is necessary. *Private surveillance videos* come from cameras placed at the entrances of semi-private spaces like offices. Individuals entering them have a purpose and access is often limited to authorized persons only. The videos may be of higher quality and are likely to have a more detailed view of the individuals. De-identification may not be essential, but could be recommended to take care of potential viewing by non-authorized people.

The privacy issues are genuine and will grow with wider adaptation of technology. Automated methods to de-identify individuals without affecting the context of the action in the video are needed to address them. It may be necessary to control the level of de-identification to cater to different situations. Some work directed towards face de-identification has been reported before. In this paper, we discuss the different issues relating to de-identification of individuals in videos. We strive to guard against algorithmic and manual identification using face, silhouette, gait, and other aspects. We also present the design of a de-identification scheme and present results on several standard and relevant videos. We also present preliminary results from a user study conducted to gauge the effectiveness of the strategy.

2   De-identification: General Framework

De-identification involves the detection and a transformation of images of individuals to make them unrecognizable. It is easy to hide the identity of individuals by replacing a conservative area around them by, say, black pixels. However, this hides most information on what sort of human activity is going on in that space, which may be important for various studies. The goal is to protect the privacy of the individuals while providing sufficient feel for the human activities in the space being imaged. There is a natural trade-off between protecting privacy and providing sufficient detail. Privacy protection provided should be immune to recognition using computer vision as well as using human vision.

2.1 Criteria for De-identification

The characteristics or features used to recognize humans in videos is the focus of a de-identification transformation, such as the following.

1. Face plays the dominant role in automatic and manual identification. Thus, the de-identification transformation should pay more attention to detect and obfuscate faces in the video more than other aspects.
2. The body silhouette or the gait are important clues available in videos which need to be obfuscated. Humans exploit them effectively and algorithmic identification using them have been developed with some success [1,2]. The silhouette can be dilated or expanded to remove its information content. Gait relates to the temporal variation of a person's arms and silhouette. Masking it needs the temporal silhouettes to be changed in a non-predictable way.
3. Other information about individuals may be critical to specific aspects of privacy, such as the race and gender. Both are hard to mask completely. Though race may relate closely to skin colour and can be masked by RGB or hue-space transformations, these destroy the naturalness of the videos in our experience. Gender is more subtle and no clearly defined manifestation has been agreed on, which makes obfuscation of gender hard.

2.2 Subverting De-identification

We now discuss ways by which the de-identification can be subverted or "attacked" to reveal the identity of individuals involved. The de-identification process has to be satisfactorily robust to these methods.

1. Reversing the transformation used for de-identification is the most obvious line of attack. The transformation should, thus, be irreversible. Blurring using convolution is susceptible to reversal by deconvolution. Frames of the de-identified video may be treated as multiple low-resolution observations when a form of blurring is used. Techniques similar to those used in super-resolution may facilitate the reversal of the blurring partially or completely. We use a blurring involving several neighbouring blocks in space and time to prevent reversal.
2. Recognizing persons from face, silhouette, gait, etc., is being pursued actively in Computer Vision. The problem may be set as a series of verification problems, given a list of people. The de-identification transformation has to be robust to the common computer vision algorithms.
3. Manual identification is another way to subvert de-identification, though it is considerably more expensive. It is not clearly known what properties humans use to identify and recognize individuals. However, general blurring and colour manipulation makes recognition highly unlikely even by humans. User study is an effective way to judge the effectiveness of the de-identification approach and to compare between multiple approaches.
4. Brute-force verification is a way to attack a de-identified video. Such attacks are possible if some knowledge of the de-identification algorithm and its parameters

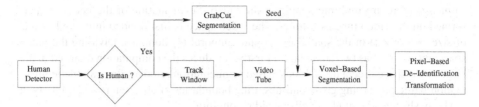

Fig. 1. Overview of the method

are available. Different combinations of algorithms and their parameters can be applied on target individuals, with comparison performed in the de-identified space. A match in the transformed space can strongly indicate a match in the original space. This way of attack cannot be prevented easily; they can only be made arbitrarily hard by the underlying combinatorics.

It should be noted that only transformations that ignore the input video can theoretically be totally safe. Brute-force attack is possible on others. Such a transformation will replace individuals in the video with a constant (say, black or white) or random colour. We rule out such methods as they destroy all information on the action performed.

3   De-identification: Proposed Approach

An overview of our method is outlined in Figure 1. The system comprises of three modules: Detect and Track, Segmentation, and De-identification.

3.1   Detect and Track

The first step is to detect the presence of a person in the scene. HOG [3] based human detector gives good results with a low miss rate. Other human detectors [4] can also be employed. To track the person in the subsequent frames, a motion compensation based segmentation is useful, which assumes that the foreground objects are small compared to the background. Hence, the dominant motion in each frame is due to the camera. Motion vectors for each pixel can be calculated using optical flow. The dominant motion is the average of motion vectors of all pixels in a frame. The foreground pixels vary significantly from the average motion.

We study the effectiveness of the de-identification process in this paper. We, therefore, concentrate on the de-identification step that follows human detection. Standard databases such as CAVIAR have the necessary ground truth information to study de-identification alone. We created such ground truth on the additional videos we used for experiments.

3.2   Segmentation

The bounding boxes of the human in every frame, provided by the ground truth, are stacked across time to generate a *video tube* of the person. Multiple video tubes are formed if there are multiple people in the video. Segmentation of the person is performed on the video tube as follows. The video space is first divided into fixed voxels of size $(x \times y \times t)$ in the spatial (x, y) and temporal (t) domains. Dividing the video space into voxels has two advantages. Firstly, it reduces the computation required in the large video space. Secondly, a block-based segmentation removes fine silhouette information while preserving gross outlines. Fine boundaries of a person reveal a lot about the body shape and gait [1,2] and can aid recognition.

Segmentation is a labeling where each voxel v is assigned a label $\alpha_v \in \{0,1\}$, where 1 is for foreground and 0 for background. For segmentation, the video tube is divided into blocks of B voxel-planes in time. One voxel-plane overlap is used between consecutive blocks to enforce continuity across the blocks. A 3D graph is constructed on these blocks in the voxel space and a mincut is performed on this graph. A rigid but blocky (because of voxelation) outline of the human is extracted by this. The energy term E associated with this graph is of the form

$$E(\underline{\alpha}, \underline{\theta}, \underline{v}) = U(\underline{\alpha}, \underline{\theta}, \underline{v}) + \lambda_1 V_1(\underline{v}) + \lambda_2 V_2(\underline{v}), \tag{1}$$

where U is the data term and V_1, V_2 are the smoothness terms corresponding to the intra-frame and inter-frame connections between two voxels respectively. $\underline{\theta} = \{\theta^0, \theta^1\}$ are two full-covariance Gaussian colour mixtures, one each for foreground and background, with K clusters each. Hence, $k \in [1, K]$, $\alpha = \{0, 1\}$ and $\theta^\alpha = \{w_k^\alpha, \mu_k^\alpha, \Sigma_k^\alpha\}$. We used $K = 6$ for the results presented here. The Gaussian Mixture Models (GMMs) are used for adequately modeling data points in the colour space.

The energy E is defined in such a way that a minimization of this energy provides us with a segmentation that is coherent across time and space. A mincut on the graph minimizes this energy function efficiently [5]. Initialization of foreground and background seeds is done by performing GrabCut [6] on the first frame with the human. The foreground and background GMMs are also initialized in this process. These GMMs later provide seeds to the graph, as well as help in defining the energy terms.

The data term U is similar to the one used by GrabCut [6], defined as $U(\underline{\alpha}, \underline{\theta}, \underline{v}) = \sum_n D(\alpha_n, \theta_k, v_n)$ where n is the number of voxels and

$$D(\alpha_n, \theta_k, v_n) = \min_{k=1 \cdots K} [-\log w_k^{\alpha_n} + \frac{1}{2} \log \det \Sigma_k^{\alpha_n} + \frac{1}{2} \bar{v}_n^T \Sigma_k^{\alpha_n -1} \bar{v}_n] \tag{2}$$

where $\bar{v}_n = v_n - \mu_k^{\alpha_n}$. The representative colour v_n for a voxel should be chosen carefully. We first compute the distance D_0 and D_1 to the background and foreground respectively for each pixel in a voxel, using pixel colour instead of v_n in Equation (2). The pixels are sorted on the ratio $\frac{D_0}{D_1}$ in the decreasing order. We choose the colour of mth pixel after sorting as the representative colour v_n. The value of m is kept low so that voxels with even a few foreground pixels are biased towards the foreground. This is important for de-identification as the foreground needs to be segmented conservatively. We also identify seed voxels for the graphcut segmentation based on D_0 and D_1. If the distance to foreground, D_1, is very low for the mth pixel, the voxel is a seed foreground. However, if the distance to background, D_0, is very low for the $(N - m)^{th}$ pixel (where N is the number of pixels in the voxel), the voxel is a seed background.

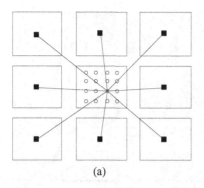 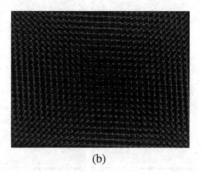

(a)   (b)

Fig. 2. (a) Distances for pixel $(3, 3)$ of a voxel from each neighbouring voxel. The distances to the neighbouring voxels in the adjacent voxel plane are calculated in a similar manner. (b) Saddle shaped vector field used for LIC.

The smoothness terms V_1 and V_2 are defined as $V(\underline{v}) = \sum_{v_p, v_q \in \underline{v}} \delta_{pq} \cdot V_{pq}$, where δ_{pq} is 1 when v_p and v_q are neighbours and 0 otherwise, and $V_{pq} = \exp^{-\beta \|v_p - v_q\|^2}$, where v_p is the mean colour of a voxel. β is the expected value calculated as $\beta = (2\mathcal{E}(\|v_p - v_q\|^2))^{-1}$, where $\mathcal{E}$ is the expectation operator [6].

3.3 De-identification

After the segmentation of the person, the next step is to apply the de-identification transformation on the human being present. Two de-identification approaches were explored. One of them is an exponential blur of pixels in a voxel.

In exponential blur, the output colour for each pixel in a foreground voxel is a weighted combination of its neighbouring voxels' average colours. All voxels within distance a participate in the computation of this colour. The weight corresponding to each voxel decreases exponentially with the distance from the voxel center to the pixel. The weights for the $(l, m, n)^{th}$ pixel of voxel v_i can be calculated $\forall v_p \in \Gamma_i$ as:

$$\gamma(l, m, n) = e^{-\frac{d^2_{(l,m,n),v_p}}{8a^2}}, \tag{3}$$

where Γ_i is the set of voxels which lie within distance a from v_i, and $d_{(l,m,n),v_p}$ is the distance of the $(l, m, n)^{th}$ pixel from the voxel center v_p. Figure 2(a) shows the distances $d_{(l,m,n)}$ in one voxel plane for the pixel $(3, 3)$. This simple blurring function ensures that there is no abrupt change in colour at the voxel boundaries. The temporal blurring of the space-time boundaries aims to remove the gait information of the individual. The amount of de-identification is controlled by varying the parameter a; more the value of a, more is the de-identification.

The second de-identification transformation is based on line integral convolution (LIC). LIC is generally used for imaging vector fields [7] on a texture. We use LIC to distort the boundaries of the person. Different vector fields can be used for achieving different effects. The gradient vector field of the texture image rotated by $90°$ gives a

Fig. 3. Results of LIC-10, Blur-4, and Blur-4 followed by an intensity space compression on three different videos, with clear frames in odd rows and de-identified frames in even rows

painterly effect to the image. We used a saddle shaped vector field (Figure 2(b)) for our experiments. LIC is applied to the foreground pixels obtained after segmentation. The amount of de-identification acquired can be controlled by the line length L, of the convolution filter.

Intensity space compression was additionally tried. The intensity values of the foreground pixels are compressed after an exponential blur or LIC. The result is boosted up by a fixed value after the compression. It provides greater de-identification, but the video loses more information. This simple technique hides the race of a person successfully. The results are presented in Figures 3 and 4.

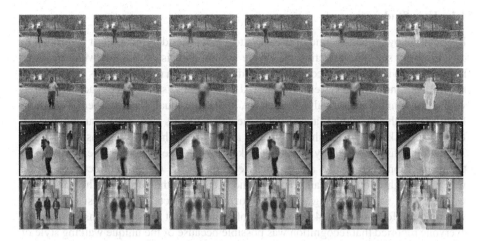

Fig. 4. The first column shows the clear frame. The next five columns show the output of Blur-2, Blur-4, LIC-10, LIC-20, and Blur-2 followed by an intensity space compression, in that order

4   Experimental Results

We implemented the above system and conducted the experiments on standard datasets like CAVIAR, BEHAVE, etc., and on our own that provide more clearly visible individuals in videos. Some of the results are shown in Figures 3 and 4. Different parameters were tried for each of the de-identification transformations; $a = 2$ and 4 for exponential blur and $L = 10$ and 20 for LIC. We divide the video into $N = 4 \times 4 \times 2$ sized voxels. m was kept as 3 (10% of N) for our experiments. Increasing the voxel size across time domain increases the blockiness across the frames. If a person is moving fast enough, it can introduce jumps in the segmented output around the boundary. More results can be seen in the video submitted as supplemental material.

   Figure 4 shows the output of different de-identification transformations on a single frame from different videos. The effect of changing the parameters of the transformations can be seen clearly. Increasing the value of a and L increases the de-identification achieved, but it results in more loss of information in a scene. In general, LIC-10 and Blur-2 are insufficient in masking the identity of people. Blur-4 and LIC-20 perform better. Body structure plays a huge role in identifying people when their faces are obfuscated beyond recognition. LIC distorts the outline of a person based on the vector field used because LIC tries to image the vector field using the person's image as a texture. However the output of LIC-20 sometimes looks unnatural and ghost-like. The intensity space compression, as shown in Figures 3 and 4, can claim to remove the race information. But it preserves the body structure of the person. This happens because the intensity values of the foreground pixels are boosted up and hence rendered visibly different from the background pixels. This trade-off can be avoided by dilating or eroding the foreground mask before applying the intensity space compression.

4.1 User Study

Recognition by humans is one of the ways to subvert de-identification. It is difficult to quantitatively state the effectiveness of the system as it is not known which features humans use to identify and recognize individuals. Hence, a user study was conducted to test the usefulness of the system. We showed 4 different sets of 6 videos each, processed with a different parameter value in each set, to 40 individuals. Half of them were quite familiar with the individuals appearing in the video. Others were only casually familiar. Users were asked to match the individuals appearing in the video against a palette of 30 photographs shown. They were also asked to state the factor that helped them in the recognition. The results are summarized in Table 1. Overall correct recognition was fairly high due to the familiarity of the users with the subjects. The gait or the walking style was also a big give-away for many subjects. The highest recognition was reported for individual 4; about 80% of the users got the correct answer. Almost everyone reported that recognition was possible because of the unique walking style of the person. For individual 2, only about 20% of the answers were correct because this person had no unique body shape or walking style. The correct answers were only from those sets in which low values of parameters for Blur and LIC were used.

Table 1. Statistics: User Study

	Familiar		Unfamiliar	
Algorithm, Parameter	Correct	Incorrect	Correct	Incorrect
Blur, $a = 2$	24	6	11	19
Blur, $a = 4$	21	9	10	20
LIC, $L = 10$	24	6	15	15
LIC, $L = 20$	23	7	13	17

4.2 Discussion

The preliminary results suggest that a high level of blurring should be used for effective de-identification. While the facial and other features can be masked adequately, the gait and other temporal characteristics are hard to mask. The amount of temporal blurring we tried was not sufficient, given some familiarity with the subjects. Our user study seems to suggest that de-identifying an individual to others familiar with him/her is a very challenging task. Without familiarity, gait and other characteristics are of low value and face plays the most important role.

5 Related Work

In the past, outlines of privacy preserving systems have been presented [8,9] to highlight the issues. These were sketches and not reports of an implemented de-identification system. Most privacy protection schemes focus on faces [10,11,12,13]. Commonly used schemes rely on methods which work well against human vision such as pixelation and blurring. [14,15] studied the effectiveness of blur filtration. Neustaedter et al. [15] concluded that blur filtration is insufficient to provide an adequate level of privacy. More recent methods such as the *k*-Same [10] and *k*-Same-Select [11] provide provable privacy and preserve data utility. Face modification has also been attempted as a way of image manipulation in [16,17,18]. The focus of these methods is seamless transfer of information from one or more input images to the target image. De-identification is a very different problem. The focus is on destroying all identifiable features from the image, which requires less effort than a seamless face substitution algorithm.

There has been very little work in the past dealing with entire human body for de-identification. Chen et al. [19] proposed a method for human body obscuring using motion history information of the edges. This method hides the identity of the actor, but it also removes all the information on the action. Park et al. [20] introduced the concept of *personal boundary* in a context adaptive human movement analysis system. Foreground pixels form multiple coherent colour blobs that constitute a human body. These blobs are used for blocking human identity. The problem with this approach is that it preserves the overall silhouette of the person which can aid recognition.

Another technique used for protecting privacy is based on segmenting the privacy information from a video and encrypting it to hide it from the end user. Different frameworks have been proposed to hide the data in the video itself, e.g., as a watermark [21] or as encrypted information in DCT blocks [22]. This information can be retrieved later on request. Prototype designs have also been proposed to provide a variable amount of control to the users over the information viewed in a video [15,21] which is a requirement of an ideal de-identification scheme.

Detecting and segmenting humans in images and videos is a very active area of research today which may help a complete de-identification system [23,24]. Recognizing humans from faces, silhouettes, gait, etc.is also an active area; success in those provides more methods a de-identification system should guard against.

6   Conclusions

In this paper, we analyzed the issues relating to de-identification of individuals in videos to protect their privacy by going beyond face recognition. We also presented a basic system to protect privacy against algorithmic and human recognition. We present results on a few standard videos as well as videos we collected that are more challenging to hide identity in. We also conducted a user study to evaluate the effectiveness of our system. Our studies indicate that gait and other temporal characteristics are difficult to hide if there is some familiarity with the subjects and the user. Blurring is a good way to hide the identity if gait is not involved. We propose to conduct further studies to evaluate the de-identification system against recognition by computer vision algorithms. That is likely to be easier than guarding against manual identification of individuals.

Acknowledgements. Partial funding was provided by the Naval Research Board of India.

References

1. Collins, R.T., Gross, R., Shi, J.: Silhouette-based human identification from body shape and gait. In: Proceedings of IEEE Conference on Face and Gesture Recognition, pp. 351–356 (2002)

2. Yoo, J.H., Hwang, D., Nixon, M.S.: Gender classification in human gait using support vector machine. In: Blanc-Talon, J., Philips, W., Popescu, D.C., Scheunders, P. (eds.) ACIVS 2005. LNCS, vol. 3708, pp. 138–145. Springer, Heidelberg (2005)
3. Dalal, N., Triggs, B.: Histograms of oriented gradients for human detection. In: CVPR (1), pp. 886–893. IEEE Computer Society, Los Alamitos (2005)
4. Tu, P., Sebastian, T., Doretto, G., Krahnstoever, N., Rittscher, J., Yu, T.: Unified crowd segmentation. In: Forsyth, D., Torr, P., Zisserman, A. (eds.) ECCV 2008, Part IV. LNCS, vol. 5305, pp. 691–704. Springer, Heidelberg (2008)
5. Boykov, Y., Jolly, M.P.: Interactive graph cuts for optimal boundary and region segmentation of objects in n-d images. In: ICCV, pp. 105–112 (2001)
6. Rother, C., Kolmogorov, V., Blake, A.: Grabcut: interactive foreground extraction using iterated graph cuts. ACM Trans. Graph. 23(3), 309–314 (2004)
7. Cabral, B., Leedom, L.C.: Imaging vector fields using line integral convolution. In: SIGGRAPH 1993: Proc. on Computer graphics and interactive techniques, pp. 263–270. ACM, New York (1993)
8. Senior, A.W.: Privacy enablement in a surveillance system. In: ICIP, pp. 1680–1683 (2008)
9. Yu, X., Chinomi, K., Koshimizu, T., Nitta, N., Ito, Y., Babaguchi, N.: Privacy protecting visual processing for secure video surveillance. In: ICIP, pp. 1672–1675 (2008)
10. Newton, E., Sweeney, L., Malin, B.: Preserving privacy by de-identifying facial images. IEEE Transactions on Knowledge and Data Engineering 17, 232–243 (2003)
11. Gross, R., Airoldi, E., Malin, B., Sweeney, L.: Integrating utility into face de-identification. In: Danezis, G., Martin, D. (eds.) PET 2005. LNCS, vol. 3856, pp. 227–242. Springer, Heidelberg (2006)
12. Gross, R., Sweeney, L., la Torre, F.D., Baker, S.: Semi-supervised learning of multi-factor models for face de-identification. In: IEEE CVPR (2008)
13. Phillips, P.: Privacy operating characteristic for privacy protection in surveillance applications, p. 869 (2005)
14. Boyle, M., Edwards, C., Greenberg, S.: The effects of filtered video on awareness and privacy. In: CSCW, pp. 1–10 (2000)
15. Neustaedter, C., Greenberg, S., Boyle, M.: Blur filtration fails to preserve privacy for home-based video conferencing. ACM Trans. Comput.-Hum. Interact. 13(1), 1–36 (2006)
16. Agarwala, A., Dontcheva, M., Agrawala, M., Drucker, S.M., Colburn, A., Curless, B., Salesin, D., Cohen, M.F.: Interactive digital photomontage. ACM Trans. Graph. 23(3), 294–302 (2004)
17. Blanz, V., Scherbaum, K., Vetter, T., Seidel, H.P.: Exchanging faces in images. Comput. Graph. Forum 23(3), 669–676 (2004)
18. Bitouk, D., Kumar, N., Dhillon, S., Belhumeur, P., Nayar, S.K.: Face swapping: automatically replacing faces in photographs. ACM Trans. Graph. 27(3), 1–8 (2008)
19. Chen, D., Chang, Y., Yan, R., Yang, J.: Tools for protecting the privacy of specific individuals in video. EURASIP Journal on Advances in Signal Processing 2007(1), 107–107 (2007)
20. Park, S., Trivedi, M.: A track-based human movement analysis and privacy protection system adaptive to environmental contexts, pp. 171–176 (2005)
21. Zhang, W., Cheung, S.C.S., Chen, M.: Hiding privacy information in video surveillance system. In: ICIP (3), pp. 868–871 (2005)
22. Cheung, S.C.S., Paruchuri, J.K., Nguyen, T.P.: Managing privacy data in pervasive camera networks. In: ICIP, pp. 1676–1679 (2008)
23. Ren, X., Berg, A.C., Malik, J.: Recovering human body configurations using pairwise constraints between parts. In: ICCV, pp. 824–831. IEEE Computer Society, Los Alamitos (2005)
24. Mori, G., Malik, J.: Recovering 3d human body configurations using shape contexts. IEEE Trans. Pattern Anal. Mach. Intell. 28(7), 1052–1062 (2006)

A Variant of the Trace Quotient Formulation for Dimensionality Reduction

Peng Wang[3,*], Chunhua Shen[1,2], Hong Zheng[3], and Zhang Ren[3]

[1] NICTA[†], Canberra Research Laboratory, Canberra, ACT, Australia
[2] Australian National University, Canberra, ACT, Australia
[3] Beihang University, Beijing, China

Abstract. Due to its importance to classification and clustering, dimensionality reduction or distance metric learning has been studied in depth in recent years. In this work, we demonstrate the weakness of a widely-used class separability criterion—trace quotient for dimensionality reduction—and propose new criteria for the dimensionality reduction problem. The proposed optimization problem can be efficiently solved using semidefinite programming, similar to the technique in [1]. Experiments on classification and clustering are performed to evaluate the proposed algorithm. Results show the advantage of the our proposed algorithm.

1 Introduction

Dimension reduction is a critical procedure for many classification and clustering algorithms, such as k-nearest-neighbors and k-means. In the literature, principal component analysis (PCA) and linear discriminant analysis (LDA) are two classical dimensionality reduction techniques. PCA projects the input data into the subspace that has maximum variance. LDA projects the input data onto a subspace by maximizing the between-class distance and minimizing the within-class variance. These two algorithms do not take constraints. In this sense, they are global learning methods. Relevant component analysis (RCA) [2], instead, is one of the important work that learns a metric from equivalence constraints. RCA can be viewed as an extension of LDA by incorporating must-link constraints and cannot-link constraints into the learning procedure. Each of these methods may be seen as devising a linear projection from the input space to a lower-dimensional output space. In [1,3] it is shown that many dimensionality reduction algorithms can be formulated in the trace quotient problem framework:

$$W^\circ = \operatorname*{argmax}_{W^\top W = \mathbf{I}_{d \times d}} \frac{\mathbf{Tr}(W^\top S_b W)}{\mathbf{Tr}(W^\top S_v W)}, \tag{1}$$

---

* Work was done when P. W. was visiting NICTA Canberra Research Laboratory and Australian National University.
† NICTA is funded by the Australian Government's Department of Communications, Information Technology, and the Arts and the Australian Research Council through *Backing Australia's Ability* initiative and the ICT Research Center of Excellence programs.

H. Zha, R.-i. Taniguchi, and S. Maybank (Eds.): ACCV 2009, Part III, LNCS 5996, pp. 277–286, 2010.

where $\mathbf{Tr}(\cdot)$ represents the matrix trace, and $\mathbf{I}_{d\times d}$ is a $d \times d$ identity matrix. S_b and S_v denote two positive semidefinite matrices, which contain the information of inter-class distances and intra-class distances, respectively. A few different methods can be used to construct those two matrices. In LDA, an approximate cost function, quotient trace,

$$\mathbf{Tr}((W^\top S_v W)^{-1}(W^\top S_b W)),$$

is maximized instead of the original quotient trace problem (1). The purpose of doing so is that the approximate cost function can be solved by generalized eigenvalue decomposition (GEVD), ending up with a close-form solution[3]. This is also a common practice for many other dimensionality reduction algorithms. S_b in LDA is defined as the within-class scatter matrix, while S_v is the between-class scatter matrix, $i.e.$,

$$S_b = \sum_c N_c(\boldsymbol{\mu}_c - \boldsymbol{\mu}_0)(\boldsymbol{\mu}_c - \boldsymbol{\mu}_0)^\top \tag{2a}$$

$$S_v = \sum_c \sum_{i\in c}(\boldsymbol{x}_i - \boldsymbol{\mu}_c)(\boldsymbol{x}_i - \boldsymbol{\mu}_c)^\top \tag{2b}$$

where $\boldsymbol{\mu}_c$ is the mean vector of class c, and $\boldsymbol{\mu}_0$ is the global mean vector; N_c is the number of vectors in class c. In the input space, $\mathbf{Tr}(S_b)$ represents the sum of distances from the mean vector of each individual class to the global mean vector. $\mathbf{Tr}(S_v)$ measures the sum of distances from each individual vector to the mean vector of its respective class. In contrast, $\mathbf{Tr}(W^\top SW)$ represents the sum of distance in the projected space. A metric learning algorithm is proffered by Xing $et~al.$ [4], aiming to maximize $squared$ inter-class distances while restrict the intra-class distances ($non\text{-}squared$)[1]. This optimization problem is shown below:

$$\underset{A}{\text{minimize}} \quad \sum_{(\boldsymbol{x}_p,\boldsymbol{x}_q)\in S}\|\boldsymbol{x}_p - \boldsymbol{x}_q\|_A^2 \tag{3a}$$

$$\text{subject to} \quad \sum_{(\boldsymbol{x}_p,\boldsymbol{x}_q)\in D}\|\boldsymbol{x}_p - \boldsymbol{x}_q\|_A \geq 1, \tag{3b}$$

$$A \succeq 0, \tag{3c}$$

where $\boldsymbol{x}_p$ and $\boldsymbol{x}_q$ are vectors in the data set; the distance metric $\|\boldsymbol{x} - \boldsymbol{z}\|_A$ is equal to $\sqrt{(\boldsymbol{x} - \boldsymbol{z})^T A(\boldsymbol{x} - \boldsymbol{z})}$; D and S are the $similarity$ set and $dissimilarity$ set, with the definition: $\{D : (\boldsymbol{x}_p,\boldsymbol{x}_q) \in D$ if $\boldsymbol{x}_p$ and $\boldsymbol{x}_q$ are dissimilar$\}$ and $\{S : (\boldsymbol{x}_p,\boldsymbol{x}_q) \in S$ if $\boldsymbol{x}_p$ and $\boldsymbol{x}_q$ are similar$\}$. This problem is convex, so a global optimum is guaranteed. Note that here a Mahalanobis metric A is learned. When A is rank-deficient, it is equivalent to reduce the dimension.

In [1], the trace quotient problem (1) is solved $directly$ through a framework based on a sequence of semidefinite programs (SDPs). Given the similarity set S and the dissimilarity set D, Shen $et~al.$ [1] shows a strategy to construct S_b and S_v different from (2a), (2b):

$$S_b = \sum_{(p,q)\in D} (\boldsymbol{x}_p - \boldsymbol{x}_q)(\boldsymbol{x}_p - \boldsymbol{x}_q)^\top, \tag{4a}$$

---

[1] If the constraints are also squared distance, the final solution will always be rank-one.

$$S_v = \sum_{(p,q)\in\mathcal{S}} (\boldsymbol{x}_p - \boldsymbol{x}_q)(\boldsymbol{x}_p - \boldsymbol{x}_q)^\top. \tag{4b}$$

The method for building the similarity and dissimilarity sets can be described as follows. For each $\boldsymbol{x}_p$, if $\boldsymbol{x}_q$ belongs to $\boldsymbol{x}_p$'s k differently-labeled neighbors, then $(\boldsymbol{x}_p, \boldsymbol{x}_q) \in \mathcal{D}$; Similarly, if $\boldsymbol{x}_q$ belongs to $\boldsymbol{x}_p$'s k' same-labeled neighbors, then $(\boldsymbol{x}_p, \boldsymbol{x}_q) \in \mathcal{S}$. In this case, $\mathbf{Tr}(S_b)$ is the sum of distances of vector pairs in the dissimilarity set, while $\mathbf{Tr}(S_v)$ is the sum of distances of vector pairs in the similarity set.

There is connection between Xing et $al.$'s method and the trace quotient problem. If similarity and dissimilarity sets are the same and (4a) and (4b) are used to construct S_b and S_v, then we have

$$\sum_{(\boldsymbol{x}_p,\boldsymbol{x}_q)\in\mathcal{S}}\|\boldsymbol{x}_p - \boldsymbol{x}_q\|_A^2 = \mathbf{Tr}(S_b A),$$

and

$$\sum_{(\boldsymbol{x}_p,\boldsymbol{x}_q)\in\mathcal{D}}\|\boldsymbol{x}_p - \boldsymbol{x}_q\|_A^2 = \mathbf{Tr}(S_v A).$$

Therefore, the optimization problem of Xing et $al.$ (Equ. (3)) is very similar to the trace quotient problem (Equ. (1)). Both algorithms are designed for the purpose of maximizing the between-class distance and at the same time minimizing the within-class distance. The results of clustering experiments verify this conclusion.

However, there are still some important differences between them. There is an additional rank constraint ($W \in \mathbb{R}^{D\times d}$) in the trace quotient problem. Therefore, the projection matrix (W) learned by [1] is orthogonal and low-dimensional, while Xing et $al.$ [4] learns a generic Mahalanobis matrix instead of a projection matrix. The optimization problem (1) can be reformulated as a series of simple SDP feasibility problems, which is much more faster than Xing et $al.$'s projected gradient descent algorithm [4].

In this work, we argue that the trace quotient formulation may not be always the best choice for dimensionality reduction. We reformulate the class separability criterion of (1). A set of different criteria are proposed, which may be better choices in some cases. We show that the resulted optimization problem can also be solved using SDP. Comparable results are obtained on various data sets for classification and clustering problems.

2   Classification Separability Criteria

The problem (1) is to optimize the class separability criterion:[2]

$$J = \frac{\mathbf{Tr}(S_b)}{\mathbf{Tr}(S_v)}, \tag{5}$$

where the numerator and the denominator are both the *global view* of the between-class distances and the within-class distances.

Now let us consider the separability for each 2-class combination individually. First, there is a matrix pair $(S_{b_{(i,j)}}, S_{v_{(i,j)}})$ for each class-pair (i,j) (i,j are both the class

---

[2] Again, we can replace $\mathbf{Tr}(S)$ with $\mathbf{Tr}(W^\top SW)$. For simplicity, we also use the matrix S to represent the scatter matrix in the projected space.

labels). The methods mentioned above can be used to construct $S_{b_{(i,j)}}$ and $S_{v_{(i,j)}}$ (only vectors of classes i and j are taken into account). Then a group of criteria are introduced to measure the separability for each class pair individually:

$$J(i,j) = \frac{\mathbf{Tr}(S_{b_{(i,j)}})}{\mathbf{Tr}(S_{v_{(i,j)}})}, \tag{6}$$

where $i > j, \forall i, j = 1, \cdots, c$, and c is the number of classes. There will be $\frac{c(c-1)}{2}$ criteria for c class data sets.

In the same way, we can also split the total classification error E into class-pairs. For class-pair (i, j), $E(i, j)$ stands for the ratio between the number of wrong predictions and the total number of predictions. All $E(i, j)$'s constitute E:

$$E = \sum_{i>j} E(i,j). \tag{7}$$

Intuitively, each $J(i, j)$ is related straightforward to the corresponding $E(i, j)$. The criteria in (6) reflect more information than the criterion (5). The best separability can be obtained when all $J(i, j)$'s are large such that each $E(i, j)$ is small.

For some multi-class cases, the criterion (5) can not measure the class separability well. The criterion in (5) mixes up all the criteria in (6) into one formula, which ignore much information about the separability. A large J may consist of some extremely small $J(i, j)$'s and some extremely large $J(i, j)$'s. Those small $J(i, j)$'s can result in a large total classification error.

3   The Trace Quotient Problems

Taking the advantage of the criteria (6), we demonstrate two trace quotient problems related to the original problem (1).

$$W^\circ = \operatorname*{argmax}_{W^\top W = \mathbf{I}_{d \times d}} \sum_{i>j} \frac{\mathbf{Tr}(W^\top S_{b_{(i,j)}} W)}{\mathbf{Tr}(W^\top S_{v_{(i,j)}} W)} \tag{8}$$

and,

$$W^\circ = \operatorname*{argmax}_{W^\top W = \mathbf{I}_{d \times d}} \min_{i>j} \frac{\mathbf{Tr}(W^\top S_{b_{(i,j)}} W)}{\mathbf{Tr}(W^\top S_{v_{(i,j)}} W)} \tag{9}$$

where $\forall i, j = 1, \cdots, c$, and c is the number of classes.

The problem (8) is to optimize the L_1 norm of $J(i, j)$'s, while the problem (9) focus on the L_∞ norm of $J(i, j)$'s. Despite its elegance and simplicity, the problem (8) is not convex. It is the sum of a bunch of quasi-convex (also quasi-concave) items. While for the problem (9), although it is convex either, it has a single minimum. The problem of minimizing the maximum of a set of quasi-convex functions has been discussed in the context of multi-view geometry [5]. For details, one may refer to [5]. So the problem (9) is proffered here, which can be transformed to a quasi-convex problem [6] and efficiently solved, using the framework presented in [1].

Algorithm 1. Bisection search

Require: δ_l and δ_u are lower and upper bounds of δ respectively, and the tolerance $\sigma > 0$.
  repeat
    $\delta = (\delta_u + \delta_l)/2$.
    Solve the feasibility problem (11a)–(11d).
    if feasible **then**
      $\delta_l = \delta$;
    else
      $\delta_u = \delta$.
    end if
  until $\delta_u - \delta_l > \sigma$

First, an slack variable δ is introduced, and the problem (9) is equal to

$$\underset{\delta, W}{\text{maximize}} \quad \delta \tag{10a}$$

$$\text{subject to} \quad \mathbf{Tr}(W^\top S_{b_{(i,j)}} W) \geq \delta \cdot \mathbf{Tr}(W^\top S_{v_{(i,j)}} W), \tag{10b}$$

$$W^\top W = \mathbf{I}_{d \times d} \tag{10c}$$

$$W \in \mathbb{R}^{D \times d}. \tag{10d}$$

where $i > j, \forall i, j = 1, \cdots, c$, and c is the number of classes.

By introducing a new variable $Z = WW^\top$ (then Z must be positive semidefinite), constraint (10b) is transformed to $\mathbf{Tr}((S_b - \delta S_v)Z) \geq 0$. Constraints (10c) and (10d) can be converted to $\mathbf{Tr}(Z) = d$ and $0 \preccurlyeq Z \preccurlyeq \mathbf{I}$. Here $\mathbf{I}$ is the identity matrix. This way our problem is reformulated to a linear fraction, therefore a quasi-convex problem, which can be solved by bisection search of δ involving a serial of SDPs.

δ° is defined as the optimal δ, which is obviously not smaller than any δ^* make the following SDP problem feasible:

$$\text{find} \quad Z \tag{11a}$$

$$\text{subject to} \quad \mathbf{Tr}((S_{b_{(i,j)}} - \delta^* S_{v_{(i,j)}})Z) \geq 0, \tag{11b}$$

$$\mathbf{Tr}(Z) = d, \tag{11c}$$

$$0 \preccurlyeq Z \preccurlyeq \mathbf{I}. \tag{11d}$$

Then, a bisection search algorithm can be adopted. Note that (11d) is not a straightforward semidefinite constraint, but it can be converted into the standard form of SDP. See [1] for how to reformulate this trace quotient problem into an sequence of SDP feasibility problems. Standard optimization packages can be used to solve the SDP problem. In our experiments, we use CVX [7] and SDPT3 [8] for all SDP problems.

We have proposed a new criterion for the dimensionality reduction problem, which is derived from the trace quotient problem in [1]. The proposed algorithm can still be efficiently solved using semidefinite programming.

4   Experiments

In this section, we carry out experiments to evaluate the performance of the proposed method on classification and clustering.

4.1   Classification

In the first classification experiment, our algorithm are evaluated on several data sets and compared with LDA and the original trace quotient algorithm in [1]. Note that our algorithm is slower when the number of classes is large because the constrains number of the optimization problem grows with the number of classes.

We first learn a projection matrix for dimensionality reduction via our algorithm and others, then a 3-NN classifier is applied on the projected metric space. Five dimensionality reduction algorithms are considered:

LDA: Fisher linear discriminant analysis.

SDP1:The algorithm solves the original trace quotient problem (1) which maximize the class separability criterion $J(i, j)$ (5) and uses the method used in LDA (2a)-(2b) to construct scatter matrices.

SDP2: The algorithm solves the variant problem (9) maximizing the minimum of a group of criteria $J(i, j)$s (6) and the method in LDA (2a)-(2b) is also used to construct scatter matrices.

SDP3: The algorithm solves the original trace quotient problem (1), however the scatter matrices are built based on the similarity and dissimilarity sets (2a)-(2b).

SDP4: The algorithm solves the variant problem (9) and uses the method (4a)-(4b) to construct scatter matrices.

Iris, Wine and Bal are small data sets from UCI machine learning repository [9], which only have three classes. These data sets are randomly sampled by a ratio of 7/3 for training and testing. USPS and ORL are both image data sets with large input dimensions. PCA is used to reduce the dimension of USPS and ORL as a preprocessing procedure for accelerating the latter computation. USPS handwriting digit data set has 10 classes (digit $0 - 9$) and 256 input dimensions(16×16 image), with predefined training and testing subsets. We only use the training set by randomly splitting this subset (20% for training and 80% for testing). The number of dimensions is reduced to 55 by PCA, preserving around 90.14% of variance. ORL face data set is made up of 400 images of faces belong to 40 individuals (10 faces per person). Each image is down-sampled from 56×46 to 28×23, and then the dimension is further reduced to 55 by PCA. The training and testing sets are obtained by 7/3 sampling for each person respectively. Table 1 summarizes the description of the data sets.

We report the classification accuracy of a 3-NN on the projected data. Table 2 reports the classification results. We find that SDP2 is slightly better than SDP1 in all data sets. In other words, when using LDA's scatter matrices, the proposed algorithm is better than the original trace quotient algorithm in [1]. Also note that LDA works very well on these data sets. For SDP3 and SDP4, the performances are comparable. No method is always better than the other on all tested data sets. The conclusion is *when using LDA's scatter matrices, the original trace quotient criterion may not be preferred.*

Table 1. Description of data sets and experimental parameters for classification.

	Iris	Wine	Bal	USPS	ORL
Train samples	105	125	438	1459	280
Test samples	45	53	187	5832	120
Classes	3	3	3	10	40
Input dimensions	4	13	4	256	644
Dimensions after PCA	4	13	4	55	42
Parameters (k, k') for SDP3	(3, 3)	(1, 5)	(3, 5)	(3, 5)	(2, 3)
Parameters (k, k') for SDP4	(3, 3)	(1, 5)	(3, 5)	(3, 5)	(2, 3)
Runs	5	5	5	5	5

Table 2. Classification accuracy of a 3-NN classifier on each data set in the form of **mean (std)**%. The final dimension is also shown.

	Iris	Wine	Bal	USPS	ORL
LDA	96.00(1.86), 2	99.25(1.03), 2	89.52(1.84), 2	92.70(0.48), 9	97.67(0.70), 39
SDP1	96.00(3.65), 3	96.23(1.89), 8	86.74(1.48), 3	94.26(0.33), 50	96.67(1.77), 39
SDP2	96.89(1.99), 3	96.60(4.70), 8	87.81(0.79), 3	94.49(0.21), 50	96.82(1.60), 39
SDP3	96.44(1.22), 3	86.04(2.15), 8	91.76(2.35), 3	95.13(0.39), 50	96.50(1.60), 39
SDP4	96.00(1.86), 3	84.34(4.62), 8	88.88(2.40), 3	94.76(0.28), 50	94.50(2.25), 39

In the second experiment, SDP1 and SDP2 are compared on the USPS digits data. We report the results in Table 3. In each run for class number c, c digits are randomly selected to form data set. We find that target dimension is more important than class number. When the target dimension is 50, the behavior of SDP1 and SDP2 are almost the same, while SDP2 is much better for 2D target dimension. Therefore, *when the target dimension is low, the trace quotient criterion tend to perform worse.*

In the third experiment, we choose digits 3, 7, 9 and 0 in USPS to form the data set. From this data set, we can see different behavior of algorithms explicitly. All the samples are treated as training data and a 2-dimensional target metric space is learned by LDA, SDP1 and SDP2. Then a 3-NN classifier is applied on the projected data.

Figure 1 illustrates the data projected into 2D by different algorithms. We can see that LDA and SDP1 can not separate digits 7 and 9, while SDP2 can separate them more clearly. Figure 2 illustrates the class separability criteria (J and $J(i, j)$) and the corresponding training errors (E and $E(i, j)$) of the data projected by LDA, SDP1 and SDP2. We can see that, although the J of SDP1 is largest (10.914) among the three algorithms, the classification result is the worst (total error: 10.252%). On the contrary, SDP2 gets the best result (total error: 3.566%) with its smallest J (3.806). It means that the criterion J can not reflect the class separability reasonably in this case. We also find that $J(7, 9)$ is extremely small in SDP1 (0.010) and LDA (0.084). In the meanwhile, $E(7, 9)$ takes the largest part in the total error E in the cases of SDP1 and LDA. There may exist over-fitting in SDP1. To maximize J, SDP1 may sacrifice some $J(i, j)$. But a extremely small $J(i, j)$ leads to an extremely large $E(i, j)$. However, $J(i, j)$s of SDP2 are more average, which makes it outperform others.

Table 3. Comparison results between SDP1 and SDP2 on USPS. For each case, the experiments are run 10 times on randomly split data.

number of classes	3 4 5 6 7 8
frequency of SDP1 wins(target dimension is 50)	4 6 5 5 5 8
frequency of SDP2 wins(target dimension is 50)	6 4 4 5 5 2
frequency of SDP1 wins(target dimension is 2)	0 3 1 1 1 4
frequency of SDP2 wins(target dimension is 2)	10 7 9 9 9 6

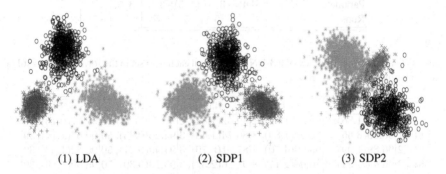

(1) LDA   (2) SDP1   (3) SDP2

Fig. 1. Subfigures (1), (2) and (3) show the data projected into 2D metric space learned by LDA, SDP1 and SDP2, respectively. $\circ, \times, +, *$ represent digits $3, 7, 9, 0$, respectively. LDA and SDP1 can not separate digits 7 and 9, while SDP2 can separate them well.

4.2 Clustering

In the clustering experiment, we run 4 algorithms on 5 UCI data sets and compare the clustering accuracies. A distance metric is learned via proposed algorithms, and then k-means clustering algorithm is applied on the metric.

We consider 4 distance metric learning algorithms, and compare these with the default Euclidean metric:

SDP5: The algorithm solving the problem (1) and using the method (4a) - (4b) to construct scatter matrices.

Xing1: The algorithm proposed by [4] (the case of full A), using the same method in SDP5 to construct the similarity and dissimilarity sets.

SDP6: The algorithm solving the problem (9) and using the method (4a)-(4b) to construct scatter matrices.

Xing2: The algorithm proposed by [4] (the case of full A), using the same method in SDP6 to construct the similarity and dissimilarity set (combine all the $S_{b_{(i,j)}}$'s, and $S_{v_{(i,j)}}$'s).

We use 5 UCI data sets to evaluate these algorithms. Each data set has more than 2 predefined labels, which is considered as the "true" clustering. Table 4 demonstrates features of data sets and parameters of algorithms.

For each run, the data set is randomly sampled by a ratio of $5/5$ (except for Soybean, which is $7/3$), then a similarity set S and a dissimilarity set D (for Xing1 and Xing2) or a inter-class scatter matrix S_b and a intra-class scatter matrix S_v (for SDP5 and SDP6)

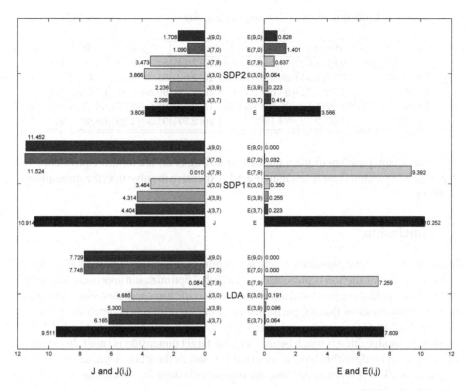

Fig. 2. Class separability criteria *vs.* training errors for the projected training data (digits 3, 7, 9, 0 in USPS data set) using the projection matrices learned by LDA, SDP1 and SDP2.

are constructed according to the training subset. Since k-means can only obtain a local optimal result, we run it 5 times for each data set and choose the best result as the final accuracy. Table 5 shows the clustering accuracy on the 5 UCI datasets. The accuracy is calculated in the way that is same as [4] (Sample(x_i, x_j) drawn from the same cluster with chance 0.5 and form different clusters with chance 0.5).

We find that all the results of SDP5 and SDP6 are better than the default Euclidean metric, and SDP5 and SDP6 have very similar performances. Compared with Xing *et al.*'s method [4], SDP5 and SDP6 also have comparable performances This verifies that

Table 4. Description of data sets and experimental parameters for clustering

	Balance	Soybean	Protein	Iris	Wine
Size of dataset	625	47	116	150	168
Training ratio	0.5	0.7	0.5	0.5	0.5
Classes	3	4	6	3	3
Input dimensions	4	35	20	4	12
Parameters (k, k') for Xing1 and SDP5	$(5, 5)$	$(3, 4)$	$(5, 5)$	$(3, 3)$	$(5, 1)$
Parameters (k, k') for Xing2 and SDP6	$(3, 2)$	$(3, 1)$	$(5, 4)$	$(5, 1)$	$(3, 5)$
Runs	10	10	10	10	10

Table 5. Clustering accurary of k-means clustering in the form of **mean (std)**%

	Balance	Soybean	Protein	Iris	Wine
Default metric	59.61(1.62)	90.54(9.15)	64.70(2.11)	87.41(1.78)	68.76(2.91)
Xing1	67.27(1.81)	96.41(6.02)	62.26(3.82)	95.36(1.79)	68.04(2.79)
SDP5	64.73(3.12)	95.60(7.13)	68.26(4.19)	90.85(3.91)	67.75(2.08)
Xing2	67.07(1.83)	96.51(4.51)	60.15(2.53)	95.93(2.27)	68.57(3.80)
SDP6	63.07(2.78)	92.19(7.44)	66.20(2.77)	91.38(4.59)	68.91(1.94)

the optimization problem of trace quotient and Xing *et al.* are almost equivalent. Note that Xing's algorithm is more computationally expensive to solve than the trace quotient problem.

5   Conclusion

In this work, we have presented a new algorithm for dimensionality reduction. A new class separability criterion is presented, and a global optimization approach is designed.

We have applied the proposed algorithm on classification and clustering. Classification experiments show that the performance of our algorithm is competitive to the one presented in [1]. Our algorithm is better when S_b and S_v are constructed by LDA. Furthermore, our algorithm is much better when the target dimension is small. In clustering experiments, our algorithm have a comparable result as the state-of-the-art [4].

Future work will focus on solving the problem (8) directly, which may lead to even better performances.

References

1. Shen, C., Li, H., Brooks, M.J.: Supervised dimensionality reduction via sequential semidefinite programming. Pattern Recogn. 41(12), 3644–3652 (2008)
2. Bar-Hillel, A., Hertz, T., Shental, N., Weinshall, D.: Learning a Mahalanobis metric from equivalence constraints. J. Mach. Learn. Res. 6, 937–965 (2005)
3. Yan, S., Tang, X.: Trace quotient problems revisited. In: Leonardis, A., Bischof, H., Pinz, A. (eds.) ECCV 2006. LNCS, vol. 3952, pp. 232–244. Springer, Heidelberg (2006)
4. Xing, E., Ng, A., Jordan, M., Russell, S.: Distance metric learning, with application to clustering with side-information. In: Proc. Adv. Neural Inf. Process. Syst. MIT Press, Cambridge (2002)
5. Kahl, F., Hartley, R.: Multiple view geometry under the L_∞-norm. IEEE Trans. Pattern Anal. Mach. Intell. 30(9), 1603–1617 (2008)
6. Boyd, S., Vandenberghe, L.: Convex Optimization. Cambridge University Press, Cambridge (2004)
7. Grant, M., Boyd, S., Ye, Y.: CVX user's guide: for cvx version 1.1. Technical report, Stanford University (2007)
8. Tütüncü, R.H., Toh, K.C., Todd, M.J.: Solving semidefinite-quadratic-linear programs using SDPT3. Math. Program. 95(2), 189–217 (2003)
9. Newman, D., Hettich, S., Blake, C., Merz, C.: UCI repository of machine learning databases (1998), http://archive.ics.uci.edu/ml/

Adaptive-Scale Robust Estimator Using Distribution Model Fitting

Thanh Trung Ngo[1], Hajime Nagahara[1], Ryusuke Sagawa[1],
Yasuhiro Mukaigawa[1], Masahiko Yachida[2], and Yasushi Yagi[1]

[1] Osaka University
[2] Osaka Institute of Technology

Abstract. We propose a new robust estimator for parameter estimation
in highly noisy data with multiple structures and without prior information on the noise scale of inliers. This is a diagnostic method that uses
random sampling like RANSAC, but adaptively estimates the inlier scale
using a novel adaptive scale estimator. The residual distribution model
of inliers is assumed known, such as a Gaussian distribution. Given a
putative solution, our inlier scale estimator attempts to extract a distribution for the inliers from the distribution of all residuals. This is
done by globally searching a partition of the total distribution that best
fits the Gaussian distribution. Then, the density of the residuals of estimated inliers is used as the score in the objective function to evaluate
the putative solution. The output of the estimator is the best solution
that gives the highest score. Experiments with various simulations and
real data for line fitting and fundamental matrix estimation are carried
out to validate our algorithm, which performs better than several of the
latest robust estimators.

1 Introduction

Robust parameter estimation is fundamental research in the fields of statistics
and computer vision. It can be applied in many estimation problems, such as
extracting geometric models in intensity images and range images, estimating
motion between consecutive image frames in a video sequence, matching images
to find their similarity, and so on. In these problems, the data contains explanatory data, which also includes leverage elements, and a large number of outliers.
The data may also contain several structures, such as various lines or planes
that appear in pictures or range images of a building. Therefore, the common
requirements for a modern robust estimator in computer vision are: robustness
to various high outlier rates (high breakdown point [1]), ability to work with
multi-structural data and good detection of inliers.

In this paper, we present a new robust estimator that has a high breakdown
point, can work with multi-structural data and estimates the correct inlier scale.
Our method relies on a novel inlier scale estimator and a density-based objective
function. The proposed inlier scale estimator finds the most Gaussian-like partition globally in the residual distribution of a putative solution. This is the main

H. Zha, R.-i. Taniguchi, and S. Maybank (Eds.): ACCV 2009, Part III, LNCS 5996, pp. 287–298, 2010.

contribution of our paper. Since we find the best inlier scale for inliers globally, smoothness of the probability density is not strictly required, and therefore, we have chosen the histogram method for fast computation.

2   Related Works

Least median squares (LMS) [1] is the most well-known robust estimator in statistics and computer vision, and can achieve a high breakdown point [1] of up to 50% of the outliers. However, in a real estimation problem, such as extracting lines from an intensity image or extracting planes from a range image, where the outlier rate is higher than 50%, the LMS cannot be used. Some estimators, however, have a higher breakdown point than 50%. The RANSAC algorithm [9] and Hough transform [10] are the most popular in this regard. If the scale of inliers is supplied, RANSAC can reach a very high breakdown point. However, the drawback of RANSAC is that it needs a user-defined threshold to distinguish inliers. The Hough transform can also achieve a very high breakdown point if it is able to manage its large voting space. Certain extensions of the LMS, such as MUSE (minimum unbiased scale estimate) [2] or ALKS (adaptive least kth order squares) [3], can be applied with high outlier rates, but these have a problem with extreme cases, such as perpendicular planes, and are sensitive to small pseudo structures. Another extension of the LMS is MINPRAN (minimize probability of randomness) [4], which requires an assumption of the outlier distribution. This assumption seems to be strict since outlier distribution is assumed with difficulty. RESC (residual consensus) [5] computes a histogram of residuals and uses several parameters to compress the histogram. The histogram power is computed as the score for the putative estimate. RESC is claimed to tolerate single structure data that contains up to 80% outliers, however, it needs many user-defined parameters to compress the histogram and to detect the inlier distribution, which reduces its adaptiveness. The pbM (projection-based M-Estimator) [6][11] is an extension of the M-Estimator that uses projection pursuit and the KDE (kernel density estimation), and can provide a breakdown point greater than 50%. However, it only works for linear residual functions, such as linear regression, or linearized residual functions. Another robust estimator that uses the KDE is the ASSC (adaptive scale sample consensus) [7]. ASSC assumes that the inliers are located within some special structure of the density distribution; practically it detects the first peak from zero and the valley next to the peak to locate the inliers. ASSC can provide a very high breakdown point, around 80%, when the correct bandwidth for the KDE is applied. ASSC has subsequently been improved, resulting in ASKC (adaptive scale kernel consensus) [8], which has an improved objective function and higher robustness in the case of high outlier rates. The bandwidth for the KDE in ASKC is computed using a scale estimate that contains approximately 10% of the smallest residuals. However, this under-smoothed bandwidth causes the ASKC estimate to have very few inliers in the case of data with a low outlier rate, and this reduces the accuracy even though the breakdown point is still high. In contrast to the pbM, ASSC or ASKC, our proposed method does not compute the inlier scale (the standard deviation of noise on the inlier residuals) directly from the estimated probability density. Since it roughly describes the true distribution and since the location of a local peak, global peak or local valley in the density estimation depends on a smoothing bandwidth, we find the best inlier scale globally by matching with a Gaussian distribution.

3   Adaptive-Scale Robust Estimator

3.1   Problem Preliminaries

Assume the estimation of a structure model with the constraint:

$$g(\boldsymbol{\theta}, \boldsymbol{X}) = 0, \tag{1}$$

where $\boldsymbol{\theta}$ is the parameter vector of the structure, and $\boldsymbol{X}$ is an explanatory data point. Our estimation problem can then be described as follows.

- *Input*: N observed data points $\boldsymbol{X_i}, i = 1..N$, including both inliers and outliers.
- *Output*: Parameter $\boldsymbol{\theta}$ that describes the data.

In a real problem, each inlier $\boldsymbol{X^t}$ is affected by an unknown amount of noise. Therefore, the actual parameter $\boldsymbol{\theta}$ cannot be recovered, and some approximation of $\boldsymbol{\theta}$ needs to be estimated. In evaluating whether an approximate estimate $\hat{\boldsymbol{\theta}}$ is good or bad, the estimator can only rely on the statistics of the error for each data point. This error is called the residual, and is a non-negative measure in the proposed method. For each model estimation problem, there are numerous ways of defining the residual function, including using the original constraint function (1). Generally, however, the residual is defined as:

$$r_{\hat{\theta}} = f(\hat{\boldsymbol{\theta}}, \boldsymbol{X}). \tag{2}$$

The standard deviation of these inlier residuals is called the *"inlier scale"*, and is denoted by $\sigma_{\hat{\theta}}$. The problem is that $\sigma_{\hat{\theta}}$ is not known, and therefore, an inlier scale estimator tries to estimate it. This estimate is denoted by $\sigma_{\hat{\theta}}^*$. Once the inlier scale has been determined, the threshold $t_{\hat{\theta}} = \tau \sigma_{\hat{\theta}}^*$ can be decided to distinguish inliers from outliers.

Given an estimate $\hat{\boldsymbol{\theta}}$, and an inlier scale $\sigma_{\hat{\theta}}$, the probability density function is denoted as $P_{\hat{\theta}}(r)$. $P_{\hat{\theta}}(r)$ is normalized using the inlier scale $\sigma_{\hat{\theta}}$ and we denote this normalized density function as $P_{\hat{\theta}}^s(\frac{r}{\sigma_{\hat{\theta}}})$. As the estimate $\hat{\boldsymbol{\theta}}$ approaches the correct value of $\boldsymbol{\theta}$, the distribution of inliers resembles more closely the ideal distribution. We call the ideal distribution when $\hat{\boldsymbol{\theta}} = \boldsymbol{\theta}$, the distribution model. The density function for the standardized distribution model, with a sample deviation of 1, is denoted as $G(\xi)$, $\xi \geq 0$. In this case, the standardized distribution model is the standard Gaussian distribution for the absolute of variables, denoted by AGD and described in Fig.1.

The proposed estimator works with data with multiple structures, and there-fore, the residual distribution $P_{\hat{\theta}}(r)$ has multiple modes. The mode near the origin is assumed to belong to the inlier structure, while the others belong to the outlier structures. Therefore, we cannot use the whole distribution model $G(\xi)$ with $0 \leq \xi < \infty$ for matching. Only the portion of $G(\xi)$ with $0 \leq \xi \leq \kappa$ is assumed as the inlier distribution model and is used for matching. κ is selected so that the range $0 \leq \xi \leq \kappa$ contains more than 95% of the population; in this study, for example, we use $\kappa = 2.5$.

3.2   Proposed Robust Estimator

In most previous works, the authors have assumed that the inlier residual distri-bution is a Gaussian distribution. This is also true for our research. We propose an estimator that uses distribution matching to find the best inlier scale from the distribution of all residuals.

Inlier Scale Estimation by Matching the Residual Distribution to the Distribution Model: The inlier scale is estimated by searching for the best fit between a segment of the residual distribution and the AGD. The segment of the residual distribution used for matching starts from zero. Then, the residual scale of the first structure is detected regardless of the outlier structures. The matching error between the density function $P_{\hat{\theta}}^s(\frac{r_{\hat{\theta}}^i}{\sigma})$ with assumed inlier scale σ and the AGD density function $G(\frac{r_{\hat{\theta}}^i}{\sigma})$ is defined by a simple minimization:

$$e_{\hat{\theta}}(\sigma) = \min_{k} \underset{0 \leq r_{\hat{\theta}}^i \leq \kappa\sigma}{Average} \{(P_{\hat{\theta}}^s(\frac{r_{\hat{\theta}}^i}{\sigma}) - kG(\frac{r_{\hat{\theta}}^i}{\sigma}))^2\}, \tag{3}$$

where k is some scale of the AGD density function, $r_{\hat{\theta}}^i$ is the ith residual and κ indicates the portion of the AGD used in the matching. Then, the best scale of inlier residuals $\sigma_{\hat{\theta}}^*$ is estimated by searching the scale that gives the smallest matching error. This is summarized as

$$\sigma_{\hat{\theta}}^* = argmin_{\sigma}\{e_{\hat{\theta}}(\sigma)\}. \tag{4}$$

Inliers are then distinguished using the threshold $t_{\hat{\theta}} = \kappa\sigma_{\hat{\theta}}^*$.

In our algorithm, to compute the probability density of the residual from an estimate $\hat{\theta}$, we apply the well-known histogram method, although the KDE can also be used. A histogram is simple and as residual sorting is not required, in contrast to most previous estimators, it gives a very low computational cost. Searching for the best inlier scale $\sigma_{\hat{\theta}}^*$ is graphically depicted in Fig.1.

Bin-width for the histogram is selected in the same way as in previous works [7][8]. A widely used bin-width [13] for robust estimators is:

$$\hat{b}_{\hat{\theta}} = (\frac{243 \int_{-1}^{1} K(\zeta)^2 d\zeta}{35N(\int_{-1}^{1} \zeta^2 K(\zeta)d\zeta)^2})^{\frac{1}{5}} \hat{s}_{\hat{\theta}}, \tag{5}$$

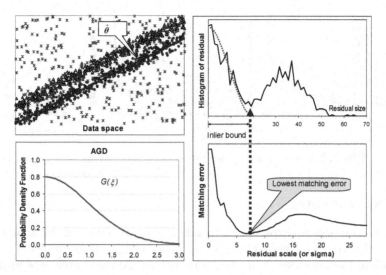

Fig. 1. Demonstration of searching the inliers scale. Data contains two actual parallel lines. The inlier scale is obtained by finding the smallest matching error.

where K is some kernel, such as the popular Gaussian kernel or Epanechnikov kernel, and $\hat{s}_{\hat{\theta}}$ is the smallest window containing 15% of the smallest residuals.

Objective Function: Inspired by the use of the KDE in the pbM-Estimator [11] and ASKC [8], we also apply it in our adaptive objective function:

$$F(\hat{\boldsymbol{\theta}}) = \frac{1}{Nh_{\hat{\theta}}} \sum_{i=1}^{N} K(\frac{r_{i,\hat{\theta}}}{h_{\hat{\theta}}}),$$ (6)

where $h_{\hat{\theta}}$ is adaptively estimated and K is a kernel such as the Gaussian kernel K_G or Epanechnikov kernel K_E. The KDE objective function evaluates how densely the residuals are distributed at zero using the kernel's window. In our case, the window of kernel K is $h_{\hat{\theta}}$, which tightly fits the estimated inliers, and therefore, the objective function gives the density measured at zero for the estimated inliers only. For K_G, $h_{\hat{\theta}} = \hat{\sigma}_{\hat{\theta}}^*$ and for K_E, $h_{\hat{\theta}} = \kappa \hat{\sigma}_{\hat{\theta}}^*$.

3.3 Estimation Algorithm Summary

We summarize the proposed algorithm below.

(a) Create a random sample and then estimate the solution parameters $\hat{\boldsymbol{\theta}}$.
(b) Estimate all the residuals of the data points given the parameters $\hat{\boldsymbol{\theta}}$.
(c) Estimate the bin-width by (5), and then compute histogram $P_{\hat{\theta}}$.
(d) Estimate the inlier scale as summarized by (4).
(e) Estimate the score using the objective function (6).
(f) Update the best solution.
(g) Repeat from (a) if not terminated.

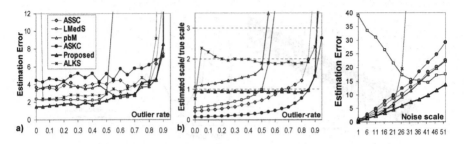

Fig. 2. Experiment on outlier rates   **Fig. 3.** Experiment on noise scales

4   Experiments

We carried out several experiments to validate our algorithm in linear and non-linear estimation problems: plane fitting, line fitting and fundamental matrix estimation. First, we used a simulation to understand the various aspects of the algorithm, and then actual experiments were performed with real data to validate the algorithm in various real situations. For the plane and line fitting (linear residual) problems, we compared our algorithm with several popular robust estimators: the pbM, LMedS, ALKS, ASSC, and ASKC. For the fundamental matrix (using non-linear residual) estimation, we used LMedS, ASSC, ASKC, and ALKS for comparison, since the pbM was originally proposed for linear robust regression problems. ALKS is very unstable when k is small, and therefore, in our experiments we only started searching for k when it was greater than 15% of the total number of data points. The Epanechnikov kernel was used in the KDE as well as the related objective functions. All algorithms were supplied with the same set of random sampling hypotheses and no optimization. For the proposed estimator, κ was selected such that the portion of the AGD for matching contained about 97% of the population; $\kappa = 2.5$ was used for all the experiments. The following criteria were used for validating the proposed estimator:

- Robustness through various outlier rates and noise scales.
- The ability to work with data with multiple structures.

4.1   Linear Fitting

In this problem, the estimator must extract the correct line or plane from a dataset that contains single or multiple structures with the appearance of random outliers. The experiments were carried out using various popular analytic simulations for the robust estimator. Given an estimate $\hat{\boldsymbol{\theta}} = (\hat{a}, \hat{b}, \hat{c}, \hat{d})$, the estimation error is defined as:

$$Error_{\hat{\theta}} = \sqrt{(a - \hat{a})^2 + (b - \hat{b})^2 + (c - \hat{c})^2 + (d - \hat{d})^2}, \qquad (7)$$

where (a, b, c, d) are ground-truth parameters. The normal vector of each plane is normalized such that $\sqrt{a^2 + b^2 + c^2} = 1$, $\sqrt{\hat{a}^2 + \hat{b}^2 + \hat{c}^2} = 1$.

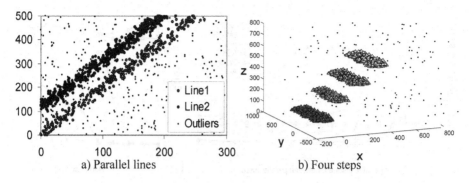

Fig. 4. Multiple data examples: (a) parallel lines and (b) data with 3D steps

Single Structure with Various Outlier Rates: We simulated a random dataset containing a random 3D plane with 500 random points within a 3D volume [0, 0, 0, 1000, 1000, 1000]. Some of the inlier points were replaced by outliers with random coordinates, thereby keeping the total number of data points as 500. The inlier points were contaminated by Gaussian noise with scale σ_G=8. The average results for 100 such datasets are shown in Fig.2. Fig.2(a) shows the estimation errors for robust estimators and Fig.2(b) shows the ratio between the estimated inlier scale and the actual inlier scale. The proposed estimators, pbM, ASSC and ASKC, have similar breakdown points, and they can work with very high outlier rates, up to 90%. However, with regards accuracy of the estimation and estimated inlier scale, the proposed estimator gives the best results. The estimated inlier scale is close to the actual inlier scale, with the ratio between them almost 1.

Single Structure with Noise Levels on Inliers: The dataset was set up in the same way as in Section 4.1 for line fitting, but the outlier rate was fixed at 60%, and the noise scale σ_G varied between 1 and 52. The average results for 100 datasets are shown in Fig.3. These results show that the performance of each estimator decreased as the noise scale increased. However, the proposed estimator was highly resistant to the high noise scale.

Parallel Lines with Varying Distances: This problem demonstrates the ability of line estimation with the appearance of multiple structures. A dataset containing two parallel lines is used in this experiment. The estimator must then discriminate the two lines and extract a line correctly from the data. The experiment was carried out with varying distances between the two parallel lines:

$$Line1 : 2x - y + d = 0, \ where \ d = 20, 30, 40, ...210$$
$$Line2 : 2x - y \quad = 0.$$

Each dataset contained 450 random points (outliers); 150 points on *line*1 and 300 points on *line*2 were generated randomly for each trial in this experiment.

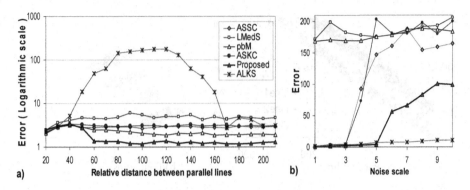

Fig. 5. Estimation errors for data (a) with parallel lines and (b) with steps

Gaussian noise with a zero mean and σ_G=8.0 was added to the points on each line, whilst keeping the range of all points within the rectangle $(0, 0, 62.5\sigma_G, 62.5\sigma_G)$. An example of a random dataset is shown in Fig.4(a) with $d = 80$. The average results from 100 trials for the estimation error and number of estimated inliers are shown in Fig.5(a). When the two lines are close together, $d = 20$, they are almost mistaken for one line, with all estimators having a similar accuracy. When the lines are further apart, the performance of ALKS is the worst, as it only manages to estimate correctly once the two lines are very far apart. Since the actual outlier rate for estimating any line is greater than 50%, LMedS produces worse results as the two lines move further apart. However, our proposed algorithm retains a similar accuracy rate irrespective of the distance between the lines. The pbM, ASSC and ASKC have the same robustness as the proposed estimator, but with lower accuracy.

Multiple Steps with Varying Noise Levels: In this experiment, step data consisting of four planes was set up as shown in Fig.4(b). The parameters of the actual planes are:

$$Plane\ 1 : z - 100 = 0$$
$$Plane\ 2 : z - 200 = 0$$
$$Plane\ 3 : z - 300 = 0$$
$$Plane\ 4 : z - 400 = 0$$

The dataset for evaluation consisted of 240 random points for each plane and 240 random outliers. Each data point on a plane was contaminated by Gaussian noise with σ_G. The experiment was carried out to test all the estimators with different values of σ_G. With larger values of σ_G, the four planes are closer and may become fused. The results are illustrated in Fig.5(b), which gives the average of the results for 100 such randomly generated datasets.

The pbM did not perform well in this experiment as it mistook the four planes for the same structure, resulting in the estimated number of inliers being about four times more than the actual number of inliers for each plane. LMedS did not perform well either, as the outlier rate is high for the estimation of

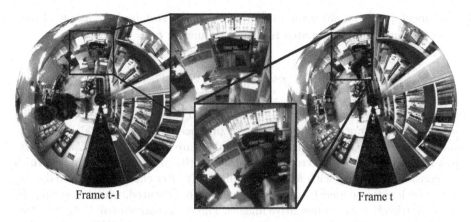

Frame t-1   Frame t

Fig. 6. One pair of images in a sequence; inliers (image features in red) and outliers (image features in green) are output by the proposed estimator

any plane. ASSC and ASKC were able to estimate correctly only at low noise levels. The proposed method was able to function correctly at slightly higher noise levels, but then it also became confused and estimated the four planes as a single plane. Since ALKS is well known for its instability and sensitivity to small pseudo structures, we limited the size of possible structures for ALKS, with the estimated structure being larger than 15% of the data. Hence, ALKS was able to function at much higher noise levels. In this case its sensitivity was an advantage.

4.2   Fundamental Matrix Estimation in Real Video Sequences

In these experiments, real video sequences were captured in an indoor environment with an omnidirectional vision sensor. Examples of the captured images are shown in Fig.6. The sensor consisted of an omnidirectional mirror, a telecentric lens and an imaging sensor. The camera was mounted on a rotary stage and controlled by a PC, which translated the camera whilst it was being rotated. For each pair of images, 200 Harris image features were detected on the first image and tracked on the second image to obtain the feature correspondence pairs using the KLT feature tracker [12] implemented in OpenCV. The fundamental matrix between a pair of consecutive images was computed using the seven point algorithm [16] with these feature correspondence pairs. The residual function is defined in [15]:

$$r = f(\boldsymbol{F}, \boldsymbol{x}, \boldsymbol{x}') = \left| \boldsymbol{x}'^T \boldsymbol{F} \boldsymbol{x} \right| \sqrt{\frac{1}{\| \boldsymbol{F} \boldsymbol{x} \|^2} + \frac{1}{\| \boldsymbol{F}^T \boldsymbol{x}' \|^2}}, \qquad (8)$$

where F is the fundamental matrix and $(\boldsymbol{x}, \boldsymbol{x}')$ a feature correspondence pair. Since we cannot compare the estimated fundamental matrix with a ground-truth fundamental matrix, we compute the error as the standard deviation of only inlier residuals of the estimated fundamental matrix $\hat{\theta}^* = \hat{F}^*$:

$$Error_{\hat{F}^*} = \sqrt{\frac{1}{M} \sum_{i=1}^{M} (r_{i,\hat{F}^*})^2}, \tag{9}$$

where M is the number of inliers. This error computation relies on how the solution fits the motion data: a better fit produces smaller residuals for inliers, and vice versa. In a simulation, the actual inliers are known and thus M is known. In a real experiment, the error is computed for the M smallest residuals (which are considered inliers), with M assigned manually after checking the actual data.

For each video sequence, about 50 images were captured, whilst ensuring the same rotation between consecutive images. The performance of all the estimators tends to deteriorate with a greater degree of rotation, since the KLT tracker is less accurate under greater rotation. Therefore, we used three video sequences with different rotation settings. These video sequences are referred to as $Video\_4deg$, $Video\_14deg$ and $Video\_18deg$ for rotation speeds of 4 degrees/frame, 14 degrees/frame, and 18 degrees/frame, respectively. We computed the error by (9) and M was set independently for each video sequence after randomly checking five pairs of images within each video sequence. The average number of true inliers and the assigned value for M for each video sequence are given in Table.1. The average errors and number of estimated inliers for 100 executions of each video sequence are given in Table.1. For low outlier rates, LMedS gave the best accuracy. However, for a high outlier rate in $Video\_18deg$, LMedS performed worst. The estimation error of the proposed method is quite similar to that of ASSC. With regard to the number of estimated inliers, the proposed method gave the best results, the number of estimated inliers was close to the actual number of inliers.

Table 1. Fundamental matrix estimation error and number of estimated inliers for real video sequences

Video sequence	Video_4deg		Video_14deg		Video_18deg	
Number of true inliers	187.7		102.7		72.2	
Assigned M	160		90		60	
Fitting error / No est. inliers						
Proposed method	0.00152	150.7	0.00377	86.4	0.00382	65.5
ASSC	0.00156	36.7	0.00377	38.7	0.00385	39.9
ASKC	0.00184	22.7	0.00474	23.6	0.00507	23.9
ALKS	0.00903	66.8	0.01955	98.7	0.02127	64.5
LMedS	0.00125	101.0	0.00349	101.0	0.00574	101.0

Fig.7 shows the estimated distributions of residuals (from both inliers and outliers) for the estimators with the sequence $Video\_18deg$. For each estimator, the distribution was computed as the average of the residual distributions for the solutions for all pairs of images. The graph shows that the distributions and the Gaussian are highly correlated regardless of the estimator.

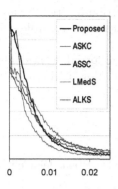

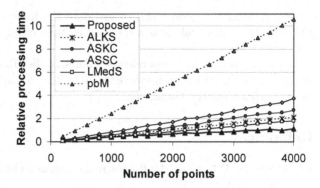

Fig. 7. Actual distribution of residuals

Fig. 8. Processing time for all estimators

4.3 Computational Cost

We simulated the relation between processing time and the number of data
points, the average results of which are shown in Fig.8. In this simulation, a
linear fitting problem for a plane was used and all the estimators were given
the same set of random samples. The graph shows that overall the proposed
estimator gives the fastest computational time, especially for large data.

5 Discussion and Conclusions

In this paper, we proposed a novel highly robust estimator for the estimation
problem in computer vision that deals with data with high outlier rates and
multiple structures. Our algorithm does not need any prior information about
the inlier scale, as this is estimated adaptively by globally searching for the
best match of the Gaussian distribution and the residual distribution. Thus, the
inlier residual distribution is tightly estimated, resulting in robustness and high
accuracy for the proposed algorithm. The validity of the proposed algorithm was
confirmed by experiments with several different estimation problems in various
situations.

Without a smoothing parameter, such as bin-width in the proposed estimator
and bandwidth in ASSC, the residual statistics are unstable, especially for a
small set of residuals. This reduces the robustness of an adaptive robust estimator, as is the case in ALKS. ALKS tends to extract smaller structures that have
a distribution similar to the Gaussian distribution. However, in a small set of
residuals, this distribution is likely to occur. Using a smoothing parameter in the
residual density estimation can make an adaptive-scale estimator more robust,
as is the case in ASSC, ASKC, and pbM. However, the problem lies in how large
this parameter should be. For example, in ASSC and ASKC, the estimated inlier scale is correlated with the bandwidth but not with the actual outlier rate.
The inlier scale is frequently underestimated for data with low outlier rates. The

proposed estimator is designed to estimate the inlier distribution tightly, and therefore the inlier scale is always close to the actual inlier scale regardless of the outlier rate.

In current method, we assume the Gaussian distribution for inlier residuals. In future, we would like to improve the algorithm for application to distribution models other than the Gaussian.

References

1. Rousseeuw, P.J., Leroy, A.: Robust Regression and Outlier Detection. John Wiley & Sons, New York (1987)
2. Miller, J.V., Stewart, C.V.: MUSE: Robust surface fitting using unbiased scale estimates. In: Proc. of CVPR, pp. 300–306 (1996)
3. Lee, K.M., Meer, P., Park, R.H.: Robust adaptive segmentation of range images. TPAMI 20, 200–205 (1998)
4. Stewart, C.V.: MINPRAN: A new robust estimator for computer vision. TPAMI 17, 925–938 (1995)
5. Yu, X., Bui, T.D., Krzyzak, A.: Robust Estimation for Range Image Segmentation and Reconstruction. TPAMI 16(5), 530–538 (1994)
6. Chen, H., Meer, P.: Robust regression with projection based M-estimators. In: ICCV, pp. 878–885 (2003)
7. Wang, H., Suter, D.: Robust Adaptive-Scale Parametric Model Estimation for Computer Vision. IEEE TPAMI 26(11), 1459–1474 (2004)
8. Wang, H., Mirota, D., Ishii, M., Hager, G.D.: Robust Motion Estimation and Structure Recovery from Endoscopic Image Sequences With an Adaptive Scale Kernel Consensus Estimator. In: CVPR 2008 (2008)
9. Fischler, M.A., Bolles, R.C.: Random Sample Consensus: A Paradigm for Model Fitting with Applications to Image Analysis and Automated Cartography. Comm. of the ACM 24, 381–395 (1981)
10. Illingworth, J., Kittler, J.: A survey of the Hough transform, Computer Vision. In: Graphics, and Image Processing (CVGIP), vol. 44, pp. 87–116 (1988)
11. Subbarao, R., Meer, P.: Beyond RANSAC: User Independent Robust Regression. In: CVPRW 2006, p. 101 (2006)
12. Shi, J., Tomasi, C.: Good Features to Track. In: Proc. of IEEE CVPR, pp. 593–600 (1994)
13. Wand, M.P., Jones, M.: Kernel Smoothing. Chapman & Hall, Boca Raton (1995)
14. Subbarao, R., Meer, P.: pbM-Estimator source code, http://www.caip.rutgers.edu/riul/research/robust.html
15. Luong, Q.T., Faugeras, O.D.: The fundamental matrix: Theory, algorithms, and stability analysis. Intl. Journal of Computer Vision 17(1), 43–75 (1996)
16. Hartley, R.I.: Projective reconstruction and invariants from multiple images. IEEE Trans. on Pattern Analysis and Machine Intelligence 16(10), 1036–1041 (1994)

A Scalable Algorithm for Learning a Mahalanobis Distance Metric

Junae Kim[1,2], Chunhua Shen[1,2], and Lei Wang[1]

[1] The Australian National University, Canberra, ACT, Australia
{junae.kim,lei.wang}@anu.edu.au
[2] NICTA, Canberra Research Laboratory, Canberra, ACT, Australia*
chunhua.shen@nicta.com.au

Abstract. A distance metric that can accurately reflect the intrinsic characteristics of data is critical for visual recognition tasks. An effective solution to defining such a metric is to learn it from a set of training samples. In this work, we propose a fast and scalable algorithm to learn a Mahalanobis distance. By employing the principle of margin maximization to secure better generalization performances, this algorithm formulates the metric learning as a convex optimization problem with a positive semidefinite (psd) matrix variable. Based on an important theorem that a psd matrix with trace of one can always be represented as a convex combination of multiple rank-one matrices, our algorithm employs a differentiable loss function and solves the above convex optimization with gradient descent methods. This algorithm not only naturally maintains the psd requirement of the matrix variable that is essential for metric learning, but also significantly cuts down computational overhead, making it much more efficient with the increasing dimensions of feature vectors. Experimental study on benchmark data sets indicates that, compared with the existing metric learning algorithms, our algorithm can achieve higher classification accuracy with much less computational load.

1 Introduction

Many visual recognition tasks can be regarded as inferring a distance metric that is able to measure the similarity of visual data in a way consistent with human perception. Typical examples include visual object categorization [1] and content-based image retrieval [2], in which a similarity metric is needed to discriminate different object classes or the relevant and irrelevant images for a given query. Classifiers, from the simple k-Nearest Neighbor (k-NN) [3] to the advanced Support Vector Machines (SVMs) [4], can be explicitly or implicitly related to a distance metric. As one of the representative classifiers, k-NN has been applied

* NICTA is funded by the Australian Government's Department of Communications, Information Technology, and the Arts and the Australian Research Council through *Backing Australia's Ability initiative* and the ICT Research Center of Excellence programs.

H. Zha, R.-i. Taniguchi, and S. Maybank (Eds.): ACCV 2009, Part III, LNCS 5996, pp. 299–310, 2010.

to a wide range of visual recognition tasks and it is the classifier that directly depends on a predefined distance metric. To make this classifier work well, an appropriate distance metric has to be applied. Previous work (*e.g.*, [5,6]) has shown that compared to using the standard Euclidean distance, employing an well-designed distance metric to measure the (dis)similarity of data can significantly boost the classification accuracy of k-NN.

In this work, we propose a scalable and fast algorithm to learn a Mahalanobis distance metric. The key issue in this task is to learn an optimal Mahalanobis matrix in this distance metric. It has been shown in the statistical learning theory [7] that increasing the margin between different classes helps to reduce the generalization error. Hence, our algorithm formulates the Mahalanobis matrix as a variable of the margin and optimizes it via margin maximization. By doing so, the learned Mahalanobis distance metric can achieve sufficient separation at the boundaries between different classes. More importantly, we address the scalability problem of learning a Mahalanobis distance in the presence of high-dimensional feature vectors, which is a critical issue of distance metric learning. As indicated in a theorem in [8], a positive semidefinite matrix (psd) with trace of one can always be represented as a convex combination of a set of rank-one matrices with trace being one. This inspired us to develop a fast optimization algorithm that works in the style of gradient descent. At each iteration, our algorithm only needs to find the largest principal eigenvector of a gradient matrix and to update the current Mahalanobis matrix. This process incurs much less computational overhead than the metric learning algorithms in the literature [9]. Moreover, thanks to the above theorem, this process automatically preserves the psd property of the Mahalanobis matrix. To verify its efficiency, the proposed algorithm is tested on a set of benchmark data sets and is compared with the state-of-the-art distance metric learning algorithms. As experimentally demonstrated, k-NN with the Mahalanobis distance learned by our algorithms attains higher classification accuracy. Meanwhile, in terms of the optimization time, our algorithm is much less affected by the increased dimensionality of feature vectors.

2   Related Work

For a given classification task, learning a distance metric aims to find a metric that makes the data in the same class close and separates those in different classes from each other as far as possible. There has been some work on distance metric learning in the literature. Xing et al. [5] propose an approach to learn a Mahalanobis distance for supervised clustering. It minimizes the sum of the distances among data in the same class while maximizing the sum of the distances among data in different classes. Their work shows that the learned metric improves clustering performance significantly. However, to maintain the psd property, they use projected gradient descent and their approach has to perform a *full* eigen-decomposition of the Mahalanobis matrix at each iteration. Its computational cost rises rapidly when the number of features increases, and this makes it less efficient in handling high-dimensional data. Goldberger et al. [10]

develop the algorithm called Neighborhood Component Analysis, which learns a Mahalanobis distance by minimizing the leave-one-out cross-validation error of the k-NN classifier on a training set. However, their algorithm leads to a non-convex optimization problem and expensive computational load. Although the work in [10] learns a Mahalanobis distance metric as ours does, it does not study and make use of the psd property of the Mahalanobis matrix. The work closest to ours is [9] in the sense that it also learns a Mahalanobis distance in the large margin framework. In their approach, the distances between each sample and its "target neighbors" are minimized while the distances among the data with different labels are maximized. A convex objective function is created and solved by using the semidefinite programming (SDP) technique. Note that they have adopted an alternating projection algorithm for solving the resulted SDP because standard interior-point methods do not scale well. At each step of iteration, similar to [5], also a full eigen-decomposition is needed. Our approach is largely inspired by their work. However, we take a different way to achieving the margin maximization and lead to a different objective function. To develop our fast algorithm, we adopt a differentiable loss function rather than the discontinuous hinge loss function in [9]. More importantly, our algorithm has a clear advantage on computational efficiency (we only need to compute the leading eigenvector) and achieves better classification performance.

3   Formulation of Our Optimization Problem

Let $\mathbf{a}_i \in \mathbb{R}^D (i = 1, 2, \cdots, n)$ denote a training sample where n is the number of training samples and D is the number of features. To learn a Mahalanobis distance, we create a set $\mathcal{S}$ which contains a group of training triplets as $\mathcal{S} = \{(\mathbf{a}_i, \mathbf{a}_j, \mathbf{a}_k)\}$, where $\mathbf{a}_i$ and $\mathbf{a}_j$ come from the same class and $\mathbf{a}_k$ belongs to a different class. A Mahalanobis distance can be defined as follows. Let $\mathbf{P} \in \mathbb{R}^{D \times D}$ denote a linear transformation and **dist** be the squared Euclidean distance in the transformed space. The squared distance between the projections of $\mathbf{a}_i$ and $\mathbf{a}_j$ is

$$\mathbf{dist}_{ij} = \|\mathbf{P}^T \mathbf{a}_i - \mathbf{P}^T \mathbf{a}_j\|_2^2 = (\mathbf{a}_i - \mathbf{a}_j)^T \mathbf{P} \mathbf{P}^T (\mathbf{a}_i - \mathbf{a}_j). \tag{1}$$

According to the class membership of $\mathbf{a}_i$, $\mathbf{a}_j$ and $\mathbf{a}_k$, we require that $\mathbf{dist}_{ik} \geq \mathbf{dist}_{ij}$ and it can be obtained that

$$(\mathbf{a}_i - \mathbf{a}_k)^T \mathbf{P} \mathbf{P}^T (\mathbf{a}_i - \mathbf{a}_k) \geq (\mathbf{a}_i - \mathbf{a}_j)^T \mathbf{P} \mathbf{P}^T (\mathbf{a}_i - \mathbf{a}_j). \tag{2}$$

It is not difficult to see that this inequality is generally not a convex constrain in $\mathbf{P}$ because the difference of quadratic terms in $\mathbf{P}$ is involved. In order to make this inequality constrain convex, a new variable $\mathbf{X} = \mathbf{P} \mathbf{P}^T$ is introduced and used through out the whole learning process. Learning a Mahalanobis distance is essentially to learn the Mahalanobis matrix $\mathbf{X}$. (2) becomes linear in $\mathbf{X}$. This is a typical technique for formulating an SDP problem whose global maximum can be efficiently computed.

3.1   Maximization of a Soft Margin

In our algorithm, the *margin* is defined as the distance between $\mathbf{dist}_{ik}$ and $\mathbf{dist}_{ij}$, that is,

$$\rho_r = (\mathbf{a}_i - \mathbf{a}_k)^T \mathbf{X}(\mathbf{a}_i - \mathbf{a}_k) - (\mathbf{a}_i - \mathbf{a}_j)^T \mathbf{X}(\mathbf{a}_i - \mathbf{a}_j),$$
$$\forall (\mathbf{a}_i, \mathbf{a}_j, \mathbf{a}_k) \in \mathcal{S}, \quad r = 1, 2, \cdots, |\mathcal{S}|. \tag{3}$$

It is maximized to identify the optimal Mahalanobis matrix $\mathbf{X}$. In the meantime, to deal with non-separable data sets and avoid over-fitting training samples, we must allow some training errors while maximizing the margin. Considering these factors, we define the objective function for learning $\mathbf{X}$ as

$$\max_{\rho, \mathbf{X}, \xi} \quad \rho - C \sum_{r=1}^{|\mathcal{S}|} \xi_r$$
$$\text{s.t.} \quad \mathbf{X} \succeq 0, \mathbf{Tr}(\mathbf{X}) = 1, \quad \xi_r \geq 0, \quad r = 1, 2, \cdots, |\mathcal{S}|,$$
$$(\mathbf{a}_i - \mathbf{a}_k)^T \mathbf{X}(\mathbf{a}_i - \mathbf{a}_k) - (\mathbf{a}_i - \mathbf{a}_j)^T \mathbf{X}(\mathbf{a}_i - \mathbf{a}_j) \geq \rho - \xi_r, \forall (\mathbf{a}_i, \mathbf{a}_j, \mathbf{a}_k) \in \mathcal{S}, \tag{4}$$

where $\mathbf{X} \succeq 0$ constrains $\mathbf{X}$ to be a psd matrix and $\mathbf{Tr}(\mathbf{X})$ denotes of trace of $\mathbf{X}$. r indexes the training set $\mathcal{S}$ and $|\mathcal{S}|$ denotes the size of $\mathcal{S}$. C is an algorithmic parameter that balances the training error and the margin. $\xi \geq 0$ is the slack variable similar to that used in the SVMs and it corresponds to the soft-margin hinge loss. Imposing $\mathbf{Tr}(\mathbf{X}) = 1$ removes the scale ambiguity because the inequality constrains are scale invariant. To simplify exposition, we define

$$\mathbf{A}^r = (\mathbf{a}_i - \mathbf{a}_k)(\mathbf{a}_i - \mathbf{a}_k)^T - (\mathbf{a}_i - \mathbf{a}_j)(\mathbf{a}_i - \mathbf{a}_j)^T. \tag{5}$$

By doing so, the last constraint in (4) can be written as

$$\langle \mathbf{A}^r, \mathbf{X} \rangle \geq \rho - \xi_r, \quad r = 1, \cdots, |S| \tag{6}$$

Note that this is a linear constrain on $\mathbf{X}$. Problem (4) is thus a typical SDP problem since it has a linear objective function and linear constraints plus a psd conic constraint. It can be solved using off-the-shelf SDP solvers. However, directly solving problem (4) using standard interior-point SDP solvers would quickly become computationally intractable with the increasing dimensionality of feature vectors. The following shows our way of developing a fast algorithm for (4).

3.2   Employing a Differentiable Loss Function

It is proven in [8] that *a psd matrix can always be decomposed as a linear convex combination of a set of rank-one matrices*. In the context of our problem, this means that $\mathbf{X} = \sum \theta_i \mathbf{Z}_i$, where $\mathbf{Z}_i$ is a rank-one matrix and $\mathbf{Tr}(\mathbf{Z}_i) = 1$. This important result inspires us to develop a gradient descent based optimization algorithm. In each iteration $\mathbf{X}$ is updated as

$$\mathbf{X}_{i+1} = \mathbf{X}_i + \alpha(\triangle \mathbf{X} - \mathbf{X}_i) = \mathbf{X}_i + \alpha \mathbf{p}_i, \quad 0 \leq \alpha \leq 1 \tag{7}$$

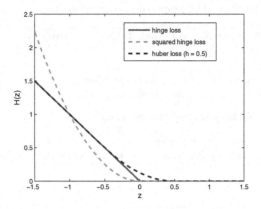

Fig. 1. The hinge loss, squared hinge loss and huber loss used in our work

where $\triangle \mathbf{X}$ is a rank-one and trace-one matrix. $\mathbf{p}_i$ is the search direction and will be introduced in Table 2.

To make a gradient descent method applicable, we need to ensure that the object function to be differentiable with respect to the variables ρ and $\mathbf{X}$.

Let f denote the objective function and ℓ be a loss function. Our optimization problem can be written as

$$f(\mathbf{X}, \rho) = \rho - C \sum_{r=1}^{|\mathcal{S}|} \ell(\langle \mathbf{A}^r, \mathbf{X} \rangle - \rho). \tag{8}$$

The above problem (4) adopts the hinge loss function which is defined as $\ell(z) = \max(0, -z)$. However, the hinge loss is not differentiable at the point of $z = 0$, and gradient-based optimization will encounter problems. In order to remove this problem, we propose to use differentiable loss functions, for example, the squared hinge loss or huber loss functions discussed below.

The squared hinge loss function can be represented as

$$\ell(\langle \mathbf{A}^r, \mathbf{X} \rangle - \rho) = \begin{cases} 0, & \text{if } (\langle \mathbf{A}^r, \mathbf{X} \rangle - \rho) \geq 0, \\ (\langle \mathbf{A}^r, \mathbf{X} \rangle - \rho)^2, & \text{if } (\langle \mathbf{A}^r, \mathbf{X} \rangle - \rho) < 0. \end{cases} \tag{9}$$

As shown in Fig. 1, this function connects the positive and zero segments smoothly and it is differentiable everywhere including the point $z = 0$. We also consider the huber loss function:

$$\ell(\langle \mathbf{A}^r, \mathbf{X} \rangle - \rho) = \begin{cases} 0, & \text{if } (\langle \mathbf{A}^r, \mathbf{X} \rangle - \rho) \geq h, \\ \frac{(h-(\langle \mathbf{A}^r, \mathbf{X} \rangle - \rho))^2}{4h}, & \text{if } -h < (\langle \mathbf{A}^r, \mathbf{X} \rangle - \rho) < h, \\ -(\langle \mathbf{A}^r, \mathbf{X} \rangle - \rho), & \text{if } (\langle \mathbf{A}^r, \mathbf{X} \rangle - \rho) \leq -h, \end{cases} \tag{10}$$

where h is a parameter whose value is usually between 0.01 and 0.5. A huber loss function with $h = 0.5$ is plotted in Fig. 1. There are three different parts in

Table 1. The proposed optimization algorithm

---

1. Randomly initialize $\mathbf{X}_0$ such that $\mathbf{Tr}(\mathbf{X}_0) = 1, \mathbf{rank}(\mathbf{X}_0) = 1$;
ε is a pre-set small value.
2. For $k = 1, 2, \ldots$
    2.1 Compute ρ_k by solving the subproblem
$$\rho_k = \arg\max_{\rho > 0} f(\mathbf{X}_{k-1}, \rho).$$
    2.2 Compute $\mathbf{X}_k$ by solving the problem
$$\mathbf{X}_k = \arg\max_{\mathbf{X} \succcurlyeq 0, \mathbf{Tr}(\mathbf{X})=1} f(\mathbf{X}, \rho_k).$$
    2.3 If $|f(\mathbf{X}_k, \rho_k) - f(\mathbf{X}_{k-1}, \rho_k)| < \varepsilon$ and $|f(\mathbf{X}_{k-1}, \rho_k) - f(\mathbf{X}_{k-1}, \rho_{k-1})| < \varepsilon$
$(k > 1)$,
       break.
3. End for.

---

the huber loss function, and they together form a continuous and differentiable function of z. This loss function approaches the hinge loss curve when $h \to 0$. Although the huber loss is a bit more complicated than the squared hinge loss, its function value increases linearly with the value of $\langle \mathbf{A}^r, \mathbf{X} \rangle - \rho$. Hence, when a training set contains outliers or sample heavily contaminated by noise, the huber loss can often give a more reasonable (milder) penalty than the squared hinge loss does. We discuss both loss functions in our experimental study. Note that by using these two loss functions, the cost function $f(\mathbf{X}, \rho)$ that we are going to optimization becomes differentiable with respect to both $\mathbf{X}$ and ρ.

4   A Fast Optimization Algorithm

The proposed algorithm maximizes the objective function iteratively, and in each iteration the two variables $\mathbf{X}$ and ρ are optimized alternatively. Note that optimizing in this alternative way will not prevent the global optimum from being obtained because $f(\mathbf{X}, \rho)$ is a convex function in both variables $(\mathbf{X}, \rho)$ and $(\mathbf{X}, \rho)$ are not coupled together. The pseudo-code of the proposed algorithm is given in Table 1. Note that ρ_k is a scalar and the step 2.1 in Table 1 can be solved directly by a simple one-dimensional maximization process. However, $\mathbf{X}$ is a psd matrix with size of $D \times D$. Recall that D is the dimensionality of feature vectors. The following section presents how $\mathbf{X}$ is efficiently optimized in our algorithm.

4.1   Compute the Mahalanobis Matrix $\mathbf{X}_k$

Let $\mathcal{P} = \{\mathbf{X} \in \mathbb{R}^{D \times D} : \mathbf{X} \succcurlyeq 0, \mathbf{Tr}(\mathbf{X}) = 1\}$ be the domain in which a feasible $\mathbf{X}$ lies. Note that $\mathcal{P}$ is a convex set of $\mathbf{X}$. As shown in Step 2.2 in Table 1, we need to solve the following maximization problem:

$$\max_{\mathbf{X} \in \mathcal{P}} f(\mathbf{X}, \rho_k), \tag{11}$$

Table 2. Compute $\mathbf{X}_k$ in the proposed algorithm

---
1. Given ρ_k and initial approximation $\mathbf{X}_k$, calculate $\nabla f(\mathbf{X}_k, \rho_k)$.
2. For $i = 1, 2, \ldots$
   2.1 Compute v_i corresponds to the largest eigen value of $\nabla f(\mathbf{X}_i, \rho_k)$.
   2.2 If the largest eigen value is less than ε, break.
   2.3 Let the search direction $\mathbf{p}_i = v_i v_i^T - \mathbf{X}_i$.
   2.4 Set $\mathbf{X}_{i+1} = \mathbf{X}_i + \alpha \mathbf{p}_i$. α is found by line search.
3. End for.
4. Set $\mathbf{X}_{k+1} = \mathbf{X}_i$.

---

where ρ_k is the output of Step 2.1. Our algorithm offers a simple and efficient way for solving this problem by automatically maintaining the positive semidefinite property of the matrix $\mathbf{X}$. It needs only compute the principal eigenvalue computation whereas the previous approaches such as the method of [9] require to carry out a full eigen-decomposition of $\mathbf{X}$.

Let $\nabla f(\mathbf{X}, \rho_k)$ be the gradient matrix of f with respect to $\mathbf{X}$ and α be a step size for updating $\mathbf{X}$. Recall that we update $\mathbf{X}$ in such a way that $\mathbf{X}_{i+1} = (1 - \alpha)\mathbf{X}_{i+1} + \alpha \triangle \mathbf{X}$, where $\mathbf{rank}(\triangle \mathbf{X}) = 1$ and $\mathbf{Tr}(\triangle \mathbf{X}) = 1$. To find the $\triangle \mathbf{X}$ that satisfies these constraints and in the meantime can best approximate the gradient matrix $\nabla f(\mathbf{X}, \rho_k)$, we need to solve the following optimization problem:

$$\max \quad \langle \nabla f(\mathbf{X}, \rho_k), \triangle \mathbf{X} \rangle$$

$$\text{s.t. } \mathbf{rank}(\triangle \mathbf{X}) = 1, \quad \mathbf{Tr}(\triangle \mathbf{X}) = 1. \tag{12}$$

Clearly *the optimal* $\triangle \mathbf{X}^\star$ *is exactly* $v_i v_i^T$ *where* v_i *is the eigenvector of* $\nabla f(\mathbf{X}, \rho_k)$ *that corresponds to the largest eigenvalue.* Hence, to solve the above optimization, we only need to compute the principal eigenvector of the matrix $\nabla f(\mathbf{X}, \rho_k)$. The step 2.2 is elaborated in Table 2. Note that $\mathbf{X}$ still retains the properties of $\mathbf{X} \succcurlyeq 0, \mathbf{Tr}(\mathbf{X}) = 1$ after this process.

Clearly, a key parameter of this optimization process is α which implicitly decides the total number of iterations. The computational overhead of our algorithm is proportional to the number of iterations. Hence, to achieve a fast optimization process, we need to ensure that in each iteration the α can lead to a sufficient reduction on the value of f. This is discussed in the following part.

4.2 Compute the Step Size α

We employ the backtracking line search algorithm in [11] to identify a suitable α. It reduces the value of α until the Wolfe conditions are satisfied. As shown in Table 2, the search direction is $\mathbf{p}_i = v_i v_i^T - \mathbf{X}_i$. The Wolfe conditions that we use are

$$f(\mathbf{X}_i + \alpha \mathbf{p}_i, \rho_i) \leq f(\mathbf{X}_i, \rho_i) + c_1 \alpha \mathbf{p}_i^T \nabla f(\mathbf{X}_i, \rho_i),$$

$$\left| \mathbf{p}_i^T \nabla f(\mathbf{X}_i + \alpha \mathbf{p}_i, \rho_i) \right| \leq c_2 \left| \mathbf{p}_i^T \nabla f(\mathbf{X}_i, \rho_i) \right|. \tag{13}$$

Table 3. The ten benchmark data sets used in our experiment

	N_{trn}	N_{val}	N_{tst}	N_{fea}	N_{fea} after PCA	N_{class}	N_{runs}
USPS	5,833	1,458	2,007	256	60	10	1
MNIST	7,000	1,500	1,500	784	60	10	1
Letter	10,500	4,500	5,000	16	16	26	1
ORLface	280	60	60	2,576	42	40	10
Twin-Peaks	14,000	3,000	3,000	3	3	11	10
Wine	126	26	26	13	13	3	10
Balance	439	93	93	4	4	3	10
Vehicle	593	127	126	18	18	4	10
Breast-Cancer	479	102	102	10	10	2	10
Diabetes	538	115	115	8	8	2	10
Face-Background	472	101	382	100	100	2	10

where $0 < c_1 < c_2 < 1$. The result of backtracking line search is an acceptable α which can give rise to sufficient reduction on the function value of f. It will shown in the experimental study that with this setting our optimization algorithm can achieve higher computational efficiency that the existing solvers.

5   Experimental Result

The goal of this experiment is to verify the efficiency of our algorithm in achieving better classification performances with less computational cost. We perform experiments on 10 data sets described in Table 3. Here, N_{train}, N_{vali}, and N_{test} denote the sizes of the training sets, validation sets, and the test sets, respectively. N_{class} is the number of class and N_{fea} shows the dimensionality of the feature vectors and "N_{fea} after PCA" is the number of features that are preserved after the Principal Component Analysis. The Wine, Balance, Vehicle, Breast-Cancer and Diabetes sets are obtained from UCI Machine Learning Repository[1], and USPS, MNIST and Letter are from libSVM[2]. For MNIST, we only use its test data in our experiment. The ORLface data is from ATT research[3] and Twin-Peaks is downloaded from Laurens van der Maaten's website[4]. The Face and Background classes (435 and 520 images respectively) in the image retrieval experiment are obtained from the Caltech-101 object database [12]. To accumulate statistics, the ORLface, Twin-Peaks, Wine, Balance, Vehicle, Diabetes and Face-Background data sets are randomly split as 10 pairs of train/validation/test subsets and experiments on those data set are repeated 10 times with each pairs.

The k-NN classifier with the Mahalanobis distance learned by our algorithm (called SDPMetric in short) is compared with the k-NN classifiers using a simple Euclidean distance ("Euclidean" in short) and that learned by the large

---

[1] Asuncion, A. Newman, D.J. (2007) UCI Machine Learning Repository [http://www.ics.uci.edu/~mlearn/MLRepository.html]. Irvine, CA: University of California, School of Information and Computer Science.

[2] C.-C. Chang and C.-J. Lin, LIBSVM: a library for support vector machines, 2001. The software is freely available at: http://www.csie.ntu.edu.tw/~cjlin/libsvm.

[3] Available at http://www.uk.research.att.com/facedatabase.html

[4] http://ticc.uvt.nl/lvdrmaaten/

margin nearest neighbor in [9] (LMNN[5] in short). Since Weinberger et al. [9] has shown that LMNN obtains the classification performance comparable to SVMs, we focus on the comparison between our algorithm and LMNN. To prepare the training set $\mathcal{S}$, we apply the 3-Nearest Neighbor method to these data sets to generate the training triplets for our algorithm and LMNN, except that the Twin-peaks and ORLface are applied with the 1-NN method. Also, the experiment compares the two variants of our proposed SDPMetric, which use the squared hinge loss (SDPMetric-S in short) and the huber loss(SDPMetric-H in short), respectively. We split each data set into 70/15/15% randomly and refer to those split sets as training, validating and testing sets except pre-separated data sets(Letter and USPS) and Face-Background which was made for image retrieval. Following [9], LMNN uses 85/15% data for training and testing. The training data is also split into 70/15% inside LMNN to be consistent with our SDPMetric. Since USPS data set has been split into training/test already, only the training data are divided into 70/15% as training and validation sets. The Letter data set is separated according to Hsu et al. [13]. As in [9], the Principal Component Analysis (PCA) is applied to USPS, MNIST and ORLface to reduce the dimensions of feature vectors.

The following experimental study demonstrates that our algorithm achieves higher classification accuracy with much less computational cost than LMNN on most of the tested data sets. The detailed test error rates and timing results are reported in Table 4 and 5. As shown, the test error rates of SDPMetric-S are comparable to those of LMNN and SDPMetric-H achieves lower misclassification error rates than LMNN and the Euclidean distance on most of data sets except Face-Background data which made as a image retrieval problem and MNIST on which SDPMetric-S achieves low error rate.

Before reporting the timing result on these benchmark data sets, we compare our algorithm with SeDuMi[6] and SDPT3[7] which are used as solvers in CVX[8]. We randomly generate 1,000 training triplets and gradually increase the dimensionality of feature vectors from 20 to 100. Fig. 2 illustrates computational time of ours, CVX/SeDuMi and CVX/SDPT3. As shown, the computational load of our algorithm almost keeps constant as the dimensionality increases. In contrast, the computational load of CVX/SeDuMi and CVX/SDPT3 rise rapidly in this course. In the case of the dimension of 100, the difference on optimization time can be as large as 800–1000 seconds. The computational time of LMNN, SDPMetric-S and SDPMetric-H are compared in Table 5. As shown, LMNN is

---

[5] Note that to be consistent with the setting in [9], LMNN here also uses the "obj=1" option and updates the projection matrix to speed up its computation. If we update the distance matrix directly to get global optimum, LMNN would be much more slower due to full eigen-decomposition at each iterations.

[6] A software package to solve optimization problems which is from http://sedumi.ie.lehigh.edu/.

[7] A software to solve conic optimization problems involving semidefinite, second-order and linear cone constraints. http://www.math.nus.edu.sg/~mattohkc/sdpt3.html

[8] Matlab Software for Disciplined Convex Programming. The CVX package is available from http://www.stanford.edu/boyd/cvx/index.html

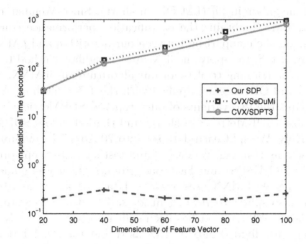

Fig. 2. Computational time vs. the dimensionality of feature vector

Table 4. 3-Nearest Neighbor misclassification error rates. The standard deviation values are in brackets.

	Euclidean	LMNN	SDPMetric-S	SDPMetric-H
USPS	5.63	**5.18**	5.28	**5.18**
MNIST	3.15	3.15	**3.00**	3.35
Letter	5.38	4.04	3.60	**3.46**
ORLface	6.00 (3.46)	5.00 (2.36)	4.75 (2.36)	**4.25 (2.97)**
Twin-Peaks	1.03 (0.21)	0.90 (0.19)	1.17 (0.20)	**0.79 (0.19)**
Wine	24.62 (5.83)	3.85 (2.72)	3.46 (2.69)	**3.08 (2.31)**
Bal	19.14 (1.59)	14.19 (4.12)	**9.78 (3.17)**)	10.32 (3.44)
Vehicle	28.41 (2.41)	21.59 (2.71)	21.67 (4.00)	**20.87 (2.97)**
Breast-Cancer	4.51 (1.49)	4.71 (1.61)	3.33 (1.40)	**2.94 (0.88)**
Diabetes	28.00 (2.84)	27.65 (3.45)	28.70 (3.67)	**27.64 (3.71)**
Face-Background	26.41 (2.72)	**14.71 (1.33)**	16.75 (1.72)	15.86 (1.37)

Table 5. Computational time per each run(seconds)

	LMNN	SDPMetric-S	SDPMetric-H
USPS	256s	111s	258s
MNIST	219s	111s	99s
Letter	1036s	6s	136s
ORLface	13s	4s	3s
Twin-peakes	595s	less than 1s	less than 1s
Wine	9s	2s	2s
Bal	7s	less than 1s	2s
Vehicle	19s	2s	7s
Breast-Cancer	4s	2s	3s
Diabetes	10s	less than 1s	2s
Face-Background	92s	5s	5s

always slower than the proposed SDPMetric which converges very fast on these data sets. Especially, on the Letter and Twin-Peaks data sets, SDPMetric shows significantly improved computational efficiency.

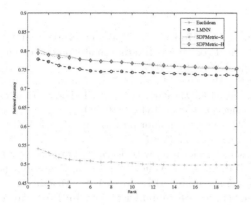

Fig. 3. Retrieval performance of SDPMetric, LMNN and the Euclidean distance

Face-Background data set consists of the two object classes, Face_easy and BACKGROUND_Google in [12], as a retrieval problem. The images in the class of BACKGROUND_Google are randomly collected from the Internet and they are used to represent the non-target class. For each image, a number of interest regions are identified by the Harris-Affine detector [14] and the visual content in each region is characterized by the SIFT descriptor [15]. A codebook of size 100 is created by using k-means clustering. Each image is then represented by a 100-dimensional histogram containing the number of occurrences of each visual word. We evaluate retrieval accuracy using each facial image in a test subset as a query. For each compared metric, the *Accuracy* of the retrieved top 1 to 20 images are computed, which is defined as the ratio of the number of facial images to the total number of retrieved images. We calculate the average accuracy of each test subset and then average over the whole 10 test subsets. Fig. 3 shows the retrieval accuracies of the Mahalanobis distances learned by Euclidean, LMNN and SDPMetric. we clearly observe that SDPMetric-H and SDPMetric-S consistently give the higher retrieval accuracy values, which again verifies their advantages over the LMNN and Euclidean distance.

6 Conclusion

We have proposed an algorithm to show how to efficiently learn the Mahalanobis distance metric with maximal margin. Enlightened by that important theorem on psd matrix decomposition, we design a gradient descent approach to update the Mahalanobis matrix with light computational load and well maintain its psd property in the whole optimization process. Experimental study on benchmark data sets and the retrieval problem verify the superior classification performance and computational efficiency of the proposed distance metric learning algorithm.

References

1. Winn, J., Criminisi, A., Minka, T.: Object categorization by learned universal visual dictionary. In: Proc. IEEE International Conference on Computer Vision, Beijing, China, pp. 1800–1807 (2005)
2. Smeulders, A.W.M., Worring, M., Santini, S., Gupta, A., Jain, R.: Content-based image retrieval at the end of the early years. IEEE Transactions on Pattern Analysis and Machine Intelligence 22(12), 1349–1380 (2000)
3. Cover, T., Hart, P.: Nearest neighbor pattern classification. IEEE Transactions on Information Theory 13, 21–27 (1967)
4. Scholkpf, B., Smola, A.: Learning with Kernels, Support Vector Machines, Regularization, Optimization, and Beyond. MIT Press, Cambridge (2002)
5. Xing, E.P., Ng, A.Y., Jordan, M.I., Russell, S.: Distance metric learning, with application to clustering with side-information. In: Proc. Advances in Neural Information Processing Systems, pp. 505–512. MIT Press, Cambridge (2003)
6. Yang, L., Sukthankar, R., Hoi, S.C.: A boosting framework for visuality-preserving distance metric learning and its application to medical image retrieval. IEEE Transactions on Pattern Analysis and Machine Intelligence 10 (November 2008)
7. Vapnik, V.: Statistical learning theory. John Wiley and Sons Inc., New York (1998)
8. Shen, C., Welsh, A., Wang, L.: PSDBoost: Matrix-generation linear programming for positive semidefinite matrices learning. In: Proc. Advances in Neural Information Processing Systems, pp. 1473–1480. MIT Press, Cambridge (2008)
9. Weinberger, K.Q., Blitzer, J., Saul, L.K.: Distance metric learning for large margin nearest neighbor classification. In: Proc. Advances in Neural Information Processing Systems, pp. 1475–1482 (2006)
10. Goldberger, J., Roweis, S., Hinton, G., Salakhutdinov, R.: Neighbourhood components analysis. In: Proc. Advances in Neural Information Processing Systems (2005)
11. Nocedal, J., Wright, S.J.: Numerical optimization. Springer, New York (1999)
12. Fei-Fei, L., Fergus, R., Perona, P.: Learning generative visual models from few training examples: an incremental bayesian approach tested on 101 object categories. In: Workshop on Generative-Model Based Vision, IEEE Conference on Computer Vision and Pattern Recognition (2004)
13. Hsu, C.W., Lin, C.J.: A comparison of methods for multi-class support vector machines. IEEE Transactions on Neural Networks 13(2), 415–425 (2002)
14. Mikolajczyk, K., Schmid, C.: Scale & affine invariant interest point detectors. International Journal of Computer Vision 60(1), 63–86 (2004)
15. Lowe, D.G.: Object recognition from local scale-invariant features. In: Proc. IEEE International Conference on Computer Vision, pp. 1150–1157 (1999)

Lorentzian Discriminant Projection and Its Applications

Risheng Liu[1], Zhixun Su[1], Zhouchen Lin[2], and Xiaoyu Hou[1]

[1] Dalian University of Technology, Dalian 116024, China
[2] Microsoft Research Asia, Beijing 100190, China
zxsu@hotmail.com

Abstract. This paper develops a supervised dimensionality reduction method, Lorentzian Discriminant Projection (LDP), for discriminant analysis and classification. Our method represents the structures of sample data by a manifold, which is furnished with a Lorentzian metric tensor. Different from classic discriminant analysis techniques, LDP uses distances from points to their within-class neighbors and global geometric centroid to model a new manifold to detect the intrinsic local and global geometric structures of data set. In this way, both the geometry of a group of classes and global data structures can be learnt from the Lorentzian metric tensor. Thus discriminant analysis in the original sample space reduces to metric learning on a Lorentzian manifold. The experimental results on benchmark databases demonstrate the effectiveness of our proposed method.

Keywords: Dimensionality reduction, Lorentzian geometry, metric learning, discriminant analysis.

1 Introduction

In recent years, the computer vision and pattern recognition community has witnessed a growing interest in dimensionality reduction. One of the most successful and well-studied techniques is the supervised discriminant analysis. We devote this paper to addressing the discriminant analysis from the perspective of Lorentzian geometry.

1.1 Related Work

Principal Component Analysis (PCA) [1] and Linear Discriminant Analysis (LDA) [2] are two most popular linear dimensionality reduction techniques. PCA projects the data points along the directions of maximal variances and aims to preserve the Euclidean distances between samples. Unlike PCA which is unsupervised, LDA is supervised. It searches for the projection axes on which the points of different classes are far from each other and at the same time the data points of the same class are close to each other. However, these linear models may fail to discover nonlinear data structures.

During the recent years, a n umber of nonlinear dimensionality reduction algorithms called manifold learning have been developed to address this issue [14][5][11][6][7][10]. However, these nonlinear techniques might not be suitable for real world applications because they yield maps that are defined only on the training data points. To compute the maps for the new testing points requires extra effort.

H. Zha, R.-i. Taniguchi, and S. Maybank (Eds.): ACCV 2009, Part III, LNCS 5996, pp. 311–320, 2010.

Along this direction, there is considerable interest in using linear methods, inspired by the geometric intuition of manifold learning, to find the nonlinear structure of data set. Some popular ones include Locality Preserving Projection (LPP) [16][9], Neighborhood Preserving Embedding (NPE) [15], Marginal Fisher Analysis (MFA) [8], Maximum Margin Criterion (MMC) [17], Average Neighborhood Margin Maximization (ANMM) [18], Semi-Riemannian Discriminant Analysis (SRDA) [4] and Unsupervised Discriminant Projection (UDP) [19].

1.2 Our Approach

Yang *et al* . [19] adapted both local and global scatters to unsupervised dimensionality reduction. They maximized the ratio of the global scatters to the local scatters. Zhao *et al* . [4] first applied the semi-Riemannian geometry to classification [4]. Inspired by prior work, in this paper, we propose a novel method, called Lorentzian Discriminant Projection (LDP), which focuses on supervised dimensionality reduction. Its goal is to discover both local class discriminant and global geometric structures of the data set. We first construct a manifold to model the local class and the global data structures. In this way, both of the local discriminant and the global geometric structures of the data set can be accurately characterized by learning a special Lorentzian metric tensor on the newly built manifold. In fact, the role of Lorentzian metric learning is to transfer the geometry from the sample space to the feature space.

The rest of this paper is organized as follows. In Section 2, we provide the Lorentzian Discriminant Projection algorithm. The experimental results of LDP approach to real-world face analysis and handwriting digits classification are presented in Section 3. Finally, we summarize our work and conclude the paper in Section 4.

2   Lorentzian Discriminant Projection

2.1   Fundamentals of Lorentzian Manifold

In differential geometry, a semi-Riemannian manifold is a generalization of a Riemannian manifold. It is furnished with a non-degenerate and symmetric metric tensor called the semi-Riemannian metric tensor. The metric matrix on the semi-Riemannian manifold is diagonalizable and the diagonal entries are non-zero. We use the metric signature to denote the number of positive and negative ones. Given a semi-Riemannian manifold $\mathbb{M}$ of dimension n, if the metric has p positive and q negative diagonal entries, then the metric signature is (p, q), where $p + q = n$. This concept is extensively used in general relativity, as a basic geometric tool for modeling the space-time in physics.

Lorentzian manifold is the most important subclass of semi-Riemannian manifold in which the metric signature is $(n - 1, 1)$. The metric matrix on the Lorentzian manifold $\mathbb{L}_1^n$ is of form

$$\mathbf{G} = \begin{bmatrix} \hat{A}_{(n-1)\times(n-1)} & 0 \\ 0 & -\check{\lambda} \end{bmatrix}, \tag{1}$$

where $\hat{\Lambda}_{(n-1)\times(n-1)}$ is diagonal and its diagonal entries and $\check{\lambda}$ are positive. Suppose that $\mathbf{r} = [\hat{\mathbf{r}}^T, \check{r}]^T$ is an n-dimensional vector, then a metric tensor $g(\mathbf{r},\mathbf{r})$ with respect to $\mathbf{G}$ is expressible as

$$g(\mathbf{r},\mathbf{r}) = \mathbf{r}^T \mathbf{G} \mathbf{r} = \hat{\mathbf{r}}^T \hat{\Lambda} \hat{\mathbf{r}} - \check{\lambda}(\check{r})^2. \tag{2}$$

Because of the nondegeneracy of the Lorentzian metric, vectors can be classified into space-like ($g(\mathbf{r},\mathbf{r}) > 0$ or $\mathbf{r} = 0$), time-like ($g(\mathbf{r},\mathbf{r}) < 0$) or null ($g(\mathbf{r},\mathbf{r}) = 0$ and $\mathbf{r} \neq 0$). One may refer to [3] for more details.

2.2 The Motivation of LDP

The theory and algorithm in this paper are based on the perspective that the discrimination is tightly related to both local class and global data structures. Our motivation of LDP are twofold: the viewpoint of Lorentzian manifold applied to general relativity and the success of considering both local and global structures for dimensionality reduction.

The Lorentzian geometry has been successfully applied to Einstein's general relativity to model the space-time as a 4-dimensional Lorentzian manifold of signature (3,1). And as will be shown later, this manifold is also convenient to model the structures of a group of classes. On one hand, we model the local class structure by the distances between each sample and its within-class neighbors. We also characterize the global data structure by the distances between each point and the global geometric centorid. Combining both local and global distances together, we naturally form a new manifold to preserve discriminant structure for data set. On the other hand, to optimize both local and global structures at the same time, we need to perform discrepancies of within-class quantities and global quantities. To do so, we introduce Lorentzian metrics which are the unique tools to integrate such kinds of dual quantities from the mathematical point of view. Therefore, the discriminant structure of the data set is initially modeled as a Lorentzian manifold where coordinates are characterized by the distances between sample pairs (each point with its within-class neighbors and the global geometric centorid). Furthermore, we use the positive part $\hat{\Lambda}$ to handle the local class structure and the negative part $-\check{\lambda}$ to model the global data structure.

To this end, learning a discriminant subspace reduces to learning the geometry of a Lorentzian manifold. Thus, supervised dimensionality reduction is coupled with Lorentzian metric learning. Moreover, we present an approach to optimize both the local discriminant and global geometric structures by learning the Lorentzian metric in the original sample space and apply it to the discriminant subspace.

2.3 Modeling Features as a Lorentzian Manifold

For supervised dimensionality reduction task, the samples can be represented as a point set $\mathcal{S}_x = \{\mathbf{x}_1, ..., \mathbf{x}_m\}$, $\mathbf{x}_i \in \mathbb{R}^n$. The class label of $\mathbf{x}_i$ is denoted by C_i and m_i is the number of points which share the same label with $\mathbf{x}_i$. As we have previously described, the goal of the proposed algorithm is to transform points from the original high-dimensional sample space to a low-dimensional discriminant subspace, i.e. $\mathcal{S}_y \subset \mathbb{R}^d$ where $d \ll n$. In this subspace, feature points belonging to the same class should have higher within-class similarity and more consistent global geometric structure. To achieve this goal, we introduce a Lorentzian manifold to model the structure of features in a low dimensional discriminant subspace.

With $\mathbf{y}_i$, $\mathcal{S}_{y_i} = \{\mathbf{y}_i, \mathbf{y}_1^i, ..., \mathbf{y}_{m_i-1}^i\}$ (points share the same class label with $\mathbf{y}_i$) and $\bar{\mathbf{y}}$ (the geometric centroid of $\mathcal{S}_y$, i.e., $\bar{\mathbf{y}} = \frac{1}{m} \sum_{i=1}^{m} \mathbf{y}_i$), a new point $\mathbf{d}_{y_i}$ is defined as:

$$\mathbf{d}_{y_i} = [d(\mathbf{y}_i, \mathbf{y}_1^i), ..., d(\mathbf{y}_i, \mathbf{y}_{m_i-1}^i), d(\mathbf{y}_i, \bar{\mathbf{y}})]^T = [\hat{\mathbf{d}}_{y_i}^T, d(\mathbf{y}_i, \bar{\mathbf{y}})]^T, \qquad (3)$$

where $\mathbf{y}_j^i \in \mathcal{S}_{y_i}$ and $d(\mathbf{y}_p, \mathbf{y}_q)$ is the distance between $\mathbf{y}_p$ and $\mathbf{y}_q$. It is easy to see that this coordinate representation can contain both local within-class similarity and global geometric structure. We consider these m_i-tuple coordinate representations as points sampled from a new manifold $\mathbb{L}_1^{m_i}$ furnished with a Lorentzian metric tensor g_l. It is straightforward to see that $g_l(\mathbf{d}_{y_i}, \mathbf{d}_{y_i})$ can be written as

$$g_l(\mathbf{d}_{y_i}, \mathbf{d}_{y_i}) = \mathbf{d}_{y_i}^T \mathbf{G}_i^l \mathbf{d}_{y_i} = tr((\mathbf{Y}_i \mathbf{D}_i)\mathbf{G}_i^l(\mathbf{Y}_i \mathbf{D}_i)^T), \qquad (4)$$

where the metric matrix $\mathbf{G}_i^l$ is real diagonal and the signature of the metric is $(m_i - 1, 1)$, $\mathbf{D}_i = [\mathbf{e}_{m_i}, -\mathbf{I}_{m_i \times m_i}]^T$ ($\mathbf{I}_{m_i \times m_i}$ is an identity matrix of size $m_i \times m_i$ and $\mathbf{e}_{m_i}$ is an all-one column vector of length m_i) and $\mathbf{Y}_i = [\mathbf{y}_i, \mathbf{y}_1^i, ...\mathbf{y}_{m_i-1}^i, \bar{\mathbf{y}}]$.

Then the total Lorentzian metric tensor can be given as:

$$\sum_{i=1}^{m} g_l(\mathbf{d}_{y_i}, \mathbf{d}_{y_i}) = tr(\mathbf{Y}\mathbf{L}\mathbf{Y}^T), \qquad (5)$$

where $\mathbf{L} = \sum_{i=1}^{m} \mathbf{B}_i \mathbf{D}_i \mathbf{G}_i^l \mathbf{D}_i^T \mathbf{B}_i^T$, $\mathbf{Y} = [\mathbf{y}_1, ..., \mathbf{y}_m, \bar{\mathbf{y}}]$ and $\mathbf{B}_i$ is a binary selection matrix of size $(m + 1) \times (m_i + 1)$ which satisfies $\mathbf{Y}_i = \mathbf{Y}\mathbf{B}_i$ [13][12].

If there is a linear isometric transformation between the low dimensional feature $\mathbf{y}$ and the original sample $\mathbf{x}$, i.e., $\mathbf{y} \to \mathbf{U}\mathbf{y} = \mathbf{x}$, we can have an optimization model:

$$\begin{cases} \arg\min_{\mathbf{U}} tr(\mathbf{U}^T \mathbf{X}\mathbf{L}\mathbf{X}^T \mathbf{U}), \\ s.t. \ \mathbf{U}^T \mathbf{U} = \mathbf{I}_{d \times d}. \end{cases} \qquad (6)$$

The linear transformation $\mathbf{U}$ that minimizes the objective function in (6) can be found as being composed of the eigenvectors associated with the d smallest eigenvalues of the following problem:

$$\mathbf{X}\mathbf{L}\mathbf{X}^T \mathbf{u} = \lambda \mathbf{u}. \qquad (7)$$

It is sufficient to note that the Lorentzian metric tensor forms the geometry of the feature structure. Thus a question naturally arises: how to learn a special Lorentzian metric tensor to furnish the newly built manifold? This is discussed in the next subsection.

2.4   Learning the Lorentzian Manifold

The Lorentzian metric matrices $\mathbf{G}_i^l$ are key to the proposed dimensionality reduction problem. We give a novel method to learn it from the sample set $\mathcal{S}_x$ and then apply it to the feature set $\mathcal{S}_y$. The metric $\mathbf{G}_i^l$ consists of two parts: the positive-definite part $\hat{\Lambda}_i$ and the negative-definite part $-\check{\lambda}_i$. In this subsection, we introduce an efficient way to learn $\hat{\Lambda}_i$ and $\check{\lambda}_i$ successively. The positive part of the Lorentzian metric tensor in the original sample space can be given as:

$$g_l^p(\hat{\mathbf{d}}_{x_i}, \hat{\mathbf{d}}_{x_i}) = \hat{\mathbf{d}}_{x_i}^T \hat{\Lambda}_i \hat{\mathbf{d}}_{x_i} = \mathbf{g}_i^T \hat{\mathbf{D}}_{x_i} \mathbf{g}_i, \tag{8}$$

where

$$\mathbf{g}_i = [\sqrt{\hat{\Lambda}_i(1,1)}, ..., \sqrt{\hat{\Lambda}_i(m_i - 1, m_i - 1)}]^T$$

and

$$\hat{\mathbf{D}}_{x_i} = \text{diag}(d(\mathbf{x}_i, \mathbf{x}_1^i)^2, ..., d(\mathbf{x}_i, \mathbf{x}_{m_i-1}^i)^2).$$

We may minimize this metric and obtain the following optimization problem:

$$\begin{cases} \arg\min_{\mathbf{g}_i} \mathbf{g}_i^T \hat{\mathbf{D}}_{x_i} \mathbf{g}_i, \\ s.t. \ \mathbf{e}_{m_i-1}^T \mathbf{g}_i = 1. \end{cases} \tag{9}$$

It is easy to check that the solution to the above problem is

$$\mathbf{g}_i = \frac{(\hat{\mathbf{D}}_{x_i})^{-1} \mathbf{e}_{m_i-1}}{\mathbf{e}_{m_i-1}^T (\hat{\mathbf{D}}_{x_i})^{-1} \mathbf{e}_{m_i-1}}. \tag{10}$$

Thus the positive-definite part $\hat{\Lambda}_i$ can be obtained as

$$\hat{\Lambda}_i(p,q) = \begin{cases} \mathbf{g}_i(p)^2 & \text{if } p = q, \\ 0 & \text{otherwise.} \end{cases} \tag{11}$$

As introduced in Section 2.1, a null (or light-like) vector $\mathbf{r}$ is the vector that vanishes the metric tensor: $g(\mathbf{r}, \mathbf{r}) = 0$. Inspired by this physical property used in general relativity, we can make the metric locally unbiased. So the negative definite part $\check{\lambda}_i$ of $\mathbf{G}_i^l$ can be determined by:

$$\sum_{j=1}^{m_i-1} \hat{\Lambda}_i(j,j) + \check{\lambda}_i = 0. \tag{12}$$

We empirically find that the discriminability will be enhanced if we choose a positive factor $\gamma \in [0,1]$ to multiply the negative part i.e., $\check{\lambda}_i \leftarrow \gamma \check{\lambda}_i$. The value of γ can be determined by cross validation.

3   Experimental Results

Experiments are conducted on Yale[1], FRGC [20] and USPS[2] databases to test the performance of LDP against the existing algorithms. For these databases, the image set of each subject is split into different gallery and probe sets, where Gm/Pn means m

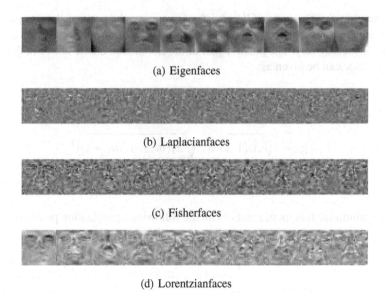

(a) Eigenfaces

(b) Laplacianfaces

(c) Fisherfaces

(d) Lorentzianfaces

Fig. 1. Eigenfaces, Laplacianfaces, Fisherfaces and our proposed Lorentzianfaces

images are randomly selected for training and the remaining n images are for testing. Such a trial is repeated 20 times.

In the face analysis (representation and recognition) problem, we want to use LDP to learn an optimal discriminant subspace which is spanned by the columns of U in (6) for face representation. The eigenvectors can be displayed as images, called the Lorentzianfaces in our approach. Using the facial images in experiment 4 of FRGC version 2 as the training set, we present the first 10 Lorentzianfaces in Figure 1, together with Eigenfaces [1], Laplacianfaces [9] and Fisherfaces [2].

We perform the discriminant subspace learning on the expressive features yielded by PCA which is classic and well-recognized preprocessing. For the PCA-based two step strategy, the number of principal components is a free parameter. In our experiments, we choose the percentage of the energy retained in the PCA preprocessing step to be 99%.

3.1   Experiments on Yale

The Yale face database was constructed at the Yale Center for the Computational Vision and Control. It contains 165 gray-scale images of 15 subjects under various facial expressions and lighting conditions such as center-light, with glasses, happy, left-light, without glasses, normal, right-light, sad, sleepy, surprised, and winking. In our experiment, we cropped each image to a size of 32×32. Figure 2 shows some cropped images in Yale database.

The average recognition rate of each method and the corresponding dimension are given in Table 1. The recognition rate curves versus the variation of dimensions are

---

[1] Available at http://cvc.yale.edu/projects/yalefaces/yalefaces.html

[2] Available at http://www.cs.toronto.edu/ roweis/data.html

Table 1. The average recognition results on Yale (G4/P7 and G6/P5) and FRGC (G3/P27 and G5/P25) databases (mean ± std %). The optimal dimension of the face subspace are given in the brackets.

Method	Yale		FRGC	
	G4/P7	G6/P5	G3/P27	G5/P25
Eigenfaces	57.6 ± 3.7 (40)	59.6 ± 5.2 (15)	48.3 ± 4.3 (120)	58.6 ± 3.5 (120)
Laplacianfaces	46.2 ± 5.2 (55)	46.4 ± 7.0 (65)	46.6 ± 3.5 (120)	57.7 ± 2.1 (120)
Fisherfaces	70.4 ± 4.8 (15)	72.7 ± 6.4 (15)	74.2 ± 5.4 (80)	87.5 ± 1.7 (75)
MMC + PCA	70.1 ± 4.5 (20)	70.5 ± 5.6 (40)	61.1 ± 7.1 (110)	78.0 ± 6.4 (85)
MFA + PCA	67.1 ± 6.0 (15)	70.1 ± 6.5 (25)	72.9 ± 5.1 (50)	85.7 ± 3.8 (65)
Lorentzianfaces	**72.9 ± 5.3 (20)**	**74.3 ± 6.2 (15)**	**80.6 ± 5.2 (60)**	**89.4 ± 2.2 (50)**

Fig. 2. Some cropped Yale facial images

illustrated in Figure 3. As can be seen, the proposed Lorentzianfaces outperforms other methods involved in this experiment.

3.2 Experiments on FRGC

Experiments are also conducted on a subset of facial data in experiment 4 of FRGC version 2 [20] that measures the recognition performance from uncontrolled images. Experiment 4 is the most challenging FRGC experiment which has 8014 single

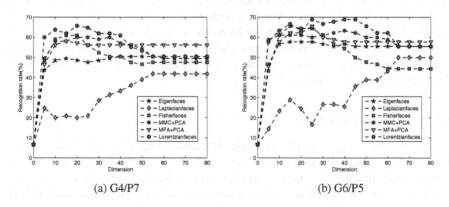

(a) G4/P7   (b) G6/P5

Fig. 3. The recognition rate curves versus the variation of dimensions on Yale database. The left figure shows the G4/P7 results and the right one shows the G6/P5 results.

Fig. 4. Some cropped FRGC version 2 facial images

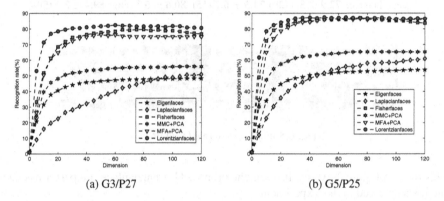

(a) G3/P27   (b) G5/P25

Fig. 5. The recognition rate curves versus the variation of dimensions on experiment 4 of FRGC version 2 database. The left figure shows the G3/P27 results and the right one shows the G5/P25 results.

uncontrolled still images of 466 subjects in the query set. We choose the first 30 images of each subject in this set if the number of images is not less than 30. Thus we get 2850 images of 95 subjects. The images are all cropped to a size of 32×32. Figure 4 shows the facial images of one subject in our experiment.

Table 1 also shows the average recognition results on experiment 4 of FRGC version 2. Figure 5 displays the recognition rate curves versus the feature space dimensions when performing these methods. One can see that Lorentzianfaces is significantly better than other methods in comparison.

3.3   Experiments on USPS

The USPS handwriting digital data includes 10 classes from "0" to "9". Each class has 1100 samples. The first 200 images of each class are chosen for our experiments. We directly apply all algorithms to the normalized data without using PCA as preprocessing. The average classification results are shown in Table 2. The performance of LDP is again better than other methods under consideration.

Table 2. The average classification results on USPS database (mean ± std %). The optimal dimension of the feature space are given in the brackets. U and S mean unsupervised and supervised methods, respectively.

Method	G30/P170	G40/P160	Type
PCA	99.27 ± 0.21 (10)	99.42 ± 0.24 (20)	U
LPP	76.29 ± 4.65 (25)	87.60 ± 10.54 (25)	U
LDA	80.23 ± 8.18 (5)	88.70 ± 7.96 (25)	S
MMC	95.04 ± 1.57 (20)	95.47 ± 0.94 (15)	S
MFA	80.81 ± 2.89 (5)	87.63 ± 2.98 (15)	S
LDP	**99.38 ± 0.18 (20)**	**99.50 ± 0.21 (15)**	S

3.4 Discussions

By conducting experiments systematically, we can find that: as in LPP and MFA, the number of neighbors (e.g., k, $\hat{k}$ and $\check{k}$) is the most important parameter. The parameter k in LPP is set to 5 in all experiments. For face recognition, the parameters $\hat{k}$ and $\check{k}$ in MFA are set to $m - 1$ (m is the number of images in the gallery set) and 210, respectively. For handwriting digits classification, we set the parameters $\hat{k}$ and $\check{k}$ to 7 and 40, respectively. The Gaussian kernel $\exp\left(-\frac{\|\mathbf{x}_i - \mathbf{x}_j\|^2}{t}\right)$ is used in LPP where we set the parameter t to 250 in our experiments.

4 Conclusions

This paper presents a novel discriminant analysis method called Lorentzian Discriminant Projection (LDP). In the first step, we construct a Lorentzian manifold to model both local and global discriminant and geometric structures of the data set. Then, an approach to Lorentzian metric learning is proposed to learn metric tensor from the original high-dimensional sample space and apply it to the low-dimensional discriminant subspace. In this way, both the local class and the global data structures can be well preserved in the reduced low-dimensional discriminant subspace. The experimental results have shown that our proposed LDP is promising.

References

1. Turk, M.A., Pentland, A.P.: Face Recognition Using Eigenfaces. In: Proc. CVPR (1991)
2. Belhumeur, P., Hespanha, J., Kriegman, D.: Eigenface vs. Fisherfaces: Recognition Using Class Specific Linear Projection. IEEE TPAMI 19, 711–720 (1997)
3. O'Neill, B.: Semi-Riemannian Geometry with Applications to Relativity. Academic Press, New York (1983)
4. Zhao, D., Lin, Z., Tang, X.: Classification via Semi-Riemannian Spaces. In: Proc. CVPR (2008)
5. Donoho, D.L., Grimes, C.: Hessian Eigenmaps: New Local Linear Embdedding Techniques for High-Dimensioanl Data. PNAS 102, 7426–7431 (2005)
6. Roweis, S.T., Saul, L.K.: Nonlinear Dimensionality Reduction by Locally Linear Embedding. Science 290, 2323–2326 (2000)

7. Tenenbaum, J.B., Silva, V.D., Langford, J.C.: A Global Geometric Framework for Nonlinear Dimensionality Reduction. Science 290, 2319–2323 (2000)

8. Yan, S., Xu, D., Zhang, B., Zhang, H.J., Yang, Q., Lin, S.: Graph Embedding and Extensions: A General Framework for Dimensionality Reduction. IEEE TPAMI 27, 40–51 (2007)

9. He, X., Yan, S., Hu, Y., Niyogi, P., Zhang, H.J.: Face Recognition Using Laplacianfaces. IEEE TPAMI 27 (2005)

10. Zhang, Z., Zha, H.: Principal Manifolds and Nonlinear Dimensionality Reduction by Local Tangent Space Alignment. SIAM Journal of Scientific Computing 26, 313–338 (2004)

11. Lafon, S., Lee, A.B.: Diffusion Maps and Coarse-Graining: A Unified Framework for Dimensionality Reduction, Graph Partitioning, and Data Set Parameterization. IEEE TPAMI 28, 1393–1403 (2006)

12. Zhao, D.: Formulating LLE Using Alignment Technique. Pattern Recogition 39, 2233–2235 (2006)

13. Zhao, D., Lin, Z., Tang, X.: Laplacian PCA and Its Applications. In: Proc. ICCV (2007)

14. Belkin, M., Niyogi, P.: Laplacian Eigenmaps and Spectral Techniques for Embedding and Clustering. In: Proc. NIPS (2001)

15. He, X., Cai, D., Yan, S., Zhang, H.J.: Neighborhood Preserving Embedding. In: Proc. ICCV (2005)

16. He, X., Niyogi, P.: Locality Preserving Projections. In: Proc. NIPS (2003)

17. Li, H., Jiang, T., Zhang, K.: Efficient Robust Feature Extraction by Maximum Margin Criterion. In: Proc. NIPS (2003)

18. Wang, F., Zhang, C.: Feature Extraction by Maximizing the Average Neighborhood Margin. In: Proc. CVPR (2007)

19. Yang, J., Zhang, D., Yang, J.Y., Niu, B.: Globally Maximizing, Locally Minimizing: Unsupervised Discriminant Projection with Applications to Face and Palm Biometrics. IEEE TPAMI 29, 650–664 (2007)

20. Phillips, P.J., Flynn, P.J., Scruqqs, T., Bowyer, K.W., Jin, C., Hoffman, K., Marques, J., Jaesik, M., Worek, W.: Overview of The Face Recognition Grand Challenge. In: Proc. CVPR (2005)

Learning Bundle Manifold by Double Neighborhood Graphs

Chun-guang Li, Jun Guo, and Hong-gang Zhang

PRIS lab., School of Information and Communication Engineering,
Beijing University of Posts and Telecommunications,
100876 Beijing, China
{lichunguang,guojun,zhhg}@bupt.edu.cn

Abstract. In this paper, instead of the ordinary manifold assumption, we introduced the bundle manifold assumption that imagines data points lie on a bundle manifold. Under this assumption, we proposed an unsupervised algorithm, named as *Bundle Manifold Embedding (BME)*, to embed the bundle manifold into low dimensional space. In BME, we construct two neighborhood graphs that one is used to model the global metric structure in local neighborhood and the other is used to provide the information of subtle structure, and then apply the spectral graph method to obtain the low-dimensional embedding. Incorporating some prior information, it is possible to find the subtle structures on bundle manifold in an unsupervised manner. Experiments conducted on benchmark datasets demonstrated the feasibility of the proposed BME algorithm, and the difference compared with ISOMAP, LLE and Laplacian Eigenmaps.

1 Introduction

In the past decade manifold learning has attracted a surge of interest in machine learning and a number of algorithms are proposed, including ISOMAP[1], LLE[2,3], Laplacian Eigenmap[4], Hessian LLE[5], Charting[6], LTSA[7], MVU[8], Diffusion Map[9] and etc. All these focus on finding a nonlinear low dimensional embedding of high dimensional data. So far, these methods have mostly been used for the task of exploratory data analysis such as data visualization, and also been successfully applied to semi-supervised classification problem[10,11].

Under the assumption that the data points lie close to a low dimensional manifold embedded in high dimensional Euclidean space, manifold learning algorithms learn the low dimensional embedding by constructing a weighted graph to capture local structure of data. Let $G(V, E, W)$ be the weighted graph, where the vertex set V corresponds to data points in data set, the edge set E denotes neighborhood relationships between vertices, and W is the weight matrix. The different methods to choose the weight matrix W will lead to different algorithms.

In the case of multiple manifolds co-exist in dataset, one should tune neighborhood size parameter (i.e. k in $k - nn$ rule, ϵ in ϵ -rule) to guarantee the constructed neighborhood graph to be connected, or to deal with each connected

H. Zha, R.-i. Taniguchi, and S. Maybank (Eds.): ACCV 2009, Part III, LNCS 5996, pp. 321–330, 2010.
© Springer-Verlag Berlin Heidelberg 2010

components individually. Neighborhood graph can be viewed as discretized representation of the underlying manifolds and the neighborhood size parameter controls the fitness to the true manifolds. Constructing neighborhood graph by a larger neighborhood size parameter will result in losing 'the details' of the underlying manifolds, due to the occurrence of 'short-cut' connections between different manifolds or the different parts of the same manifold (when the manifold with high curvature). On the other hand, treating each connected component individually will lose the information of correspondence between different components so that the panorama of the global geometry of observation data set cannot be obtained.

In this paper, instead of the global manifold assumption, we suggest that it is more appropriate to imagine data points to lie on a bundle manifold, when one faces the task to visualize the image dataset in which may consists of multiple classes. For example, facial images of a certain person, under the pose changing and expression variation, in which the different expressions relate to different classes, span a bundle manifold. Under the bundle manifold assumption, to make the embedding faithful, it is needed to preserve the subtle local metric structures. We propose a naive way to visualize the subtle structure of bundle manifold, named as Bundle Manifold Embedding (BME). By incorporating the intrinsic dimension as apriori information, BME can discover the subtle substructure in an unsupervised manner. Experiments conducted on benchmark datasets validated the existence of subtle structure, and demonstrated the feasibility and difference of the proposed BME algorithm compared with ISOMAP, LLE and Laplacian Eigenmaps.

1.1   The Related Work

In computer vision, object images with continuous pose variations can be imagined to lie close to a Lie group[12]. Ham et al.[13] reported that different databases may share the same low-dimensional manifold and the correspondence relationship between different data sets can be learned by constructing unit decomposition. Lim et al.[14] presented a geometric framework on the basis of quotient space for clustering images with continuous pose variation. Recently, Ham and Lee[15] assumed a global principal bundle as the model of face appearance manifold for facial image data set with different expressions and pose variation. And they also proposed a factorized isometric embedding algorithm to extract the substructure of facial expressions and the pose change separately.

In this paper, following the way consistent with Ham and Lee[15], we suppose that in some multi-class dataset data points lie on bundle manifold and each class-specific manifold relates to an orbit. Under the bundle manifold assumption, we will discuss how to develop manifold learning algorithm to discover the subtle substructure of bundle manifold.

2   The Proposed Algorithm: Bundle Manifold Embedding

The principle of learning manifold is to preserve the local metric structure when obtain the low dimensional embedding. In the case of bundle manifold assumption,

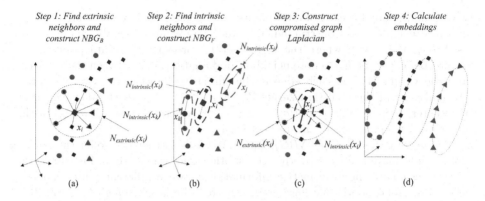

Fig. 1. Illustration for the proposed BME algorithm

however, there are extra subtle substructures, that is, the orbit structure. Therefore the local metric structures on bundle manifold consist of two aspects: (a) local metric between different orbits, and (b) local metric within each orbit. To obtain the faithful embedding of bundle manifold, two kinds of local metric need to be preserved as much as possible.

We propose to construct two neighborhood graphs: NBG_B and NBG_F, where NBG_B is used to represent the local metric structure between orbits, and NBG_F is used to capture the subtle substructure for each orbit (an orbit is likely corresponding to data points within each class, also can be viewed as fibre manifold). By means of spectral graph approach on combination of the weight matrices of two neighborhood graphs, the low dimensional embedding can be obtained.

Given data set $X = \{x_i, x_i \in R^m, i = 1, ..., n\}$, where m is the dimensionality of the observation space and n is the number of data points in data set X. First of all, we need to interpret a little of the two concepts: ***extrinsic neighbors*** and ***intrinsic neighbors***, denoted as $N_{extrinsic}$ and $N_{intrinsic}$, respectively. An illustration is given in Fig. 1 (a) and (b). For a data point $x_i \in X$, its extrinsic neighbors $N_{extrinsic}(x_i)$ can be selected by the ambient space metric, that is, Euclidean metric; whereas the intrinsic neighbors $N_{intrinsic}(x_i)$ of $x_i \in X$ are defined to be able to capture the subtle substructure of each orbit. In fact the extrinsic neighbors are the same as in the common manifold learning algorithms; whereas the intrinsic neighbors need to be selected along each orbit. The later is the key to discover the subtle structure of bundle manifold.

The proposed bundle manifold embedding algorithm consists of four steps as illustrated in Fig. 1, and will be depicted in the next subsections.

2.1   Find Extrinsic Neighbors and Construct Extrinsic Neighborhood Graph NBG_B

For each data point $x_i \in X$, we select the extrinsic neighbors $N_{extrinsic}(x_i)$ by Euclidean distance. We prefer to choose $k - nn$ rules rather than ϵ ball rule for its simplicity to determine the local scale parameter. And then a weighted graph with n nodes, one for each of data points, and a set of edges connecting each of extrinsic neighbors, is constructed. Denoted the extrinsic neighborhood graph as $NBG_B(V, E_B, W)$, where the vertex set V correspond to data points, the undirected edges set E_B denote neighborhood relationships between the vertices and the weight W_{ij} on each edge is the similarity between the two vertexes. We make use of the Gaussian kernel $W_{ij} = e^{-\|x_i - x_j\|/\sigma_i \sigma_j}$ with adaptive scale parameter $\sigma_i = \|x_i - x_i^k\|$ and $\sigma_j = \|x_j - x_j^k\|$, where x_i^k and x_j^k are the k-th nearest neighbors of x_i and x_j, respectively.

The neighborhood graph $NBG_B(V, E_B, W)$ is constructed to offer the background information for discovering the subtle structure of orbits, instead of to directly calculate the local metric information between different orbits. Therefore the neighborhood scale parameter k need to be large enough to guarantee the connectivity of extrinsic neighborhood graph $NBG_B(V, E_B, W)$. The neighborhood relationship defined by Euclidean distance can be used to preserve the 'global structure' within local neighborhood[1], see Fig. 1(a).

2.2   Find Intrinsic Neighbors and Construct Intrinsic Neighborhood Graph NBG_F

The subtle substructure in bundle manifold is orbits (also called fibers) of the structure group. For multi-class data set, Euclidean distance cannot distinguish such a subtle local metric structure, so that it often failed to find the orbit structure. In order to select intrinsic neighbors in an unsupervised way, we need a new metric, which can discern the subtle difference between different orbits.

Under the bundle manifold assumption, each orbit is controlled by structure group (a Lie group), and it is also a smooth manifold. Therefore we can suppose that each data point and its neighbors lie on a locally linear patch of the smooth manifold within each orbit and define the intrinsic neighbors by local linear structure. Based on neighborhood graph $NBG_B(V, E_B, W)$, we characterize the local geometry of these patches by nonnegative linear coefficients that reconstruct each data point x_i from its k neighbors x_i^j where $j \in N_{extrinsic}(x_i)$, $N_{extrinsic}(x_i)$ is the index set of k extrinsic neighbors of x_i. Here we need to solve a set of quadratic programming problems: for $x_i \in X, i = 1, \ldots, n$

$$\begin{aligned} \min_{a_{ij}} \varepsilon(a_{ij}) &= \|x_i - \sum_{j \in N_{extrinsic}(x_i)} a_{ij} x_i^j\|^2 \\ s.t. \sum_{j \in N_{extrinsic}(x_i)} a_{ij} &= 1 \\ a_{ij} &\geq 0 \end{aligned} \tag{1}$$

where a_{ij} are the nonnegative local linear reconstructing coefficients. For $j \notin N_{extrinsic}(x_i)$, a_{ij} are set to zero. Notice that weight matrix A constructed in such a manner is consistent with convex LLE[3].

---

[1] Under the bundle manifold assumption, the local subtle structure is orbit structure. Euclidean distance cannot distinguish the subtle orbit structure. Therefore, the neighborhood computed by Euclidean distance can be used as reference information to capture the global structure of neighborhood.

Given the nonnegative reconstructing coefficients matrix A, constructing the intrinsic neighborhood graph $NBG_F(V, E_F, A)$ is straightforward. Taking the intrinsic dimension d of data set as apriori information, we keep the $d+1$ largest nonnegative reconstructing coefficients and set those minor coefficients to zero. This is our recipe to find the exact intrinsic neighbors. The nonnegative coefficients are treated as affinity measure to find the intrinsic neighbors and those dominant coefficients indicate a reliable subtle neighborhood relationship of each orbit.

In fact, the intrinsic neighborhood graph $NBG_F(V, E_F, A)$ is refinement of the extrinsic neighborhood graph and can be derived from $NBG_B(V, E_B, W)$ by removing those edges related to minor reconstructing coefficients a_{ij}. The remaining $d+1$ dominant positive coefficients will span simplex with dimension d. These simplex can reveal the subtle intrinsic structure hiding in bundle manifold, that is, help us to reveal those orbit structures or class-specific manifolds. In the virtue of this recipe, the obtained intrinsic neighborhood graph can distinguish the subtle local structures.

2.3 Construct the Generalized Graph Laplacian

We denote L_B as the normalized graph Laplacian of $NBG_B(V, E_B, W)$, where $L_B = D^{-1/2}(D - W)D^{-1/2}$, D is diagonal matrix with entries $D_{ii} = \sum_j W_{ij}$. On the other hand, we denote $L_A = A^T A$, in which L_A is a nonnegative symmetric matrix for capturing the subtle substructure from $NBG_F(V, E_F, A)$. To obtain the faithful embedding of bundle manifold, both the local metric within each orbit, and the local metric between different orbits need to be preserved. Therefore we need to make use of both information from $NBG_B(V, E_B, W)$ and $NBG_F(V, E_F, A)$ to form an affinity relationship matrix. For simplicity, we linearly combine the normalized graph Laplacian matrix L_B and the nonnegative symmetric matrix L_A as follows:

$$U = (1 - \gamma)L_B + \gamma L_A \qquad (2)$$

where $\gamma(0 \leq \gamma < 1)$ is a tradeoff parameter. In the extreme case, $\gamma = 0$, it turned out to be Laplacian Eigenmap[4], in which the subtle substructure information from orbit is ignored. The more γ tends to 1, the more the subtle substructure is emphasized.

The matrix U is nonnegative, symmetric[2], and carries two aspects of local metric information. We treat U as affinity weight matrix to construct a generalized graph Laplacian $\tilde{L}$ for embedding the data points into low dimensional space, in which $\tilde{L} = U - \tilde{D}$ and $\tilde{D}$ is diagonal matrix with entries $\tilde{D}_{ii} = \sum_j U_{ij}$.

2.4 Embed into Low Dimensional Space

Under the assumption that data points lie on bundle manifold, mapping data points from high-dimensional space into low dimensional space must keep the

---

[2] The weight matrix W need to be symmetric.

local metric both on orbits and between orbits as much as possible. The constructed generalized graph Laplacian $\tilde{L}$ above is ready for such a purpose.

Suppose that the embedding is given by the $n \times q$ matrix $Y = [y_1, y_2, \ldots, y_n]^T$ where the i-th row provides the embedding coordinates of the i-th data point. As in Laplacian Eigenmap[4], we formulated a quadratic optimization problem as following:

$$\min \varepsilon(Y) = \frac{1}{2} \sum_{i,j} \{U_{ij} \|y_i - y_j\|^2\} = trace(Y^T \tilde{L} Y)$$

$$s.t.\ \ Y^T \tilde{D} Y = I \tag{3}$$
$$Y^T \tilde{D} \mathbf{1} = \mathbf{0}$$

where $y_i \in R^q$ is q-dimensional row vector, I is identity matrix, $\mathbf{1} = [1, 1, \ldots, 1]^T$ and $\mathbf{0} = [0, 0, \ldots, 0]^T$. Apparently, the optimization problem in (3) is a generalized eigenvector problem as:

$$\tilde{L}\mathbf{f} = \lambda \tilde{D}\mathbf{f} \tag{4}$$

Let $\mathbf{f}_0, \mathbf{f}_1, \ldots, \mathbf{f}_q$ be the solution of equation (4), and ordered them according to their eigenvalues in ascending order:

$$\tilde{L}\mathbf{f}_0 = \lambda_0 \tilde{D}\mathbf{f}_0$$
$$\tilde{L}\mathbf{f}_1 = \lambda_1 \tilde{D}\mathbf{f}_1$$
$$\cdots$$
$$\tilde{L}\mathbf{f}_q = \lambda_q \tilde{D}\mathbf{f}_q \tag{5}$$

where $0 = \lambda_0 \leq \lambda_1 \leq \ldots \leq \lambda_q$. We remove the eigenvector $\mathbf{f}_0$ corresponding to eigenvalue 0 and employ the next q eigenvectors to obtain the embedding Y as $Y = [y_1, y_2, \ldots, y_n]^T = [\mathbf{f}_1, \mathbf{f}_2, \ldots, \mathbf{f}_q]$ in q-dimensional Euclidean space.

3   Experimental Results

In this section we will demonstrate data visualization experiments on the benchmark data sets. The proposed BME algorithm is compared with ISOMAP, LLE, and Laplacian Eigenmaps. The parameter k is chose $k = 20$ for all algorithms in all experiments and the intrinsic dimension d used in BME is set to $d = 1$.

The first set of experiments are conducted on a selected data subset COIL-4, which consists of image samples from four classes (i. e. object-3, object-5, object-6 and object-19) of COIL-20[16]. The four classes of objects are the most similar four classes of object images in COIL-20. The manifold embedded in each class of COIL-20 is homeomorphism to circle (i.e. S^1).

As can be seen from Fig. 2 in panels (a), (b) and (c), ISOMAP, LLE, and Laplacian Eigenmap all failed to find the subtle class-specific manifold substructures. The results obtained by the proposed BME algorithm are given in Fig. 2 panels (d), (e) and (f) with different tradeoff parameter $\gamma = 0.90, 0.95, 0.99$. It is obvious that the subtle class-specific manifold substructures are discovered by BME algorithm.

In Fig. 2 panel (d) and (e), however, it can be observed that data points of the three classes of object-3, object-6 and object-19 are still piled together. We gathered those piled data points of the three classes (object-3, object-6 and

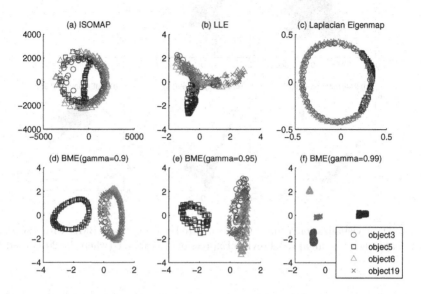

Fig. 2. Data visualization results that compared the proposed BME with ISOMAP, LLE, Laplacian Eigenmap on COIL-4 data set (where k=20 is used for all algorithms)

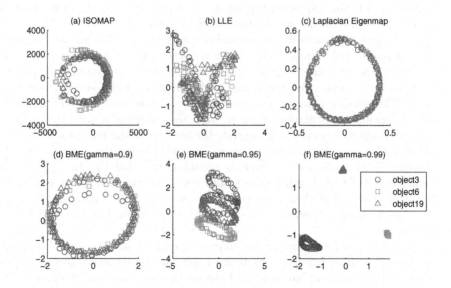

Fig. 3. Data visualization results that compared the proposed BME with ISOMAP, LLE, Laplacian Eigenmap on COIL-3 (where k=20 is used for all algorithms)

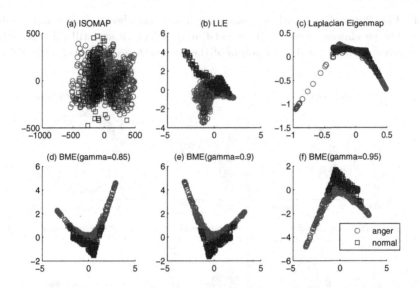

Fig. 4. Data visualization results that compared the proposed BME with ISOMAP, LLE, Laplacian Eigenmap on FreyfaceExpression-2 data set (where k=20 is used for all algorithms)

object-19) in Fig. 2 panel (d) and (e) to form data set COIL-3. It is interesting to further visualize the data in COIL-3. Therefore we conduct the second set of experiments on dataset COIL-3. The results are presented in Fig. 3. The ISOMAP, LLE and Laplacian Eigenmap still failed; whereas the proposed BME algorithm can reveal the subtle substructures distinctly.

From the data visualization results above, we can draw the conclusion that the tradeoff parameter γ controls the clearness of the discovered subtle substructure. The larger the parameter γ is, the more consideration is taken into the intrinsic neighborhood graph, and it will lead to focusing on subtle substructure much more. The smaller parameter γ corresponds to take into consideration more the background information, that is, from the extrinsic neighborhood graph. An over-large γ, however, will degrade the corresponding relationship between different class-specific manifolds, and will result in losing the faithfulness of the obtained subtle substructure. Strictly speaking, the global geometric structure hiding in the COIL-4 and COIL-3 data sets may not be exactly a principal bundle manifold, but then using such an assumption will remind us to capture the true geometric structure carefully and help us to explore the 'real feature' of data set.

The third set of experiments are conducted on Frey face data set[3]. We manually sorted the Frey face dataset into five expressions categories ('anger', 'happy', 'sad', 'tongue_out' and 'normal') and choose the two most similar classes of expressions ('anger' and 'normal') as the FreyfaceExpression-2 dataset for data

---

[3] http://www.cs.toronto.edu/~roweis/data.html, B. Frey and S. Roweis

visualization. There are continuous pose variation in both 'anger' and 'normal' expressions. Therefore the two expression manifolds will share the similar one-dimensional subtle structure. The experimental results are displayed in Fig. 4. We can find that the BME is superior to the other algorithms that it can reveal the subtle substructure.

Finally we need to mention about the parameters k, d and γ in BME. The neighborhood scale parameter k need to be large enough to guarantee the connectivity of extrinsic neighborhood graph to provide reference information. For the explorative data analysis task, one can try the intrinsic dimension d from one to the estimated intrinsic dimension by those significant nonnegative local linear reconstruction coefficients. In addition, the parameter γ may be selected from some typical values, such as 0.85, 0.90, 0.95, 0.99 and etc.

4 Concluding Remarks and Discussion

In this paper we suggest that the true global geometric structure of some datasets is likely bundle manifold, not a single manifold, and also presented a naive unsupervised algorithm, BME, for visualizing the subtle structure. Experiments on benchmark data sets demonstrated the feasibility of the proposed BME algorithm. We believe that the principal bundle manifold assumption and the proposed bundle manifold embedding algorithm are beneficial to deeply understand the global intrinsic geometry of some image datasets.

Under bundle manifold assumption, an interesting question arose that what is the exact meaning of the estimated intrinsic dimensionality. Perhaps we need redefine the task of intrinsic dimension estimation due to the exitance of orbit structures. In the proposed algorithm, however, the information used is only the local metric at each of orbits and the locality on bundle manifold. The sharing intrinsic structure among orbits has not been employed yet. Therefore the more sophisticated means to learning the bundle manifold will be investigated in future.

Acknowledgments. This work was partially supported by National High-Tech Research and Development Plan of China under Grant No. 2007AA01Z417 and the 111 project under grand No.B08004.

References

1. Tenenbaum, J.B., Silva, V., Langford, J.C.: A global geometric framework for nonlinear dimensionality reduction. Science 290(5500), 2319–2323 (2000)
2. Roweis, S.T., Saul, L.K.: Nonlinear dimensionality reduction by locally linear embedding. Science 290(5500), 2323–2326 (2000)
3. Saul, L.K., Roweis, S.T.: Think globally, fit locally: unsupervised learning of low dimensional manifolds. Journal of Machine Learning Research 4, 119–155 (2003)
4. Belkin, M., Niyogi, P.: Laplacian eigenmaps for dimensionality reduction and data representation. Neural Computation 15(6), 1373–1396 (2003)

5. Donoho, D.L., Grimes, C.: Hessian eigenmaps: Locally linear embedding techniques for high-dimensional data. Proc. Natl. Acad. Sci. USA 100(10), 5591–5596 (2003)
6. Brand, M.: Charting a manifold. In: NIPS, vol. 15. MIT Press, Cambridge (2003)
7. Zhang, Z., Zha, H.: Principal manifolds and nonlinear dimensionality reduction by local tangent space alignment. SIAM Journal of Scientific Computing 26(1), 313–338 (2004)
8. Weinberger, K., Packer, B., Saul, L.: Unsupervised learning of image manifolds by semidefinite programming. In: CVPR 2004, vol. 2, pp. 988–995 (2004)
9. Coifman, R.R., Lafon, S., Lee, A.B., Maggioni, M., Nadler, B., Warner, F., Zucker, S.W.: Geometric diffusions as a tool for harmonic analysis and structure definition of data: Diffusion maps. Proc. of the Natl. Academy of Sciences 102, 7426–7431 (2005)
10. Belkin, M., Niyogi, P.: Semi-supervised learning on riemannian manifolds. Machine Learning 56(1-3), 209–239 (2004)
11. Wang, F., Zhang, C.: Label propagation through linear neighborhoods. IEEE Transactions on Knowledge and Data Engineering 20(1), 55–67 (2008)
12. Rao, R., Ruderman, D.: Learning lie groups for invariant visual perception. In: NIPS, vol. 11. MIT Press, Cambridge (1999)
13. Ham, J., Lee, D., Saul, L.: Semisupervised alignment of manifolds. In: AI & STAT, pp. 120–127 (2005)
14. Lim, J., Ho, J., Yang, M.-H., Lee, K.-C., Kriegman, D.J.: Image clustering with metric, local linear structure and affine symmetry. In: Pajdla, T., Matas, J.G. (eds.) ECCV 2004. LNCS, vol. 3021, pp. 456–468. Springer, Heidelberg (2004)
15. Hamm, J., Lee, D.D.: Separating pose and expression in face images: A manifold learning approach. Neural Information Processing – Reviews and Letters 11, 91–100 (2007)
16. Nene, S.A., Nayar, S.K., Murase, H.: Columbia object image library (coil-20). Technical Report CUCS-005-96, Columbia University (1996)

Training Support Vector Machines on Large Sets of Image Data

Ignas Kukenys, Brendan McCane, and Tim Neumegen

University of Otago, Department of Computer Science
Dunedin, New Zealand
{ignas,mccane,tneumege}@cs.otago.ac.nz

Abstract. Object detection problems in computer vision often present a computationally difficult task in machine learning, where very large amounts of high-dimensional image data have to be processed by complex training algorithms. We consider training support vector machine (SVM) classifiers on big sets of image data and investigate approximate decomposition techniques that can use any limited conventional SVM training tool to cope with large training sets. We reason about expected comparative performance of different approximate training schemes and subsequently suggest two refined training algorithms, one aimed at maximizing the accuracy of the resulting classifier, the other allowing very fast and rough preview of the classifiers that can be expected from given training data. We show how the best approximation method trained on an augmented training set of one million perturbed data samples outperforms an SVM trained on the original set.

1 Introduction

Problems in computer vision often deal with large sets of high-dimensional image data, making the machine learning tasks involved computationally expensive. Even with moderate sets of data, straightforward implementations of learning algorithms can quickly exceed time and memory limitations. In cases where the amount of data is purposely very large, even advanced exact solutions can struggle to complete in acceptable time.

A Support Vector Machine (SVM) is a binary classification technique which is successfully used in computer vision systems. The training of an SVM is a quadratic programming problem and there is a great ongoing effort to improve the optimization algorithms and adapt them to work with large sets of training data. A number of incremental approaches have been developed that attempt to solve the optimization problem by iteratively working on a heuristically chosen subset of the training data. Decomposition algorithm by Osuna et al. [1] and chunking by Vapnik [2] work on a subset of fixed size and choose samples that most violate the optimization conditions. The Sequential Minimal Optimization (SMO) algorithm by Platt [3] optimizes just two samples at a time to arrive at the global solution and can be modified to only keep a limited 'working-set' in mind [4]. Incremental SVM learning method by Cauwenberghs and Poggio [5] and its adaptation for online learning [6] iteratively update the current optimal solution to include the next sample. All of these methods strive to find the exact

H. Zha, R.-i. Taniguchi, and S. Maybank (Eds.): ACCV 2009, Part III, LNCS 5996, pp. 331–340, 2010.
© Springer-Verlag Berlin Heidelberg 2010

solution of the original optimization problem for the entire training set, and scale poorly as they try to guarantee optimization conditions for all of the training samples.

Other approaches to very large datasets include ways to scale down the training data, as in the hypersphere approach of Katagiri and Abe [7], or the development of truly approximate alternatives to SVM training, like the Core Vector Machines of Tsang et al. [8]. However to this day widely spread implementations of the SVM algorithms normally include one of the exact incremental flavours of training and are quite limited in the amounts of data they can successfully be used on. This fact makes approximate decomposing approaches still attractive: by considering the limited SVM implementation as a basic 'black-box' tool that can summarize small parts of the training data, one can attempt to build different training schemes that try to extract the best possible classifiers within the limitations. An example of such approach is the incremental training proposed by Syed et al. [9].

In this paper we attempt to introduce a framework for reasoning about the accuracy of training schemes built using SVMs of limited size. We describe two algorithms with those assumptions in mind, an incremental scheme which is similar in spirit to chunking algorithms and attempts to optimize classifier accuracy by extracting as many support vectors as possible, and a reduction scheme which aims at fast shrinking of the training set by removing the samples that are less likely to be support vectors. We demonstrate the methods on the face detection problem and show how to use very large sets of artificially generated variations of the samples to produce a more accurate classifier with a limited SVM implementation.

2   Object Detection with Support Vector Machines

A support vector machine classifier is a function:

$$f(x) = \sum_{i=1}^{N} y_i \alpha_i K(x_i, x) + b, \qquad (1)$$

where $sgn(f(x))$ is the classification label for query $x \in R^n$, $X \equiv \{x_i, y_i\}$ is the training set with $x_i \in R^n$, class label $y_i \in \{\pm 1\}$, and cardinality $N = |X|$. $K(x_1, x_2)$ is the kernel function such that $K(x_1, x_2) = \langle \phi(x_1) \cdot \phi(x_2) \rangle$ for some mapping $\phi : R^n \to F$ from input space R^n to a potentially high-dimensional space F where the two classes become linearly separable. Weights α_i and offset b are results of the training, and for problems where good generalization is attainable, the majority of samples x_i will have weight $\alpha_i = 0$ and thus can be ignored in the application stage, while those with $\alpha_i > 0$ are referred to as *support vectors* and provide an approximate description of the training data.

In object detection applications an SVM can be trained to distinguish between object and non-object (background) images. For the face detection problem, typically thousands of images of fixed dimensions representing the object and the background are flattened into vectors containing colour or grayscale intensity values of pixels. The vectors are then assigned class labels, and using an appropriate kernel function (Gaussian Radial Basis Function, $K(x, y) = exp(-||x - y||^2/\sigma^2)$, is a commonly used choice) a decision function can be trained that uses a subset of training images for classification.

Even for small image patches of e.g. 20×20 pixels that result in 400-dimensional vectors, there is usually a very large number of potential examples that represent the object in question. If available examples of the object are limited, it is common to augment the training set with artificially generated variations, for example small linear transformations (shifts, rotations, etc.) of the data [2][8], and emulated lighting conditions or viewing angles [10]. Several such varying properties used together can result in several orders of magnitude increase in the number of samples in the training set.

Most of the SVM training algorithms perform at their best when the entire training set and its kernel matrix (containing the values $K(x_i, x_j)$) is cached for fast access. With a straightforward setup however, a moderate size problem of ten thousand 400-dimensional samples takes up over 800 Megabytes of RAM to cache (assuming 8 byte double values for $K(x_i, x_j)$) and a single training run even on a modern machine can take hours.

For image detection problems such as face detection, the set of positive examples is usually quite large (for modern applications, 10000 at least), and the set of negative examples is often extremely large (at least 100000), and if faster training algorithms were available, could easily be made larger still. It is generally not feasible to train a full SVM on such large training sets, especially when the dimensionality of the data is also high, hence the need for better approximate algorithms.

3 Properties of Subset Trained SVMs

We consider the case where an implementation of an SVM training algorithm can be run on at most $M_{max} \ll N$ samples in an acceptable time. This section derives properties of different subset selection methods which will allow us to motivate the algorithms in Section 4.

We use the following definitions.

Definition 1. $svm(A)$: *used to indicate the support vector machine classifier (support vectors and their weights) resulting from using an SVM training algorithm on input set A. We also consider the size of an SVM, $|svm(A)|$ to be the number of support vectors in the machine.*

Definition 2. $sv(A)$: *used to indicate the support vectors of an SVM trained on input set A. By definition, $sv(A) \subseteq A$.*

Definition 3. $r(svm(A))$: *the theoretical accuracy of an SVM trained on input set A ($0 \leq r \leq 1$ with 1 indicating a perfect classifier).*

Definition 4. $\hat{r}(svm(A))$: *the estimated accuracy of an SVM trained on input set A.*

Definition 5. $\bar{r}(svm(A))$: *the expected accuracy of an SVM trained on a random subset $A \subseteq X$, with $|A| = M$. $\bar{r}$ could be computed as the average $\hat{r}$ over all subsets.*

In the following, we assume that any SVM training algorithm will obey Axiom 1.

Axiom 1
$$r(svm(A)) \leq r(svm(B)), if\ A \subseteq B$$

Proposition 1 (Smaller)

$$\bar{r}(svm(A)) \leq \bar{r}(svm(B)), A, B \subseteq X, if\, |A| \leq |B|.$$

Proof. Recall that $\bar{r}(svm(A))$ is the expected accuracy of an SVM computed over all possible subsets of size $|A|$, and since $|A_i| \leq |B_j|$, it follows that for any i there exists j such that $A_i \subseteq B_j$, and for any j there exists i such that $B_j \supseteq A_i$. From Axiom 1, it follows that for each subset A_i, there exists B_j such that $\hat{r}(svm(A_i)) \leq \hat{r}(svm(B_j))$. Conversely, for each subset B_j, there exists A_i such that $\hat{r}(svm(B_j)) \geq \hat{r}(svm(A_i))$. Therefore it follows that $\bar{r}(svm(A)) \leq \bar{r}(svm(B))$.

Proposition 1 confirms the intuitive belief that to maximise the expected accuracy of an approximate SVM training scheme we should choose the largest subset possible.

The following three propositions seek to establish an ordering for different training data decomposition schemes.

Proposition 2 (Reduction)

$$\bar{r}(svm(sv(A) \cup sv(B))) \leq \bar{r}(svm(A \cup B))$$

Proof. From $sv(A) \subseteq A$, $sv(B) \subseteq B$, it follows that:

$$sv(A) \cup sv(B) \subseteq A \cup B,$$

and the proposition follows from Proposition 1.

Proposition 3 (Incremental)

$$\bar{r}(svm(sv(A) \cup B)) \leq \bar{r}(svm(A \cup B))$$

Proof

$$sv(A) \subseteq A$$
$$sv(A) \cup B \subseteq A \cup B$$

and the proposition follows from Proposition 1.

Proposition 4 (Reduction versus Incremental)

$$\bar{r}(svm(sv(A) \cup sv(B))) \leq \bar{r}(svm(sv(A) \cup B))$$

Proof

$$sv(A) \cup sv(B) \subseteq sv(A) \cup B$$

and the proposition follows from Proposition 1.

Notice that these decomposition schemes can be applied recursively, which leads to the decomposition algorithms outlined in the following section. For splitting the data into two subsets, we have the following ordering from the above propositions:

$$\bar{r}(svm(sv(A) \cup sv(B))) \leq \bar{r}(svm(sv(A) \cup B)) \leq \bar{r}(svm(A \cup B))$$

If we were to split into three subsets, the following ordering would result (stated without proof, but straightforward to prove):

$$\bar{r}(svm(sv(A) \cup sv(B) \cup sv(C))) \leq \bar{r}(svm(sv(A \cup B) \cup sv(C)))$$
$$\bar{r}(svm(sv(A \cup B) \cup sv(C))) \leq \bar{r}(svm(sv(A \cup B) \cup C))$$
$$\bar{r}(svm(sv(A \cup B) \cup C)) \leq \bar{r}(svm(sv(A) \cup B \cup C))$$
$$\bar{r}(svm(sv(A) \cup B \cup C)) \leq \bar{r}(svm(A \cup B \cup C))$$

4   Approximate Decomposition Training

4.1   Incremental Validating Scheme

Proposition 3 can be applied in a straightforward manner to implement the algorithm proposed by Syed et al. [9] that was shown to produce classifiers with minimum to no penalty in accuracy for a variety of datasets. In this approach the support vectors from the previous training step (the current model) are merged with the next chunk of data to train the next classifier. The limitation of this algorithm is that there is no simple way to limit the size of the training set a priori, which can lead to unacceptably long training times or exceed the capabilities of the SVM implementation at hand.

We propose a revised version of the algorithm that uses the incremental approach, with two main differences. Firstly, we keep the size of the training subset constant, so it doesn't exceed the maximum capability of the SVM implementation. Secondly, when choosing the data for the next iteration of training, we validate the data samples with the current classifier and only pick the ones that are misclassified. This is partly inspired by the 'bootstrapping' approach that is often used to obtain 'hard' non-object (background) data, where the negative samples that the current solution fails to discard can be used to improve the classifier. This is also similar to what exact chunking algorithms do internally, minus the requirement that the optimization criteria must be satisfied for the entire training set - here the samples that were picked for a round of training and did not become support vectors get dropped from the training set.

1. Input: data set X and constant M.
   Output: an SVM, S_{inc}.
2. Set $j = 1$.
3. Remove a random subset $X^1 \subset X, |X^1| = M$ from X:

$$X = X \setminus X^1$$

4. Train an SVM for X^1:

$$S^1 = svm(X^1)$$

5. Do
    (a) Use the support vectors from the previous classifier:

$$X^{j+1} = sv(X^j)$$

    (b) Fill the subset with misclassified samples:
        While $|X^{j+1}| < M$
        i. Pick next $x_i \in X$
        ii. If $S^j(x_i) \neq y_i$ then $X = X \setminus \{x_i\}$, $X^{j+1} = X^{j+1} \cup \{x_i\}$
    (c) Train the next iteration of the SVM:

$$S^{j+1} = svm(X^{j+1})$$

    (d) $j = j + 1$
    While $|S^j| < M$ and $|X^j| > |S^{j-1}|$
    (stop when the training buffer is full of support vectors or all remaining samples
    are classified correctly).
6. The last SVM trained is the final decision function:

$$S_{inc} = S^j$$

The benefit of this approach is that a potentially large number of training samples are
never directly used in the training steps, yet are validated to classify correctly. In our
observations, if M is larger than the size of the SVM that would result from training
on the entire set X, $M > |svm(X)|$, the algorithm will produce a classifier of similar
complexity as the full solution and will terminate by validating all of the remaining
training samples. Otherwise, a set of M support vectors will emerge that another round
of training is not able to reduce, giving a reasonably good classifier for size M.

4.2   Reduction Scheme

We propose the following algorithm based on the idea of iteratively dividing the training set. The data is recursively replaced by support vectors obtained by applying the
reduction method with a small size $\bar{M}$ on the current data set, until the remaining data
set is either smaller than the target size M, or further reduction steps fail to remove any
more samples.

1. Input: data set X^1 and constants M and $\bar{M}$.
   Output: an SVM, S_{red}.
2. $j = 1$
3. Do:
    (a) Split the training data into chunks of size $\bar{M}$:

$$D^j = \{d_i^j | d_i^j \subset X^j, |d_i^j| = \bar{M}, d_i^j \cap d_k^j = \phi\}$$

    (b) Train an SVM for every chunk and merge all resulting support vectors and
        consider them the new training set:

$$X^{j+1} = \bigcup_i sv(d_i^j)$$

(c) $j = j + 1$

While $|X^j| > M$ and $|X^j| < |X^{j-1}|$

(stop when remaining data reaches manageable size or the set cannot be reduced further).

4. If $|X^j| \leq M$, train the final function on the final training set:

$$S_{red} = svm(X^j)$$

otherwise pick a random subset $\bar{X} \subset X^j, |\bar{X}| = M$:

$$S_{red} = svm(\bar{X})$$

From Proposition 4, this algorithm is expected to give less accuracy than the incremental scheme:

$$\bar{r}(S_{red}) \leq \bar{r}(S_{inc}) \leq r(svm(X)) \tag{2}$$

However by choosing a smaller division size $\bar{M}$ the algorithm can be forced to quickly reduce the large data set into a manageable subset consisting of 'most representative' samples. We next show how these training schemes compare in practical experiments.

5   Results

5.1   Comparison

Dataset. To compare the different training schemes, we used image data from our face detection project. 20×20 pixel patches of grayscale images containing human eyes (figure 1) were used as positive samples and random background image patches were used as negative samples. We ran these experiments using a set of 1407 images containing 2456 eye objects.

The data set was augmented with variations of every eye object, where we added one pixel shifts of the object window in 8 directions, resulting in 22104 positive samples of the eye object. The same number of random background patches from the same images were used as the negative samples, giving us a large training set of 44208 samples.

Experiments. To measure the accuracy of the resulting classifiers, we chose to evaluate on the entire training set, denoting by $\hat{r}$ the percentage of samples in the training set that a given decision function classifies correctly. We ran the training schemes varying

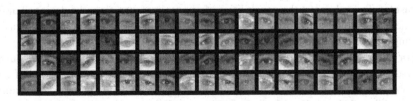

Fig. 1. Example subset of the training data: 20x20 pixel patches containing human eyes

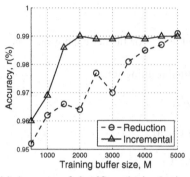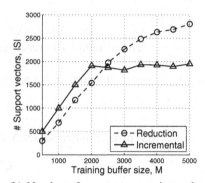

(a) Accuracy of classifiers obtained using different training schemes.

(b) Number of support vectors in resulting classifiers.

Fig. 2. Accuracy and complexity on the comparison set

the subset size parameter M between 500 and 5000 samples, a practical limit of available hardware resources. SVM parameters for the Gaussian kernel width ($\sigma = 6.3$ for normalized data) and constraint bound $C = 10$ were assumed to be problem specific and were fixed at values known to work well for the data set. For every resulting decision function we recorded the overall time taken and the accuracy $\hat{r}$. For the reduction scheme we used $\bar{M} = 0.1M$.

Figure 2(a) shows the accuracies of the classifiers obtained using the different methods. The results are consistent with the expected order (Equation 2) - the reduction scheme is less accurate, while the incremental scheme becomes more accurate early on. The conclusion is that the largest possible training subset size M should be used where maximizing the accuracy is desired.

Figure 2(b) shows the complexity of the resulting classifiers in terms of the number of support vectors. Notably there seems to be a limit to how complex the solutions for the given training set can get when using the incremental method. If this method indeed picks 'better' support vectors, it could indicate how complex an exact solution for the given large problem might be.

The time taken to train a classifier using the different approaches is shown in figure 3(a). The reduction approach is a clear winner if a small $\bar{M}$ size is chosen.

5.2   A Million Sample Dataset

Datasets. To further test the capabilities of approximate training, we designed an experiment that attempts to utilize a training set of one million samples, a task infeasible if using exact SVM training.

For the training set, we took 1571 images of human faces (multiple image sources, around 1000 different subjects, varying lighting conditions), containing a total of 2500 eye objects (obstructed or closed eyes not included). We then augmented the training set by adding shifts of the object window in four directions (×5), two slightly smaller and one slightly larger crop for each location (×4), and nine image rotations between

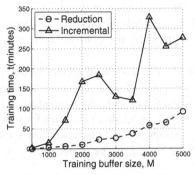 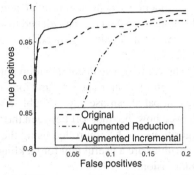

(a) Time taken to train the classifiers on the comparison set.

(b) ROC curves of the classifiers on the 1M set.

Fig. 3. Training times (comparison set) and ROC curves (1M set)

$-20°$ and $20°$ at each position ($\times 10$), giving us $500K$ samples of an eye object. We then extracted $500K$ random background patches from the same images, resulting in a training set of one million samples.

For the evaluation set, we took a different set of 505 images containing 801 eye objects that we used as positive evaluation samples and extracted 16020 random background patches from the images for the negative samples.

Experiments. To have a baseline, we first trained an SVM classifier using just the original 2500 positive samples and bootstrapping for negative samples over the $500K$ set of background patches. The overall training time was 3.5 hours and the resulting decision function had 1598 support vectors.

We then trained a classifier using the incremental validating scheme, using the buffer size of $M = 5000$. 16 cycles of training took a total of 17.5 hours and used up (validating or training) $350K$ of the samples before saturating the training buffer with support vectors, resulting in a decision function with 5000 support vectors. The reduction scheme with $\bar{M} = 500$ on the other hand took only 10.5 hours and discarded $957K$ samples. A decision function trained on a random subset of 5000 from the remaining $43K$ had 3896 support vectors.

Figure 3(b) shows the ROC curves for the two augmented set functions compared to the original one, calculated over the evaluation set. The approximate incremental function trained on the augmented set shows a better characteristic than the original. To further support this, we ran the functions as object detector scanners over the evaluation images. The conventional classifier found 93.5% percent of known eyes in the images, while the incremental classifier from the augmented set found 98.8% percent.

6   Conclusions and Future Work

When faced with a large learning problem and an SVM implementation of limited capabilities, approximate training strategies can be used to obtain an approximate solution.

The reduction scheme can provide a quick feel of the redundancy in the problem data, checking if the data can be reduced to a manageable size, while the incremental scheme can extract a classifier of maximum complexity dictated by the available computing resources.

The approximate decomposition approaches to SVM training allowed us to quickly train approximate decision functions over very large sets of data. The two schemes we compared can use any available SVM implementation as its basic component. We showed how the trade-off between the training time and the resulting accuracy for both algorithms can be controlled using the subset size parameter, and discussed how such algorithms are a useful tool for tackling large real-life SVM learning problems in computer vision.

Having a fast way to train SVM classifiers on large sets of data allows us to look into ways of increasing the accuracy of our face detecting classifiers. We are now able to augment our training sets with variations of the sample data, increasing the amount of data by several orders of magnitude, and judge which variations give a worthy improvement, despite the penalty of the approximate training.

References

1. Osuna, E., Freund, R., Girosi, F.: Training support vector machines: an application to face detection, pp. 130–136 (1997)
2. Vapnik, V.N.: Statistical Learning Theory. Wiley-Interscience, Hoboken (1998)
3. Platt, J.C.: Using analytic QP and sparseness to speed training of support vector machines. In: Kearns, M.S., Solla, S.A., Cohn, D.A. (eds.) Advances in Neural Information Processing Systems, vol. 11. MIT Press, Cambridge (1999)
4. Joachims, T.: Making large-scale support vector machine learning practical. In: Advances in kernel methods: support vector learning, pp. 169–184 (1999)
5. Cauwenberghs, G., Poggio, T.: Incremental and decremental support vector machine learning. In: NIPS, pp. 409–415 (2000)
6. Laskov, P., Gehl, C., Kruger, S., Muller, K.R.: Incremental support vector learning: Analysis implementation and applications. Journal of Machine Learning Research 7, 1909–1936 (2006)
7. Katagiri, S., Abe, S.: Incremental training of support vector machines using hyperspheres. Pattern Recognition Letters 27(13), 1495–1507 (2006)
8. Tsang, I.W., Kwok, J.T., Cheung, P.M.: Core vector machines: Fast svm training on very large data sets. J. Mach. Learn. Res. 6, 363–392 (2005)
9. Syed, N., Liu, H., Sung, K.: Incremental learning with support vector machines (1999)
10. Heisele, B., Serre, T., Poggio, T.: A component-based framework for face detection and identification. International Journal of Computer Vision 74(2), 167–181 (2007)

Learning Logic Rules for Scene Interpretation Based on Markov Logic Networks

Mai Xu and Maria Petrou

Electrical and Electronic Engineering Department, Imperial College London,
Exhibition Road, London, SW7 2BT, United Kingdom
{Mai.Xu06,Maria.Petrou}@imperial.ac.uk

Abstract. We propose a novel logic-rule learning approach for the Tower of Knowledge (ToK) architecture, based on Markov logic networks, for scene interpretation. This approach is in the spirit of the recently proposed Markov logic networks of machine learning. Its purpose is to learn the soft-constraint logic rules for labelling the components of a scene. This approach also benefits from the architecture of ToK, in reasoning whether a component in a scene has the right characteristics in order to fulfil the functions a label implies, from the logic point of view. One significant advantage of the proposed approach, rather than the previous versions of ToK, is its automatic logic learning capability such that the manual insertion of logic rules is not necessary. Experiments of building scene interpretation illustrate the promise of this approach.

1 Introduction

The aim of scene interpretation is to classify the objects in a scene and then associate with each class of object a semantic label. Recent years have seen considerable literature on this topic, including [1] [2] [3] [4]. Recently, an exciting development of scene interpretation has focused on graphical models such as Bayesian networks [5] and Markov random fields (MRF) [6]. However, most of these approaches are based on **statistical learning**, and hence they rely heavily on the availability of sufficient training data.

To avoid such a deficiency, the Tower of Knowledge (ToK) scheme was proposed in [7] [8] [9], either in the form of a non-iterative algorithm or an iterative algorithm, to combine logic rules with the statistical properties of each class of object, for 3D scene interpretation. Applying logic in scene interpretation [10] [11] [12] has been around for a couple of decades. However, the exploration of object functionalities, incorporated in the logic rules, was proposed for the first time by the architecture of ToK [7], as we know that objects, in particular man-made objects, exist with their own functionalities to fulfil human need. The logic rules of ToK are used to discover whether an object has the right characteristics in order to fulfil the functions a label implies from the logic point of view.

Previous versions of ToK assume that the logic rules have been programmed into the computer vision system, and thus they lack automatic learning capabilities.This paper proposes a Markov logic network based (MLN-based) ToK for

H. Zha, R.-i. Taniguchi, and S. Maybank (Eds.): ACCV 2009, Part III, LNCS 5996, pp. 341–350, 2010.
© Springer-Verlag Berlin Heidelberg 2010

self-learning the set of rules in the form of first-order logic. Instead of assuming that all (descriptor/functionality) units of the same level are independent as in the previous versions of ToK, we use logic rules to express that the units of the same level may depend on each other for reasoning on the units from neighboring levels. This scheme still offers the advantages of the recursive ToK on generalising more accurately from sparse data, and at the same time uses FOIL (First Order Inductive Learner) to learn the logic rules.

Our method benefits from the most recent successes of Markov logic networks (MLNs) [13] in the machine learning community for learning and making inference by combining first-order logic and probabilistic graphical models in a single representation. MLNs combine logic and probabilities to soften the hard-constraint logic rules, by attaching weights to logic rules and viewing them as templates for features of an MRF. So, they are used in this paper for enhancing the architecture of ToK, in which logic rules, are normally used to impose a label with soft constraints. The next section reviews the architecture of ToK.

2   Brief Overview of ToK

The ToK architecture provides a rational way of labelling the objects of a scene by considering the rules between the functionalities of objects and their descriptors. The architecture of ToK, as schematically proposed in [7], is shown in Figure 1. In this figure, ToK consists of four levels: image, semantic, functionality and descriptor levels. The image level belongs to low level vision. Features extracted from images are the units of this level and the input to ToK. The other three levels belong to high level vision. The nouns of the semantic level are the names of the objects, i.e. labels (e.g. "balcony","window"). The remaining two levels are those of the functionalities and the descriptors, which may be seen as the implicit logic representations of object models. The verbs of the functionality level are functionalities of the objects such as "to stand in" and "to look out". A functionality may be fulfilled, if the object has certain characteristics. These are captured at the descriptor level. Examples of these units are "having enough space for a person" and "there is an opening on the wall". The units in the descriptor level can interrogate the sensors and the images to verify that a required descriptor applies to an object. This way, the vertical connections of the scheme encode implicitly the generic models of objects, seen not in isolation or as static entities, but in the context of what they are used for and what their generic characteristics are.

The original ToK architecture [8] [9] assumes that the units of functionalities/descriptors are independent of each other for the inference of a specific label. These units, in practice, are dependent as far as the inference is concerned. Thus, in order to avoid such a disadvantage of the previous ToK approaches, we apply MLN in this paper to model the architecture of ToK. The reason why MLN is applied, instead of other rule-based learning methods, is that the hard constraints of logic rules can be softened in MLN by learning the weights of each logic rule. This is applicable to the ToK architecture since each logic rule in the

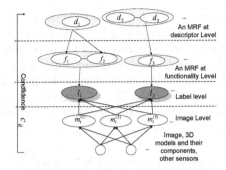

Fig. 1. ToK for labelling object a_i. The units in this figure stand for the measurements M_i, labels L, functionalities F and descriptors D. The arrows represent the transfer of information from evidence to queries.

ToK architecture has different probability to hold as discussed previously. Next, we shall show the details of the MLN-based method for scene interpretation.

3   The Proposed MLN-Based Approach

Based on the architecture of ToK, the problem of scene interpretation may be seen as assigning label $l_j \in L$ to object $a_i \in A$, according to each functionality $f_k \in F$ and descriptor $d_l \in D$. This problem will be solved by the inference of probabilities of assigning l_j to a_i represented by $l_j(a_i)$ (simplified to be l_{ij}), via the proposed MLN model in Section 3.3. For such inference, we have to learn the rules in Section 3.2 and their weights in Section 3.4. First, we need to review the basic idea of MLN in Section 3.1, as the foundation of the proposed method.

3.1   Basic Idea of MLN

In order to introduce MLN, it is necessary first to have a look at the notation and expression of logic rules [14], in the form of **first-order logic**. Assume that there is a logic rule: $F_h \leftarrow F_{e1} \wedge \ldots \wedge F_{en}$. In this logic rule, F_h as **postcondition**, is implied by **preconditions** $F_{e1}, \ldots, F_{en}$ which may be seen as evidence. Each precondition/postcondition is called a **literal**. Assigning values to possible literals, such as $f_3(a_1) = 1$ and $l_2(a_1) = 0$, defines a **possible world**. Similarly, assigning a value to each logic rule , such as $l_2(a_1) \leftarrow f_3(a_1)$, is called a **grounding**. Considering the logic rule in ToK, the above logic rules may be rewritten in the form of XOR (exclusive or, $\veebar$) shown in Table 1, which is slightly different from the equivalent form of first-order logic rules in [14].

However, in some cases, the logic rules may hold with their own probabilities. Consider the logic rule $l_2 \leftarrow f_3$ in Figure 1. We know that for an object to be a "door" ($= l_2$), it has to be able to "let people to go through" ($= f_3$) such that f_3 is a requirement for l_2. Then, one may say that if we observe functionality f_3, we have a non-zero probability of this object being l_2. In other words, the hard logic rule is changed into a soft one implying a label with some probability, probably lower than 1, as the object through which people can go may or may not be s door (soft classifier). MLN was proposed [13] to soften the hard constraints of logic rules, and therefore can be applied in our approach for the soft classifier.

In MLN [13], MRF is applied to model logic rules by considering the literals of logic rules as binary nodes of an MRF. Considering each logic rule R_i as a clique of an MRF with weight w_i, the probability of a possible world x may be computed by MLN as,

$$P(X = x) = \frac{1}{Z} \exp \left(\sum_{i=1}^{R} w_i n_i(x) \right) \tag{1}$$

where R is the number of logic rules involved in MLN and $n_i(x)$ is the number of true groundings of logic rule R_i. Z is a normalising constant to make $\sum_{x \in \mathcal{X}} P(X = x) = 1$, in which $\mathcal{X}$ consists of all x. In our model of MLN, X stands for the combinations of values assigned to the label of an object and the preconditions for this label, and x stands for a particular combination of values X. For example, a particular x may be $x = \{l_2(a_1) = 1, f_3(a_1) = 1\}$. $n_i(x)$ is 1 if x makes rule R_i true, else it is 0. In addition, w_i is the weight of rule R_i. So, $P(X = x)$ is the probability for combination of values x to arise.

Then, for a specified logic rule, the probability that the postcondition F_h is true may be queried given the already known MLN M and preconditions as the evidence, expressed by $F_e = \{F_{e1}, \ldots, F_{en}\}$. We may obtain such a probability as:

$$P(F_h|F_e, M) = \frac{P(F_h \wedge F_e|M)}{P(F_e|M)} = \frac{\sum_{x \in \mathcal{X}_{F_h} \cap \mathcal{X}_{F_e}} P(X = x|M)}{\sum_{x \in \mathcal{X}_{F_e}} P(X = x|M)} \tag{2}$$

where $\mathcal{X}_{F_h}/\mathcal{X}_{F_e}$ is the set of worlds in which F_h/F_e holds. $P(X = x|M)$ may be computed by using (1).

Let us cite an example for showing how (2) works. Assume that the previous logic rule for $\forall a_i, l_2(a_i) \leftarrow f_3(a_i)$ is a classifier with weight w for recognising doors. As another expression, this rule is equivalent to $l_2(a_i) \veebar \neg f_3(a_i)$, which is an expression of XOR: an object is either a door, or it is something not allowing people to go through. For component a_1, this leads to four possible worlds $\{l_2(a_1) = 1, f_3(a_1) = 1\}$, $\{l_2(a_1) = 1, f_3(a_1) = 0\}$, $\{l_2(a_1) = 0, f_3(a_1) = 1\}$ and $\{l_2(a_1) = 0, f_3(a_1) = 0\}$. If we observe a person going trough component a_1 (i.e. $f_3(a_1) = 1$), there will be only two worlds: $\{l_2(a_1) = 1, f_3(a_1) = 1\}$ and $\{l_2(a_1) = 0, f_3(a_1) = 1\}$. Given Table 1, $\{l_2(a_1) = 1, f_3(a_1) = 1\}$ makes the logic rule true, and $\{l_2(a_1) = 0, f_3(a_1) = 1\}$ makes it false. According to (1) and (2), it is easy to obtain $P(l_2(a_1) = 1|f_3(a_1) = 1) = \frac{p(l_2(a_1)=1, f_3(a_1)=1)}{p(l_2(a_1)=0, f_3(a_1)=1) + p(l_2(a_1)=1, f_3(a_1)=1)}$ $= \frac{\frac{1}{Z} e^w}{\frac{1}{Z} + \frac{1}{Z} e^w} = \frac{e^w}{e^w + 1}$.

3.2   The Learning Method of Logic Rules

In order to construct the ToK architecture described in Section 2, the logic rules for scene interpretation have to be learnt first. Before learning such logic rules,

Table 1. Truth table of logic rule: $F_h \leftarrow F_{e1} \wedge \ldots \wedge F_{en}$

postcondition F_h	preconditions $F_{e1} \wedge \ldots \wedge F_{en}$	logic rule $F_h \veebar \neg\{F_{e1} \wedge \ldots \wedge F_{en}\}$
1	1	1
1	0	0
0	1	0
0	0	1

we decide to treat the functionality units of the ToK architecture in our approach as the latent units, and then consider the descriptors as preconditions and the labels as postconditions for the logic rules. Therefore, we take the descriptors and labels of each object in the training dataset as input to the learning method. The labels and descriptors of objects from the training dataset, have to be annotated before training.

Then, an logic programming method, FOIL [15], is applied in our proposed approach to learn the logic rules of recognising the components of scenes. FOIL begins with the most general preconditions (the empty preconditions), and then recursively learns literals to specialise the rule for the postcondition until it avoids all negative examples. However, in order to accommodate the soft constraints of logic rules, the original FOIL is modified as summarised in Table 2. In this table, FOIL selects the precondition with the most gain, defined as

$$Gain(d_l, New\_Rule) \equiv p_1 \left(\log \frac{p_1}{p_1 + n_1} - \log \frac{p_0}{p_0 + n_0} \right) \tag{3}$$

where p_0 and n_0 are numbers of positive and negative examples satisfying logic rule: New_Rule, and p_1 and n_1 are numbers of positive and negative examples after adding precondtion d_l to New_Rule. In addition, min_gain is defined as the threshold of minimum gain for adding a new precondition. See [15] for more details.

3.3 The Proposed MLN Inference Model for Scene Interpretation

This subsection focuses on applying MLN and the learnt logic rules for interpreting scenes given the problem and notation stated at the beginning of Section 3. Now, consider the inference model of MLN from the viewpoint of ToK architecture. The architecture, as shown in Figure 1, has labels as the query nodes of MLN, and functionalities as latent nodes. The descriptors, as preconditions of all logic rules leading to l_{ij} (more than one rule for some label categories), are the evidence for the query. Therefore, the model of MLN, denoted as M, may be obtained through the rule learning method in Section 3.2 and weight learning method in Section 3.4. Then, the *Markov blanket* of l_{ij}, denoted by $MB(l_{ij})$, is set up to involve the descriptors of all logic rules ($\bigcap_{t=1}^{F} R_t$) leading to label l_j for component a_i, which have been learnt in Section 3.2. Then, (2) may be extended to accommodate $MB(l_{ij})$. a_i is thereby labelled as l_j with probability

$$P(l_{ij} = 1 | MB(l_{ij}), M) = \frac{\sum_{x \in (l_{ij}=1) \cap MB(l_{ij})} P(x|M)}{\sum_{x \in MB(l_{ij})} P(x|M)} \tag{4}$$

Table 2. Summary of the FOIL algorithm

- **Input:** Training dataset in which attributes are descriptors and targets are labels.
- **Output:** A set of logic rules to predict the labels for a scene.
- Rule set $R \leftarrow \Phi$

For each category of $l_j \in \mathbf{L}$
- $P \leftarrow$ Those positive examples the labels of which are l_j
- $N \leftarrow$ Those negative examples the labels of which are not l_j
- $D' \leftarrow$ Possible descriptor set, with $\forall d'_l \in D'$ satisfied by members of P

  While $D' \neq \Phi$
  - New_rule: $l_j \leftarrow$ Empty descriptor
  - $N' \leftarrow N$

    While $N' > 0$
    - $D_{Candidate}$: Generate candidate new descriptors from D' for New_rule by searching for the descriptors which are satisfied by the maximum number of examples in P.

      If $\max_{d_l \in D_{Candidate}} Gain(d_l, New\_rule) < min\_gain$, **Then Break**
    - $d_{best} \leftarrow \operatorname{argmax}_{d_l \in D_{Candidate}} Gain(d_l, New\_rule)$
    - Append d_{best} to preconditions of New_rule
    - $N' \leftarrow$ Subset of N' that satisfies preconditions of New_rule
    - $D' \leftarrow$ Subset of D' that excludes d_{best}

      If $D_{Candidate} = \Phi$, **Then Break**

    End
  - $R \leftarrow R \cup New\_rule$

  End

End

According to (1) and (4), $P(l_{ij} = 1|MB(l_{ij}), M)$ can be rewritten as

$$P(l_{ij} = 1|MB(l_{ij}), M) = \frac{P(l_{ij} = 1, MB(l_{ij}), M)}{P(l_{ij} = 0, MB(l_{ij}), M) + P(l_{ij} = 1, MB(l_{ij}), M)}$$

(5)

$$= \frac{e^{\sum_{t=1}^{F} w_t f_t(l_{ij}=1, MB(l_{ij}))}}{e^{\sum_{t=1}^{F} w_t f_t(l_{ij}=0, MB(l_{ij}))} + e^{\sum_{t=1}^{F} w_t f_t(l_{ij}=1, MB(l_{ij}))}}$$

where with the observed descriptors as preconditions stored in $MB(l_{ij})$, $f_t(l_{ij} = 1, MB(l_{ij}))$ is the binary value of the feature corresponding to the tth logic rule being true or not, when labelling component a_i as l_j. Similarly, $f_t(l_{ij} = 0, MB(l_{ij}))$ is the binary value corresponding to the tth logic rule being true or not, when labelling the component as non-l_j. w_t is the weight associated with the tth logic rule. It can be learnt by the method of the next subsection.

Next, the problem of scene interpretation on the basis of MLN is reduced to computing $f_t(l_{ij} = 1, MB(l_{ij}))$ and $f_t(l_{ij} = 0, MB(l_{ij}))$ with relevant descriptors. Here, we assume that $D_{ijt} = \{d_{ijt}^{(1)}, \ldots, d_{ijt}^{(m)}\}$ is the set of descriptors of the tth logic rule in $MB(l_{ij})$ leading to l_{ij}, where $D_{ijt} \subseteq D$ that is the set of all descriptors. According to Section 3.1, logic rule $l_{ij} \leftarrow d_{ijt}^{(1)} \wedge \ldots \wedge d_{ijt}^{(m)}$ can be rewritten in the form of exclusive logic as $l_{ij} \veebar \neg(d_{ijt}^{(1)} \wedge \ldots \wedge d_{ijt}^{(m)})$. Therefore, it can be obtained that in (5) $f_t(l_{ij} = 1, MB(l_{ij})) = 1$ and $f_t(l_{ij} = 0, MB(l_{ij})) = 0$, iff $d_{ijt}^{(1)} \wedge \ldots \wedge d_{ijt}^{(m)} = 1$. Then, $f_t(l_{ij} = 1, MB(l_{ij}))$ and $f_t(l_{ij} = 0, MB(l_{ij}))$ may be derived, given the observed D_{ijt}.

However, the above descriptors may be estimated with soft constraints. As introduced in [8], the descriptors observed for a particular object have associated confidences with which they apply to the object. The confidence of descriptor d_l being true for a_i may be computed and normalised [8] [9] through $c_{il} = \frac{1}{\max p(\tilde{\mathbf{M}}_\mathbf{i}|d_l)} p(\tilde{\mathbf{M}}_\mathbf{i}|d_l)$, where $\tilde{\mathbf{M}}_\mathbf{i}$ is used to indicate the measurements we need to verify the descriptors for a_i. Then, the confidence of $d_{ijt}^{(1)} \wedge \ldots \wedge d_{ijt}^{(m)} = 1$ may be written as $C_{ijt} = \prod_v c_{ijt}^{(v)}$, where $c_{ijt}^{(v)}$ is the confidence that descriptor $d_{ijt}^{(v)}$ is true. Therefore, we can obtain the confidences of $f_t(l_{ij} = 1, MB(l_{ij})) = 1$ and $f_t(l_{ij} = 0, MB(l_{ij})) = 0$, and further rewrite (5) as,

$$P(l_{ij} = 1|MB(l_{ij}), M, \tilde{\mathbf{M}}_\mathbf{i})$$
$$= \frac{\prod_{t=1}^{F}\{\prod_v c_{ijt}^{(v)} e^{w_t} + (1 - \prod_v c_{ijt}^{(v)})e^0\}}{\prod_{t=1}^{F}\{\prod_v c_{ijt}^{(v)} e^0 + (1 - \prod_v c_{ijt}^{(v)})e^{w_t}\} + \prod_{t=1}^{F}\{\prod_v c_{ijt}^{(v)} e^{w_t} + (1 - \prod_v c_{ijt}^{(v)})e^0\}} \tag{6}$$

for the probability of assigning l_j to a_i. Based on (6), we may label object a_i by

$$l(a_i) = \underset{l_j \in L}{\operatorname{argmax}} P(l_{ij} = 1|MB(l_{ij}), M, \tilde{\mathbf{M}}_\mathbf{i}) \tag{7}$$

3.4   Learning the Weights of the Logic Rules

Now, the only task left for scene interpretation is learning the weights of the logic rules. Here, we use a gradient ascent algorithm [13] to learn weights $\{w_1, w_2, \ldots w_t, \ldots\}$ of the logic rules learnt in Section 3.2. Assume that $\mathbf{X} = \{\mathbf{l}^*, \mathbf{D}^*\}$ is the training dataset, where $\mathbf{l}^*$ is the label set of the training data, and $\mathbf{D}^*$ is its corresponding descriptor set. Then, the gradient conditional log-likelihood is

$$\frac{\partial}{\partial w_i} \log P_w(\mathbf{l}^*|\mathbf{D}^*) \tag{8}$$

$$= n_i(\mathbf{l}^*, \mathbf{D}^*) - \sum_s \{P_w(l_s^* = 1|\mathbf{D}^*)f_i(l_s^* = 1, \mathbf{D}^*) + P_w(l_s^* = 0|\mathbf{D}^*)f_i(l_s^* = 0, \mathbf{D}^*)\}$$

where $n_i(\mathbf{l}^*, \mathbf{D}^*)$ is the number of true groundings of the ith logic rule (i.e. the number of training examples satisfying the ith rule) in dataset $\mathbf{X}$. For l_j involved in the ith rule, $l_s^* = 1$ means that label $l^*(a_s)$ of each object a_s in $\mathbf{l}^*$ is forced to be l_j (i.e. $l_{sj}^* = 1$), and $l_s^* = 0$ likewise means that each $l_{sj}^* = 0$, while $\mathbf{D}^*$ remains unchanged. $f_i(\cdot)$ is the binary value of the ith logic rule being true or not. $P_w(l_s^*|\mathbf{D}^*)$ is $P(l_s^*|\mathbf{D}^*)$ computed using current weight vector $w = \{w_1, \ldots, w_t, \ldots\}$ and (5), by

$$P_w(l_s^*|\mathbf{D}^*) = \frac{\exp(\sum_{t=1}^{F} w_t f_t(l_s^*, \mathbf{D}^*))}{\exp(\sum_{t=1}^{F} w_t f_t(l_s^* = 0, \mathbf{D}^*)) + \exp(\sum_{t=1}^{F} w_t f_t(l_s^* = 1, \mathbf{D}^*))} \tag{9}$$

Given (8) and (9), w_i may be updated iteratively through gradient ascent:

$$w_{i,k} = w_{i,k-1} + \eta \frac{\partial}{\partial w_i} \log P_w(\mathbf{l}^*|\mathbf{D}^*)|_{w_{k-1}} \tag{10}$$

where $w_{i,k}$ is the value of w_i in iteration k and η (= 0.01 in the next section) is the learning rate of gradient ascent. Each weight may be initialized to be 0. For more detail about weight learning of logic rules see [13].

4   Experimental Results

To validate the proposed approach, we performed experiments on a variety of building scenes to recognise four classes of components: windows, doors, balconies and pillars. The domain of building scene interpretation is shown in Table 3. Using the rule learning (Section 3.2) and weight learning (Section 3.4) methods, all logic rules and their weights were obtained in Table 4 by learning from the training dataset, which consists of only 5 buildings with 131 components, randomly selected from database [16]. Here, we used the annotation tool [16] to generate the labels and descriptors of these training components.

We have extensively evaluated the proposed approach for labelling 700 components of the 3D reconstructed models of 12 buildings from databases [16] and [17]. The 3D models for testing were reconstructed and represented according to [18]. We used the annotation tool, available at [16], to manually segment the 3D components. Moreover, the confidence of each descriptor being true, as introduced in Section 3.3, can be set in this specific 3D scene (building) interpretation task by using the method described in [8] [9].

Table 3. Domain of knowledge for Building Scene interpretation based on Figure 1

Level	English expression	Units
Label	Window	l_1
	Door	l_2
	Balcony	l_3
	Pillar	l_4
Functionality	Lets people look out	f_1
	Lets light in	f_2
	Lets people walk out	f_3
	Lets people stand in	f_4
	Makes building stable	f_5
Descriptor	It is glass-like	d_1
	The bottom of the component touches the ground	d_2
	It is high enough for human size	d_3
	The top of the component touches a flat plane	d_4
	The width is large enough for human size	d_5
	There are some opening components next to it	d_6

Table 4. The learnt logic rules and their weights for building scene interpretation

Labels	Logic rules	Weight
Window	$l_1 \leftarrow d_1$	2.97
	$l_1 \leftarrow d_3 \wedge d_2$	−5.27
Door	$l_2 \leftarrow d_3 \wedge d_2$	1.06
Balcony	$l_3 \leftarrow d_5 \wedge d_6$	2.91
Pillar	$l_4 \leftarrow d_4$	3.22

Fig. 2. The images of buildings for the scene interpretation task. All these data are from the eTRIMS [16] and IMPACT[17] databases.

Table 5. The confusion matrix of the results of 3D scene interpretation using MLN-based ToK-original ToK-recursive ToK. The running time of these three approaches, for labelling all 700 components, is 39.68-28.97-1070.41 seconds.

	Window(Results)	Door(Results)	Balcony(Results)	Pillar(Results)
Window (Ground Truth)	**538-538-533**	7-6-11	0-1-1	0-0-0
Door (Ground Truth)	0-3-9	**65-62-53**	0-0-0	0-0-3
Balcony (Ground Truth)	2-1-1	0-0-0	**26-27-27**	0-0-0
Pillar (Ground Truth)	0-0-0	4-16-9	0-0-0	**58-46-53**

Then, we implemented the original, recursive and MLN-based versions of ToK on all 12 buildings shown in Figure 2, in order to evaluate the performance of the proposed MLN-based approach. Table 5 shows the confusion matrix of labelling all 700 components of the 12 buildings. From this table, it can be seen that the proposed approach with labelling error 1.9% outperforms the recursive ToK (error rate: 4.9%) and the original ToK (error rate: 3.9%). The original ToK requires a large set of training data (more than 200 buildings with over 5000 components), yet only about 2.5% of these training data are required by the MLN-based ToK. Also, note that the MLN-based ToK does not operate an iterative algorithm as the recursive ToK does, and therefore saves computational time as illustrated in Table 5. However, the most important attraction of MLN-based ToK is that it is able to **automatically** learn the logic rules instead of using the human knowledge to insert them in advance into the computer as the original or recursive ToK requires.

5   Conclusions

In this paper, we proposed an MLN-based ToK approach for scene interpretation. The success of ToK implies that scene interpretation can be built on the inference of the causal dependencies between the functionalities of objects and their descriptors. In contrast to the original ToK, the proposed approach has three major parts. First, an inductive logic programming method has been extended to learn the logic rules between labels and descriptors of objects. Second, the weights of these rules have been learnt by gradient ascent search. Third, based on ToK, MLN may recognise the components of a scene, given the already learnt logic rules and their corresponding weights. In conclusion, the proposed approach automatically learns the soft-constraint logic rules to label the components of a scene by MLN. This allows the approach to benefit from the advantage of using sparse data for learning, and at the same time avoid the need of the previous versions of ToK all logic rules to have to be inserted into the algorithm manually. In addition, experimental results showed that our approach is superior to both the original and recursive ToKs.

References

1. Neumann, B., Möller, R.: On scene interpretation with description logics. Image and Vision Computing 26(1), 82–101 (2008)
2. Sudderth, E.B., Torralba, A., William, F.T., Willsky, A.S.: Describing visual scenes using transformed objects and parts. International Journal of Computer Vision 77(1-3), 291–330 (2008)
3. Thomas, A., Ferrari, V., Leibe, B., Tuytelaars, T., Schiele, B., Gool., L.V.: Towards multi-view object class detection. In: Proceedings of CVPR, pp. 1589–1596 (2006)
4. Heitz, G., Gould, S., Saxena, A., Koller, D.: Cascaded classification models: Combining models for holistic scene understanding. In: Proceedings of NIPS (2008)
5. Fei-fei, L., Perona, P.: A Bayesian hierarchical model for learning natural scene categories. In: Proceedings of CVPR, pp. 524–531 (2005)
6. Komodakis, N., Tziritas, G., Paragios, N.: Fast approximately optimal solutions for single and dynamic MRFs. In: Proceedings of CVPR, pp. 1–8 (2007)
7. Petrou, M.: Learning in computer vision: some thoughts. In: Rueda, L., Mery, D., Kittler, J. (eds.) CIARP 2007. LNCS, vol. 4756, pp. 1–12. Springer, Heidelberg (2007)
8. Petrou, M., Xu, M.: The tower of knowledge scheme for learning in computer vision. In: Proceedings of DICTA 2007, pp. 85–91 (2007)
9. Xu, M., Petrou, M.: Recursive tower of knowledge for learning to interpret scenes. In: Proceedings of BMVC (2008)
10. Yakimovsky, Y., Feldman, J.: A semantics-based decision theory region analyzer. In: Proceedings of IJCAI, pp. 580–588 (1973)
11. Ohta, Y.: Knowledge-based interpretation of outdoor natural color scenes. Pitman Publishing (1985)
12. Han, F., Zhu, S.: Bottom-up/top-down image parsing with attribute graph grammar. IEEE Transactions on Pattern Analysis and Machine Intelligence 31(1), 59–73 (2009)
13. Richardson, M., Domingos, P.: Markov logic networks. Machine Learning 62(1-2), 107–136 (2006)
14. Mitchell, T.M.: Machine Learning, 1st edn. McGraw-Hill Higher Education, New York (1997)
15. Quinlan, J.R., Cameron-Jones, M.,, R.: Foil: A midterm report. In: Brazdil, P.B. (ed.) ECML 1993. LNCS, vol. 667, pp. 3–20. Springer, Heidelberg (1993)
16. IST06: E-training for interpreting images of man-made scenes,
    http://www.ipb.uni-bonn.de/projects/etrims/
17. IMPACT: The image processing for automatic cartographic tools project,
    http://www.robots.ox.ac.uk/~impact
18. Dick, A.R., Torr, P.H.S., Cipolla, R.: Modelling and interpretation of architecture from several images. International Journal of Computer Vision 60(2), 111–134 (2004)

Efficient Classification of Images
with Taxonomies

Alexander Binder[1], Motoaki Kawanabe[1,2], and Ulf Brefeld[2]

[1] Fraunhofer Institute FIRST, Kekuléstr. 7, 12489 Berlin, Germany
{alexander.binder,motoaki.kawanabe}@first.fraunhofer.de
[2] TU Berlin, Franklinstr. 28/29, 10587 Berlin, Germany
brefeld@cs.tu-berlin.de

Abstract. We study the problem of classifying images into a given, pre-determined taxonomy. The task can be elegantly translated into the structured learning framework. Structured learning, however, is known for its memory consuming and slow training processes. The contribution of our paper is twofold: Firstly, we propose an efficient decomposition of the structured learning approach into an equivalent ensemble of local support vector machines (SVMs) which can be trained with standard techniques. Secondly, we combine the local SVMs to a global model by re-incorporating the taxonomy into the training process. Our empirical results on Caltech256 and VOC2006 data show that our local-global SVM effectively exploits the structure of the taxonomy and outperforms multi-class classification approaches.

1 Introduction

Recognizing objects in images is one of the most challenging problems in computer vision. Although much progress has been made during the last decades, performances of state-of-the-art computer vision systems are far from the recognition rates of humans.

There are of course many natural explanations why humans outperform artificial recognition systems. However, an important difference between them is that humans effectively use background knowledge and incorporate semantic information into their decision making; their underlying representation is highly structured and allows for assessing co-occurrences to estimate the likeliness of events. By contrast, artificial recognition systems frequently rely on shallow or flat representations and models. The number of object recognition systems exploiting those co-occurrences or semantic relations between classes is rather small.

We believe that incorporating semantics into the object recognition process is crucial for achieving high classification rates. In this paper, we focus on tasks where the semantics is given *a priori* in form of a class-hierarchy or taxonomy. In general, incorporating a taxonomy into the learning process has two main advantages: Firstly, the amount of extra information that is added to the system details inter-class similarities and dependencies which can enhance the detection

H. Zha, R.-i. Taniguchi, and S. Maybank (Eds.): ACCV 2009, Part III, LNCS 5996, pp. 351–362, 2010.

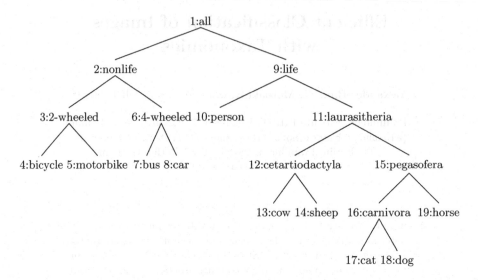

Fig. 1. The VOC2006 taxonomy

performance. Secondly, the complexity of the task is spread across the taxonomy which can be exploited by simpler learning techniques.

There have been many publications dealing with *learning* class-hierarchies, for instance on the basis of delayed decisions [1], dependency graphs and co-occurrences [2,3], greedy margin-trees [4], and by incorporating additional information [5]. By contrast, we focus on classifying images into a *pre-determined* taxonomy. The task fits into the structural learning framework [6,7] which has recently gained much attention in the machine learning community and which has already been successfully applied to document classification with taxonomies [8].

However, the structural framework is computationally costly in terms of training time and memory consumption. We propose an efficient decomposition of the structural objective into several binary optimization tasks. The local models can be trained efficiently in parallel and converge to the same solution as their structural analogon. We furthermore show how to incorporate global taxonomy information into the training process of the local models by re-scaling the impact of images according to their location in the class-hierarchy. Empirically, we show on VOC2006 and Caltech256 data sets that our local-global SVM effectively exploits the structure of the taxonomy and outperforms multi-class classification approaches.

The remainder of this paper is structured as follows. Section 2 introduces the formal problem setting and Section 3 briefly reviews structural learning. We present our main theorem detailing the decomposition of the structured approach into local models in Section 4 where we also address the problem of assembling local models on a global level. We report on empirical results in Section 5 and Section 6 concludes.

2   Problem Setting

We focus on the following problem setting where we are given n pairs $\{(x^{(i)}, y^{(i)})\}$, $1 \leq i \leq n$, where $x^{(i)} \in \Re^d$ denotes the vectorial representation of the i-th image which can be represented in higher dimensions by a possibly non-linear mapping $\phi(x^{(i)})$. The latter gives also rise to a kernel function on images, given by $k(x, x') = \langle \phi(x), \phi(x') \rangle$. The set of labels is denoted by $Y = \{c_1, c_2, \ldots, c_k\}$. For simplicity, we focus on multi-class classification tasks, where every image is annotated by an element of Y. However, our approach can easily be generalized to the multi-label setting, where an image can be annotated with several class labels.

In addition, we are given a taxonomy T in form of an arbitrary directed graph (V, E) where $V = (v_1, \ldots, v_{|V|})$ and $Y \subset V$ such that classes are identified with leaf nodes, see Figure 1 for an example. We assume the existence of a unique root node. The set of nodes on the path from the root node to a leave node y is defined as $\pi(y)$. Alternatively, the set $\pi(y)$ can be represented by a vector $\kappa(y)$ where the j-th element is given by

$$\kappa_j(y) = \begin{cases} 1 : v_j \in \pi(y) \\ 0 : otherwise \end{cases} \quad 1 \leq j \leq |V|, \; y \in Y$$

such that the category *sheep* in Figure 1 is represented by the vector

$$\kappa(\text{sheep}) = (1, 0, 0, 0, 0, 0, 0, 0, 1, 0, 1, 1, 0, 1, 0, 0, 0, 0, 0)'.$$

The goal is to find a function f that minimizes the generalization error $R(f)$,

$$R(f) = \int_{\Re^d \times Y} \delta(y, f(x)) dP(x, y),$$

where $P(x, y)$ is the (unknown) distribution of images and annotations. As in the classical classification setting, we address this problem by searching a minimizer of the empirical risk that is defined on a fixed *iid* sample from P

$$R_{emp}(f) = \sum_{i=1}^{n} \delta \left(y^{(i)}, f(x^{(i)}) \right). \tag{1}$$

The quality of f is measured by an appropriate, symmetric, non-negative loss function $\delta : Y \times Y \to \Re_0^+$ detailing the distance between the true class y and the prediction. For instance, δ may be the common 0/1 loss, given by

$$\delta_{0/1}(y, \hat{y}) = \begin{cases} 0 : & y = \hat{y} \\ 1 : & \text{otherwise.} \end{cases} \tag{2}$$

When learning with taxonomies, the distance of y and $\hat{y}$ with respect to the taxonomy is fundamental. For instance, confusing a *bus* with a *cat* is more severe than mixing-up the classes *cat* and *dog*. We'll therefore also utilize a taxonomy-based loss function reflecting this intuition by counting the number of nodes between the true class y and the prediction $\hat{y}$,

$$\delta_T(y, \hat{y}) = \sum_{j=1}^{|V|} |\kappa_j(y) - \kappa_j(\hat{y})|. \tag{3}$$

For instance, the taxonomy-based loss between categories *horse* and *cow* in Figure 1 is $\delta_T(\text{horse}, \text{cow}) = 4$ because

$$\pi(\text{cow}) \text{ xor } \pi(\text{horse}) = \{\text{cow, cetartiodactyla, pegasofera, horse}\}.$$

3   Learning in Joint Input-Output Spaces

The taxonomy-based learning task matches the criteria for learning in joint input-output spaces [6,7] where one learns a function

$$f(x) = \underset{y}{\operatorname{argmax}} \langle w, \Psi(x, y) \rangle \tag{4}$$

that is defined jointly on inputs and outputs. The mapping $\Psi(x, y)$ is often called the joint feature representation and for learning taxonomies given by the tensor product [8]

$$\Psi(x, y) = \phi(x) \otimes \kappa(y) = \begin{pmatrix} \phi(x)[[v_1 \in \pi(y)]] \\ \phi(x)[[v_2 \in \pi(y)]] \\ \vdots \\ \phi(x)[[v_{|V|} \in \pi(y)]] \end{pmatrix}.$$

Thus, the joint feature representation subsumes the structural information and explicitly encodes paths in the taxonomy. To minimize the empirical risk in Equation (1), parameters w can be optimized with conditional random fields (CRFs) [9] or structural support vector machines (SVMs) [6,7]. Following the latter and using the formulation by [10,11] we obtain the optimization problem in Equation (5).

$$\min_{w, \xi} \quad \frac{1}{2}\|w\|^2 + C \sum_{i=1}^{n} \sum_{\bar{y} \neq y^{(i)}} \xi_{\bar{y}}^{(i)}$$

$$\text{s.t.} \quad \forall i, \ \forall \bar{y} \neq y^{(i)} : \quad \langle w, \Psi(x^{(i)}, y^{(i)}) - \Psi(x^{(i)}, \bar{y}) \rangle \geq \delta(y^{(i)}, \bar{y}) - \xi_{\bar{y}}^{(i)} \tag{5}$$

$$\forall i, \ \forall \bar{y} \neq y^{(i)} : \quad \xi_{\bar{y}}^{(i)} \geq 0.$$

The above minimization problem has one constraint for each alternative classification per image. Every constraint is associated with a slack-variable $\xi_{\bar{y}}^{(i)}$ that acts as an upper bound on the error δ caused by annotating the i-th image with label $\bar{y}$. Once, optimal parameters w^* have been found, these are used as plug-in estimates to compute predictions for new and unseen examples using Equation (4). The computation of the argmax can be performed by explicit enumeration of all paths in the taxonomy.

Note that the above formulation differs slightly from [6,7] where every instance is associated with only a single slack variable representing the most strongly violated constraint for each image. Although, Equation (5) can be optimized with standard techniques, the number of categories in state-of-the-art object recognition tasks can easily exceed several hundreds which renders the structural approaches infeasible. As a remedy, we will present an efficient decomposition of the structural optimization problem in the next section.

4   Local-Global Support Vector Learning

In this section we present the main contribution of this paper. Firstly, we devise a decomposition of the structural approach in Equation (5) into several local models in Section 4.1. Secondly, we show how to combine the local models globally by incorporating the structure of the taxonomy into the learning processes in Section 4.2.

4.1   An Efficient Local Decomposition

The idea is to learn a binary SVM using the original representation $\phi(x)$ for each node $v_j \in V$ in the taxonomy instead of solving the whole problem at once with an intractable structural approach. To preserve the predictive power, the final binary SVMs need to be assembled appropriately according to the taxonomy. Essentially, our approach boils down to training $|V|$ independent binary support vector machines such that the score $f_j(x) = \langle \tilde{w}_j, \phi(x) \rangle + \tilde{b}_j$ of the j-th SVM centered at node v_j serves as an estimate for the probability that v_j lies on the path y of instance x, i.e., $Pr(\kappa_j(y) = 1)$. It will be convenient to define the auxiliary label function $z_j(y)$ by

$$z_j(y) = \begin{cases} +1 : \text{if } \kappa_j(y) = 1 \\ -1 : \text{otherwise.} \end{cases} \tag{6}$$

An image $x^{(i)}$ is therefore treated as a positive example for node v_j if this very node lies on the path from the root to label $y^{(i)}$ and as a negative instance otherwise. In Figure 1 for instance, we have $z_{\text{life}}(\text{cow}) = 1$ but $z_{\text{life}}(\text{bus}) = -1$.

Using Equation (6), we resolve the *local-SVM* optimization problem that can be split into $|V|$ independent optimization problems, effectively implementing a one-vs-rest classifier for each node.

$$\min_{\tilde{w}_j, \tilde{b}_j, \tilde{\xi}_j} \quad \frac{1}{2} \sum_{j=1}^{|V|} \|\tilde{w}_j\|^2 + \sum_{j=1}^{|V|} \tilde{C}_j \sum_{i=1}^{n} \tilde{\xi}_j^{(i)}$$

$$\text{s.t.} \quad \forall i, \forall j : \quad z_j(y^{(i)})(\langle \tilde{w}_j, \phi(x^{(i)}) \rangle + \tilde{b}_j) \geq 1 - \tilde{\xi}_j^{(i)} \tag{7}$$

$$\forall i, \forall j : \quad \tilde{\xi}_j^{(i)} \geq 0.$$

At test time, the prediction for new and unseen examples is computed similarly to Equation (4). Denote the local-SVM for the j-th node by f_j then the score for class y is simply the sum of all nodes lying on the path from the root to the leave y,

$$\hat{y} = \underset{y \in Y}{\text{argmax}} \sum_{j: \kappa_j(y) = 1} f_j(x). \tag{8}$$

The following theorem shows that the above approach is equivalent to the structural SVM in Equation 5.

Theorem 1. *If $C = \tilde{C}_j$ for $1 \leq j \leq |V|$ and $\delta(y, \bar{y})$ in Equation (5) is the 0/1 loss (Equation (2)) then the optimization problems in Equations (5) and (7) are equivalent.*

The proof is shown in the Appendix and relies on projecting combinatorial variables $\bar{y}$ onto nodes, hence reducing the number of possible events significantly to only a binary choice: either a node lies on a path or not. Along with the number of combinatorial outcomes, the training times reduce significantly. Another appealing aspect of this result is that the $|V|$ support vector machines can be trained efficiently in parallel. This property is also preserved when re-incorporating the taxonomy information as is shown in the next section. Moreover, model selection can be applied to the training process of each model separately which may lead to highly adapted local models with optimal trade-off C_j parameters (and potentially also kernel parameters) while its structural counterpart allows only for a single parameter C. In the next section we will show how to combine the local SVMs of optimization problem (7) globally by introducing example-specific costs.

4.2   Incorporating Global Misclassification Costs

The previous section shows how to decompose the structural approach into independent, binary problems. Although, the taxonomy is still necessary for scoring paths at prediction time (Equation (8)), the training processes of the binary SVMs is independent of any taxonomy information.

We now show how to incorporate taxonomy information into the training process of the local models. The intuition behind our approach is to reweight images by their taxonomy-distance. That is, we intend to penalize confusions of classes that have a large distance with respect to the taxonomy. On the other hand we are willing to accept misclassifying instances of nearby classes.

To be precise, we identify the cost $c_j(x^{(i)})$ at node v_j for a negative example as the number of nodes on the path from the j-th node to the true output; that is, $c_j(x^{(i)}) = \delta_T(v_j, y^{(i)})$. For instance, in Figure 1, the associated costs with an instance (x, bus) at the node *life* are $c_{\text{life}}(x) = 4$. The costs for positive examples are given by the costs of all negative instances for balancing reasons,

$$c_j(x) = \frac{1}{n_j^+} \sum_{i: z_j(y^{(i)}) = -1} c_j(x^{(i)}),$$

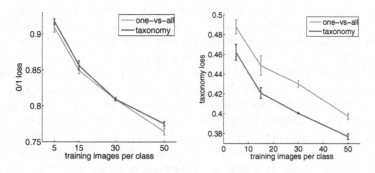

Fig. 2. Results for Caltech256. 0/1 loss and Taxonomy loss of local-global-SVM.

where n_j^+ is the number of positive examples at node v_j. Given the weights c_j, these can be augmented into the training process according to [12]. The *local-global* SVM optimization problem can be stated as follows,

$$\min_{\tilde{w}_j, \tilde{b}_j, \tilde{\xi}_j} \quad \frac{1}{2} \sum_{j=1}^{|V|} \|\tilde{w}_j\|^2 + \sum_{j=1}^{|V|} \tilde{C}_j \sum_{i=1}^{n} c_j(x^{(i)}) \tilde{\xi}_j^{(i)}$$

$$\text{s.t.} \quad \forall i, \forall j : \quad z_j(y^{(i)})(\langle \tilde{w}_j, \phi(x^{(i)}) \rangle + \tilde{b}_j) \geq 1 - \tilde{\xi}_j^{(i)} \tag{9}$$

$$\forall i, \forall j : \quad \tilde{\xi}_j^{(i)} \geq 0.$$

That is, if $c_j(x^{(i)}) \gg 1$ then the importance of the i-th input is increased while $c_j(x^{(i)}) \ll 1$ decreases its impact on the objective function. Thus, input examples that are associated with large costs $c_j(x)$ are likely to be classified correctly while accepting misclassifications associated with small costs.

5   Empirical Results

We compare our local-global SVMs empirically with the one-vs-rest SVM which is contained as a special case of our approach and furthermore equivalent to employing a flat taxonomy, where the root is directly connected to all leave nodes.

We experiment on the Caltech256 [13] and on the VOC2006 [14] data sets.

5.1   Data Sets

The Caltech256 data set comes with 256 object categories plus a clutter class; we focus on the 52 animal classes. This reduces the number of images to 5895; the smallest class has 80, the largest 270 elements. Each image is annotated with precisely one class label. We construct 5 sets of training, holdout, and test splits and deploy a taxonomy with approximately 100 nodes from biological systematics as underlying class-hierarchy. The left panel of Figure 3 shows the loss $\delta_T(y, \hat{y})$ based on our taxonomy. Here blue color denotes categories which are close in taxonomy distance while red pairs are far apart. For example, the classes 40–52 belong to a sub-group which is far from the cluster 18-39.

The VOC2006 dataset comprises 5,304 images containing in total 9507 annotated objects from 10 categories. The smallest class consists of 354 and the largest contains 1341 examples. We prepare 5 different training, holdout, and test splits by drawing images randomly to preserve the same number of class labels as proposed by the VOC2006 challenge. Thus, our training sets vary in their sizes and comprise between 2,500 and 3,000 instances. Although VOC2006 is a multi-label task, we treat the data set as a multi-class classification task by comparing for each class and each image belonging to that class the class label to the class of the maximum score. The taxonomy is shown in Figure 1.

5.2   Feature Extraction and Combination

We employ pyramid histograms [15] of visual words [16] (PHOW) for pyramid levels 0,1 over grey, opponent color 1 and 2 channels, which results in six different features. For every color channel, 1200 visual words are computed by hierarchical k-means clustering on SIFT features [17] from randomly drawn images. For VOC2006, the underlying SIFT features are extracted from a dense grid of pitch six. For Caltech256 the images have been pre-scaled to have 160,000 pixels, while their aspect ratios have been preserved. We apply a χ^2-kernel for every PHOW feature [18]. The kernel width parameter is initialized with the mean of the χ^2 distances over the respective training splits [2]. The final kernel K is then computed by the product of the six χ^2-kernels, $K = \left(\prod_{i=1}^{6} K_i \right)^{\lambda}$, where λ controls the width of the product kernel.

5.3   Experimental Setup

Model selection is performed for the SVM trade-off parameter C in the range $C \in [6^{-2}, 6^4]$ and for the kernel parameter λ in the interval $\lambda \in [3^{-7}, 3^2]$. For experiments with the taxonomy loss δ_T (Equation (3)) we also apply δ_T for finding the optimal parameters in the model selection. All other experiments use the 0/1-loss analogon. We deploy class-wise losses at each node to balance extreme class ratios for all methods. In our binary classification setting, this reduces to the computing the average of the loss on the positive class $\ell(+1)$ and that of the negative class $\ell(-1)$. The final value is then given by $\ell = \frac{1}{2}(\ell(+1) + \ell(-1))$. We use the model described in Section 4.2 and refer to it as *local-global SVM*.

5.4   Caltech256

Figure 2 shows the results for varying numbers of training images per class for combining the training of local-global SVMs (right). As expected, the error of all methods decrease with the sample size. As expected, there is no significant

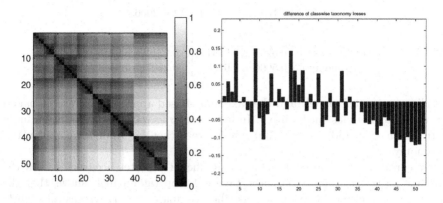

Fig. 3. (Left panel) The taxonomy loss $\delta_T(y, \hat{y})$ for the Caltech256 experiment. (Right panel) The expected taxonomy loss for each class.

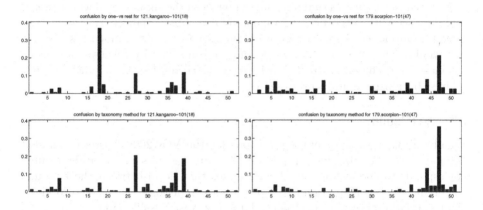

Fig. 4. Confusion probabilities for classes kangaroo (left) and scorpion (right)

difference between a one-vs-all SVM and our local-global SVM in terms of 0/1 loss. By contrast, the local-global SVM significantly outperforms the shallow basline in terms of taxonomy loss δ_T. This effect is due to incorporating the taxonomy structure into the training process of local-global SVMs.

To interpret this result, we compute average confusion matrices detailing $P(\hat{y}|y)$ over 5 repetitions for 50 training images per class. We compute the average taxonomy loss with respect to the confusion probabilities for each object class, i.e., $\sum_{\hat{y}} \delta_T(y, \hat{y}) P(\hat{y}|y)$. The right panel of Figure 3 shows the differences of the average taxonomy losses between our method and the one-vs-rest baseline. Negative values in this plot indicate that our method reduces the taxonomy loss of the corresponding classes. We observe that the local-global SVM effectively reduces the taxonomy loss for a large number of classes. However, there also exist classes such as *toad* (4), *ostrich* (9), and *kangaroo* (18) for which the error increased. To investigate this finding, we compared confusion probabilities of the

Table 1. Error-rates for VOC2006

	δ_{01}	δ_T
one-vs-rest	0.5257 ± 0.0131	0.2714 ± 0.0050
taxonomy	0.5006 ± 0.0126	0.2507 ± 0.0042

baseline (upper left panel) and the taxonomy-based approach (lower left panel) for the *kangaroo* class in Figure 4. In fact, *kangaroo* was substantially confused with *llama* (27) and *raccoon* (39) which are rather far from *kangaroo* in our taxonomy.

By contrast, our approach achieves significantly better accuracies than the baseline on the *scorpion* (47) class. Figure 4 (top right panel) shows that the taxonomy model increases confusions when compared to one versus all slightly between scorpion and Arthropoda like *crab* (44) which are relocated in the higher fourty indices and are biologically close to scorpions while it reduces confusions for example to *kangaroo* (18), *raccoon* (39) and *toad* (4).

Our analysis indicates that a mismatch between the similarity in feature space and distance with respect to the taxonomy can substantially harm the classification performance. Thus to improve learning with pre-determined taxonomies, one would either have to (i) remove these mismatches by reverse engineering the class-hierarchy or to (ii) design features which resolve this conflict. We will address both aspects in future research.

5.5 VOC2006

Finally, Table 1 shows average precisions for the VOC2006 data set. The left column shows the 0/1 loss (Equation (2)) and the loss in the right column corresponds to the average number of nodes that lie in-between the true and the predicted class (Equation (3)). For both loss functions, the local-SVM yields significantly lower error-rates than a flat one-vs-rest classification.

6   Conclusions

We presented an efficient approach to classification of images with underlying taxonomies. Our method grounds on decomposing structural support vector machines into local, binary SVMs that can be trained in parallel. Furthermore, we employed taxonomy-based costs for images to incorporate the taxonomy into the learning process. Significant contributions like [1,19] compared taxonomy models to flat ones using *0/1-loss*. Empirically, we observed our local-global SVMs to effectively benefit from the underlying taxonomy with respect to *taxonomy loss*: our approach was always equal or better than its shallow multi-class counterpart that cannot make use of taxonomy information.

Acknowledgements. This work was supported in part by Federal Ministry of Economics and Technology of Germany under the project THESEUS (01MQ07018) and by the FP7-ICT Programme of the European Community, under the PASCAL2 Network of Excellence, ICT-216886.

References

1. Marszalek, M., Schmid, C.: Constructing category hierarchies for visual recognition. In: Forsyth, D., Torr, P., Zisserman, A. (eds.) ECCV 2008, Part IV. LNCS, vol. 5305, pp. 479–491. Springer, Heidelberg (2008)
2. Lampert, C.H., Blaschko, M.B.: A multiple kernel learning approach to joint multi-class object detection. In: Proceedings of the 30th DAGM symposium on Pattern Recognition (2008)
3. Blaschko, M.B., Gretton, A.: Learning taxonomies by dependence maximization. In: Advances in Neural Information Processing Systems (2009)
4. Tibshirani, R., Hastie, T.: Margin trees for high-dimensional classification. JMLR 8, 637–652 (2007)
5. Marszalek, M., Schmid, C.: Semantic hierarchies for visual object recognition. In: Proceedings of the IEEE Conference on Computer Vision and Pattern Recognition (2007)
6. Taskar, B., Guestrin, C., Koller, D.: Max–margin Markov networks. In: Advances in Neural Information Processing Systems (2004)
7. Tsochantaridis, I., Joachims, T., Hofmann, T., Altun, Y.: Large margin methods for structured and interdependent output variables. Journal of Machine Learning Research 6, 1453–1484 (2005)
8. Cai, L., Hofmann, T.: Hierarchical document categorization with support vector machines. In: Proceedings of the Conference on Information and Knowledge Management (2004)
9. Lafferty, J., Zhu, X., Liu, Y.: Kernel conditional random fields: representation and clique selection. In: Proceedings of the International Conference on Machine Learning (2004)
10. Weston, J., Watkins, C.: Multi–class support vector machines. Technical Report CSD-TR-98-04, Department of Computer Sciences, Royal Holloway, University of London (1998)
11. Har-Peled, S., Roth, D., Zimak, D.: Constraint classification for multi–class classification and ranking. In: Advances in Neural Information Processing Systems (2002)
12. Brefeld, U., Geibel, P., Wysotzki, F.: Support vector machines with example dependent costs. In: Lavrač, N., Gamberger, D., Todorovski, L., Blockeel, H. (eds.) ECML 2003. LNCS (LNAI), vol. 2837, pp. 23–34. Springer, Heidelberg (2003)
13. Griffin, G., Holub, A., Perona, P.: Caltech-256 object category dataset. Technical Report 7694, California Institute of Technology (2007)
14. Everingham, M., Zisserman, A., Williams, C.K.I., Gool, L.V.: The 2006 pascal visual object classes challenge (voc2006) results (2006)
15. Lazebnik, S., Schmid, C., Ponce, J.: Beyond bags of features: Spatial pyramid matching for recognizing natural scene categories. In: IEEE Computer Society Conference on Computer Vision and Pattern Recognition, New York, USA, June 2006, vol. 2, pp. 2169–2178 (2006)
16. Csurka, G., Bray, C., Dance, C., Fan, L.: Visual categorization with bags of keypoints. In: Workshop on Statistical Learning in Computer Vision, ECCV, Prague, Czech Republic, May 2004, pp. 1–22 (2004)
17. Lowe, D.: Distinctive image features from scale invariant keypoints. International Journal of Computer Vision 60(2), 91–110 (2004)

18. Zhang, J., Marszalek, M., Lazebnik, S., Schmid, C.: Local features and kernels for classification of texture and object categories: A comprehensive study. International Journal of Computer Vision 73(2), 213–238 (2007)
19. Griffin, G., Perona, P.: Learning and using taxonomies for fast visual categorization. In: IEEE Conference on Computer Vision and Pattern Recognition, CVPR (2008)

Appendix: Proof of Theorem 1

Proof: We show the equivalence of the unconstraint objective functions. We first note that the dual representation of the structural parameter vector is given by $w = \sum_{i,\bar{y}\neq y_i} \alpha(i,\bar{y})(\Psi(x_i,y_i) - \Psi(x_i,\bar{y}))$. Since nodes are treated independently and the κ_j are orthogonal, we have

$$\|w\|^2 = \left\| \sum_{i=1}^{n} \sum_{\bar{y}\neq y^{(i)}} \alpha(i,\bar{y}) \left(\Psi(x^{(i)},y^{(i)}) - \Psi(x^{(i)},\bar{y}) \right) \right\|^2$$

$$= \sum_{j=1}^{|V|} \left\| \sum_{i=1}^{n} \sum_{\bar{y}\neq y^{(i)}} \alpha(i,\bar{y})\, \phi(x^{(i)}) \left(\kappa_j(y^{(i)}) - \kappa_j(\bar{y}) \right) \right\|^2$$

$$= \sum_{j=1}^{|V|} \left\| \sum_{i=1}^{n} \tilde{\alpha}_j(i)\, z_j(i)\, \phi(x^{(i)}) \right\|^2$$

$$= \sum_{j=1}^{|V|} \|w_j\|^2,$$

for $\tilde{\alpha}_j(i) = \sum_{\bar{y}\neq y^{(i)}} \alpha(i,\bar{y})|\kappa_j(y^{(i)}) - \kappa_j(\bar{y})|$. Note that the pseudo labels in Equation (6) can alternatively be computed by $z_j(i) = \text{sign}(\sum_{\bar{y}\neq y^{(i)}} \kappa_j(y^{(i)}) - \kappa_j(\bar{y}))$. For the sum of the slack variables, we define the non-negativity function $(t)_+ = t$ if $t > 0$ and 0 otherwise and proceed as follows:

$$\sum_{i=1}^{n} \sum_{\bar{y}\neq y^{(i)}} \xi_{\bar{y}}^{(i)} = \sum_{i=1}^{n} \sum_{\bar{y}\neq y^{(i)}} \left(1 - \langle w, \Psi(x^{(i)},y^{(i)}) \rangle + \langle w, \Psi(x^{(i)},\bar{y}) \rangle \right)_+$$

$$= \sum_{j=1}^{|V|} \sum_{i=1}^{n} \sum_{\bar{y}\neq y^{(i)}} \left(1 - \langle w_j, \phi(x^{(i)}) \rangle \left[\kappa_j(y^{(i)}) - \kappa_j(\bar{y}) \right] \right)_+$$

$$= \sum_{j=1}^{|V|} \sum_{i=1}^{n} \left(1 - z_j(i)\langle \tilde{w}_j, \phi(x^{(i)}) \rangle \right)_+$$

$$= \sum_{j=1}^{|V|} \sum_{i=1}^{n} \tilde{\xi}_j^{(i)},$$

where w_j denotes the j-th block of $w = (w_1, \ldots, w_{|V|})$ and is given by

$$\tilde{w}_j = w_j | \sum_{i,\bar{y}\neq y^{(i)}} \kappa_j(y^{(i)}) - \kappa_j(\bar{y})|.$$

This concludes the proof.   □

Adapting SVM Image Classifiers to Changes in Imaging Conditions Using Incremental SVM: An Application to Car Detection

Epifanio Bagarinao[1], Takio Kurita[1], Masakatsu Higashikubo[2], and Hiroaki Inayoshi[1]

[1] Neuroscience Research Institute
National Institute of Advanced Industrial Science and Technology
Tsukuba City, Ibaraki, 305-8568 Japan
{epifanio.bagarinao,takio-kurita,h.inayoshi}@aist.go.jp
[2] Sumitomo Electric Industries, Ltd.
Shimaya, Konohana-ku, Osaka, 554-0024 Japan
higashikubo@sei.co.jp

Abstract. In image classification problems, changes in imaging conditions such as lighting, camera position, etc. can strongly affect the performance of trained support vector machine (SVM) classifiers. For instance, SVMs trained using images obtained during daylight can perform poorly when used to classify images taken at night. In this paper, we investigate the use of incremental learning to efficiently adapt SVMs to classify the same class of images taken under different imaging conditions. A two-stage algorithm to adapt SVM classifiers was developed and applied to the car detection problem when imaging conditions changed such as changes in camera location and for the classification of car images obtained during day and night times. A significant improvement in the classification performance was achieved with re-trained SVMs as compared to that of the original SVMs without adaptation.

Keywords: incremental SVM, car detection, constraint training, incremental re-training, transfer learning.

1 Introduction

The effective training of support vector machine (SVM) usually requires a large pool of training datasets. However, gathering datasets for SVM learning takes longer times and needs more resources. Once trained, SVM classifiers cannot be easily applied to new datasets obtained from different conditions, although of the same subject. For instance, in image classification problems, changes in imaging condition such as lighting, camera position, among others, can strongly affect the classification performance of trained SVMs making the deployment of these classifiers more challenging.

Consider for example the detection of cars in images from cameras stationed along highways or roads as a component of an intelligent traffic system (ITS). The problem is to detect the presence of cars in sub-regions within the camera's field of view.

H. Zha, R.-i. Taniguchi, and S. Maybank (Eds.): ACCV 2009, Part III, LNCS 5996, pp. 363–372, 2010.

To solve this problem, one can start collecting images from a given camera, extract training datasets from these images, and train an SVM for the detection problem. After training, the SVM could work perfectly well for images obtained from this camera. However, when used with images taken from other cameras, the trained classifier could perform poorly because of the differences in imaging conditions. The same can be said of SVMs trained using images obtained during daylight and applied to classify images taken at night.

One solution to this problem is to train SVMs for each camera or imaging condition. But this can be very costly, requires significant resources, and takes a longer time. An ideal solution is therefore to be able to use an existing large collection of training datasets to initially train an SVM and adapt this SVM to the new conditions using a minimal number of additional training sets. This involves transferring knowledge learned from the initial training set to the new conditions.

This problem is related to the topic of transfer learning (for instance [1-3]). Closely related to this work is that of Dai and colleagues [3]. They presented a novel transfer learning framework allowing users to employ a limited number of newly labeled data and a large amount of old data to construct a high-quality classification model even if the number of the new data is not sufficient to train a model alone. Wu and Dietterich [4] also suggested the use of auxiliary data sources, which can be plentiful but of lower quality, to improve SVM accuracy. The use of unlabeled data to improve the performance on supervised learning tasks has also been proposed by Raina, et al.[5].

In this paper, we investigate the use of incremental SVM [6-7] to improve the classification of the same class of images taken under different imaging conditions. We assumed the existence of a large collection of labeled images coming from a single camera that could be used as starting training samples. Two training methods based on incremental SVM are employed for the initial training. One is the standard incremental approach, henceforth referred to as *non-constraint training*. The other one is *constraint training*, which imposes some limitations on the accepted support vectors during the learning process. After training, SVMs are adapted by means of incremental re-training to the new imaging condition using only a small number of new images. This is the transfer learning stage. The algorithms used will be detailed in the next section. In our experiments, we used images captured from cameras stationed along major roads and highways in Japan. Sub-images containing cars or background (road) were extracted and their histogram of oriented gradient (HOG) [3] computed. HOG features were then used as training vectors for SVM learning.

2   Materials and Method

In this section, we first give a brief discussion of the standard incremental SVM approach (non-constraint training). The constraint training method is then presented in the next subsection and finally incremental re-training is discussed.

2.1   Incremental SVM

Incremental SVM [6-7] learning solves the optimization problem using one training vector at a time, as opposed to the batch mode where all the training vectors are used at once. Several methods had been proposed, but these mostly provided only approximate solutions [9-10]. In 2001, an exact solution to incremental SVM was proposed by Cauwenberghs and Poggio (CP) [6]. In the CP algorithm, the Kuhn-Tucker (KT) conditions on all previously seen training vectors are preserved while "adiabatically" adding a new vector to the solution set.

To see this, let $f(\mathbf{x}) = \sum_{i=1}^{n} \alpha_i y_i K(\mathbf{x}_i, \mathbf{x}) + b$ represents the optimal separating function with training vectors $\mathbf{x}_i$ and corresponding labels $y_i = \pm 1$. The KT conditions can be written as (see [1] for more details):

$$g_i = f(\mathbf{x}_i) y_i - 1 = \begin{cases} \geq 0, & \alpha_i = 0 \\ = 0, & 0 < \alpha_i < C, \\ \leq 0, & \alpha_i = C \end{cases} \tag{1}$$

$$h = \sum_{i=1}^{n} \alpha_i y_i \equiv 0, \tag{2}$$

with C being the regularization parameter, the α_i's are the expansion coefficients, and b the offset. The above equations effectively divides the training vectors into three groups, namely, margin support vectors ($g_i = 0$), error support vectors ($g_i < 0$), and non-support vectors ($g_i > 0$).

In the CP algorithm, a new training vector is incorporated into the solution set by first setting its α-value to 0, and then its g-value is computed using Eq. (1). If it is greater than 0, then the new training vector is a non-support vector and no further processing is necessary. If not, the training vector is either an error vector or a support vector and the initial assumption that its α-value is 0 is not valid. The α-value is then recursively adjusted to its final value while at the same time preserving the KT conditions on all existing vectors. For a detailed discussion, refer to Ref. [6]. In this paper, the use of the original CP algorithm for training is referred to as non-constraint training as compared to constraint training, which will be discussed next. We also used an in-house implementation of this algorithm using C to support incremental SVM learning.

2.2 Constraint Training

Supposed we have an initial training set labeled as $\mathbf{X} = \{(\mathbf{x}_1, y_1), (\mathbf{x}_2, y_2), ..., (\mathbf{x}_n, y_n)\}$ where n is significantly large. In our problem, the training vector $\mathbf{x}_i$ represents the HOG features from images coming from a given camera, while the label y_i can either be 'with car' (1) or 'no car' (0). Also, let $\mathbf{Z} = \{(\mathbf{z}_1, y_1), (\mathbf{z}_2, y_2), ..., (\mathbf{z}_m, y_m)\}$ denotes another dataset taken from another camera and $m \ll n$. We defined constraint training as the selection of an appropriate set of support vectors from $\mathbf{X}$ that maximizes the classification performance of an SVM using dataset $\mathbf{Z}$ as test set. It should be noted that the support vectors of $\mathbf{X}$ do not necessarily give an optimal classification of $\mathbf{Z}$ as will be shown in the results. However, there may exist a subset of $\mathbf{X}$ with support vectors that can lead to an optimal classification of $\mathbf{Z}$. Finding this subset is the aimed of constraint training.

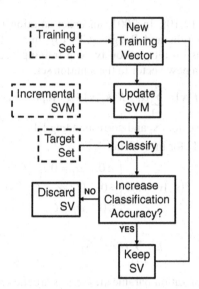

Fig. 1. Incremental SVM-based constraint training: 1) Get a new training vector from the training set **X**. 2) Update existing SVM using incremental approach. 3) Test updated SVM using target dataset **Z**. 4) If classification accuracy increases, keep the support vector (SV); otherwise, discard it. 5) Repeat (1) until all training vectors are processed.

There are several ways to implement constraint training. An example is to randomly extract subsets from **X**, train SVMs using these subsets, and select the subset which gives the maximum classification accuracy of **Z**. In this paper, we used incremental SVM and employed the algorithm outlined in Fig. 1. The algorithm follows from that of the non-constraint case except for an additional constraint, which is given as follows. As each new training vector is added, a classification test using a target dataset (**Z** in the notation above) is performed. A newly computed support vector is included into the running solution set if it increases the classification accuracy of the evolving SVM; otherwise, support vectors that tend to decrease the classification accuracy are discarded. The algorithm ensures that only support vectors that increase the classification accuracy of the target set are included in the final SVM. This effectively realigns the separating function of **X** to give an optimal separation of samples from **Z**, without using any sample from the latter. The final set of support vectors is the desired subset of **X**.

2.3 Incremental Re-training

In constraint training, only samples from the initial training set **X** are used during training. Samples from the target set **Z** are not included in the training process. In incremental re-training, the trained SVM is updated using this limited number of samples. See Fig. 2. The basic idea is that an SVM is already trained using dataset **X** via either non-constraint or constraint training method. After this initial training, samples from dataset **Z** are incrementally incorporated into the trained SVM to adapt

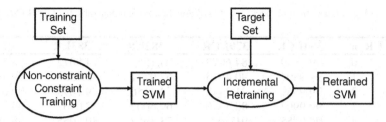

Fig. 2. With incremental re-training, an SVM is trained using an initial training set either via non-constraint or constraint approach, then is re-trained using the target set by means of incremental SVM

it to the new dataset. This is the transfer learning phase. The final result is an adapted SVM with a much improved classification performance of the class of feature vectors represented by the target dataset **Z**.

3 Results

Five cameras stationed at five different locations along major roads in Japan were used to capture images of passing vehicles. For each camera image, 16 x 16 sub-images containing cars and no cars were extracted. These selected images were then converted into HOG features using an 8 x 8 overlapping blocks with 4 pixels overlap giving a total of 9 blocks. The direction of gradient in each block was divided into 8 effectively converting each 16 x 16 image into a 72-dimensional feature vector.

From this, five groups of datasets were formed and labeled as follows: 379LCR (58,453 feature vectors), 382LR (56,405 feature vectors), 383LR (50,058 feature vectors), 122LR (12,762 feature vectors), and 384LCR (61,214 feature vectors). Images from 379LCR, 382LR, and 383LR were taken during daytime, while that from 122LR and 384LCR were obtained at night. Each dataset was then divided into 10 subsets. For each subset, an SVM was trained and then tested using the other subsets. The optimal SVM kernel (selected from linear, polynomial, RBF, and sigmoid kernels) and the associated kernel parameters were chosen using a cross validation approach with a grid search method in the parameter space. Each subset can have different optimal kernel and kernel parameters.

In our first experiment, we looked into the classification performance of SVMs trained using the non-constraint approach. The within group classification performance where SVMs were trained and tested using datasets belonging to the same group was evaluated. For instance, an SVM trained using 379LCR_0 was used to classify 379LCR_n, where n = 1, ..., 9. We also tested cross group classification performance where SVMs trained from one group were used to classify data from another group.

The classification performance for different SVMs trained using subsets of 384LCR are shown in Table 1. The first column indicates the subset used to train the SVM, while the rest of the columns show the classification accuracy. The second column is the result for within group classification, while columns 3 to 6 are the

Table 1. Classification accuracy (%) of SVMs trained using subsets of 384LCR

384LCR_n	384LCR	379LCR	382LR	383LR	122LR
0	99.9739	84.6013	75.1565	74.8072	98.5896
1	99.9804	90.4915	67.9231	75.1508	99.8433
2	99.9869	91.2442	72.4156	79.7095	99.8668
3	99.9902	88.5310	69.6002	77.0167	99.8198
4	99.9755	91.1023	73.3942	80.6065	99.7649
5	99.9739	90.5240	73.3907	80.7084	99.7649
6	99.9771	91.4256	72.7755	80.2269	99.7963
7	99.9820	91.2152	80.9450	86.7913	99.8041
8	99.9902	90.1887	70.3555	77.6399	99.8590
9	99.9788	91.6240	77.9559	83.3593	99.8746

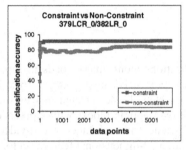 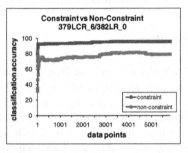

Fig. 3. Classification accuracy during constraint (red plots) and non-constraint (green plots) training as the number of incorporated samples is increased. In both panels, 382LR_0 was used as the target/test set, while 379LCR_0 (left) and 379LCR_6 (right) as the training sets.

results for cross group classification. For within group classification, the classification accuracy is significantly high (more than 99%). The same performance can be said for the other datasets not shown. On the other hand, the performance for cross group classification varies depending on the dataset used as test set. For some dataset, the performance can be as high as 99% (e.g., table 1, column 6), while for others, it can be lower than 70% (e.g., table 1, column 4). 384LCR-based SVMs are poor classifiers for 382LR or 383LR (both daytime datasets), but performed relatively well in classifying 379LCR (daytime dataset) or 122LR (nighttime datasets).

For the next experiment, we examined whether it is possible to improve cross group classification accuracy using constraint training. We also compared the accuracy of the constraint method with that of the non-constraint method for cross group classification during incremental learning. The results are shown in Fig. 3. For non-constraint training, the classification accuracy of the target set fluctuates as the number of support vectors increases. This is shown in the green plots of both panels. Since constraint training considers only support vectors that can increase the classification accuracy of the target set, the plots shown in red are always increasing. Interestingly, the classification accuracy with constraint training exceeded that of the

Table 2. Classification accuracy (%) of SVMs trained with constraint and using subsets of 379LCR as training sets and 382LR_0 as target set

379LCR_n	379LCR	382LR	383LR	384LCR	122LR
0	91.2186	91.0664	93.3217	90.6786	93.3004
1	86.4113	94.7753	93.5515	95.9650	97.7198
2	86.3121	93.6920	92.0253	92.6275	96.4739
3	86.3172	93.9863	92.7764	97.9841	98.8011
4	79.6931	93.3215	92.1611	94.1419	96.3329
5	78.2252	92.8127	92.7164	92.4756	95.2359
6	87.0819	95.2256	93.7712	92.8742	96.4582
7	83.0770	93.3481	93.4796	96.1463	96.0586
8	86.0674	88.6038	91.3760	98.4415	97.4220
9	88.8885	95.1299	94.4924	97.0056	98.0959

Table 3. Classification accuracy (%) results for incremental re-training. Subsets of 379LCR were used as training sets and 384LR_0 as the target set

379LCR_n	Incremental Retraining			
	Constraint		Non-constraint	
n	379LCR	384LCR	379LCR	384LCR
0	89.0613	99.9951	99.6750	99.9935
1	90.9996	99.9886	99.7109	99.9935
2	93.0765	99.9935	99.6613	99.9902
3	96.0669	99.9706	99.7006	99.9951
4	90.9329	99.9967	99.7793	99.9967
5	90.6660	99.9967	99.8084	99.9918
6	82.0351	98.6686	99.7536	99.9886
7	92.5308	99.9984	98.8777	99.4527
8	90.9466	99.9951	99.7827	99.9918
9	97.9693	99.9918	99.6921	99.9820

non-constraint case even with this simple condition. By imposing this constraint to the learning process, the performance of the evolving SVM as a classifier of the target set is considerably improved.

Table 2 shows the classification performance of the trained SVMs with constraint. Two effects can be observed. As expected, the cross group classification accuracy generally increases for all datasets considered. This is particularly true for the target dataset, which in this case is 382LR, with more or less 10% increase in accuracy (column 3). On the other hand, a corresponding decrease in the within group classification accuracy can also be observed (column 2). But this is just expected since constraint training is designed to optimize the classification of the target set, which may not result in an optimal solution for the original training set.

We next used incremental re-training to include the limited number of target dataset into the training process and evaluated the classification performance of the resulting SVMs. Both the use of non-constraint and constraint approaches for initial training was investigated. The results are summarized in Table 3. Here, subsets of 379LCR were used as initial training sets and the resulting SVMs were incrementally re-trained using 384LR_0. With incremental re-training, the classification accuracy of the target dataset (384LCR) jumps to more than 99%, a significant improvement compared to the cross group classification performance. Moreover, for non-constraint initial training, the classification accuracy of the initial training dataset (379LCR) remains high.

To evaluate the number of additional training vectors needed to raise the classification accuracy during retraining, we performed classification test for each newly added support vectors as the SVM evolved. We randomly shuffled the order the additional training vectors are incorporated into the training process and took the average of the classification result. Representative plots are shown in Fig. 4. The left panel shows the classification performance of an SVM initially trained using 379LCR_0, and then incrementally re-trained using 382LR_0. On the other hand, 384LCR_0 was used for re-training in the right panel. Both panels showed that the constraint approach for initial training (blue plots) made the trained SVMs adapt faster (less additional training samples) to the new datasets as compared to the use of non-constraint approach for initial training. In both cases, only a small number of target vectors are needed to adapt the SVMs to the new datasets.

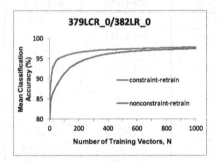 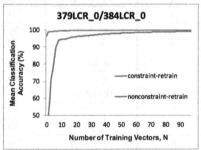

Fig. 4. Classification accuracy as a function of the number of target samples incorporated into the incremental re-learning process. The SVMs were initially trained using 379LCR_0 and then incrementally retrained using 382LCR_0 (left panel) and 384LCR_0 (right panel). Both constraint (blue plots) and non-constraint (red plots) approaches for initial training were evaluated.

4 Discussion

Support vector machines are robust classifiers for datasets they are initially trained. Changes to some of the conditions where the initial datasets were acquired could significantly affect the classifiers' performance. The case currently considered is the detection of cars in images from cameras stationed along major roads. From the results presented, differences in lighting conditions from one location to the other can significantly affect the classification performance of SVMs trained using only dataset from one location (see Table **1**). This presents a significant problem in the deployment of these classifiers. Training an SVM for each location can mitigate this limitation for small deployment. But for large scale application, this can be very costly, requires significant resources, and takes a longer time, and therefore, impractical.

In this paper, we have demonstrated a practical approach to overcome this limitation. The approach requires that an initial collection of dataset, possibly from a single camera, be available. For new deployment, a small number of additional images can be taken, which can then be used to adapt an existing classifier to the new imaging condition via transfer learning. Since the approach is based on incremental SVM, it is also possible to do on-line learning. The general idea is that from the initial collection, a subset can be selected that optimizes the classification accuracy of the new dataset using constraint training. The resulting SVM can then be incrementally re-trained using the additional (target) dataset to further improve its classification performance.

The result in Table 2 shows the efficacy of the constraint approach to extract subsets from the initial training set which can maximize the classification accuracy of the target set. Although the classification accuracy of the initial dataset decreases, this is immaterial since the final goal is the improvement in the classification of the new dataset for deployment purposes. The extracted subsets can then be combined with the target set via incremental re-training to further improve the classification of the target set as shown in Table 3. This has the advantage of faster adaptation of the trained SVM to the new datasets. On the other hand, using non-constraint approach for initial training does not only improve the classification of the target set, but also preserve the accuracy of the initial dataset (see Table 3). This is important if we don't want to lose the classification accuracy of the initial training set such as the case when re-training the SVM to accommodate day and night time images. In both cases, the achieved improvement requires only several hundreds of additional datasets, which can be readily obtained. The cost involved and the resources required will therefore be minimal.

The use of incremental SVM here is critical. With incremental SVM, additional training vectors can be added to the learning process without retraining from scratch. Given that training is the most computationally intensive task in the classification problem, incremental SVM can provide a significant saving in training time. It also enables us to evaluate the contribution of the newly added vectors to the classification performance of the evolving SVM. As an application, we were able to constraint the support vectors that can be included into the solution set in terms of their contribution to the classification accuracy. This in turn allowed us to select only subsets within the initial training dataset that are useful for the optimization of the target set. Moreover, the training process itself involves the selection process. And with an additional incremental re-training, the target dataset can be easily incorporated into the final SVM.

In conclusion, we have demonstrated the combined use of non-constraint/constraint initial training and incremental re-training to adapt SVM image classifiers to changes in imaging conditions. When applied to the car detection problem, significant improvement in the classification accuracy was achieved validating the efficacy of the method. The small number of additional datasets required for re-training makes the approach cost effective and practical for use in large deployment, such as in intelligent traffic systems, as the additional cost and needed resources are minimal.

References

[1] Thrun, S., Mitchell, T.M.: Learning one more thing. In: Proceedings of the 14th International Joint Conference on Artificial Intelligence (1995)

[2] Caruana, R.: Multitask learning. MachineLearning 28(1), 41–75 (1997)

[3] Dai, W., Yang, Q., Xue, G.-R., Yu, Y.: Boosting for Transfer Learning. In: Proceedings of the 24th International Conference on Machine Learning (2007)

[4] Wu, P., Dietterich, T.: Improving SVM Accuracy by Training on Auxiliary Data Sources. In: Proceedings of the 21st International Conference on Machine Learning (2004)

[5] Raina, R., Battle, A., Lee, H., Packer, B., Ng, A.: Self-taught Learning: Transfer Learning from Unlabeled Data. In: Proceedings of the 24th International Conference on Machine Learning (2007)

[6] Cauwenberghs, G., Poggio, T.: Incremental and Decremental Support Vector Machine Learning. In: Leen, T.K., Dietterich, T.G., Tresp, V. (eds.) Advances in Neural Information Processing Systems, vol. 13, pp. 409–415. MIT Press, Cambridge (2001)

[7] Laskov, P., Gehl, C., Kruger, S., Muller, K.R.: Incremental Support Vector Learning: Analysis, Implementation and Application. Journal of Machine Learning Research 7, 1909–1936 (2006)

[8] Dalal, N., Triggs, B.: Histograms of Oriented Gradients for Human Detection. In: Conference on Computer Vision and Pattern Recognition (2005)

[9] Ralaivola, L., d'Alché-Buc, F.: Incremental support vector machine learning: A local approach. In: Dorffner, G., Bischof, H., Hornik, K. (eds.) ICANN 2001. LNCS, vol. 2130, pp. 322–329. Springer, Heidelberg (2001)

[10] Kivinen, J., Smola, A.J., Williamson, R.C.: Online learning with kernels. In: Diettrich, T.G., Becker, S., Ghahramani, Z. (eds.) Advances In Neural Information Processing Systems (NIPS 2001), pp. 785–792 (2001)

Incrementally Discovering Object Classes Using Similarity Propagation and Graph Clustering

Shengping Xia[1] and Edwin R. Hancock[2]

[1] ATR Lab, School of Electronic Science and Engineering,
National University of Defense Technology, Changsha, Hunan, P.R.China 410073
[2] Department of Computer Science, University of York, York YO10 5DD, UK
erh@cs.york.ac.uk

Abstract. We are interested in incrementally discovering the set of object classes present in a scalable database of images. This paper describes a graph-based framework for learning the set of object classes in a weakly supervisedly manner. Rather than making use of the "Bag-of-Features (BoF)" approach widely used in current work on object recognition, we represent each image by a graph using a group of selected local invariant features. Using local feature matching and iterative Procrustes alignment, we perform graph matching and compute a similarity measure. Borrowing the idea of query expansion, we develop a similarity propagation based graph clustering (SPGC) method. Using this method class specific clusters of the graphs can be obtained. Such a cluster can be generally represented by using a higher level graph model whose vertices are the clustered graphs, and the edge weights are determined by the pairwise similarity measure. Experiments are performed on a dataset, in which the number of images increases from 1 to 50K and the number of objects increases from 1 to over 500. Some objects have been discovered with total recall and a precision 1 in a single cluster.

1 Introduction

Suppose we are given a database of images which contain frequent occurrences of a set of unknown objects. In this paper we are interested in discovering a set of models that can describe the individual objects from a scalable image database in an incremental manner.

In the statistical text analysis community, latent topic models such as probabilistic Latent Semantic Analysis (pLSA) [1] and Latent Dirichlet Allocation (LDA) [2] have had significant impact as methods for "semantic" clustering. Given a collection of documents, with each document represented by a "Bag-of-Words (BoW)" vector, the models are able to learn common topics such as "biology" or "astronomy".

Given the success of these models, several papers in computer vision [3][4][5] have applied them to the visual domain, replacing text words with visual features [6][7]. This approach is usually referred to as the "Bag-of-Features (BoF)" method. Rather than discovering topics, the BoF method aims to discover visual categories, such as cars or bikes in the image database. However, in the visual domain there are strong geometric relations within images, which do not exist in the text domain. There have been several attempts to learn visual categories in an unsupervised manner by jointly modeling the

H. Zha, R.-i. Taniguchi, and S. Maybank (Eds.): ACCV 2009, Part III, LNCS 5996, pp. 373–383, 2010.

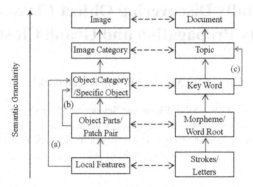

(a) Bag of Features based Specific Object Recognition or Object Categorization;

(b) Visual Parts/Phrases based Specific Object Recognition or Object Categorization;

(c) Bag of Words based Topic Discovery Method

Fig. 1. An analogy between image and text document in semantic granularity

appearance of local patches and their spatial arrangement [8][9]. Examples include the rotation, translation and scale invariant pLSA (RTSI-pLSA) model proposed by Li et al [8] and the geometric LDA (gLDA) model proposed by Philbin et al [9]. These methods can be regarded as extensions of the basic BoF based method. However, there are three basic problems which may compromise their modeling or recognition performance: a) local invariant features in the vision domain do not operate at the same semantic level as words in text domain; b) local features are not object specific; and c) visual vocabulary need to be incrementally adapted as more data becomes available. Before offering solutions to these problems, we explore them in further depth.

Firstly, if we compare the text domain BoW and the visual domain BoF, then it becomes clear that the BoF does not operate at the same semantic level as the BoW. A word in BoW is a single word, a term or a phrase. Every keyword (e.g. cup or car) normally has at least one high level semantic meaning. However, a visual feature usually does not posses semantic meaning. For convenience of comparisons, we draw an analogy between image based object discovery and text based topic discovery. Figure 1 shows the semantic granularities of images and documents, and indicates the analogies that we draw between their constituent elements. From the diagram it is clear that "topic discovery" and "visual object recognition" or "categorization" do not belong to the same semantic level. "Visual object recognition" might at best correspond to the problem on how to recognize words according to a group of letters, strokes, morphemes or word roots that are placed in a particular arrangement.

Secondly, most of the local invariant features or visual words are not object or class specific. To provide an illustration, we have trained a large clustering tree of over 2 million selected 128-dimensional SIFT (Scale Invariant Feature Transforms) [10] descriptors extracted from over 50K images and spanning more than 500 objects. There are 25334 leaf nodes in the clustering tree and the center vector of each leaf node corresponds to a quantized visual word. With an increasing number of objects, a single visual word may appear in hundreds of different objects. By contrast, a group of local features for an image object together with their collective spatial arrangement, are usually of a high level semantic meaning. The co-occurrence of the features with a specific spatial arrangement is object specific.

The third significant issue is that it is difficult to incrementally select a suitable number of visual words to construct a BoF when we increase the number of images and objects present. As the number of objects present increases, it is difficult to maintain a stable model. Alternatively, a visual vocabulary might not be static but instead evolve over time when new images are added to the database.

Although the BoF method has demonstrated impressive levels of performance and provide arguably the most successful paradigm for object discovery and recognition, because of the shortcomings listed above, in this paper we offer an alternative to the BoF model. We regard a group of local features together with their spatial arrangement as a visual entity. If such a visual entity is of a certain semantic meaning, e.g. corresponding to a car, then it is placed at the word-level in text domain. Since each visual entity is represented by structured data, a more versatile and expressive representational tool is provided by attributed graphs. Hence we simply term such a visual entity as a graph, which takes the place of a BoF based vector. We thus demonstrate how to implement object discovery and recognition without using the BoF model.

Most of the successful BoF based approaches [7][11][12][13] include the following ingredients: a) an image representation, b) a spatial verification and similarity measure, c) clustering of feature descriptors, and d) a search engine. Our method also has similar ingredients. In Section 2, we provide an overview of the corresponding basic ingredients for our method, and point out the differences with that of the BoF based approach. In Section 3, we propose an object discovery and model learning method. We present experimental results in Section 4 and conclude the paper in Section 5.

2 Ingredients of a Scalable Search Engine

Image representation. We first scale each training image to an identical size, and then select a subset of visually salient local features. For simple description, we just present the experiment on SIFT in the following. But we emphasize our methods could be adapted to alternative families of local invariant feature extractors or any combinations. For an image, those SIFT features that are robustly matched with the SIFT features in similar images can be regarded as salient representative features. Motivated by this, a method for ranking SIFT features has been proposed in [14]. Using this method, the SIFT features of an image I are ranked in order according to their decreasing matching frequency. We select the $\mathcal{T}$ top ranked SIFT features, denoted as $\mathcal{V}=\{V^t, t = 1, 2, ..., \mathcal{T}\}$, where $V^t = ((\overrightarrow{X^t})^T, (\overrightarrow{D^t})^T, (\overrightarrow{U^t})^T)^T$. Here, $\overrightarrow{X^t}$ is the location, $\overrightarrow{D^t}$ is the direction vector and $\overrightarrow{U^t}$ is the set of descriptors of a SIFT feature. In our experiments, $\mathcal{T}$ is set to 40. If there are less than this number of feature points present then all available SIFT features in an image are selected.

For the reasons given in Section 1, we regard the above selected local features together with their spatial arrangement as a semantic visual entity, which is placed at the word-level in text domain. This kind of structured data can be represented by using attributed graphs G [15] (hereafter simplified as graphs). We can obtain a set of graphs $\mathbb{G}$ $=\{G_l, l = 1, 2, ..., N\}$ from a set of images.

Pairwise graph matching for spatial verification and similarity measure. As shown in [7][11][13], the recognition or retrieval results can be significantly improved using the geometry of spatial feature arrangement to verify consistency. Here the idea is to re-rank an initial list of matching candidates by estimating geometric transformations, e.g. affine homographies, between the query image image and each of the top-ranking candidates. The re-ranking score is computed from the number of verified inliers, and outliers are excluded.

In our approach, on the other hand, each image is represented by a graph. As a result the spatial verification problem becomes one of pairwise graph matching (PGM). We perform PGM with the aim of finding a maximum common subgraph (MCS) between two graphs G_l and G_q, and the result is denoted as $MCS(G_l,G_q)$. There are a plethora of available methods for finding matching features consistent with a given set of geometric constraints, and the problem has been proven to be NP-hard. RANSAC provides one popular set of methods, however their implementation is slow [16]. In [17], pairwise graph matching is achieved by combining SIFT feature matching and iterative Procrustes alignment. The method can not only be used to align the feature points, but can also be used to discard those features that do not satisfy the spatial arrangement constraints. Given $MCS(G_l,G_q)$ obtained by PGM, they define a similarity measure between the graphs G_l and G_q as follows:

$$R(G_l,G_q) = \|MCS(G_l,G_q)\| \times (\exp(- e(X_l,X_q)))^\kappa. \tag{1}$$

Here a) $\|MCS(G_l,G_q)\|$ is the cardinality of the MCS of G_l and G_q, b) κ is the number of roughly mismatched feature pairs by SIFT matching, which is used to amplify the influence of the geometric dissimilarity between X_l and X_q, and c) X_l and X_q are respectively the position coordinates in graphs G_l and G_q corresponding to the vertexes of $MCS(G_l,G_q)$.

This similarity measure is significantly different from the BoF similarity measure which is based on the L1 or L2 distance between vectors [7][11][18][13], and captures both the similarity of local appearance and global spatial consistency.

Clustering of feature descriptors. For BoF based methods, the vector quantization of feature descriptors has been used by Sivic and Zisserman [7]. Here small vocabularies were generated using the k-means clustering method. It was subsequently shown in [12][18][13] that for large scale cases a more discriminative vocabulary is necessary. In [18], hierarchical k-means (HKM) and in [13] a KD-forest approximation were explored as possible refinements of the method. The aim of using these clustering methods is to obtain the visual vocabulary for construction of a BoF vector. Each image is then represented by a high dimensional tf-idf (Term Frequency-Inverse Document Frequency) [12][18][13] weighted BoF vector.

Although we represent images by graphs, we still require means of clustering the local feature descriptors. We use a SOM neural net based tree clustering method (termed a RSOM tree) proposed in [19] for learning a large corpus of SIFT descriptors. The RSOM tree can be incrementally trained since it utilizes a self-organizing divide-and-conquer architecture. It is also important to stress that though the leaf nodes in an RSOM tree are a quantization of the descriptors, we do not regard such a quantization as a visual vocabulary. We simply use the RSOM tree to efficiently retrieve candidate matching graphs, in the manner detailed in the following paragraphs.

Search engine. Given a graph set $\mathbb{G} = \{G_q, q = 1, 2, ..., N\}$, for each graph $G_l \in \mathbb{G}$, and the remaining graphs in the set ($\forall G_q \in \mathbb{G}$), we obtain the pairwise graph similarity measures $R(G_l, G_q)$ defined in Equation (1). Using the similarity measures we rank the graphs G_q in decreasing order. The K top-ranked graphs are defined as the generalized K-nearest neighbor graphs (KNNG) of graph G_l, denoted as $\mathbb{K}\{G_l\}$.

With increasing size of the graph dataset, it becomes time consuming to obtain $\mathbb{K}\{G_l\}$ if a sequential search strategy is adopted. Fortunately, for a large graph set, most of the similarity measures are low. For a single graph G_l, if we can efficiently find a subset $\mathbb{G}'$ with significant similarity values as a pre-filtering stage, then we only need to perform pairwise graph matching on this subset. To this end, we use the above mentioned RSOM clustering tree.

To obtain $\mathbb{K}\{G_l\}$ for each sample graph using a trained RSOM tree we proceed as follows. Given a graph G_l, we find the winner of the leaf nodes for each descriptor of this graph and define the union of all graphs for the winners as follows:

$$UG\{G_l\} = \{ G_q \mid U_q^j \in G_q, U_q^j \in WL\{U_l^t\}, U_l^t \in G_l\}. \tag{2}$$

where $WL\{U_l^t\}$ is the winner of the leaf nodes for descriptor U_l^t. The frequency of graph G_q, denoted as H_q, represents the number of roughly matched descriptors between two graphs. Since we aim to obtain $\mathbb{K}\{G_l\}$, we need not process all graphs in the set $UG\{G_l\}$. We rank the graphs in $UG\{G_l\}$ according to decreasing frequency H_q. From the ranked list, we select the first K graphs, denoted by $\mathbb{K}'\{G_l\}$ as follows:

$$\mathbb{K}'\{G_l\} = \{ G_q \mid G_q \in UG\{G_l\}, H_q > H_{q+1}, q = 1, 2, ..., K.\}. \tag{3}$$

For each graph G_q in $\mathbb{K}'\{G_l\}$, we obtain the similarity measure according to Equation (1) and then $\mathbb{K}\{G_l\}$ can be obtained. Using this method, we can efficiently obtain $\mathbb{K}\{G_l\}$. As a result, it is not necessary to use a search engine constructed from BoF vectors, which is the usual practice in the text domain. Hence, the method can be easily adapted to incremental learning settings.

3   Object Discovery and Model Learning

This section commences by presenting a new graph clustering method developed by borrowing the widely used idea of query expansion from text query. We then explain how the method can be used to discover object classes and learn object class models.

3.1   Similarity Propagation Based Graph Clustering

In the text retrieval literature, a standard method for improving performance is query expansion, where a number of the highly ranked documents from the original query are reissued as a new query. This allows the retrieval system to use relevant terms not present in the original query. In [11][13], query expansion was imported into the visual processing domain. Spatial constraints between the query image and each result allows for an accurate verification of each returned image. This has the effect of suppressing false positives, which typically limit the effectiveness of text-based query expansion. These verified images can then be used to learn a latent feature model to enable the controlled construction of expanded queries. The simplest query expansion method that offers good performance is the so-called "average query expansion". Here a new query is constructed by averaging a number of document descriptors. The documents used for the expanded query are taken from the top-ranked verified results from the original query.

Our query expansion method is based on the RSOM tree and the set $\mathbb{K}\{G_l\}$ for each graph, obtained in the training stage. The method is based on a pairwise similarity propagation algorithm for graph clustering (SPGC). Stated simply, the method is as follows. A group of graphs are referred to as siblings of a given graph G_l provided they satisfy the following condition:

$$S\{G_l\} = \{G_q \in \mathbb{K}\{G_l\} \mid R(G_l, G_q) \geq R_\tau\} \triangleq S_{R_\tau}\{G_l\}. \tag{4}$$

We use the definition to recursively obtain the family tree for the graph G_l, and this is formally defined as follows.

Family Tree of a Graph (**FTOG**): For any given similarity threshold R_τ, an FTOG of G_l with k generations and denoted as $M\{G_l, k\}$, is defined as follows:

$$M\{G_l, k\} = M\{G_l, k - 1\} \bigcup_{G_q \in L\{G_l, k-1\}} S_{R_\tau}\{G_q\}. \tag{5}$$

where, if $k = 1$, $L\{G_l, 1\} = L\{G_l, 0\} \bigcup S\{G_l\}$ and $M\{G_l, 0\} = \{G_l\}$; and the process stops when $M\{G_l, k\} = M\{G_l, k + 1\}$. An FTOG, whose graphs satisfy the restriction defined in Equation (4), can be regarded as a cluster of graphs. However, it must be stressed that this is not a clustering method based on a central prototype. Instead, graphs are clustered using the similarity propagation strategy.

3.2 Weakly Supervised Object Discovery and Model Learning

The clustering process is controlled by the threshold R_τ. By varying the parameter, we can represent images using canonical graphs constructed from a number of selected local invariant features so that most of the graphs belonging to an identical object form a single FTOG. An example FTOG obtained from a large dataset is shown in Figure 2, where $R_\tau = 7.8$.

In this case, the FTOG is class specific. From the perspective of fault tolerance, the precision does not necessarily need to be 100%.

According to our experiments, if $R_\tau \geq 10.0$ is large then the corresponding FTOG will have high precision (close to 1). With this setting, we can obtain a number of disjoint FTOG's from a large graph dataset (in each FTOG, there are at least 2 graphs.). We use these FTOG's as cluster seeds. For each FTOG, in a weak supervision stage, we manually assign a groundtruth object label (or name) to a cluster. We can also manually adjust the threshold to obtain a better cluster containing more graphs belonging to the

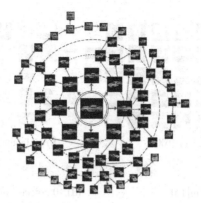

Fig. 2. A sample FTOG obtained by using SPGC. A dataset of over 50,000 images contains 72 images of a car, appearing with viewpoint variations of $0^o - 360^o$. Using SPGC, we can obtain an FTOG only containing all the 72 images as shown in this figure.

same object class. We denote the similarity threshold for the corresponding FTOG's as $R_{\tau_1}(M_l\{G_q\})$. In this way each cluster corresponds to an object class discovered from the data, and the corresponding FTOG is the class model. However, a single object may be split between multiple clusters.

If we regard each graph in an FTOG as a vertex in a higher level graph, for a pair of vertexes an edge, weighted by the similarity measure, is defined iff their similarity measure is subject to the given similarity constraint, an FTOG can be further regarded as a class specific graph (CSG) model.

Given that c FTOGs have been detected for a single object-class in a dataset, i.e. $\exists G_{l_i}, i = 1, 2, ..., c$, subject to $M\{G_{l_i}, g\} \cap M\{G_{l_j}, g\} = \emptyset, i \neq j, i, j \in \{1, 2, ..., c\}$, then we uniquely label the corresponding FTOG's as $L_1, L_2, ..., L_c$. We denote the set of clusters for a single discovered object model as follows:

$$C_{R_\tau} = \{ M_{R_\tau}\{G_l, \infty\}\} \triangleq \{ M_l \mid l \in \{L_1, L_2, ..., L_c\} \}. \tag{6}$$

A set of class specific FTOGs of an object can also be regarded as class specific graph models and still termed CSG model. Ideally a single object has one corresponding FOTG, that is $c = 1$. However, in an incremental learning setting, each object will tend to have more then one FTOG. With an increasing size of the dataset it is likely that two disjoint FTOG's will become merged when intermediate graphs are encountered. In an incremental learning setting, a new graph G_l is added to its discovered model according to the following rules:

1. If $\exists$ more than one graph G_q, s.t. $R(G_l, G_q) \geq R_{\tau_0}$, G_l is processed as a redundant duplicate graph of G_q, in our settings, $R_{\tau_0} = 18$.

2. If $\exists G_{q_0}$, s.t. $R(G_l, G_{q_0}) \geq R_{\tau_1}(M_l\{G_{q_0}\})$, G_l is incremented as an irreducible graph of $M_l\{G_{q_0}\}$; If there is another graph $G_{q_1} \in M_l\{G_{q_1}\}$, $M_l\{G_{q_0}\}$ and $M_l\{G_{q_1}\}$ come from different classes, G_l then is marked as an ambiguous graph. If $M_l\{G_{q_0}\}$ and $M_l\{G_{q_1}\}$ belong to the same class, then we merge these two FTOG's.

3. If $\max\{R(G_l, G_q)\} < R_{\tau_1}(M_l\{G_q\})$, create a new FTOG $M_l\{G_l\}$.

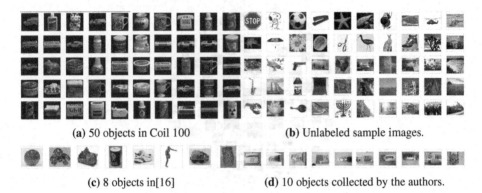

(a) 50 objects in Coil 100   (b) Unlabeled sample images.

(c) 8 objects in[16]   (d) 10 objects collected by the authors.

Fig. 3. Image data sets. a: 3600 images of 50 objects in COIL 100, labeled as A1~A50; b: 29875 unlabeled images from many other standard datasets, e.g. Caltech101 [3] and Google images, covering over 450 objects and used as negative samples; c: 161 images of 8 objects used in [16], labeled as C1 to C8; d: 20000 images of 10 objects collected by us, labeled as D1 to D10. For each of the objects in D1 to D9, we collect 1500 images which traverse a large variation of imaging conditions, and similarly 6500 images for D10. For simple description, the 4 dada sets are denoted as A to D. The objects in Figure 3a,Figure 3c and Figure 3d are numbered from left to right and then from top to bottom as shown in the corresponding figures, e.g. A1 to A50 in Figure 3a. As a whole, the 68 objects are also identified as Object 1 to Object 68.

Once a CSG model is trained, for a test graph G_l, we can obtain $K_\tau\{G_l\}$ and use a k-nearest neighbor weighted voting recognition strategy, using the similarity measure $R(G_l, G_q)$ as a weight.

4   Experimental Results

We have collected 53536 training images, some examples of which are shown in Figure 3, as training data. The data spans more than 500 objects including human faces and natural scenes. For each of these images, we extract ranked SIFT features using the method presented in [14]. Of these at most 40 highly ranked SIFT features are selected to construct a graph. We have collected over 2,140,000 SIFT features and 53536 graphs for the training set. We have trained an RSOM clustering tree with 25334 leaf nodes for the SIFT descriptors using the incremental RSOM training method. In this stage, we have also obtained $K\{G_l\}$ for each of the graphs. We use the 68 objects (detailed in Fig. 3) and the 31 human faces (detailed in Fig. 4) to test our object class discovery method.

(1) Object discovery. The object discovery results for the 68 object problem are shown in Fig. 4, it is clear that for most of the objects sampled under controlled imaging conditions, ideal performance has been achieved. For 35 objects in COIL 100, 35 models are individually discovered with total recall and precision of unit in one FTOG. For 13 objects, 6 models are discovered. Each group of objects in Fig. 5 (A)(B)(C)(D) are actually identical in shape but color. Since it only uses gray scale information in SIFT, our method fails in this case. We hence regard these objects in the four groups as being correctly discovered according to shape.

ID \ Par	1~50 Except 3, 39	3	39	51	52	53	54	55	56	57	58	59	60	61	62	63	64	65	66	67	68
N_i	72	72	72	29	20	16	16	16	16	28	20	1500	1500	1500	1500	1500	1500	1500	1500	1500	6500
N_d	72	64	66	22	16	15	15	16	16	27	20	1491	1483	1500	1500	1500	1475	1487	1500	1467	6488
p	1.0	1.0	1.0	1.0	1.0	1.0	1.0	1.0	1.0	1.0	1.0	1.0	1.0	1.0	1.0	1.0	1.0	1.0	1.0	1.0	1.0
r	1.0	.875	.917	.759	.80	.938	.938	1.0	1.0	.964	1.0	.994	.989	1.0	1.0	1.0	.983	.991	1.0	.978	.998
N_c	1	2	2	3	1	3	3	3	3	4	2	6	8	4	5	3	9	3	3	4	1

Fig. 4. Results of object discovery

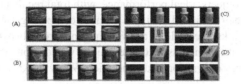

Fig. 5. 6 groups of objects are overlapping-clustered into 6 clusters

In the above table, ID is the Object ID; N_i is the number of the initial images of an object; N_d is the number of images discovered by using our method; N_d^+ is the number of correctly discovered images; p is the precision defined as N_d^+/N_d; r is recall defined as N_d^+/N_i. N_c is the number of discovered clusters of each object.

Unfortunately, in most practical situations, the images of an object are likely to be obtained with large variations of imaging conditions and are more likely to be clustered into several FTOGs. As a result, each object gives rise to multiple clusters. For objects 51 to 58 there are no more than 30 images with large variations in viewing conditions, and the images are not representative enough to perform ideal recognition. However, for objects 59 to 68, the images clustered together are sufficient to form an effective object model which can be used for recognition. For object 68, since there are thousands of images, the different views form a single cluster.

It is worth pointing out that all of these experiments are implemented in an incremental learning setting. We commenced by using 3600 images of 50 objects in the COIL 100 database as the first batch of images. From which, the models of these 50 objects are discovered. With the increase of additional training images, the discovered models of the 50 objects have not been changed. We than trained a second batch of samples containing instances of Object 51 to Object 68, and their corresponding models are discovered. The number of images is than increased to over 50K by including the category of Caltech faces and over 450 other objects. From this data we attempt to discover the face class. Compare to the up-to-date BoF based methods, the size of the RSOM clustering tree is dynamic, the scale of the image corpus is also dynamic. The discovered model keeps stable and can be refined in the incremental settings.

5   Conclusion

In this paper, we propose a scalable framework for learning object classes (object discovery). The method is graph-based and makes use of the RSOM tree clustering of local feature descriptors and graph clustering using similarity propagation (SPGC). As such it is therefor distinct from current state-of-the-art "Bag-of-Feature" based methods. We represent each bag of features of an image together with their spatial configuration using a graph instead of a BoF vector. We use our similarity propagation clustering method to extend the widely used query expansion strategy to graph representations of images. One significant feature of our model is that it can be placed in an incremental setting and used to expand the set of objects and refine the corresponding object models. We perform experiments on large image datasets. As an example here, the number of images increases from 1 to over 50K, and the number of objects increases from 1 to over 500. For some of the objects, ideal performance, with total recall and precision of unity in one cluster, has been achieved. Using a parallel computing environment, e.g. PC-clusters or local networks, the scale of our system can be readily extended to huge size. Using the object models learned using our technique we can potentially simultaneously effect object detection, recognition and annotation. We will explore these problems in future work.

References

1. Hofmann, T.: Unsupervised learning by probabilistic latent semantic analysis. Machine Learning 43, 17–196 (2001)
2. Blei, D., Ng, A., Jordan, M.: Latent dirichlet allocation. In: NIPS (2002)
3. Fei-Fei, L., Perona, P.: A bayesian hierarchical model for learning natural scene categories. In: CVPR (2005)
4. Sivic, J., Russell, B.C., Efros, A.A., Zisserman, A., Freeman, W.: Discovering object categories in image collections. In: ICCV (2005)
5. Russell, B.C., Efros, A.A., Sivic, J., Freeman, W.T., Zisserman, A.: Using multiple segmentations to discover objects and their extent in image collections. In: CVPR (2006)
6. Csurka, G., Bray, C., Dance, C., Fan, L.: Visual categorization with bags of keypoints. In: Workshop on Statistical Learning in Computer Vision, ECCV, pp. 1–22 (2004)
7. Sivic, J., Zisserman, A.: Video google: A text retrieval approach to object matching in videos. In: ICCV, pp. 1470–1477 (2003)
8. Li, Y., Wang, W., Gao, W.: A robust approach for object recognition. In: Zhuang, Y.-t., Yang, S.-Q., Rui, Y., He, Q. (eds.) PCM 2006. LNCS, vol. 4261, pp. 262–269. Springer, Heidelberg (2006)
9. Philbin, J., Sivic, J., Zisserman, A.: Geometric lda: A generative model for particular object discovery. In: BMVC (2008)
10. Lowe, D.: Distinctive image features from scale-invariant key points. IJCV 60(2), 91–110 (2004)
11. Chum, O., Philbin, J., Sivic, J., Isard, M., Zisserman, A.: Total recall: Automatic query expansion with a generative feature model for object retrieval. In: ICCV (2007)
12. Nister, D., Stewenius, H.: Scalable recognition with a vocabulary tree. In: CVPR (2006)
13. Philbin, J., Chum, O., Isard, M., Sivic, J., Zissermans, A.: Object retrieval with large vocabularies and fast spatial matching. In: CVPR (2007)
14. Xia, S.P., Ren, P., Hancock, E.R.: Ranking the local invariant features for the robust visual saliencies. In: ICPR 2008 (2008)
15. Chung, F.: Spectral graph theory. American Mathematical Society (1997)

16. Rothganger, F., Lazebnik, S., Schmid, C., Ponce, J.: 3d object modeling and recognition using local affine-invariant image descriptors and multi-view spatial constraints. IJCV 66(3), 231–259 (2006)
17. Xia, S., Hancock, E.: 3D object recognition using hyper-graphs and ranked local invariant features. In: da Vitoria Lobo, N., Kasparis, T., Roli, F., Kwok, J.T., Georgiopoulos, M., Anagnostopoulos, G.C., Loog, M. (eds.) S+SSPR 2008. LNCS, vol. 5342, pp. 117–126. Springer, Heidelberg (2008)
18. Jegou, H., Harzallah, H., Schmid, C.: A contextual dissimilarity measure for accurate and efficient image search. In: CVPR (2007)
19. Xia, S.P., Liu, J.J., Yuan, Z.T., Yu, H., Zhang, L.F., Yu, W.X.: Cluster-computer based incremental and distributed rsom data-clustering. ACTA Electronica sinica 35(3), 385–391 (2007)

Image Classification Using Probability Higher-Order Local Auto-Correlations

Tetsu Matsukawa[1] and Takio Kurita[2]

[1] University of Tsukuba,
1-1-1 Tennodai, Tsukuba, Japan
[2] National Institute of Advanced Industrial Science and Technology,
1-1-1 Umezono, Tsukuba, Japan
{t.matsukawa,takio-kurita}@aist.go.jp

Abstract. In this paper, we propose a novel method for generic object recognition by using higher-order local auto-correlations on probability images. The proposed method is an extension of bag-of-features approach to posterior probability images. Standard bag-of-features is approximately thought as sum of posterior probabilities on probability images, and spatial co-occurrences of posterior probability are not utilized. Thus, its descriptive ability is limited. However, using local auto-correlations of probability images, the proposed method extracts richer information than the standard bag-of-features. Experimental results show the proposed method is enable to have higher classification performances than the standard bag-of-features.

1 Introduction

Genetic object recognition technologies are important for automatic image search. Despite many methods have been researched until now, the performance is still inferior to human recognition system.

The most popular approach for generic object recognition is bag-of-features [3], because of its simplicity and effectiveness. Bag-of-features is originally inspired from text recognition method "bag-of-words", and uses orderless collection of quantized local features. The main steps of bag-of-features are : 1) Detection and description of image patches. 2) Assigning patch descriptors to a set of predetermined codebooks with a vector quantization algorithm. 3) Constructing a bag of features, which counts the number of patches assigned to each codebook. 4) Applying a classifier by treating the bag of features as the features vector, and thus determine which category to assign to the image.

It is known that the bag of features method is robust for background clutter, pose changes, intra-class variations and produces good classification accuracy. However, several problems are existed for applying to image representation. To solve these problems, many methods are proposed. Some of these methods are spatial pyramid binning to utilize location informations [7], higher level codebook creation based on local co-occurrence of codebooks [1][13][18], improvement of codebook creation[9][10][11] and region of interest based matching [14].

H. Zha, R.-i. Taniguchi, and S. Maybank (Eds.): ACCV 2009, Part III, LNCS 5996, pp. 384–394, 2010.

In this paper, we present a novel improvement of bag-of-features. The main novelty of the proposed method is to utilize probability images for feature extraction. The standard bag-of-features is approximately thought as a method so called "sum of posterior probabilities" on probability images. So the method does not utilize local co-occurrence on probability images. We applied higher-order local auto-correlations on probability images, thus richer information of probability images can be extracted. We call this image representation method as "Probability Higher-order Local Auto-correlations (PHLAC)". PHLAC has desirable property for recognition, namely shift-invariance, additivity and synonymy [19] invariance. We show this image representation method PHLAC has the significantly better classification performance than the standard bag-of-features.

The proposed method gives the different direction of improvement to the currently proposed methods of bag-of-features (e.g. Correlation of codebooks, improvement of clustering and spatial pyramid binning), so this method can be combined with those methods in the future.

2   Related Work

The image feature extraction using local co-occurrence is recognized as an important concept [6] for recognition. Recently, several methods have been proposed using correlation. These are categorized to feature level co-occurrence and codebook level co-occurrence. The examples of feature level co-occurrence are local self similarity [12] and GLAC [5]. We can use these features in the codebook creation process, then the codebook level co-occurrence and the feature level co-occurrence is thought as another concept. The examples of codebook level co-occurrence are correlations [13] and Visual Phrases [18]. When using codebook level co-occurrence, we need large number of dimensions, e.g. in proportion to codebook size × codebook size when we consider only co-occurrence of two codebooks. Thus, features selection method or dimension reduction method is necessary and current researches are focused on how to mining frequent and distinctive codebook sets [17][18][19]. The expressions of co-occurrence using a generative model have also been proposed [1] [16]. But, these methods require a complex latent model and expensive parameter estimations. On the other hand, our method can be easy implemented and is relatively low dimension but effective for classifications, because it is based on auto-correlations on posterior probability images. The methods which give posterior probability to a codebook have also been proposed [15][14], but these methods are not using auto-correlation of codebooks.

3   Probability High-Order Local Auto-Correlations

3.1   Probability Images

Let I be an image region and $r = (x, y)^t$ be a position vector in I. The image patch whose center is r_k are quantized to M codebook $\{V_1,...,V_M\}$ by local feature extraction and vector quantization algorithm $VQ(r_k) \in \{1,...,M\}$. These steps are same as the standard bag-of-features [7]. Posterior probability $P(c|V_m)$ of category $c \in \{1, ..., C\}$ is assigned to each codebook V_m using image patches on training images. Several forms of estimating posterior probability can be taken. (a) Codebook plausibility. The posterior probability is estimated by Bayes' theorem as follows.

$$P(c|V_m) = \frac{P(V_m|c)P(c)}{P(V_m)}, \tag{1}$$

where, $P(c) = 1/C$, $P(V_m)$=(# of V_m)/(#of all patches), $P(V_m|c)$ = (# of class c $\wedge$ V_m)/(# of class c patches). Here, $P(c)$ is common constant, so set to 1.

(b) Codebook uncertainty. In our method, the probability is not restricted to the theoretical definition of probability. The pseudo probability which indicates the degree of supporting to each category from a codebook is considered. Codebook uncertainty is the percentage of class c in given codebook. This is defined as follows.

$$P(c|V_m) = \frac{P(V_m|c)P(c)}{\sum_{c=1}^{C} P(V_m|c)}. \tag{2}$$

(c) SVM weight. The weight of each codebook when learning by one-against-all linear SVM [4] is used to define pseudo probability. Assume we use K local image patches from one image, then the histogram of bag-of-features $\boldsymbol{H} = (H(1), ..., H(M))$ becomes as follows.

$$H(m) = \sum_{k=1}^{K} \begin{cases} 1 & if \ (VQ(\boldsymbol{x_k}) = m) \\ 0 & otherwise \end{cases}. \tag{3}$$

Using the histogram of bag-of-features, the classification function of one-against-all linear SVM becomes as follows.

$$arg \max_{c \in C} \{f_c(\boldsymbol{H}) = \sum_{m=1}^{M} \alpha_{c,m} H(m) + b_c\}, \tag{4}$$

where, $\alpha_{c,m}$ is the weight for each histogram bins and b_c is the learned threshold. We transform the weight of each histogram to non-negative by $\alpha_{c,m} \leftarrow \alpha_{c,m} - min\{\boldsymbol{\alpha_c}\}$ and normalize it by $\alpha_{c,m} \leftarrow \frac{\alpha_{c,m}}{\sum_{m=1}^{M} \alpha_{c,m}}$. Then we can obtain the pseudo probability by SVM weight as follows.

$$P(c|V_m) = \frac{\alpha_{c,m} - min\{\boldsymbol{\alpha_c}\}}{\sum_{m=1}^{M}(\alpha_{c,m} - min\{\boldsymbol{\alpha_c}\})}. \tag{5}$$

We used SVM weight as pseudo probability because the proposed method becomes a complete extension of the standard bag-of-features when using this pseudo probability (Sec. 3.3).

In this paper, we assume to use grid sampling of local features [7] per p pixel interval, because of simplicity. We denote the set of sample points as I_p and we call the map of (pseudo) posterior probability of codebook of each local

Fig. 1. Probability images (codebook plausibility): Original image, probability of BIKE(left), probability of CAR(middle), probability of PEOPLE(right). This probability image is calculated by 2 pixel interval (p=2), for easy understanding the original images are resized to the same size to probability images. The actual size of the original images are larger than the probability images by p×p pixels. Local features and codebook are same as those used in experiment.

regions as a probability image. Examples of probability images are shown in Fig. 1. White color shows the high probability. The data are comes from IG02 used in the following experiment. The number of categories is 3 (BIKE, CAR and PEOPLE). It is noticed the human-like contours are appeared in PEOPLE probability.

3.2   PHLAC

We call HLAC features [6] on this probability images as PHLAC. The definition of Nth order PHLAC is as follows.

$$R(c, a_1, ..., a_N) = \int_{I_p} P(c|V_{VQ(r)}) P(c|V_{VQ(r + a_1)}) \cdots P(c|V_{VQ(r + a_N)}) dr.$$

(6)

In practice, Eq.(6) can take so many forms by varying the parameters N and a_n. In this paper, these are restricted to the following subset: $N \in \{0, 1, 2\}$ and $a_{nx}, a_{ny} \in \{\pm \Delta r \times p, 0\}$. By eliminating duplicates which arise from shifts, the mask patterns of PHLAC becomes as shown in Fig. 2. This mask pattern is the same as 35 HLAC mask patterns [6]. Thus, PHLAC inherits the desirable properties of HLAC for object recognition, namely shift-invariance and additivity. Although PHLAC does not have scale-invariance, we can deal with scale changes by using several size of mask patterns.

By calculating correlations in local regions, PHLAC becomes to robust against small spatial difference and noise. There are several alternatives of preprocessing

---

Algorithm 1. PHLAC computation

Training Image :
1) Create codebook by local features and clustering algorithm (e.g. SIFT + K means).
2) Configure posterior probability of each codebook {plausibility, uncertainly, SVM}.
Training and Test Image :
3) Create C posterior probability images by p pixel interval.
4) Preprocessing posterior probability images (local averaging).
5) Calculate HLAC on posterior probability images by sliding HLAC mask patterns.

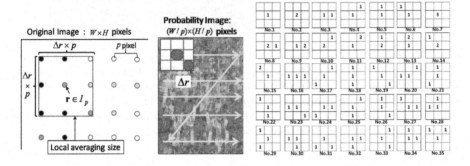

Fig. 2. PHLAC: local averaging size(left), extracting process(middle) and mask patterns(right).The number {1,2,3} of mask patterns show the frequency for which its pixel value is used for product in Eq.(6).

of these local regions such as {max, average, median}. We found average is the best for other settings. Thus the practical formulation of PHLAC is given by

$$0^{\text{th}}\text{order} \quad R_{N=0}(c) = \sum_{r \in I_p} L_a(P(c|V_{VQ(r)})) \tag{7}$$

$$1^{\text{st}}\text{order} \quad R_{N=1}(c, a_1) = \sum_{r \in I_p} L_a(P(c|V_{VQ(r)}))L_a(P(c|V_{VQ(r + a_1)}))$$

$$2^{\text{nd}}\text{order} \quad R_{N=2}(c, a_1, a_2) = \sum_{r \in I_p} L_a(P(c|V_{VQ(r)}))L_a(P(c|V_{VQ(r + a_1)}))$$

$$L_a(P(c|V_{VQ(r + a_2)})),$$

where L_a means local averaging on a $(\Delta r \times p) \times (\Delta r \times p)$ region centered on r(Fig. 2). Actually, PHLAC are obtained by HLAC calculation on local averaged probability image (see Algorithm.1.). PHLAC are extracted from probability images of all categories, thus the total number of features of PHLAC becomes $35 \times C$. There are two possibilities of classification using PHLAC image representations. One is the classification using all PHLAC of all categories (PHLAC$_{ALL}$) and the other is using one categories PHLAC for each one-against-all classifiers (PHLAC$_{CLASSWISE}$). We compare these methods in the following experiments.

3.3   Interpretation of PHLAC

Bag-of-features(0th) + local auto-correlations(1st + 2nd): If we use SVM weights as pseudo probabilities, then 0-th order of PHLAC becomes the same as the classification by the standard bag-of-features using linear-SVM. Because $\mathbf{H}$ is a histogram (see Eq.(3)), Eq.(4) is rewritten as follows.

$$arg \max_{c \in C} \{ \sum_{k=1}^{K} \alpha_{c, VQ(r_k)} + b_c \} \tag{8}$$

$$= arg \max_{c \in C} \{ \sum_{k=1}^{K} (\alpha_{c, VQ(r_k)} - min\{\boldsymbol{\alpha}_c\}) + K min\{\boldsymbol{\alpha}_c\} + b_c \} \tag{9}$$

$$= arg \max_{c \in C} \{ A_c R_{N=0}(c) + B_c \}, \tag{10}$$

where $A_c = \sum_{m=1}^{M} (\alpha_{c,m} - min\{\boldsymbol{\alpha}_c\})$, $B_c = K min\{\boldsymbol{\alpha}_c\} + b_c$. (In this transformation from Eq.(9) to Eq.(10), the relationship $R_{N=0}(c) = \sum_{k=1}^{K} \frac{\alpha_{c,VQ(r_k)} - min\{\boldsymbol{\alpha}_c\}}{A_c}$ is used.) This equation shows that the classification by the standard bag-of-features is possible by using only 0-th order of PHLAC and the learned parameters A_c and B_c. (Exactly, this was assumed no-preprocessing in the calculation of PHLAC). This is the case that SVM weight is used as pseudo probability, but it is expected other probabilities have also similar property. Because the histogram of the standard bag-of-feature is created by not utilizing local co-occurrences, the 0th order of PHLAC is thought as almost the one-against-all bag-of-features classifications. Higher order features of PHLAC have richer information of probability images (e.g. the shape of local probability distributions). Thus, if any commonly existed patterns are contained in the specific classes, this representation can be expected to achieve better classification performance than the standard bag-of-features.

The relationship of the standard bag-of-features and PHLAC classification is shown in Fig.3. In our PHLAC classification, we train additional classifier using 0th order PHLAC $\{R_{N=0}(1), ..., R_{N=0}(C)\}$ and higher order PHLAC as feature vector. Thus, the only 0-th order $PHLAC_{SVM}$ can achieve better performance than the standard bag-of-features.

Synonymy invariance: The synonymous codebooks are the codebooks which have similar posterior probabilities [18]. PHLAC calculates directly on the probability images, the same features can be extracted even a local appearance is exchanged to other appearances whose posterior probabilities are same. This synonymy invariance is important for creating compact image representations [19].

4   Experiment

We compared the classification performances of the standard bag-of-features and PHLAC using two commonly used image datasets: IG02[8] and fifteen natural scene categories [7].

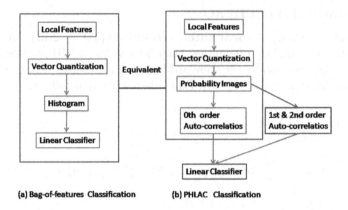

(a) Bag-of-features Classification   **(b) PHLAC Classification**

Fig. 3. Schematic comparison of the standard bag-of-features classification with our proposed PHLAC classification

To obtain reliable results, we repeated the experiments 10 times. Ten random subsets were selected from the data to create 10 pairs of training and test data. For each of these pairs a codebook was created by using k-means clustering on training set. For classification, a linear SVM was used by one-against-all. As implementation of SVM, we used LIBSVM. Five-fold cross-validation on the training set was used to tune parameters of SVM. The classification rate we report is the average of the per-class recognition rates which in turn are averaged over the 10 random test sets.

As local features, we used a SIFT descriptor [2] sampled on a regular grid. The modification by the dominant orientation was not used and computed on 16×16 pixel patch sampled every 8 pixels ($p = 8$). In the codebook creation process, all features sampled every 16 pixel on all training images were used for k-means clustering. As normalization method, we used L2-norm normalization for both the standard bag-of-features and PHLAC. In PHLAC, the features were L2 normalized by each auto-correlations order. Below we denote the classification of PHLAC using probability by codebook plausibility as $PHLAC_{Plau}$, PHLAC using pseudo probability by codebook uncertainty as $PHLAC_{Unc}$ and SVM weight as $PHLAC_{SVM}$. Note that although the SVM of standard bag-of-features is used for Eq.(5) of $PHLAC_{SVM}$, the result of 0th order $PHLAC_{SVM}$ is different from the result of standard bag-of-features from the reason mentioned in Sec 3.3.

4.1   Result of IG02

At first, we used IG02 [8](INRIA Annotations for Granz-02) dataset which contains large variations of target size. The classification task is to classify the test images to 3 categories, CAR, BIKE and PEOPLE. The number of training images of each category is 162 for CAR, 177 for BIKE and 140 for PEOPLE. The number of test images is same as training images. We resampled 10 sets of training and test sets

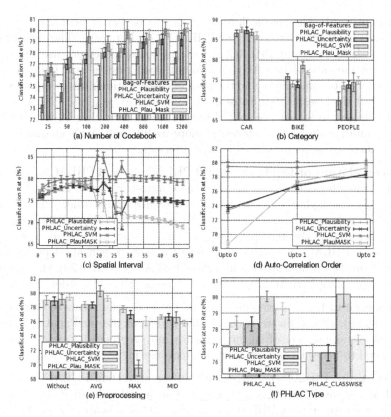

Fig. 4. Recognition rates of IG02. The basic setting is codebook size = 400 ((b)-(f)), Spatial Interval Δr= 12 ((a),(b),(d)-(f)) and PHLAC$_{ALL}$ ((a)-(e)).

from all images. Image size is 640×480 pixels or 480×640 pixels. Maraszalek at el prepared mask images which indicates target object locations. We also attempted to estimate probability of Eq.(1) by using only target object region's local features. We denote this PHLAC features as PHLAC$_{Plau-MASK}$. The experimental results are shown in Fig. 4.

Overall performance: As basic settings we used spatial interval Δr=12 and PHLAC$_{ALL}$. In all codebook size, all types of PHLAC achieves higher classification performances than the standard bag-of-features (Fig.4(a).). PHLAC$_{SVM}$ achieves higher classification rates than PHLAC$_{plau}$ and PHLAC$_{Unc}$. By using mask images for estimating probability, the performance of PHLAC$_{plau}$ becomes better when the codebook size is larger than 400.

Recognition rates per category: The classification rates of PHLAC becomes higher than the standard bag-of-features almost all cases (Fig.4(b).). Especially, the classification rates of PEOPLE are higher than the standard bag-of-features in any settings of PHLAC. This is because human-like contours which are shown in Fig.1 are appeared in human's regions and not existed in other images.

Spatial interval: The spatial interval seems to be better near $\Delta r=12$ (12×8 = 96 pixel) in all settings except for PHLAC$_{SVM}$ (Fig.4(c).). The classification rates of PHLAC$_{Plau}$ and PHLAC$_{Unc}$ become lower as to increase the spatial interval. In the case of PHLAC$_{SVM}$, classification rates is still high when the spatial interval becomes large and the peak of classification rates is appeared near $\Delta r=20$. But the classification rates in $\Delta r=20$, PHLAC$_{Plau}$ and PHLAC$_{Unc}$ become to be low, so we set the spatial interval as to $\Delta r=12$ as basic settings. In practice, multi-scale spatial interval is more useful than single spatial interval, because there are several optimal spatial intervals.

Auto-correlation order: In the case of PHLAC$_{Plau}$ and PHLAC$_{Unc}$, the classification rates become higher as to increase auto-correlation order (Fig.4(d)). PHLAC$_{SVM}$ is higher classification performance than other PHLAC only 0-th order auto-correlations. This is the reason of high classification rates of PHLAC$_{SVM}$ in the large spatial intervals. Using up to 2nd order auto-correlations, PHLAC$_{SVM}$ also can achieve the best classification performance. Especially in the optimal spatial interval of PHLAC$_{SVM}$($\Delta r=20$), the 2nd order auto-correlation of PHLAC$_{SVM}$ were 5.01% better than 0th order (Fig.4(c)).

Preprocessing: In local averaging and no preprocessing seems to be comparable in Fig.4(e). But when we tried another codebook size and spatial intervals, the local averaging were often outperformed no preprocessing cases. Thus, we recommend to using local averaging for preprocessing.

PHLAC type: PHLAC$_{ALL}$ are better performance than PHLAC$_{CLASSWISE}$ in PHLAC$_{Plau}$ and PHLAC$_{Unc}$ (Fig.4(f)). On the other hand PHLAC$_{SVM}$ are better in the case of using PHLAC$_{CLASSWISE}$. This indicates the dimension for training of each SVM can be reduced to 35 dimension when using PHLAC$_{SVM}$.

4.2 Result of Scene-15

Next we performed experiments on Scene-15 dataset [7]. The Scene-15 dataset consists of 4485 images spread over 15 categories. The fifteen categories contain 200 to 400 images each and range from natural scene like mountains and forest to man-made environments like kitchens and office. We selected 100 random images per categories as a training set and the remaining images as the test set. We used PHLAC$_{ALL}$ and experimentally set spatial interval as to $\Delta r = 8$. Some examples of dataset images and probability images are shown in Fig.5. Recognition rates of scene 15 are shown in Fig.6. In Scene-15, PHLAC achieves higher recognition performances than the standard bag-of-features classification in all categories and all number of codebook. In this dataset, PHLAC$_{Plau}$ and PHLAC$_{Unc}$ indicates higher accuracy than PHLAC$_{SVM}$. In the case of codebook size is 200, PHLAC$_{Plau}$ gives more than 15% higher recognition rate.

In our experimental settings, classification rates of the standard bag-of-features using histogram intersection kernel [7] is 66.31($\pm$ 0.15)% in codebook size 200 and PHLAC$_{Plau}$ achieves 69.48 ($\pm$ 0.27) % by using linear SVM. While Lazabnik reported 72.2($\pm$ 0.6) % on the standard bag-of-features, this difference is caused

office   opencountry   forest   mountain

industrial   coast   bedroom   highway

Fig. 5. Example of Scene15. Probability image shows probabilities of own category.

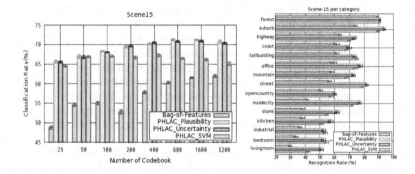

Fig. 6. Recognition Rates of Scene15: per codebook size (left) and per category when codebook size is 200(right)

by the difference of implementations such as feature extractions and codebook creations. The proposed method and the standard bag-of-features use the same codebook and features through in our experiments.

5   Conclusion

In this paper, we proposed an image description method using higher-order local auto-correlations on probability images called "Probability Higher-order Auto Correlations(PHLAC)". This method is regarded as an extension of the standard bag-of-features for improving the limitation of spatial information by utilizing co-occurrence of local spatial pattern in posterior probabilities. This method has shift-invariance and additivity as in HLAC [6]. Experimental results show the proposed method achieved higher classification performance than the standard bag-of-features in average 2 % and 15 % in the case of IG02 and Fifteen Scene Dataset respectively using 200 codebooks. We think combinations with other method (e.g. spatial binning and correlation features) probably improve the performance by the proposed probability auto-correlations scheme.

References

1. Agarwal, A., Triggs, B.: Multilevel Image Coding with Hyperfeatures. International Journal of Computer Vision 78, 15–27 (2008)
2. Lowe, D.G.: Distinctive image features from scale-invariant keypoints. International Journal of Computer Vision 60, 91–110 (2004)
3. Csurka, G., Dance, C.R., Fan, L., Willamowski, J., Bray, C.: Visual Categorization with Bag of Keypoints. In: European conference on computer vision 2004 workshop on Statistical Learning in Computer Vision, pp. 59–74 (2004)
4. Vapnik, V.: Statistical Learning Theory. John Wiley & Sons, Chichester (1998)
5. Kobayashi, T., Otsu, N.: Image Feature Extraction Using Gradient Local Auto-Correlations. In: Forsyth, D., Torr, P., Zisserman, A. (eds.) ECCV 2008, Part I. LNCS, vol. 5302, pp. 346–358. Springer, Heidelberg (2008)
6. Otsu, N., Kurita, T.: A new scheme for practical flexible and intelligent vision systems. In: IAPR Workshop on Computer Vision (1988)
7. Lazebnik, S., Schmid, C., Ponce, J.: Beyond bags of features: Spatial pyramid matching for recognizing natural scene categories. In: IEEE Conference on Computer Vision and Pattern Recognition, pp. 2169–2178 (2006)
8. Marszalek, M., Schmid, C.: Spatial Weighting for Bag-of-Features. In: IEEE Conference on Conputer Vision and Pattern Recognition, vol. 2, pp. 2118–2125 (2006)
9. Jurie, F., Triggs, B.: Creating efficient codebooks for visual recognition. In: IEEE International Conference on Computer Vision, vol. 1, pp. 604–610 (2005)
10. Nowak, E., Jurie, F., Triggs, B.: Sampling strategies for bag-of-features image classification. In: Leonardis, A., Bischof, H., Pinz, A. (eds.) ECCV 2006. LNCS, vol. 3954, pp. 490–503. Springer, Heidelberg (2006)
11. van Gemert, J.C., Geusebroek, J.-M., Veenman, C.J., Smeulders, A.W.M.: Kernel Codebooks for Scene Categorization. In: Forsyth, D., Torr, P., Zisserman, A. (eds.) ECCV 2008, Part III. LNCS, vol. 5304, pp. 696–709. Springer, Heidelberg (2008)
12. Shechtman, E., Irani, M.: Matching local self-similarities across images and videos. In: IEEE Conference on Computer Vision and Pattern Recognition, pp. 511–518 (2007)
13. Savarse, S., Winn, J., Criminisi, A.: Discriminative Object Class Models of Appearance and Shape by Correlatons. In: IEEE Conference on Computer Vision and Pattern Recognition, pp. 2033–2040 (2006)
14. Bosch, A., Zisserman, A., Munoz, X.: Image classification using random forests and ferns. In: IEEE International Conference on Computer Vision, pp. 1–8 (2007)
15. Shotton, J., Johnson, M., Cipolla, R.: Semantic texton forests for image categorization and segmentation. In: IEEE Conference on Computer Vision and Pattern Recognition, pp. 1–8 (2008)
16. Wang, X., Grimson, E.: Spatial Latent Dirichlet Allocation. In: Proceedings of Neural Information Processing Systems Conference, NIPS (2007)
17. Quack, T., Ferrari, V., Leibe, B., Van Gool, L.: Efficient mining of frequent and distinctive feature configurations. In: IEEE International Conference on Computer Vision (2007)
18. Yuan, J., Wu, Y., Yang, M.: Discovery of Collocation Patterns: from Visual Words to Visual Phrases. In: IEEE Conference on Conputer Vision and Pattern Recognition (2007)
19. Zheng, Y.-T., Zhao, M., Neo, S.-Y., Chua, T.-S., Tian, Q.: Visual Synset: Towards a Higher-level Visual Representation. In: IEEE Conference on Computer Vision and Pattern Recognition (2008)

Disparity Estimation in a Layered Image for Reflection Stereo

Masao Shimizu*, Masatoshi Okutomi, and Wei Jiang**

Graduate School of Science and Engineering, Tokyo Institute of Technology, Japan

Abstract. By watching the reflection in the glass window, one can often observe a two-layered image consisting of a front-surface reflection from a glass and a rear-surface reflection through the glass. The transparent glass plate reflects and transmits the incident light from its front surface. The transmitted light is then reflected from the rear surface and is transmitted again to the air through the front surface. These two light paths create a layered image comprising two identical images with a specific displacement depending on the object range. Estimating the object range requires the accurate detection of the image shift in the layered image. This paper presents a study of the shift estimation method using Fourier transformation of the layered image. The maximum location in the Fourier transform of the Fourier power spectrum of the layered image indicates the image shift. Experimental results demonstrate the effectiveness of the method compared with a method using an autocorrelation function.

1 Introduction

A transparent glass plate has two surfaces: frontal and rear. These surfaces both reflect and transmit rays from an object. A camera receives rays that have been reflected by the glass surfaces from the object if the object and the camera are on the same side of the glass plate. In this situation, the image includes two nearly identical scenes that have been reflected from the frontal surface and the rear surface. Figure 1 presents an example of a resultant layered image. The displacement between the two reflections is observable especially if the object is close to the glass and if the glass plate is thick.

Few papers describe multiple reflections at surfaces of a transparent glass plate. Miyazaki and Ikeuchi [9] modeled internal reflections in a transparent object with polarization to estimate the object shape. Diamant and Schechner [3] proposed a regularized optimization method to recover scenes, but they assume that the displacement in reflected scenes is constant in the image, independent of the object distances. Shimizu and Okutomi [12],[13] used displacement to

---

* His current affiliation is the College of Science and Technology, Nihon University, Japan.
** His current affiliation is the State Key Lab. of Industrial Control Technology, Zhejiang University, Hangzhou, China.

H. Zha, R.-i. Taniguchi, and S. Maybank (Eds.): ACCV 2009, Part III, LNCS 5996, pp. 395–405, 2010.
© Springer-Verlag Berlin Heidelberg 2010

Fig. 1. The glass reflection shown here produces a layered image: the right image is a magnification of the left

estimate the scene depth. They designated the depth estimation configuration as reflection stereo. To estimate the displacement, they use the autocorrelation function along with a positional constraint in the layered image on the condition that the camera and the transparent plate are calibrated.

The reflection stereo is a type of monocular stereo rig with a narrow baseline. Monocular methods are categorizable as multi-view [6], multi-image [4], and multi-exposure [11] methods. The reflection stereo belongs to the last category.

This paper presents a study of the shift estimation method using a Fourier transform of the layered image. A periodic variation in the Fourier power spectrum of a layered image will be observed corresponding to the amount and direction of the image shift. Therefore, the Fourier transform of the Fourier power spectrum can detect the cycle and direction by finding its peak location.

This paper is organized as follows. Section 2 briefly explains basic principles of the reflection stereo range measurement. Section 3 presents three methods to estimate the shift in the layered image: autocorrelation, cepstrum, and the proposed method. In section 4, we validate the effectiveness of the proposed method using some experiments with a real image. Section 5 concludes this paper with some relevant remarks.

2   Reflection Stereo

This section briefly explains basic information related to the reflection stereo [12] range measurement.

Figure 2 portrays two light paths from an object to the camera optical center. A transparent glass plate reflects and transmits the incident light on

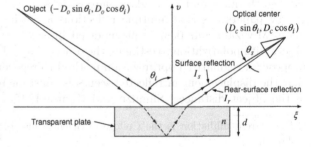

Fig. 2. Geometry of the reflection stereo apparatus

its front surface. The transmitted light is then reflected from the rear surface and is transmitted again to the air through the front surface. These two light paths have an angle disparity θ_s that depends on the relative refractive index n of the plate, the plate thickness d, the incident angle θ_i, and the object distance D_o.

The fundamental relation between the angle disparity θ_s and the distance D_o is explainable as the reflection and refraction of light in a plane including the object, the optical center, and the normal vector of the plate (the plane of incidence). A two-dimensional (2D) ξ-v coordinate system is set with its origin at the reflecting point on the surface. The following equation can be derived by projecting the object position $(-D_o \sin \theta_i, D_o \cos \theta_i)$ and the optical center position $(D_c \sin \theta_i, D_c \cos \theta_i)$ to ξ-axis.

$$D_o + D_c = d \frac{\sin (2 (\theta_i - \theta_s))}{\sin \theta_s \sqrt{n^2 - \sin^2 (\theta_i - \theta_s)}} \tag{1}$$

The angle disparity θ_s is obtainable by finding the displacement in the layered image. Then the object distance D_o is derived from Eq. (1). The displacement has a constraint which describes a correspondent position in the rear-surface image moving along a constraint line with respect to the position in the image. The constraint reduces the search to 1D, just as for stereo vision with the epipolar constraint. The angle disparity takes the minimum value $\theta_s = 0$ when $D_o = \infty$ if the plate is manufactured perfectly as a parallel planar plate. In other words, the two layers will perfectly overlap for a far distant object.

3   Disparity Estimation

3.1   Autocorrelation

The autocorrelation function $R_a(\tau)$ of a function $f(x)$ is defined as

$$R_a(\tau) = \lim_{T \to \infty} \frac{1}{2T} \int_{-T}^{T} f(x) f(x - \tau) dx. \tag{2}$$

It is an even function with respect to τ; it takes the maximum value at $\tau = 0$. Some local maxima will be detected if $f(x)$ is not a random function.

Let $f(x)$ be a 1D function representing the pixel values on a constraint line. In the case of the layered image, it can be written as $f(x) = I(x) + gI(x - \Delta)$, where $I(x)$ and g denote a reflected image and a "gain" difference, respectively, and Δ represents a shift between them. Autocorrelation function $R_a(\tau)$ of $f(x)$ is written as a sum of the following autocorrelation functions of image $I(x)$.

$$R_a(\tau) = (1 + g^2) R_I(\tau) + g R_I(\tau + \Delta) + g R_I(\tau - \Delta) \tag{3}$$

The image shift Δ can be found by determining the second local maximum[1] of the autocorrelation function $R_a(\tau)$.

---

[1] The second and third maxima in Eq. (3) equally appear if the integral interval in Eq. (2) is infinite. But in real implementations, the autocorrelation is computed with a limited range. This results in asymmetrical second and third peaks in Eq. (3).

The integral range is limited to a finite region of interest in real situations. In addition, the autocorrelation function is evaluated in discrete locations along the constraint line; then the sub-sampling peak location is estimated using an interpolation.

The peak shape of the autocorrelation function $R_I(\tau)$ depends on the spatial frequency response of the image $I(x)$; the second peak location can not be found if the region has a weak texture[2].

3.2   Cepstrum

The cepstrum is the spectrum of the logarithm of the spectrum of a time or spatial domain signal[3] [2],[10]. The cepstrum domain designated as the quefrency is not both the frequency and the spatial domain, but it corresponds perfectly to the spatial domain of the original signal. The cepstrum has been used for measurement of the delay time in an audio signal, image blur restoration [1], or correspondence search in stereo images [8],[16].

The shift estimation in the layered image can be considered as the same problem to estimate the delay time in an audio signal with echo; the cepstrum method is applicable.

The cepstrum of the 1D layered image $f(x) = I(x) + gI(x - \Delta)$ is obtainable as shown below.

$$\mathcal{F}\left[\log |\mathcal{F}[f(x)](u)|^2\right](\chi) = \mathcal{F}\left[\log \left|\mathcal{F}[I(x)](u)\left(1 + ge^{-j\Delta u}\right)\right|^2\right](\chi) =$$

$$\mathcal{F}\left[\log |\mathcal{F}[I(x)](u)|^2\right](\chi) + 2\pi \log(1 + g^2)\delta(\chi) + \frac{2g}{1 + g^2}\pi\delta(\chi \pm \Delta) +$$

$$\mathcal{F}\left[\sum_{m=2}^{\infty} \frac{(-1)^{m+1}}{m}\left(\frac{2g}{1 + g^2}\cos \Delta u\right)^m\right](\chi) \quad (4)$$

Therein, the Fourier transform of a spatial domain function $f(x)$ denotes $\mathcal{F}[f(x)](u)$. Furthermore, u denotes a variable in the frequency domain. The Fourier transform is performed using a discrete Fourier transform for a digital image. The variable in the secondary Fourier transform χ denotes the quefrency.

The first term in Eq. (4) depends on the spatial frequency response of the image $I(x)$. The second term is a delta function at the origin; these terms are unnecessary to estimate the shift. The third term is two delta functions corresponding to the shift amount. The fourth term indicates negligible multiple maxima at an integral multiple of the shift. It is notable that the shift in the layered image should be found by detecting a delta function in the quefrency

---

[2] Note that the reflection stereo can estimate the object distance using the peak location in the autocorrelation function of the layered image, even if the object does not have a specular reflection. The secondary peak requires only that the object has some textures.

[3] As an extension of the cepstrum, the complex cepstrum is the **inverse** Fourier transform of the complex logarithm of the Fourier transform of a signal. An informative survey can be found in [10].

domain. The peak can be very sharp; the sub-pixel peak location might fail to be estimated accurately.

3.3 Proposed Method

The proposed method is inspired by the cepstrum, but without taking the logarithm of the power spectrum, and with some pre-processing and post-processing to estimate an accurate sub-pixel shift. A periodic variation in the Fourier power spectrum of a layered image will be observed corresponding to the amount and direction of the image shift. The Fourier transform of the Fourier power spectrum detects the cycle and direction by finding its peak location.

In a way similar to that described in previous subsections, the sum of two identical signals $I(x)$ with shift Δ models the layered image in 1D along a constraint line as $f(x) = I(x) + gI(x - \Delta)$. The ratio g denotes the brightness difference between the layered images.

As the pre-processing in the proposed method, a high-pass filter (HPF) is applied to the layered image signal by substructing the low-frequency component from the original signal as

$$f'(x) = (1 - N(\sigma^2, x)) \otimes (I(x) + gI(x - \Delta)), \tag{5}$$

where $N(\sigma^2, x)$ and symbol $\otimes$ respectively signify a Gaussian function with variance σ^2 and convolution operation, as follows.

$$N(\sigma^2, x) = e^{-\frac{x^2}{2\sigma^2}} \tag{6}$$

$$\mathcal{F}[N(\sigma^2, x)](u) = \sqrt{2\pi}\sigma e^{-\frac{\sigma^2 u^2}{2}} \tag{7}$$

Then, taking the Fourier transform of Eq. (5) as

$$\begin{aligned}
\mathcal{F}[f'(x)](u) &= \mathcal{F}\left[1 - N(\sigma^2, x)\right](u)\mathcal{F}\left[I(x) + gI(x - \Delta)\right](u) \\
&= \mathcal{F}\left[1 - N(\sigma^2, x)\right](u)\mathcal{F}[I(x)](u)\left(1 + ge^{-j\Delta u}\right) \\
&\triangleq HPI(u)\left(1 + ge^{-j\Delta u}\right) \\
&= HPI(u)\left(1 + g(\cos \Delta u - j\sin \Delta u)\right) \\
&= HPI(u)\left((1 + g\cos \Delta u) - jg\sin \Delta u\right), \tag{8}
\end{aligned}$$

where $HPI(u)$ denotes a Fourier transform of high-pass filtered $I(x)$, the power spectrum of Eq. (8) becomes obtainable as

$$|\mathcal{F}[f'(x)](u)|^2 = |HPI(u)|^2 \left(1 + g^2 + 2g\cos \Delta u\right). \tag{9}$$

The Fourier transform of Eq. (9) is

$$\begin{aligned}
\mathcal{F}\left[|\mathcal{F}[f'(x)](u)|^2\right](\chi) &= (1 + g^2)\mathcal{F}\left[|HPI(u)|^2\right](\chi) \\
&\quad + g\mathcal{F}\left[|HPI(u)|^2\right](\chi + \Delta) + g\mathcal{F}\left[|HPI(u)|^2\right](\chi - \Delta), \tag{10}
\end{aligned}$$

where χ denotes the quefrency.

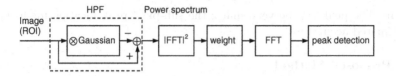

Fig. 3. Processing flow of the proposed method

Equation (10) shows the existence of three peaks in the quefrency domain. As is true with the cepstrum, the second and the third terms correspond to the shift in the layered image. The constraint in the spatial domain is applicable to the quefrency domain without modification. Figure 3 presents the processing flow.

The shape around the maximum in Eq. (10), $\mathcal{F}\left[|HPI(u)|^2\right](\chi)$, cannot be determined analytically because it includes the original signal. However, the high-pass filter and the weight in the frequency domain (described in the next subsection) allow its approximation as a 2D Gaussian function. The results of the discrete Fourier transform comprise a set of data at discrete locations. Nine values around the secondary peak are used to estimate the sub-quefrency peak location by fitting them to a 2D Gaussian (also see the next subsection).

3.4   Implementation Details

Eliminating the Low-frequency Component: This pre-processing is done by applying high-pass filtering to the original layered image before taking the Fourier transform. As described in [5], this pre-processing has the following two effects.

1. The power of the low-frequency component in images is much greater than the high-frequency component, but the low-frequency component does not contribute to estimation of the correspondence location in the layered image.

2. The 2D FFT computation for the discrete Fourier transform assumes that the finite region for the computation is an infinite series of patches. A discontinuity at the patch edges influences the results. Reduction of the low-frequency components decreases the discontinuity at the region edges.

Weighting in the frequency domain after the first Fourier transform can also reduce the low-frequency component in the layered image. However, this weighting has no effect on **2.** above. Therefore in this case, a weighting in the spatial domain before the Fourier transform is required, such as Blackman–Harris windowing [7]. This windowing in the spatial domain decreases the effective area in the region of interest (ROI); it enlarges the ROI and increases the computational time.

Weighting in the Frequency Domain: High-pass filtering pre-processing increases the noise effect in the whole process by reducing the low-frequency component. To reduce the noise effect caused by an unnecessary high-frequency component, a weight is applied in the frequency domain after the first Fourier transform.

The weighting has the following two effects: it reduces the noise effect caused by high frequency, and it forms the shape around the peak location in Eq. (10). In the proposed method, the Fourier transform of 2D Gaussian used for the weighting to form the peak shape is also a 2D Gaussian. This shape forming has efficacy for estimating the sub-quefrency (it is the same as the sub-pixel) estimation by fitting a continuous 2D Gaussian to the obtained discrete samples.

We have performed many experiments using both synthetic and real images to confirm the pre-processing and weighting ($\sigma = 0.4$ in Eq. (7)) effects to estimate the correspondence in the layered image (not shown in the paper).

Using the Constraint: The quefrency domain has the same dimensions of the spatial domain. The constraint in the spatial domain is applicable with no modification to the quefrency domain.

Results of the discrete Fourier transform comprise a set of values at discrete locations in the quefrency domain; searching along the constraint line in a fractional unit is impossible.

As depicted in Fig. 4, nine values around the second peak are searched along the constraint line from the peak candidates, which include rounding to integer locations from the constraint line ($\otimes$ marks) and their surrounding nine integer locations ($\circ$ marks).

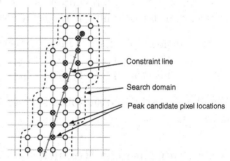

Fig. 4. Search range limitation by a constraint

Sub-Pixel Disparity Estimation: An accurate sub-pixel disparity is indispensable for practical range estimation in a very narrow baseline in the reflection stereo configuration. A sub-pixel peak location is estimated using a 2D Gaussian fitting with nine values around the peak location, as depicted in Fig. 5.

The following 2D quadratic

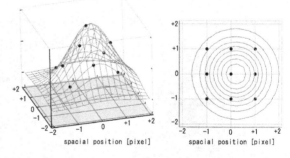

Fig. 5. 2D Gaussian fitting

function fitting is used for the 2D Gaussian fitting, after taking the logarithm of the value of the secondary Fourier transform $r(\cdot)$.

$$S(x,y) = Ax^2 + Cy^2 + Dx + Ey + F \tag{11}$$

The sub-pixel peak location estimated by fitting the 2D quadratic function is obtainable as follows [14].

$$(d_x, d_y) = \left(-\frac{D}{2A}, -\frac{E}{2C}\right) \tag{12}$$

The A, C, D, and E is obtainable by the following using nine values centered at (p, q), which is the maximum location found among the candidates.

$$
\begin{aligned}
A &= \left(\rho_{mm} - 2\rho_{zm} + \rho_{pm} + \rho_{mz} - 2\rho_{zz} + \rho_{pz} + \rho_{mp} - 2\rho_{zp} + \rho_{pp}\right)/6 \\
C &= \left(\rho_{mm} + \rho_{zm} + \rho_{pm} - 2\rho_{mz} - 2\rho_{zz} - 2\rho_{pz} + \rho_{mp} + \rho_{zp} + \rho_{pp}\right)/6 \\
D &= \left(-\rho_{mm} + \rho_{pm} - \rho_{mz} + \rho_{pz} - \rho_{mp} + \rho_{pp}\right)/6 \\
E &= \left(-\rho_{mm} - \rho_{zm} - \rho_{pm} + \rho_{mp} + \rho_{zp} + \rho_{pp}\right)/6
\end{aligned}
\tag{13}
$$

Therein, $\rho_{..}$ is an abbreviation of the following logarithms of the secondary Fourier transform results at the corresponding locations.

$$
\begin{aligned}
\rho_{mm} &= \log r(p-1, q-1) & \rho_{zm} &= \log r(p, q-1) & \rho_{pm} &= \log r(p+1, q-1) \\
\rho_{mz} &= \log r(p-1, q) & \rho_{zz} &= \log r(p, q) & \rho_{pz} &= \log r(p+1, q) \\
\rho_{mp} &= \log r(p-1, q+1) & \rho_{zp} &= \log r(p, q+1) & \rho_{pp} &= \log r(p+1, q+1)
\end{aligned}
\tag{14}
$$

Finally, the estimated sub-pixel shift in the layered image is obtainable as $(p + d_x, q + d_y)$.

4   Experimental Results

4.1   Comparison with Autocorrelation

Figures 6(a) and 6(b) respectively present the object (about 25 cm height) and a layered image. Figures 7(a) and 7(b) respectively show the autocorrelation

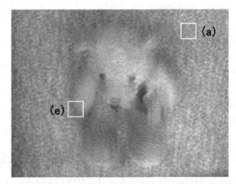

(a) Object from oblique view point   (b) Observed complex image

Fig. 6. The object and layered image reflected at a transparent plate

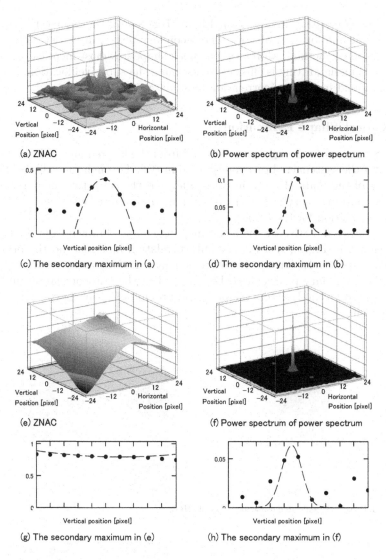

Fig. 7. Autocorrelation and the proposed method

function and the proposed method for region (a) in Fig. 6(b). The ROI size is 49×49 [pixel] and the search range is ± 24 [pixel] for the autocorrelation function. The ROI size for the proposed method is 48×48 [pixel]. Figures 7(c) and 7(d) respectively portray the intersection of the secondary peak in Figs. 7(a) and 7(b). A quadratic and a Gaussian function are fitted respectively to the function values. The sub-pixel location of the secondary peak is clearly detected in both methods for this ROI.

Figures 7(e) and 7(f) respectively portray the autocorrelation function and the proposed method for region (e) in Fig. 6(b). Figure 7(h) depicts the intersection of the secondary peak in Fig. 7(f). Figure 7(g) shows the intersection of Fig. 7(e) at the same location of 7(h). The secondary peak can be detected clearly in the proposed method. Moreover, the peak shape is almost identical with Fig. 7(d); the Gaussian fitting is effective to estimate the sub-pixel location. No peak could be found in the autocorrelation function at that location.

4.2   Object Shape Estimation

Figure 8 presents the range maps obtained from the layered image shown in Fig. 6(b), after the system calibration described in [13]. Through the calibration, the thickness of the plate (10 mm in catalogue) and the refractive index (typically 1.49 for consumer acrylic plate) are estimated simultaneously with the plate angle and position for the camera.

Figures 8(a) and 8(b) are the resultant range maps obtained from the layered image shown in Fig. 6(b) using the autocorrelation function and the proposed method, respectively. The whiteout region in Fig. 8(a) depicts the region in which the secondary peak cannot be detected in the autocorrelation function. The proposed method detects the peak and provides slightly sharper edges than autocorrelation.

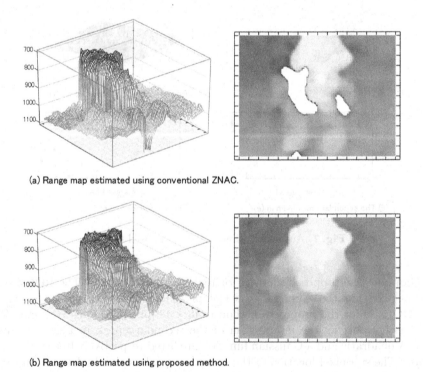

(a) Range map estimated using conventional ZNAC.

(b) Range map estimated using proposed method.

Fig. 8. 3D measurement results

5   Conclusions

This paper proposed a method to estimate the shift in the layered image using Fourier transformation. The method was applied to range estimation using the reflection stereo configuration. Experimental results represented the effectiveness of the method compared with a method using autocorrelation function. Future studies will investigate texture recovery of the layered image and real-time computation of the reflection stereo.

References

1. Cannon, M.: Blind deconvolution of spatially invariant image blurs with phase. Acoustics, Speech, and Signal Processing 24(1), 58–63 (1076)
2. Childers, D.G., Skinner, D.P., Kemerait, R.C.: The cepstrum: a guide to processing. Proc. of the IEEE 65(10), 1428–1443 (1977)
3. Diamant, Y., Schechner, Y.Y.: Overcoming visual reverberations. In: CVPR (2008)
4. Gao, C., Ahuja, N.: A refractive camera for acquiring stereo and super-resolution images. In: CVPR, pp. 2316–2323 (2006)
5. Gennery, D.B.: Determination of optical transfer function by inspection of frequency-domain plot. Journal of the Optical Society of America 63(12), 1571–1577 (1973)
6. Gluckman, J.M., Nayar, S.K.: Catadioptric stereo using planar mirrors. IJCV 44(1), 65–79 (2001)
7. Harris, F.J.: On the use of windows for harmonic analysis with the discrete Fourier transform. Proc. of the IEEE 66(1), 51–83 (1978)
8. Lee, D.J., Krile, T.F., Mitra, S.: Power cepstrum and spectrum techniques applied to image registration. Applied Optics 27(6), 1099–1106 (1988)
9. Miyazaki, D., Ikeuchi, K.: Shape estimation of transparent objects using inverse polarization ray tracing. PAMI 29(11), 2018–2029 (2007)
10. Oppenheim, A.V., Schafer, R.W.: From frequency to quefrency: a history of the cepstrum. IEEE Signal Processing Magazine 21(5), 95–106 (2004)
11. Pachidis, T.P., Lygouras, J.N.: Pseudo-stereo vision system: a detailed study. Journal of Intelligent and Robotic Systems 42(2), 135–167 (2005)
12. Shimizu, M., Okutomi, M.: Reflection stereo – novel monocular stereo using a transparent plate. In: Canadian conference on computer and robot vision, CRV (2006)
13. Shimizu, M., Okutomi, M.: Calibration and rectification for reflection stereo. In: CVPR (2008)
14. Sun, C.: Fast algorithms for stereo matching and motion estimation. In: Australia–Japan Advanced Workshop on Computer Vision, pp. 38–48 (2003)
15. Whitted, T.: An improved illumination model for shaded display. Communications of the ACM 23(6), 343–349 (1980)
16. Yeshurun, Y., Schwartz, E.L.: Cepstral filtering on a columnar image architecture: a fast algorithm for binocular stereo segmentation. PAMI 11(7), 759–767 (1989)

Model-Based 3D Object Localization Using Occluding Contours

Kenichi Maruyama, Yoshihiro Kawai, and Fumiaki Tomita

National Institute of Advanced Industrial Science and Technology
Central 2, 1–1–1, Umezono, Tsukuba, Ibaraki 305–8568, Japan
{k.maruyama,y.kawai,f.tomita}@aist.go.jp

Abstract. This paper describes a method for model-based 3D object localization. The object model consists of a triangular surface mesh, model points, and model geometrical features. Model points and model geometrical features are generated using contour generators, which are estimated by the occluding contours of projected images of the triangular surface mesh from multiple viewing directions, and they are maintained depending on the viewing direction. Multiple hypotheses for approximate model position and orientation are generated by comparing model geometrical features and data geometrical features. The multiple hypotheses are limited by using the viewing directions that are used to generate model geometrical features. Each hypothesis is verified and improved by using model points and 3D boundaries, which are reconstructed by segment-based stereo vision. In addition, each hypothesis is improved by using the triangular surface mesh and 3D boundaries. Experimental results show the effectiveness of the proposed method.

1 Introduction

Model-based 3D object localization is an important issue in computer vision. For metallic or plastic industrial objects and the indoor environments, it is difficult to obtain stable dense 3D data using an area-based stereo method or a laser rangefinder, because the objects often lack texture information and/or shiny. Therefore, a 3D-3D matching method using dense 3D data [1] is unsuitable in such environments. In dealing with such environments, the use of edge information is effective. Several edge-based methods including object tracking [2,3], object localization [4,5], have been proposed. These methods adopt a 2D-3D matching algorithm, which uses 2D image(s) and a 3D object model. As one approach to achieving greater robustness for such environments, edge-based 3D-3D matching algorithms, which use 3D edge information and a 3D object model, have been proposed. For example, Sumi et al. [6,7] created object models from range data that have a lattice data structure. This modeling enables one to estimate a model's contour generators rapidly, however, there is a problem in that modeling for concave objects is difficult. Maruyama et al. [8] created object models from triangular surface meshes. This method dealt with various objects including free-form objects and concave objects, however, this algorithm requires

H. Zha, R.-i. Taniguchi, and S. Maybank (Eds.): ACCV 2009, Part III, LNCS 5996, pp. 406–415, 2010.

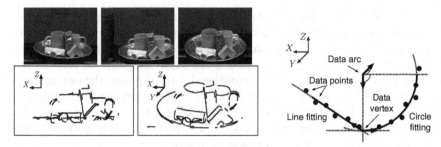

Fig. 1. Reconstruction of 3D data. (Top row: input stereo images, Bottom row: reconstructed 3D boundaries

Fig. 2. Geometrical features

a great deal of computational cost to obtain model points that are dynamically updated in an iterative localization process according to viewing direction.

In this paper, to overcome these problems, we propose a method for rapid model-based 3D object localization. Object model features are generated from a triangular surface mesh according to the viewing directions, which are discretely set. These features are maintained according to the viewing direction. This modeling allows easy parallel processing, in addition, by using the viewing directions that are used in model geometrical features generation, the number of combinations of features between the model and reconstructed 3D boundaries is reduced. The error in the matching caused by discrete modeling is resolved by searching corresponding triangles for 3D boundaries. To show the effectiveness of the proposed method, we present the results of experiments for various objects.

2 3D Reconstruction

We use segment-based stereo vision [6] for the reconstruction of 3D boundaries. Geometrical features are generated by fitting a line or a circle to reconstructed segments. The geometrical features consist of vertexes and arcs, which have two tangent vectors. As a feature, vertexes have an angle between two tangent vectors, and arcs have radius. The top row of Figure 1 shows an example of input stereo images, The bottom row of Figure 1 shows reconstructed 3D boundaries. Figure 2 shows an example of geometrical features.

3 Object Model

An object model consists of a triangular surface mesh, model points and model geometrical features.

The triangular surface mesh reflects the whole shape of the object. This is used to generate model points and model geometrical features, as well as to improve position and orientation in the fine adjustment process described later. Each triangle consists of three vertexes and a normal vector, and has information on adjacent triangles.

Model points and model geometrical features are used to estimate approximate model position and orientation. As shown in Figure 3, they are generated and maintained according to viewing direction, which discretely sets every face of a geodesic dome. This method enables the prior execution of some operations that require a great deal of computational cost, including the estimation of contour generators and hidden-line removal. This discreteness in modeling may cause an error in the matching. However, we believe that any such errors can be remedied in the fine adjustment process. The procedure of generating model points and model geometrical features is as follows.

1. Project a triangular surface mesh onto a 2D image according to viewing direction $W_i (i = 1, \cdots, N_v)$, where N_v is the number of viewing directions.
2. Extract contours of the projected image. The extracted contours are segmented [6]. Then, the 3D position for each contour point is calculated [8].
3. Generate model vertexes and model arcs by fitting a line or a circle to 3D segments. Model points are sampled on the 3D segments at equal intervals.
4. Calculate the distance between each model point and centroid of each triangle. For each model point, the index of the triangle that has the minimum distance is stored as the corresponding triangle. In addition, a normal vector corresponding to the triangle is stored as the normal vector of the model point.
5. Repeat 1 through 4 for each viewing direction.

Contour generators that are used to generate model points and model geometrical features can be estimated from a triangular surface mesh without projection onto a 2D image.Because the generated data geometrical features used in this research are dependent on the segmentation of contours on 2D images, we consider that model geometrical features are generated by the same operation as the data geometrical features. Therefore, we adopt the method stated previously.

4   Localization

Localization consists of two processes: initial matching and fine adjustment. Initial matching generates multiple hypotheses for the approximate model position and orientation using each model according to viewing direction. Fine adjustment improves each hypothesis generated in initial matching. The model's position and orientation are expressed as a 4×4 matrix $T = \begin{bmatrix} R & t \\ 0\ 0\ 0 & 1 \end{bmatrix}$, where R is a 3×3 rotational matrix and t is a 3×1 translation vector that moves an object model.

4.1   Initial Matching

Initial matching is independently carried out for each model according to the viewing direction. Here, we describe a case using model M_d, whose viewing direction is W_d. First, R and t are calculated by comparing model geometrical

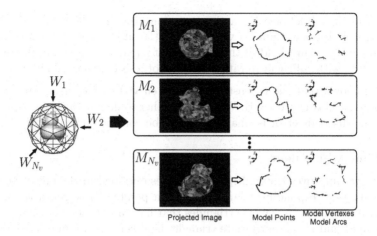

Fig. 3. Generation of model points and model geometrical features

features and data geometrical features [6]. By this comparison, multiple hypotheses with different T are generated. This comparison can be very fast. However, the later processes require a great deal of computational cost because they are based on an iterative process. To reduce computational costs, each hypothesis is verified using R and t at this stage.

The centroid of a triangular surface mesh P_{Mc} is moved and the viewing direction W_d is rotated according to the following formulas:

$$P'_{Mc} = RP_{Mc} + t, W'_d = RW_d. \tag{1}$$

If this hypothesis is similar to the true position and orientation, the vector from camera position O to P'_{Mc} and W'_d are almost the same. To reflect this conjecture, hypotheses that have the angle between $\left(P'_{Mc} - O\right)$ and W'_d is less than θ_W are adopted, where θ_W is a threshold.

Next, each hypothesis is verified and improved using an iterative method based on the Iterative Closest Point (ICP) algorithm [9,10]. The procedure is as follows:

1. Search data points corresponding to model points using their normal vectors [6]. Let $\{M_i\}, \{D_i\} (i = 1, \cdots, n_p)$ be a pair of model point and corresponding data point, where n_p is the number of correspondences. If the distance between a model point and a data point exceeds a threshold θ_{Id}, the pair is excluded from the pairs of correspondences.
2. Estimate T' that moves P_{M_i} to P_{D_i} by the least squares method, which minimizes the following error $\varepsilon(t)$:

$$\varepsilon^2(t) = \sum_{i=1}^{n_p} \left| R' P_{M_i} + t' - P_{D_i} \right|^2, \tag{2}$$

where t is the number of iteration.

3. Update the model position and orientation using $T = T'T$.
4. Repeat 1 through 3 until a variation of $\varepsilon(t)$ satisfies $|\varepsilon(t-1) - \varepsilon(t)| < \theta_{Ic}$, where θ_{Ic} is a threshold. If the variation of $\varepsilon(t)$ does not satisfy the previous equation with sufficient iteration, this hypothesis is wrong and it is excluded.

It is well known that the reconstruction of a curved surface using stereo vision involves a measuring error [11]. We do not bother to deal with this error because we assume that this error is small enough to be considered as insignificant.

4.2   Fine Adjustment

This process improves the multiple hypotheses obtained in the initial matching by searching corresponding triangles for data points. To search a corresponding triangle rapidly, we traverse triangles that have adjacency information. This search could find an inappropriate triangle, however, we can find a warmer triangle by using iterative process based on the ICP algorithm. The procedure is as follows:

1. Calculate matrix $T'' = T^{-1}$ that moves the data points.
2. Move data points $\{D_i\}$ according to T''.
3. Search the triangle that has the minimum distance between data point P_{D_i} and the triangle's centroid.
   (a) Decide the vertex $v_m(m = 1, 2, 3)$ that has the maximum distance between P_{D_i} and the three vertexes on the current corresponding triangle F. Initial corresponding triangle is stored during the model generation process.
   (b) Calculate the distance between P_{D_i} and the centroid $P_{F_{next}}$ which is an adjacent triangle to F and is an opposite-side triangle to v_m. If the distance $|P_{D_i} - P_{F_{next}}|$ is larger than that $|P_{D_i} - P_F|$, then go to 4.
   (c) Update the corresponding triangle $F = F_{next}$, then go back to 3a.
4. Search the corresponding model point on the triangle F for P_{D_i}.
   Case Fig 4(a): Calculate $P_{M_i'}$, which is the foot point perpendicular from the data point P_{D_i} using N which is the normal vector of F. If $P_{M_i'}$ exists on the triangle F, $P_{M_i'}$ is the model point.
   Case Fig 4(b): Calculate $P_{M_i'}$, which is the foot point perpendicular from P_{D_i} to each edge $e_j(j = 1, 2, 3)$. If $P_{M_i'}$ exists on the edge e_j, $P_{M_i'}$ is the model point.
   Case Fig 4(c): If a model point that satisfies the previous two conditions does not exist, $P_{M_i'}$ is $v_k(k = 1, 2, 3)$, which has the minimum distance between P_{D_i} and P_{v_k}.
   Verification: If the distance between $P_{M_i'}$ and P_{D_i} exceeds a threshold θ_{Fd}, the pair is excluded from the pairs of correspondences.
5. Estimate T''' that moves P_{D_i} to $P_{M_i'}$ by using the similar Eq. (2). Here, let $\xi(t)$ be the error, n_p' be the number of correspondences.
6. Update the model position and orientation by $T'' = T'''T''$.
7. Repeat 2 through 6 until the variation of $\xi(t)$ is less than θ_{Fc}, where θ_{Fc} is a threshold.
8. Calculate $T = T''^{-1}$ that moves an object model.

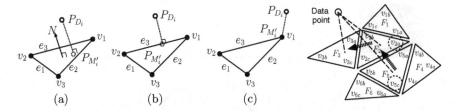

Fig. 4. Correspondence between data point and triangle   **Fig. 5.** Mesh traversing

Figure 5 shows an example of mesh traversing. In Figure 5, a circle with a dashed line shows a vertex that has the maximum distance with a data point at each triangle. In this example, triangles are traversed as follows: the first step is from F_5 to F_2, the next step is from F_2 to F_3.

4.3   Rank for Hypothesis

Each hypothesis is given a score based on the number of both the 3D corresponding points and the 2D corresponding points. The procedure for searching 2D correspondences is as follows:

The triangular surface mesh is projected onto the 2D image according to a hypothesis T, and the contours of the projected image are extracted. A normal vector for the each point of the contours is calculated [6]. The surrounding neighborhood is traced in the direction of the normal vector for each contour point on the 2D image, which stores edge information for an input image. If an edge point is found within the trace-length threshold and the normal vectors are similar, the edge point is the corresponding point for the contour point. This process is carried out for each input image, and a total score $s = n'_p + w\,(n_L + n_R + n_V)$ is calculated, where n_V, n_R, n_V is the number of correspondences of each input image, and w is a weight for 2D correspondences. w is experimentally set to 0.5. After scores for all hypotheses are calculated, the hypothesis which has the largest s is selected.

Figure 6 shows an example for Figure 1 with a cup model. Figure 6 (Left) shows the contours of the projected image and the direction of the normal vectors. In Figure 6(Right), the large black dots show corresponding points on a 2D image. The score of Figure 6(a) is $317.5 = 56 + 261.5$ and that of Figure 6(b) is $109 = 56 + 53$. Therefore, the hypothesis in Figure 6(a) has a high priority.

4.4   Parallel Processing

Our localization algorithm allows parallel processing because initial matching is executed independently for each model according to the viewing direction. Fine adjustment also is executed independently for each hypothesis. In this paper, we implement parallel processing by means of a simple partition. Namely, let N_t be the number of partitions, 1 CPU handles N_v/N_t models in initial matching and handles N_f/N_t hypothesis in fine adjustment, where N_f is the number of hypotheses obtained by initial matching.

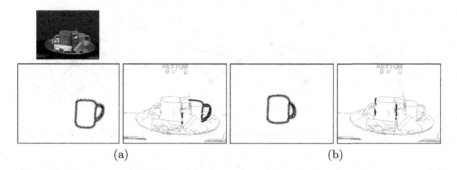

Fig. 6. Correspondence search on image (top row: input left stereo image. bottom row: contours and normal vectors, corresponding point).

Fig. 7. Object models (Top Row: block, snack 1, snack 2, snack 3, bottle 1, bottle 2. Bottom Row: bottle 3, "rocker-Arm", "igea", cup, phone, duck)

Fig. 8. Experimental setup

5   Experiments

To evaluate the effectiveness of the proposed method, experiments are carried out for various objects. Each input image has 640×480 pixels with 256 gray-level resolution. The models used in this research are shown in Figure 7. The triangular surface meshes for block, snack 1, snack 2 and snack 3 are created using commercial CAD software. The "rockerArm" and "igea" are courtesy of Cyberware. The duck, cup, phone, bottle 1, bottle 2 and bottle 3 are created from real objects using range data measured by a laser rangefinder. Using a 3D printer, we created real 3D objects of "rockerArm" and "igea". The experimental setup is shown in Figure 8. We use three CCD cameras with 25 mm lenses, and a desktop PC with Dual Intel Xeon E5440 with 3 GB RAM. Parallel processing of the proposed method is implemented using the POSIX thread library.

Figure 9 shows localization results with green contours obtained by projecting the model onto a left stereo image. Table 1 shows the computational costs in Figure 9, where M_v, M_c are the numbers of vertexes and circles; D_v, D_c are those of the data; H_I is the number of hypotheses without limitation in Sect. 4.1, H_W is the number with limitation in Sect. 4.1, H_F is after initial matching; T is the execution time (seconds). The parameters are: $\theta_{Ic} = 0.01$, $\theta_{Fc} = 0.01$, $\theta_{Id} = 7$ (mm), $\theta_{Fd} = 5$ (mm). These parameters are decided experimentally. θ_W

is: 90 (deg.) in the case $N_v = 20$; 60 (deg.) in the case $N_v = 80$; 40 (deg.) in the case $N_v = 320$. These parameters are decided according to the angle between adjacent viewing directions in the model generation process. The results show that the proposed method can be executed rapidly and robust for both occlusion and cluttered environments.

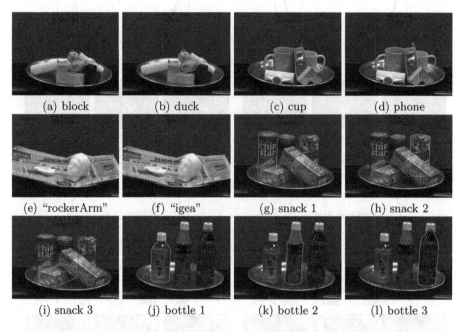

(a) block   (b) duck   (c) cup   (d) phone

(e) "rockerArm"   (f) "igea"   (g) snack 1   (h) snack 2

(i) snack 3   (j) bottle 1   (k) bottle 2   (l) bottle 3

Fig. 9. Experimental results

Table 1. Computational costs and number of hypotheses in Figure 9

	N_v	M_v	M_c	D_v	D_c	H_F	H_W	H_I	T
(a)	20	1420	1486	60	80	497	11792	34730	3.07
(b)	80	284	0	60	80	697	2386	2398	2.21
(c)	20	350	362	121	134	371	8141	11703	4.64
(d)	80	1122	956	121	134	994	11336	29222	3.60
(e)	80	1132	1162	107	156	1489	14355	41365	2.83
(f)	320	1608	1910	107	156	731	53282	241975	6.46
(g)	20	176	190	152	164	462	6235	9643	3.54
(h)	20	300	0	152	164	292	2383	2395	2.57
(i)	20	216	0	152	164	613	2469	2503	2.48
(j)	20	354	428	115	156	250	10804	17327	4.19
(k)	20	428	390	115	156	96	9282	13983	4.70
(l)	20	488	448	115	156	119	11127	16844	4.53

Table 2. Standard deviation of R_x, R_y, Z, r in Figure 10

	R_x	R_y	Z	r
	[deg.]		[mm]	
block	0.54	0.72	0.22	0.57
duck	0.88	1.04	0.32	1.26
"igea" 1	1.83	1.79	0.62	1.47
"igea" 2	4.08	2.38	0.73	1.83

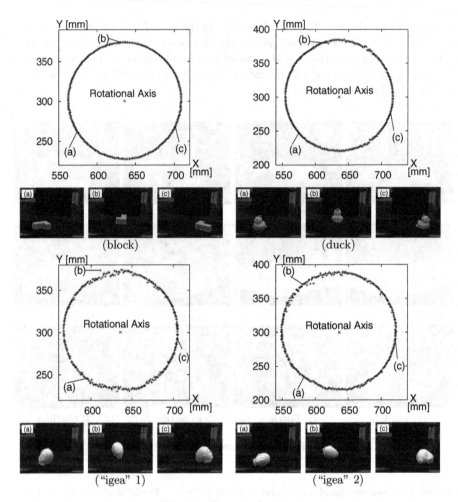

Fig. 10. Error evaluation

To evaluate the accuracy of the position and orientation, we conduct experiments using a turntable [6,8]. We use a block, duck and "igea". For "igea", we set up two poses. As shown in Figure 8, the rotational stage of the turntable is set up parallel with the X-Y plane of the world-coordinate system. An object is placed on the rotational table and rotated through 360 degrees in increments of 1 degree. Figure 10 shows the motion of the centroid for each model in the X-Y coordinates and the localization result for points (a), (b) and (c). In this experiment, the standard deviation of rotation angles around the X-axis and Y-axis, the Z-position and r, which is the distance between a centroid of a model and the rotational axis of the table, should be constant. Table 2 shows the standard deviation of R_x, R_y, Z and r. The results show that the proposed method has a high enough accuracy for a robot manipulator to pick up an object.

6   Conclusion

This paper described a method for model-based 3D object localization. Object model features were generated and maintained according to viewing directions that were discretely set. By using the viewing directions that were used in object modeling, we reduced the number of combination of features between a model and the reconstructed 3D boundaries. Errors in matching caused by discrete modeling were improved by searching corresponding triangles for 3D boundaries. The proposed localization algorithm and object modeling allowed parallel processing. Experimental results for various objects showed the effectiveness of the proposed method. In the future, we will reduce computational cost by reducing the number of features.

References

1. Johnson, A.E., Hebert, M.: Using spin images for efficient object recognition in cluttered 3D scenes. IEEE Trans. on PAMI 21(5), 433–449 (1999)
2. Li, G., Tsin, Y., Genc, Y.: Exploiting occluding contours for real-time 3D tracking: A unified approach. In: Proc. ICCV 2007 (2007)
3. Drummond, T., Cipolla, R.: Real-time visual tracking of complex structures. IEEE Trans. on PAMI 24(7), 932–946 (2002)
4. Kotake, D., Satoh, K., Uchiyama, S., Yamamoto, H.: A fast initialization method for edge-based registration using an inclination constraint. In: Proc. ISMAR 2007, pp. 239–248 (2007)
5. Sethi, A., Renaudie, D., Kriegman, D., Ponce, J.: Curve and surface duals and the recognition of curved 3D objects from their silhouettes. Int. J. of Computer Vision 58(1), 73–86 (2004)
6. Sumi, Y., Kawai, Y., Yoshimi, T., Tomita, F.: 3D object recognition in cluttered environments by segment-based stereo vision. Int. J. of Computer Vision 46(1), 5–23 (2002)
7. Sumi, Y., Ishiyama, Y., Tomita, F.: 3D localization of moving free-form objects in cluttered environments. In: Proc. ACCV 2004, vol. I, pp. 43–48 (2004)
8. Maruyama, K., Kawai, Y., Tomita, T.Y. F.: 3D object localization based on occluding contour using STL CAD model. In: Proc. 19th ICPR, TuBCT8.41 (2008)
9. Besl, P.J., McKay, N.D.: A method for registration of 3-D shapes. IEEE Trans. on PAMI 14(2), 239–256 (1992)
10. Chen, Y., Medioni, G.: Object modeling by registration of multiple range image. Image and Vision Computing 10(3), 145–155 (1992)
11. Vaillant, R., Faugeras, O.D.: Using external boundaries for 3-D object modeling. IEEE Trans. on PAMI 14(2), 157–173 (1992)

A Probabilistic Model for Correspondence Problems Using Random Walks with Restart

Tae Hoon Kim, Kyoung Mu Lee, and Sang Uk Lee

Dept. of EECS, ASRI, Seoul National University, 151-742, Seoul, Korea
thkim@diehard.snu.ac.kr, kyoungmu@snu.ac.kr, sanguk@ipl.snu.ac.kr

Abstract. In this paper, we propose an efficient method for finding consistent correspondences between two sets of features. Our matching algorithm augments the discriminative power of each correspondence with the spatial consistency directly estimated from a graph that captures the interactions of all correspondences by using Random Walks with Restart (RWR), one of the well-established graph mining techniques. The *steady-state* probabilities of RWR provide the global relationship between two correspondences by the local affinity propagation. Since the correct correspondences are likely to establish global interactions among them and thus form a strongly consistent group, our algorithm efficiently produces the confidence of each correspondence as the likelihood of correct matching. We recover correct matches by imposing a sequential method with mapping constraints in a simple way. The experimental evaluations show that our method is qualitatively and quantitatively robust to outliers, and accurate in terms of matching rate in various matching frameworks.

Keywords: Random Walks with Restart, feature correspondence, sequential matching.

1 Introduction

Feature correspondence is one of the fundamental problems of computer vision and lies at the core of many applications including 3D reconstruction and object recognition. To solve this problem, several approaches [9][3][7] have been proposed. One approach is to formulate the matching problem as an integer quadratic programming, like [9][3]. However, the method of Maciel et al. [9] is based on a non-optimal minimization technique with non-polynomial complexity, and the method by Berg et al. [3] is more suitable only for the case of allowing several features to match the same feature. The other one is to use a spectral technique for finding consistent correspondences between two sets of features, like [7]. Leordeanu et al. [7] used the principal eigenvector of the pairwise affinity matrix corresponding to its largest eigenvalue as the information about how strongly the matching candidates belong to the optimal set. However, their results depend mainly on the properties of the affinity matrix such as the number of links adjacent to each correspondence in local neighborhood system. Moreover, it is difficult to control the scale of each individual appearance-based matching score compared with the geometric affinities in a principal manner.

H. Zha, R.-i. Taniguchi, and S. Maybank (Eds.): ACCV 2009, Part III, LNCS 5996, pp. 416–425, 2010.
© Springer-Verlag Berlin Heidelberg 2010

In this paper, we introduce an efficient probabilistic method for solving various correspondence problems. We propose to estimate the likelihood that each candidate corresponds to the consistent correspondences between two sets of features by the Random Walks with Restart (RWR) [6][11], one of the well-established graph mining techniques. Namely, this likelihood of one matching candidate is defined as the weighted sum of all the *steady-state* probabilities between that candidate and other candidates in the RWR framework. We finally recover the optimal matches from the estimated likelihoods by simply adopting a sequential method with mapping constraints, as in the work of Leordeanu et al. [7]. Our matching framework has various advantages over [7] as follows. First, since RWR, similarly to the graph-based semi-supervised learning [13], has the ability to estimate the global relevance between pairs of correspondences by the local affinity propagation, our proposed likelihood of each correspondence represents its confidence by considering global interactions among highly consistent correspondences. Second, we easily define the combination of two properties: the discriminative power of each individual correspondence and the pairwise geometric affinities, in a probabilistic framework. Finally, our approach can be applied to various correspondence problems between points, regions, or interest points [8][10][12]. In case of non-discriminative features like points, the only pairwise geometric information helps in finding the correct correspondences. When discriminative features like regions or interest points are employed, both the geometric relations and each individual appearance-based matching score can be utilized for improving the performance.

2 Proposed Algorithm

Feature matching is to find the optimal set L^{opt} of well-matched pairs in a candidate set $L = \{l_n\}_{n=1,...,N}$ of the initial feature correspondences $l_n = (x_n, x_{n'})$, where the features x_n and $x_{n'}$ are extracted in two sets X and X' respectively. Let e be the event of a candidate be matched. We intend to estimate the likelihood $\theta_n = p(l_n|e)$ that the candidate l_n is a correct match. We finally recover the optimal matches L^{opt} from the total likelihoods $\{\theta_n\}_{n=1,...,N}$ by simply imposing a sequential method with mapping constraints.

2.1 Likelihood Estimation

The likelihood θ_n can be obtained by

$$\theta_n = \sum_{l_k \in \bar{L}} p(l_n|l_k, e)p(l_k|e) = \sum_{l_k \in \bar{L}} \pi_n^k \eta_k, \tag{1}$$

where $\bar{L} \subset L$ is a set of the seed correspondences. All candidates are generally used as seeds, $\bar{L} = L$. However, if there are many outliers with very similar appearances, it is more effective to use only a few correspondences, that are likely to exist in the optimal set L^{opt}, as seeds. Each likelihood θ_n is modeled by a mixture of distributions $\pi_n^k = p(l_n|l_k, e)$ from each seed $l_k \in \bar{L}$ which has an initial seed distribution $\eta_k = p(l_k|e)$. The distribution π_n^k indicates the geometric relevance score between a candidate l_n and a seed l_k. In this work, we propose to use the RWR *steady-state* probability based on the pairwise local affinities, as similar to the segmentation framework of Kim et al. [6]. Compared with traditional graph distances (such as shortest path, maximum flow), this *steady-state* probability can capture the whole relationship between two candidates. The seed distribution η_k corresponds to the weight of the seed l_k. Namely, it means how well the features' descriptors of the seed l_k match to each other. In brief, our matching algorithm combines the discriminative power of each correspondence with the global geometric interactions in a probabilistic framework. Now, we describe our proposed distributions π_n^k and η_k in detail.

Estimating Pairwise Relationship of Correspondences. Let us consider an undirected weighted graph $G = (L, E)$, where each node $l_n \in L$ uniquely identifies a feature correspondence, and each edge $e_{nm} \in E$ spanning between two nodes $l_n, l_m \in L$ is determined by the neighborhood system. Each weight $w_{nm} \in W$ is assigned to the edge e_{nm}, and measures how compatible the features (x_n, x_m) in a set X are with $(x_{n'}, x_{m'})$ in the other set X' by the computation of the geometric consistency between two correspondences $l_n = (x_n, x_{n'})$ and $l_m = (x_m, x_{m'})$. The affinity matrix $\mathbf{W} = [w_{nm}]_{N \times N}$ may be differently designed according to various applications. We will introduce various pairwise affinity models in Section 3 in more detail.

Now, we propose to use the *steady-state* probability of RWR, that captures the whole relationship between a candidate l_n and a seed l_k in this graph G, via the geometric affinity π_n^k in (1). Suppose that a random walker starts from a seed l_k, and iteratively transmits to its neighborhood with the probability that is proportional to the edge weight between them. Also at each step, it has a restarting probability λ to return to the seed l_k. After convergence, we obtain the *steady-state* probability that the random walker will finally stay at the node l_n. Since this *steady-state* probability considers all possible paths between the two correspondences l_n and l_k, it is suitable measure for the distribution π_n^k in (1). By setting a vector $\boldsymbol{\pi}^k = [\pi_n^k]_{N \times 1}$, RWR can be formulated as follows [6][11].

$$\boldsymbol{\pi}^k = (1 - \lambda)\mathbf{P}\boldsymbol{\pi}^k + \lambda \boldsymbol{h}^k, \qquad (2)$$

where $\boldsymbol{h}^k = [h_n^k]_{N \times 1}$ is the seed indicating vector with $h_n^k = 1$ if $n = k$ and 0 otherwise, and the transition matrix $\mathbf{P}$ is the adjacency matrix $\mathbf{W}$ row-normalized: $\mathbf{P} = \mathbf{D}^{-1} \times \mathbf{W}$, where $\mathbf{D} = diag(d_1, ..., d_N)$, $d_n = \sum_{m=1}^{N} w_{nm}$. The random walker positioned at each correspondence l_n is returned with the restarting probability λ. With smaller λ, the current state becomes more emphasized and more propagated to its neighborhoods. We empirically set $\lambda = 0.01$ for all experiments.

Estimating Initial Seed Weights. A seed weight η_k in (1) means how well matched both features of the seed correspondence l_k are. Let $\hat{\boldsymbol{\eta}} = [\hat{\eta}_k]_{N \times 1}$ be the seed weight vector with $\hat{\eta}_k = \eta_k$ if $l_k \in \bar{L}$ and 0 otherwise. This vector $\hat{\boldsymbol{\eta}}$ can be differently designed according to the feature types for the specific applications.

In case of non-discriminative features such as points, there are no initial scores on the individual correspondences. In this case, we use the principal eigenvector of the pairwise affinity matrix $\mathbf{W}$ as in the work of Leordeanu et al. [7]. Their work is to find the optimal solution $u^* = argmax_u(u^T\mathbf{W}u)$ that maximizes the inter-cluster score $S = \sum_{l_n, l_m \in L} w_{nm}$. By the Raleigh's ratio theorem, this solution u^* is the principal eigenvector of $\mathbf{W}$. Since the eigenvector u^* denotes the unary scores that represent how strongly each correspondence belongs to the optimal set, it is defined as our seed weight vector $\hat{\eta} = u^*$ ($|\hat{\eta}| = 1$).

For discriminative features like regions or interest points [8][10][12], we use the following seed weight $\hat{\eta}_k$ based on the Euclidean distance between two features x_k and $x_{k'}$ of each seed l_k with feature properties v_k and $v_{k'}$.

$$\hat{\eta}_k = \begin{cases} exp\left(-\|v_k - v_{k'}\|/2\sigma_w^2\right) & l_k \in \bar{L} \\ 0 & otherwise, \end{cases} \tag{3}$$

where σ_w is the variance of the total feature properties. In this work, all candidates are used as seeds, $\bar{L} = L$. Although each seed weight provides a proper information about how well the features' descriptors match, it does not give absolute confidence under difficult conditions such as nonrigid deformation, occlusion and illumination changes. So, if we can choose only a few reliable seeds instead of all candidates under uncertain conditions, they can help in finding better correspondences. For example, we can select the refined seeds $\bar{L}$ by adding an additional condition that the distance to the first nearest neighbor is closer than 0.7 times the distance to the second one. This constraint can be generally used for extracting more discriminative correspondences.

Overview of Our Probabilistic Model. Based on the RWR formulation in (2), the total likelihoods $\{\theta_n\}_{n=1,...,N}$ in (1) can be written in a vector form, $\theta = [\theta_n]_{N \times 1}$ such that

$$\theta = (1 - \lambda)\mathbf{P}\theta + \lambda\hat{\eta} = \lambda(\mathbf{I} - (1 - \lambda)\mathbf{P})^{-1}\hat{\eta}. \tag{4}$$

Since a small neighborhood system is used for the transition matrix $\mathbf{P}$, the matrix $(\mathbf{I} - (1 - \lambda)\mathbf{P})$ in (4) is very large ($N \times N$) but quite sparse. Therefore its inversion is practically feasible by efficient numerical methods. For example, the MATLAB division operator '\' (which we used in our experiments) serves as a very efficient tool in finding the inversion of such large sparse matrix.

2.2 Finding Optimal Correspondences

We finally choose the well-matched pairs L^{opt} from the estimated likelihoods θ in (4). Algorithm 1 describes the selection procedure of correct matches, which is similar to the greedy algorithm of Leordeanu et al. [7] for finding the solution of the correspondence problem. We start by first selecting l_n^* ($= argmax_{l_m \in L}\theta_m$) that has the maximum likelihood as a correct correspondence, because it is the one we are most confident of being correct. Namely, we assign l_n^* into L^{opt}. Next we have to reject all other candidates that are in conflict with l_n^* by user-defined

---
Algorithm 1. Sequential Matching Estimator

1: Accept a correct pair l_n^* of maximum likelihood θ_n and insert it into L^{opt}.
2: Reject all other candidates that are in conflict with l_n^* by user-defined constraints.
3: Choose the next correct match l_n^* as the one with the next highest likelihood except the rejected or accepted candidates.
4: (*Optional*) If l_n^* is incompatible with the inliers $l_m \in L^{opt}$ such that $max_{l_m \in L^{opt}} w_{nm} < \gamma$, reject it and go to **step 3**.
5: Accept a correct pair l_n^* and insert it into L^{opt}.
6: If all candidates are not either rejected or accepted, go to **step 2**.

---

constraints. In our experiment, we reject all candidates of the form $(x_n, \cdot)$ or $(\cdot, x_{n'})$. Note that here the user could use different constraints. We accept the next correct match l_n^* as the one that has the next highest likelihood among the remained candidates. In this accept step, we can *optionally* use the additional rejecting constraint in Algorithm 1.4, where the pairwise affinity score w_{nm} is used for deciding the optimality of l_n^*. Since this constraint is based on the concept that the matches in L^{opt} have a tendency to smoothly change the local geometric deformation between the neighboring ones, we can easily find the optimal set L^{opt} regardless of the real sets with many outliers. We then continue by rejecting the pairs in conflict with the newly accepted one l_n^*. We repeat this procedure of accepting new match, until all candidates are either rejected or accepted. We finally produce the set L^{opt} of correct matches.

3   Experiments

We present experiments which demonstrate the performance of our approach to feature matching. In this section, we applied our algorithm to several different correspondence problems according to the feature types including Point Matching, Region Matching and Interest Point Matching. These problems have different affinity matrices **W** and seed weight vectors $\hat{\eta}$ in (4).

Point Matching. We evaluate the robustness of our algorithm according to the deformation and the ratio of outliers to inliers on the task of finding correspondences between 2D point sets, like in [7]. For quantitative evaluation, we study the case when the deformation noise is added by a Gaussian distribution with zero mean. We generate date sets of 2D model points X by randomly selecting N^i inliers in a given plane. We obtain the corresponding inliers in X' by disturbing independently the N^i points from X with white Gaussian noise $N(0, \sigma_e^2)$. The parameter σ_e controls the degree of the deformations between two sets X and X'. Next we randomly add N^o point outliers in X and X', respectively, with the same random uniform distribution over the x-y coordinates. The total number of points in X (or X') is $N^p = N^i + N^o$. The size of L is $N = N^p \times N^p$ since all possible correspondences are used as candidates. In this experiment, we score the performance according to the variation of the deformation parameter σ_e and the number of outliers N^o.

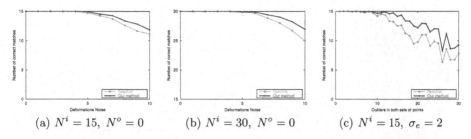

Fig. 1. Comparison of our method with spectral method ('Spectral') [7] for point matching. (a) and (b) show the number of the correct matches according to the variation of deformation noise σ_e. (c) compares the number of the correct matches according to the variation of the number of outliers N^o.

For estimating the likelihoods $\boldsymbol{\theta}$ in (4), the affinity matrix $\mathbf{W} = [w_{nm}]_{N \times N}$ is defined by the following pairwise score w_{nm} between two candidates $l_n = (x_n, x_{n'})$ and $l_m = (x_m, x_{m'})$ [7]. Note that a feature x_n has the x-y position vector f_n.

$$
w_{nm} = \begin{cases} 4.5 - \frac{(\mathcal{D}_{nm} - \mathcal{D}_{n'm'})^2}{2\sigma_d^2} & if \ |\mathcal{D}_{nm} - \mathcal{D}_{n'm'}| < 3\sigma_d \\ 0 & otherwise, \end{cases} \tag{5}
$$

where the functions $\mathcal{D}_{nm} = \|f_n - f_m\|$ and $\mathcal{D}_{n'm'} = \|f_{n'} - f_{m'}\|$ output the Euclidean distances between the pairs of points. The parameter σ_d controls the sensitivity of the weight on deformations. The larger σ_d, the more deformations in the data we can accommodate, also the more pairwise relationships between wrong matches will get positive scores. We initially set $\sigma_d = 5$. Since points X and X' are non-discriminative and there are no information on the individual correspondences, the principal eigenvector of the affinity matrix $\mathbf{W}$ is used as the seed weights $\hat{\eta}$. We finally produce the optimal set L^{opt} from these likelihoods $\boldsymbol{\theta}$ by Algorithm 1 without the optional step 4.

Fig. 1 shows the performance curves of our method vs. the spectral method [7] as we vary the deformative noise σ_e from 0 to 10 (in steps of 1), the number of inliers N^i from 15 to 30, and the number of outliers N^o from 1 to 30 (in steps of 1). Both methods ran on the same problem sets over 30 trials for each value of the varying parameter. We compared the performances of these two methods by counting how many matches agree with the ground truth. Compared with the spectral method [7] that depends mainly on neighborhood system to each candidate, our method increases the confidence of all correspondences by considering the whole relationship between the candidates.

Region Matching. In the task of finding region correspondences like [4], this experiment gives the average performances of the algorithms according to the variation of the region properties. For quantitative evaluation, we studied the case when the color noise was added by a Gaussian distribution with zero mean. We generated date sets of $N^c \times N^c$ grid regions X with random colors, as shown

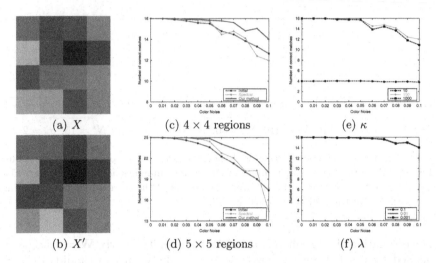

Fig. 2. Comparison of our method with the 'Initial' method and the 'Spectral' method [7] for region matching. (a) and (b) show the synthetic examples with 4×4 grid regions in X and X', respectively. (c) and (d) compare the number of the correct matches according to the variation of the color noise σ_c. In case of 4×4 region matching, (e) and (f) check the sensitivities of the 'Spectral' method and 'Our' method according to the variation of the parameters κ in (7) and λ in (4), respectively.

in Fig. 2(a). We obtained the corresponding regions in X' by supporting the adjacency relations in X. We then disturbed independently the colors of the regions in X' with white Gaussian noise $N(0, \sigma_c^2)$, as shown in Fig. 2(b). The parameter σ_c controls the degree of the color variance between two sets X and X'. The total number of regions in X is $N^p = N^c \times N^c$. The size of candidates L is $N^p \times N^p$, since all possible combinations were used as candidates. In this experiment, we scored the performance according to the color variance σ_c.

For estimating the likelihoods $\boldsymbol{\theta}$ in (4), the pairwise affinity score w_{nm} between two candidates $l_n = (x_n, x_{n'})$ and $l_m = (x_m, x_{m'})$ was defined under the basic and simple concept that a correspondence preserves adjacency relations in the image space, as follows.

$$w_{nm} = \begin{cases} 1 & if \ (x_n, x_m) \in \aleph \ and \ (x_{n'}, x_{m'}) \in \aleph' \\ 0 & otherwise, \end{cases} \tag{6}$$

where the adjacency relation $(x_n, x_m) \in \aleph$ (or $(x_{n'}, x_{m'}) \in \aleph'$) exists if regions x_n (or $x_{n'}$) and x_m (or $x_{m'}$) share a common boundary as in the work of Hedau et al. [4]. We simply generated the seed weights $\hat{\boldsymbol{\eta}}$ for all correspondences $\bar{L} = L$ by using the 3-dimensional color values as the feature property $v(\cdot)$ in (3). We initially set $\sigma_w = 0.25$ in (3). We finally produced the optimal set L^{opt} by Algorithm 1 without the optional step 4.

Fig. 2(c) and (d) compare the performance curves of our method with the 'Initial' method and the 'Spectral' method [7] as we varied the color noise σ_c

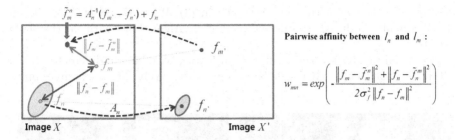

Fig. 3. Introducing our geometric affinity score w_{nm} between two correspondences $l_n = (x_n, x_{n'})$ and $l_m = (x_m, x_{m'})$ for affine covariant features. Each feature x_n has the x-y position vector f_n. Each candidate l_n has the local affine transformation matrix $\mathbf{A}_n$ between two features x_n and $x_{n'}$, estimated by [8][10][5]. We initially set $\sigma_f = 0.5$.

from 0 to 0.1 (in steps of 0.01), the number of matched regions N^p from 16 to 25. We compared the performances of these three methods over 30 trials by counting how many matches agreed with the ground truth. Note that the 'Initial' method is the same as Algorithm 1 with the seed weights $\hat{\boldsymbol{\eta}}$, instead of the likelihoods $\boldsymbol{\theta}$. It was included for testing the qualities of the seed weights $\hat{\boldsymbol{\eta}}$ itself. Although the pairwise affinity w_{nm} in (6) for region matching only considers the adjacency relation, our method achieved better performance than other methods.

For discriminative features, the 'Spectral' method [7] uses a new weight matrix $\mathbf{\Pi}$, instead of $\mathbf{W}$, as follows.

$$\mathbf{\Pi} = \mathbf{W} + \kappa \cdot diag(\hat{\boldsymbol{\eta}}), \qquad (7)$$

where the parameter κ controls the scale of the scores $\hat{\boldsymbol{\eta}}$ of each individual correspondence compared with the geometric affinity $\mathbf{W}$. With larger parameter κ, the discriminative power of each correspondence is more emphasized than pairwise relations. Fig. 2(e) shows that the performance of the 'Spectral' method is very sensitive to the parameter κ. We empirically set $\kappa = 100$. Our method also needs one parameter: the restarting probability λ in (4). However, compared with the 'Spectral' method, our method finds better correspondences with little performance changes according to the variation of λ, as shown in Fig. 2(f).

Interest Point Matching. We generally use the interest points, extracted by the affine covariant region detectors [8][10][12], as features. We choose a candidate set L of the N feature correspondences with the condition that the descriptors are the nearest neighbors. Note that here the user could use different constraints for generating L. In this experiment, we used both affine covariant region detectors: the MSER detector [12] and the Hessian Affine detector [10] to obtain larger candidates L. The pairwise affinity w_{nm} was defined as the spatial configuration between the neighboring feature correspondences, and based on the Euclidean distances between the pairs of features as shown in Fig. 3. This affinity matrix $\mathbf{W}$ well represents the pairwise geometric relationships under non-rigid deformations. The seed weights $\hat{\boldsymbol{\eta}}$ were obtained by using the SIFT descriptor [8] as the feature property $v(\cdot)$ in (3). We initially set $\sigma_w = 0.2$ in (3). We finally produced the optimal set L^{opt} by Algorithm 1 with the threshold $\gamma = 0.9$.

Fig. 4 and Fig. 5 show the results of our feature matching in different dataset: ETHZ toys dataset and ICCV2005 datasets, respectively. These examples prove

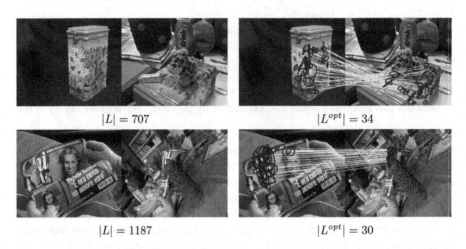

$|L| = 707$ $|L^{opt}| = 34$

$|L| = 1187$ $|L^{opt}| = 30$

Fig. 4. Results of our feature matching in ETHZ toys dataset [1]: The original color images (the left column) and the matched features (right column)

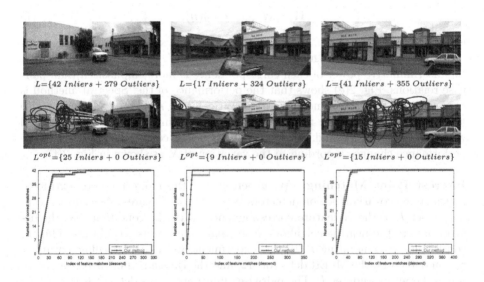

$L=\{42\ Inliers + 279\ Outliers\}$ $L=\{17\ Inliers + 324\ Outliers\}$ $L=\{41\ Inliers + 355\ Outliers\}$

$L^{opt}=\{25\ Inliers + 0\ Outliers\}$ $L^{opt}=\{9\ Inliers + 0\ Outliers\}$ $L^{opt}=\{15\ Inliers + 0\ Outliers\}$

Fig. 5. Results of our feature matching between two scenes sharing overlapping fields of view in ICCV2005 datasets [2]. The matched features between each pair of the color images, displayed in the top row, are presented in the middle row. The graphs in the bottom row show the accumulated number of correct pairs in a high likelihood order.

that our method produces well-matched pairs under difficult conditions such as nonrigid deformation and many outliers.

4   Conclusions

This paper presents a novel probabilistic framework for various correspondence problems. In this work, we design the likelihood of each correspondence as the weighted sum of all the RWR *steady-state* probabilities between feature correspondences. This likelihood efficiently represents the confidence of each candidate by considering the whole relations between two candidates in small neighborhood system. We finally obtain the optimal matches by a simple sequential method with mapping constraints. our method is qualitatively and quantitatively robust to noise and outliers in various matching frameworks. Our future work will include the candidate growing approach, instead of the fixed candidates L.

Acknowledgement

This research was supported in part by the IT R&D program of MKE/IITA (2008-F-030-01), and in part by the Defense Acquisition Program Administration and Agency for Defense Development, Korea, through IIRC (UD070007AD).

References

1. ETHZ Toys Datatset,
   http://www.vision.ee.ethz.ch/~vferrari/datasets.html
2. ICCV2005 Dataset, http://research.microsoft.com/iccv2005/contest/
3. Berg, A.C., Berg, T., Malik, J.: Shape Matching and Object Recognition using Low Distortion Correspondences. In: CVPR, pp. 26–33 (2005)
4. Hedau, V., Arora, H., Ahuja, N.: Matching Images Under Unstable Segmentations. In: CVPR, pp. 1–8 (2008)
5. Kannala, J., Rahtu, E., Brandt, S.S., Heikkilä, J.: Object Recognition and Segmentation by Non-Rigid Quasi-Dense Matching. In: CVPR, pp. 1–8 (2008)
6. Kim, T.H., Lee, K.M., Lee, S.U.: Generative Image Segmentation Using Random Walks with Restart. In: Forsyth, D., Torr, P., Zisserman, A. (eds.) ECCV 2008, Part III. LNCS, vol. 5304, pp. 264–275. Springer, Heidelberg (2008)
7. Leordeanu, M., Hebert, M.: A Spectral Technique for Correspondence Problems Using Pairwise Constraints. In: ICCV, pp. 1482–1489 (2005)
8. Lowe, D.G.: Distinctive Image Features from Scale-Invariant Keypoints. IJCV 60(2), 91–110 (2004)
9. Maciel, J., Costeira, J.: A Global Solution to Sparse Correspondence Problems. PAMI 25(2), 187–199 (2003)
10. Mikolajczyk, K., Schmid, C.: Scale & Affine Invariant Interest Point Detectors. IJCV 60(1), 63–86 (2004)
11. Pan, J.Y., Yang, H.J., Faloutsos, C., Duygulu, P.: Automatic Multimedia Crossmodal Correlation Discovery. In: KDD, pp. 653–658 (2004)
12. Tuytelaars, T., Gool, L.V.: Matching Widely Separated Views based on Affine Invariant Regions. IJCV 59(1), 61–85 (2004)
13. Zhou, D., Bousquet, O., Lal, T.N., Weston, J., Scholkopf, B.: Learning with Local and Global Consistency. In: NIPS, pp. 321–328 (2004)

Highly-Automatic MI Based Multiple 2D/3D Image Registration Using Self-initialized Geodesic Feature Correspondences

Hongwei Zheng, Ioan Cleju, and Dietmar Saupe

Computer and Information Science, University of Konstanz
Fach M697, 78457 Konstanz, Germany
{firstname.surname}@uni-konstanz.de

Abstract. Intensity based registration methods, such as the mutual information (MI), do not commonly consider the spatial geometric information and the initial correspondences are uncertainty. In this paper, we present a novel approach for achieving highly-automatic 2D/3D image registration integrating the advantages from both entropy MI and spatial geometric features correspondence methods. Inspired by the scale space theory, we project the surfaces on a 3D model to 2D normal image spaces provided that it can extract both local geodesic feature descriptors and global spatial information for estimating initial correspondences for image-to-image and image-to-model registration. The multiple 2D/3D image registration can then be further refined using MI. The maximization of MI is effectively achieved using global stochastic optimization. To verify the feasibility, we have registered various artistic 3D models with different structures and textures. The high-quality results show that the proposed approach is highly-automatic and reliable.

1 Introduction

Multiple 2D/3D image registration and mapping is a key problem in computer vision that shows up in a wide variety of applications such as medical image analysis, object tracking, recognition and visualization. In practice, due to the less information about intra- and inter-correspondences for captured multiple images and the 3D model, the problem of multiple 2D/3D image registration is highly ill-posed. The MI measure based 2D/3D image registration methods take only intensity values into account without considering spatial geometric information. The error of initial correspondences may easily lead to a blunder in the final registration. Therefore, it is often that the initial spatial correspondences are manually determined by users, which is non-efficient and time consuming.

This paper presents a novel approach for highly-automatic MI based texture registration using self-initialized geodesic feature correspondences. Given a 3D shape model and multiple images, we perform this approach in three main steps with respect to the search of initial spatial correspondences, the estimation of projective transformation of multiple views, and the refinement of texture registration. At first, we extract local features of surfaces on a 3D shape. However,

H. Zha, R.-i. Taniguchi, and S. Maybank (Eds.): ACCV 2009, Part III, LNCS 5996, pp. 426–435, 2010.
© Springer-Verlag Berlin Heidelberg 2010

direct geometric feature extraction on 3D shapes is difficult. The reason is that the scale-variability of geometric structures on scanned 3D models are simplified due to discrete 3D coordinate point-clouds or triangulated surfaces on 3D models, shown in Fig. 1. Traditional work extract feature descriptors using only surface and curvature smoothing based on 3D coordinates lacking canonical scale analysis. The important discriminative information encoded in the scale-variability of intrinsic geometric structures are easily ignored. Recent work on the scale-variability of images as a 2D projection of 3D objects [1], scale invariant features in the discrete scale space for 2D images [2], and scale-dependent 3D geometric features [3] have been studied intensively. Inspired from these work, we present a comprehensive framework for analyzing and extracting local feature descriptors using the constructed multiple normal maps in geometric scale-spaces.

Secondly, the projective transformation of correspondences for image-to-image 2D/2D and image-to-model 2D/3D are estimated using sparse geometric features and related camera parameter estimation procedures. The key idea underlying the correspondence between a 3D shape and images is that multiple 2D normal images are the 2D projections of geometric surfaces on a 3D shape. The converted multiple normal maps encode the rich geometric information within the spatial distribution of each local features that are sparsely distributed on the normal images using geodesic distance measure. The self-initial correspondences are estimated in two steps with respect to 2D/2D and 2D/3D correspondences. Furthermore, a maximization of MI method [4], [5] is extended for refining multiple 2D/3D image registration using self-initialized geodesic feature correspondences.

Our approach has several advantages. First, the approach is highly-automatic and efficient, facilitating the human supervision and the search of initial correspondences to geometric 3D models with varying geometric complexity. One only needs to define the group of input images according to their surface representations on the 3D shapes. The best position of given multiple viewed images to the 3D surface is determined using self-initialized correspondences. Second, sparse geometric features based initial correspondence does not require camera captured images to contain the entire 3D object for the purpose of silhouette extraction [6], or shape outline extraction. Third, the approach allows sparse geometric feature correspondences and entropy MI based optimization to be integrated for solving a practical problem in a reliable and optimal way.

The rest of the paper is organized as follows. Section 2 presents the concepts of multiple normal images of a 3D shape model. Section 3 describes the geodesic measure and sparse geometric feature extraction. Section 4 formulates the global stochastic optimization based maximization of MI. Implementation details and experimental results are presented in Section 5.

2   Multiple Normal Image Representation of a 3D Model

Given a triangular mesh model of a 3D object, a original mesh M is parameterized to a planar domain D. The parametrization $p : D \to M$ is a bijective mapping from a discrete set of planar points to the mesh vertex set. Normally,

Fig. 1. $a|b|c|d$. (a) A partial point-clouds 3D model. (b) Shaded 3D model. (c) Normals on the 3D model. (d) 2D mesh parameterization with fixed boundary of this 3D model.

parameterizing a mesh to a planar domain does not preserve the angles and the surface area of faces on the mesh. Some changes in the angles and surface area are considered as distortions. Minimizing the parameterization distortion is a challenging problem [7], [8], [9]. For example, in Fig. 1(d), we parameterize one 2D mesh image that encodes the original 3D model.

Although the geometric properties can be encoded via 3D coordinates and curvatures, the surface normals have been demonstrated as a suitable base representation, shown in Fig. 1(c). It allows us to use Gaussian filtering on the 3D shape without influencing the topology of 3D shapes. The normal directions are critical for detecting 3D features. To implement it, we project the surface normal of each vertex of the 3D model and then interpolate those values in the planar domain using barycenter coordinates within each triangular face to obtain a dense normal map. The resulting normal map is a geometric 2D image representation of the original 3D shape (or part of the shape) that is independent of the resolution of its 3D model. To achieve accurate representation of geometric surfaces on a 3D shape to one or multiple normal images, we define the transformation in terms of geodesic distances instead of the traditional Euclidean distances.

The generated one or multiple normal maps cannot exactly represent the original 3D shape due to the distortion of parameterization. For example, the distance between any two points in the normal map is not equivalent to the corresponding relative geodesic distance on the 3D model. To construct 2D surface representation of the original shape, the correct relative geodesic distances between any two points on the normal map is necessary. Therefore, the distortion is computed for each point in the normal map. Given a point $v \in D$ that maps to a 3D mesh vertex $\Psi(v)$, we define its distortion $\xi(v)$ in the equation $\xi(v) = \frac{1}{|adj(v)|} \sum_{u \in adj(v)} \frac{\|v-u\|}{\|\Psi(v)-\Psi(u)\|}$, where $adj(v)$ is a set of vertices adjacent to v. The local distortion is a measure of the average change in the length of the edge adjacent to a vertex. The large $\xi(v)$, the more the adjacent edges have been stretched in the parameterization around v. We then construct a dense map of distortion values in this way. The resulting distortion map is to approximate the geodesic distances between any two points in the normal map.

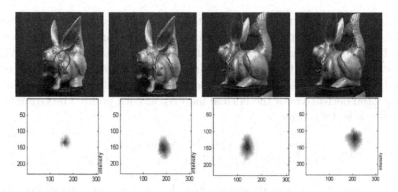

Fig. 2. $\frac{a|b|c|d}{e|f|g|h}$. Geodesics Gaussian distribution on embedded surfaces in 3D spaces. (a)(b)(c)(d) The boundary of geodesic Gaussian kernel with a radius. (e)(f)(g)(h) The distribution of geodesic gaussian kernels with a given radius.

3   Geodesics Measure and Feature Corners Extraction

To achieve initial correspondence searching, we have to define the right feature spaces. To detect salient feature corners for matching, we first derive the first order and second order partial derivatives of the normal map N_σ. Novel feature corners can then be derived using these partial derivatives using geodesics distance as the distance metric which can accurately represent the local surface geometry in scale-space. Given a 2D isotropic Gaussian centered at a point $u \in D$, we define the value of geodesic Gaussian kernel at a point v, then the boundary of geodesic support region on a intensity surface in 3D space. The geodesic Gaussian kernel is derived as $G_{geod}(v, u, \sigma) = \frac{1}{2\pi\sigma^2} \exp\left[-\frac{d_{geod}(v,u)^2}{2\sigma^2}\right]$, where $d_{geod} : R^2 \times R^2 \to R$ is the geodesic distance between the 3D surface points $\Psi(v)$ and $\Psi(u)$. The geodesic distance between two 3D points is defined as the discretized line integral $d_{geod}(v, u)$ in the distortion map, which can be computed as $d_{geod}(v, u) \approx \sum_{v_i \in \Omega(v,u)} \frac{\xi(v_i)^{-1} + \xi(v_{i+1})^{-1}}{2} \|v_i - v_{i+1}\|$, where $\Omega(u, v) = [v_1, v_2, \cdots, v_n, u]$ is a list of points sampled on the surface between v and u. The density of this geodesic sampling determine the quality of the approximation of the original geodesic distance. Using the geodesic Gaussian kernel, the normal at point u for scale level σ as $N_\sigma(u) = \sum_{v \in F} N(v)G_{geod}(v; u, \sigma)/\|\sum_{v \in F} N(v)G_{geod}(v; u, \sigma)\|$, where F is a set of points in a window centered at u. The window size is also defined in terms of geodesic distance and is proportional to the standard deviation σ at each scale level. In our implementation, we change the size of the window from the center point while evaluating each point's geodesic distance from the center to correctly estimating the distribution of similar "high" points. Note that the geodesic Gaussian kernel can be performed for the image embedded surface with the 3rd coordinate of intensity in 3D space. Fig. 2 shows the non-isotropic boundary distribution of geodesic Gaussian kernel with a scale σ for an embedded surface in 3D spaces. It has the same effects on the normal maps which can be smoothed using the geodesic Gaussian kernel in different scales.

Based on these properties, we extract the geometric meaningful feature corners on the normal maps so that we can find the correspondence points between normal maps and the photographs of the real object in the next step. We are interested in detecting the geometric corners which can also be detected on the related 2D photographs. Firstly, we compute the Gram matrix $\mathcal{R}$ of the first order partial derivatives of the normal map N_σ at each point. The Gram matrix at a point u is defined as

$$\mathcal{R}(u;\sigma) = \sum_{v\in W} \begin{bmatrix} N_\sigma^s(v)^2 & N_\sigma^s(v)N_\sigma^t(v) \\ N_\sigma^s(v)N_\sigma^t(v) & N_\sigma^t(v)^2 \end{bmatrix} G_{geod}(u,v)] \qquad (1)$$

Where N_σ^s and N_σ^t are the horizontal first derivatives and vertical first derivatives in the tangential plane on the normal map. The normal map encodes rich geometric information parameterized from the 3D model. Then, using a principle of corner extraction [10], we extract corners from normal maps using the likelihood of a corner as the corner response following $\mathcal{P}(u;\sigma) = \det(\mathcal{R}(u;\sigma)) - \tau\text{Trace}(\mathcal{R}(u;\sigma))^2$, where τ is a tunable parameter. Once the corners are detected in 2D they can be mapped back to the original 3D model. Since the 2D normal map is dense, the corresponding location of the corners in 3D are independent of the input 3D model's triangulation.

4   Maximization of MI Based Registration Refinement

Let x be an arbitrary point on the surface of the 3D model that is visible in the texture image $I(x)$, and $T(x)$ is the 3D-2D projective transformation. The intensity value in the image $I(T(x))$ depends on the radiance in the scene, the (bidirectional reflectance distribution function) BRDF of the surface in x, and the normal to the surface $N(x)$. The dependance of the intensity $I(T(x))$ on the surface normal $N(x)$ can be estimated using the MI (redefining x as a random variable), i.e., the entropy of the "normal-intensity" $\mathcal{M}[N(x), I(T(x))]$. If we consider a random variable x, its entropy $\mathcal{H}(x)$ can be estimated from two independent samplings of x. One sampling is used to estimate the probability density function with the Parzen window method, which is then evaluated on the second sampling. The MI between $N(x)$ and $I(T(x))$ is estimated from small sub-samplings of the data (order of tens of points). When the image $I(T(x))$ and the model $N(x)$ are optimally aligned, the mutual information $\mathcal{M}$ is maximized.

Based on this principle, Viola and Wells [4] proposed a method based on Parzen windows [11] to estimate the MI and its differential with respect to $T(x)$,

$$\mathcal{M}[N(x), I(T(x))] = \mathcal{H}[N(x)] + \mathcal{H}[I(T(x))] - \mathcal{H}[N(x), I(T(x))] \qquad (2)$$

where $\mathcal{M}$ is MI and $\mathcal{H}$ entropy. Note that $\mathcal{H}[N(x)]$ does not depend on the transformation $T(x)$. Due to the small random sub-sampling of data, the estimation of the MI gradient is stochastic. Recently, Cleju and Saupe [5] extended this formulation to support multiple image registration. Except the image-to-model MI which is defined in the same way as [4], additional image-to-image MI objective function are defined using the full color space. The MI between images I_1 and I_2, associated with the transforms T_1 and T_2, is defined as:

$$\mathcal{M}[I_1(T_1(x)), I_2(T_2(x))] = \mathcal{H}[I_1(T_1(x))] + \mathcal{H}[I_2(T_2(x))] - \mathcal{H}[I_1(T_1(x)), I_2(T_2(x))]$$

The main advantage of the formulation is that the new objective functions bring the surface BRDF in the global optimization criterion. In this function, the image-to-image MI is defined from the chrominance components I and Q of the YIQ color space. The image-to-image MI is parameterized by the projective transformations associated with both images, and it is maximized when both images are aligned to the model. The stochastic gradient estimation follows the same procedure as for the image-to-model MI.

For the joint refinement and optimal registration of several images to a 3D model, we use a multi-objective optimization method [5] that is defined as a linear combination of the elementary MI functions with non-negative weights. In this method, firstly, when all images are aligned and the registration refined to the model, all objective functions are maximized. If only the image-to-model MI functions are considered, each set of camera parameters corresponds to one objective function. In this case the iterative gradient-based optimization updates each set of parameters in the direction of the corresponding gradient. Secondly, when all image-to-image MI functions are considered, we estimate several gradients for the parameters of each camera, corresponding to the MI with the model and with other overlapping images. In each iteration we must choose the direction for optimization based on the these gradients.

5   Implementation and Experimental Results

We present the implementation in detail. Sequentially, we describe the intermediate and final registration results in our experiments for the proposed approach.

5.1   Self-initialized Correspondence Using Sparse Features

In this step, we estimate initial correspondence for both image-to-image and image-to-model matching. We have implemented the proposed geodesic feature corner extraction method on the normal maps which is parameterized from the 3D shape models. Then we present automatic initial correspondence results for image-to-image and image-to-model via certain related matching algorithms and a camera self-calibration method. Finally, we further optimize the extrinsic parameters of the cameras and refine the registration results using the MI based global stochastic optimization framework.

Firstly, the projective transformation T is computed by estimating camera model. The optimization model does not make assumptions on the projective transformation T, and consequently on the camera model. In our implementation we consider the pinhole camera model [12] with four distortion coefficients (two for radial distortion and two for tangential distortion). Since multiple views of photographs have been taken around the real 3D object, any two uncalibrated

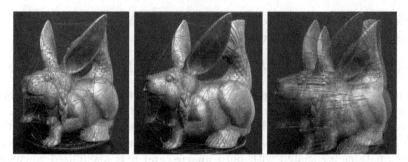

Fig. 3. $a|b|c$ Initial correspondence searching of pairwise texture images. (a)(b) Two captured texture images for the real 3D object with detected and triangulated feature corners. (c) Unsupervised searching of initial feature correspondence between pairwise texture images (a) and (b) using the GASAC method.

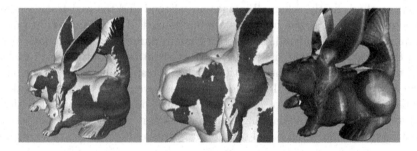

Fig. 4. $a|b|c$ (a) Project two images to the 3D model using the self-initialized feature correspondence. (b) Zoom in (a). (c) After projective transformation, these texture images are initially mapped to the surface of the 3D model. Note that these two images were taken with different illuminations (one texture image was taken using flashlight).

image consequences can be used to estimate the fundamental camera matrix and epipolar lines for pairwise image-to-image matching [13]. The intrinsic parameters field-of-view, optical center, and distortions, were self-calibrated using Zhang's method [14] which are used as initial value for constructing image-to-model correspondence. Any of projective transformation parameters are further refined and optimized using the MI based multiple objective functions. In our experiments, we consider the intrinsic parameters fixed and we optimize only the extrinsic parameters. The rotation matrix is parameterized by axis-angle form for its advantages over Euler angles in the iterative optimization [15].

Secondly, image-to-image 2D/2D correspondences are self-initialized using an extended RANSAC algorithm. The initial correspondence for 2D/2D matching is to determine the relative orientation of the images. The self-initialization is estimated using the methods in multiple view geometry [13], [12]. We have estimated the fundamental matrix and the epipolar lines for describing the projective relative orientation of uncalibrated images. To handle the large number of highly resolving images, the computationally intensive RANSAC algorithm for robust

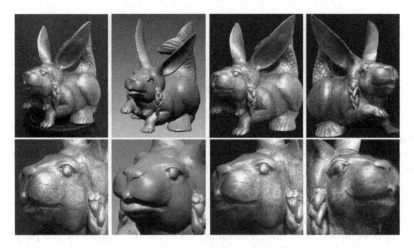

Fig. 5. $\frac{a|b|c|d}{e|f|g|h}$ High-fidelity 2D/3D texture registration results using the suggested method. (a)(e) Camera photo for the real 3D object. (b)(f) The scanned 3D model. (c)(g) and (d)(h) Final results of multiple image registration on the 3D model.

outlier detection has been replaced by a faster evolutionary approach called Genetic Algorithm Sampling Consensus GASAC [16]. The initial correspondence value and results of the feature based matching are shown in Fig. 3.

Furthermore, image-to-model 3D/2D correspondence are estimated based on estimated camera parameters and additional camera calibration. To find initial correspondence value between the 3D shape and the given texture images, we have extracted and utilized the obtained geodesic feature descriptors using normal maps of the 3D shape. We convert the 3D/2D matching problem to a 3D/3D one. Similar to the ICP algorithm [17], the search of initial correspondence is to estimate a paired-point matching transformation based on geodesic feature points and then apply the transformation to one side of the registration. We have scanned several artistic 3D objects with metal surface and reflection. In Fig. 4(a) and (b), we can see some images are initially projected to the surface on the 3D model without any projective transformation processing using sparsely distributed correspondent feature points. After the projective transformation using self-calibrated transformation parameters, shown in Fig. 4(c), several images with different illuminations are mapped on the surface of the 3D shape model after refined projection and registration.

5.2   Color Image Registration and Comparison of Other Approaches

The multiple image registration can be refined and tuned using the maximization of mutual information. If a patch of the surface is visible in two images after self-initialized correspondence, we will simply say that the images overlap. We define image-to-image MI functions for each overlap. In [18], a 3D model with reflectance values mapped on its surface was registered to color images using the method [4]. Here, we extend the objective function for fully color information

Fig. 6. $a|b|c|d$ High-fidelity 2D/3D texture registration results using the suggested method. (a) Photograph. (b) The scanned 3D model. (c)(d) Final results of multiple image registration using the suggested method. Look from different viewpoints.

of the images to the registration objective functions. In our implementation we defined the image-to-image MI from the chrominance components I and Q of the YIQ color space. The image-to-image MI is parameterized by the projective transformations associated with both images, and it is maximized when both images are aligned to the model. The gradient estimation follows the same procedure as for the image-to-model MI. Fig. 5 and Fig. 6 show the refined final registration results using the suggested approach.

In the refinement period of registration, the maximization of MI does not need the existence of any 3D-2D feature information (including visible outlines in the image) after self-initialized correspondence. The refinement of global stochastic optimization does not make assumptions on the unknown parameters of the rendering function. It is robust to various illumination conditions and even to occlusions. Compare to other registration algorithms, our accuracy is significantly better than the one reported in [19], mean projection error of 5-6 pixels for 3072×2304 pixel images. One restriction when using the MI objective function is that the value of the global maximum cannot be estimated. In contrast, when registration is refined and further optimized with point correspondences, for instance, the global optimum corresponds to 0 projection error. The whole software system has been implemented in Cpp language based on SUSE 10.3 Linux system. In Fig. 5, the full registration and refinement of six images takes 10 minutes using an AMD Athlon Dual-Core 4600+ 2GB PC.

6   Conclusions

In this paper, we have suggested a new approach for reliable and highly-automatic multiple image registration using self-initialized geodesic feature correspondences. To improve the robustness and automation of MI based multiple 2D/3D image registration, the integration of self-initialized geodesic feature correspondence can support accurate initial value for further global stochastic optimization based maximization of MI. Furthermore, we have demonstrated that the normal maps of the 3D model in scale space encode rich geometric information for geodesic feature extraction. In particular, we have combined and utilized both advantages from sparse features and entropy MI in an integrated framework. A thorough evaluation and several high-fidelity registered 3D point based models show that the proposed approach has more flexibilities for highly-automatic and reliable multiple image registration.

Acknowledgments

The work was supported by the DFG GK 1042 "Explorative Analysis and Visualization of Large Information Spaces" at the University of Konstanz in Germany.

References

1. Witkin, A.P.: Scale-space filtering. In: Proc. Int. Joint Conf. Artif. Intell., IJCAI Karlsruhe, pp. 1019–1021 (1983)
2. Lowe, D.G.: Distinctive image features from scale-invariant keypoints. International Journal of Computer Vision 60(2), 91–110 (2004)
3. Novatnack, J., Nishino, K.: Scale-dependent 3D geometric features. In: IEEE Eleventh International Conference on Computer Vision (2007)
4. Viola, P.A.: Alignment by maximization of mutual information. Technical Report AITR-1548 (1995)
5. Cleju, I., Saupe, D.: Stochastic optimization of multiple texture registration using mutual information. In: Hamprecht, F.A., Schnörr, C., Jähne, B. (eds.) DAGM 2007. LNCS, vol. 4713, pp. 517–526. Springer, Heidelberg (2007)
6. Lensch, P., Heidrich, W., Seidel, H.P.: Automated texture registration and stitching for real world models. In: Pacific Graphics (2000)
7. Floater, M.S., Hormann, K.: Surface parameterization: a tutorial and survey, pp. 157–186. Springer, Heidelberg (2005)
8. Yoshizawa, S., Belyaev, A., Seidel, H.-P.: A fast and simple stretch-minimizing mesh parametrization. In: Int. Conf. on Shape Modeling and Applications (2004)
9. Eck, M., DeRose, T., Duchamp, T., Hoppe, H., Lounsbery, M., Stuetzle, W.: Multiresolution analysis of arbitrary meshes. In: ACM SIGGRAPH 1995, pp. 173–182 (1995)
10. Förstner, W.: A feature based correspondence algorithm for image matching. Int. Arch. Photogrammetry Remote Sensing 26(3), 150–166 (1986)
11. Duda, R.O., Hart, P.E.: Pattern Classification, 2nd edn. Wiley Interscience, Hoboken (2000)
12. Faugeras, O.: Three-Dimensional Computer Vision: A Geometric Viewpoint. MIT Press, Cambridge (1993)
13. Hartley, R.I., Zisserman, A.: Multiple View Geometry in Computer Vision, 2nd edn. Cambridge University Press, Cambridge (2004)
14. Zhang, Z.: Parameter estimation techniques: A tutorial with application to conic fitting. Journal of Image and Vision Computing 15(1), 59–76 (1997)
15. Taylor, C.J., Kriegman, D.J.: Minimization on the lie group SO(3) and related manifolds. Technical report, Dept. of E.E. Yale University (1994)
16. Rodehorst, V., Hellwich, O.: Genetic algorithm sample consensus (GASAC) - a parallel strategy for estimation. In: 25 Years of RANSAC in CVPR (2006)
17. Penney, G.P., Edwards, P.J., King, A.P., Blackall, J.M., Batchelor, P.G., Hawkes, D.J.: A stochastic iterative closest point algorithm. In: Niessen, W.J., Viergever, M.A. (eds.) MICCAI 2001. LNCS, vol. 2208, p. 762. Springer, Heidelberg (2001)
18. Nishino, K., Sato, Y., Ikeuchi, K.: Appearance compression and synthesis based on 3D model for mixed reality. In: IEEE Int. Conf. Computer Vision, pp. 38–45 (1999)
19. Jank, Z., Chetverikov, D.: Photo-consistency based registration of an uncalibrated image-pair to a 3D model using genetic algorithm. In: 3DPVT, pp. 616–622 (2004)

Better Correspondence by Registration

Shufei Fan[1], Rupert Brooks[2], and Frank P. Ferrie[1]

[1] Center for Intelligent Machines, McGill University
Montreal, Canada
{fansf, ferrie}@cim.mcgill.ca
[2] Industrial Materials Institute, National Research Council Canada
Montreal, Canada
rupert.brooks@imi.cnrc-nrc.gc.ca

Abstract. Accurate image correspondence is crucial for estimating multiple-view geometry. In this paper, we present a registration-based method for improving accuracy of the image correspondences. We apply the method to fundamental matrix estimation under practical situations where there are both erroneous matches (outliers) and small feature location errors. Our registration-based method can correct feature locational error to less than 0.1 pixel, remedying localization inaccuracy due to feature detectors. Moreover, we carefully examine feature similarity based on their post-alignment appearance, providing a more reasonable prior for subsequent outlier detection. Experiments show that we can improve feature localization accuracy of the MSER feature detector, which recovers the most accurate feature localization as reported in a recent study by Haja and others. As a result of applying our method, we recover the fundamental matrix with better accuracy and more efficiency.

1 Introduction

Most current methods for establishing epipolar geometry between two uncalibrated views use correspondences between point features detected in each image. Each correspondence provides one linear equation to be used in estimating the fundamental matrix. This process is affected by error in two main ways. First, not all matches between features reflect real correspondence between objects in the 3D scene, and it is necessary to filter out the false matches before attempting to estimate the fundamental matrix. The erroneous matches (outliers) are singled out using robust estimation methods such as M-estimator [1] and random sampling algorithms [2][3]. These methods, however, discard the valuable information about correspondence quality contained in the similarity score between the two points, in effect assuming that all matched pairs have an equal chance of being a mismatch. Some recent works [4][5] mitigated this shortcoming by considering this similarity quality and achieved improved results. The second issue is, how to accurately recover the epipolar geometry assuming we are working with inlying feature matches. In practical applications, errors in the position of the matched point centriods are unavoidable. A feature's geometric properties, such as location and shape, are determined by its appearance in a single

H. Zha, R.-i. Taniguchi, and S. Maybank (Eds.): ACCV 2009, Part III, LNCS 5996, pp. 436–447, 2010.

image. Under wide-baseline conditions, these properties are highly volatile due to factors such as image noise, occlusion, image quantization error, *etc.* Hence, even correctly corresponding features can not be precisely related by the ground truth two-view geometry. This is echoed by the recent work by Haja *et al.* [6]. They showed that different feature detectors exhibit significantly different localization accuracy in position and feature shape. They have also found this positional accuracy is proportional to feature scale, which agrees with intuition. Various numerical schemes [7][8] have been proposed for high accuracy fundamental matrix computation, under the assumption that the locational errors of each feature are Gaussian. Also, Georgel *et al.* [9] implicitly corrected this error by introducing a photometric cost to their pose estimation framework.

We present a method for improving point correspondences that improves both the robustness and accuracy of fundamental matrix estimation by advancing in both of the above areas. We achieve this by an intensity based alignment of the local patches around each matched feature point. For each of the initial putative matches, we locally adjust the position and shape of the feature in one image according to the appearance of its counterpart in the other image. Consequently, we will have a better characterization of the feature similarity and the features are better localized towards the image of a common 3D structure. This improved similarity and localization will enable a more effective robust outlier rejection. At the same time, we obtain a more accurate fundamental matrix by directly correcting the source of the inaccuracy: feature location errors.

The remainder of the paper is organized as follows. In Section 2 we discuss related work on fundamental matrix estimation. After describing our registration-based refinement in Section 3.1, we layout the procedure for the improved fundamental matrix estimation in Section 3.2. The effectiveness of the proposed correspondence refinement is validated in Section 4. This paper concludes with a discussion of other possible applications and future work.

2   Related Work

The fundamental matrix is the algebraic representation of the epipolar geometry, the intrinsic projective geometry between two views. Encapsulating this two-view geometry, the fundamental matrix $\mathbf{F}$ constrains corresponding image points with a linear equation

$$\mathbf{m}'^{\top}\mathbf{F}\mathbf{m} = 0, \tag{1}$$

for any pair of matching points $\mathbf{m} \longleftrightarrow \mathbf{m}'$ in two images, where $\mathbf{m} = (x, y, 1)$, $\mathbf{m}' = (x', y', 1)$ are homogeneous representations of point image-coordinates, and $\mathbf{F}$ is a 3×3 matrix with 7 degrees of freedom.

Being linear in the elements of $\mathbf{F}$, Equation (1) can be used to estimate $\mathbf{F}$ by linear least squares regression, as long as we have a sufficient number of correspondences in general position. However, most automated methods for selecting matched point pairs suffer from having some amount of false matches mixed in with the correct matches, which can cause serious errors in the regression process. Thus most methods for **F**-estimation proceed in two stages, estimating initial **F** using a robust method to filter out erroneous matches, and then re-estimating **F** precisely using the matches deemed correct.

2.1 Robust Fundamental Matrix Estimation

Robust methods are designed to deal with estimation problems where a portion of the data is completely erroneous. Representative works are M-Estimators [1], least median of squares [10], and random sampling approaches (*e.g.* [2][3]). However, each of these operates under the assumption that each input datum is equally likely to be erroneous. In the image matching problem discussed here, additional information is available to estimate the quality of the matches being used to estimate **F**.

The PROSAC algorithm by Chum and Matas [5] and the Guided-MLESAC algorithm of Tordoff and Murray [4] introduced some domain-specific priors into the random sampling scheme. That is, they incorporated information about the quality of the point matches into the random sampling process. These schemes, which we call *prior-influenced random sampling*, demonstrate significant gain in computational efficiency and robustness. PROSAC is of particular interest because of its mild *not-worse-than-random* assumption and its computational efficiency. It draws samples on progressively larger subsets consisting of top-ranked correspondences. Their ranking is based on such similarity measures as Euclidean distance of discrete cosine transform (DCT) coefficients [11] or ratio of SIFT distances [12]. The confidence in the solution is guaranteed by a RANSAC-equivalent termination criterion.

2.2 Precise Fundamental Matrix Estimation

Even once a set of correct matches has been selected, the equations implied by Equation (1) cannot be satisfied exactly due to the noise in the point positions. Precise fundamental matrix estimation (abbreviated as **F**-estimation) is often cast as a minimization problem, minimizing either an algebraic residual or some geometric distance. From the algebraic perspective, it can be solved either linearly by the Orthogonal Least Squares Regression algorithm [1], or by nonlinear iterative estimation methods [13]. When approached as a geometrical minimization problem, the objective function bears some meaningful geometrical distance. It can be either reprojection errors of corresponding points (Golden method [14]), or the perpendicular geometric distances of points to a certain conic (Sampson distance [15]), or the distance of a point to its epipolar line [16].

3 Our Approach

Robust **F**-estimation methods rely therefore on the possibility of making a clear distinction between outliers and inliers. However, the errors in feature alignment have a tendency to blur this distinction. As these errors increase, all components of the system degrade. First, the similarity scores used to rank points are less reliable, which makes the *prior-influenced random sampling* less effective. Second, the initial **F** estimated by the robust methods are of poorer quality, which leads to more difficulty categorizing inliers from outliers. In fact, the inlier/outlier categorization is inherently less reliable, as the errors on inlying matches tend to be larger. Finally the resulting precisely estimated **F** is less accurate, as its accuracy is ultimately determined by the accuracy of the point matches used as input to the minimization algorithm.

We propose to improve their alignment by local registration. This will produce two immediate results. The first is a more accurate localization of the matched points. This effectively reduces the noise level of the points. The second is a better similarity measure of the matches because of this reduction in position and shape discrepancy.

Robust outlier rejection will benefit from these results. The improved similarity provides a more reliable prior for the *prior-influenced random sampling* schemes. In the meantime, the reduced noise in position will give rise to a stronger positive vote if a correct model is being tested by a random sampling method. Thus, one would expect the inliers to be detected more efficiently and with better success rate. Finally, precise **F**-estimation will also benefit from the improved feature localization.

3.1   Localization Refinement by Registration

Most feature points used in image matching applications achieve a level of transformation invariance by incorporating some transformation information into their description. Following the convention introduced by Mikolajczyk *et al.* [17], we define an Maximally Stable Extremal Region (MSER) [18], i, by a centroid, $\boldsymbol{x}_{c_i}(x_i, y_i)$, as well as three parameters, a_i, b_i, c_i, describing an elliptical region around the centroid. A correspondence between a pair of points then implies that these elliptical regions correspond to each other. An affine transformation ϕ which matches one ellipse onto the other can be computed by determining three or more equivalent points on each ellipse and solving for the affine transformation parameters that map the points from one ellipse to the other.

For each correspondence, our registration-based refinement tries to find the optimal affine transform ϕ_{opt} based on pair-wise appearances and to re-align the corresponding features accordingly. This registration is implemented in two steps, ϕ-*initialization* and ϕ-*optimization*.

ϕ-Initialization. This step establishes an initial affine transform ϕ_{init} with which to start registration, based on an approximate patch alignment. With each feature ellipse being defined by five parameters $(x_i, y_i, a_i, b_i, c_i)$, one cannot infer a six parameter affine transform ϕ between a pair of features without resorting to the use of more information such as image appearances. By mapping bounding rectangles of the two ellipses, we establish an approximate transform ϕ_{init} and leave the accurate ϕ-estimation to the optimization step.

Specifically, the ellipse for each point satisfies the quadratic form

$$[\boldsymbol{x} - \boldsymbol{x_c}] \, A \, [\boldsymbol{x} - \boldsymbol{x_c}] = 1; \quad A = \begin{bmatrix} a & b \\ b & c \end{bmatrix}. \tag{2}$$

It is known that the lengths of the semimajor and semiminor axes of the ellipse are given by the square roots of the eigenvalues, $(\lambda_{max}, \lambda_{min})$, of A^{-1}, and the direction of each axis is given by the corresponding eigenvector, (v_{max}, v_{min}). The major axis thus intersects the ellipse at $p_{1,2} = x_c \pm \sqrt{\lambda_{max}} \cdot v_{max}$, and the minor axis intersects the ellipse at $p_{3,4} = x_c \pm \sqrt{\lambda_{min}} \cdot v_{min}$.

To simplify initialization, we assume the bounding rectangles of two features i and j correspond to each other. If the length (width) of the bounding rectangle i still maps to length (width) of the bounding rectangle j, these rectangles are related by a *restricted* affine transform with 5 degrees of freedom (dof): a translation (2 dof), a rotation (1 dof), and re-scaling along the length/width of the rectangle (2 dof). The affine transformation parameters, $\phi_{init} = \{\phi_1, ...\phi_6\}$ mapping rectangle i onto rectangle j can then be found by solving the linear equation:

$$\begin{bmatrix} p_{j_1} & p_{j_2} & p_{j_3} & p_{j_4} \\ 1 & 1 & 1 & 1 \end{bmatrix} = \begin{bmatrix} \phi_1 & \phi_2 & \phi_3 \\ \phi_4 & \phi_5 & \phi_6 \\ 0 & 0 & 1 \end{bmatrix} \cdot \begin{bmatrix} p_{i_1} & p_{i_2} & p_{i_3} & p_{i_4} \\ 1 & 1 & 1 & 1 \end{bmatrix}. \tag{3}$$

There is a 180 degree ambiguity in the direction of the major axis. We resolve it assuming that the correct transformation will involve the smaller amount of rotation. This heuristic is in accordance with the way digital photographs are taken - usually, we hold cameras roughly vertical to the floor/ground and we do not make big camera rotation around the optical axis. If camera rotations can be large, this can easily be fixed, in the ϕ-*optimization* step, by trying both directions.

ϕ-**Optimization.** We optimize the transformation ϕ using direct or intensity based registration. Intensity based registration approaches solve for a smooth transformation between images (or image patches) by maximizing a similarity measure defined on the pixel intensities (see, *e.g.* [19] for details). Specifically, one image, I_{mov}, is warped by some parameterized transformation to match the other one, I_{fix}, and the similarity is evaluated. The correct registration is considered to be the one that maximizes the similarity between the images. The registration problem is thus expressed as an unconstrained optimization problem

$$\phi_{opt} = argmax_\phi S(I_{fix}, I_{mov}(W(x, \phi))). \tag{4}$$

In our case, we use the normalized correlation coefficient as the similarity measure S and use the affine transformation (ϕ in Equation (3)) as the warping function $W(x, \phi)$. We solve this optimization problem using a trust-region Newton-Raphson optimization method. Details of this type of optimization may be found in [20].

3.2   Improved Fundamental Matrix Estimation

Algorithm (1) gives an outline of our proposed method for automatically compute epipolar geometry between two images. The input to the algorithm is simply the image pair; and the output is the estimated $\mathbf{F}$ and a set of correct matches. The key difference between this algorithm and previous approaches is the *Correspondence refinement* step, where we refine the localizations of each pair of correspondences. However, it is worth pointing out that our approach can be applied to any multiple-view geometry estimation method that follows this basic pattern.

We use the MSERs as our features and their putative correspondences are established by nearest-neighbor classification of their SIFT descriptors [17]. The Sampson distance is used as the distance function for both the PROSAC consensus testing and the final iterative $\mathbf{F}$-estimation. The Sampson measure is found to give adequate accuracy in the $\mathbf{F}$-estimation [1][14].

Algorithm 1. Compute the fundamental matrix between two images.

Data: stereo images I_l, I_r

begin

    1. **Features:** Extract affine invariant features in each image.

    2. **Putative correspondences:** Compute a set of feature matches based on similarity of their SIFT Descriptors.

    3. **Correspondence refinement:** For each putative match, re-align the position and shape of the feature in one image (I_r) according to match appearances.

    4. **PROSAC robust estimation:** Progressively enlarge sample pool, starting with most promising candidates. In the end, PROSAC chooses the $\mathbf{F}$ with the largest number of inliers.

    5. **Non-linear estimation:** Re-estimate $\mathbf{F}$ from all inliers by minimizing the Sampson cost function.

end

Result: Fundamental Matrix $\mathbf{F}$, the set of inlier matches.

---

4   Experiments

We evaluated our method on three aspects. The first aspect was feature localization accuracy, the second was robust outlier rejection, and the third was the accuracy of the final $\mathbf{F}$ estimated. We experimented on four standard image sets: the *House, Corridor, Valbonne* and *Shed.* [1] The images are presented in Figure (1) and show the estimated epipolar lines. Among them, the *House* and *Corridor* have ground truth $\mathbf{F}$ and correspondences for localization accuracy analysis.

4.1   Test on Feature Localization Accuracy

It was reported that the MSER [18] is the most accurate in feature localization [6], thus we worked on the MSER features to see if further accuracy improvement was indeed achieved.

---

[1] The *House, Corridor* and *Valbonne* were retrieved from
http://www.robots.ox.ac.uk/~vgg/data1.html.

(a) House   (b) Valbonne   (c) Corridor   (d) Shed

Fig. 1. Image sets with estimated epipolar lines

Error Measure. Since our application here was estimating $\mathbf{F}$, we measured the error of feature positions using the epipolar geometry. We focused on the accuracy of positions only since the shape wasn't relevant in our $\mathbf{F}$-estimation.

We measured the deviation of the matched points with the distance between a point's epipolar line and the matching point in the other image $d(\mathbf{x}'_i, \mathbf{F}\mathbf{x}_i)$, where $d(\mathbf{x}, \mathbf{l})$ is the distance in pixels between a point $\mathbf{x}$ and a line $\mathbf{l}$ (both in homogeneous coordinates). The more precise the matched points are localized, the smaller this distance (or error) is. To ensure that each image received equal consideration, we examined statistics of the set of errors in both images

$$D = \{d(\mathbf{x}'_i, \mathbf{F}\mathbf{x}_i), d(\mathbf{x}_i, \mathbf{F}^\top \mathbf{x}'_i) | \forall i \in [1, 2, ..., N]\}, \tag{5}$$

where N is the number of inlier matches.

Note that although the deviation of a point from its epipolar line doesn't exactly measure its displacement on a 2D image, it can be used as an adequate approximation. By definition, the error $d(\mathbf{x}'_i, \mathbf{F}\mathbf{x}_i)$ measures the deviation of points only in the direction perpendicular to the epipolar lines. A more precise measure is that used in the work by Haja *et al.* [6], where they examined match localization accuracy by measuring the region overlap errors based on carefully estimated ground truth homographies. However, their overlap measure is very restrictive: one is limited to planar scenes where all features lie on the same plane; while the measure here is suitable for real-life 3D scenes containing complex structures. When the errors in point positions are equally possible in all directions (as is always the case), it is often adequate.

Results on Localization Accuracy. On the image sets *House* and *Corridor*, we compared the sets of errors D of three point sets using ground truth fundamental matrix $\mathbf{F}_{truth}$: the *Oxford points*, the *original points*, and the *refined points*. The *Oxford points* are ground truth point matches provided along with the image set. The *original points* are the MSER features selected as inlying matches. And the *refined points* are the inlier subset of our registration-refined MSER features. Both of the above two point sets were selected using the PROSAC algorithm.

Figure (2) shows the error of the *refined points* is statistically lower than other point sets on both *House* and *Corridor*. On the *House* dataset, for example, *refined points* have an error median of 0.1 pixel; the values for *original points* and *Oxford points* are 0.14 and 0.25 respectively. Since the ground truth points were hand-selected by visual inspection, their localization could be inaccurate, thus, the error of the *Oxford points* ended up being the largest. This also explains why our registration-based refinement can lead to an even better localization accuracy.

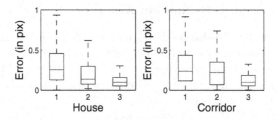

Fig. 2. Accuracy Comparison Using Ground Truth (F_{truth}). For each of *House* and *Corridor*, we show error boxplots of three different point sets, the *Oxford points* (represented by 1 on the x-axes), *original points* (2) and *refined points* (3). Along the y-axis, the units are in pixels. For each point set, the red line in the center of the box is the error median and the upper and lower horizontal lines of the box represent the top quartile and bottom quartile.

4.2   Improvement on Robust Inlier Detection

We applied Algorithm (3.2) on the image sets and obtained results on robust inlier detection. Table (1) shows the average number of inliers detected and samples drawn of different point sets over 100 experiments.

Table (1) reveals that refinement can improve robust inlier detection in two ways. First, it encourages more inliers to be detected. This is because some small inaccuracies of feature location were improved, thus some of the previously classified outliers were corrected. This correction is particularly important when the overall match count is low - we do not want to lose any matches due to false-negatives. Second, it drastically reduces the amount of samples needed to

Table 1. The Comparison of the number of inliers detected and the number of samples drawn on the set of original vs. refined matches

Methods	#Total matches	#Inlier matches		#Sample trials	
		original matches	refined matches	original matches	refined matches
House	77	55	62	16	13
Valbonne	26	16	18	32	8
Corridor	66	45	54	31	7
Shed	47	34	35	30	10

find the correct solution. Using the PROSAC scheme on both point sets, fewer samples are drawn from the *refined points* to detect the inliers. This trend is consistent over all data. Part of the reason is more accurate locations will facilitate identifying the correct model (in this case, fundamental matrix **F**) more quickly, *i.e.* avoid being distracted by minor inaccuracies. Another factor is that the registration provides better similarity scores for the match ranking of PROSAC. This sample count reduction is more obvious when the inlier percentage is low, as in *Valbonne, Shed,* and *Corridor.*

4.3   Improvement on F-Estimation Accuracy

The statistics on the set of distances D (Equation (5)) are also commonly used in measuring **F**-estimation accuracy [14]. We estimated **F** using the different point sets and then measured the resulting errors. The same procedure, iteratively re-weighted least squares minimization using Sampson distance [1], was used for estimating the **F** on all point sets.

In Figure (3), we show the errors of *original points* versus *refined points* on the four images. The *refined points* consistently achieved better accuracy than the *original points.* Between 21% and 67% reduction in error median was achieved by the proposed method. In the case of *Valbonne* (plot for *Valbonne* in Figure (3)), if we were to directly compare the errors here against that presented in Table 3 of [18], we would see no significant improvement. The reason is although both used the *Valbonne* sequence, they selected *different* images of the sequence. Also, their set of correspondences were obtained differently: first they estimated a "rough EG"; then more and better correspondences were obtained using "guided-matching" with a very narrow threshold. This *narrowing* of threshold effectively ensured that only those better-localized matches be selected. Their "guided-matching" effectively added more accurate matches and deleted bad ones; while our method worked on available matches and made them better. Both strategies are useful; in practice, one can combine them for a further improved result.

4.4   Computing Time

Running time of the proposed method is dependent on many factors, *e.g.* the number of putative matches, accuracy in their original alignment, *etc.* Our method spends extra time on local patch optimization but needs less time on robust outlier rejection.

Our current implementation of the algorithm is a mixture of Matlab scripts and C++ binaries, and its running time is not particularly informative. However, we have timed the registration components of the algorithm. The local patch optimization consists of an initialization, mainly involving pre-computing image derivatives, which only needs to be done once per image pair, and the optimization of each patch. Running single core on a 1.8GHz Intel Core Duo processor, the initialization times ranged between 0.32–0.72s (depending on the

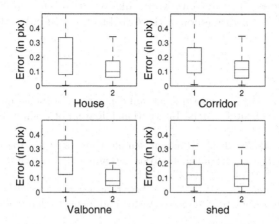

Fig. 3. Accuracy Comparison of F-estimation. Error boxplots of different point sets on four image sets. 1 and 2 on the x-axes represent the *original points* and *refined points* respectively. The lower the error (along y-axis) is, the more accurate is the F-estimation. The red lines indicate the error medians.

size of the image), and the optimization time averaged 11.5ms per patch. Considering that both parts of the algorithm can be easily parallelized, the processing time of an integrated algorithm could be expected to be reasonable.

5   Discussion and Conclusion

We proposed a method for improving the quality of correspondences by local patch registration. This registration further improves localization accuracy of feature detectors and produces a better measure of feature's similarity. In the context of robust fundamental matrix estimation, our method enables a more effective outlier rejection and obtains a more accurate fundamental matrix.

It is reasonable to expect this improvement in feature localization accuracy since information of both images is utilized, whereas in the feature detection one decides feature localization based on only a single image. This idea of registration-based correspondence refinement can also be used in other tasks involving multiple-view correspondence, since this gain in localization accuracy is always desired. The effect of our method on the MSERs implies that the F-estimation can always benefit from the refinement even if one use other features, since most popular features have more room for improvement than MSERs [6].

Another gain from this registration that can be explored is the improvement in the local mapping implied by the feature shape parameters. Certain approaches, such as [21], have used this shape information to assist in F-estimation using only a few feature correspondences. Improving the accuracy of this local mapping could enhance the applicability of this type of approach.

Acknowledgement. The authors would like to thank Dr. Ondrej Chum and Professor Jiri Matas for discussion with regard to the PROSAC algorithm.

References

1. Torr, P., Murray, D.: The development and comparison of robust methods for estimating the fundamental matrix. International Journal of Computer Vision 24(3), 271–300 (1997)
2. Fischler, M.A., Bolles, R.C.: Random sample consensus: a paradigm for model fitting with applications to image analysis and automated cartography. Communications of the ACM 24(6), 381–395 (1981)
3. Torr, P., Zisserman, A.: MLESAC: A new robust estimator with application to estimating image geometry. Computer Vision and Image Understanding 78(1), 138–156 (2000)
4. Tordoff, B., Murray, D.: Guided-MLESAC: Faster image transform estimation by using matching priors. IEEE Transactions on Pattern Analysis and Machine Intelligence 27(10), 1523–1535 (2005)
5. Chum, O., Matas, J.: Matching with PROSAC: Progressive sample consensus. In: Proceedings of Computer Vision and Pattern Recognition, pp. I: 220–226 (2005)
6. Haja, A., Jahne, B., Abraham, S.: Localization accuracy of region detectors. In: Proceedings of Computer Vision and Pattern Recognition, June 2008, pp. 1–8 (2008)
7. Kanatani, K., Sugaya, Y.: High accuracy fundamental matrix computation and its performance evaluation. IEICE Transactions on Information and Systems E90-D(2), 579–585 (2007)
8. Chojnacki, W., Brooks, M., van den Hengel, A., Gawley, D.: A new constrained parameter estimator for computer vision applications. Image and Vision Computing 22(2), 85–91 (2004)
9. Georgel, P., Benhimane, S., Navab, N.: A unified approach combining photometric and geometric information for pose estimation. In: Proceedings of British Machine Vision Conference, pp. 133–142 (2008)
10. Rousseeuw, P.: Robust Regression and Outlier Detection. Wiley, Chichester (1987)
11. Obdrzalek, S., Matas, J.: Image retrieval using local compact DCT-based representation, pp. 490–497 (2003)
12. Lowe, D.G.: Distinctive Image Features from Scale-Invariant Keypoints. International Journal of Computer Vision 60(2), 91–110 (2004)
13. Bookstein, F.L.: Fitting conic sections to scattered data. Computer Graphics and Image Processing 9(1), 56–71 (1979)
14. Hartley, R.I., Zisserman, A.: Multiple View Geometry in Computer Vision, 2nd edn. Cambridge University Press, Cambridge (2004)
15. Weng, J., Huang, T., Ahuja, N.: Motion and structure from two perspective views: Algorithms, error analysis, and error estimation. IEEE Transactions on Pattern Analysis and Machine Intelligence 11(5), 451–476 (1989)
16. Luong, Q., Deriche, R., Faugeras, O., Papadopoulo, T.: On determining the fundamental matrix: Analysis of different methods and experimental results (1993)
17. Mikolajczyk, K., Tuytelaars, T., Schmid, C., Zisserman, A., Matas, J., Schaffalitzky, F., Kadir, T., Van Gool, L.: A comparison of affine region detectors. International Journal of Computer Vision 65(1-2), 43–72 (2005)

18. Matas, J., Chum, O., Urban, M., Pajdla, T.: Robust wide baseline stereo from maximally stable extremal regions. Image and Vision Computing 22(10), 761–767 (2004)
19. Modersitzki, J.: Numerical Methods for Image Registration. Numerical Mathematics and Scientific Computation. Oxford University Press, Oxford (2004)
20. Conn, A.R., Gould, N.I.M., Toint, P.L.: Trust-Region Methods. Society for Industrial and Applied Mathematics and Mathematical Programming Society (2000)
21. Riggi, F., Toews, M., Arbel, T.: Fundamental matrix estimation via TIP - transfer of invariant parameters. In: Proceedings of the International Conference on Pattern Recognition, Hong Kong, August 2006, pp. 21–24 (2006)

Image Content Based Curve Matching Using HMCD Descriptor

Zhiheng Wang[1], Hongmin Liu[1], and Fuchao Wu[2]

[1] School of Computer Science and Technique, Henan Polytechnic University,
Jiaozuo, China
[2] National Laboratory of Pattern Recognition, Institute of Automation,
Chinese Academy of Sciences Beijing, China
wzhenry@eyou.com

Abstract. Curve matching plays an important role in many applications, such as image registration, 3D reconstruction, object recognition and video understanding. However, compared with other features(such as point, region) matching, it has made little progress in recent years. In this paper, we investigate the problem of automatic curve matching only from their neighborhood appearance. A novel descriptor called HMCD descriptor is proposed for this purpose, which is constructed by the following three steps: (1) Curve neighborhood is divided into a series of overlapped sub-regions with the same size; (2) Curve description matrix (CDM) is formed by characterizing each sub-region into a vector; (3) HMCD descriptor is built by computing the first four order Moments of CDM column vectors. Experimental results show that HMCD descriptor is highly distinctive and very robust for curve matching on real images.

Keywords: Curve matching; Curve descriptor; HMCD descriptor.

1 Introduction

Compared to point matching [1,2] and region matching [3], little progress has been made in curve matching (including line matching) in recent years, which is due to several reasons [4], such as inaccuracy of endpoint locations, geometric constraint can not be easily available, support regions of different curves have different size. Only a few methods for curve matching are reported in literature until now. For images of planar surfaces, Lourakis [5] proposed an approach using "2 lines + 2 points" projective invariants for line matching. Herbert [4] presented a novel method for automatic matching in color images. The main drawback of this method is its heavy reliance on color information. While color provides a very strong cue for discrimination, it may fail in the case where color feature is not distinctive, such as on gray images or remote sensing images. Schmid and Zisserman [6,7] applied geometrical constraints (epipolar geometry, one parameter family of homographies and curvature of curves) and cross correlation for line matching and curve matching. Grouping matching strategy proposed by Deng and Lin [8] has the advantage that more geometric information can be

H. Zha, R.-i. Taniguchi, and S. Maybank (Eds.): ACCV 2009, Part III, LNCS 5996, pp. 448–455, 2010.
© Springer-Verlag Berlin Heidelberg 2010

available for removing ambiguities, and such method can cope with more significant camera motion. However, it often has high complexity and is sensitive to topological connections or inaccuracy of endpoints. Mikolajczyk and Zisserman [9] also proposed a curve descriptor by generalizing SIFT point descriptor and Orrite [10] developed continuity Hausdorff distance for matching partially occluded curves invariant under projective transformation. Most existing methods for curve matching either require prior knowledge or are limited to some specific scenes, such as geometries between images or planar scenes.

This paper is focus on automatic curve matching without any prior knowledge, and a descriptor called Harris Moment curve descriptor (HMCD) is developed only based on local appearance. Compared with previous approaches, HMCD has two advantages: (1) It is an automatic method that can work without known any constraints, (2) It can be applicable to general conditions. The remainder of this paper is organized as follows. Section 2 introduces the strategy of partitioning curve neighborhood into sub-regions. In section 3 each sub-region is characterized into a feature vector. Section 4 elaborates the construction of HMCD descriptor and section 5 provides the experiments. Section 6 is the conclusions.

2   Partition of Curve Neighborhood

In this paper, we propose a novel and effective scheme to summarize curve neighborhoods with different size into vectors with the same dimension. As shown in figure 1, for a pixel $\mathbf{P}_i$ on a curve, denote its gradient direction as $\mathbf{d}_{ni}$ and the direction orthogonal to $\mathbf{d}_{ni}$ anticlockwise as $\mathbf{d}_{ti}$, then a rectangular region centered at $\mathbf{P}_i$ and along with $\{\mathbf{d}_{ni}, \mathbf{d}_{ti}\}$ is defined as pixel support region(PSR). Denote the PSRs defined by all the pixels on the curve along curve as $G_1, G_2, ..., G_N$ (Assuming the curve consists of N pixels), then the union of all these PSRs is called

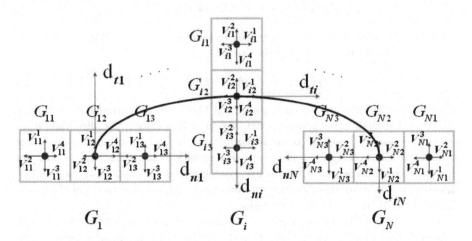

Fig. 1. Schematic figure of HMCD computation.(This figure shows the situation of 3 subregions is used for each PSR, whereas in this paper 9 is used.)

the curve support region(CSR). In order to characterize CSR in more detail, each PSR is divided into M sub-regions with the same size along the direction $\mathbf{d}_{ni}$: $G_i = G_{i1} \bigcup G_{i2}, ..., \bigcup G_{iM}$. It is noted that determination of the direction $\mathbf{d}_{ni}$ is significant for ensuring rotation invariance, otherwise, some ambiguity could occur when deciding the order of $G_{i1}, G_{i2}, ..., G_{iM}$.

3 Sub-region Representation

In this section, we characterize each sub-region into a description vector using a rotation invariant Harris feature. The original Harris self-related matrix can be expressed as [11] ($\nabla \mathbf{f} = [\nabla x, \nabla y]$ denotes the sample gradient):

$$\mathbf{H}(x,y) = \begin{pmatrix} \nabla_x \cdot \nabla_x & \nabla_x \cdot \nabla_y \\ \nabla_x \cdot \nabla_y & \nabla_y \cdot \nabla_y \end{pmatrix} \tag{1}$$

Since that gradient vector is not rotation invariant,to achieve rotation invariance, we use the coordinate system determined by $\{\mathbf{d}_{ni}, \mathbf{d}_{ti}\}$ to express sample gradient in each PSR. The new coordinate of a sample gradient can be expressed: $\nabla' \mathbf{f} = [\nabla_n, \nabla_t] = [\nabla \mathbf{f} \cdot \mathbf{d}_{ni}, \nabla \mathbf{f} \cdot \mathbf{d}_{ti}]$. This is similar to that of SIFT which rotates each gradient relative to the orientation of keypoint. Then, rotation invariant Harris Matrix can be expressed as:

$$\mathbf{H}'(x,y) = \begin{pmatrix} \nabla_n \cdot \nabla_n & \nabla_n \cdot \nabla_t \\ \nabla_n \cdot \nabla_t & \nabla_t \cdot \nabla_t \end{pmatrix} \tag{2}$$

Denote two eigenvalues of the matrix $\mathbf{H}'$ as α, β respectively, the sum of the eigenvalues can be computed from the trace of $\mathbf{H}'$ and their product can be computed from the determinant of $\mathbf{H}'$:

$$Tr(\mathbf{H}') = \alpha + \beta, \ Det(\mathbf{H}') = \alpha \cdot \beta \tag{3}$$

Then, the following two features are used as rotation invariant Harris feature for each sample in support region of the curve:

$$h_1 = Tr(\mathbf{H}'), h_2 = sign(Det(\mathbf{H}')) \cdot \sqrt{|Det(\mathbf{H}')|} \tag{4}$$

After computing feature for each sample, a Gaussian weighting function, with scale equal to half the curve support region width (along the direction $\mathbf{d}_{ni}$), is used to assign a weight to each sample in the curve support region. The purpose of such a weighting is to give less emphasis to importance of samples that are far from the curve, which are most effected by mis-registration errors. Another reason is to avoid sudden changes of descriptor due to small change in the position of the curve support region.

In order to reduce boundary effect, each sample feature is distributed into two adjacent sub-regions along the direction $\mathbf{d}_{ni}$ by the following means: for a sample whose two nearest neighborhood sub-regions are G_{ij} , $G_{i(j+1)}$, if it has distances d_1, d_2 from the central lines (parallel to $\mathbf{d}_{ti}$) of the two sub-regions respectively, the sample feature is weighted by $w_1 = d_2/(d_1 + d_2)$, $w_2 = d_1/(d_1 + d_2)$ and then distributed into G_{ij} , $G_{i(j+1)}$ respectively.

Denote the features distributed into a sub-region G_{ij} as $\{(h_1, h_2)^T\}$, accumulate these features according to their signs, then a feature vector with a dimension of 4 can be formed: $\mathbf{V}_{ij} = (V_{ij}^1, V_{ij}^2, V_{ij}^3, V_{ij}^4)^T$ (As shown in figure 1), where,

$$V_{ij}^1 = \sum_{h_1 > 0} h_1, \quad V_{ij}^2 = \sum_{h1 < 0} -h_1, \quad V_{ij}^3 = \sum_{h_2 > 0} h_2, \quad V_{ij}^4 = \sum_{h_2 < 0} -h_2$$

It is not difficult to see that $\mathbf{V}_{ij}$ is invariant to image rotation, we call it the description vector of the sub-region G_{ij}.

4   HMCD Descriptor

By the description vectors of sub-regions of a curve C, we define a $4M \times N$ matrix, called curve description matrix (CDM):

$$\mathbf{CDM}(C) = \begin{pmatrix} \mathbf{V}_{11} & \mathbf{V}_{12} & \cdots & \mathbf{V}_{1N} \\ \mathbf{V}_{21} & \mathbf{V}_{22} & \cdots & \mathbf{V}_{2N} \\ \cdots & \cdots & \cdots & \cdots \\ \mathbf{V}_{M1} & \mathbf{V}_{M2} & \cdots & \mathbf{V}_{MN} \end{pmatrix} \triangleq (\mathbf{V}_1, \mathbf{V}_2, ..., \mathbf{V}_N) \quad (\mathbf{V}_i \in R^{4M}) \qquad (5)$$

CDM contains most structural information of curve support region. However, it can not be considered as a curve descriptor since its size still varies with curve length. To achieve descriptors independent of curve length, the first four order moments are used, and a vector with $16M$ dimensions can be attained here: $(\mathbf{M}_1^T, \mathbf{M}_2^T, \mathbf{M}_3^T, \mathbf{M}_4^T)$, where,

$$\mathbf{M}_1 = \frac{1}{N} \sum_i^N (\mathbf{V}_i - \mathbf{M}(\mathbf{V})), \mathbf{M}_2 = \frac{1}{N} \sum_i^N (\mathbf{V}_i - \mathbf{M}(\mathbf{V}))^2$$

$$\mathbf{M}_3 = \frac{1}{N} \sum_i^N (\mathbf{V}_i - \mathbf{M}(\mathbf{V}))^3, \mathbf{M}_4 = \frac{1}{N} \sum_i^N (\mathbf{V}_i - \mathbf{M}(\mathbf{V}))^4$$

$$\mathbf{M}(\mathbf{V}) = \frac{1}{N} \sum_i^N \mathbf{V}_i$$

Then, in order to make the descriptor invariant to linear changes of illumination, these Moment vectors are normalized to unit norm respectively. Finally, by concatenating these vectors into a single vector, a descriptor called Harris Moment-based curve descriptor (HMCD) can be attained here:

$$\mathbf{HMCD}(C) = \left(\frac{\mathbf{M}_1^T}{\|\mathbf{M}_1\|} \frac{\mathbf{M}_2^T}{\|\mathbf{M}_2\|} \frac{\mathbf{M}_3^T}{\|\mathbf{M}_3\|} \frac{\mathbf{M}_4^T}{\|\mathbf{M}_4\|} \right)^T \in R^{16M} \qquad (6)$$

To reduce the influence of non-linear illumination, for the same reason as [1], each value of the unit vector is limited no larger than 0.2, which means that matching the magnitudes for large gradients is no longer as important, and that the distribution of orientations has greater influence. After restraining the maximum value of each dimension, HMCD is re-normalized to unit norm as a whole and the ultimate descriptor is achieved.

5 Experiments

In this section, we test the performance and robustness of HMCD by using it for curve and line matching on real image pairs.

Setup: HMCD descriptor with 144 dimensions is used here, which is computed by using 9 sub-regions with size of 5×5 pixels for each PSR. Euclidean distance between descriptors is used as the metric, and NNDR (Nearest and Next Distance Ratio) which has become the most popular criterion for point matching, is used as our curve matching criterion. Besides using the NNDR criterion of 0.8, a simple global threshold of 0.55 is also used in experiments.

Curve segmentations are detected by using the Canny edge detector and then removing junctions in edges. Line segments used in experiments are extracted using the method proposed in [4]: firstly Canny edge detector is used to extract edges, then edges are split at points with high curvature. Finally segments with length less than 20 pixels are discarded and lines are fitted to the split edges using the least squares technique.

Results: Figure 2 shows four examples of HMCD-based curve matching. For pair (a), there exists a rotation and a little viewpoint change between two images. 98 curves are matched and all the matches are correct (b). On the second pair (c) of two fresco images, 175 curves are matched and 2 match is incorrect (d).The two images in pair (e) are captured under different viewpoint and obviously large affine distortion exists between them. 93 curves are matched and 5 matches is incorrect (f). As for the last pair (g), 92 curves are matched and 6 match is incorrect (h).

As a special case of curve, lines can certainly be matched by HMCD descriptor proposed in this paper. Figure 3 provides four results of line matching. The two images in the first three groups (a)(c)(e) are captured under different viewpoints, which results in rotation and affine changes. It can be seen from the results, HMCD can be competent for robust line matching under rotation and affine changes. As for the last image pair, it can be seen from the result (h) that, though there exists obvious occlusion between two images, HMCD can still work effectively with a high correct ratio.

The experiments illustrate that HMCD performs great and robust for both curve matching and line matching. Comparatively, HMCD can attain a higher correct ratio for curve matching than for line matching, and this can be explained by that curves usually have support regions with richer texture than lines.

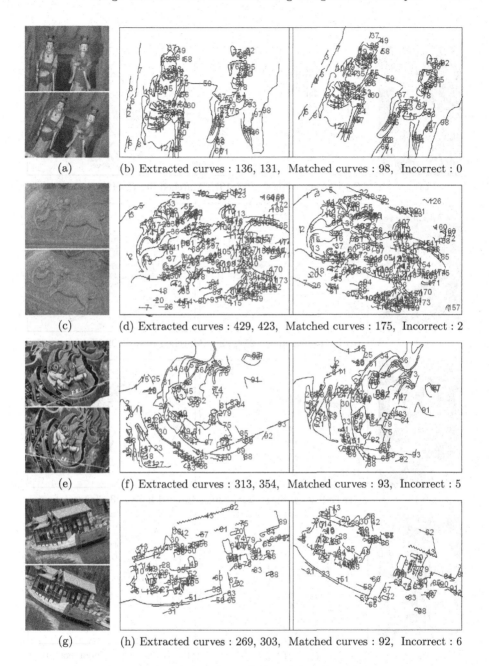

(a)

(b) Extracted curves : 136, 131, Matched curves : 98, Incorrect : 0

(c)

(d) Extracted curves : 429, 423, Matched curves : 175, Incorrect : 2

(e)

(f) Extracted curves : 313, 354, Matched curves : 93, Incorrect : 5

(g)

(h) Extracted curves : 269, 303, Matched curves : 92, Incorrect : 6

Fig. 2. Curve matching results using HMCD descriptor (Image pairs (c)(g) are provided by [2], the size of all images is 640 × 480)

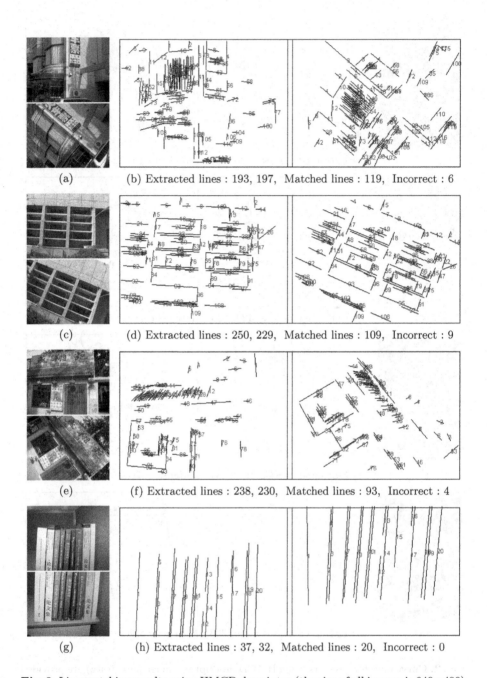

(a)

(b) Extracted lines : 193, 197, Matched lines : 119, Incorrect : 6

(c)

(d) Extracted lines : 250, 229, Matched lines : 109, Incorrect : 9

(e)

(f) Extracted lines : 238, 230, Matched lines : 93, Incorrect : 4

(g)

(h) Extracted lines : 37, 32, Matched lines : 20, Incorrect : 0

Fig. 3. Line matching results using HMCD descriptor (the size of all images is 640×480)

6   Conclusions

This paper reports a novel and robust descriptor for curve matching (including line matching), which can be used for automatic wide baseline stereo matching. The main contribution of this work is that our HMCD based matching is fully automatic, and can work without any prior knowledge about the scene or camera positions. The experiments show that HMCD descriptor is very effective and robust for curve and line matching. Up to now, our HMCD descriptor is not scale-invariant,and making multi-scales analysis will be one of our future work directions.

References

1. Lowe, D.G.: Distinctive image features from scale-invariant key-points. International Journal of Computer Vision 60(2), 91–110 (2006)
2. Mikolajczyk, K., Schmid, C.: A performance evaluation of local descriptors. IEEE Transactions on Pattern Analysis and Machine Intelligence 60(2), 91–110 (2006)
3. Mikolajczyk, K., Tuytelaars, T., Schmid, C., Zisserman, A.: A comparison of affine region detectors. International Journal of Computer Vision 27(10), 1615–1630 (2005)
4. Herbert, B., Vittorio, F., Luc, V.G.: Wide-Baseline Stereo Matching with Line Segments. In: IEEE International Conference on Computer Vision and Pattern Recognition (2005)
5. Lourakis, M.I.A., Halkidis, S.T., Orphanoudakis, S.C.: Matching Disparate Views of Planar Surfaces Using Projective Invariants. Image and Vision Computing 18(9), 673–683 (2005)
6. Schmid, C., Zisserman, A.: Automatic line matching across views. In: IEEE International Conference on Computer Vision and Pattern Recognition (1997)
7. Schmid, C., Zisserman, A.: The geometry and matching of lines and curves over multiple views. International Journal of Computer Vision 40(3), 199–233 (2000)
8. Deng, Y., Lin, X.Y.: A Fast Line Segment Based Dense Stereo Algorithm Using Tree Dynamic Programming. In: Leonardis, A., Bischof, H., Pinz, A. (eds.) ECCV 2006. LNCS, vol. 3953, pp. 201–212. Springer, Heidelberg (2006)
9. Mikolajczyk, K., Zisserman, A., Schmid, C.: Shape Recognition with Edge-Based Features. In: British Machine Vision Conference (2003)
10. Orrite, C., Herrero, J.E.: Shape Matching of Partially Occluded Curves Invariant Under Projective Transformation. Computer Vision and Image Understanding 93(1), 34–64 (2004)
11. Harris, C., Stephens, M.: A combined corner and edge detector. In: Proceeding 4th Alvey Vision Conference (1988)

Skeleton Graph Matching Based on Critical Points Using Path Similarity

Yao Xu, Bo Wang, Wenyu Liu, and Xiang Bai

Department of Electronics and Information Engineering,
Huazhong University of Science and Technology, Wuhan, 430074, China
{quickxu,wangbo.yunze}@gmail.com, {liuwy,xbai}@hust.edu.cn

Abstract. This paper proposes a novel graph matching algorithm based on skeletons and applies it to shape recognition based on object silhouettes. The main idea is to match the critical points (junction points and end points) on skeleton graphs by comparing the geodesic paths between end points and junction points of the skeleton. Our method is motivated by the fact that junction points can carry information about the global structure of an object while paths between junction points and end points can represent specific geometric information of local parts. Our method yields the promising accuracy rates on two shape datasets in the presence of articulations, stretching, boundary deformations, part occlusion and rotation.

Keywords: Skeleton, skeleton graph, graph matching, shape recognition, path similarity.

1   Introduction

Image matching is a fundamental aspect of many problems in computer vision, including object or scene recognition, solving for 3D structure from multiple images, stereo correspondence, and moving tracking [1]. In this paper, we focus on shape matching based on skeletal path similarity. Recent few years have witnessed a popular way in which skeleton is involved in the image matching problems. Integrating geometrical and topological feature of the object, skeleton (or Medial Axis) [2] plays an important role as a shape descriptor for object recognition. However, the fact that the topological structure of skeleton trees or graphs of similar objects may be completely different probably remains the most challenging aspect due to the sensitivity of skeletonization. This fact is illustrated in Figure 1,the objects from the same class may have different skeleton graph because of the instability of the critical points (junction points and endpoints). Thus some nontrivial edit operations (cut, merge, et al.) are inevitable to match skeleton graphs or trees. This paper presents a novel scheme for skeleton-based shape similarity measure. The proposed method is based on the similarity of shortest paths between end points and junction points of the pruned skeletons [3] to overcome the limitations mentioned above.

H. Zha, R.-i. Taniguchi, and S. Maybank (Eds.): ACCV 2009, Part III, LNCS 5996, pp. 456–465, 2010.

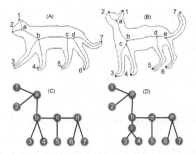

Fig. 1. Visually similar shapes in (A) and (B) have very different skeleton graph in (C) and (D)

As a preprocess for skeleton matching, we do the merge operation on the junction points of each skeleton based on their local context similarity. Then, the junction points and end points of different skeletons are matched in one-to-one correspondence with minimal cost, and the redundant junction points are not considered (cut operation on junction points). The penalty cost will be added for each redundant endpoint in order to compute the final shape similarity.

In section 2, the background of the related methods will be discussed. The way to match shapes based on the similarity of the skeleton paths between endpoints and junction points is introduced in section 3 and section 4. In section 5, the experimental results and analysis on two different datasets have been provided. At last, conclusion and future work are drawn out in section 6.

2   Related Work

The skeleton-based recognition methods are usually based on the graph or tree representation of the skeletons. Since the skeleton or medial axis is always organized into an Attributed-Relation Graph(ARG), the similarity between two objects can be measured by matching their ARGs. Zhu and Yuille [4] matched the skeleton graphs of objects using a branch-bounding method that was limited to motionless objects. Shock graph was a kind of ARG proposed by Siddiqi et al. [5], which was based on Shock Grammar. The distance between subgraphs was measured by comparing the eigenvalues of their adjacency matrices. Sebastian et al. have presented a scheme to compute the edit distance between the shock graphs [6]. Liu et al. [7,8] can deal with the problem when the two shapes have different amount of junction points in their skeleton graph. Demirci et al. transform weighted graphs into metric trees for accurate matching [9]. Aslan and Tari proposed an unconventional approach to shape recognition using unconnected skeletons in the course level [10]. Bai et al. proposed a method to match ARGs based on the shortest paths between endpoints [11]. The approach does not require any editing of the skeleton graph, however, only endpoints were used for matching in their framework without using the explicit structure of parts.

Motivated by the skeletal path representation [11], our proposed method utilizes the shortest paths between all the pairs of end points and junction points to represent a context of local structures. Utilization of merge or cut operation similar to [8] in matching phase is used for finding the optimal correspondence between the critical points on different shapes.

3   Shape Representation with Skeleton Paths

In this paper, all the skeletons for shape matching are extracted and pruned by the method introduced in [3].

A critical point (endpoint/junction point) can be called a node (end node /junction node) in a skeleton graph, and the shortest paths between every pair of nodes are represented as sequence of radii of the maximal disks at corresponding skeleton points [11]. If there is no other junction node on the path between an end node and a junction node, the end node and the junction node is said to be connected. The shortest path between a pair of end nodes on a skeleton graph is called a **end-to-end path**. The path between an end node and the nearest junction node on a skeleton graph is called a **junction-to-end path**. In addition,the path between different junction nodes is called a **junction-to-junction path**. We show a few example skeleton paths in Fig 2. Let sp denotes a skeleton path. We sample the path sp with M equidistant points, which are all skeleton points. Let $R(t)$ denotes the radius of the maximal disk at the skeleton point with index t in sp. Let L denotes the length of sp, R denotes a vector of the radius of the maximal disks centered at the M sample skeleton points on sp:

$$R = (R(t))_{t=1,2,\ldots,M} = (r_1, r_2, \ldots, r_M) \tag{1}$$

In our method, the radius $R(S)$ is approximated with the values of the distance transform $DT(s)$ at each skeleton point s. Suppose there are N_0 pixels in the

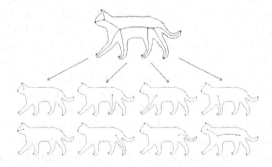

Fig. 2. Some of local paths (in red) in the cat's skeleton

original shape S. To make the proposed method invariant to the scale, $R(S)$ is normalized in the following way:

$$R(S) = \frac{DT(s)}{\frac{1}{N_0} \sum_{i=1}^{N_0} DT(s_i)} \qquad (2)$$

where $s_i(i = 1, 2, \ldots, N_0)$ varies over all N_0 pixels in the shape. The shape dissimilarity between two paths is called a path distance. If R and R' denote the vectors of radius of two paths sp and respectively, L and L' denote the lengths of the two paths sp and respectively, then the path distance pd between sp and textslsp' is:

$$pd(sp, sp') = \sum_{i=1}^{M} \frac{(r_i - r_i')^2}{r_i + r_i'} + \alpha \frac{(L - L')^2}{|L + L'|} \qquad (3)$$

Where α is a weight factor. In order to make the representation scale invariant, the path lengths are normalized.

4 Matching Nodes Using Skeleton Paths

Compared to the method in [11] that only used the end-to-end skeleton paths for matching the correspondence between end nodes, we match both junction nodes and end nodes using path similarity. The basic idea here is to match the junction nodes first using path similarity, then end nodes are matched using path similarity based on the correspondence of junction nodes. This is reasonable, since junction points always contain the important structure information for connecting the local meaningful parts of an object, and matching end nodes are easy when the correct correspondence of junction points are obtained. However, a challenging problem is the fact that junction nodes may not be stable, see example in Fig. 1. In order to solve this problem we do the merging operations based on the path contexts of junction nodes before matching process and the cut operations in matching process. In total, our method consists of two steps: mergence of junction nodes, matching critical nodes.

4.1 Mergence of Junction Nodes

We assume there are N junction nodes in a skeleton. The cost to merge two junction nodes V_i and V_j is defined as following:

$$cost(V_i, V_j) = \sum_{k=1}^{N} pd(sp_{i,k}, sp_{j,k}) \qquad (4)$$

where $sp_{i,k}$, $sp_{j,k}$ denote the junction-to-end paths between every end node and junction nodes V_i and V_j, and k is the index of the end nodes in a counterclockwise direction. And the merging condition is as following:

$$cost(V_i, V_j) < N * \delta \qquad (5)$$

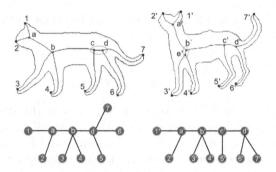

Fig. 3. The merge of junction nodes of two cats skeletons

where δ is a small value as a threshold. Any pair of junction nodes that satisfy the condition (5) are merged. Fig 3 illustrates an example of the merging process above. As Fig 3 shows, junction nodes c and d are merged as a single junction node d because they satisfy condition (5), so are b' and e'. In our implementation, we didn't merge the junction nodes c and d to one node actually. Instead only one of them will be selected for junction nodes matching.

4.2 Matching Critical Nodes

Let G and G' denote two graphs to be matched, and let the numbers of the junction nodes in G and G' be K and N, respectively. Here we assume $K \leqslant N$. It is easy to know that there are $C_N^K * K!$ kinds of matching cases and our aim is to obtain the optimal one-to-one matching with the minimal cost. In the case that the two graphs have different numbers of junction nodes, cut operation will be implemented by neglecting the redundant junction nodes. Specifically, we eliminate the junction nodes which are not matched. For example, there are one junction nodes V_1 in G, two junction nodes V_1', V_2' in G' , so 2 kinds of possible matching cases exist:

$$V_1 \longleftrightarrow V_1' \text{ or } V_1 \longleftrightarrow V_2'$$

In the former, V_2' is eliminated and in the latter one V_1' is eliminated. Of course, in most cases,more complex matching situations will occur. In Fig 4, after matching junction nodes and cut operation(in this case, the junction point d has been eliminated), critical points (in this case a,b,c) are obtained. Then, we get the common structure of the matched skeletons,and the critical nodes are in one-to-one correspondence.

For any pair of matched junction nodes V and V',suppose the numbers of end nodes adjacent to V and V' are m and n respectively. We assume $m \leqslant n$. Thus there are $C_n^m * m!$ kinds of matching choices. In this way, we can get U kinds of possible matching choices. Each matching choice has a matching cost and our aim is to obtain the one with the minimal cost. Assume there are P_k matched paths and Q_k unmatched paths in the kth matching choice(k is the index of matching choices), hence our model can be represented as following:

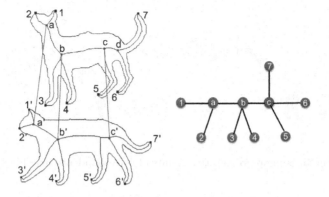

Fig. 4. Critical points achieved after junction node matching

$$\arg\min\left(cost_k\right), k = 1, 2, ..., U$$

$$cost_k = (1 + Q_k/P_k) \sum_{i=1}^{P_k} pd(sp_i, sp_i') \tag{6}$$

where sp_i and sp_i' represent skeleton paths in the graphs to be matched, Q_k/P_k functions as a penalty factor if unmatched skeleton paths exist.

5   Experiments

In this section, we evaluate the performance of the proposed method in two parts: matching the critical nodes in the skeleton graphs, and the recognition performance of our method on two standard shape databases.

5.1   Correspondence Matching

To verify the accuracy of our method, shapes of various objects are matched and some representative results are shown. Besides the matching of two horses in Fig 5.(A) ,we test our method on several other examples. Since the structure of the horse is similar to the cat, our matching process finds the correct correspondence shown in Fig 5.(B). Fig 6 illustrates that the proposed method works well in the presence of articulation. Fig 7 also shows some matching results in the presence of occlusion or part missing. In Fig 7.(A) there is protrusion on the back of a cat, and in Fig 7.(B) two legs of a horse were removed. It demonstrates that the proposed method is able to obtain a correct correspondence even if parts of a shape are altered.

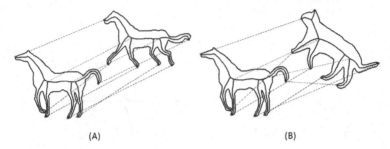

Fig. 5. Some representative results of correspondence matching

Fig. 6. The correspondence in the presence of articulation

Fig. 7. The correspondence in the presence of occlusion or part missing

5.2   Robustness of Recognition

To evaluate the recognition performance of the proposed method, we test it on Aslan and Tari's two databases [10]. The first dataset includes 14 classes of articulated shapes with 4 shapes in each class, as shown in Fig 8. We use each shape in this database as a query. Several representative results are shown in Fig 9, where five most similar shapes are shown for the queries. Below each shape is the cost to match with the query. For each query, a perfect result should have three most similar shapes in the same class as the query. The distance in red marks an error where this is not the case.Encouragingly, the recognition rate on this dataset is 99.4% since there are only 1 errors in 168 query results. Moreover, we can easily observe that the wrong result is very similar to the query. For this dataset, we use parameters $M = 50, \alpha = 45$.

Fig. 8. Alan and Tari database [10] with 56 shapes

Table 1. Retrieval results on Alan and Tari 56 database [10]

Algorithm	1st	2nd	3rd
IDSC+DP [12]	53	51	38
Path Similarity [11]	55	55	53
Ours	56	56	55

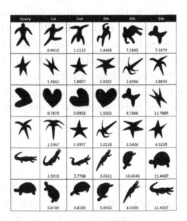

Fig. 9. Selected results of the proposed method on Alan and Tari database [10].Distance in red is the only error.

In Table 1, the result by the proposed method is compared to the result by other two recent shape matching methods. The proposed method performs better both than Inner Distance [12] in non-rigid deformations and Path Similarity [11], since we use the information of the junction nodes explicitly.

Our method is also tested on another bigger database provided by Aslan and Tari [13]. The database consists of 180 shapes which have 30 classes with 6 shapes in each class. For each shape, we check whether the 5 closest matches are in the same class as the query. Some typical results are shown in Fig 10. In the whole database, there are only 24 errors in 900 query results, so the recognition rate is 97.3%. The numbers of correct shapes for all 900 queries among the 1st,

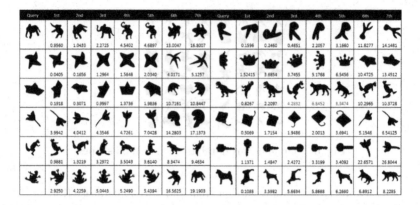

Fig. 10. Selected results of the proposed method on Tari'180 database [10]. Distance in red are errors

2nd, 3rd,4th, 5th closest matches are 180,179,174,175,168. Here, parameters are $M = 50, \alpha = 55$. We now analyze the computational complexity of the proposed method. Let M_i be the number of end nodes in the graph G_i, and let N_i be the number of junction nodes in G_i. Since the implementations in section 4.2 and 4.3 cost the most time, the time complexity of our method is approximately $O(M_i! * N_i!)$. However, since the number of junction nodes N_i has usually been significantly reduced to less than 7 after the merging process in section 4.1, the average time for matching per pair of shapes is very small. In this experiment, it is only 0.8 second.

6   Conclusion

In this paper, we propose a novel method to match skeleton graphs. The most important contribution is the merge and cut operation on junction nodes of skeleton graphs. The effect of these operations is the introduction of the structural information of the skeleton, which is very helpful in matching. As a result, our method is simple and efficient in correspondence matching even in the presence of occlusion and articulation. The experiment shows that the merge and cut process of junction nodes in our method have advantages over the method based only on path similarity. However, in our framework we didn't consider the case for many-to-one matching, which may be a limitation. In the future, our work will focus on classification based on the construction and unsupervised learning of tree union of skeletons.

Acknowledgement

This work was in part supported by Education Ministry Doctoral Research Foundation of China (No. 20070487028) and NSFC (No. 60873127). Xiang Bai was supported by MSRA Fellowship.

References

1. Lowe, D.G.: Distinctive image features from scale-invariant keypoints. IJCV 60, 91–110 (2004)
2. Blum, H.: Biological shape and visual science. J. Theor. Biol. 38, 205–287 (1973)
3. Bai, X., Latecki, L.J., Liu, W.Y.: Skeleton pruning by contour partitioning with discrete curve evolution. IEEE Trans. PAMI 29, 449–462 (2007)
4. Zhu, S.C., Yuille, A.L.: Forms: A flexible object recognition and modeling system. IJCV 20, 187–212 (1996)
5. Siddiqi, K., Shkoufandeh, A., Dickinson, S., Zucker, S.: Shock graphs and shape matching. In: ICCV, pp. 222–229 (1998)
6. Sebastian, T.B., Klein, P.N., Kimia, B.B.: Recognition of shapes by editing their shock graphs. IEEE Trans. PAMI 26, 550–571 (2004)
7. Liu, T., Geiger, D.: Approximate tree matching and shape similarity. In: ICCV, pp. 456–462 (1999)
8. Geiger, D., Liu, T., Kohn, R.: Representation and self-similarity of shapes. IEEE Trans. PAMI 25, 86–99 (2003)
9. Demirci, F., Shokoufandeh, A., Keselman, Y., Bretzner, L., Dickinson, S.: Object recognition as many-to-many feature matching. IJCV 69, 203–222 (2006)
10. Aslan, C., Tari, S.: An axis based representation for recognition. In: ICCV, pp. 1339–1346 (2005)
11. Bai, X., Latecki, L.J.: Path similarity skeleton graph matching. IEEE Trans. PAMI 30, 1282–1292 (2008)
12. Ling, H., Jacobs, D.W.: Shape classification using inner-distance. IEEE Trans. PAMI 29, 286–299 (2007)
13. Baseski, E., Erdem, A., Tari, S.: Dissimilarity between two skeletal trees in a context. Pattern Recognition 42, 370–385 (2009)

A Statistical-Structural Constraint Model for Cartoon Face Wrinkle Representation and Generation

Ping Wei, Yuehu Liu, Nanning Zheng, and Yang Yang

Xi'an Jiaotong University, 710049 Xi'an, China
tradic@163.com, liuyh@mail.xjtu.edu.cn,
nnzheng@mail.xjtu.edu.cn, yyang@aiar.xjtu.edu.cn

Abstract. This paper presents a statistical-structural constraint model to represent and generate cartoon face wrinkles. A weighted constraint cost is defined to measure constraint of age, facial structure and parameter on wrinkles. Then wrinkle generation model is built in the sense of minimum constraint cost. Through clustering, age constraint and its parameters are learned from wrinkle samples with respect to regions and age group. According to facial structure, region-center wrinkles are computed to realize structural constraint on wrinkles. Having obtained the two constraints and parameters, generation model is optimized to produce wrinkles. Experimental results have demonstrated validity of the model.

Keywords: Cartoon face wrinkle, age, facial structure.

1 Introduction

Facial cartoon[1][2] is an interesting rendering form for human face, which has been widely used in multimedia world. They use concise elements like shape, curve, and contour to render face[1][2]. However, most of them fail to pay enough attention to wrinkles that are essentially important for expressing rich variances of face. Proper wrinkles can largely enhance expressive effect of cartoon face. Thus, adding proper wrinkles to cartoon face is necessary as well as significant work.

There are two challenges for this work. First, direct information provided by cartoon face is sparse. Usually, only facial structure information like shape and contour is available. Second, wrinkle itself has no regular forms. Wrinkle formation is a complex process that is affected by various factors like aging and facial muscle movement[3][4], which lead to high non-structure and uncertainty of wrinkles' attributes. How to represent wrinkle and simulate formation with sparse facial information are two key problems for wrinkle generation.

This paper presents a statistical-structural constraint method to represent and generate cartoon face wrinkles. Wrinkle curve is represented with feature points and PCA model[5][6]. Similar to the AAM[6], constraint cost is defined, which characterize constraint of age, facial structure and parameter. Wrinkle generation model is built in the sense of minimum constraint cost. Age constraint and parameters are learned from wrinkle samples through statistic and clustering. Structural constraint and parameters

H. Zha, R.-i. Taniguchi, and S. Maybank (Eds.): ACCV 2009, Part III, LNCS 5996, pp. 466–474, 2010.
© Springer-Verlag Berlin Heidelberg 2010

are computed according to facial structure. Having realized the two constraint models, generation model is optimized to produce cartoon face wrinkles.

2 Related Work

Modeling Wrinkles. Amounts of work have been done to model wrinkles. Zijian Xu et al[7] divide face to 16 zones to process facial details and wrinkles. They build a dictionary of wrinkle primitives learned from labeled wrinkle patches using clustering. Using inference and optimization, facial details and wrinkles are reconstructed on realistic or sketchy faces. To add proper wrinkles to aging faces, Jinli Suo et al[8] divides face plane into 8 zones and builds wrinkle database using labeled wrinkle curves for each age group and facial zones. Yu Zhang[9]determine 3D expressive wrinkle's shape and amplitude based on face anatomy model. Yin Wu et al [10] simulates 3D wrinkles through changing attributes of facial layers based on muscle movement. Though those methods achieve good results in their applications, they are inapplicable to generate cartoon face wrinkles with sparse information of cartoon face.

Representing Shapes. The ASM[5] use feature points to represent shape of objects, and align shape vector to form shape models. The AAM[6] use PCA method to parameterize facial shape, then build fit function to represent prior position constraint, which is optimized to reconstruct face. Zijian Xu et al[7] represent facial details as parameters of image primitive type, rotation, translation, scale, etc. Jinli Suo et al[8] represent wrinkle geometry with parameters of wrinkle number, position, orientation and scale.

3 Wrinkle Representation and Generation Model

Wrinkle representation and generation are closely related. In this section, we first build representation of wrinkles. Based on that, the generation model is given.

Due to biologic property of human face, wrinkles in different regions of face have different forms. So, face plane is always divided into subregions[7][8]. We improve the subdivision in paper [7][8] and redefine 11 wrinkle regions on face according to the facial contour feature points manually labeled or extracted using the ACM[11]. They are shown in figure 1.

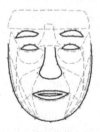

Fig. 1. Facial wrinkle regions

As one muscle structure may influence different types of wrinkles, some subregions may overlap. The significance of wrinkle regions is that they provide a representation of facial structure related to wrinkle distribution.

Following the shape representation method of the ASM[5] and AAM[6], and wrinkle position representation way of paper[7][8], we use feature points vector to typify wrinkle curve data and PCA method to parameterize it. Suppose $(x_1, y_1), (x_2, y_2), ...(x_N, y_N)$ are N nearly even-spaced coordinates points on wrinkle curve, and the shape vector is $\mathbf{w} = (x_1, x_2...x_N, y_1, y_2...y_N)^T$. Using PCA method, $\mathbf{w}$ is parameterized as:

$$\mathbf{v} = (\mathbf{b}, t_x, t_y, \theta, s) \tag{1}$$

where $\mathbf{b}$ is a vector that typify coefficients of trained wrinkle shape bases. t_x, t_y, θ and s respectively typify translation of x and y direction, rotation, and scale of similarity transformation that align the original wrinkle $\mathbf{w}$ to a reference wrinkle with least squares solution[5].

$\mathbf{v}$ is parameterized representation of wrinkles. Wrinkle data $\mathbf{w}$ can be reconstructed with PCA method and similarity transformation from $\mathbf{v}$.

Aging and facial muscle movement are two key factors that lead to facial wrinkles[3][4]. Muscle movement can be reflected through facial structure. So, a wrinkle is constrained by age feature and facial structure. Suppose $\mathbf{w}_A$, $\mathbf{w}_R$ and μ respectively typifies the parameter of constraint of age, facial structure and wrinkle parameters. Similar to AAM[6], we define constraint cost to measure constraint effect on wrinkles. The cost $C(\mathbf{v})$ is:

$$C(\mathbf{v}) = \alpha D_A(\mathbf{w}_v, \mathbf{w}_A) + \beta D_R(\mathbf{w}_v, \mathbf{w}_R) + \gamma D_P(\mathbf{v}, \mu) \tag{2}$$

where α, β, γ is positive weighting factors, $\mathbf{w}_v$ is wrinkle data that is reconstructed from $\mathbf{v}$. $D_A(\cdot)$, $D_R(\cdot)$ and $D_P(\cdot)$ are distance measurement between two vectors.

The smaller the cost is, the better the constraint effect is. Thus, the wrinkle $\mathbf{v}^*$ in the sense of minimum constraint cost is:

$$\mathbf{v}^* = \arg\min C(\mathbf{v}) \tag{3}$$

$D_A(\mathbf{w}_v, \mathbf{w}_A)$ and $D_R(\mathbf{w}_v, \mathbf{w}_R)$ respectively reflects age and facial structure constraint. $D_P(\mathbf{v}, \mu)$ typifies constraint of parameters. In the following section, we will learn and compute the constraints on wrinkles.

4   Learning Constraint of Age

Wrinkles on different faces in the same age group have common characteristics. For instance, they usually distribute around a center. This center characterizes distinct distributive feature of wrinkles in an age group. We define this 'center' as age-center wrinkle. Age-center wrinkle can be learned from wrinkle curve samples that are labeled on facial images of the same age group. Before learning, rude samples are aligned to reference face according to wrinkle regions with similarity transformation.

4.1 Learning Age-Center Wrinkles

Burt et al[12] compute average face image of each age bracket as central features of the faces in this age bracket. Similar to that, we use age-center wrinkles to reflect age constraint on wrinkles. They are learned from wrinkle samples in the same wrinkle regions of different faces in the same age group. Wrinkles with common distributive features are supposed to be clustered from samples. Translation parameter of each wrinkle is used to cluster wrinkle samples. Translation parameter $l = (t_x, t_y)$ typifies relative translation to reference wrinkle from the wrinkle whose scale and rotation are aligned. It can cluster wrinkles with similar position and direction considering that wrinkles in the same class have similar positions, directions and scales.

Clustering is operating with respect to age group and wrinkle regions. Suppose there are Q facial images in the same age group A. All wrinkle samples in wrinkle region R of the j-th face is: $\mathbf{V}_j = \{(\mathbf{b}_i, t_{xi}, t_{yi}, \theta_i, s_i), i = 1...M_j\}(j = 1, 2...Q)$, where M_j is the number of wrinkles. Through clustering, the wrinkle samples are classified into K clusters according to translation parameters $l = (t_x, t_y)$. K can be set according to experience. Clusters with too small samples (for example, less than 2) are regarded as noise and discarded.

Suppose the K clusters are $G_i : \{\mathbf{w}_j^i, j = 1, 2...M_{Gi}\}(i = 1, 2, ...K)$, where $\mathbf{w}_j^i$ is wrinkle sample of cluster G_i, and $M_{Gi}(i = 1, 2...K)$ is the number of samples in the i-th cluster. The average values of wrinkles in each cluster are denoted as $\Omega_A = [\omega_1, \omega_2, ...\omega_K]$. Ω_A is just the age-center wrinkle matrix. $\omega_i(i = 1, 2, ...K)$ is the average value of i-th cluster, which represents the i-th age-center wrinkle in region R of age group A. Figure 2 shows part of wrinkle samples on right cheek of old people, and figure 3 illustrates results of clustering those wrinkle samples, where data points are connected for clarity.

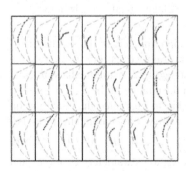
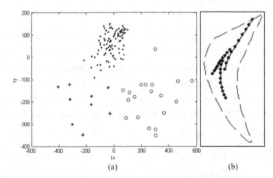

(a)   (b)

Fig. 2. Wrinkle samples (drawn on the region of mean face)

Fig. 3. Learning age-center wrinkles. (a) Translation parameters and clustering. (b) Age-center wrinkles.

4.2 Measurement of Age Constraint on Wrinkles

Age-center wrinkle Ω_A typify the mean distribution of an age group A, and characterize age constraint on wrinkles. For a wrinkle $\mathbf{w}$ of age group A, similar to AAM[6], measurement of age constraint is rewritten as:

$$D_A = (\mathbf{w} - \boldsymbol{\omega}_A)^{\mathrm{T}} \Sigma_A^{-1} (\mathbf{w} - \boldsymbol{\omega}_A) \tag{4}$$

where $\boldsymbol{\omega}_A$ is one of the elements of Ω_A, i.e. age-center wrinkle. Σ_A^{-1} is weighting matrix, and Σ_A can be trained as variance from wrinkle samples.

5   Computing Constraint of Facial Structure

Age-center wrinkles characterize common distributive feature of wrinkles in an age group. Due to discrepancy of individual face, wrinkles are different on various faces even in the same age group. This fact reflects constraint of various facial structures on wrinkles. According to biomechanics, wrinkle forms when muscle contracts[13]. Repeated movement of muscle fibres will cause everlasting wrinkles. Essentially, wrinkles are also fibers that are constrained by neighbor fibres. The closer they are, the stronger the constrained effect is. Figure 4 simply shows analysis of a wrinkle $\mathbf{w}$. E_1 and E_2 are projection of the wrinkle on edges of muscle fibers.

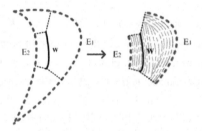

Fig. 4. Facial structure constraint on wrinkles. Red thick dashed lines typify muscle fibre edges, black dashed lines typify projection operation. Orange dot dash lines typify muscle fibres.

Edges of wrinkle regions defined in section 3 are approximately in the similar direction of muscle fibres, so we can take the edges as constraint edges. For an assumptive wrinkle $\mathbf{w}$, it distributes around a center that is determined by constraint edges of facial structure. Though the constrained correlation between the edges and the 'center' may be complex, we can approximate it with linear relationship to guarantee the condition on edges. Suppose E_1 and E_2 have the same data form with $\mathbf{w}$. Positional distances between $\mathbf{w}$ and E_1, E_2 are defined as $d_1 = \| l - l_1 \|_2$, and $d_2 = \| l - l_2 \|_2$, where $l = (t_x, t_y)$, $l_1 = (t_{x1}, t_{y1})$, $l_2 = (t_{x2}, t_{y2})$ are respectively translation parameters of $\mathbf{w}$, E_1 and E_2. According to above analysis, region-center wrinkle with respect to $\mathbf{w}$ is defined as:

$$\boldsymbol{\omega}_R = \frac{d_2}{d_1 + d_2} E_1 + \frac{d_1}{d_1 + d_2} E_2 \tag{5}$$

Wrinkle distributes around its region-center wrinkle under constraint of facial structure, and therefore $\boldsymbol{\omega}_R$ reflects the constraint of facial structure on wrinkles. Similar to D_A, measurement of facial structure constraint is:

$$D_R = (\mathbf{w} - \boldsymbol{\omega}_R)^{\mathrm{T}} \Sigma_R^{-1} (\mathbf{w} - \boldsymbol{\omega}_R) \tag{6}$$

where Σ_R^{-1} is weighting matrix. $\boldsymbol{\omega}_R$ is the region-center wrinkle.

6 Wrinkle Generation and Experimental Results

Having obtained age and facial structure constraint, we can generate wrinkles on cartoon face. Substituting (4) and (6) into (3), $\mathbf{v}^*$ is given as:

$$\mathbf{v}^* = \arg\min\{\alpha(\mathbf{w} - \boldsymbol{\omega}_A)^{\mathrm{T}} \Sigma_A^{-1} (\mathbf{w} - \boldsymbol{\omega}_A) + \beta(\mathbf{w} - \boldsymbol{\omega}_R)^{\mathrm{T}} \Sigma_R^{-1} (\mathbf{w} - \boldsymbol{\omega}_R) \\ + \gamma(\mathbf{v} - \mu)^{\mathrm{T}} \Sigma_v^{-1} (\mathbf{v} - \mu)\} \tag{7}$$

where μ is average value of parameterized wrinkle samples, and Σ_v^{-1} is weighting matrix. $\mathbf{w}$ is reconstructed from $\mathbf{v}$, and $\boldsymbol{\omega}_R$ is computed according to $\mathbf{w}$. They are both the function of $\mathbf{v}$.

Due to the nonlinear operation in computing region-center wrinkle, we adopt a simplex search method[14] to optimize formula (7). Though it may not give global optimizing values, it can still be the optimal method if a good initial value is selected.

6.1 Data Preparation and Training

We have collected 100 facial images of young, middle-aged and old people respectively. In order to learn center wrinkles and variances of wrinkle samples, we manually label wrinkle curves on the 300 images. Those wrinkle regions in which the appearance frequency of wrinkle is less than 25% are removed. The data in those regions are regarded as noise data for a specific age. For example, in 100 samples of middle-aged people, there are only less 20 faces that appear little wrinkles in the region between eyebrows. Eventually, 1643 wrinkle samples with respect to 11 regions and 3 age groups are collected.

We assume that Σ_A and Σ_R are equal diagonal matrix, which are learned from wrinkle samples. Σ_v are assumed as diagonal matrix. μ is mean value of parameterized wrinkles. Σ_v and μ are learned from parameterized wrinkles. $\boldsymbol{\omega}_A$ is obtained in clustering. $\boldsymbol{\omega}_R$ is a variable related to $\mathbf{w}$, which is computed following $\mathbf{w}$.

It must be noted that generated wrinkle data with the model are discrete coordinate points of wrinkles as defined in section 3. The wrinkle curves are drawn by connecting those points.

6.2 Experiment 1: Wrinkle Adjustment by Facial Structure

Region-center wrinkle presents regulated forms of a known wrinkle under the constraint of facial structure. It can be used to adjusting abnormal wrinkles on a specific face, which is important in cartoon wrinkle rendering. For an assumptive abnormal wrinkle, the adjusted wrinkle is computed with formula (5).

Figure 5 shows assumptive wrinkles $\mathbf{w}$ on left cheek on a specific face and its adjusted wrinkles. We can see that adjusted wrinkles are more realistic and beautiful.

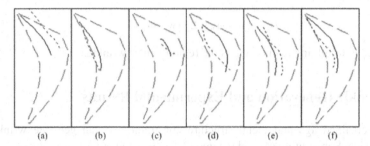

Fig. 5. Wrinkle adjustment by facial structure.(a)(b) Position adjustment.(c)(d) Abnormal shape adjustment.(e)(f) Smoothing irregular wrinkles. Red dashed lines typify facial wrinkle regions. Blue dot lines typify original wrinkles, and black real lines typify adjusted wrinkles.

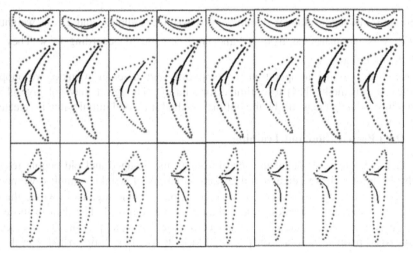

Fig. 6. Personalized wrinkles on various facial structures. The first line is generated wrinkles in left lower eyelid region. The second line is in the right cheek, and the third line is in the left outer canthus. Red dot lines typify the facial structure, and black real lines are wrinkles.

6.3 Experiment 2: Personalized Wrinkles on Different Faces

Wrinkles on different faces exhibit various forms even in the same age group. The generated wrinkles by our model can present rich variances in different facial structures. Here, we assume $\alpha = \beta = \gamma = 1$. Figure 6 shows some results in different facial structures of old people. The wrinkles exhibit personalities in different facial structures, which prove validity of our model.

6.4 Experiment 3: Generation of Cartoon Face Wrinkles

Figure 7 shows generated wrinkles in faces of three different age. In experiment, we assume $\alpha = \beta = \gamma = 1$. We first use the Personal Facial Cartoon Generation System[1][15] to generate sketchy and texture cartoon face, as Figure 7(b) and (d) shows, then add optimal wrinkles generated by our model. The figures show that generated wrinkles are vivid and expressive.

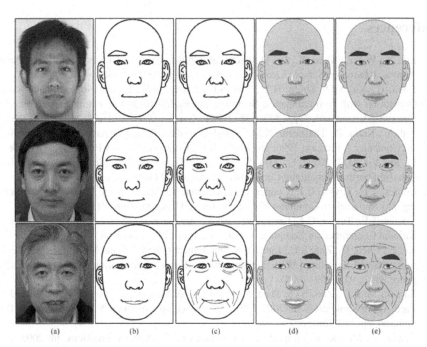

Fig. 7. Generation of cartoon face wrinkles.(a)Original facial images.(b) Sketchy cartoon face without wrinkles.(c) Sketchy cartoon face with wrinkles. (d)Texture cartoon face without wrinkles. (e) Texture cartoon face with wrinkles.

7 Discussion and Conclusion

We have presented a statistical-structural constraint model for cartoon face wrinkle representation and generation. Experimental results are expressive. This model can be used in facial aging, wrinkle extraction, facial expression and so on.

There are some limitations of this model, which are also the future work we should do. For the reason that the same number of generated wrinkles in the same age group and some times similarity of wrinkle regions of different people face, whole appearance of wrinkles on different faces in the same age group seem similar sometimes. Second, our model aims at adding 'proper' wrinkles for specific cartoon face. It is not proof of nature laws but approximation or intimation. Thus, added wrinkles are not always the same completely with wrinkles in the natural situation.

Aiming at those limitations, we will further research methods of generating more personalized and realistic wrinkles.

Acknowledgement

This work was supported by the NSF of China (No. 60775017) and the Research Fund for the Doctoral Program of Higher Education of China (No. 20060698025). The author would like to thank those teachers and students whose photos are used as experimental samples. The authors would also like to thank Zejian Yuan, Yang Wu and Wei Hu for their useful suggestions.

References

1. Liu, Y., Wu, Z., Shao, Y., Jia, D.: Face Cartoon Rendering-A Unified Cartoon Rendering Approach based on Sample Learning. In: Asia Graph 2008, pp. 146–149 (2008)
2. Chen, H., Xu, Y.Q., Shum, H.Y., Zhu, S.C., Zheng, N.N.: Example-based Facial Sketch Generation with Non-parametric Sampling. In: Eighth IEEE International Conference on Computer Vision, vol. 2, pp. 433–438 (2001)
3. Wu, Y., Kalra, P., Thalmann, N.M.: Simulation of Static and Dynamic Wrinkles of Skin. In: Computer Animation 1996, pp. 90–97. IEEE Computer Society Press, Geneva (1996)
4. Li, M., Yin, B.C., Kong, D., Luo, X.: Modeling Expressive Wrinkles of Face For Animation. In: Fourth International Conference on Image and Graphics, pp. 874–879 (2007)
5. Cootes, T.F., Taylor, C.J., Cooper, D.H., Graham, J.: Active Shape Models - Their Training and Application. Computer Vision and Image Understanding 61(1), 38–59 (1995)
6. Cootes, T.F., Taylor, C.J.: Constrained Active Appearance Models. In: Eighth IEEE International Conference on Computer Vision, vol. 1, pp. 748–754 (2001)
7. Xu, Z., Chen, H., Zhu, S.C., Luo, J.: A Hierarchical Compositional Model for Face Representation and Sketching. IEEE Transactions on Pattern Recognition and Machine Intelligence 30(6), 955–969 (2008)
8. Suo, J., Min, F., Zhu, S.C., Shan, S., Chen, X.: A Multi-Resolution Dynamic Model for Face Aging Simulation. In: 2007 IEEE Conference on Computer Vision and Pattern Recognition, pp. 1–8 (2007)
9. Zhang, Y.: Muscle-driven modeling of wrinkles for 3D facial expressions. In: 2008 IEEE International Conference on Multimedia & Expo., pp. 957–960 (2008)
10. Wu, Y., Thalmann, N.M., Thalmann, D.: A plastic-visco-elastic model for wrinkles in facial animation and skin aging. In: Second Pacific Conference on Computer Graphics and Applications, pp. 201–214 (1994)
11. Blake, A., Isard, M.: Active Contours: The Application of Techniques from Graphics, Vision, Control Theory and Statistics to Visual Tracking of Shapes in Motion. Springer, London (1998)
12. Burt, D.M., Perrett, D.I.: Perception of Age in Adult Caucasian Male Faces: Computer Graphic Manipulation of Shape and Colour Information. Proceedings of the Royal Society of London 259, 137–143 (1995)
13. Fung, Y.: Mechanical Properties of Living Tissues. Springer, New York (1993)
14. Lagarias, J.C., Reeds, J.A., Wright, M.H., Wright, P.E.: Convergence Properties of the Nelder-Mead Simplex Method in Low Dimensions. SIAM Journal of Optimization 9(1), 112–147 (1998)
15. Liu, Y., Su, Y., Wu, Z., Yang, Y.: Nature Face: A Cartoon Face Producer for Mobile Content Service. In: 1st International Workshop on Mobile Multimedia Processing, Florida (2008)

Spatially Varying Regularization of Image Sequences Super-Resolution

Yaozu An[1], Yao Lu[1], and Zhengang Zhai[1,2]

[1] Beijing Laboratory of Intelligent Information Technology, School of Computer,
Beijing Institute of Technology, Beijing 100081 China
[2] Air Defense Forces Command College, Zhengzhou 450052 China
{bitanyz,vis_yl,zz_gang}@bit.edu.cn

Abstract. This paper presents a spatially varying super-resolution approach that estimates a high-resolution image from the low-resolution image sequences and better removes Gaussian additive noise with high variance. Firstly, a spatially varying functional in terms of local mean residual is used to weight each low-resolution channel. Secondly, a newly adaptive regularization functional based on the spatially varying residual is determined within each low-resolution channel instead of the overall regularization parameter, which balances the prior term and fidelity residual term at each iteration. Experimental results indicate the obvious performance improvement in both PSNR and visual effect compared to non-channel-weighted method and overall-channel-weighted method.

Keywords: Super resolution, spatially varying weight, adaptive regularization functional, local mean residual.

1 Introduction

Due to imaging system's physical constraints, it is difficult to obtain high-resolution images in some applications. Super-resolution is a very good approach to resolve this problem. Super-resolution is to form a higher resolution image by means of multiple low-resolution images of the same scene or object and its applications can be widely found in a broad range of image and video processing task such as aerial photo, medical imaging, video surveillance etc [1].

Super resolution is an ill-posed problem and a number of estimation results satisfy the constraints of the observation model. The Tikhonov regularization formulation is an important research method to formulate the inverse problem well-posed and find the optimized solution, which can incorporate prior information easily. The choice of regularization parameter is the central issue and plays a very important role in the reconstruction process. So far, a number of approaches have been developed to address this problem, such as generalize cross validation (GCV) [6][7] and L-Curve [8]-[10]. However, the determination of the regularization parameter needs the prior knowledge about signal and noise and additional computation in a separate first step. The main disadvantage of using a constant regularization parameter is that edges cannot be preserved well when regularization is based on a smoothness assumption.

H. Zha, R.-i. Taniguchi, and S. Maybank (Eds.): ACCV 2009, Part III, LNCS 5996, pp. 475–484, 2010.
© Springer-Verlag Berlin Heidelberg 2010

To overcome this difficulty, References [2][3] modify regularization parameter itera-tively using an adaptively regularization functional at the same time with the restored image. An adaptive method based on different degree of registration error is used to determine the regularization parameter automatically in each low-resolution channel, which not only incorporates auto channel information but also cross channel informa-tion [4]. Reference [5] proposed a MAP-based image resolution enhancement with overall weight in terms of the cross-channel fidelity to each low-resolution image.

The disadvantage of non-channel-weighted regularization method is that the data residual term drops the difference of each channel's contribution and each low-resolution channel has an equal and constant weight during the entire reconstruction process. The overall-channel-weighted regularization method takes into account the difference of each channel's contribution but ignores the difference of different re-gions in one channel, such as the textured regions and the smoothing regions. We present a spatially varying super-resolution approach based on local mean residual, which can give different weights and regularization parameters in different regions and better removes the additive noise with high variance.

The rest of the paper is organized as follows. In section 2, the observation model is briefly presented; In section 3, we introduce the spatially varying super-resolution approach based on local mean residual with adaptive weights and regularization pa-rameters in different regions; Experimental result and discussion are presented in section 4, and conclusions are shown in section 5.

2   Observation Model

In most cases, the image degradation model can be described by a linear process. Assume that p observed low-resolution images, each of size $N_1 \times N_2$ and l_k represents the kth measured low-resolution image. The deterministic high-resolution image h is of size $LN_1 \times LN_2$ and L is the down-sampling factor. All vectors are ordered lexico-graphically and the degradation model can be represented by:

$$l_k = DBFh + n_k, k = 1,2,...,p \ . \tag{1}$$

where n_k represents random Gaussian zero mean noise with variance σ_k^2. F, B and D represent respectively geometric warp operation, space invariant blur operation and decimation operation.

Assume no prior information of the noise variance for each channel, and as in [4], the registration error noise has a Gaussian type pattern, and its standard deviation is proportional to the degree of the registration error. Reference [5] takes into account the registration error and gives different fidelity to each low-resolution channel. Hence the so-called inverse problem in (1) can be formulated using multi-channel method:

$$\hat{h} = \underset{h}{\operatorname{argmin}} \left\{ \sum_{k=1}^{p} \alpha_k \left(\left\| l_k - DBFh \right\|^2 + \lambda_k(h) \left\| Ch \right\| \right) \right\}, k = 1,2,...,p \ . \tag{2}$$

where $\left\| l_k - DBFh \right\|^2$ is the residual term of the kth low-resolution channel which enforces faithfulness of the solution to the data, and $\left\| Ch \right\|^2$ is the regularization term representing a prior information about the high-resolution image which measures the image singularity and enforces smoothness on the solution. $\lambda_k(h)$ is the regularization parameter within the kth low-resolution channel, and α_k is weight coefficient of the kth low-resolution channel. C denotes two-dimensional Laplacian high-pass filter.

3 Spatially Varying Regularization Reconstruction

The basic idea behind the proposed method is not only taking into account the difference of each channel's contribution but also considering the difference of different regions' contribution within one channel. For example, the local mean residual in the textured regions is larger than the one in the smoothing regions. So we propose a spatially varying super-resolution approach based on local mean residual, which can adaptively weight different regions in different channel and give different regularization parameter in different regions in one channel.

3.1 Spatially Varying Weight for Each Low-Resolution Channel

According to the properties in [5], the cross-channel weight is inversely proportional to the residual norm $\left\| l_k - DBFh \right\|^2$:

$$\alpha_k = \frac{p}{\sum\limits_{s=1}^{p} \left\{ \frac{1}{\left\| l_s - DBFh \right\|^2} \right\} \left\| l_k - DBFh \right\|^2} \quad \text{s.t.} \quad \sum\limits_{k=1}^{p} \alpha_k = p . \tag{3}$$

where p is the number of the low-resolution images. Equation (2) is non-channel-weighted regularization method when the weight coefficient of each low-resolution channel α_k equals to 1.

The purpose of this section is to show that a relatively simple modification of the above methods yields a spatially varying weight for each low-resolution channel. And the modified method can better remove the additive noise with high variance while preserve the texture information of the image. To obtain a spatially varying scheme, we generalize the residual term by imposing a mean window to get a piecewise local residual constraint. Let us define a measure first to which we refer as local residual:

$$R_k(x,y) = \sum\limits_{\bar{x}=1}^{N} \sum\limits_{\bar{y}=1}^{N} \left(l_k(\bar{x},\bar{y}) - \hat{l}(\bar{x},\bar{y}) \right)^2 w_{(x,y)}(\bar{x},\bar{y}) . \tag{4}$$

where $\hat{l}(\bar{x}, \bar{y})$ is the corresponding degradation of the high-resolution image in each channel and $R_k(x, y)$ is the local mean of the data residual term with size of $N_1 \times N_2$. $w_{(x,y)}(\bar{x}, \bar{y}) = w(|\bar{x} - x|, |\bar{x} - x|)$ is a normalized and radially symmetric smoothing window and subjects to

$$\sum_{\bar{x}=1}^{N} \sum_{\bar{y}=1}^{N} w_{(x,y)}(\bar{x}, \bar{y}) = 1 . \tag{5}$$

So the weight coefficient of each low-resolution channel $\alpha_k(x, y)$ can be rewritten as

$$\alpha_k(x, y) = \frac{p}{\sum_{s=1}^{p} \left\{ \frac{1}{R_k(x, y)} \right\} R_k(x, y)} . \tag{6}$$

In order to make the coordinates identical, we multiply R_k by D^T

$$LR_k = D^T R_k . \tag{7}$$

where LR_k is the nearest interpolation up-sample of R_k with size of $LN_1 \times LN_2$. Equation (6) can be represented as

$$\alpha_k(x, y) = \frac{p}{\sum_{s=1}^{p} \left\{ \frac{1}{LR_k(x, y)} \right\} LR_k(x, y)} . \tag{8}$$

3.2 Spatially Varying Regularization Functional in Each Low-Resolution Channel

A set theoretical (ST) approach [14][15] is used to formulate the image super-resolution problem. Assume the solution to (1) is smooth and this is achieved by

$$\|Ch\|^2 \leq E^2 . \tag{9}$$

where E^2 is a prescribed constant, which restricts the bound of the high frequency of the high-resolution image h. Similarly, the noise n_k is assumed to belong to the sets

$$\|n_k\|^2 = \|l_k - DBFh\|^2 \leq e_k^2 . \tag{10}$$

where e_k^2 is proportional to the variance of the noise in the kth low-resolution chan-nel. If both bounds e_k^2 and E^2 are known, $\lambda_k(h) = (e_k / E)^2$ is used to compute the regularization parameter. But in practical cases, it is difficult to obtain an accurate estimate of them. So $\left\| l_k - DBFh \right\|^2$, which is the data residual in the kth channel, can be used to replace the numerator of the regularization functional. And the denominator is also replaced by $\left\| Ch \right\|^2$, then we can get a new regularization functional

$$\lambda_k(h) = \frac{\left\| l_k - DBFh \right\|^2}{\left\| Ch \right\|^2} \tag{11}$$

The regularization functional controls the weight of the regularization term and regulates the proportion between the data residual term and the regularization term. When it becomes larger, the edge of the reconstructed image is blurrier, and reversely, the reconstructed image is shown much noisier. So we should take into account the different effect of the regularization functional on the difference regions in the high-resolution image. A newly adaptive regularization functional based on the spatially varying residual is proposed to control each low-resolution channel instead of the overall regularization functional. We replace the numerator of Equation (11) with LR_k in order to make the coordinates identical, which is the up-sample of local residual of each low-resolution channel R_k. And in order to prevent the denominator from becoming zero we use the maximum of the regularization term to replace the denominator. The regularization functional is described as

$$\lambda_k(x, y) = \frac{LR_k(x, y)}{\max(\left\| Ch(x, y) \right\|^2)} \ . \tag{12}$$

The gradient descent optimization algorithm can be used to reconstruct the high-resolution image by minimizing the cost function (2). The expected high-resolution h can be updated iteratively beginning with an initial estimate of the high-resolution image $\hat{h}^0$ which is obtained using nearest interpolation from a low-resolution image and moves toward the optimum image as

$$\hat{h}^{m+1} = \hat{h}^m + \beta \left(\sum_{k=1}^{p} \alpha_k \left\{ F^T B^T D^T \left(l_k - DBF \hat{h}^m \right) + \lambda_k (\hat{h}^m) C^T C \hat{h}^m \right\} \right), m = 0,1,2,\dots \ . \tag{13}$$

until convergence is reached. The parameter β in (13) represents the step size at each iteration and m is the iteration number.

4   Experimental Result and Discussion

To test the performance of our proposed spatially varying weight image sequences super-resolution algorithm, we adopted test image "Lena" with size of [512×512] to do numerical experiment for a synthetic test. 16 low-resolution images were created by translating, blurring and down-sampling with a factor of 4 in each dimension and added by zero mean Gaussian white noise. The blur operation B was [5×5] Gaussian kernel with variance 2. The decimation operation D was [4×4] averaging and the two-dimensional Laplacian operator was used for C. The weight coefficient $\alpha_k(x, y)$ of the low-resolution channel was obtained by Equation (8), and the regularization parameter $\lambda_k(x, y)$ was determined by Equation (12). 4 cases listed in Table 1, were used to test the validity of our algorithm. The first low-resolution image was chosen as reference image and the relative motions with other images were estimated using Lucas-kanade method. Nearest interpolation of the first frame was chosen as the first estimate of high-resolution image. The algorithm was carried out for 50 iterations or it got convergent with the criterion $E^2 = \left\| h^{n+1} - h^n \right\|^2 / \left\| h^n \right\|^2 < 10^{-6}$. The window size used to compute the local mean residual take an important role in the reconstruction process. Fig. 1 shows the PSNR of Case 4 in different window size. We can see it can not get better results when the window size between 9 and 11.

Table 1. Four cases of synthetic test using "Lena"

	p=16: number of low-resolution images	σ_k^2
Case 1	16 frames of "Lena" with size of [128×128]	2^2
Case 2	16 frames of "Lena" with size of [128×128]	10^2
Case 3	16 frames of "Lena" with size of [128×128]	15^2
Case 4	16 frames of "Lena" with size of [128×128]	20^2

Table 2. PSNR of the "Lena" using the four methods

PSNR	Case 1	Case 2	Case 3	Case 4
Bilinear	25.42	24.12	23.30	22.36
Non-channel-weighted method	27.48	26.71	25.92	24.96
Overall-channel-weighted method	27.85	26.80	25.85	24.76
Our proposed method	27.29	27.07	26.69	26.29

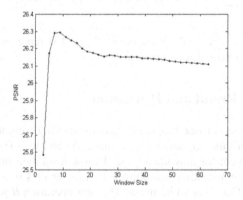

Fig. 1. The PSNR of "Lena" test with different window size in Case 4

(a)   (b)

(c)   (d)

Fig. 2. Results of case 2. (a) Bilinear interpolation of reference image; (b) Non-channel-weighted method; (c) Overall-channel-weighted method; (d) Our proposed method.

The performance of the proposed algorithms was quantitatively evaluated by measuring the PSNR. It is defined by $PSNR = 10\log_{10}\left\{\left(255^2 \times N\right)\big/\left\|\hat{h} - h\right\|^2\right\}$, where N is the total number of pixels in the high-resolution image, and $\hat{h}$ and h are the estimated high resolution image and the original image respectively. For comparison, the PSNR of the restored images for "Lena" using Bilinear, Non-channel-weighted method, Overall-channel-weighted method and our proposed method are demonstrated in Table 2 respectively. The window size we use is 9. From Case1 to Case 4, the superiority of our proposed method is better and better compared with other methods, and especially in Case 4 with standard deviation of 20. The results of Case 2, Case 3 and Case 4 are shown in Fig. 2, Fig. 3 and Fig. 4.

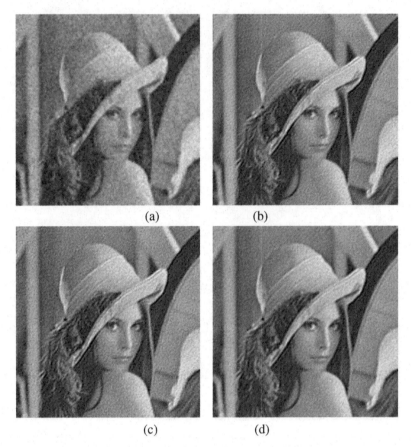

(a)   (b)

(c)   (d)

Fig. 3. Results of case 3. (a) Bilinear interpolation of reference image; (b) Non-channel-weighted method; (c) Overall-channel-weighted method; (d) Our proposed method.

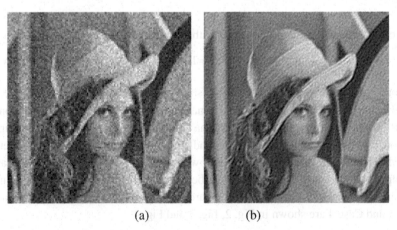

(a)   (b)

Fig. 4. Results of case 4. (a) Bilinear interpolation of reference image; (b) Non-channel-weighted method; (c) Overall-channel-weighted method; (d) Our proposed method.

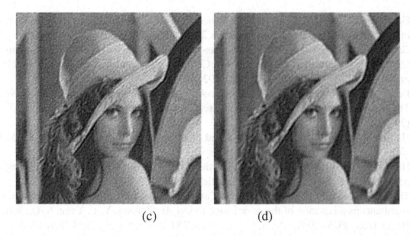

(c)   (d)

Fig. 4. (*continued*)

5 Conclusion

In this paper, we have presented a spatially varying functional to update the weight of each low-resolution channel, and simultaneously determine the within-channel regularization functional adaptively based on the partly restored image at each iteration step. The weight coefficients act as the cross-channel fidelity to each low-resolution image in terms of the local mean residual, while the regularization functional works as balance between the fidelity term and the prior term for each channel. The experimental results demonstrate the validity of our proposed algorithm, which better remove the additive noise with high variance and perform a better reconstruction.

Acknowledgements

This paper is partially supported by the Beijing Key Discipline Construction Program.

References

1. Park, S.C., Park, M.K., Kang, M.G.: Super-resolution image reconstruction: A technical overview. IEEE Signal Process Magazine 20(3), 21–36 (2003)
2. Kang, M.G., Katsaggelos, A.K.: General choice of the regularization functional in regularized image restoration. IEEE Transactions on Image Processing 4, 594–602 (1995)
3. Leung, C.M., Lu, W.S.: A multiple-parameter generalization of the tikhonov-miller regularization method for image restoration. In: 27th Annual Asilomar Conference on Signals, Systems, and Computers, vol. 2, pp. 856–860 (1993)
4. Lee, E.S., Kang, M.G.: Regularized Adaptive High- Resolution Image Reconstruction Considering Inaccurate Sub-pixel Registration. IEEE Transactions on Image Processing 12(7), 826–837 (2003)
5. He, H., Kondi, L.P.: Resolution enhancement of video sequences with adaptively weighted low-resolution images and simultaneous estimation of the regularization parameter. In: Int. Conf. Acoustics, Speech and Signal Processing, vol. 3(5), pp. 213–216 (2004)

6. Golub, G.H., Heath, M.T., Wahba, G.: Generalized cross-validation as a method for choosing a good ridge parameter. Technometrics 21(2), 215–223 (1979)
7. Galatsanos, N.P., Katsaggelos, A.K.: Cross-validation and other criteria for estimating the regularization parameter. In: International Conference Acoustics, Speech and Signal Processing (ICASSP 1991), vol. 4, pp. 3021–3024 (1991)
8. Bose, N.K., Lertrattanapanich, S., Koo, J.: Advances in superresolution using L-curve. In: The IEEE International Symposium on Circuits and Systems, Sydney, vol. 2, pp. 433–436 (2001)
9. Hansen, P.C.: Analysis of discrete ill-posed problems by means of the L-curve. SIAM Review 34(4), 561–580 (1992)
10. Hansen, P.C., O'Leary, D.P.: The use of the L-curve in the regularization of discrete ill-posed problems. SIAM Journal on Scientific Computing 14(6), 1487–1503 (1993)
11. Tian, J., Ma, K.K.: Markov chain Monte Carlo super- resolution image reconstruction with simultaneous adaptation of the prior image model. In: Zhuang, Y.-t., Yang, S.-Q., Rui, Y., He, Q. (eds.) PCM 2006. LNCS, vol. 4261, pp. 287–294. Springer, Heidelberg (2006)
12. Kang, M.G., Katsaggelos, A.K.: Simultaneous Multichannel Image Restoration and Estimation of the Regularization parameters. IEEE Trans. Image Processing, 774–778 (1997)
13. Gilboa, G., Sochen, N., Zeevi, Y.Y.: Texture Preserving Variational Denoising Using an Adaptive Fidelity Term. In: Proc. VLSM 2003, Nice, France (2003)
14. Katsaggelos, A.K., Biemond, J., Schafer, R.W., Mersereau, R.M.: A regularized Iterative Image Restoration Algorithm. IEEE Transactions on Signal Processing 39(4), 914–929 (1991)
15. Kang, M.G., Katsaggelos, A.K.: Simultaneous iterative restoration and evaluation of the regularization parameter. IEEE Trans. Signal Processing 40, 2329–2334 (1992)

Image Search Result Summarization with Informative Priors*

Rui Liu[1,2], Linjun Yang[2], and Xian-Sheng Hua[2]

[1] Tsinghua University, Beijing, 100084, P.R.China
liu-r07@mails.tsinghua.edu.cn
[2] Microsoft Research Asia, Beijing, 100190, P.R.China
{linjuny,xshua}@microsoft.com

Abstract. Though current commercial image search engines provide effective ways to retrieve the relevant images, they are ineffective for users to find the desired from the retrieved hundreds of results, especially for ambiguous queries. In this paper, we propose to summarize the search results by several representative images. We argue that the relevance and image quality are two important measures for a user friendly summarization since image search results are normally noisy with some low-quality images. The two factors, which can be regarded as informative prior of whether an image is a good summary candidate, are modeled into Affinity Propagation framework. User studies demonstrate that our proposed method is able to produce a user friendly summary, in terms of relevance, diversity, and coverage.

1 Introduction

Though image search engine provides a convenient tool for users to retrieve the desired images from the large amount of images on the Web, users are often difficult to find the interesting ones from the returned results due to the excessive amount of images for users' browsing. Image search result summarization, which selects the representative images from the results for presentation, can alleviate users from browsing all the returned images.

Consider the situation where a user issues a query "apple" and the search engine returns hundreds of images sorted by relevance. As shown in Fig.1, the images returned for query "apple" range from apple food to Apple Inc. products, even to apple shape rock. It is very inefficient for users to browse all the images to find the desired ones. Actually, when several topics for "apple" are presented, users are able to obtain their targets more conveniently, as shown in Fig.2.

There are some prior works on automatically determining the image summaries from an image collection [1][2][3][4][5]. Simon et al. [1] formulate the problem of scene summarization as an optimization problem by taking the image coverage and diversity into consideration and then describe a greedy algorithm to solve it. Kennedy et al. [2] focus on landmark summarization. They

---

* This work was performed when Rui Liu was visiting Microsoft Research Asia as a research intern.

H. Zha, R.-i. Taniguchi, and S. Maybank (Eds.): ACCV 2009, Part III, LNCS 5996, pp. 485–495, 2010.

Fig. 1. Top 35 images for the query "apple", retrieved by Microsoft Live Search

employ K-Means to cluster the images into visually similar groups, and then select images from the clusters according to some heuristic criteria including visual coherence and interest point connections. Fan et al. [3] compute an optimal partition based on a mixture-of-kernels and use a sampling algorithm to select representative images. Yang et al. [4] propose a greedy method to recommend canonical images. They first adopt visual words to represent the visual features in the scene, and then iteratively pick up the images which cover the most informative visual words as many as possible. Another related work is from Raguram et al. [5]. They work on clustering Flickr photos by utilizing image content and the associated tags to summarize general queries, such as "love", "CLOSEUP" and so on.

Although the above methods, referred to as image collection summarization (ICS), are effective to select representative images from a collection, they are not optimal to summarize image search results. There are several reasons. One is that the image search engines often return some noisy images which should not be contained in the summarization result. Hence, selecting images primarily by coverage and diversity, as most of the ICS methods do, is not a good strategy in the noisy circumstances. For example, as shown in Fig.3, it is very possible to select a "green map" (the third image from the left) that is obviously not favored by users when only coverage and diversity are considered. The second reason is that the relevance obtained from the search engine is useful prior information for images to be selected as summaries. However, most of the ICS methods did not take this into consideration. The third reason is that the image quality in the summarization result is important for users' experience. The low-quality images such as the rightmost in Fig.3 are non-informative for users if they occur in the summaries, since users cannot get the "complex" idea from such small-sized thumbnails. Our study shows that user experience significantly suffers from low quality summaries, and even cannot tolerate any thumbnail images with low resolution.

In this paper we proposed Image Search Result Summarization (ISRS) to address these problems, as illustrated in Fig.4. Informally, we define the image search result summarization as a problem of extracting the most "important"

Fig. 2. A human summary for "Apple", which contains the images of "red apple", "apple logo", "apple iPhone", "apple tree", and "apple pie"

Fig. 3. A machine summary for "Apple" when only coverage and diversity are used

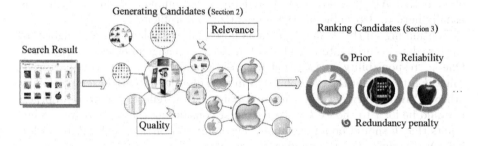

Fig. 4. Image Search Result Summarization System

images of search results. Important images mean that they are relevant to queries, attractive to users, and representative for the different subtopics. To achieve these goals, first, we investigate human summaries and employ several criteria such as relevance and quality to capture human's perception of image summaries. We take the initial rank returned by the search engine as the relevance information. Several features including dynamic range, color entropy, brightness, blur and contrast are employed to train a quality model. In order to select the representative images with little redundancy, we cluster the images to find the exemplars using Affinity Propagation and then greedily select summaries from the exemplars according to several criteria such as relevance, quality, reliability and redundancy penalty. The experimental results show that our proposed method can give an excellent summarization for image search results.

The rest of the paper is organized as follows. Section 2 introduces a clustering step to extract the summary candidates. Section 3 discusses a ranking step to select top-ranked images from the candidate set until the desired number is met. Section 4 describes the various experiments and shows the results. Finally, the paper concludes with Section 5.

2   Generating Summary Candidates

For each image in the search result, we first estimate the relevance and quality, which will be combined as the prior whether the image should be selected as a summary. Then we select exemplars by using Affinity Propagation (AP) algorithm [6] with the prior to generate the candidates for summarization.

2.1   The Clustering Approach

To start with, we will briefly introduce Affinity Propagation (AP), which is an exemplar-based clustering algorithm developed by Frey and Dueck [6]. The reason that we employ AP clustering method lies in two folds. First, it is difficult for other clustering methods to take the relevance and quality factors into account as a prior, while AP algorithm enables us to assign the prior for each image. The other is that AP does not require predefining the number of clusters, which is usually hard to determine for the summarization problem.

Considering all the N data points as potential exemplars, the AP algorithm clusters data according to two kinds of message exchanged between data points. One is "responsibility" $r(i,k)$, sent from data point i to k, reflecting how well-suited k is to serve as the exemplar for i in view of other potential exemplars. The other is "availability" $a(i,k)$, sent from point k to i, reflecting how appropriate it would be for i to choose k as its exemplar considering the support from other points that k should be an exemplar. The computational cost of AP algorithm is $O(N^2T)$ where T is the number of iterations.

One of the inputs to the AP algorithm is the similarity matrix of the N data points. The other is the preference, which can be regarded as the prior for each image to be selected as an exemplar. With the preference, AP algorithm does not need to specify the number of clusters. In the output of AP clustering algorithm, every data point i has its corresponding exemplar k, which means the image I_i can be represented by I_k, and we denote this as $S(I_i) = I_k$.

2.2   Scoring Preference

In this section, several criteria are proposed to measure the prior of an image to be contained in a summary, which are natural to be incorporated into AP framework. The preference for each image as an exemplar is estimated via a linear model of the relevance $R(I_i, q)$ and quality $Q(I_i)$:

$$Prior(I_i, q) = w_1 R(I_i, q) + w_2 Q(I_i) + c \qquad (1)$$

where I_i is the i-th image in the search result, q is a given query, and c is a constant.

In the following we will detail the estimation of relevance and quality respectively.

Percentage of all possible representative images

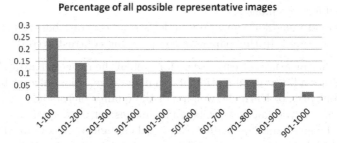

Fig. 5. Percentage of representative images (average over the 26 queries) that falls in different intervals of the initial rank

Relevance. The basic idea to estimate relevance is to use the initial rank, which records the ranked position of each image returned by the search engine directly. In order to verify that the rank is useful, we perform a simple experiment. We manually label 26 queries in order to find out all the representative images, and then compute the percentage of representative images (average over the 26 queries) that falls in different intervals of the initial rank. As can be seen from Fig.5, those representative images in top 100 take up one quarter of the total representative images and far outnumber those in the other intervals. Meanwhile, the number of representative images decreases significantly along the rank. This fact reveals that the top ranked images are more likely to be representative images than those bottom ones, which suggests that relevance is one of the important factors that influence a human's decision to select summary images and that the rank provided by search engines is a good indication of the "true" relevance.

Given N retrieved images under a specified query q, the relevance score for each image I_i is defined as:

$$R(I_i, q) = 1 - Pos(I_i, q)/N, i = 1, \ldots, N. \qquad (2)$$

where $Pos(I_i, q)$ is the position of the image I_i in the search result.

Quality. Images presenting a good appearance are likely to attract more attentions. Good appearance means both clear view and high aesthetics. Here we adopt a set of features that are effective in describing the quality of an image to predict whether an image has a good appearance.

Dynamic Range. Dynamic range is used for denoting the luminance range of a scene being photographed. The value is computed by the ratio between the maximum and minimum measurable light intensities.

Color Entropy. We use color entropy proposed in [7] to describe the colorlessness of the image content.

Brightness. A large amount of low-quality images are photographed with insufficient lights. We calculate this factor according to [7].

Blur. The blur algorithm that we adopt is proposed in [8], and has been proven to work well for web images.

Contrast. Good images are generally under strong contrast between the subject and the background. In this paper we compute the contrast according to [8].

Each quality measure returns a score for each of the images. The quality factor $Q(I_i)$ is further a linear combination of dynamic range, color entropy, brightness, blur and contrast. To learn the weights of the quality factors automatically, we first construct a training set by labeling images into low-quality (Fuzzy and unpleasant images), middle-quality (Not good enough to be contained in a summary), and high-quality (Good looking and easy to understand). Because each image's relative order is important in our task, ranking support vector machine [9] is used to train the quality model.

Once the relevance and quality are defined, the summary candidates are then generated by employing AP clustering method. After the clustering step, we now turn to the ranking process.

3   Ranking and Selecting Summary Candidates

In this section, we aim at selecting the most "competitive" images to form a summary. Competitiveness is a measure to minimize the redundancy while maximize both the candidate's prior confidence and reliability.

Prior. The prior of an exemplar is assigned by the $Prior(I_i, q)$ (See Eq. 1) to measure the importance of the image I_i for query q.

Reliability. We design this measure to describe how reliably an exemplar would be selected as a summary, based on the visual consistency property. The intuition is based on the observation that the neighbors of a reliable exemplar will locate in the same cluster as the exemplar, on the other hand, the neighbors of an unreliable exemplar will scatter around other clusters. Suppose we have M generated exemplars by $\chi = \{x_1, x_2, \ldots, x_M\}$, and N images, whose pairwise similarity matrix is denoted by W. For a particular exemplar x_i, we obtain its K-Nearest-Neighbors (KNN) $P = \{p_1, p_2, \ldots, p_K\}$. Let $p_j^{x_i}$ be one of exemplar x_i's KNN. The reliability of x_i is computed as the following:

$$NNC(x_i) = \frac{1}{K} \sum_{j=1}^{K} \delta(p_j^{x_i}, x_i) \tag{3}$$

where

$$\delta(p_j^{x_i}, x_i) = \begin{cases} 1, \ S(p_j^{x_i}) = x_i, i = 1, \ldots, M, j = 1, \ldots, K. \\ 0, \ else \end{cases} \tag{4}$$

That is to say, if $p_j^{x_i}$ links to the exemplar x_i, then I_j contributes one to $NNC(x_i)$, else it contributes zero.

Redundancy penalty. Some queries often contain significant number of similar images with the same topic. Take "apple" for example, a large portion of the returned images are "apple logo". However, these images are often clustered into multiple groups. In order to avoid such redundancy to achieve a diversified summary, we punish the images which are similar to previously selected images. For an image I_i, the redundancy penalty is computed by:

$$Redundancy(I_i) = \max_{I_j \in A} Sim(I_i, I_j) \qquad (5)$$

where A is the image set composed of already selected ones.

Afterwards, the prior, reliability and redundancy penalty scores are aggregated by linear combination, to produce the overall score:

$$Score(I_i, q) = \beta_1 Prior(I_i, q) + \beta_2 NNC(I_i) - \beta_3 Redundancy(I_i) \qquad (6)$$

where I_i is an exemplar and $\beta_1, \beta_2, \beta_3$ are the weight parameters that can be set empirically.

In each iteration, we greedily select the exemplar I_i with the highest $Score(I_i, q)$. The iterative process ends until the required number of images is met, and the selected images are finally taken as our summarization results.

4   Experiments

In this section, we present the experimental results of our summarization approach, based on a number of user studies and comparisons.

4.1   Data Preparation and Parameters

In our experiment, 26 queries with totally 24,010 images are crawled from Live Image Search before 2008/8/8. Each query returns approximately 1000 images. We filter out the bad images, for example, the images with the aspect ratio greater than 4 or lower than 1/4, because such kinds of images are not suited for presentation in the summary.

We extract three kinds of low-level features developed in [10] to represent images from different perspectives, such as color (24-dimension Attention Guided Color Signature), shape (324-dimension Histogram of Gradient, 45-dimension Multi-Layer Rotation Invariant EOH), and texture (192-dimension Daubechies Wavelet). Adaptive visual similarity measure is used to combine all the image features to generate the similarity matrix. Detailed algorithm is described in [10].

Following the methods in Section 2.2.2, we calculate the overall measure to characterize the quality of a thumbnail. We label all the images of the 26 queries, where 20% are labeled as high-quality images, and 23% as low-quality images. RankSVM with linear kernel [9] is used to learn the quality model. 13 queries are selected as the training set and the other 13 as the test set for evaluating the quality model and the summarization result.

4.2   Evaluation Design and Procedure

20 invited participants aged between 20 and 30 with different professional knowledge, took part in our study. To evaluate the proposed summarization approach,

we conduct a two step user study by these participants. Firstly, we ask these participants to scan the images in each query so that they will be familiar with the topics. Secondly, we ask them to score the summary for each query.

We implement a rank-only baseline and a quality-only baseline, which both use AP framework. The rank-only baseline considers only the relevance of an image in the phrase of assigning preference, and the quality-only baseline considers only the quality of the image. For the purpose of comparing our method, we further implement two image summarization baseline systems: Top5, which takes the top five images in the retrieved results as summary [4], and APSP, obtained by AP clustering sharing the same preference value.

Since it is usually difficult to have people agree on which images should be selected to compose a "gold" summary, the use of multiple criteria for evaluation could help alleviate this problem [2, 4]. Our evaluation is based on ten different popular queries among the test set. Summaries on each query are generated by the methods shown in Table 1, each of which contains five images. For each summary, we ask users to answer the following questions:

Relevance: How many images in the summary are relevant to the topic (0-5)?
Coverage: How well does this summary represent the retrieved images (0-5)?
Diversity: How many different topics are there in the summary (1-5)?

4.3   Results

To begin with, we evaluate the different measures used in the proposed method, i.e., rank and quality as detailed in Section 2, and try to analyze how such measures affect the summarization result. Table 1 summarized the average performance of our method with only one of the measures and the combination. As can be seen, the combination (M3) of two measures achieves the best score. This implies that various factors are all useful and can complement each other. As well, we can see that M2 (rank-only) performs better than M1 (quality-only), especially on relevance.

Now we compare the proposed methods (M3) with the other two baselines, Top5 and APSP as shown in Table 1. M3 achieves the best results in terms of coverage and diversity, and the relevance is comparable to Top5. Unsurprisingly, since APSP does not consider the rank and quality measures, it performs poorly. Since M3 takes diversity into consideration it is reasonable that the relevance is

Table 1. Performance comparison statistics

Methods	Relevance	Coverage	Diversity
APSP	3.835	3.205	3.05
Top5	4.54	3.425	2.785
M1(quality-only)	3.65	3.05	2.83
M2(rank-only)	4.285	3.38	2.935
M3(combination)	4.405	3.675	3.415

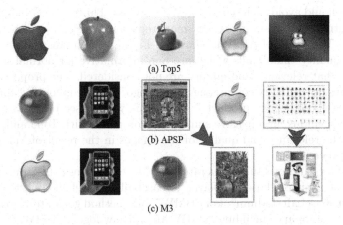

(a) Top5

(b) APSP

(c) M3

Fig. 6. The different summarization results for "apple"

(a) Baseball

(b) BMW

(c) Birds

(d) Anne Hathaway

Fig. 7. Example summaries generated by our method

slightly lower than Top5. This also demonstrates that the rank obtained from search engine is really a useful factor to model relevance in the summarization.

The summaries for "apple" generated by Top5, APSP, and M3 are illustrated in Fig.6. As can be shown, Top5 is able to provide relevant images for "apple", however, the diversity and representativeness is not considered. Firstly, two "apple logo" and two "fresh apple" are presented in the top images while a good summary should avoid such redundancy. Second, a "Think Linux" image appears in the rightmost of the summary, yet, more representative images would be a better choice. The result of APSP as shown in Fig. 6(b), contains irrelevant images and poor-quality thumbnails which are non-informative for normal users. This is because that relevance and quality are not considered. The proposed method M3 achieve the summary comprising "apple logo", "apple iphone", "apple fruit", "apple tree", and "apple products". From this we can see that M3 generate a more diverse and comprehensive summaries compared with Top5 and APSP. In addition, the relevance and quality of the images in the result of M3 are better than the others.

Fig.7 shows more results generated by M3. For "Baseball", our summary contains the topic of "baseball player", "baseball", "baseball clipart", "baseball bats", and "baseball stadium". For "BMW", our method generates a high-quality and diverse summary, including "BMW X6", "Bmw logo", "BMW Z4", "BMW Serie 1", as well as "BMW Isetta". Other results for queries "Birds" and "Anne Hathaway" are also shown in Fig.7.

5   Conclusion

We propose a novel approach to summarize image search results by taking the relevance and quality as a prior. It mainly consists of two steps: a clustering step and a ranking step. In the clustering step, we generate the summary candidates based on a clustering method with the priors of relevance and quality. In the ranking step, the summary is obtained by selecting the top candidates which are ranked according to the prior, reliability and redundancy penalty. User studies conducted on several popular queries show that the proposed method can achieve a user friendly summarization in terms of relevance, diversity and coverage.

References

1. Simon, I., Snavely, N., Seitz, S.M.: Scene summarization for online image collections. In: International Conference on Computer Vision, pp. 1–8 (2007)
2. Kennedy, L., Naaman, M.: Generating diverse and representative image search results for landmarks. In: International World Wide Web Conference, pp. 297–306 (2008)
3. Fan, J., Gao, Y., Luo, H., Keim, D.A., Li, Z.: A novel approach to enable semantic and visual image summarization for exploratory image search. In: Proceeding of the 1st ACM international conference on Multimedia information retrieval, pp. 358–365 (2008)
4. Yang, Y., Wu, P., Lee, C., Lin, K., Hsu, W.H., Chen, H.: Contextseer: Context search and recommendation at query time for shared consumer photos. ACM Multimedia, 199–208 (2008)
5. Raguram, R., Lazebnik, S.: Computing iconic summaries of general visual concepts. In: Proc. of IEEE CVPR Workshop on Internet Vision, pp. 1–8 (2008)
6. Frey, B.J., Dueck, D.: Clustering by passing messages between data points. Science 315(5814), 972–976 (2008)

7. Mei, T., Hua, X., Zhu, C., Zhou, H., Li, S.: Home video visual quality assessment with spatiotemporal factors. IEEE Transactions on Circuits and Systems for Video Technology 17(6), 699–706 (2007)
8. Luo, Y., Tang, X.: Photo and video quality evaluation: Focusing on the subject. In: Forsyth, D., Torr, P., Zisserman, A. (eds.) ECCV 2008, Part III. LNCS, vol. 5304, pp. 386–399. Springer, Heidelberg (2008)
9. Joachims, T.: Training linear svms in linear time. In: Proceedings of the ACM Conference on Knowledge Discovery and Data Mining, pp. 729–732 (2006)
10. Cui, J., Wen, F., Tang, X.: Real time google and live image search re-ranking. ACM Multimedia, 727–736 (2008)

Interactive Super-Resolution through Neighbor Embedding

Jian Pu[1], Junping Zhang[1,*], Peihong Guo[2], and Xiaoru Yuan[2]

[1] Shanghai Key Lab of Intelligent Information Processing
School of Computer Science, Fudan University, Shanghai 200433, China
[2] Key Laboratory of Machine Perception (Ministry of Education)
School of EECS, Peking University, Beijing 100871, China

Abstract. Learning based super-resolution can recover high resolution image with high quality. However, building an interactive learning based super-resolution system for general images is extremely challenging. In this paper, we proposed a novel GPU-based Interactive Super-Resolution system through Neighbor Embedding (ISRNE). Random projection tree (RPtree) with manifold sampling is employed to reduce the number of redundant image patches and balance the node size of the tree. Significant performance improvement is achieved through the incorporation of a refined GPU-based brute force kNN search with a matrix-multiplication-like technique. We demonstrate 200-300 times speedup of our proposed ISRNE system with experiments in both small size and large size images.

1 Introduction

Learning based super-resolution, which recovers the high resolution (HR) by learning the relationship between HR training images and low resolution (LR) counterparts, attracts much attention recently. Comparing with other methods, learning based super-resolution is capable of extracting more image/patch information from a collection of image pairs or image patch pairs and supports higher magnification factors with fewer LR images [1].

Freeman *et al.* [2] constructed a Markov network to connect the LR and HR image patches, followed by employing Bayesian belief propagation to allocate HR counterparts. However, artistic style is exhibited in the recovered HR image [3]. Assuming local geometry preservation for both high- and low-dimensional manifold, Chang *et al.* [4] proposed single image super-resolution through neighbor embedding (SRNE). Wei *et al.* [5] improved SRNE by extracting visual primitives and removing the noisy patches by validation (NEVPM). Yang *et al.* [6] investigated the selection of neighbor factors from the perspective of compressed sensing and Su *et al.* [7] studied the influence of patches from the viewpoint of neighborhood preservation. Furthermore, efficient face super-resolution methods has been proposed by employing a hallucination algorithm and its variants [8,9,10]. These algorithms are efficient because they employ linear PCA algorithm to project all the LR images into a low-dimensional subspace [8].

---

* Corresponding author.

H. Zha, R.-i. Taniguchi, and S. Maybank (Eds.): ACCV 2009, Part III, LNCS 5996, pp. 496–505, 2010.

It is worth noting that although many refinements have been proposed, the performance issue of learning based super-resolution, which plays a crucial role in its practical applications, is not well studied yet. It is very challenging to build an interactive (a few frames per second) learning-based method which can learn from hundreds of thousands of image patches or training images.

To attack the aforementioned issue, we propose Random Projection tree (RPtree) [11] with manifold sampling to reduce the total number of image patches and balance the tree structure. Then a refined GPU-based kNN search is employed to find the neighboring patches from the nodes of RPtree. Thirdly, we perform SRNE for the recovery of high-resolution test image patches. Finally, we introduce a global reconstruction constrain for further improving the image quality of high-resolution images. We successfully build an interactive super-resolution with neighboring embedding system (ISRNE) without compromising the image quality, even achieving a slightly better quality than the previous SRNE. Our experiments indicate that ISRNE not only demonstrates a remarkable improvement over performance, but also shows a superior scalability to existing methods.

The rest of the paper is organized as follows. In Sect. 2, we describe our interactive SRNE in details. We report the experiment results and discuss the limitation of the ISRNE in Sect. 3, followed by a conclusion in Sect. 4.

2 Interactive Super-Resolution through Neighbor Embedding (ISRNE)

To construct an interactive super-resolution system, we devote our efforts on the parallelization of two crucial steps of SRNE. These steps are: (1) All the image patches are separately reconstructed by neighbor embedding which has a closed-form solution; (2) The neighboring patches of each test patch are searched by kNN. It is worth noting that in this paper, we do not consider the parallelization of NEVPM, a refined version of SRNE since NEVPM comprises some steps which are hard to be paralleled [5]. For self-containness, we give a brief introduction on SRNE before the discussion of our approach.

2.1 Super-Resolution through Neighbor Embedding

A key assumption in SRNE is that the local geometries of image patches are similar in two distinct HR and LR feature spaces. Therefore, an HR counterpart of an LR image patch can be recovered using a collection of HR training patches.

We denote $\mathbf{y}_s$ and $\mathbf{x}_s$ be the training patches from HR images and its LR counterparts respectively. The optimal reconstruction weights of each patch $\mathbf{x}_t$ from LR test images is obtained by minimizing the local reconstruction error [4]:

$$\epsilon = \min \| \mathbf{x}_t - \sum_{\mathbf{x}_s \in \mathcal{N}_{\mathbf{x}_t}} \omega_{\mathbf{ts}} \mathbf{x}_s \|^2, \quad \mathbf{x}_t, \mathbf{x}_s \in \mathbb{R}^d \tag{1}$$

subject to the constraints $\sum_{\mathbf{x}_s \in \mathcal{N}_{\mathbf{x}_t}} \omega_{\mathbf{ts}} = 1$ and $\omega_{\mathbf{ts}} = 0$ for any $\mathbf{x}_s \notin \mathcal{N}_{\mathbf{x}_t}$, where $\mathcal{N}_{\mathbf{x}_t}$ is the neighborhood of $\mathbf{x}_t$ given neighbor factor k. Denote $\mathbf{G} = (\mathbf{x}_t \mathbf{1}^T - \mathbf{X}_s)^T$

$(\mathbf{x}_t \mathbf{1}^T - \mathbf{X}_s)$, Equation (1) can be optimized by solving a linear system equation $\mathbf{GW} = 1$, s.t. $\sum_{\mathbf{x}_s} \mathbf{w}_{ts} = 1$. Thus, the HR patch $\mathbf{y}_t$ is attained as follows:

$$\mathbf{y}_t = \sum_{\mathbf{x}_s \in \mathcal{N}_{\mathbf{x}_t}} \omega_{\mathbf{ts}} \mathbf{y}_s, \qquad \mathbf{y}_s \in \mathbb{R}^D. \tag{2}$$

where $\mathbf{y}_s$ is the HR counterpart of LR image patch $\mathbf{x}_s$.

In the last step above, we can either simply average the values in the overlapped regions between adjacent patches, or employ other more sophisticated methods (e.g. one pass algorithm) to enforce inter-patch relationship.

To achieve efficient parallelization of SRNE, we introduce RPtree with manifold sampling.

2.2   Random Projection Tree with Manifold Sampling

RPtree, a variant of the k-d tree, hierarchically partitions data of D dimension into pieces in a manner which only depends on the intrinsic low-dimensional manifold [11]. The advantages of utilizing RPtree are that: (1) RPtree consumes less time ($O(n)$) to construct than PCA tree ($O(n log n)$) [11], given n data points; (2) Unlike k-d tree, RPtree can deal with high-dimensional data (≥ 30) which are often seen in super-resolution domain; (3) RPtree won't bring a detrimental effect on the SRNE performance, since the manifold assumption of RPtree is the same as that of neighbor embedding [4].

RPtree is built in a streaming manner [12] in which the following statistics at each internal node of the tree are maintained and updated as new data arrives.

$$\mu_i \leftarrow (1 - \alpha_i)\mu_{i-1} + \alpha_i x_i$$

$$\sigma_i^2 \leftarrow (1 - \alpha_i)\sigma_{i-1}^2 + \alpha_i (x_i - \mu_i)^2.$$

where μ_i and σ_i^2 denote the mean value and the corresponding variance in the ith iterative times, respectively. Parameter $\alpha_i (\leq 1/i)$ is a weighted factor, and x_i means a new sample. The details can be seen in [12].

With this way, Freund et al. [11] proved that if data in C are of intrinsic dimension d, the average diameter of any descendant cell ($\leq d$ levels below) of C will be less than half of the average diameter of C with constant probability, picking any cell C in the RP tree. However, this theorem is not sufficient to assure the even partition of RPtree especially when the data is distributed unevenly, which is the case in natural image patches. Since the background patches are quite similar, most of such patches will be assigned to few nodes. To reduce the difference of distribution density between the background and foreground patches, we introduce manifold sampling in order to balance the RPtree. Given d dimensional n data points $\mathbf{x}_i (i = 1, ..., n)$, specifically, we approximate the geodesic distance between data points $\mathbf{x}_i$ and $\mathbf{x}_j$, which are lying close together (their Euclidean distances $dist(\mathbf{x}_i, \mathbf{x}_j)$ is less than a given threshold ϵ or one of the K nearest neighbors of $\mathbf{x}_j$ of $\mathbf{x}_j$), can be approximated. For data points lying far apart, we then approximate the geodesic distance by the shortest path distance which is formulated as follows:

$$dist(\mathbf{x}_i, \mathbf{x}_j) = \min\{dist(\mathbf{x}_i, \mathbf{x}_j), dist(\mathbf{x}_i, \mathbf{x}_k) + dist(\mathbf{x}_k, \mathbf{x}_j)\} \quad \forall k, 0 \leq k \leq n$$

Once the approximated geodesic distances between sample pairs in the high dimensional space are calculated, we can directly use these distance values to decimate redundant points in the manifold. We also prove an error upper bound of manifold sampling for super-resolution as follows:

$$\frac{\|\Delta\mathbf{y}\|}{\|\mathbf{y}\|} \leq \frac{4\epsilon}{\|\mathbf{P}\|} + \frac{r\epsilon}{\|\mathbf{y}\|},$$

where $\mathbf{P}^T\mathbf{P} = \mathbf{G}$, and r denotes the super-resolution factor. It indicates that we can guarantee the difference between the original SR results and correspond one with manifold sampling is small by carefully choosing ϵ. Due to limited space, we put the proof into the supplementary.

2.3   GPU Acceleration

The complexity of the brute force kNN algorithm reaches an order of $O(nmd + nmlogm)$, where m represents for the number of query data points and, n for the number of reference data points, and d is the dimensionality of the data points. To reduce computational cost, Garcia *et al.* [13] proposed a fast kNN search scheme based on a brute force GPU algorithm and obtained a remarkable increase in performance. However, a naïve implementation of GPU acceleration has very low efficiency due to large amount of un-coalesced memory access and bank conflicts. In our approach, we develop a matrix-multiplication-like algorithm, to compute the distances.

Denoting the query points as $\mathbf{X}_t(x_{t_{ij}})_{m \times d}$ and the reference points as $\mathbf{X}_s(x_{s_{ij}})_{n \times d}$, the squared distance matrix $\mathbf{D}(dist_{ij}^2)_{m \times n}$ can then be calculated:

$$\mathbf{D} = \mathbf{X}_t \odot \mathbf{X}_s^T,$$

where $\odot$ denotes the operator between two matrices, and is defined by:

$$dist_{ij}^2 = \mathbf{x}_{t_i} \cdot \mathbf{x}_{s_j} = \sum_{k=1}^{d}(\mathbf{x}_{t_{i_k}} - \mathbf{x}_{s_{j_k}})^2.$$

Above approach is very similar to the matrix multiplication between $\mathbf{X}_t$ and $\mathbf{X}_s^T$, except that the computing kernel is modified. We can very conveniently cope with the computation utilizing currently available parallel matrix multiplication algorithms to obtain significant performance improvement. An illustration of this operation is shown in Fig. 1.

As the neighborhood number k is relatively small in our application, we employ insertion sort for best performance [13]. Unlike Bishop *et al.*'s method [14], we needn't perform dimension reduction which is required for k nearest neighbor search on k-d tree. We further propose a combination of GPU-based kNN and RPtree with manifold sampling to speed up queries. In Sect. 3, we show that there is no negative impact on the the quality of restoration.

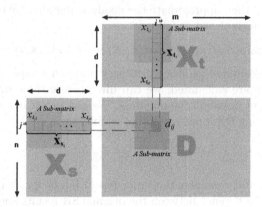

Fig. 1. Matrix-mulitplication-like operation between $\mathbf{X_t}(x_{t_{ij}})_{m \times d}$ and $\mathbf{X_s}(x_{s_{ij}})_{n \times d}$. We follow the method of matrix multiplication to compute the distance matrix, with the computing "kernel" modified.

2.4   Global Reconstruction Constrain

In super-resolution domain, there are two important criteria to evaluate the recovered HR quality. One is the recovery of high frequency, the other is the consistency of LR and HR images. To keep the consistency, generally speaking, a global reconstruction constrain which means the simulated downsampling of the reconstructed HR image $\mathbf{Y}$ is the same as the LR image $\mathbf{X}$ should be considered as follows:

$$\mathbf{X} = D_S H \mathbf{Y}$$

where H represents a blurring filter, and D_S the downsampling operator.

As the consistency of LR and HR images are not always satisfied when patch by patch restoration is employed, Liu *et al.* [15] first proposed a two step method to combine the local nonparametric and global parametric model. In ISRNE, we utilize the back-projection method (BP) which has been studied by Yang *et al.* [6] as a post-processing procedure to enhance the consistency.

Back-projection algorithm is an iterative procedure for estimating unknown scenes. Given an estimation of the super resolution image, a simulated imaging process yields a set of low-resolution images which are compared with the observed low resolution images. The super-resolution estimation is then modified so as to reduce the error between the observed and simulated images. The process is terminated when the error is less than a predetermined level, or after a given number of iterations. The iterative procedure is formally described as follows:

$$\hat{\mathbf{Y}}^{(t+1)} = \hat{\mathbf{Y}}^{(t)} + \mathbf{H}^{BP}\left(\mathbf{X} - \hat{\mathbf{X}}^{(t)}\right)$$
$$= \hat{\mathbf{Y}}^{(t)} + \mathbf{H}^{BP}\left(\mathbf{X} - D_S H \hat{\mathbf{Y}}^{(t)}\right)$$

where $\mathbf{H}^{BP}$ is a back-projection operator which is an approximation to the inverse of the operator $D_S H$, t is the iterative times.

3   Experiments

In order to evaluate the effectiveness of ISRNE, experiments are carried out on two image sets of different scales. The smaller training set is from Chang *et al.*'s paper [4] as in Fig. 2, and the larger one consists of 370 images are collected from a well-known COREL database.

In the experiments, we will magnify the input image by a factor of 4. In the LR images, we always use 3×3 LR patches, with overlap of 2 pixel between adjacent patches, corresponding to 12×12 patches with overlap of 8 pixels for the HR images. Like SRNE [4], the neighbor factor k is set to be 5 and the features (first-order and second-order gradient) are extracted directly from the illuminance component of LR images since humans are more sensitive to illuminance changes.

The computer used for the evaluation is an Intel Core 2 Duo E7200 2.53GHz with 2GB of DDR2 memory PC2-5300 (2×1GB dual-channel memory). The graphics card used is an NVIDIA GeForce 8800 GT with 512MB of DDR3 memory. NVIDIA CUDA 2.0 is employed for GPU computation.

We first evaluate the effectiveness of RPtree with manifold sampling using the small training set. The tree height is set to be 4, which is a tradeoff between the tree search and node search cost. To remove the randomness of RPtree, the output, *i.e.* the number of patches in each node, of 10 times are recorded. The sum of node frequencies of the 10 repetitions is reported as in Fig. 3. It is easy to see from Fig. 3 that the distribution of these patches on the tree nodes are highly imbalanced. Furthermore, there always exists a "big" node in the tree, which contains almost half of the total patches. For example, the frequency of a node owing the number of points in $[4000, 6000]$ is equal to 10. It is not difficult to observe that such patches are sampled from the background. After manifold sampling is employed, the imbalance is greatly reduced as shown in Fig. 3. It indicates that the proposed RPtree with manifold sampling indeed remove redundant patches and improve the balance of RPtree.

As shown in Fig. 4, we compare our method with neighbor embedding (SRNE) [4] and back projection. It is easy to notice that the forehead hair and double eye of the girl utilizing ISRNE are more clear than those using SRNE. Furthermore, ISRNE has lower RMSE for the recovery of HR image than SRNE, and is comparable to SRNE+BP method and sparse representation method [6] which needs several hours to get the result. It indicates that while the main goal of the proposed ISRNE is to

Fig. 2. Small training set

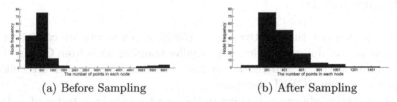

(a) Before Sampling   (b) After Sampling

Fig. 3. The distribution of data in `RPtree`. The vertical axis means the times of a node of `RPtree` owing the number of points in some interval.

Fig. 4. 4× recovery of low resolution image. The root mean squared errors (RMSEs) are shown in the Brackets, from left to right: LR, `SRNE` (0.0387), `SRNE` + BP (0.0368), `Sparse Representation` (0.0357), `ISRNE` (0.0369), Ground truth.

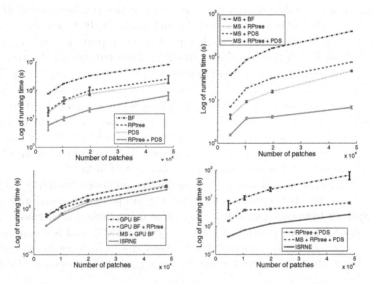

Fig. 5. A performance comparison on the super-resolution with different search methods for images with different resolutions

attain interactivity, the recovered image quality is not sacrificed, even better than that of the previous one (*e.g.* `SRNE`) in some cases.

To evaluate the performance of `ISRNE`, we compare it with several state-of-the-art acceleration methods including: Brute force kNN search (`BF`), `RPtree`, partial distance search acceleration (`PDS`) [16], and the combination of manifold sampling with the former three methods. Furthermore, we also study the performance of

Fig. 6. 4× recovery of low resolution image using the big training set. For each scene, the left one is the LR image and the right one is recovered by ISRNE. From left to right, top and bottom, the RMSE errors of these four test images are: 0.0827, 0.0583, 0.0643, and 0.0734, respectively. In the middle, there are close-ups of the four images.

Table 1. Running time (RT) of ISRNE in seconds, from top to bottom: RT for prepro-cessing, RT for kNN search, RT for weights calculation, RT for reconstruction, RT for postprocessing and the total RT

	Test 1	Test 2	Test 3	Test 4
T_{pre} (s)	9.490	9.450	9.420	9.400
T_{kNN} (s)	1.930	1.890	1.760	1.870
T_w (s)	0.115	0.118	0.117	0.118
T_{resto}(s)	0.161	0.160	0.162	0.166
T_{post} (s)	0.107	0.107	0.103	0.107
Total	11.803	11.725	11.500	11.560

three variants of the proposed ISRNE algorithm by neglecting either manifold sampling or RPtree, or both. The training images are the small training set as in Fig. 2. The test images of increasing sizes include one image from Chang *et al.*'s paper [4] and three images downloaded from Internet. To remove the randomicity of RPtree, all the methods related to RPtree are repeated 10 times and the corresponding means and standard deviations of the computational times are reported in Fig. 5.

It can be seen from Fig. 5 that compared with other methods, ISRNE has the best performance, and the acceleration ratio of BF is increased with the resolution of the test images. Furthermore, RPtree and manifold learning are two comparable and complementary methods which can further accelerate the refined GPU-based kNN procedure. When the size of images are smaller than 500×348, the running time is less than 1 second which is a basic requirement to build an interactive super-resolution system. While the "MS+RPtree+PDS" made a remarkable improvement in the aspect of acceleration, it is hard for PDS to design an alternatively parallelized one due to its serial computation nature.

Finally, we attempt to figure out how many training/test patches will hinder the interactive property of ISRNE. Therefore, we extract $131,523$ patches from $2,156,360(5828 \times 370)$ raw patches which are generated from the mentioned large training image set. The test set consists of four images from Corel test set without overlapping with the large training set. The HR test images (of size 384×256) recovered by ISRNE are shown in Figures 6, and running time analysis are tabulated in Table 1. Compared with the LR images, we can observe that (1) the wall of Roman relics becomes cleaner; (2) the faces of these horses become smoother and a little bit recognizable; (3) some buildings on the mountain are shown up; (4) the food details in the dish is distinguishable and the edges of the dish is cleaner. Note that most of the running time is spent on pre-processing, especially on transferring all the $131,523$ patches into memory. The time for kNN search and neighbor embedding is only about 2 second, while other aforementioned learning methods for super-resolution never run through such tough tests.

4   Conclusion

With the combination of RPtree with manifold learning and the refined GPU-based kNN search, an interactive super-resolution through neighbor embedding is proposed. Experiments on both small-scale images and large-scale images indicate that the proposed ISRNE not only remarkably accelerates the procedure of super-resolution but also enhances the image quality of recovered high-resolution images well. Note that although the kNN search time grows with the training patches and test patches, a more powerful hardware will greatly neutralize the side effect. Meanwhile, this scheme can easily be applied to other patch based search and replace problems like image denoising, inpainting, texture transfer, and transparency separation.

There are a few issues that require a thorough investigation. Since RPtree can construct a tree much more efficient than other tree-based algorithms, we will investigate how to dynamically update the training patches to further refine the performance of ISRNE in the future. Furthermore, we would like to generalize the proposed framework to other learning based super-resolution method.

Acknowledgements

This research was sponsored by the 973 Program (No. 2010CB327900 and No. 2009CB320903), 863 Project (2007AA01Z176), NSFC 60635030 and Key Project of Chinese Ministry of Education (No. 109001).

References

1. Lin, Z.C., He, J.F., Tang, X.O., Tang, C.K.: Limits of learning-based superresolution algorithm. In: Proceedings of IEEE CVPR, pp. 1–7 (2007)
2. Freeman, W.T., Pasztor, E.C., Carmichael, O.T.: Learning low-level vision. International Journal of Computer Vision 40(1), 25–47 (2000)

3. Freeman, W.T., Jones, T.R., Pasztor, E.C.: Example based superresolution. IEEE Computer Graphics and Applications 22(2), 56–65 (2002)
4. Chang, H., Yeung, D.Y., Xiong, Y.: Super-resolution through neighbor embedding. In: Proceedings of IEEE CVPR, pp. 275–282 (2004)
5. Wei, F., Yeung, D.Y.: Image hallucination using neighbor embedding over visual primitive manifolds. In: Proceedings of IEEE CVPR, pp. 1–7 (2007)
6. Yang, J.C., Wright, J., Ma, Y., Huang, T.: Image super-resolution as sparse representation of raw image patches. In: Proceedings of IEEE CVPR, pp. 1–8 (2008)
7. Su, K., Tian, Q., Xue, Q., Sebe, N., Ma, J.: Neighborhood issue in single-frame image super-resolution. In: Proceedings of IEEE ICME, pp. 1122–1125 (2005)
8. Gunturk, B.K., Batur, A.U., Altunbasak, Y., Hayes III, M.H., Mersereau, R.M.: Eigenface-domain super-resolution for face recognition. IEEE Trans. Image Proc. 12(5), 597–606 (2003)
9. Liu, C., Shum, H.Y., Freeman, W.T.: Face hallucination: Theory and practice. International Journal of Computer Vision 75(1), 115–134 (2007)
10. Baker, S., Kanade, T.: Limits on super-resolution and how to break them. IEEE Trans. PAMI 24(9), 1167–1183 (2002)
11. Freund, Y., Dasgupta, S., Kabra, M., Verma, N.: Learning the structure of manifolds using random projections. In: NIPS, pp. 473–480 (2008)
12. Dasgupta, S., Freund, Y.: Random projection trees and low dimensional manifolds. Technical Report CS2007-0890, UCSD (2007)
13. Garcia, V., Debreuve, E., Barlaud, M.: Fast k nearest neighbor search using gpu. In: CVPR Workshop on Computer Vision on GPU, pp. 1–7 (2008)
14. Bishop, C.M., Blake, A., Marthi, B.: Super-resolution enhancement of video. In: Proceedings 9th International Conference on Artificial Intelligence and Statistics (2003)
15. Liu, C., Shum, H.Y., Zhang, C.S.: A two-step approach to hallucinating faces: Global parametric model and local nonparametric model. In: Proceedings of IEEE CVPR, pp. 192–198 (2001)
16. Qiao, Y.L., Pan, J.S., Sun, S.H.: Improved partial distance search for k nearest-neighbor classification. In: Proceedings of IEEE ICME, vol. 2, pp. 1275–1278 (2004)

Scalable Image Retrieval Based on Feature Forest

Jinlong Song[1], Yong Ma[2], Fuqiao Hu[1], Yuming Zhao[1], and Shihong Lao[2]

[1] Shanghai Jiao Tong University, Shanghai, China
{sjl321,fqhu,arola_zym}@sjtu.edu.cn
[2] Core Technology Center, Omron Corporation, Kyoto, Japan
{ma,lao}@ari.ncl.omron.co.jp

Abstract. Vocabulary tree-based method is one of the most popular methods for content-based image retrieval due to its efficiency and effectiveness. However, for existing vocabulary tree methods, the retrieval precision in large scale image database has never been acceptable especially for image datasets with high variations. In this paper, we propose a novel tree fusion framework: Feature Forest, utilizing and fusing different kind of local visual descriptors to achieve a better retrieval performance. In the offline-learning stage, our framework first establishes different feature vocabulary trees based on different features and uses the average covariance to build vocabulary tree adaptively. In the online-query stage, we use the ratio of the resulting score to the standard score to fuse retrieval results of each vocabulary tree adaptively. The evaluations show the effectiveness of our approach compared with single vocabulary-tree based methods on different databases.

1 Introduction

For content based image retrieval system, the quality of retrieval result depends highly on two factors: one is whether the extracted feature of image is representative or not, the other is whether the online retrieval is efficient and effective, which is especially important for large scale image database. For the former, some excellent features have been proposed in recent years, such as sift, Speed Up Robust Feature [11], Histogram of Oriented Gradient [10], but they also have their respective limitations for different image contents. As to the retrieval method, the key idea of current retrieval methods is to partition the feature space as well as possible in the offline stage though their partition methods are different. [12, 13] use a variation of supervised learning methods to train the bag of words with positive and negative labels, [14, 15] use hashing algorithm to bucketing the descriptors and [3, 5, 6, 8] use hierarchical k-means to train the descriptor vectors into visual words. And on query stage, voting for the images which are near to the query feature is adapted by all methods above.

Vocabulary tree method has been proved feasible for scalable image retrieval and it was first proposed in [5]. Based on this structure, [3] propose distance-weighted scoring scheme to make the scoring strategy more reasonable and [8] used the adaptive forests to replace vocabulary tree with fixed structure. However, [3] brings up the memory and speed problem. [8] used capacity constraint to determine whether to create next level or not. Inspired by this method, we propose to use average

H. Zha, R.-i. Taniguchi, and S. Maybank (Eds.): ACCV 2009, Part III, LNCS 5996, pp. 506–515, 2010.
© Springer-Verlag Berlin Heidelberg 2010

covariance to replace the capacity constraint and it can solve two cases, which [8] can't solve. What's more important is that the methods based on vocabulary tree all utilize just one feature. However, single feature may be inadequate to describe different visual properties of the images, especially for scalable images and [1] has realized the problem and pointed out that for multi-class object categorization, multiple features and different combinations of features are needed. To overcome the inadequacy of using signal type of feature, we propose the Feature Forest, which consist of several vocabulary trees trained with different type of visual features. In the offline-training stage, our proposed method first establishes different feature vocabulary trees, the structure of which is adaptively constructed using our own rule, which is described in section 3.2. In the online stage, we use the ratio of the resulting score to the standard score to fuse retrieval results of each vocabulary tree adaptively. The contribution of our work is as follows:

1. Using average covariance of the node as guide line to determine whether such feature space needs to be clustered into sub-space.
2. Proposing a novel framework: feature forest, which can fuse the query results of each vocabulary tree adaptively.

The rest of the paper is organized as follows. Section 2 presents related works on vocabulary tree and object recognition technology. Section 3 briefly reviews vocabulary tree framework and our extended work. Section 4 describes the framework of Feature Forest and a sample feature forest. Section 5 shows experimental result. Finally, we provide conclusions and a plan for feature work in Section 6.

2 Related Work

Content based image retrieval is a discipline of considerable value on both practical application and research. In recent years, some effective methods have been proposed, such as the Multiple Instance Learning, Local Sensitive Hashing and Vocabulary Tree. Based on these methods, a lot of extended work also has been done.

Our work is more relative to vocabulary tree based methods. In 2003, Sivic and Zisserman [6] proposed a text retrieval method for object matching in video. Descriptors extracted from local affine invariant regions are quantized into visual words, which are clustered by k-means into several classes. The collection of visual words is used in Term Frequency Inverse Document Frequency (TF-IDF) scoring of the relevance of an image to the query. The scoring is accomplished using inverted files. The effect of this method is very good but it does not fit for scalable retrieval. Based on this method, David Nister and Henrik Stewenius [5] propose the famous vocabulary tree. They use hierarchical k-means, which could quickly compute very large vocabularies. But the structure of vocabulary tree is fixed and it can't part the feature space adaptively. K. Grauman and T. Darrell [7] propose vocabulary tree guided feature pyramid to approximate correspondences in high dimensions. It has the same shortcoming as method [5]. Tom Yeh propose an adaptive vocabulary forests methods [8], which adapts a vocabulary forest and automatically keeps existing histogram pyramid database entries up-to-date in a forward file system. Tom Yeh has considered the problem in [5, 7], but its rule of whether to continue to partition is decided by the data number in the node. Different from adaptive method in [8], our rule is based on the average covariance of the node, which is more reasonable. The detailed explanation will be given in section 3.2. In order to score more reasonable, [3] propose an additional weight based on the distance for scoring in the same vocabulary. Though it stores the compressed PCA instead of original data, it still costs a lot of memory, because it needs to load in all the compressed training data and spend added time to calculate the weights for each voting. Another common shortcoming of above methods is that they have not considered the problem proposed in [1]. Only using single feature for a large database with high diversity is an important constraint for the retrieval precision. Feature forest just hammers at solving this problem. The experiment shows the effectiveness of our approach compared with single vocabulary tree on different databases.

3 Vocabulary Tree

3.1 Review of Vocabulary Tree Structure

Given a scalable image database, it extracts descriptors from all the training image and use the hierarchical k-means to train a vocabulary tree. The tree is determined level by level, up to some maximum number of levels L, and each division into k parts is only defined by the distribution of the descriptor vectors that belong to the parent quantization cell. The feature space will be parted into sub-spaces on different level. The leaf node will write down the ID of descriptors. ID indicates the descriptor comes from which image. This is used in hierarchical Term Frequency Inverted Document Frequency (TF-IDF) scoring of the relevance of an image to the query. In order to make the score be more suitable for the combination of feature forest, we use the pyramid match kernel [2].

$$\kappa^L(X,Y) = \Gamma^L + \sum_{l=0}^{L-1} \frac{1}{2^{L-l}}\left(\Gamma^l - \Gamma^{l+1}\right) = \frac{1}{2^L}\Gamma^0 + \sum_{l=1}^{L}\frac{1}{2^{L-l+1}}\Gamma^l \tag{1}$$

$\kappa^L(X,Y)$ is the score of image Y in database for query image X, Γ^L is the number of features from image Y, passing the same node with features from image X at level l

.

On the online stage: each descriptor from the query image is simply propagated down the tree by at each level comparing the descriptor vector to the k candidate cluster centers and choosing the closest one. The score for each database image is calculated with (1) and query results will be ranked according to the score.

3.2 Extended Work for Vocabulary Tree

[8] has proved that adaptive structure can work better than the fixed vocabulary tree structure. They construct the adaptive tree by constraining the capacity of the node. It can insure that each node has an appropriate number of features and avoid voting for

the weak matching feature. Different from the work done in [8], our adaptive rule is based on the average variance. Whether the feature space need to be clustered into k sub-space is determined by the covariance of the cluster. When the average is less than the threshold, we will stop clustering, otherwise, we will divide the node into k sub-spaces. The threshold is determined by the average covariance of the total data.

$$\theta = \kappa \frac{1}{BranchNum^N} TotalAverVar \qquad (2)$$

N is the level number. TotalAverVar is covariance of all data in root node of the tree. For some image database, we need to multiple κ (most time it is less than 0.5) to make the effect better.

When the data number in a node is small but sparse or the data number is large but compact, using number of the node to determine whether it is need to be divided into sub-space will fail. In this case, our rule is more reasonable, because it is according to compact degree of the cluster but to the feature number in the cluster. Adaptive structure can avoid missing vote for the perfect matching feature and avoid voting for the weak matching feature.

4   Building Feature Forest

It is important to note that the visual properties of various images are different, so it is difficult to use one feature to characterize all types of images well. B.Libe [1] has concluded that for multi-class object categorization, multiple features and different combination of features are needed to get a better result. For scalable image retrieval, the image contents vary a lot, so a single feature may be suitable to characterize some images, but it can't suitable for all the images. Fig.5 gives a visible interpretation. For some querying images, single feature trees fail to give an acceptable query results, but the feature forest, combined two single trees, gives a better result. So we need to characterize the image from different viewpoints for image retrieval, especially for scalable image retrieval.

In order to solve the above mentioned problems of vocabulary-tree, we propose a new structure, Feature Forest, to fuse several vocabulary trees built upon different features and combine these trees adaptively.

4.1   Tree Fusion

4.1.1   Weight Tuning
The essence of the scoring strategy of (1) is to measure the number of matching point of two images. For one feature, the visual similarity degree of two images is proportional to the matching point number. So the higher the query resulting score, the better the query result. Based on above analysis, the rationale of finding an optimal weight for each built feature tree relies on how to find an optimal measurement for its query result score. For a feature tree A, if the relative score of the querying result is higher than that of feature tree B, it indicates that the querying result of tree A is better than tree B. So when fusing the tree, we need to give a larger

weight for tree A. How to get the relative score? Firstly, we define a standard score for each feature tree and here the standard score for feature tree i is defined as the statistical average score of K query images, which have a good querying results.

In online-query stage, for each feature tree, we use the ratio of its query score to its standard score to indicate the effect of the query result. The higher the ratio, the better the query results of this feature tree. The standard score is calculated with (3). For a query image k, we note M_{ijk} as the score of top j rank in the retrieval results of feature tree i and M_{ij_aver} as the standard score of top j rank in feature tree i.

$$M_{ij\_aver} = \sum_{k=1}^{K} M_{ijk} \bigg/ K \tag{3}$$

Once getting the average score for top j rank in feature tree i, we use the average ratio of top N rank to make the weight more stable. The weight w_i for feature tree i is calculated as follows:

$$w_i = \sum_{j=0}^{N} \left(M_{ij} / M_{ij\_aver} \right) \bigg/ N \tag{4}$$

For a query image, if the ratio of query result score to the standard score is small in one feature tree, the weight for this tree is relatively small. If the w_i is smaller than 1, the query result is worse than standard query result, otherwise, the query result is better than standard query result.

4.1.2 Retrieval
In the test phase, the scales of scores for different features are different. In order to combine the score of different feature tree together; we need to normalize the score of each feature to [0,1]:

$$M_{ij}' = \frac{M_{ij}}{\sum_{j=0}^{N} M_{ij}} \tag{5}$$

Here N is the number of database images. By now, we have gotten the resulting score and the weight of each feature tree and we have also normalized the score to make it can be combined together. For a query image, the final score of each database image can be calculated by (6)

$$S_k = \sum_{i=1}^{m} w_i S_{ik}' \tag{6}$$

m is the number of feature tree. $S_{ik}^{'}$ is the score of image k in tree i. The value of $S_{ik}^{'}$ equals to the corresponding $M_{ij}^{'}$ with the same image ID. S_k is the final score of image k in image database.

4.2 Image Representation and Two Tree Fusion

4.2.1 Image Representation

It is crucial that using different type of visual feature to characterize image content from different viewpoints and resolution scales, such as color, texture and shape. For our Feature forest, using same type of visual features can only bring nearly same weights for different tree structures, which is less meaningless to utilize the advantage of Feature Forest. Such as building a feature forest with sift and Speed Up Robust Feature, is meaningless, because they are the same type feature. So only using complementary features can fully achieve the superior effect of feature forest.

In this paper, we use Histogram of Oriented Gradient (HOG) feature, and Speed Up Robust Feature (SURF) to build the feature forest. On one hand, HOG Feature is dense feature, which can match similar regions better and SURF feature is sparse feature. On the other hand, SURF is a texture feature to some extent and HOG contain partial color information and shape information.

SURF has an approximate effect compared to SIFT, but its speed is much faster than SIFT. It is based on sums of 2D Haar wavelet responses and makes an efficient use of integral images. As basic image features it uses a Haar wavelet approximation of the determinant of Hessian blob detector. In order to get a higher retrieval speed, we use SURF with 64 dimensions, and extract about 500 features for each image. HOG descriptors describe the distribution of intensity gradients or edge directions of local object appearance and shape within an image. In this paper, the histogram is calculated for each cell with size 2*2 and the direction is divided into 9 bins. The combination of these histograms then represents the descriptor. To have better invariance in illumination or shadowing result, we normalized the local histograms by the intensity across a larger region 3*3. The final HOG feature is 81 dimensions.

4.2.2 Tree Fusion

If we extract about 3000 feature with 128 dimensions per image for both SURF and HOG. The query time of feature forest would be twice of the query time in [3]. In that

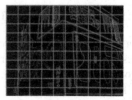

Fig. 1. Left: Original image. Middle: Detected interest points. This kind of scenes shows clearly the nature of the features from Hessian-based detectors. Right: Calculated gradient image. HOG feature is calculated in each region and normalized in block.

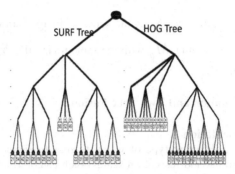

Fig. 2. For simplicity, we just give a sample picture of feature forest structure, consisting of 2 trees. SURF tree is 3 levels and 3 branch and HOG tree is 3 levels and 4 branches.

case, the feature forest would be less meaningful. So we only extract about 400 SURF with 64 dimension and about 500 HOG features with 81 dimensions by controlling the parameters. Then each image has about 900 features in all and the feature dimension is less than 81. So the query image would be less than that in [3]. The levels and branches of each tree can be determined according to the number of the feature.

In the experiment, the structure of SURF tree and HOG tree are all 5 levels and 10 branches. Because we have utilized the rule in section 3.2, some of the branches in the tree stop in the middle level, just like some node in Fig. 2.

5   Experimental Results

Our experiments results are based on 3 standard databases: UKY [17], ZuBuD [18], famous_landmark [16] and a stamp database. For the first 3 database, they all contains m objects and each object contains n images of different viewpoints resulting in m*n images. ZuBuD contains 201*5 images, UKY (first 250 objects) contains 250*4 images and famous_landmark contains 102*10 images.

ZuBuD and UKY database are relative easy for image retrieval task compared to famous_landmark. In ZuBuD and UKY, the variations for same object are viewpoint, rotation, lighting condition, and sheltering. But in famous_landmark dataset, the changes are more complicated and some images for same object have background changes.

5.1   Single Vocabulary Tree Performance

In order to show effectiveness of our improved vocabulary tree structure, we firstly test the single vocabulary tree on UKY database under the same experimental condition in [3, 5]. In [3, 5], they take the first 500 images (125 objects) from the UKY database and 125 views were put into the training database. Another 125 different views, but of the same object were used for query. For the retrieval quality we count the number of correct best matches (top-1 rank).

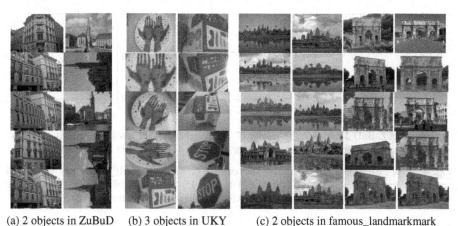

(a) 2 objects in ZuBuD   (b) 3 objects in UKY   (c) 2 objects in famous_landmarkmark

Fig. 3. Each object has 5, 4, 10 relevant images separately in (a) (b) (c). The relevant images are different viewpoint of the same object.

Table 1. VT: vocabulary tree. Retrieval quality on database with125 images (subset of UKY dataset) compared to the standard approach. Although the result with the standard approach is already very good it can still be improved with adaptive create next level in section 3.2.

Method	Retrieval quality
Standard VT	0.814
Our VT	**0.840**

5.2 Feature forests Performance

For each of the three databases, we train HOG vocabulary tree, SURF vocabulary tree and feature forest for the three databases, separately. As to query, we index each image of the database. The performance is weighted by precision:

$$precision = \frac{|\{relevant\ images\} \cap \{images\ retrievaled\}|}{|\{images\ retrievaled\}|} \qquad (7)$$

The lowest precision of feature forest is 38.63%, 85.63%, 89.16% for famous_landmark, UKY, ZuBuD, separately. In 3 databases, the precision of feature forest is always higher than single SURF and HOG vocabulary tree. ZuBuD is a relative easy database for image retrieval and the single SURF can reflect its contents well, so the feature forest method doesn't improve too much compared to SURF tree. But for UKY and famous_landmark, image contents are more diverse. In this case, the performance of feature forest is visible. The precision gain for UKY database at top 4 is 8.2% and the precision gain for famous_landmark database is 4.13% at top 10. Fig. 5 shows some examples of feature forest compared to single vocabulary tree.

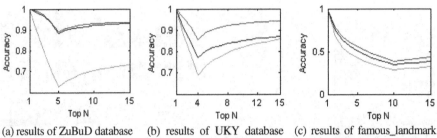

(a) results of ZuBuD database   (b) results of UKY database   (c) results of famous_landmark
relevant image number is 5   relevant image number is 4   relevant image number is 10

Fig. 4. In (a), (b), (c), the curve shows the retrieval precision of SURF vocabulary tree, HOG vocabulary tree and feature forest from Top 1 to Top 15. The green, blue and red curve is the retrieval precision of HOG vocabulary tree, SURF vocabulary tree and feature forest, separately.

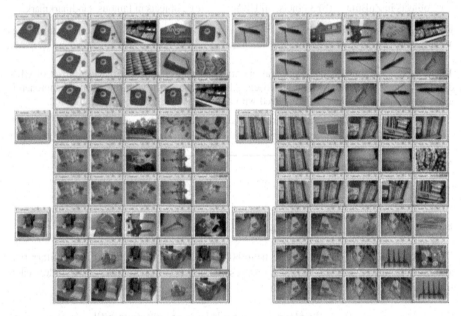

Fig. 5. For each of the image, the 1rd, 2rd, 3rd are the retrieval results of HOG, SURF and the feature forest, separately. Obviously, feature forest gives the best querying result.

6 Conclusion and Future Work

In this paper, we introduce a novel tree fusion framework: Feature Forest, utilizing different kind of local visual descriptors to achieve a better retrieval performance. In the offline-learning stage, our framework first establishes different feature vocabulary trees based on different features and uses the average covariance to determine whether to create the next level. In the online-query stage, we use the ratio of the resulting score to the average score to fuse retrieval results from each vocabulary tree. The final results are combined adaptively from each feature tree according to their ratio. The evaluations show our method outperform other original vocabulary tree method under the same experimental conditions. In the future, we will test on the feasibility to incorporate more than two kinds of features into our Feature Forest structure. Our final goal is to build a feature forest consisting of several feature trees and each feature tree is trained with the least but most important features to boost the query speed. Though the feature tree trained with less features may have weaker performance, we just want to utilize such weak feature tree to construct a strong feature forest, which is similar to boosting algorithm in some extent.

References

1. Leibe, B., Schiele, B.: Analyzing contour and appearance based methods for object categorization. In: IEEE Computer Vision and Pattern Recognition (CVPR) (2003)
2. Lazebnik, S., Schmid, C., Ponce, J.: Beyond Bags of Features: Spatial Pyramid Matching for Recognizing Natural Scene Categories. In: IEEE Computer Vision and Pattern Recognition, CVPR (2006)
3. Frauendorfer, F., Wu, C., Frahm, J.-M., Pollefeys, M.: Visual Word based Location Recognition in 3D models using Distance Augmented Weighting. In: 3D Data Processing Visualization and Transmission(3DPVT) (2008)
4. Siggelkow, S.: Feature histograms for content-based image retrieval, Ph.D. dissertation Freiburg, Germany: Univ. Freiburg, Dept. Computer Sci. (2002)
5. Nister, D., Stewenius, H.: Scalable Recognition with a Vocabulary Tree. In: IEEE Computer Vision and Pattern Recognition (CVPR), Washington, DC, USA, pp. 2161–2168 (2006)
6. Sivic, J., Zisserman, A.: Video Google: A text retrieval approach to object matching in videos. In: International Conference on Computer Vision, ICCV (2003)
7. Grauman, K., Darrell, T.: Approximate correspondences in high dimensions. In: Advances in Neural Information Processing Systems (NIPS) (2006)
8. Adaptive Vocabulary Forests for Dynamic Indexing and Category Learning. In: International Conference on Computer Vision, ICCV (2007)
9. Mikolajczyk, K., Tuytelaars, T., Schmid, C., Zisserman, A.: A Comparison of Affine Region Detectors. International Journal of Computer Vision (IJCV) (2005)
10. Dalal, N., Triggs, B.: Histograms of Oriented Gradients for Human Detection. In: IEEE Computer Vision and Pattern Recognition (CVPR) (2005)
11. Bay, H., Tuytelaars, T., Van Gool, L.: SURF: Speeded Up Robust Features. In: Leonardis, A., Bischof, H., Pinz, A. (eds.) ECCV 2006. LNCS, vol. 3951, pp. 404–417. Springer, Heidelberg (2006)
12. Dietterich, T.G., Lathrop, R.H., Lozano-Perez, T.: Solving the Multiple-Instance Problem with Axis-Parallel Rectangles. Artificial Intelligence Journal 89 (1997)
13. Maron, O., Ratan, A.: A framework for multiple-instance learning. In: Neural Information Processing Systems (NIPS), p. 10
14. Andoni, A., Indyk, P.: Near-Optimal Hashing Algorithms for Approximate Nearest Neighbor in High Dimensions. Communications of the ACM 51, 117–122 (2008)
15. Andoni, A., Datar, M., Immorlica, N.: Locality-Sensitive Hashing Scheme Based on p-Stable Distributions. MIT Press, Cambridge (2006)
16. http://people.csail.mit.edu/tomyeh/homepage/software/index.html
17. http://www.vis.uky.edu/~stewe/ukbench/
18. http://www.vision.ee.ethz.ch/showroom/zubud/index.en.html

Super-Resolution of Multiple Moving 3D Objects with Pixel-Based Registration

Takuma Yamaguchi[1], Hiroshi Kawasaki[2], Ryo Furukawa[3],
and Toshihiro Nakayama[1]

[1] Research Center, The Nippon Signal Co., LTD,
1836–1 Oaza Ezura, Kuki, Saitama 346–8524 Japan
{ymgc-tkm,nkym-ts}@signal.co.jp
[2] Department of Information and Computer Sciences, Saitama University,
Shimo-Okubo 255, Sakura-ku, Saitama, 338–8570 Japan
kawasaki@cgv.saitama-u.ac.jp
[3] Department of Computer Science, Hiroshima City University,
Ozuka-higashi 3-4-1, Asaminami-ku, Hiroshima, 731–3194 Japan
ryo-f@cs.hiroshima-cu.ac.jp

Abstract. In this paper, we propose a super-resolution technique for multiple independently moving 3D objects from a single camera, the camera is also allowed to move freely. Previous techniques were mostly focused on planar objects, and it was difficult to realize super-resolution for the scene containing 3D objects, due to significant appearance changes caused by objects' motion and viewpoint changes. In this paper, we propose a new technique which can solve the above mentioned problems by applying pixel-based registration instead of planar based registration, which are commonly used in the previous 3D super-resolution techniques. Since the technique is pixel-wise and is not required to divide the scene into planar patches, it can be applied to images containing objects with complex shapes or non-rigid objects, to which applying planar approximation is difficult.

1 Introduction

Recently, a number of super-resolution techniques are proposed and commercialized, because the higher resolution of images are, the more stable and accurate the results become in tracking, surveillance and other vision problems. Although there are many attempts to develop a sensor with high resolution, a super-resolution technique is still important, because there is a limit on integration degree on a chip.

In terms of super-resolution techniques, reconstructing a high-resolution image from multiple low-resolution images is intensively researched [1,2]. In those techniques, it is assumed that scenes are either static or dynamic, but consist of single depth or planar objects with little motion, and the camera is also assumed to be static. With such assumptions, registration between frames can be simplified and it can be done with sufficient accuracies with 2D affine or homography

H. Zha, R.-i. Taniguchi, and S. Maybank (Eds.): ACCV 2009, Part III, LNCS 5996, pp. 516–526, 2010.
© Springer-Verlag Berlin Heidelberg 2010

transformation using just a limited number of correspondences. However, for applying techniques to more general purposes, it is necessary to allow 3D scenes containing multiple independently moving objects, non-rigid motion objects (*e.g.* cloths), etc. With existing super-resolution techniques, it is difficult to achieve this, because of significant appearance changes caused by objects' motion and viewpoint changes. To perform super-resolution for such objects or scenes, 3D information should be considered.

There have been several studies targeting super-resolution of 3D objects and scenes [4,5,6]. Tung *et al.* [4] have applied super-resolution technique to construct a high-resolution 3D video[3]. Their target is a person wearing the special cloth which changes its shapes drastically with his/her motion. To cope with such non-rigid 3D object, they first constructed 3D shape using voxel curving technique, and then, divided captured frames into triangular patches to approximate planar surfaces of the object. Similarly, Sei *et al.* [5] have succeeded in performing super-resolution for 3D scenes by dividing the scene with several patches, however, in their method, it is necessary to assign the initial patches manually. Mudenagudi *et al.* [6] used several cameras to reconstruct 3D scene to apply super-resolution techniques to 3D scenes. These previous works are based on approximating 3D objects by triangular patches, and thus, accurate and dense 3D reconstruction is required; it is still a basic and open problem for computer vision research.

In this paper, we propose a super-resolution technique for 3D objects without conducting an explicit planar approximation of object surfaces. More specifically, our method adopts a pixel-wise registration instead of planar based registration which is common in previous techniques. To achieve this, first, we extract a sufficient number of planes as the candidate planes, one of which all the pixels belong to, and then, estimate which plane a pixel belongs to for all the pixels; Note that our technique allows missing planes or wrong assignments of pixels. Since this process does not use explicit scene approximation using triangular patches, our method can be performed even for independently moving 3D objects and non-rigid objects.

The contributions of the proposed method can be summarized in the following three points: (1) Super-resolution method for 3D objects based on pixel-wise registration without the need for explicit planar approximation is proposed. (2) The method is robust against noise and outlier related to the corresponding points of the input images. (3) The technique can be performed even for scenes containing multiple moving objects and non-rigid objects.

2   Pixel-Wise Super-Resolution Technique

2.1   Outline

In previous works, triangular patches are used for super-resolution of 3D objects. A difficult problem of this approach is how to generate triangular patches; where registration becomes incorrect if a single created patch crosses multiple planes. In [7], an optimization is implemented with respect to the position of the created patches, and the resulting method is effective. However, this method

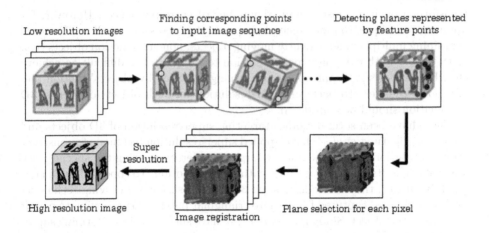

Fig. 1. Outline of our super-resolution technique

requires feature points near plane boundaries and this is usually difficult because of aperture problem. Since registration accuracy of a triangular patch depends on accuracy of correspondences between frames, wrong correspondences of even one vertex cause failure of registration and super-resolution processes of relevant patches.

In this paper, we propose a super-resolution technique without dividing scenes into triangular patches. Fig. 1 shows the outline of our technique. Our technique can be largely divided into two steps, such as registration step and super-resolution step. The registration step is composed of the following three sub-steps: (1) tracking corresponding points between input images, (2) retrieving groups of feature points which reside in the same plane (section 2.2), and (3) selecting the optimum group for each pixel by finding the minimum error value of the average of the re-projection error for all frames (section 2.3). Super-resolution process is implemented using the registration results based on MAP (Maximum A Posterior) formulation (section 2.4).

2.2   Estimating Candidate Planes with Feature Point Tracking

A number of studies have already been reported related to the extraction of planes from the scene for the purpose of 3D reconstruction [8,9]. In these studies, planar areas are extracted by clustering feature points. If it was possible to perform highly accurate planar approximation of all objects in the image including curved planes and moving objects, it would be possible to implement registration process with regard to super-resolution process. However, it is difficult to perform the accurate plane approximation because tracking of feature points are easily affected by outliers, aperture problem and view-dependent appearance changes.

In this paper, we propose a super-resolution technique based on pixel-wise registration which is less affected than a patch-based plane approximation technique

---

Algorithm 1. Candidate plane estimation

1: X is defined as a set of all corresponding feature points across input frames.
2: $P(x)$ is defined as a predicate that is true if point x have been unselected and unlabeled.
3: **while** $\exists x \in X; P(x)$ **do**
4:    Select a feature point $a(\subseteq \{x \in X; P(x)\})$ and the k nearest neighbor points $b(\subseteq X)$ (in this paper $k := 7$).
5:    $A^{(0)} := \phi$, $A^{(1)} := a \cup b$, $i := 1$
6:    **while** $A^{(i)} \neq A^{(i-1)}$ **do**
7:       Compute the homography matrix $\mathcal{H}$ of $A^{(i)}$ for each frame.
8:       $A^{(i+1)} := \phi$
9:       **for** $\forall y \in X$ **do**
10:          **if** Adequateness of the $\mathcal{H}$ for $y \geq threshold$ **then**
11:             $A^{(i+1)} := A^{(i+1)} \cup y$
12:          **end if**
13:       **end for**
14:       $i := i + 1$
15:    **end while**
16:    $A^{(i)}$ is one of groups of feature points residing in the same plane.
17: **end while**

---

described above. More specifically, instead of dividing the scene into triangular patches, candidate planes are first extracted, each of which is defined by a group of feature points included in a single plane, and then, all pixels are assigned to one of them. Therefore, the method assumes that sufficient number of candidate planes are extracted to approximate the 3D scene; to fullfill the requirement, extraction of planes as much as possible from all the combination of feature points is one simple solution. On the other hand, the smaller the number of candidate planes is, the more efficient the computation is; therefore, we propose an efficient method to reduce the number of candidate planes to approximate the 3D scene by using the knowledge that the neighboring feature points usually belong to the same plane. This process is described as Algorithm 1 as follows:

In Step 10, the adequateness is judged by the number of the frames with which the average of the re-projection error of all the correspondent points using $\mathcal{H}$ is less than the threshold value (0.2 pixel in our case).

In Fig. 2, three groups are obtained, where the black points represent the feature points which are already calculated or assigned to some planes, and the white points represent unselected and unlabeled points.

2.3 Pixel-Wise Registration by Minimization of Re-projection Error

Since the candidate planes (groups of feature points each of which is included in a single plane) extracted by the aforementioned method are represented as groups of feature points rather than explicit patches, the correspondence points of each pixel is not determined at this stage. Since transformation parameters of

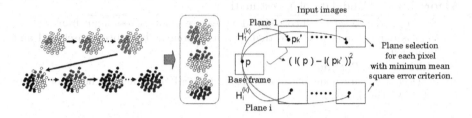

Fig. 2. Candidate plane detection   **Fig. 3.** Plane detection for each pixel

each candidate plane between frames are calculated in the previous step, pixelwise correspondences can be estimated by assigning each pixel to one of the candidate planes by minimizing the re-projection error using the parameters.

In this paper, the homography matrices obtained from the candidate planes are used as transformation parameters. Then, the differences of intensity for each pixel from the base frame to all other frames are computed, the average of the differences are stored for each planes, and the pixel is assigned to the plane for which the value of the average of the differences is the minimum. The actual calculation is as follows. By denoting the number of input frames as N, the homography matrix (as obtained from the i-th candidate plane, $i.e.$, the i-th group of feature points) of the base frame onto the k-th frame as $\mathcal{H}_i^{(k)}$, and the respective intensity levels of arbitrary points from the base frame and the k-th frame as $I(\cdot)$ and $I^{(k)}(\cdot)$, respectively, the following equation is obtained for each pixel in the base frame.

$$\hat{i}\boldsymbol{p} = \arg\min_i \left[\frac{\sum_{k=1}^{M} \left\{ I(\boldsymbol{p}) - I^{(k)}(\mathcal{H}_i^{(k)}\boldsymbol{p}) \right\}^2}{M} \right] \tag{1}$$

Here, $M(\le N)$ denotes the number of frames for which the pixels were effective before the projection (in other words, the pixels were within the image), and $\boldsymbol{p}$ represents a coordinate vector. By finding the minimum projection difference, each pixel is assigned to plane $\hat{i}\boldsymbol{p}$; Note that since we can reject pixels whose difference obviously are large, our method can handle occlusion. The selection process is shown in Fig. 3.

Finally, registration of each pixel is conducted by projecting the pixel of k-th frame onto the base frame using the transformation matrix $\{\mathcal{H}_i^{(k)}\}^{-1}$. If $\hat{i}$ derived from Eq. (1) of each pixel in the base frame and the plane number i of the corresponding pixel coincide, those pixels are adopted as corresponding pixels. As a result, the corresponding position in the base frame of each pixel from each frame is obtained with subpixel accuracy. Since there is a high possibility that neighborhood pixels reside in the same plane, the initial results are smoothed out by using a mode-filter for 24 neighboring pixels in this paper.

2.4   Super-Resolution Calculation from Pixel-Wise Registration

Super-resolution is a technique to reconstruct high-resolution images by using multiple low-resolution images. A large number of studies related to super-resolution have been published, among which the most prominent ones utilize a formulation based on MAP (Maximum A Posterior) [1,2]. The popular MAP based method is also used in this paper. Taking x as a high-resolution image vector, y as an input image vector and N as the number of input frames, the MAP formulation is given by:

$$\hat{x} = \arg\min_{x} \left\{ \sum_{k=1}^{N} ||y_k - \mathrm{DB}_k\mathrm{W}_k x||^2 + \lambda||\mathrm{C}x||^2 \right\} \qquad (2)$$

Here, the matrix representing the subsampling is denoted as D, the matrix representing the PSF (Point Spread Function) as B_k and the matrix representing the motion of the scene or the camera as W_k. In addition, C denotes the matrix representing prior regarding the high-resolution image, and λ is a parameter denoting the level of contribution of the prior. In this regard, optimization methods such as the conjugate gradient method are used in the actual estimation of high-resolution images.

The formulation of Eq. (2) has a problem of efficiency. Therefore, the following formulation based on a simple approximation is used.

$$\hat{x} = \arg\min_{x} \left\{ \sum_{j=1}^{P} w_j(m_j - b_j x)^2 + \lambda||\mathrm{C}x||^2 \right\} \qquad (3)$$

Here, m_j and w_j denote the averaged pixel value and the number of pixels contained in the j-th pixel of the high-resolution image in the case where each pixel from the input images is projected onto the high-resolution image, and P denotes the number of pixels of the high-resolution image x. Furthermore, PSF is assumed to be constant for all frames, and the PSF kernel corresponding to the j-th pixel is denoted as b_j.

3   Experiments

In the experiments, we conducted three types of techniques to compare the results.

1. The proposed method
2. MAP based super-resolution technique assuming a *single depth*
   For registration, a homography matrix of each frame onto the base frame is computed.
3. MAP based super-resolution based on Delaunay *triangulation* [10].

For registration, 2D affine transformation matrices are obtained from the three points defining each of the resulting patches, and the position of each pixel in the base frame is subsequently computed.

For all the experiments, we captured the scene using a USB camera (Logitech QuickCam Pro 9000) with grayscale and size 300×300 pixels, and used 41 frames as the input where the 21st frame were defined as the base frame. Feature extraction and tracking are conducted by using KLT tracker [11].

For super-resolution calculation, we defined several parameters empirically as follows. A Gaussian kernel ($\sigma = 1.8$) was used as PSF kernel, MRF (Markov Random Field) of 4 neighboring pixels were assumed for the regularization terms in Eq. (3), and the matrix C corresponds to the convolution with the Laplacian kernel be $\{(0, 1, 0), (1, -4, 1), (0, 1, 0)\}$. The contribution of the regularization terms λ was set to 0.3. The scale of both the vertical and the horizontal axis for the high-resolution image was set to 4 times larger than that of the input images.

3.1   Super-Resolution of Images of 3D Objects

In this experiment, scenes were static and the camera was moved drastically. Because of the dynamic camera motion, appearance of the scene was significantly different, depending on captured frames as shown in Fig. 4(a) and 5(a).

First, we captured the scene with multiple planar objects and conducted super-resolution techniques. Fig. 4 shows the input image sequence and the super-resolution results. In Fig. 4(d), we can observe a super-resolution effect only on a limited part with the *single depth* technique, whereas all parts are improved by the *triangulation* and our techniques. However, when we see the boundary of the planes, apparent artifacts are observed with the *triangulation* technique, which did not appear with our technique. The results of the search for planes performed with the proposed method and the results of selecting a plane for each pixel are shown in Fig. 7. We can confirm that our technique successfully assigns all pixels to correct planes and the smoothing process allows for reducing noise generated as a result of failures in the plane selection process.

Next, we captured the scene with a curved object and conducted super-resolution techniques. Fig. 5(a) show the input sequence and Fig. 5(c)–(e) show the results. The result of the selection of candidate planes is shown in Fig. 8. In this experiment, we can observe a super-resolution effect only on a limited part with the *single depth* technique, whereas all parts are improved by the *triangulation* and our techniques. However, because of tracking error of feature points, apparent artifacts are observed with the *triangulation* technique in some parts, which did not appear with our technique.

Finally, we compared the PSNR (Peak signal to noise ratio) of the three methods using simulation data (Fig. 6 (a) and (b).). The super-resolution results and the PSNR are shown in Fig. 6 (c) to (e). The results show that the proposed method improved the PSNR with approx. 1[db] (*triangulation*) and 3[db] (*single depth*).

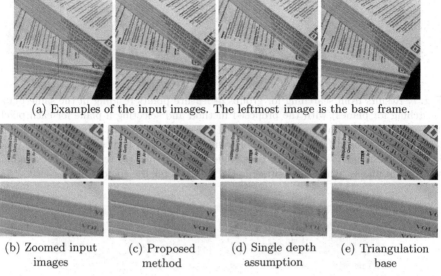

(a) Examples of the input images. The leftmost image is the base frame.

(b) Zoomed input images   (c) Proposed method   (d) Single depth assumption   (e) Triangulation base

Fig. 4. Input images containing multiple planar objects and the super-resolution results

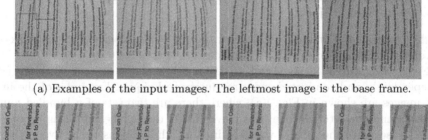

(a) Examples of the input images. The leftmost image is the base frame.

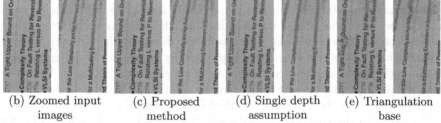

(b) Zoomed input images   (c) Proposed method   (d) Single depth assumption   (e) Triangulation base

Fig. 5. Input images containing curved surface objects and the super-resolution results

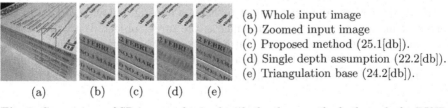

(a)   (b)   (c)   (d)   (e)

(a) Whole input image
(b) Zoomed input image
(c) Proposed method (25.1[db]).
(d) Single depth assumption (22.2[db]).
(e) Triangulation base (24.2[db]).

Fig. 6. Comparison of SR images obtained with the three methods through the PSNR

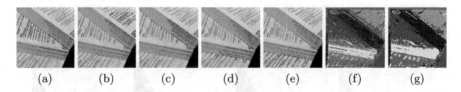

(a)	(b)	(c)	(d)	(e)	(f)	(g)

Fig. 7. Results from searching for groups of feature points residing in the same plane (searching for planes) with the proposed method and selecting a plane for each pixel. The groups of red points in (a)–(e) represent the groups of feature points corresponding to candidate planes. (f)–(g) shows the results of selecting planes for each pixel, and (a)–(e) correspond to red, green, blue, yellow and purple. (f) represents the original selection of planes, while (g) represents the results after the smoothing.

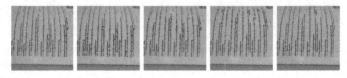

Fig. 8. Results of the search for candidate planes for objects containing curved planes

3.2 Super-Resolution of Images Containing Moving Objects and Non-rigid Objects

In this experiment, dynamic scenes were captured by the moving camera. Objects were both rigid and non-rigid.

First, we captured the scene consisted of multiple planar objects which moved independently and conducted super-resolution techniques. Examples of the input images are shown in Fig. 9(a), where there are two sets of a bundled four booklets and one set(right one) was moved freely during the capturing process. In this case, since the camera was held in hand, the motions of the two objects were independent to each other. The results are shown in Fig. 9(c)–(e). Since it is impossible to take into account multiple moving objects by assuming a single depth, entire parts are blurred in the result as shown in Fig. 9(d). With the method based on *triangulation*, it was better than *single depth*, however, tracking error and wrong triangulation resulted in also significant artifacts as shown in Fig. 9(e). To the contrary, with the proposed method, although small color artifacts are observed in some areas where there is no texture, it is clear that the overall resolution is improved (Fig. 9(c)).

Next, we performed an experiment by using a non-rigid moving object. In the experiment, we captured an waving flag as the target object. With the best of our knowledge, no other method can achieve super-resolution for such scenes. Since the proposed method is based on pixel-wise registration, we can confirm that the results were drastically improved by our method as shown in Fig. 10.

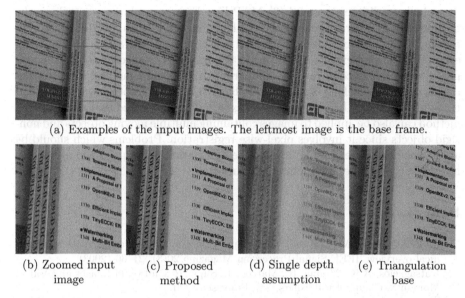

(a) Examples of the input images. The leftmost image is the base frame.

| (b) Zoomed input image | (c) Proposed method | (d) Single depth assumption | (e) Triangulation base |

Fig. 9. Input images containing moving objects and the super-resolution results

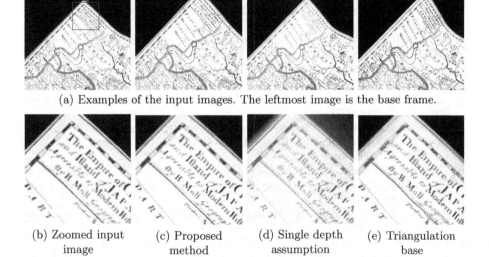

(a) Examples of the input images. The leftmost image is the base frame.

| (b) Zoomed input image | (c) Proposed method | (d) Single depth assumption | (e) Triangulation base |

Fig. 10. Input images containing non-rigid objects and the super-resolution results

4   Summary

In this paper, we proposed a super-resolution technique for independently moving 3D objects with pixel-based registration. The proposed method can be divided into three parts. (1) Plane candidates extraction step, (2) assignment of each pixel to a plane candidate step, and (3) MAP based super-resolution step. Since the technique does not require an explicit plane extraction such as triangulation of the scene, the method does not affected by the feature extraction and tracking error. With several experiments using actual images, the effectiveness of the proposed method was confirmed by comparing the proposed method with conventional methods, such as the methods based on single depth assumption and triangulate patches. In addition, it was experimentally verified that the proposed method can also be applied to images containing multiple moving objects and non-rigid objects since it involves pixel-wise registration. Problems which should be approached in future research involve the application of the proposed method to motion blur and objects with intensity variation.

References

1. Park, S.C., Park, M.K., Kang, M.G.: Super-resolution image reconstruction: a technical overview. IEEE Signal Processing Magazine 20(3), 21–36 (2003)
2. Katsaggelos, A.K., Molina, R., Mateos, J.: Super Resolution of Images and Video. Morgan & Claypool Publishers, San Francisco (2007)
3. Matsuyama, T., Wu, X., Takai, T., Wada, T.: Real-Time Dynamic 3D Object Shape Reconstruction and High-FidelityTexture Mapping for 3D Video. IEEE Trans. Circuits and Systems for Video Technology CSVT–14(3), 357–369 (2004)
4. Tung, T., Nobuhara, S., Matsuyama, T.: Simultaneous super-resolution and 3D video using graph-cuts. In: Proc. IEEE Conf. Comput. Vision Pettern Recog., Anchorage, AK, USA (2008)
5. Sei, S., Saito, H.: Super-resolved image synthesis from uncalibrated camera with unknown motion. In: IAPR Workshop on Machine Vision Applications (MVA 2002), Nara, December 2002, pp. 420–423 (2002)
6. Mudenagudi, U., Gupta, A., Goel, L., Kushal, A., Kalra, P.: Super resolution of images of 3D scenens. In: Proc. Asian Conf. Comput. Vision, Tokyo, Japan, November 2007, pp. 85–95 (2007)
7. Morris, D.D., Kanade, T.: Image-consistent surface triangulation. In: Proc. IEEE Conf. Comput. Vision Pattern Recog., Hilton Head, SC, U.S.A., June 2000, vol. 1, pp. 332–338 (2000)
8. Zucchelli, M., Santos-victor, J., Christensen, H.I.: Multiple plane segmentation using optical flow. In: Proc. British Machine Vision Conf., September 2002, pp. 313–322 (2002)
9. Dick, A., Torr, P., Cipolla, R.: Automatic 3d modelling of architecture. In: Proc. British Machine Vision Conf., pp. 372–381 (2000)
10. Bern, M.W., Eppstein, D.: Mesh generation and optimal triangulation. In: Du, D.Z., Hwang, F.K.M. (eds.) Computing in Euclidean Geometry, pp. 23–90. World Scientific, Singapore (1992)
11. Tomasi, C., Kanade, T.: Detection and Tracking of Point Features, Carnegie Mellon University Technical Report CMU-CS-91-132 (April 1991)

Human Action Recognition Using Pyramid Vocabulary Tree

Chunfeng Yuan[1], Xi Li[1], Weiming Hu[1], and Hanzi Wang[2]

[1] National Laboratory of Pattern Recognition, Institute of Automation, CAS, Beijing, China
{cfyuan,lixi,wmhu}@nlpr.ia.ac.cn
[2] School of Computer Science, University of Adelaide, SA 5005, Australia
wang.hanzi@gmail.com

Abstract. The bag-of-visual-words (BOVW) approaches are widely used in human action recognition. Usually, large vocabulary size of the BOVW is more discriminative for inter-class action classification while small one is more robust to noise and thus tolerant to the intra-class invariance. In this pape, we propose a pyramid vocabulary tree to model local spatio-temporal features, which can characterize the inter-class difference and also allow intra-class variance. Moreover, since BOVW is geometrically unconstrained, we further consider the spatio-temporal information of local features and propose a sparse spatio-temporal pyramid matching kernel (termed as SST-PMK) to compute the similarity measures between video sequences. SST-PMK satisfies the Mercer's condition and therefore is readily integrated into SVM to perform action recognition. Experimental results on the Weizmann datasets show that both the pyramid vocabulary tree and the SST-PMK lead to a significant improvement in human action recognition.

Keywords: Action recognition, Bag-of-visual-words (BOVW), Pyramid matching kernel (PMK).

1 Introduction

Human action recognition has been received more and more attentions due to its crucial values in smart surveillance, human-computer interface, video indexing and browsing, automatic analysis of sports events, and virtual reality. However, there exist many difficulties with human action recognition, including occlusion, illumination changes, as well as geometric variations in scale, rotation, and viewpoint.

In general, the action recognition approaches can be roughly classified as the template-based and the appearance-based approaches [1]. For the template-based approaches, there exist two sorts of templates. The first sort of templates directly use several key frames or segmented patches of the input videos, as described in [6, 8]. The second sort of templates are obtained by linear or nonlinear transformation of the input videos. For example, Rodriguez et al. [9] combine a sequence of training images into a single composite template by a MACH filter. For the appearance-based approaches, local features or global (or large-scale) features are employed to represent the videos.

H. Zha, R.-i. Taniguchi, and S. Maybank (Eds.): ACCV 2009, Part III, LNCS 5996, pp. 527–537, 2010.

Fig. 1. Interest points localization of ten action video sequences in Weizmann dataset. Each red point corresponds to a video patch associated with a detected interest point. One key frame is shown for each video and all interest points detected in that video are overlapped on the key frame.

Generally, local spatio-temporal features are more robust to noise, occlusion and action variation than large-scale features.

Recently, several state-of-the-art action recognition approaches [2, 3, 4, 5, 17, 19] use the BOVW to exploit local spatio-temporal features. Typically, these approaches firstly generate a vocabulary of visual words and then characterize videos with the histograms of visual word counts. It is obvious that the vocabulary plays a decisive role in the process of action recognition. A good vocabulary should not only discriminate the inter-class invariance but also tolerant the intra-class invariance of objects or actions. It is common to choose an appropriately large vocabulary size [4, 10]. However, the large size of vocabulary may introduce a sparse histogram for each video, yield more noise and reduce the discriminability of vocabulary. On the other side, if the vocabulary size is small, it may cause over-clustering and high intra-class distortion. Motivated by these observations, we propose a novel architecture of vocabulary – *the pyramid vocabulary tree* which combines the vocabularies of different sizes and exploits a larger and more discriminative vocabulary efficiently. In addition, it is very fast to project new features on the tree. With pyramid vocabulary tree, video sequences are hierarchically represented as the multi-resolution histograms of the vocabulary tree.

Moreover, it is well known that the BOVW approaches are geometrically unconstrained. Therefore, there are many algorithms intending to combine the geometrical information with BOVW. Some approaches [13, 15] uniformly divide the 3D space into the spatio-temporal grids and then compute the histogram of local features in each grid. However, in the human action videos, the interest points are usually detected in some local regions while most other regions contain no interest points (as illustrated by Fig.1). Inspired by this observation, we cluster the interest points in the spatio-temporal space, which forms several cluster centers. At each cluster center we compute the histogram of the local features. Based on the spatio-temporal cluster centers, we propose a sparse spatio-temporal pyramid matching kernel (called SST-PMK) to measure the similarities between video sequences. In SST-PMK, the histogram used for representing the video is more compact and robust than that in [13, 15]. Therefore the distance computed by SST-PMK is more reliable. Besides, the SST-PMK satisfies the Mercer's condition and can be directly used as the SVM kernel to perform action recognition.

In general, we propose a novel framework based on the sparse spatio-temporal representation of the pyramid vocabulary tree for action recognition. The pyramid tree is built to model the local features, and also prepares a hierarchical structure for computing SST-PMK. Moreover, SST-PMK effectively integrates the distances obtained from all levels of the pyramid vocabulary tree to compute the similarities between video sequences with a very fast speed.

The remainder of the paper is organized as follows. Section 2 describes how to generate the pyramid vocabulary tree. Section 3 introduces SST-PMK and then combines it with the SVM classifier. Section 4 reports experimental results. Section 5 concludes the paper.

2 Pyramid Vocabulary Tree

The Pyramid vocabulary tree is built by hierarchically clustering a large set of training descriptor vectors. The building process of the pyramid vocabulary tree is illustrated in Fig. 2. First of all, the training descriptor vectors are clustered into k visual words to build the coarsest level 0 (i.e. the conventional BOVW). Subsequently, we split each visual word at the coarsest level 0 into two ones, resulting in a finer vocabulary level. In this case, the vocabulary tree grows in a hierarchical coarse-to-fine manner. Meanwhile, the number of its leaf nodes increases in an exponential manner.

In the following sections, we briefly describe the generation of BOVW and the building of the pyramid vocabulary tree in details.

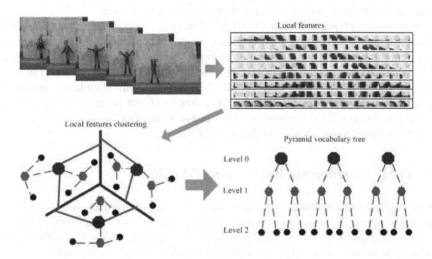

Fig. 2. The building process of the proposed pyramid vocabulary tree

2.1 The Generation of BOVW

A large set of local features are used in the unsupervised training of the tree. Capturing local features includes two relatively independent steps: detecting cuboids and describing cuboids. In recent years, a number of detectors and descriptors have been proposed for human action recognition. All can be used in our recognition framework. In this paper, we employ the Dollár et al.'s detector [7] to detect cuboids at every frame of each video and use the PCA-SIFT descriptor [14] to describe the detected cuboids. Dollár et al. [7] detector improves the 3D Harris detector by applying Gabor filtering to the temporal domain. The outputs of the detector are the location, the scale, and the dominant orientation of each interest point. We extract a cuboid at a given scale centered at every interest point with a size which is s times of its scale (s is set to be 6 in this paper). Then, PCA-SIFT descriptor applies Principal Components Analysis (PCA) to the normalized gradient vector which is formed by flattening the horizontal and vertical gradients of all the points in the cuboid.

Subsequently, a K-means clustering process is run on the obtained PCA-SIFT features. As a result, k cluster centers are treated as k visual words at Level 0. Other clustering methods, such as spectral clustering [21] or Maximization of Mutual Information (MMI) [22], can also be two alternatives instead of the K-means clustering.

2.2 The Pyramid Vocabulary Tree

After building the 0th level of the tree, the training features are partitioned into k groups, where each group consists of the features closest to a particular visual word. Then the training features of each group are clustered into two new visual words at a new level. Therefore each visual word at 0th level is split into two new visual words at level 1. This splitting is reasonable because the visual words at level 0 are highly compact after clustering. In this way, the tree grows till the maximum number of levels L is reached. The vocabulary size of each level is doubled than its upper level.

In the online phase, each new PCA-SIFT feature is compared to k candidate cluster centers at level 0 and assigned to the nearest words. Then the result is propagated to the next level in order that we only need to compare the descriptor vector to the 2 children cluster centers and choose the closest one. Level by level, the new feature is projected to the tree very fast. Furthermore, in the computational complexity aspect, the quantization of new PCA-SIFT features requires $k+2L$ dot products in our approach. However, it needs $2^L k$ dot products for the conventional BOVW in a non-hierarchical manner with the same vocabulary size at the Lth level.

3 SVM Classification Based on SST-PMK

With the pyramid vocabulary tree, each video can be represented as a multi-level visual word histogram. To effectively measure the similarity of two visual word histograms, we present a sparse spatio-temporal pyramid matching kernel (called SST-PMK) in this section. Moreover, SST-PMK can serve as a kernel for SVM classification.

3.1 The Sparse Spatio-temporal Pyramid Matching Kernel (SST-PMK)

The pyramid matching kernel (PMK) proposed by Grauman and Darrell [11] is an effective kernel to measure the similarity of two multi-resolution histograms and it has been successfully applied to object recognition. However, one potential problem with the PMK [11] is that it does not consider the spatio-temporal information. From Fig.1, it can be seen the geometrical distribution of interest points is regularly varying among different action classes, and thus spatio-temporal information is very helpful for improving the action recognition accuracy. Therefore, we take into account the spatio-temporal information of interest points while computing PMK. This is the contribution of our SST-PMK.

The other observation in Fig.1 is that interest points are not uniformly distributed in the image and some regions contain no interest points. Without considering this observation, the SPM [13] uniformly partitions the whole image into 2D grids in the spatial space (i.e., the image coordinate) and the STPM [15] uniformly partitions the whole video into 3D grids in the spatial and temporal space. These two methods do not effectively assign grids, which leads to a large number of grids and some of the grids do not contain any interest points. Moreover, both SPM and STPM require a preprocessing step for normalizing the size of images or videos. In contrast, the grids obtained by SST-PMK are sparse and discriminative, without normalizing videos beforehand. Fig. 3 shows the hierarchical structure of SST-PMK. The following lists the specific procedure of constructing the SST-PMK.

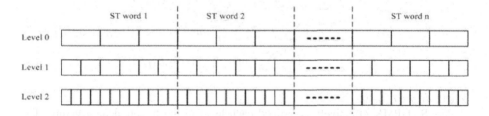

Fig. 3. The hierarchical structure of SST-PMK for each video. The geometrical information of interest points is combined with the pyramid vocabulary tree to represent the videos.

At first, the spatio-temporal vectors of interest points are clustered to produce spatio-temporal words (i.e. ST word i in Fig. 3 $1 \leq i \leq n$). The 3-D data set formed by these vectors is divided into several subsets. The ST words are derived from the center of subsets.

Then, for each video, we compute the histograms of its descriptor vectors (i.e. PCA-SIFT features) at each ST word and each level. And then we concatenate the obtained histograms into a vector $H = [H_1, \ldots, H_L]$, where H_l represents the histogram at level l. And $H_l = [h_{l\text{-}ST\,1}, \ldots, h_{l\text{-}ST\,n}]$, where $h_{l\text{-}ST\,i}$ is the histogram for ST word i at level l. That is, we build a hierarchical structure as Fig.3 for each video and represent the video as a histogram vector.

Given the corresponding histogram vectors X and Y of two videos, the SST-PMK computes a weighted histogram intersection in the hierarchical structure as illustrated in Fig. 3. At each level l, the histogram intersection is defined as the sum of the minimal value at each bin:

$$I(X_l, Y_l) = \sum_m \min(X_l(m) - Y_l(m))$$
$$= \sum_{i=1}^{2^l k} \min(x_{l-ST1}(i) - y_{l-ST1}(i)) + \cdots + \sum_{i=1}^{2^l k} \min(x_{l-STn}(i) - y_{l-STn}(i)) \quad (1)$$
$$= \sum_{j=1}^n \sum_{i=1}^{2^l k} \min(x_{l-STj}(i) - y_{l-STj}(i))$$

where x_{l-STj} is an element of X and represents the histogram of the video for ST word j at the level l, and $x_{l-STj}(i)$ denotes the count of the ith bin of x_{l-STj}. The number of the newly matched pairs N_l induced at level l is the difference between successive levels' histogram intersections:

$$N_l = I(X_l, Y_l) - I(X_{l+1}, Y_{l+1}) \quad (2)$$

Because level L is the finest level, we compute the number of matches N_l from level L to level 0 just opposite to the building process of the pyramid vocabulary tree. The resulting kernel K is obtained by the weighted sum over the number of matches N_l occurred at each level, and the weight associated with level l is set to (2^{l-L}):

$$K(X,Y) = \sum_{l=0}^L \frac{1}{2^{L-l}} (I(X_l, Y_l) - I(X_{l+1}, Y_{l+1}))$$
$$= \sum_{l=0}^{L-1} \frac{1}{2^{l+1}} I(X_{L-l}, Y_{L-l}) + \frac{1}{2^L} I(X_0, Y_0)$$
$$= \sum_{j=1}^n \left(\sum_{l=0}^{L-1} \frac{1}{2^{l+1}} \sum_{i=1}^{2^{L-l}k} \min(x_{(L-l)-STj}(i) - y_{(L-l)-STj}(i)) \right) \quad (3)$$
$$+ \frac{1}{2^L} \sum_{i=1}^k \min(x_{0-STj}(i) - y_{0-STj}(i))$$

where $X_{L+1} = Y_{L+1} = 0$.

The SST-PMK effectively combined each level in the hierarchical structure. The newly matched pairs at coarser level, which are not matched ones at its finer level, are also considered in the SST-PMK. This corresponds to some cases in action recognition, such as the same class actions performed by different persons, and the same class actions performed by one person at many times. If these intra-class actions are not regarded as match at fine level, they are still able to be treated as match at coarser level. Therefore, according to the pyramid tree and SST-PMK, our approach can overcome the variations between intra-class objects or actions.

3.2 SVM Classification

We adopt the algorithm in [16] to train SVM for human action recognition. From equation (3), we obtain the following equation:

$$K(X,Y) = \sum_{j=1}^n K_A(X_{STj}, Y_{STj}) \quad (4)$$

$$K_\Delta(X_{STj}, Y_{STj}) = \sum_{l=0}^{L-1} (\frac{1}{2^{l+1}} \sum_{i=1}^{2^{L-l}k} \min(x_{(L-l)-STj}(i) - y_{(L-l)-STj}(i)))$$
$$+ \frac{1}{2^L} \sum_{i=1}^{k} \min(x_{0-STj}(i) - y_{0-STj}(i)) \tag{5}$$

$K_\Delta(X_{STj}, Y_{STj})$ is actually a pyramid matching kernel (PMK) [11]. In [11] it is proved that PMK is a Mercer kernel and a positive semi-definite kernel. Given that Mercer kernels are closed under addition, equation (4) shows that SST-PMK is a Mercer kernel. Therefore, SST-PMK distance between videos is directly incorporated into the kernel function of the SVM classifier.

4 Experiments

The proposed action recognition approach directly manipulates the unsegmented input image sequences, which aims to recognize low-level actions such as walking, running, and hand clapping. Note that our recognition system does not require any preprocessing step. In contrast, there is a common limitation in [12, 18, 20]: a figure centric spatio-temporal volume or silhouette for each person must be specified and adjusted with a fixed size in advance. However, object segmentation and tracking is hard to implement in itself.

We test our approach on the Weizmann dataset [23]. The Weizmann human action dataset contains 10 different actions including Walking, Running, Jumping, Galloping sideways, Bending, One-hand waving, Two-hands waving, Jumping in place, Jumping

	bend	Jack	Jump	Pjump	run	side	Skip	Walk	Wave1	Wave2
bend	1.00	.00	.00	.00	.00	.00	.00	.00	.00	.00
Jack	.00	1.00	.00	.00	.00	.00	.00	.00	.00	.00
Jump	.00	.00	.67	.00	.00	.00	.33	.00	.00	.00
Pjump	.00	.00	.00	1.00	.00	.00	.00	.00	.00	.00
run	.00	.00	.00	.00	.89	.00	.11	.00	.00	.00
side	.00	.00	.00	.00	.00	1.00	.00	.00	.00	.00
Skip	.00	.00	.33	.00	.00	.00	.67	.00	.00	.00
Walk	.00	.00	.00	.00	.00	.00	.00	1.00	.00	.00
Wave1	.00	.00	.00	.00	.00	.00	.00	.00	1.00	.00
Wave2	.00	.00	.00	.00	.00	.00	.00	.00	.00	1.00

Fig. 4. The confusion matrix of our approach on the Weizmann action dataset

Jack and Skipping. One representative frame from each action category is shown in Fig.1. There are 93 samples in total. The resolution of the videos is 320x240 pixels and the frame rate is 15fps.

We perform the leave-one-out cross-validation to evaluate the competing algorithms. The red line is obtained by the proposed approach, the blue one is the ordinary BOVW approach, and the black one is the PMK approach without considering the spatio-temporal information.

In all experiments we use the videos of the first five persons to learn the bag of visual words. In each run, the videos of 8 actors are used as the training set and the remaining videos of one person are used as the testing set. There is no overlap between the training set and the testing set. We run the algorithms 9 times and report the average results.

In our approach, the three-level pyramid vocabulary tree is used to model local features. The number of visual words is set to 160 at the coarsest level (i.e. level 0) and 640 at the finest level (i.e. level 2). The geometrical information of the interest points is clustered into 10 centers. We use SST-PMK as the SVM kernel. Fig. 4 shows the confusion matrix of our approach on the Weizmann dataset. Each row of the confusion matrix corresponds to the ground truth class, and each column corresponds to the assigned cluster. It shows that our approach works much better on the actions with large movements, but it does not achieve desirable results for the actions of small difference. The recognition accuracy for the actions with large movements is 100%, such as "bend", "Jack", "Pjump", "side", "walk", "wave1", and "wave2". The actions "Jump", "Run", and "Skip" are similar to each other, and thus may be a little confused with each other.

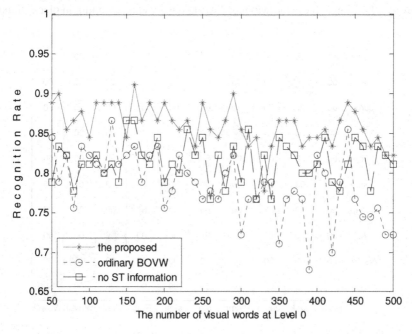

Fig. 5. Recognition accuracy obtained by the three approaches vs. vocabulary size in Level 0

4.1 The Comparison of Three Approaches

In order to demonstrate the advantages of the pyramid vocabulary tree and the proposed SST-PMK, we compare two other approaches with our approach. In the first approach, we use only one vocabulary (i.e. conventional BOVW) and the remaining settings are all the same as our approach. Since there is only one level, the SST-PMK degenerates to the sum of the two histogram intersection:

$$I(X,Y) = \sum_{i=1}^{nk_L} \min(X(i), Y(i)) \tag{6}$$

where n is the number of ST words, and k_L is equal to the vocabulary size of level L in our approach. Therefore in the first approach, equation (6) is used as the kernel of SVM classification. For the second approach, we do not consider the geometrical information, i.e., PMK is used for SVM classification. Moreover, we run the three approaches using different vocabulary sizes. Fig.5 draws the recognition accuracy curve of the three approaches vs. the vocabulary size k at level 0. Fig.5 shows that our approach gains the highest recognition accuracy at most cases. For $k=[50, 60, ..., 500]$, our approach is on average 7.63% higher than the first approach, and 4.66% higher than the second approach. It demonstrates that both the pyramid vocabulary and the geometrical information of the interest points are helpful for the action recognition.

4.2 Kernel Comparison of SVM

We also compare the proposed SST-PMK with other four popular kernels used in SVM: linear kernel $x'*y$, polynomial kernel $(g*x'*y)^3$, radial basis function (RBF) $exp(-g\|x-y\|^2)$, and sigmoid kernel $tanh(g*x'*y)$. The same experimental configurations are used for all five kernels. Moreover, in the SVM classifier [16], C-Support Vector Classification (C-SVC) is employed and two kernel parameters (c and g) are considered. Different kernel parameters are used to estimate the recognition accuracy:

$$c = [2^{-5}, 2^{-4}, \cdots, 2^{25}], \quad g = [2^{-15}, 2^{-14}, \cdots, 2^3]$$

Table 1. Comparisons between the proposed SST-PMK and the four popular kernels for SVM classifier

	Linear	Polynomial	RBF	Sigmoid	**SST-PMK**
Bend	1	0.6667	1	1	1
Jack	1	0.4444	1	1	1
Jump	**0.8889**	0.4444	0.6667	0.5556	0.6667
Pjump	0.8889	0.4444	1	1	1
Run	0.6667	0.5556	0.8889	0.8889	**0.8889**
Side	1	0.1111	1	1	1
Skip	**0.6667**	0.4444	**0.6667**	0.4444	**0.6667**
Walk	0.7778	0.2222	0.8889	1	1
Wave1	1	0.2222	1	1	1
Wave2	1	0.6667	1	1	1
Average	0.8889	0.4222	0.9111	0.8889	**0.9222**

More specifically, since the linear kernel and SST-PMK just have one parameter c, we try 31 different c values and report the best results. For the other three kernels (polynomial kernel, RBF, and sigmoid kernel) have two parameters c and g, we try $31 \times 19 = 589$ combinations. Table 1 shows the experimental results using the five kernels based approaches. Polynomial kernel based approach achieves the worst results, and the average accuracy of other three kernels (Linear kernel, Sigmoid kernel, and RBF) based approaches is a little lower than ours. Our approach achieves the best recognition performances, and it outperforms the other four kernels for nine actions of ten.

5   Conclusion

In this paper, we develop a novel framework which can recognize low-level actions such as walking, running, and hand clapping from unsegmented video sequences. This paper has the following two contributions. First, to the best of our knowledge, the vocabulary is built into pyramid tree topology in human action recognition for the first time. Second, we propose SST-PMK, which takes advantages of geometrical information of local features, to compute the similarities between video sequences. SST-PMK improves PMK by clustering the spatio-temporal information of interest points. Experiments show the effectiveness and robustness of the proposed approach.

Acknowledgment

This work is partly supported by NSFC (Grant No. 60825204, 60672040, 60705003) and the National 863 High-Tech R&D Program of China (Grant No. 2006AA01Z453, 2009AA01- Z318).

References

1. Aggarwal, J.K., Park, S.: Human motion: modeling and recognition of actions and interactions. In: Second International Symposium on 3D Data Processing, Visualization and Transmission, September 6-9, pp. 640–647 (2004)
2. Schuldt, C., Laptev, I., Caputo, B.: Recognizing Human Actions: A Local SVM Approach. In: ICPR, pp. 32–36 (2004)
3. Laptev, I., Marszałek, M., Schmid, C., Rozenfeld, B.: Learning realistic human actions from movies. In: CVPR (2008)
4. Niebles, J., Wang, H., Fei-Fei, L.: Unsupervised Learning of Human Action Categories Using Spatial Temporal Words. IJCV, 299–318 (2008)
5. Yan, K., Sukthankar, R., Hebert, M.: Efficient Visual Event Detection using Volumetric Features. In: ICCV, pp. 166–173 (2005)
6. Weinland, D., Boyer, E.: Action Recognition using Exemplar-based Embedding. In: CVPR (2008)
7. Dollár, P., Rabaud, V., Cottrell, G., Belongie, S.: Behavior Recognition Via Sparse spatiotemporal Features. In: 2nd Joint IEEE International Workshop on Visual Surveillance and Performance Evaluation of Tracking and Surveillance, pp. 65–72 (2005)
8. Lv, F., Nebatia, R.: Single View Human Action Recognition using Key Pose Matching and Viterbi Path Searching. In: CVPR (2007)

9. Rodriguez, M.D., Ahmed, J., Shah, M.: Action MACH A Spatio-temporal Maximum Average Correlation Height Filter for Action Recognition. In: CVPR (2008)
10. Fulkerson, B., Vedaldi, A., Soatto, S.: Localizing Objects With Smart Dictionaries. In: Forsyth, D., Torr, P., Zisserman, A. (eds.) ECCV 2008, Part I. LNCS, vol. 5302, pp. 179–192. Springer, Heidelberg (2008)
11. Grauman, K., Darrell, T.: Pyramid match kernels: Discriminative classification with sets of image features. In: Proc. ICCV (2005)
12. Fathi, A., Mori, G.: Action Recognition by Learning Mid-level Motion Features. In: CVPR (2008)
13. Lazebnik, S., Schmid, C., Ponce, J.: Beyond bags of features: Spatial pyramid matching for recognizing natural scene categories. In: CVPR, pp. 2169–2178 (2006)
14. Yan, K., Sukthankar, R.: PCA-SIFT: A More Distinctive Representation for Local Image Descriptors. In: CVPR, pp. 506–513 (2004)
15. Choi, J., Jeon, W.J., Lee, S.C.: Spatio-Temporal Pyramid Matching for Sports Videos. In: Proceedings of ACM International Conference on Multimedia Information Retrieval (MIR) (2008)
16. Chang, C., Lin, C.: LIBSVM: a library for SVMs (2001)
17. Liu, J., Ali, S., Shah, M.: Recognizing Human Actions Using Multiple Features. In: CVPR (2008)
18. Jia, K., Yeung, D.: Human Action Recognition using Local Spatio-Temporal Discriminant Embedding. In: CVPR (2008)
19. Perronnin, F.: Universal and Adapted Vocabularies for Generic Visual Categorization. PAMI 30(7), 1243–1256 (2008)
20. Wang, L., Suter, D.: Recognizing Human Activities from Silhouettes: Motion Subspace and Factorial Discriminative Graphical Model. In: CVPR (2007)
21. Wang, Y., Jiang, H., Drew, M.S., Li, Z., Mori, G.: Unsupervised Discovery of Action Classes. In: CVPR, pp. 1654–1661 (2006)
22. Liu, J., Shah, M.: Learning Human Actions via Information Maximazation. In: CVPR (2008)
23. http://www.wisdom.weizmann.ac.il/~vision/SpaceTimeActions.html

Auto-scaled Incremental Tensor Subspace Learning for Region Based Rate Control Application

Peng Zhang[1], Sabu Emmanuel[1], Yanning Zhang[2], and Xuan Jing[1]

[1] Nanyang Technological University, 639798, Singapore
{zh0036ng,asemmanuel}@ntu.edu.sg, jingxuan@pmail.ntu.edu.sg
[2] Northwestern Polytechnical University, 710072, Xi'an, China
ynzhang@nwpu.edu.cn

Abstract. In this paper, we proposed a method that employs the auto-scaled incremental eigenspace learning to locate the salient distortion areas continually in the video to serve the purpose of region based rate control application. Compared to other locating methods, the auto-scaled incremental eigenspace learning locating method can achieve locating the salient distortion areas robustly and accurately, and specifically in real-time. In addition, for the case that there exists the overlap/occlusion between different salient distortion areas, the proposed method can also obtain accurate location information which could make the region based rate control and bit allocation to reach higher efficiency in many applications. The experiment results of the proposed algorithm demonstrate the subject visual quality of the video has been improved greatly.

Keywords: Incremental tensor subspace, Region based, Tracking.

1 Introduction

For region based coding methods, popular resolutions are based on employing image segmentation algorithms to identify the shapes and locations of the *ROI* inside the video frame. In recent years, a large number of research works [1] [2] have been proposed for *ROI* segmentation and rate control based on motion, texture and color segmentation. The main challenge of these segmentation algorithms is to reduce the processing time in order to meet the requirement of low delay in real time applications. Song *et al.* [1] proposed a simple yet effective moving region segmentation algorithm based on morphological processing techniques. Because this method also considers removing background noise to simplify the segmentation result, it is inevitable for it to be with high computational complexity.

Tang *et al.* want to resolve the efficient problem from another point of view, they found that visual foreground and background analysis is not that radically useful for rate control algorithms, while the resolution for such questions should consider taking advantage of the visual distortion sensitivity *(VDS)*, which is

H. Zha, R.-i. Taniguchi, and S. Maybank (Eds.): ACCV 2009, Part III, LNCS 5996, pp. 538–547, 2010.
© Springer-Verlag Berlin Heidelberg 2010

the capability of human vision to detect distortion in video/image sequence. Upon such idea, Tang et al. proposed their work in [2], in this work, the model proposed by Ma et al. [3] was adopted due to its low computational complexity and reasonable performance. However, this texture structure model also can not avoid the heavy processing cost although it is better compared with the work of Song et al. For the region based coding, it is not obliged to obtain the binary mask or the segmented ROI for the following work. The location information of ROI is generally enough. Therefore, one idea that uses efficient and accurate tracking algorithms may be more effective in locating the ROI because for the general tracking algorithms, the speed requirement is always a prior consideration.

Object tracking mainly aims at locating the position of the interest objects frame by frame and marking the regions where these objects are in each video frame. The main challenge of the object tracking is to deal with the intrinsic and extrinsic appearance variations of the tracking regions. Thus, how to effectively model the appearance variations becomes a key to the solution of the object tracking problems. In recent years, a lot of research works have been done [4] [5]for the object tracking based on target appearance modeling and using the eigenspace analysis for object tracking has been demonstrated to be effective by many works. Black and Jepson [6] proposed an algorithm by utilizing the representation of pre-trained view-based eigenspace and a robust error norm to model the appearance variations. Their algorithm makes the assumption of subspace constancy in motion estimation instead of using the assumption of brightness constancy in optical flow based techniques. However, the robust performance of this algorithm is at the cost of large amount of off-line training images that may cover as much possible appearance variation (due to viewing angle or illumination) from which to construct the eigenbasis. This requirement can not be always fulfilled for many general applications. A more flexible mixture model via online EM to explicitly model the appearance change during tracking was recently proposed by Fleet et al. [4]. Although their algorithm has good discriminability between the variations of pose, illumination and expression, its treatment of the pixels in the target region makes it fail when background pixels are modeled other than foreground during tracking.

In order to treat the tracking target as an abstract "thing" other than independent pixels, Lim et al. proposed their online incremental learning algorithm for robust visual tracking in [5] because it has been widely accepted that the distortion in the video under various environments can be effectively described and represented in low dimensional linear spaces, which is named Tensor Subspace Analysis TSA [7]. Lim's algorithm also need learning, but this learning is an online process without training phase because it learns the eigenbasis during the object tracking process. The efficient subspace update mechanism facilitates this algorithm successfully track the object under varying pose and illumination conditions. However, this robust tracking algorithm may also drift from target under some circumstances, such as target scale or size is small or changing greatly. Based on the work of Lim, Li et al. [8] and Zhang et al. [9] respectively proposed their algorithm for object tracking, however neither of these works shows the results of the multiple object tracking when there exists the occlusion case.

In this paper, we proposed our auto-scaled incremental tensor subspace analysis to track/locate the regions of interest in the video frame for the region based coding applications. The paper is arranged as following: section 2 presents the auto-scaled incremental tensor locating algorithm. Section 3 describes the region-based rate control by using tracked location, and section 4 is our experiment results. Finally, our paper concludes in section 5.

2   Auto-scaled Incremental Eigenspace Tracking

The algorithm of incremental eigenspace tracking is proposed as an extension of the work of sequential Karhunen-Loeve (*SKL*) [10] by using an incremental *PCA* mechanism, which can update the eigenbasis as well as mean. Suppose we have a $d \times n$ data matrix $\mathcal{A} = \{\mathbf{I}_1, \mathbf{I}_2, ..., \mathbf{I}_n\}$, each column $\mathbf{I}$ is an observation, which is a d dimensional vector of image, the SVD of $\mathcal{A}$ can be represented as $\mathcal{A} = U \Sigma V^\top$. If there is a new observation $\mathcal{B} = \{\mathbf{I}_1, \mathbf{I}_2, ..., \mathbf{I}_m\}$ coming, which is a $d \times m$ matrix, let $\mathcal{C} = \begin{bmatrix} \mathcal{A} \, \mathcal{B} \end{bmatrix}$ to be the concatenation of $\mathcal{A}$ and $\mathcal{B}$, then the SVD of $\mathcal{C}$ can be represented as follows:

$$\mathcal{C} = \begin{bmatrix} \mathcal{A} \, \mathcal{B} \end{bmatrix} = \left(\begin{bmatrix} U \, \tilde{\mathcal{B}} \end{bmatrix} \tilde{U} \right) \tilde{\Sigma} \left(\tilde{V}^\top \begin{bmatrix} V^\top & 0 \\ 0 & I \end{bmatrix} \right) \tag{1}$$

In this equation, $\tilde{\mathcal{B}}$ is the component of $\mathcal{B}$ orthogonal to U, the $\tilde{U}$ and $\tilde{V}^\top$ come from the SVD of matrix $\tilde{U} \tilde{\Sigma} \tilde{V}^\top = \begin{bmatrix} \Sigma & U^\top \mathcal{B} \\ 0 & \tilde{\mathcal{B}}^\top \mathcal{B} \end{bmatrix}$. If we denote the means of $\mathcal{A}, \mathcal{B}, \mathcal{C}$ as $\bar{I}_\mathcal{A}, \bar{I}_\mathcal{B}, \bar{I}_\mathcal{C}$ and scatter matrices (defined as the outer product of the centered data matrix) as $\mathcal{S}_\mathcal{A}, \mathcal{S}_\mathcal{B}, \mathcal{S}_\mathcal{C}$, the problem caused by time-varying mean of the new coming data of the *SKL* algorithm can be corrected by using the following equation:

$$\mathcal{S}_\mathcal{C} = \mathcal{S}_\mathcal{A} + \mathcal{S}_\mathcal{B} + \frac{nm}{n+m}(\bar{I}_\mathcal{B} - \bar{I}_\mathcal{A})(\bar{I}_\mathcal{B} - \bar{I}_\mathcal{A})^\top \tag{2}$$

The mean of the $\mathcal{C}$ can be computed as $\bar{I}_\mathcal{C} = \frac{n}{n+m}\bar{I}_\mathcal{A} + \frac{m}{n+m}\bar{I}_\mathcal{B}$. If there is a forgetting factor f, $\bar{I}_\mathcal{C}$ can be modified as $\bar{I}_\mathcal{C} = \frac{fn}{fn+m}\bar{I}_\mathcal{A} + \frac{m}{fn+m}\bar{I}_\mathcal{B}$.

Then the tracking process is controlled by using a variant type of condensation algorithm [11]. Given a set of observed images $\mathcal{I}_t = \{\mathbf{I}_1, \mathbf{I}_2, ..., \mathbf{I}_t\}$, the estimation of the hidden data variable $\mathbf{X}_t$ which describe the affine motion transformation of the target at time t can be computed by

$$p(\mathbf{X}_t | \mathcal{I}_t) \propto p(\mathbf{I}_t | \mathbf{X}_t) \int p(\mathbf{I}_t | \mathbf{X}_{t-1}) p(\mathbf{X}_{t-1} | \mathcal{I}_{t-1}) d\mathbf{X}_{t-1} \tag{3}$$

Here, the affine motion transformation $\mathbf{X}_t$ is composed of six parameters including x, y translation x_t, y_t, rotation angle θ_t, scale s_t, aspect ratio α_t and skew ϕ_t direction at time t. Each parameter of $\mathbf{X}_t$ is assumed to be modeled independently by a Gaussian distribution from the state $\mathbf{X}_{t-1}$, then the frame-wise motion is represented as an affine transformation as:

$$p(\mathbf{X}_t|\mathbf{X}_{t-1}) = \mathcal{N}(\mathbf{X}_t; \mathbf{X}_{t-1}, \Psi) \tag{4}$$

Where Ψ is a diagonal covariance matrix whose elements are the corresponding variances of affine parameters $\{\sigma_x^2, \sigma_y^2, \sigma_\theta^2, \sigma_s^2, \sigma_\alpha^2, \sigma_\phi^2\}$. We assume that the variance of each affine parameter does not change over time except the scale σ_s^2. With the dynamic changing values of the scale parameter σ_s^2, it is possible to track the object regions with higher precision because let the moving objects to keep its shape or size constantly during tracking is not always reasonable for the realistic situation. Enlightened by the work of [12], we incorporate the automatic blob scale computation algorithm of Collins [13] to estimate the scale of the affine transformation parameter changing.

For the image features that are blob-sized and the like, the work of Lindeberg [12] uses the Laplacian as the differential operator, which is a multi-resolution image analysis based on convolution with Laplacian-of-Gaussian *(LoG)* filters at varying scales when the Gaussian scale space is employed, and the *LoG* is defined as $LoG(x; \sigma) = \frac{2\sigma^2 - \|x\|^2}{2\pi\sigma^6} e^{\frac{-\|x\|^2}{2\sigma^2}}$. Then, the corresponding blob features at different scales can be found as the form (x_0, σ_0) where local maxima is achieved spatially and in scale. Different from Lindeberg, Collins replaces the *LoG* scale space with the Difference-of-Gaussian *(DoG)* [13] because it has been demonstrated that the filter of *LoG* can be approximated by a difference of two centered Gaussian with the scales related by $\sigma_2/\sigma_1 = 1.6$. Thus *DoG* has the form as:

$$DoG(x; \sigma) = G(x; 0, \sigma_1) - G(x; 0, \sigma_2)$$
$$= \frac{1}{2\pi\sigma^2/1.6} e^{\frac{-\|x\|^2}{2\sigma^2/1.6}} - \frac{1}{2\pi\sigma^2(1.6)} e^{\frac{-\|x\|^2}{2\sigma^2(1.6)}} \tag{5}$$

The reason for choosing the *DoG* instead of *LoG* is that the efficient computation methods of generating Gaussian convolution pyramids is available, which is very important and useful for the real time application. Another reason is that we assume that each parameter of the affine transformation from is according to an independent Gaussian distribution especially for the position and scale change. It should be pointed out that the *DoG* operator does not approximate the *LoG* as the traditional form of $DoG(x) \approx LoG(x)$ but equal with a constant scale factor as $DoG(x)/LoG(x) \approx c$, the intuitionistic representation of the scale space is in Fig. 1.

We then apply this feature selection theory to propose our auto-scaled incremental eigenspace tracking when tracking area estimation can be described as blobs through changes in covariance of the tracking parameter samples. The auto-scaled mechanism can be described as: at any given scale σ_0, we use a spatial filter $DoG(x, \sigma_0)$ as the 2D marginal kernel $H(x, \sigma) = \sigma_0$. Then each estimated weight sample image patch where each pixel is proportional to the

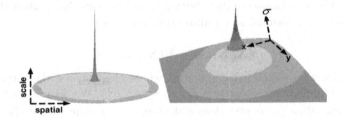

Fig. 1. *DoG* spatial kernels at different scales

likelihood that it belongs to the object be tracked is convolved with a scale-space filter bank of a set of *DoG* filters at multiple different scales. The result is a three dimensional scale space representation in the manners of representing blobs having different spatial position and scale estimated parameters.

Accurately, the set of kernel scales around the current scales σ_0 is defined as:

$$\{\sigma_s = \sigma_0 \times b^s, for - n \leq s \leq n\} \tag{6}$$

Where $b > 1$ specifies the base of a logarithmic coordinate scale and n is the limited range of scales to compute around the current scale σ_0. In the work of Collins, he recommend to use the values: $b = 1.1$ and $n = 2$, while in proposed method, we choose $b = 1.15, n = 3$. Also, a filter bank of spatial shadow kernels is also defined, each is for different scale σ_s and is define as a *DoG* kernel around each estimated object position parameter (x_0, y_0).

$$H_x(x, s) = DoG[diag(1/w, 1/h)(x - x_0), \sigma_s] \tag{7}$$

The w and h is the width and hight of the spatial kernels. During the implementation and experiment, the each current scale σ_0 is considered as a constant. It is obvious that the *DoG* is a linear composition of the Gaussians, therefore with the assumption that $\sigma_1 = \sigma_s/1.6$ and $\sigma_2 = 1.6\sigma_s$, the expected spatial kernel can be defined also as a combination of Gaussians:

$$K_x(x, s) = G(x; x_0, \sigma_1)/\sigma_1^2 - G(x; x_0, \sigma_2)/\sigma_2^2 \tag{8}$$

For the scale kernel, locking one estimated location (x_0, y_0) and looking for the best scale σ_s. Then the value of $\sum_x H_x(x, s)w(x)$ is computed in the range of scales $-n \leq s \leq n$.

3   Region-Based Rate Control by Using Tracked Location

Generally, the region based rate control [1] [14] [2] [15] in video coding is to enhance the coding quality of *ROI* by allocating more bits to this region or decrease the quantization parameter (QP) for *ROI*. As a result, the subjective visual quality of the reconstructed video can be greatly improved. We also adopt this strategy into our scheme. H.264/AVC [16] is so far the most efficient standard for video compression which achieves much higher coding efficiency than previous ones. This is because that H.264/AVC employs more advanced approaches in the coding procedure. *Li et al.* in *JVT-G012* [17] proposed an adaptive rate control frame work for H.264/AVC and it has been adopted by the Joint Video Team. This single-pass rate control method is based on the classic quadratic rate-quantization (R-Q) model and a linear model for mean absolute difference (MAD) prediction. According to *JVT-G012*, there are three levels of rate control, which include group of picture (GOP) level, frame level and the basic unit level. Note that the basic unit can be one macroblock *(MB)* or a group of MBs. In this work, we focus on MB level rate control, which will incorporate our tracking results from the previous section.

4   Experiment Results

The Fig. 2 and Fig. 3 show the comparison between the tracking results without and with the automatic scale changing. The left column is the tracking results by using incremental eigenspace learning [18], while right column is the tracking results of proposed auto-scaled incremental eigenspace tracking algorithm. In our experiment, we use the database of PETS2006 and the experiment results show for multiple moving object tracking with the blob scale changing, the proposed tracking algorithm is more robust and have higher locating accuracy.

Fig. 4 shows the *ROI* obtained by our tracking algorithm for three typical video sequences: Hall, Stefan and Coastguard. In our MB level rate control, if

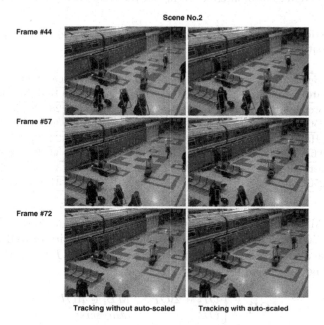

Fig. 2. Tracking results comparison (using the PETS2006)

Fig. 3. Tracking results comparison (using the PETS2006)

Fig. 4. Tracking regions-of-interest serving for the region-based rate control purpose

Table 1. Performance comparison for JVT-G012 rate control and proposed region based rate control scheme

Sequence		Actual Bitrate	Average PSNR(dB)		
(Bitrate, framerate)	Algorithm	(Kbps)	Overall	ROI	Non-ROI
Stefan CIF	JVT-G012	257.07	28.57	28.52	28.59
(256k, 30fps)	Proposed	256.34	27.68	30.91	27.30
Hall CIF	JVT-G012	96.36	35.23	32.08	35.83
(96k, 30fps)	Proposed	96.27	34.63	33.39	34.80
Coastguard CIF	JVT-G012	256.28	30.32	30.76	30.23
(256k, 30fps)	Proposed	255.89	29.68	31.95	29.41

the current MB overlaps with the *ROI*, it will be classified as *ROI-MB* otherwise it is a *Non-ROI-MB*. In order to improve the coding quality of ROI in a frame, the QP value of the *ith* MB determined by the original *JVT-G012* MB level rate control will be further adjusted as follows:

$$QP_i = \begin{cases} QP_i - \Delta QP & MB_i \in ROI \\ QP_i & otherwise \end{cases}$$

(a) Uncompressed frame

(b) Overall:	**29.16 dB**
ROI:	**28.39 dB**
Non-ROI:	**29.36 dB**

(c) Overall:	**28.93 dB**
ROI:	**30.35 dB**
Non-ROI:	**28.67 dB**

Fig. 5. Coding results for 4th frame of Stefan: (a) Uncompressed frame, (b) original rate control and (c) with region based rate control

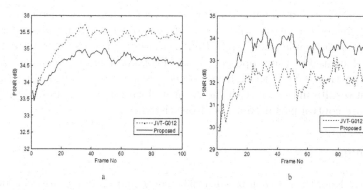

a   b

Fig. 6. Frame by frame comparison for Hall sequence. (a) Overall PSNR (b) PSNR for ROI region.

where $\Delta QP = 2$ is adopted as a quality adjustment factor in our scheme. Actually, the QP adjustment scheme is not limited to the H.264 rate control. It can be applied to the MB level rate control for any other video coding standard.

We have implemented our proposed algorithm to the H.264/AVC reference software JM11 [19]. The original rate control algorithm *JVT-G012* in JM11 was used as a benchmark for comparison. The experiments were conducted using the first 100 frames of three CIF (352x288) test video sequences with various target bit rates. In our experiments, the frame coding structure was IPPP and the rate-distortion-optimization (RDO) was enabled in motion estimation and mode decision. In motion estimation, we set the number of reference frames to be one and selected the search range of 16. We have configured all other encoder parameters to be the same for both methods.

Table 1 tabulates test results of the actual bit rate, the average luminance PSNR for the overall sequence, the *ROI* and the Non-ROI areas for both rate control schemes. From the table we find that both algorithms can achieve accurate output bit rate. It is observed that by using our proposed region based rate control method, the PSNRs for *ROI* have been greatly improved for all test sequences by up to 2.4 dB while the overall PSNR degradation is within 1 dB. Fig. 5 shows the coding results of the 4*th* frame of Stefan. As can be seen, the visual quality of the *ROI*, which is the tennis player has been significantly improved while the quality degradation in *Non-ROI* area is not noticeable. In addition, Fig. 6 illustrates frame by frame comparisons for Hall sequence. Similar results have been observed for other two sequences. Although some degradation is introduced to *Non-ROI*, based on our observation it is almost invisible to the human perception. Thus the overall subjective visual quality is greatly improved by incorporating the tracking algorithm into region-based rate control scheme.

5   Conclusion

In this paper, we proposed using the auto-scaled incremental eigenspace tracking method to locate the regions-of-interest *(ROI)* to serve the purpose of region based rate control applications. The *ROI* in the video frames can be accurately tracked and located by the proposed auto-scaled incremental eigenspace tracking method even the scale of the interest object is small or changes rapidly. The experiment results show that with the accurate location information of the *ROI*, the final rate control performance is also satisfying.

References

1. Song, H., Kuo, C.: A region-based h.263+ codec and its rate control for low vbr video. IEEE Transactions on Multimedia 6(3), 489–500 (2004)
2. Tang, C., Chen, C., Yu, Y., Tsai, C.: Visual sensitivity guided bit allocation for video coding. IEEE Transactions on Multimedia 8(1), 11–18 (2006)
3. Ma, Y., Lu, L., Zhang, H., Li, M.: A user attention model for video summarization, pp. 533–542 (2002)
4. Jepson, A., Fleet, D., El-Maraghi, T.: Robust online appearance models for visual tracking. IEEE Transactions on Pattern Analysis and Machine Intelligence 25(10), 1296–1311 (2003)

5. Lim, J., Ross, D., Lin, R., Yang, M.: Incremental learning for visual tracking. In: Advances in Neural Information Processing Systems (NIPS), vol. 17, pp. 793–800 (2005)
6. Black, M., Jepson, A.: Eigentracking: Robust matching and tracking of articulated objects using a view-based representation. International Journal of Computer Vision 26(1), 63–84 (1998)
7. He, X., Cai, D., Niyogi, P.: Tensor subspace analysis. In: Advances in Neural Information Processing Systems, vol. 18, pp. 499–506 (2006)
8. Li, X., Hu, W., Zhang, Z., Zhang, X., Luo, G.: Robust visual tracking based on incremental tensor subspace learning. In: IEEE International Conference on Computer Vision, October 2007, pp. 1–8 (2007)
9. Zhang, X., Hu, W., Maybank, S., Li, X.: Graph based discriminative learning for robust and efficient object tracking. In: IEEE International Conference on Computer Vision, October 2007, pp. 1–8 (2007)
10. Levy, A., Lindenbaum, M.: Sequential karhunen-loeve basis extraction and its application to images. IEEE Transactions on Image processing 9, 1371–1374 (2000)
11. Isard, M., Blake, A.: Condensation – conditional density propagation for visual tracking. International Journal of Computer Vision 29(1), 5–28 (1998)
12. Lindeberg, T.: Feature detection with automatic scale selection. International Journal of Computer Vision 30(2), 79–116 (1998)
13. Collins, R.: Mean-shift blob tracking through scale space. In: IEEE Conference on Computer Vision and Pattern Recognition, June 2003, vol. 2, pp. II–234–240 (2003)
14. Sun, Y., Ahmad, I., Li, D., Zhang, Y.Q.: Region-based rate control and bit allocation for wireless video transmission. IEEE Transactions on Multimedia 8(1), 1–10 (2006)
15. Sun, Y., Ahmad, I.: A robust and adaptive rate control algorithm for object-based video coding. IEEE Transactions on Circuits and Systems for Video Technology 14(10), 1167–1182 (2004)
16. Wiegand, T., Sullivan, G., Bjontegaard, G., Luthra, A.: Overview of the h.264/avc video coding standard. IEEE Transactions on Circuits and Systems for Video Technology 13(7), 560–576 (2003)
17. Li, Z., Pan, F., Lim, K., Feng, G., Lin, X., Rahardaj, S.: Adaptive basic unit layer rate control for jvt. Joint Video Team Doc. JVT-G012 (2003)
18. Ross, D., Lim, J., Lin, R., Yang, M.: Incremental learning for robust visual tracking. International Journal of Computer Vision 77(1-3), 125–141 (2008)
19. JM reference Software, http://iphome.hhi.de/suehring/tml/download

Visual Focus of Attention Recognition in the Ambient Kitchen

Ligeng Dong[1], Huijun Di[1], Linmi Tao[1], Guangyou Xu[1], and Patrick Oliver[2]

[1] Key Lab on Pervasive Computing, Department of Computer Science and
Technology, Tsinghua University, Beijing, China
{dongligeng99,ajon98}@mails.thu.edu.cn,
{linmi,xgy-dcs}@tsinghua.edu.cn
[2] Culture Lab, Computing Science, Newcastle University, Newcastle Upon Tyne, UK
p.l.olivier@ncl.ac.uk

Abstract. This paper presents a model for visual focus of attention
recognition in the Ambient Kitchen, a pervasive computing prototyping environment. The kitchen is equipped with several blended displays
on one wall and users may use information presented on these displays
from multiple locations. Our goal is to recognize which display the user is
looking at so that the environment can adjust the display content accordingly. We propose a dynamic Bayesian network model to infer the focus
of attention, which models the relation between multiple foci of attention, multiple user locations and faces captured by the multiple cameras
in the environment. Head pose is not explicitly computed but measured
by a similarity vector which represents the likelihoods of multiple face
clusters. Video data are collected in the Ambient Kitchen environment
and experimental results demonstrate the effectiveness of our model.

1 Introduction

Attention awareness is an important component of many pervasive computing
applications [1], including assisted daily living and understanding and retrieval
of meeting records. Visual focus of attention (VFOA) refers to the object or
location that a person is focusing his visual attention on. In human-computer
interaction (HCI), by recognizing a user's VFOA, a system can infer a user's
interest or intention in response to which an appropriate situated service can be
provided. In this paper, we investigate the problem of inferring a user's VFOA in
the Ambient Kitchen. The Ambient Kitchen is a kitchen environment equipped
with a heterogeneous array of sensors and displays, including several projected
displays on the walls to show situated information, including recipes and food
preparation guidance. In a typical scenario, before the user starts to prepare
food, different recipes appear on different displays. By inferring the user's VFOA,
the system can know which display the user is attending to, and by comparing
the time spent looking at different displays, infer the recipe that the user is
most interested in. As a result, proactive services can be provided to the user,
e.g. displaying more detailed food preparation guidance according to the recipe
of interest.

H. Zha, R.-i. Taniguchi, and S. Maybank (Eds.): ACCV 2009, Part III, LNCS 5996, pp. 548–559, 2010.

VFOA is related to both head pose and eye gaze. However, psychological research has demonstrated that in many cases head pose is a sufficient cue to estimate a user's VFOA [2]. This is fortunate as the facial images captured in the Ambient Kitchen are of a resolution that is too low to be used to estimate eye gaze accurately. We have also taken into account a number of factors specific to the kitchen environment in the design of our solution to the VFOA recognition problem in the Ambient Kitchen. Firstly, in the kitchen, when a user is preparing food in front of the counter a user may stand at different locations and there are several visual targets that might be the focus of attention. Consequently, the relation between the user's position and the target's location has to be taken into account in inferring the focus of attention. Secondly, in order to capture the user's face and body at different locations, we have placed three cameras inside the wall on which the displays are projected. Different cameras may capture different poses of the faces, and it is desirable, if possible, to make use of information from these multiple cameras. Finally, the user's head pose ranges from a frontal pose to a full profile pose. Consequently, our approach must be able to track faces with large pose variations and estimate the VFOA accordingly.

In recent years there has been an increase in interest in estimating visual focus of attention. Stiefelhagen [3] studied the VFOA of participants in meetings both with an omni-direction camera on the table, and later from multi-view far field cameras [4]. Ba [5] and Otsuka [6] also worked on head pose tracking and inferring VFOA in meetings in different meeting room settings. However, in the meeting situation, participants are sitting at fixed locations and exhibit only limited bodily movement. Smith [7] studied the VFOA problem in an outdoor environment in which passers-by look at an advertisement (a single target) on a wall. Zhang [8] also monitored the VFOA in outdoor settings but only estimated near frontal head poses for which each pose is considered a VFOA.

Our research is the first attempt to estimate the VFOA in the kitchen setting. Previous research usually addresses VFOA problems either using a fixed viewer location with multiple targets, or multiple user locations with a single target. However, in our application, there are multiple user locations and multiple targets. Conventional approaches also usually invoke specialized mechanisms to estimate the head pose, either 3D models which require accurate and robust feature tracking, or 2D appearance models which need a training set for the pose models. The low-resolution images available in our setting mean that 3D model based methods are not applicable. Due to the generalization problem, and the fact that we lack ground truth head pose data, 2D appearance based pose models trained using other databases are also not appropriate. However, since our goal is to estimate the VFOA rather than head pose, we are interested in whether it is possible to infer the VFOA using face images without explicitly computing head pose. Previous work mostly uses single camera information although in [4] multi-camera information is used to estimate head pose and VFOA is estimated according to the computed head pose. However, if the head pose is not explicitly computed, it is desirable to integrate multi-camera information directly for VFOA recognition.

We propose a principled solution using a dynamic Bayesian network (DBN) model. The inference of the multiple VFOAs is formulated as the maximum a posteriori (MAP) problem. The current VFOA is deduced from multiple camera information, i.e. the faces captured by different cameras. The head pose is not explicitly computed but measured by a similarity vector that represents the likelihoods of multiple face clusters, and we take the similarity vector as a hidden variable. Since the head pose captured by a camera is determined not only by the current VFOA but also by the location of the head, we also introduce the face location to the model. The model observations include the face images and face locations in all cameras.

The remainder of the paper is organized as follows. The application environment is described in Sect. 2. Our DBN model and model inference are presented in Sects. 3 and 4. The experimental results are described in Sect. 5, and finally, conclusions and a discussion of further work are presented in Sect. 6.

2   Application Environment

Our Ambient Kitchen [13] is a high fidelity prototype for exploring the design of pervasive computing algorithms and applications for everyday environments. The environment integrates projectors, cameras, RFID tags and readers, object mounted accelerometers [14], and underfloor pressure sensing using a combination of wired and wireless networks. Figure 1(a) shows the physical set-up of the kitchen. On the wall of the Ambient Kitchen, there are four displays that show a range of information, e.g. recipes and food preparation guidance. Our task is to find out which display the user is looking at, i.e. the user's VFOA, when the user is preparing food at the counter.

Due to the limited filed of view of the cameras, three cameras have been embedded in the wall immediately above the counter so that the face of the user will always be captured when the user is standing in front of any display (which are projected above the counter). The cameras are located between the boundaries of two projected displays so that they do not interfere with the projected content. Figure 1(b,c) shows the layout of the displays and cameras, and the images captured by three cameras when a user is looking at a display.

To simulate the action of looking at a display we placed paper markers at the center of each display and asked subjects to look at these markers. Subjects were asked to look at each marker for a short time in a specified sequence while three cameras captured video data simultaneously. Strictly speaking, the user might stand at any location in front of the counter. However, according to our observations and experience, in a real kitchen, users prefer to stand at one of a few relatively fixed locations when preparing food. Since the displays on the wall show the recipes and guidance, we assumed that the preferred locations for the user corresponded to positions in front of each display. Therefore, to simplify the data collection, we split the area in front of the counter into three areas according to the locations of the displays, and asked subject to stand in these areas for the data collection sessions.

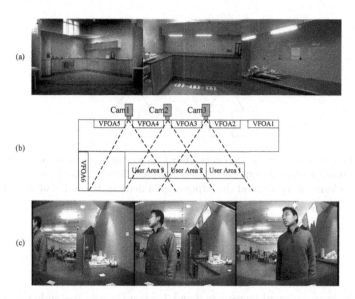

Fig. 1. (a) The Ambient Kitchen, the four displays on the walls, and the markers; (b) the layout of the VFOAs, cameras and areas; (c) the images captured by 3 cameras when the user is standing in area 2

3   The DBN Model for VFOA Recognition

3.1   Model Overview

We used a dynamic Bayesian network (DBN) model to address the visual focus of attention recognition problem, as is illustrated in Fig. 2. In the model, the hidden variable F_t denotes the user's focus of attention at time t. The possible values of F_t are the M possible VFOAs. The hidden variable C_t^i denotes the face cluster of face images captured by camera i at time t. The possible values of C_t^i are the K face clusters. The observation variable Z_t^i denotes the face captured by camera i at time t. And the observation variable L_t^i denotes the horizontal face location in the image captured by each camera. In our model, we neglect the influence of the user's height. The DBN model describes the probabilistic relationships among the variables and reflects their stochastic dependencies. The face cluster C_t^i is governed by the VFOA F_t and the location L_t^i. That means when a user is standing at a fixed location and looking at a specific object, the possible face cluster C_t^i captured by camera i will be determined and the face observations Z_t^i will be dependent on the face cluster C_t^i. Note that the head pose estimation is solved in an implicit way by taking the face cluster as the hidden state variable C_t^i.

Note also that i denotes the index of different cameras and F will be inferred according to the multi-camera information, since when the user is standing in areas 2 and 3, he will be captured by two cameras. In some cases, it would be difficult to compute the user's VFOA using the image from a single camera, a

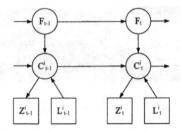

Fig. 2. The dynamic Bayesian network model for visual focus of attention recognition. Squares represent observations and circles represent hidden variables. The subscript t denotes the frame number, and the superscript i denotes the index of the camera.

Fig. 3. The faces captured by camera 2 and 3, when the user is standing in area 2 and looking at VFOA 1 and 2

problem that is addressed by the use of multiple cameras. As illustrated in Fig. 3, the user is standing area 2, looking at VFOA1 and VFOA2 respectively. The images from camera 2 are very similar and relatively difficult to distinguish as compared to the images from camera 3 (which are quite distinct). Consequently, the information from two cameras can be combined to obtain considerably more accurate results.

3.2   Elements of the Model

According to the model, the joint distribution of all variables is given by:

$$P(F_{1:T}, C_{1:T}^{1:R}, L_{1:T}^{1:R}, Z_{1:T}^{1:R}) = \prod_{t=1}^{T} P(F_t|F_{t-1}) \prod_{i=1}^{R} P(C_t^i|C_{t-1}^i, L_t^i, F_t) P(Z_t^i|C_t^i). \quad (1)$$

$P(F_t|F_{t-1})$ models the temporal transition probabilities of a user's VFOA and is defined to enforce temporal smoothness. When a user is looking at a target, he will tend to look at the target for a relatively short time and then move to another target.

$P(C_t^i|C_{t-1}^i, L_t^i, F_t)$ models the probabilistic dependencies of C_t^i on the VFOA F_t , the face location L_t^i and the face cluster C_{t-1}^i in last frame. This is the core of the model, which captures the relations among multiple VFOAs, multiple user locations and faces captured by multiple cameras. Suppose the user's face is at a fixed location L_t^i and looking at a specific target F_t, the possible face cluster C_t^i captured by camera i will be determined. This probability matrix will be obtained according to the training data. To enforce the temporal smoothness of face cluster C, $P(C_t^i = k|F_t, L_t^i, C_{t-1}^i = k)$ will be increased by α and then normalized to be a probability distribution.

$P(Z_t^i|C_t^i)$ denotes the face observation likelihood. Given the face cluster C_t^i, this term is the probability that face observation Z_t^i will be generated by the face cluster. We formulate the likelihood as:

$$P(Z_t^i|C_t^i = k) = exp(-d^2(Z_t^i, M_k)/\sigma^2)/\Lambda, \tag{2}$$

where Λ is a normalization term, M_k denotes the image subspace of the face cluster $C_t^i = k$ and $d(Z_t^i, M_k)$ denotes the distance of the image Z_t^i to the image subspace M_k (e.g. the residual error of the image if represented by the subspace). Suppose there are K face clusters, then for each observation we can obtain a similarity vector S whose length is K, where $S_k = P(Z_t^i|C_t^i = k)$. The details of the observation model are described in the next subsection.

3.3   The Observation Model

Our system is initialized using a multi-view face detector with which faces are tracked using a combination of face detection and online template update tracking. We train our multi-view face detectors in a manner similar to [9] and [10]; for a given frame, faces are detected near the face location in the previous frame. If no face is detected, online template updating is employed to maintain the tracking [11].

After we identify the face box, we compute the similarity vector that represents the likelihoods of the face produced by multiple face clusters. The term $P(Z_t^i|C_t^i)$ represents the face observation likelihood, which is formulated in (2). Due to the lack of ground truth head pose data, we do not have predefined or trained face clusters in advance. Instead, we build the face clusters directly from our video data. When users are standing at a fixed location l and looking at a specific object f, the possible face poses captured by camera i are determined and poses of different people are treated as similar. We denote the collection of face images captured in this manner as $C(l, f, i)$. Suppose we divide the user locations into N regions, and that there are M VFOAs and R cameras, in total there will be $M \times N \times R$ face clusters. Note that the intrinsic face poses of different face clusters defined in this way may be similar if the relative geometrical relations of $C(l, f, i)$ are similar. Hence the likelihood that a face produced by face clusters with similar poses will also be similar. The obtained face clusters are taken as the hidden variable. In our experiment, face clusters are modeled by PCA subspaces.

3.4   Parameter Learning and Setting

For the dynamics of VFOA, we set $P(F_t = i|F_t = i) = P_f$, and spread the remaining transition probability to other VFOAs as $P(F_t = j, j \neq i|F_t = i) = \frac{1-P_f}{M-1}$. Usually P_f is set to a value near to 1.0 and in our study, we set it to 0.8.

$P(C_t^i|C_{t-1}^i, L_t^i, F_t)$ is trained by counting the frequencies of the observations belonging to a face cluster with the a fixed F and L. F is the manually labeled ground truth VFOA, and L are the observations computed from the training image sequences. We first assume that C_t is independent of C_{t-1} and after counting is finished, we increase the probability $P(C_t^i = j | C_{t-1}^i = j, L_t^i, F_t)$ by β to introduce smoothness between face clusters, and then we normalize the probability matrix (β is set to 0.2). The number of locations L_t^i in the image of each camera is set as 3 corresponding to the three user areas.

$P(Z_t^i | C_t^i)$ denotes the face observation likelihood. A similarity vector S is computed as the measurement of the observation. In effect we are not making a deterministic decision and the parameter in (2) is adjusted to make the highest value of the similarity vector lie at around α (which is set to 0.4 in our experiment). If no face is detected, we set the similarity vector $S = \frac{1}{K}$, meaning that the similarity with each face cluster is equal.

4   Model Inference

The VFOA recognition problem is formulated as the inference of our model. Given the observations Z and L, we want to infer the values of hidden random variables F and C. In other words, our objective is to maximize the following joint distribution:

$$(\hat{F}, \hat{C}) = arg \max_{F,C} P(F, C, Z, L). \tag{3}$$

We use approximate inference techniques [12] which minimize a "free energy" cost function. Free energy measures the accuracy of a simpler probability distribution $Q(h)$ which is used to approximate the true posterior distribution $P(h|v)$. Here, h and v represent the hidden variables (F, C) and observations (Z, L) respectively. The distribution $Q(h)$ that is closest to $P(h|v)$ is then used for computing the estimates of our objective. The distribution is defined as:

$$Q(h) = \prod_{t=1}^{T} Q(F_t | F_{t-1}) \prod_{i=1}^{R} Q(C_t^i | C_{t-1}^i, F_t). \tag{4}$$

Following [12], the free energy in our problem is given by:

$$E = \int_h Q(h) ln \frac{Q(h)}{P(h, v)}. \tag{5}$$

Given the states of the hidden variables F, C in time $t - 1$, by minimizing E w.r.t. $Q(C_t^i | C_{t-1}^i, F_t)$ and $Q(F_t | F_{t-1})$, we get:

$$\frac{\partial E_t}{\partial Q(C_t^i | C_{t-1}^i, F_t)} = 0 => Q(C_t^i | C_{t-1}^i, F_t) \propto P(C_t^i | C_{t-1}^i, L_t^i, F_t) P(Z_t^i | C_t^i), \tag{6}$$

$$\frac{\partial E_t}{\partial Q(F_t | F_{t-1})} = 0 => Q(F_t | F_{t-1}) \propto P(F_t | F_{t-1}) \prod_{i=1}^{R} \prod_{C_{t-1}^i=1}^{K}$$

$$\sum_{C_t^i=1}^{K} (P(C_t^i | C_{t-1}^i, L_t^i, F_t) P(Z_t^i | C_t^i))^{Q(C_{t-1}^i | F_{t-1})}. \tag{7}$$

In (7), $Q(C_{t-1}^i | F_{t-1})$ can be computed by:

$$Q(C_t^i | F_t) = \int_{F_{t-1}, Q_{t-1}^i} Q(C_t^i | C_{t-1}^i, F_t) Q(C_{t-1}^i | F_{t-1}) Q(F_{t-1}). \qquad (8)$$

Then the probability distributions can be computed iteratively by:

$$Q(F_t) = \int_{F_{t-1}} Q(F_t | F_{t-1}) Q(F_{t-1}), \qquad (9)$$

$$Q(C_t^i) = \int_{F_t} Q(C_t^i | F_t) Q(F_t). \qquad (10)$$

The output of the model inference will be the VFOA with the highest probability:

$$VFOA = arg \max_{F_t} Q(F_t). \qquad (11)$$

5   Experiments

We collected data from 8 subjects. The subjects were asked to look at different markers from three different locations (areas in front of the counter) while three cameras captured video data of the subjects simultaneously. As a result we collected 24 sets of video (25 fps) and with 3 video clips, one for each of the cameras, in each video set. The length of each video varied from 25 to 30 seconds. The video resolution was 360×288 for which a face typically occupied a region of around 40×40 pixels. To establish the ground truth for the focus of attention, we manually annotated the video data with the marker number and the start and end time of the act of looking at each marker. We performed the model inference on the whole video data set, but only the video data with the ground truth VFOA was used for face cluster training, model parameter training and the evaluation. All the faces were histogram equalized to reduce the influence of illumination differences and were normalized by zero mean and unit norm.

5.1   Face Image Clusters

Examples of tracked faces are given in Fig. 4(a), where every two rows contains the images of a different subject. The first row contains the original tracked faces and the second row shows the corresponding mean image of the face cluster with the highest probability. As can be seen, the mean image of the most similar face cluster is similar to the true face pose, which qualitatively demonstrates the effectiveness of our approach. We can see that the tracked faces are not exactly aligned and in the model we do not compute the accurate pose but use a similarity vector as a "soft" measure. Our goal is to use observations that are not well aligned to infer the VFOA.

When users are in area 1, the faces are visible to only camera 3, while in areas 2 and 3, the faces are visible to two cameras. So in our experiment, the number of face clusters is $5 \times 6 = 30$. For each cluster, we randomly selected 10 face images for each subject to make up the training set. PCA subspace models are then trained for each cluster. The mean for each cluster is shown in Fig. 4(b).

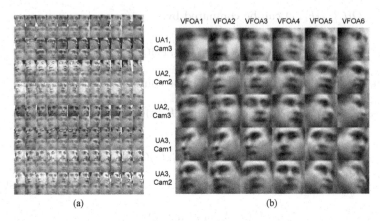

VFOA1   VFOA2   VFOA3   VFOA4   VFOA5   VFOA6

UA1, Cam3

UA2, Cam2

UA2, Cam3

UA3, Cam1

UA3, Cam2

(a)   (b)

Fig. 4. (a) The tracked faces and the mean of the corresponding face clusters; (b) the mean images of all face clusters

Table 1. The result of VFOA recognition with same training and test set

Area	VFOA1	VFOA2	VFOA3	VFOA4	VFOA5	VFOA6
1	100.00	99.78	100.00	97.87	98.47	100.00
2	100.00	89.00	94.33	97.25	95.89	98.32
3	100.00	92.21	86.61	93.72	97.71	98.50

5.2   VFOA Recognition

We ran two experiments to evaluate the effectiveness and generality of the face image representation and the model. In the first experiment, we used the data for 8 subjects as the training and test set. In the second experiment, we performed leave-one-out cross-validation, i.e. we used data for 7 subjects as the training set and data for the other subject as the test set, and ran 8 rounds using each subject as a test. The training set is used to train the face clusters and the model parameters, and the test set is used to infer the VFOA. The results of the two experiments are shown in Table 1 and 2 respectively. The recognition accuracy is computed as the proportion of correctly recognized frames in all the video segments using the manual annotation as the ground truth. For the second experiment, we only considered the result of the test set video and the results of 8 rounds are used to compute the overall recognition accuracy.

The accuracy shown in Table 1, is a direct result of using the same training and test set. The lower accuracy achieved in the second experiment can be explained by the large variations of face appearance and illumination between different subjects. We can see that when the user is standing in area 1 and looking at VFOA 4, 5 and 6, the accuracy is particularly low and the VFOAs are wrongly recognized as the neighboring VFOAs. This is because VFOA 4, 5 and 6 are relatively distant from area 1 and are close to each other. As a result

Table 2. The result of VFOA recognition using leave-one-out cross-validation

Area	VFOA1	VFOA2	VFOA3	VFOA4	VFOA5	VFOA6
1	97.22	98.01	64.86	53.52	45.70	58.46
2	91.70	80.45	95.57	81.50	46.47	87.31
3	81.16	46.12	70.77	99.78	64.86	74.31

Table 3. The average accuracy when user is in areas 2 and 3, looking at 6 VFOAs

Area 2	Accuracy	Area 3	Accuracy
Cameras 2 & 3	80.50	Cameras 1 & 2	72.83
Camera 2 only	68.29	Camera 1 only	52.84
Camera 3 only	74.91	Camera 2 only	63.49

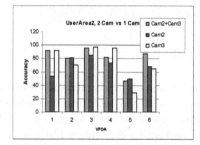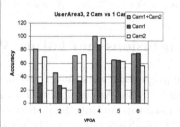

Fig. 5. Comparisons between multi-camera and single-camera configuration with user in area 2(left) and area 3(right). The horizontal axis is the VFOA index, and the vertical axis is the recognition accuracy.

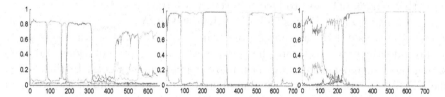

Fig. 6. The inference process. The horizontal axis is the frame number and the vertical axis is the VFOA probability. The lines of different colors denote different VFOAs.

when users attend to VFOAs 4, 5 and 6, they tend not to rotate their heads significantly, sometimes only adjusting eye gaze to change VFOA (in the videos where VFOA 4, 5 and 6 are wrongly recognized the subjects clearly exhibit this kind of behavior). Another factor that impacts on the accuracy is that the faces captured by camera 3 when looking at VFOA 4, 5 and 6 are all close to being in full profile and are very difficult to discriminate. A similar situation occurs for VFOA 5 when viewed from area 2 and for VFOA 2 when viewed from area 3.

To evaluate the impact of multi-camera information fusion, we also estimated the VFOA using the model with single camera information. When the user is standing in area 1, only one camera has a clear view of the subject and we therefore do not include these results in our evaluation. The remaining results for areas 2 and 3, are shown in Fig. 5 and show that most of the time, the results for the multi-camera are better than that for a single camera. For multi-camera information, good results can be obtained for any VFOA. Table 3 lists the average accuracy for different VFOAs when the user is standing in areas 2 and 3. This demonstrates that multi-camera information produces acceptable results for all the possible situations.

Some example inference processes are depicted in Fig. 6. The three figures from left-to-right represent the inference results of video data for one subject standing in areas 1, 2 and 3 respectively. The different colored lines denote the probability of different VFOAs. The line with the highest probability at a certain frame indicates the recognized VFOA at that frame. It can be seen that when the user is standing in area 1 and looking at VFOAs 4, 5 and 6, the probability of the best VFOA is lower than when looking at VFOAs 1, 2 and 3.

6   Conclusions and Future Work

We have proposed a multi-layer probabilistic model for visual focus of attention recognition in the Ambient Kitchen. The model can integrate and model the relation between multiple foci of attention, multiple user locations and faces captured by multiple cameras. The focus of attention is computed by maximizing the posterior probabilities of the hidden variables of the model. The head pose is not explicitly computed but measured using a similarity vector that is computed by comparing the tracked face with multiple face clusters. We have collected video data in the Ambient Kitchen environment and our experimental results show that our model can produce sufficiently accurate results.

Currently, when the user is looking at distant VFOAs, the recognition performance decreases due to the similar appearances of face images. For future work, we are intending to investigate the use of better image presentations and combining motion information to discriminate neighboring VFOAs. In this paper, the VFOAs are constrained to be one of six targets on the wall of the Ambient Kitchen. In the future, we will extend the VFOAs to a larger set of targets (e.g. different locations on the counter) and we will evaluate our method in a real food preparation process. Although the model has been evaluated in the Ambient Kitchen, it is also applicable to other application environments, e.g. finding out which products in a shop window passers-by are looking at.

Acknowledgments. This work is supported by the National Science Foundation of China under grants No. 60673189 and No. 60433030.

References

1. Roda, C., Thomas, J.: Attention aware systems: Theories, applications, and research agenda. Computers in Human Behavior 22, 557–587 (2006)
2. Langton, S.R.H., Watt, R.J., Bruce, V.: Do the Eyes Have it? Cues to the Direction of Social Attention. Trends in Cognitive Sciences 4(2), 50–58 (2000)
3. Stiefelhagen, R.: Tracking Focus of Attention in Meetings. In: Proc. Fourth IEEE Conf. Multimodal Interfaces (2002)
4. Voit, M., Stiefelhagen, R.: Deducing the Visual Focus of Attention from Head Pose Estimation in Dynamic Multi-view Meeting Scenarios. In: ACM and IEEE International Conference on Multimodal Interfaces (ICMI 2008), Chania, Crete, Greece, October 20-22 (2008)
5. Ba, S.O., Odobez, J.M.: A Study on Visual Focus of Attention Recognition from Head Pose in a Meeting Room. In: Renals, S., Bengio, S., Fiscus, J.G. (eds.) MLMI 2006. LNCS, vol. 4299, pp. 75–87. Springer, Heidelberg (2006)
6. Otsuka, K., Sawada, H., Yamato, J.: Automatic Inference of Cross-modal Nonverbal Interactions in Multiparty Conversations. In: Proc. of ACM 9th Int. Conf. Multimodal Interfaces (ICMI 2007), Nagoya, Japan, November 2007, pp. 255–262 (2007)
7. Smith, K., Ba, S.O., Perez, D.G., Odobez, J.M.: Tracking the multi person wandering visual focus of attention. In: Proceedings of the 8th international conference on Multimodal interfaces, Banff, Alberta, Canada, November 2-4 (2006)
8. Zhang, H., Toth, L., Deng, W., Guo, J., Yang, J.: Monitoring Visual Focus of Attention via Local Discriminant Projection. In: Proceedings of ACM International Conference on Multimedia Information Retrieval (2008)
9. Viola, P., Jones, M.: Rapid Object Detection Using a Boosted Cascade of Simple Features. In: Proceedings of IEEE Conference on Computer Vision and Pattern Recognition, pp. 511–518 (2001)
10. Jones, M., Viola, P.: Fast multi-view face detection. Technical Report TR2003-96, MERL (June 2003)
11. Ross, D., Lim, J., Lin, R.-S., Yang, M.-H.: Incremental Learning for Robust Visual Tracking. International Journal of Computer Vision (2007)
12. Frey, B., Jojic, N.: A comparison of algorithms for inference and learning in probabilistic graphical models. IEEE Trans. Pattern Analysis and Machine Intelligence 27(9), 1–25 (2005)
13. Olivier, P., Monk, A., Xu, G., Hoey, J.: Ambient Kitchen: designing situated services using a high fidelity prototyping environment. In: Proceedings of 2nd International Conference on Pervasive Technologies Related to Assistive Environments, Workshop on Affect and Behaviour Related Assistance in Support for the Elderly, Corfu, Greece (June 2009)
14. Pham, C., Olivier, P.: Slice and Dice: Recognizing food preparation activities using embedded accelerometers. In: Proceedings of the 3rd European Conference on Ambient Intelligence (AmI 2009), Salzburg, Austria (2009)

Polymorphous Facial Trait Code

Ping-Han Lee[1], Gee-Sern Hsu[2], and Yi-Ping Hung[3]

[1] Graduate Institute of Computer Science and Information Engineering,
National Taiwan University
[2] Department of Mechanical Engineering,
National Taiwan University of Science and Technology
[3] Graduate Institute of Networking and Multimedia,
National Taiwan University

Abstract. The recently proposed Facial Trait Code (FTC) formulates the component-based face recognition problem as a coding problem using Error-Correcting Code. The development of FTC is based on the extraction of local feature patterns from a large set of faces without significant variations in expression and illumination. This paper reports a new type of FTC that encompasses the faces with large expression variation and under various illumination conditions. We assume that if the patches of a local feature on two different faces look similar in appearance, this pair of patches will also show similar visual patterns when both faces change expressions and are under different illumination conditions. With this assumption, we propose the *Polymorphous Facial Trait Code* for face recognition under illumination and expression variations. The proposed method outperforms the original Facial Trait Code substantially in solving a strict face verification problem, in which only one facial image per individual is available for enrolling to the gallery set, and the probe set consists of facial images with strong illumination and expression variations.

1 Introduction

Local features are commonly considered effective for face recognition. Different feature extraction methods result in different descriptors of local features. Liao and Li [1] extracted 17 local features using the Elastic Graph Matching (EGM), and each of these 17 features had its own specific spot on a face, for example, the corners of eyes, the ends of eyebrows, and the centers of lips. Deformable graphs and dynamic programming were used in [2] to determine eyes, nose, mouth, and chin. A two-level hierarchical component classifier was proposed in [3] to locate 14 feature patches in a face, and [4] showed that face recognition using these 14 feature patches outperformed the same recognition method but using the whole face as the feature. Ivanov et. al. [5] extended this study by experimenting with a few different recognition schemes using the same set of 14 feature patches. Recently, an iterative growing process was proposed to further improve the localization of these 14 feature patches, leading to a two-layered identification approach proven to perform well in identifying faces with large pose and illumination variations [6]. Few have different perspectives toward the

H. Zha, R.-i. Taniguchi, and S. Maybank (Eds.): ACCV 2009, Part III, LNCS 5996, pp. 560–569, 2010.

definition of such local features, as the features are *perceivable* to our nature, and many feature-based approaches have yielded promising performance.

It has been shown in [7] that patterns exist in many of the unperceivable features and can be extracted, and the extracted patterns can be used to decompose and encode a face. The unperceivable features with patterns good for discriminating faces are called *facial traits*, and the associated face coding scheme is called the *Facial Trait Code*. Through empirical observations, we found that the variations across human faces can be categorized into two types: the *inherent* variation and the *external* variation, the former is the variation caused by the inherent difference between people, while the latter is the variation caused by different conditions, such as illumination conditions or facial expressions, under which facial images are taken. In [7], the facial patterns are extracted based on a large collection of facial images called the **FTC face set**, and basically it contains faces taken under the inherent variation only. Hence the patterns extracted can be regarded as the *inherent patterns* that best discriminate between different people. However, if we take faces under both inherent and external variations into account, [7] will extract a mixture of *inherent* and *external patterns*. The external patterns, which capture the variation in external conditions such as illumination and facial expressions, are useless for discriminating different people. Without a proper mechanism, these external patterns will cripple the FTC for face recognition problem.

In this paper, we propose a novel Facial Trait Code, called **Polymorphous Facial Trait Code**, or **POLYFTC** for short, that handles the inherent and external patterns in a systematic way. The construction of the POLYFTC involves a two-stage pattern extraction scheme that extracts *inherent patterns* and their associating *external patterns* hierarchically. The corresponding elaborated encoding and decoding schemes are also proposed, which jointly recognize human faces under variations in illumination conditions and facial expressions robustly. This paper will begin with an introduction to the Facial Trait Code in Section 2, followed by the development of the Polymorphous Facial Trait Code in Section 3. A comparative study on the face recognition performance using the POLYFTC and other algorithms will be reported in Section 4. The conclusion and contribution of our study will be summarized in Section 5.

2   Facial Trait Code

The original version of the Facial Trait Code (FTC) is reported in [7], and is summarized in this section.

2.1   Facial Trait Extraction and Associated Codewords

One can specify a local patch on a face by a rectangle bounding box $\{x, y, w, h\}$, where x and y are the 2-D pixel coordinates of the bounding box's upper-left corner, and w and h are the width and height of this bounding box, respectively. If the bounding box is moved from left to right and top to bottom in the face with various sizes of steps, denoted by Δx and Δy pixels in each direction, and if w and h can change from some small values to large values, we will end up with an exhaustive set of local patches across the face. The number of the patches grows with the size range of the patches and the reduction in the step size. With an extensive experimental study on the size range and step, [7] ended up with slightly more than a couple thousands of patches for a face with 80x100 pixels in size. In the following, we assume M patches in total obtained from a face.

A large collection of facial images, called the **FTC face set**, is needed for FTC construction. Assuming K faces available from the FTC face set, and all faces aligned by the centers of both eyes, the above running box scheme will give a stack of K patch samples in each patch. To cluster the K patch samples in each patch stack, the Principal Component Analysis (PCA) is firstly applied to extract the features. Considering the case that the K facial images can be from L individuals ($L \leq K$, i.e., one individual may have multiple facial samples), for each patch stack the Linear Discriminant Analysis (LDA) is then applied to determine the L most discriminant low dimensional patch features for the L individuals. It is assumed that the L low dimensional patch features in each patch stack can be modeled by a Mixture of Gaussian (MoG), then the unsupervised clustering algorithm proposed by Figueiredo and Jain [8] can be applied to identify the MoG patterns in each patch stack. Assuming M patch stacks are available, this algorithm can cluster the L low dimensional patch features into k_i clusters in the i-th patch stack, where $i = 1, 2, ..., M$. The k_i clusters in the i-th patch stack were considered the patterns existing in this patch stack, and they are called the **patch patterns**.

A scheme is proposed in [7] that selects some combination of the patches with their patch patterns able to best discriminate the individuals in the FTC face set by their faces. This scheme first define a matrix, called **Patch Pattern Map** (PPM), for each patch. PPM shows which individuals' faces reveal the same pattern at that specific patch. Let PPM_i denote the PPM for the i-th patch, $i = 1, 2, ..., M$. PPM_i will be $L \times L$ in dimension in the case with L individuals, and the entry at (p, q), denoted as $PPM_i(p, q)$, is defined as follows: $PPM_i(p, q) = 0$ if the patches on the faces of the p-th and the q-th individuals are clustered into the same patch pattern, and $PPM_i(p, q) = 1$ otherwise.

Given N patches and their associated PPM_i's stacked to form a $L \times L \times N$ dimensional array, there are $L(L-1)/2$ N-dimensional binary vectors along the *depth* of this array because each PPM_i is symmetric matrix and one can only consider the lower triangular part of it. Let $v_{p,q}$ ($1 \leq q < p \leq L$) denote one of the N-dimensional binary vectors, then $v_{p,q}$ reveals the local similarity between the p-th and the q-th individuals in terms of these N local patches. More unities in $v_{p,q}$ indicates more differences between this pair of individuals, and on the contrary, more zeros shows more similarities in between.

The binary vector $v_{p,q}$ motivated the authors in [7] to apply the Error Correcting Output Code (ECOC) [9] to their study. If each individual's face is encoded using the most discriminant patches, defined as the **facial traits**, then the induced set of $[v_{p,q}]_{1 \leq q < p \leq L}$ can be used to define the minimum and maximum

Hamming distance among all encoded faces in the corresponding code space. The $v_{p,q}$ with the least (most) of unities gives the minimum (maximum) Hamming distance. To maximize the robustness against possible recognition errors in the decoding phase, authors in [7] proposed an Adaboost algorithm to maximize the d_{min}, the minimum Hamming distance, for the determination of the facial traits from the overall patches.

Assuming N facial traits selected from the the overall M patches, and each with trait patterns *symbolized* by $1, 2, ..., k_i$, $i = 1, 2, ..., N$, one can now define the codewords in FTC. Each codeword is of length N and n-ary where n is the largest number of the trait patterns found in one single trait. In summary, given a large collection of faces as the FTC face set, one can define N facial traits, $\sum_{i=1}^{N} k_i$ trait patterns, and $\prod_{i=1}^{N} k_i$ faces (or FTC codewords).

2.2   FTC Encoding and Decoding

With a pre-selected length of the FTC codeword, N, the FTC face set defines N facial traits of different sizes, orientations, and locations, and also the patterns in each facial trait. Each facial trait pattern is tagged with a number, which will be used as a symbol in the FTC codeword. In the FTC encoding, a given face is firstly decomposed into N patches according to the specifications given by the N facial traits, and each patch is then classified into a specific facial trait pattern and numbered as the pattern tag. An ordinary classifier can be used for the patch classification. The authors in [7] applied a Nearest-Neighbor classifier based on feature vectors resulting from LDA. The given face is therefore encoded into a n-ary FTC codeword of length N.

In practice the images in the *gallery set* are firstly encoded into **gallery codes**. Given a probe, an image from the *probe set*, it is also firstly encoded into a **probe code**. The FTC **decoding** matches this probe code against all gallery codes, and finds the 'closest' one using the Hamming distance as the measure.

Given two codewords $\mathbf{g}_c = [g_1 g_2 ... g_N]$ and $\mathbf{p}_c = [p_1 p_2 ... p_N]$, the Hamming distance can be easily interpreted using the code difference $\mathbf{d}_c = [d_1 d_2 ... d_N]$ where

$$d_i = \begin{cases} 0 & if \ p_i = g_i \\ 1 & otherwise. \end{cases}$$

Then the Hamming distance between $\mathbf{g}_c$ and $\mathbf{p}_c$ is given by the following,

$$D(\mathbf{g}_c, \mathbf{p}_c) = \sum_{i=1}^{N} d_i. \tag{1}$$

3   Polymorphous Facial Trait Code

As stated in Introduction, human facial images are taken under *inherent* and *external* variations. The original FTC [7] considered mainly facial images taken under only the inherent variation. Although it was reported to be effective in identifying faces under inherent variations, it is expected to have degraded performance when faces taken under external variations are involved, owing to no mechanism was proposed to handle such a situation.

In this paper we propose a novel Facial Trait Code that handles the inherent and external patterns in a systematic way, and robustly recognizes faces taken under variations in illumination conditions and facial expressions. We begin with dividing the FTC face set into two disjoint subsets, the *Trait Extraction Set* and the *Trait Variation Set*, respectively. The **Trait Extraction Set** consists of a large number of frontal facial images taken under the *inherent* variation only (i.e. taken with neural expression and evenly distributed illumination). The **Trait Variation Set** consists of facial images taken under both *inherent* and *external* variations. Assume the Trait Extraction and Variation Set has n_E and n_V facial images, respectively, the following sections give the construction of the proposed POLYFTC.

3.1   The First Stage of Clustering: Extraction of Inherent Patterns

For each of the M patches defined in Section 2.1, we extract its trait patterns following the procedures described in [7]. Instead of using the whole FTC Face Set, as is the case in [7], we use facial images in the *Trait Extraction Set* only. Assuming that the inherent variation across faces in the Trait Extraction Set follows a Gaussian Mixture model, the **first stage of clustering** extracts the corresponding *inherent patterns*. Then, based on the extracted patterns, we select the N most discriminative facial traits out of M patches using the Adaboost-based algorithm proposed in [7]. Assume each facial trait has k_i patterns, $i = 1 \sim N$. For each of the i-th facial trait, this step clusters the total n_E patch samples in the Trait Extraction Set into k_i disjoint subsets, denoted as $E_{i,j}$, $j = 1 \sim k_i$, which is the collection of patch samples cropped from faces belong to the j-th inherent pattern in the Trait Extraction Set.

3.2   The Second Stage of Clustering: Extraction of External Patterns

$E_{i,j}$ is defined in the Trait Extraction Set, which contains faces with only inherent variation. We denote $V_{i,j}$ as the counterpart of $E_{i,j}$ in the Trait Variation Set, and $V_{i,j}$ contains patch samples whose identities are all in $E_{i,j}$. We define $P_{i,j}$ as the union of $E_{i,j}$ and $V_{i,j}$, and it contains patch samples belong to the same inherent pattern, but are taken under various external variations.

In our study, we found that when the patches of a local feature on two different faces are clustered into the same inherent pattern, this pair of patches will also show similar visual patterns when both faces are taken under the same *external variation* (e.g. when both faces change expressions, or when they are taken under another illumination condition). Based on this observation, we assume that the external variation across patch samples belong to the same inherent pattern also follows a Gaussian Mixture model, and the **second stage of clustering** upon these patch samples extracts the corresponding *external patterns*. Fig. 1

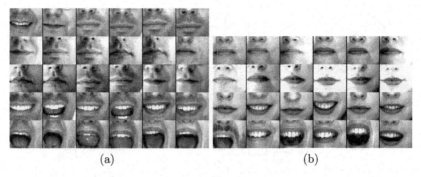

(a)   (b)

Fig. 1. See text

(a) illustrates an example of the clustering result. Patch samples in this figure belong to the same inherent pattern, and those in the same row are clustered as the same external pattern. From this figure, it appears that when different people have the same inherent mouth pattern, their mouths taken under the same illumination condition look similar (Figure 1 (a), the second row shows left-lit samples and the third row shows right-lit samples), or with different expressions (the fourth row for smiling and the fifth row for shouting). For the same local feature, Fig. 1 (b) illustrates patch samples belong to another inherent pattern.

3.3 Polymorphous Patterns for Illumination and Expression Robust Encoding

The proposed POLYFTC aims to encode human faces with their inherent variations maximized, while this encoding process is made invariant to external variations. We define a **Polymorphous Pattern** as a set of *external patterns* belong to the same *inherent pattern*. The Facial Trait Code using the polymorphous patterns is thus called the **Polymorphous Facial Trait Code**. Recall that the FTC encoding transforms a facial image into a codeword. Each digit location in the FTC codeword is a pattern tag of the associating facial trait, and this pattern tag is the classification result of a trait-specific classifier. When we apply polymorphous patterns, this encoding process needs to be modified. The following gives the elaborated POLYFTC encoding scheme.

1. For the i-th facial trait, assume the above construction results in k_i polymorphous patterns, each consists $k_{i,j}$ external patterns. $j = 1 \sim k_i$. The total number of external patterns exist in the i-th trait is thus $K_i = \sum_{j=1}^{k_i} k_{i,j}$. We relabel all the n, $n = n_E + n_V$, patch samples in the whole FTC face set using their external pattern tags, and it gives K_i classes.
2. Perform LDA on these n patch samples based on their external patterns labels.
3. Train a K_i-class Support Vector Machine (SVM) using the resulting LDA feature vectors.

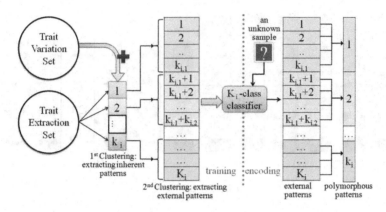

Fig. 2. The flow chart of the polymorphous pattern extraction and encoding

4. Repeat step 1 through 3 for all the N facial traits to complete the POLYFTC training stage.
5. In the POLYFTC encoding stage, a facial image is spatially decomposed into N local patch samples. For each patch sample, the corresponding trait-specific SVM classifies it into one of total K_i external patterns, and the resulting external pattern tag gives the polymorphous pattern tag it belongs to.
6. The resulting N polymorphous pattern tags are concatenated to form a N-digit codeword, which is the POLYFTC encoding result.

The training and encoding of the proposed POLYFTC are illustrated in Fig. 2. The POLYFTC decoding, required for the face recognition application, is the same with that of the FTC.

4   Experimental Results

To demonstrate the effectiveness of the proposed algorithm, we conducted several experiments on the AR face database [10]. There are 126 different people (70 men and 56 women) in the AR database. Each person participated in two sessions, separated by two weeks (14 days). We include one neutral faces (Fig. 3 (a)), three faces taken under three different facial expression (Fig. 3 (b),(c) and (d)), and three faces taken under three different illumination conditions (Fig. 3 (e),(f) and (g)). These faces are aligned with the centers of two eyes, converted to gray scale images, and resized to 80-by-100 pixels.

We compared the performance of the proposed algorithm with two baseline algorithms, Eigenface [11] and Fisherface [12], the LBP approach [13], and the original FTC [7]. Note that instead of using the nearest neighbor classifier for trait pattern classification [7], in this work we applied the Support Vector Machine[1] (SVM), and it gives about 10% boost in identification accuracy. For both

---

[1] For both FTC and POLYFTC implemented in this paper.

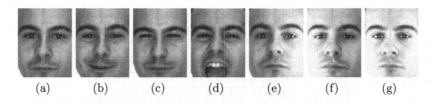

Fig. 3. Samples of faces from the AR database

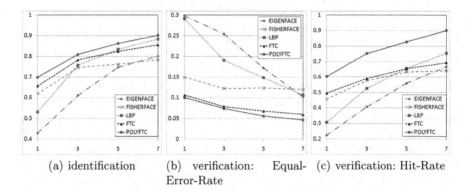

(a) identification   (b) verification: Equal-   (c) verification: Hit-Rate
Error-Rate

Fig. 4. Performance of different algorithms. The y-axis is the accuracy and the x-axis is the SPP.

FTC and POLYFTC, 64 facial traits are selected to form 64-digit codewords. Both the identification and verification results are reported.

4.1 Test Protocol and Performance Comparison

We randomly select 63 identities from 126 ones with their samples to form the *training set*. The facial samples belong to the remaining 63 identities taken during the first session form the *gallery set*, and those taken during the second session form the *probe set*. Face recognition algorithms are trained using samples in the training set, and they are not allowed to alter their models afterward. The facial images in the gallery set are enrolled, and images in the probe set are identified or verified against the gallery identities. The number of sample per person (**SPP** for short) in the gallery set is considered as a factor, it ranges from 1 to 7. SSP=1 presents a very strict protocol, in which only one image is enrolled, and it may be taken under strong illumination variation or slight facial expressions.[2] Meanwhile, the probe set includes images under all the kinds of variations.

Fig. 4 (a) shows the identification results; (b) shows the Equal Error Rates in verification problem; (c) shows the Hit Rates when the False Alarm Rate equals to 0.01. Each data point in these figures is the averaged result over 20 rounds of

---

[2] We do not use Fig. 3 (d) for enrolling, since in practice it is rarely the case.

Table 1. Summary of the performance of algorithms

SPP	7			1		
algorithm	Ident	HIT	EER	Ident	HIT	EER
EIGEN [11]	0.80	0.67	0.102	0.42	0.22	0.298
FISHER [12]	0.78	0.64	0.118	0.62	0.46	0.149
LBP [13]	0.88	0.75	0.106	0.53	0.31	0.291
FTC [7]	0.85	0.69	0.056	0.66	0.49	0.106
POLYFTC	**0.90**	**0.90**	**0.046**	**0.70**	**0.60**	**0.099**

random identity selection. Note that the performance of the Eigenface and LBP approaches decrease dramatically when SPP decreases, as expected, since the two algorithms do not learn any feature that is invariant to within-person variation in appearance. Obviously the proposed POLYFTC outperforms all other algorithms consistently. Note that POLYFTC outperforms FTC substantially for the verification problem in Fig. 4 (c). The reason is that the minimum pairwise codeword distance, or d_{min}, among the gallery codewords for POLYFTC is typically around 50, while it is around 14 for FTC in our experiment, and it means that codewords of different identities are far more well separated in the POLYFTC code space than those in the FTC code space. Table 1 gives the summary of the performance of all the algorithms under SPP equals 1 and 7.

5   Conclusion and Future Work

In this paper we propose a new type of the Facial Trait Code [7]. The proposed algorithm applies a more sophisticated two-stage clustering scheme to extract inherent and external patterns of human facial parts. The inherent patterns capture the genuine variation in human facial appearance, while the external patterns capture the variations caused by illumination or facial expressions. The proposed algorithm yields promising recognition results for faces under illumination and expression variations. An it achieves significant better verification performance than the original Facial Trait Code.

The introduction of external patterns makes the proposed POLYFTC applicable to the *facial expression recognition* problem, since the POLYFTC encoding actually recognizes the external patterns besides the polymorphous pattern. Our future work will develop an algorithm that simultaneously recognizes the facial expression, illumination condition and identity of a given face.

References

1. Liao, R., Li, S.Z.: Face recognition based on multiple facial features. In: Proc. of the 4th IEEE Int. Conf. on Automatic Face and Gesture Recognition, pp. 239–244. Dekker Inc. (2000)
2. Ahlberg, J.: Facial feature extraction using deformable graphs and statistical pattern matching. In: Swedish Symposium on Image Analysis, SSAB (1999)

3. Heisele, B., Thomas, S., Sam, P., Poggio, T.: Hierarchical classification and feature reduction for fast face detection with support vector machines. Pattern Recognition 36(9), 2007–2017 (2003)
4. Heisele, B., Ho, P., Wu, J., Poggio, T.: Face recognition: component-based versus global approaches. CVIU 91(1), 6–12 (2003)
5. Ivanov, Y., Heisele, B., Serre, T.: Using component features for face recognition. In: FGR 2004, p. 421 (2004)
6. Heisele, B., Serre, T., Poggio, T.: A component-based framework for face detection and identification. IJCV 74(2), 167–181 (2007)
7. Lee, P.H., Hsu, G.S., Chen, T., Hung, Y.P.: Facial trait code and its application to face recognition. In: Bebis, G., Boyle, R., Parvin, B., Koracin, D., Remagnino, P., Porikli, F., Peters, J., Klosowski, J., Arns, L., Chun, Y.K., Rhyne, T.-M., Monroe, L. (eds.) ISVC 2008, Part II. LNCS, vol. 5359, pp. 317–328. Springer, Heidelberg (2008)
8. Figueiredo, M., Jain, A.: Unsupervised learning of finite mixture models. PAMI 24, 381–396 (2002)
9. Dietterich, T.G., Bakiri, G.: Solving multiclass learning problems via error-correcting output codes. Journal of Artificial Intelligence Research 2, 263–286 (1995)
10. Martinez, A., Benavente, R.: The ar face database. Technical Report 24, CVC (1998)
11. Turk, M., Pentland, A.: Eigenfaces for recognition. Journal of Cognitive Neuroscience 3(1), 71–86 (1991)
12. Belhumeur, P., Hespanha, J., Kriegman, D.: Eigenfaces vs. fisherfaces: Recognition using class specific linear projection. PAMI 19(7), 711–720 (1997)
13. Ahonen, T., Hadid, A., Pietikainen, M.: Face description with local binary patterns: Application to face recognition. PAMI, 2037–2041 (2006)

Face Recognition by Estimating Facial Distinctive Information Distribution

Bangyou Da, Nong Sang, and Chi Li

Institute for Pattern Recognition and Artificial Intelligence
Huazhong University of Science and Technology
Wuhan, Hubei 430074, China

Abstract. Several studies of psychophysics have shown that the eyes or the mouth seem to be an important cue in human face perception, and the nose plays an insignificant role, this means that there exists a distinctive information distribution of faces.This paper presents a novel approach for face recognition by combining the Local Binary Patterns (LBP) based face descriptor and the distinctive information of faces. First, we give a quantitative estimation of the density for each pixel in fronted face image by combining Parzen-window approach and Scale Invariant Feature Transform (SIFT) detector, which is taken as the measure of the distinctive information of the faces. Second, we integral the density function in the sub-window region of face to gain the weights set which is used in the LBP based face descriptor to produce weighted Chi square statistics. As an elementary application of the estimation of distinctive information of face, the proposed method is tested on the FERET FA/FB image sets and yields a recognition rate of 98.2% contrast to the 97.3% which is produced by the method adopted by Ahonen.

Keywords: Face Recognition, Parzen-window, SIFT, LBP.

1 Introduction

Face recognition is possibly one of the first cognitive process used by human to recognize familiar people and attracts much attention due to its potential values for applications as well as theoretical challenges. A key issue in face recognition is finding efficient descriptors for facial appearance. Up to now, many holistic representation approaches have been introduced, including Principal Component Analysis (PCA)[1], Linear Discriminant Analysis (LDA)[2], Independent Component Analysis (ICA)[3]. PCA is commonly referred to as the "eigenface" method; it finds a set of the most representative projection vectors so that the projected samples retain most information about original samples in the sense of the least mean squared reconstruction error. ICA captures both second and higher order statistics and projects the input data onto the basis vectors that are as statistically independent as possible. LDA uses the class information and finds a set of vectors that maximize the between-class scatter while minimizing the within-class scatter.

H. Zha, R.-i. Taniguchi, and S. Maybank (Eds.): ACCV 2009, Part III, LNCS 5996, pp. 570–580, 2010.
© Springer-Verlag Berlin Heidelberg 2010

A main shortage of holistic methods is the sensitivity of the variations in different factors such as pose, illumination etc. On the other hand, the local descriptors have gained more attention due to their robustness to challenge such factors. In 2004, Ahonen et al. introduced a new approach for face recognition based on Local Binary Pattern features[4], which uses both shape and texture information to represent the face images. In their approach, a face image is divided into small regions from which the Local Binary Pattern (LBP) histogram[5] are extracted and concatenated into a single feature histogram efficiently representing the face image. In the end, the recognition is performed using a nearest neighbor classifier in the computed feature space with Chi square as a dissimilarity measure. From then on, many studies based on LBP features were investigated [6,7,8,9].

The performance of the LBP-based algorithm largely depends upon the weights set of facial parts. The weights set is determined by the inherent property of face which is suggested by the studies of psychophysics that the eyes or the mouth seem to be an important cue in human face perception, and the nose plays an insignificant role[10,11,12]. To make use of this property of face for recognition, several empiric approaches were introduced, which include getting weights by performing recognition experiments on a training set[4], or learning suitable weights based on Fisher separation criterion[7]. Another method utilizes Adaboost technique to find more appropriate facial parts and their weights[6].

In this paper we propose a novel generative approach which is different from the methods adopted in[4,6,7], to find the weights of different facial parts. First, according to the research of psychophysics, we give a quantitative estimation of the density for each pixel in fronted face image by combining Parzen-window approach and Scale Invariant Feature Transform (SIFT) local interest point detector, which is taken as the measure of the distinctive information of the faces. Second, we integral the density function in the sub-window region of face to gain the weights set which is used in the LBP based face descriptor to produce weighted Chi square statistics. As an elementary result, the proposed method is tested on the FERET FA/FB image sets and yields a recognition rate of 98.2% contrast to the 97.3% which is produced by the method adopted in[4].

The rest of this paper is organized as follows: In section 2, the Local Binary Patterns are introduced. In section 3, the estimation of distinctive information probability density of face is proposed and used in LBP based face description. And the experiment results on the FERET database is given in section 4. In section 5, we present the conclusion and future work.

2   Face Description with LBP

2.1   Local Binary Pattern

The original LBP operator, introduced by Ojala et al.[5], is a powerful means of texture description. The operator labels the pixels of an image by thresholding the 3×3-neighbourhood of each pixel with the center value and considering the result as a binary number. Then the histogram of the labels can be used as a texture descriptor.

The basic operator was extended to use neighborhoods of different sizes [5]. Using circular neighborhoods and bilinearly interpolating the pixel values allow any radius and number of pixels in the neighborhood. For neighborhoods we will use the notation (P, R) which means P sampling points on a circle of radius of R.

Another important extension to the original operator is to use uniform patterns[5]. A Local Binary Pattern is called uniform if it contains at most two bit-wise transitions from 0 to 1 or vice versa when the binary string is considered circular. Ojala reported that in their experiments with texture images, uniform patterns account for a bit less than 90% of all patterns when using the $(8, 1)$ neighborhood and for 70% in $(16, 2)$ neighborhood.

In this paper, according to [5], we use the following notation for the LBP operator: $LBP_{P,R}^{u2}$. Where the subscript represents using the operator in a (P, R) neighborhood. Superscript $u2$ stands for using only uniform patterns and labeling all remaining patterns with a single label.

A histogram of the labeled image $f_l(x, y)$ can be defined as:

$$H_i = \sum_{x,y} I\{f_l(x, y) = i\}, \quad i = 0, \ldots, k-1 \tag{1}$$

in which k is the number of different labels produced by the LBP operator and

$$I\{A\} = \begin{cases} 1, & \text{A is true} \\ 0, & \text{A is false} \end{cases}$$

2.2 LBP Based Face Description

In [4], Ahonen et al. presented that the face area can be divided into small regions from which Local Binary Pattern (LBP) histograms are extracted and concatenated into a single, spatially enhanced feature histogram efficiently representing the face image. For this purpose, the face image is divided into regions $R_0, R_1 \ldots R_{m-1}$ (see Fig.1) and the spatially enhanced histogram is defined as

$$H_{i,j} = \sum_{x,y} I\{f_l(x, y) = i\} \cdot I\{(x, y) \in R_j\}, \quad i = 0, \ldots, k-1, j = 0, \ldots, m-1 \tag{2}$$

Meanwhile, regarding the psychophysics studies that some facial regions contain more useful information than others in terms of distinguishing between people, Ahonen presented a weighted Chi square statistics as follow to build a dissimilarity measure of face.

$$\chi_\omega^2(S, M) = \sum_{i,j} \omega_j \cdot \frac{(S_{i,j} - M_{i,j})^2}{S_{i,j} + M_{i,j}} \tag{3}$$

In which S and M are two histograms, and ω_j is the weight for region j. See Fig.1 for the illustration of face descriptor, more details can be seen in [4].

An important issue is how to find the weights of different local face region. In [4], Ahonen presented the following procedure to find the weights ω_j for

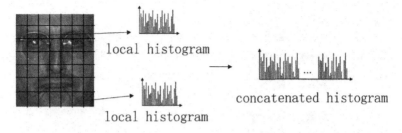

concatenated histogram

local histogram

Fig. 1. LBP face description with concatenated histogram

the weighted χ^2 statistic: a training set was classified using only one of the sub-windows at a time. The recognition rates of corresponding windows on the left and right half of the face were averaged. Then the windows whose rate lay below the 0.2 percentile of the rates got weight 0 and windows whose rate lay above the 0.8 and 0.9 percentile got weights 2.0 and 4.0, respectively. The other windows got weight 1.0. Hereinafter we will give a generative method to determine the weights set of face region by estimating the distinctive information density of face.

3   Density Estimation of Distinctive Information of Face

3.1   Estimating Density by Parzen-Window Approach

From the view of object classification, the face image can be considered as a class with consistent texture in almost same scale (see Fig2). A normal human face always has the same facial components on certainly position. Given exact position of eyes, the position of other facial components such as nose, mouth, is determined. Such geometry property of face is exactly the foundation of the registration of face image. So, we can consider thousands of aligned face images as a unified class.

Previous studies of psychophysics have shown that different facial parts play different role for face perception[10,11,12]. It is obvious that the more significant role the facial parts play, the more distinctive information facial parts contain. In the view of detecting local interest point, it is reasonable to induce that the significant facial parts of face image region will detect more local interest points. In this regard, we can draw a conclusion that the position of local interest points indicate the significance of facial parts. Furthermore, the local interest points detected from thousands of aligned face images can be treated as equal role (see Fig.4).

The studies of psychophysics means that there exists a true two dimensional probability distribution density $p(\mathbf{X})$ of the distinctive information on the face image, and the local interest points can be considered the samples drawn independently and identically distributed (i.i.d.), according to the probability law $p(\mathbf{X})$ of face image by local interest point detector. Here we can regard the

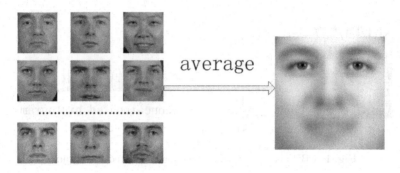

Fig. 2. The unified structure of face. In this illustration, the right blur image is created by averaging thousands of aligned face images with fixed scale and pose as left column. The face images are got from face database of University of Notre Dame[13].

detector as a sampler. The purpose is to estimate the probability density function $p(\boldsymbol{X})$ by using the locations and scales of local interest points.

In fact, until now we have no idea of the form of the underlying probability density function $p(\boldsymbol{X})$. Fortunately, the nonparametric procedures such as Parzen-window approach can be used with arbitrary distributions and without the assumption that the forms of the underlying densities are known. Furthermore, in this study, we have two advantages. First, we are essentially assured of convergence to a complicated target density with enough samples more than 200,000. Second, the dimensionality of the density is limited to two dimensions, and somewhat avoid "curse of dimensionality".

To specify the problem, suppose we have n samples $\boldsymbol{X}_1, \boldsymbol{X}_2, ..., \boldsymbol{X}_n$ of two dimensions, in which $\boldsymbol{X}_i = (x_{i_1}, x_{i_2})$. It is well known that the Parzen-window estimate function is below.

$$p_n(\boldsymbol{X}) = \frac{1}{n} \sum_{i=1}^{n} \frac{1}{V_n} \phi(\frac{\boldsymbol{X} - X_i}{h_n}) \qquad (4)$$

Where $\phi(\boldsymbol{X})$ is the window function, h_n is the window width. And V_n is the volume of tiny local region, here we can set $V_n = h_n^2$. In fact, the form of the window function can be arbitrary, but an appropriate function is the zero-mean, unit-variance normal density. Let the window function as follows:

$$\phi(x, y) = \frac{1}{2\pi} e^{-\frac{x^2 + y^2}{2}} \qquad (5)$$

Here we suppose $\boldsymbol{X} = (x, y)$. Thus $p_n(\boldsymbol{X})$ is an average of normal densities centered at the samples as follows:

$$p_n(\boldsymbol{X}) = \frac{1}{n} \sum_{i=1}^{n} \frac{1}{2\pi h_n^2} e^{-\frac{(x - x_{i_1})^2 + (y - x_{i_2})^2}{2h_n^2}} \qquad (6)$$

The real density function can be expressed as an average of functions of X and the samples X_i. In essence, each sample contributing to the estimation in accordance with its distance from X.

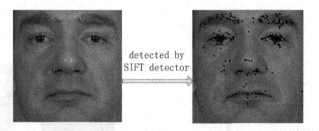

detected by
SIFT detector

Fig. 3. The local interest point(keypoint) detected by SIFT detector

3.2 Local Interest Point Detector

As described above, the local interest point detector can be seen as a sampler which samples the local interest point according probability law $p(\boldsymbol{X})$ of distinctive information of face image. Thus it is important to choose the appropriate detector to extracting the local interest point.

In the 2004, David Lowe presented a method to extract distinctive invariant features from images named Scale Invariant Feature Transform (SIFT)[14]. The method includes both detector and descriptor. In this paper, we choose the SIFT detector to extract the local interest point. There are two reasons for selecting SIFT detector. First, the SIFT detector produces the scale invariant local interest points (called keypoints in the SIFT framework) which could contain multi-scale distinctive information, another merit of SIFT detector is that there are large numbers of local interest points can be extracted from typical images (See Fig.3). In this paper, the SIFT keypoints is detected with Lowe's code[1]. More details about SIFT detector can be seen in [14].

3.3 Finding Weights Set of Facial Parts

As discussed in [4], the effective face description can be discribed as the weighted Chi square statistics. By using probability density $p(\boldsymbol{X})$ of the distinctive information of the face, for the divided regions $R_0, R_1, \ldots, R_{m-1}$ (see Fig.6), the weights can be calculated as follows:

$$\omega_j = \int_{R_j} p(\boldsymbol{X})d\boldsymbol{X}, \quad j = 0, \ldots, m - 1 \tag{7}$$

Then the dissimilarity measure of face can be rewritten as follows:

$$\chi_\omega^2(S, M) = \sum_{i,j} \frac{(S_{i,j} - M_{i,j})^2}{S_{i,j} + M_{i,j}} \cdot \int_{R_j} p(\boldsymbol{X})d\boldsymbol{X}, \quad j = 0, \ldots, m - 1 \tag{8}$$

The keypoints detected by SIFT detector include parameters such as position, scale, and orientation. In this study, we consider the position as the coordinates of samples detected from face image by SIFT detector, and the scale as the

---

[1] Available at http://www.cs.ubc.ca/lowe/keypoints/

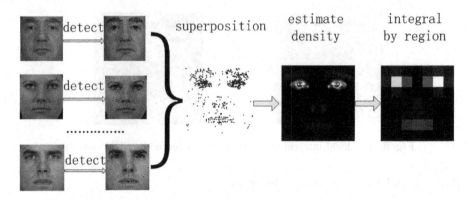

Fig. 4. Procedure of estimating distinctive information density. First we detect thousands of aligned face image and gain hundred of thousand keypoints, then we superposition all keypoints in one image. Second, we estimate the density $p(\boldsymbol{X})$ by Parzenwindow approach, the right image was integral by $p(\boldsymbol{X})$ in sub-window of face.

scope the samples affects. For this consideration, we set the keypoint scale as the window width h_n of the window function and the keypoint position as the samples X_i. By detecting thousands of aligned face image, we gain more than 200000 samples X_i which are huge enough to converge to the true density of distinctive information. The estimation procedure can be seen in Fig.4.

4   Experiments and Results

4.1   Finding Weights Set of Face

Note that the distinctive information distribution of face is the inherent property of face and independent of face database. To explain this fact, we estimate the density function $p(\boldsymbol{X})$ in the face database of University of Notre Dame[13], and perform the face recognition in the FERET face database.

The face database consists of 2292 images acquired under different lighting and expression conditions. The lighting configuration includes "FERET style lighting"(also called "LF") and "mugshot lighting"(also called "LM"). For each subject and illumination condition, two images are taken: one is with neutral expression, which will be called "FA", and the other image is with a smiling expression, which will be called "FB". According to the lighting and expression, there are four categories: (a) FA expression under LM lighting ($FA|LM$), (b) FB expression under LM lighting ($FB|LM$), (c) FA expression under LF lighting ($FA|LF$) and (d) FB expression under LF lighting ($FB|LF$). In this study, the estimation procedure is performed on neutral expression dataset includes ($FA|LM$) and ($FA|LF$).

To compare with the weights set got from the method adopted in [4], we divide the face image into 7x7 windows (see Fig.6).

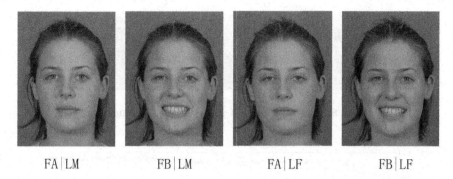

FA|LM   FB|LM   FA|LF   FB|LF

Fig. 5. Face images under different lighting and facial expression conditions

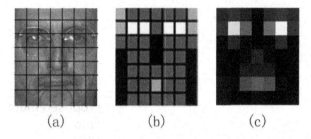

(a)   (b)   (c)

Fig. 6. (a) An example of a face image divided into 7x7 windows. (b) The weights set produced by method adopted in [4]. (c) The weights set produced by proposed method.

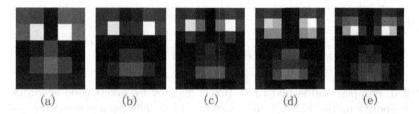

(a)   (b)   (c)   (d)   (e)

Fig. 7. Different block of face image. (a) 5x5 windows (b) 6x6 windows (c) 7x7 windows (d) 8x8 windows (e) 9x9 windows.

In fact, the proposed method can be used to calculate weight in sub-region of face image with arbitrary dividing manner. (See Fig.7). This flexibility is a useful property which can be used for future works.

4.2   Face Recognition on FERET FA/FB Image Sets

The proposed method is tested on the FERET FA/FB image sets[15]. There are totally 3,737 images in the training set of FERET database. All images are

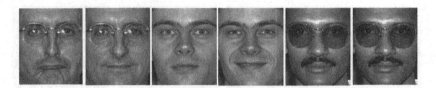

Fig. 8. Some examples of preprocessed face images

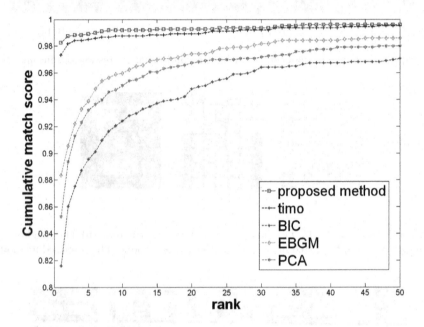

Fig. 9. Rank curves for the FB probe sets

rectified, cropped and scaled to 77 pixels high by 67 pixels wide according to the eye positions the FERET database provided. The preprocessed images are illustrated in Fig.8. Several comparative experiments were tested on the probe set FB with the gallery FA of the FERET database. There are 1196 images in FA, 1195 images in FB, and all exactly the subjects have exactly one image in both FA and FB. The rank curves of the final recognition results are plotted in Fig.9. It should be noted that the CSU implementations of the algorithms whose results we introduce here do not achieve the same figures as in original FERET test due to some modifications in the experimental setup [16].

To compare with method adopted in [4], we divide the face image into 7x7 windows. Our approach has achieved the upper bound recognition performance shown in Fig.9. While Ahonen's method gets a recognition rate of 97.3% on FERET FA/FB image sets, our approach delivers a slightly better recognition rate of 98.2%.

5   Discussion and Conclusion

Different form previous methods, this paper presents a generative method, which is originally inspired by the studies of psychophysics that different facial parts play different role in face perception, to find the weights set which can be used in LBP based face representation. This method extracts the inherent property of the face by estimating the distinctive information density of face. Experimental results on FERET FA/FB image set show that our method achieves a slightly better recognition rate of 98.2% than Ahonen's approach.

Future work includes studying more effective methods for dividing the facial image into local regions and finding multi-scale representation of the face. Another important topic is to look for effective methods to fuse different spectrum face image such as visual and infrared spectrum by using the distinctive information density.

Acknowledgments. This work was supported by the National Natural Science Foundation of China under contract 60672162, the Program for New Century Excellent Talents in University CNNCET-05-06417. The authors would also thank to generous support from Tom Gong, DIS in Princeton, NJ, USA.

References

1. Turk, M., Pentland, A.: Eigenfaces for Recognition constraints. IJ. Cognitive Neuroscience 3(1), 71–86 (1991)
2. Etemad, K., Chellappa, R.: Discriminant Analysis for Recognition of Human Face Images. J. Optical Soc. Am. 14, 1724–1733 (1997)
3. Bartlett, M.S., Movellan, J.R., Sejnowski, T.J.: Face recognition by independent compo-nent analysis. IEEE Trans Neural Networks 13, 1450–1464 (2002)
4. Ahonen, T., Hadid, A., Pietikainen, M.: Face Recognition with Local Binary Patterns. In: Pajdla, T., Matas, J.G. (eds.) ECCV 2004. LNCS, vol. 3021, pp. 469–481. Springer, Heidelberg (2004)
5. Ojala, T., Pietikainen, M., Maenpaa, M.: Multiresolution gray-scale and rotation invariant texture classification width local binary patterns. IEEE Transactions on Pattern Analysis and Machine Intelligence 24, 971–987 (2002)
6. Zhang, G., Huang, X., Li, S.Z., Wang, Y., Wu, X.: Boosting Local Binary Pattern (LBP)-Based Face Recognition. In: Li, S.Z., Lai, J.-H., Tan, T., Feng, G.-C., Wang, Y. (eds.) SINOBIOMETRICS 2004. LNCS, vol. 3338, pp. 179–186. Springer, Heidelberg (2004)
7. Zhang, W., Shan, S., Gao, W., Chen, X., Zhang, H.: Local Gabor Binary Pattern Histogram Sequence (LGBPHS): A Novel Non-Statistical Model for Face Representation and Recognition. In: Proc. IEEE Int'l Conf. Computer Vision, pp. I: 786–I: 791 (2005)
8. Rodriguez, Y., Marcel, S.: Face Authentication Using Adapted Local Binary Pattern Histograms. In: Leonardis, A., Bischof, H., Pinz, A. (eds.) ECCV 2006. LNCS, vol. 3954, pp. 321–332. Springer, Heidelberg (2006)
9. Li, S.Z., Chu, R., Ao, M., Zhang, L., He, R.: Highly Accurate and Fast Face Recognition Using Near Infrared Images. In: Proc. Int'l Conf. Advances in Biometrics, pp. 151–158 (2006)
10. Sadr, J., Jarudi, I., Sinha, P.: The role of eyebrows in face recognition. Perception 32, 285–293 (2003)

11. Davies, G., Ellis, H., Shepherd, J.: Cue saliency in faces as assessed by the Photofit technique. Perception 6, 263–269 (1977)
12. Young, A.W., Hellawell, D., Hay, D.C.: Configurational information in face perception. Perception 16, 747–759 (1987)
13. Biometrics Database Distribution, The Computer Vision Laboratory, Univ. of Notre Dame (2002), http://www.nd.edu/cvrl/
14. Lowe, D.: Distinctive image features from scale-invariant keypoints. Int. Journal of Computer Vision 60(2), 91–110 (2004)
15. Phillips, P.J., Moon, H., Rauss, P.J., Rizvi, S.: The FERET evaluation methodology for face recognition algorithms. IEEE Transactions on Pattern Analysis and Machine Intelligence 22(10) (October 2000)
16. Bolme, D.S., Beveridge, J.R., Teixeira, M., Draper, B.A.: The CSU face identification evaluation system: Its purpose, features and structure. In: Third International Conference on Computer Vision Systems, pp. 304–311 (2003)

Robust 3D Face Recognition Based on Rejection and Adaptive Region Selection

Xiaoli Li and Feipeng Da

Key Laboratory of Measurement and Control for
Complex System of Ministry of Education, Research Institute of Automation,
Southeast University, Nanjing 210096, China
{lixiaoli,dafp}@seu.edu.cn

Abstract. We present an efficient 3D face recognition algorithm and demonstrate its performance on the FRGC v2.0 data set. The pose of a 3D face is automatically corrected based on the nose tip and principle component analysis(PCA). The facial curve in the nose region is used to eliminate a large number of dissimilar faces in the gallery at an early stage. Facial curves in the regions of forehead and cheeks are used to produce a mapping of facial deformation caused by expressions. The remaining faces after rejection are then verified using a region-based matching approach. This approach adaptively selects regions which are relatively steady based on the deformation mapping, and matches them separately. At last, the results are fused using the sum rule. Promising experimental results are achieved on FRGC v2.0 data set.

Keywords: 3D face recognition, PCA, deformation mapping, region-based matching.

1 Introduction

Face recognition is a challenging problem because of the ethnic diversity of faces and variations caused by expressions, gender, pose, illumination and makeup. Most previous studies of the face recognition exploited 2D images. But 2D face recognition is sensitive to illumination and pose[1]. Therefore, researchers are now investigating other data acquisition modalities of the face to overcome these limitations. One of the most promising modalities is the 3D shape of the face and 3D face recognition is considered to be invariant to illumination and pose[2].

Most of the 3D face recognition systems treat the 3D face surface as a rigid surface. But actually the face surface is deformed by different expressions. Therefore, systems that treat the face as a rigid surface are prone to fail when dealing with face with expressions. The involvement of facial expression has become an important challenge in 3D face recognition systems. Chang et al. [3] use multiple overlapping nose regions and obtain increased performance relative to using the whole-frontal-face region. In the work by Mian et al. [4], the nose and the forehead regions are separately matched by iterative closest point(ICP) [5] algorithm, then their scores are fused. Such approaches, however, don't make full use of the discriminative information that exists in the entire face.

H. Zha, R.-i. Taniguchi, and S. Maybank (Eds.): ACCV 2009, Part III, LNCS 5996, pp. 581–590, 2010.
© Springer-Verlag Berlin Heidelberg 2010

In the work by Wang [6], the rigid parts of facial surface are dynamically extracted by selecting a part of nearest points pairs to calculate dissimilarity measure during registration of facial surfaces. Faltemier et al. [7] select 28 different regions around the face, and then perform score-based fusion on the individual region match scores. Both of the methods use ICP to perform image matching, and achieve good performance. But the time consumption is large because all of the face regions should be matched between scans.

Considering that face is usually deformed in different way under different expressions, some researchers combine facial expression categorisation with face recognition [8], [9], [10]. In the work by Cook [8], images are manually allocated to three groups based on expression, and then a part-face recognition system based on subspace projection methods is constructed. Martinez [10] creates 6 regions of the face and defines the weight of each region for three distinct expressions in a train set, and then the weights are used for recognition. However, both of the methods above assume expression of the face is known. In [9] an automated variant of this approach is detailed. A "happy face" recognition system is used to aid the face recognition.

Beumier and Acheroy [11] extract several facial profiles and compare them for recognition. The main advantages of this method are its high speed and low storage needs and it is reported that the central profile shows the major distinctiveness [12].

In this paper, we present an robust 3D face recognition method using rejection and adaptive region selection. The pose of a 3D face is automatically corrected using a novel approach based on the nose tip and principle component analysis(PCA) [13]. Facial curves in nose, forehead and cheek regions are extracted and compared. Facial curve in the nose region is matched to reject unlikely faces, and curves in other regions are matched to produce a facial deformation mapping for expressions. Then, the appropriate sub-regions which are more resilient to expressions can be selected based on the deformation mapping and matched using ICP algorithm. Final similarity score is the sum of elementary scores given by each region. Fig.1 shows the block diagram of our method.

The rest of this paper is organized as follows: Section 2 explains our automatic 3D face detection and normalization algorithm. In Section 3, comparisons

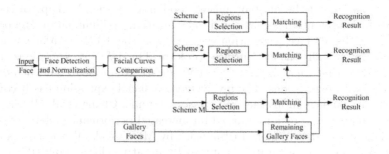

Fig. 1. Block diagram of our algorithm

between facial curves are presented. Section 4 gives details of our adaptive region selection scheme. Section 5 lists and compares the recognition results of our algorithm with others. Conclusion and future work are discussed in Section 6.

2 Face Detection and Normalization

2.1 Face Preprocessing

We perform our experiments on FRGC v2.0 dataset [16]. There are missing and outlier points in many images in FRGC, which will deteriorate the recognition accuracy, so the images are firstly denoised for future processing. Small holes in the face are firstly filled by locating "missing" points which are surrounded by four or more "good" points. The x, y, and z coordinates of the missing point are interpolated from its valid neighbors. Then, spikes caused by outlier points are removed, and the outlier points are defined as the one whose distance is greater than a threshold from any one of its neighboring points.

2.2 Face Detection

Since faces in the FRGC v2.0 dataset are mostly acquired from the shoulder level up(See Fig.2(a)), the faces should be localized. It is well known that the location of nose is around the centroid of the face, so the nose tip is firstly detected. The nose tip is detected using a coarse to fine approach as follows. An initial nose tip is found using the curvature and geometric constraint. At first, the curvature and shape index [14] at each point on the face is calculated to find possible nose tip candidates, labeled $S1_{nt}$. Then, the centroid of the pointcloud of the face is calculated, and the points in the $S1_{nt}$ whose distance is smaller than a threshold from the centroid are selected to form a more accurate nose tip candidate, labeled $S2_{nt}$. Finally, the centroid of the candidate points $S2_{nt}$ is chosen as the initial nose tip location.

A sphere of radius r centered at the initial nose tip is then used to crop the 3D face. A constant value of $r = 90mm$ is selected in this paper. This process crops an ellipsoid region, as shown in Fig.2(b).

(a)   (b)   (c)

Fig. 2. (a) The original face. (b) The cropped face. (c) The cropped face with PCS.

2.3   Face Normalization

It can be found that the shape of the cropped face is approximately an ellipsoid. Three eigenvectors can be obtained after PCA is used to the pointcloud of the face, and the vertical and horizontal orientation are the eigenvectors of two largest eigenvalues and the face normal is the smallest eigenvector. Therefore, the pose of a face can be normalized using PCA.

Taking eigenvector corresponding to the largest eigenvalue as the Y axis, and eigenvector corresponding to the smallest eigenvalue as the Z axis, we define a new right-hand coordinate system. This coordinate system is called the pose coordinate system(PCS), and it represents the head pose and depends only on the points distribution of the facial surface. The original facial surface is then transformed to the PCS. The final nose tip is determined as the point with the largest z value. In order to avoid the influence by hair, the final nose tip is selected in a smaller regions centered at the initial nose tip. The origin of PCS is then transformed to the location of the final nose tip. All the faces in the PCS have the same pose, so the face is normalized, as shown in Fig.2(c).

3   Comparison Based on Facial Curves

3.1   Facial Curves Extraction

Facial surface is often deformed by expressions. Generally speaking, the mouth is the most affected by expressions, whereas the nose is the least affected. Smile expression leads to shape deformation of mouth and cheek, surprise affects mouth, sad even changes the shape of forehead area slightly and the upper part of the face is more stable. Considering that the nose is the most static region and the forehead and cheeks will deform in certain case, we choose facial curve in the nose to form rejection classifier, facial curves in the forehead and cheeks to map facial deformations, and finally 4 vertical and 4 horizontal curves which are located in the regions of nose, forehead and cheeks are extracted (Shown in Fig.3).

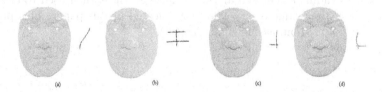

(a)   (b)   (c)   (d)

Fig. 3. Facial curves. (a) Facial curve $p_{(1)}$, (b) Facial curves $p_{(2)}, p_{(3)}, p_{(4)}$, (c) facial curves $p_{(5)}, p_{(6)}$, (d) facial curves $p_{(7)}, p_{(8)}$.

A facial curve is defined as the intersection of a plane with the surface of a face. Since all the faces embedded in the PCS have the same pose and the geometric distribution of facial features is almost the same, we extract facial curves based on the coordinate information.

3.2   Comparison Based on Facial Curves

Once all of the curves have been extracted, matching is performed using ICP algorithm. ICP establishes correspondences between the closest points of two sets of 3D points and minimizes the distance error between them by applying a rigid transformation to one of the sets. This process is repeated iteratively until the distance error reaches a minimum saturation value. The similarity is measured by the average distance between two curves.

Facial curve in the nose region is used to reject unlikely faces in the gallery, and curves in other regions are used to produce the deformation mapping of the face. Firstly, facial curve in the nose region of a probe is matched to all of the galleries, and the matching process results in a vector of similarity scores $s_{p_{(1)}}$ of size N ,where N is the size of the gallery. Gallery faces whose similarity score is above a threshold δ_{reject} are rejected. Then, other 7 facial curves of the probe are matched to the remaining gallery faces, and vectors of similarity scores $s_{p_{(i)}}, (i = 2, 3, ..., 8)$, can be obtained, and the size of each $s_{p_{(i)}}$ is N', where N' is the size of the remaining galleries and $N' < N$. The ratio of distance error between the seven facial curves and facial curve in the nose is calculated using

$$\Delta s_{p_{(i)}} = s_{p_{(i)}}/s_{p_{(1)}}, \tag{1}$$

where $i = 2, 3, ..., 8$. The facial deformation can be scaled by $\Delta s_{p_{(i)}}$. We assume that the higher the value of $\Delta s_{p_{(i)}}$, the larger deformation is presented in the corresponding region. So regions for recognition are selected based on the value of $\Delta s_{p_{(i)}}$, which will be discussed in detail in Subsection 4.2.

In the process of rejection a threshold $\delta_{reject} = 0.8$ is selected so that 69% of the gallery faces are rejected, and the verification rate of the rejection classifier is 98.1% for probes with all expressions. In this paper, a C++ implementation of the rejection classifier on a Intel Core Duo 2.34GHz machine with 1.0 GB of memory machine takes 3.07 seconds for matching a probe with a gallery of 466 faces and only 145 faces are remained to be processed in the next stage, which shortens the recognition time largely and the average matching time for all the facial curves is 9.77s.

4   Face Recognition

4.1   Part-Face Methodology

Face recognition techniques typically employ a monolithic representation of the face during recognition, however, approaches which decompose the face into sub-regions have shown considerable promise [3,4]. Lower part of the face is usually affected by opening mouth and mustache, so only upper part of the face is used in this paper. We consider 4 regions in the upper part of the face by a set of predefined implicit functions (See Fig.4).

Fig. 4. Matching surface extraction for four probe and gallery surfaces. (a) Probe A (probe surface in a forehead region), (b) Probe B (probe surface in a left cheek region), (c) Probe C (probe surface in a right cheek region), (d) Probe D (probe surface in a nose region), and (e) a gallery surface.

4.2   Adaptive Region Selection Scheme

Given that the deformation mapping caused by expressions can be obtained by the comparison of facial curves, we propose an adaptive region selection scheme which selects regions based on facial deformation mapping produced by facial curves. We assume that the higher the value of $\Delta s_{p_{(i)}}$, the larger deformation is presented in the region in which the ith curve is located. Hence, the deformation of each region can be scaled by the corresponding similarity score ratio $\Delta s_{p_{(i)}}$ as

$$\Delta s_{ProbeA} = \frac{\Delta s_{p_{(2)}} + \Delta s_{p_{(3)}} + \Delta s_{p_{(4)}}}{3}, \tag{2}$$

$$\Delta s_{ProbeB} = \frac{\Delta s_{p_{(5)}} + \Delta s_{p_{(6)}}}{2}, \tag{3}$$

$$\Delta s_{ProbeC} = \frac{\Delta s_{p_{(7)}} + \Delta s_{p_{(8)}}}{2}. \tag{4}$$

The nose is almost invariant under all expressions, so Probe D is always selected. Other regions are selected only when the corresponding deformation $\Delta s_{ProbeA}, \Delta s_{ProbeB}, \Delta s_{ProbeC}$ is less than a threshold δ_{deform}. In this paper, threshold δ_{deform} is the key for region selection. Here, we obtain the optimal δ_{deform} from the training set: $\delta_{deform} = 2.0$. All the experiments in Section 6 are carried out with the optimal parameter.

By identifying images in which deformation is present, the recognition precess can place more emphasis on those regions which are least affected. Through looking at the distortions on a region by region basis, this system configuration can scale to any number of facial expressions without requiring the use of expression specific recognition systems as in [9]. Comparing with the work by Wang [6], only regions which are useful for recognition are matched in this paper, which can improve the efficiency of recognition. Comparing with systems such as [3,4], more useful information are used for recognition in our paper.

4.3   Face Matching and Results Fusion

Once regions have been selected, the ICP algorithm is running on each probe to the remaining galleries. In order to accelerate the ICP algorithm, the neighbor search algorithm [15] is used. The final recognition results are fused using sum rule, which is given by

$$s_i = \sum_{j=1}^{K} s_{ji}, \tag{5}$$

where $i = 1, 2, \ldots, N'$, K is the number of regions and N' is the number of remaining faces in the gallery. The identity corresponding to the smallest s is supposed to be the recognition result.

5   Experiments and Analysis

FRGC v2.0 data set includes 4007 3D face images of 466 distinct human subjects with from 1 to 22 images per subject. This currently represents the largest 3D face database publicly available to biometrics researchers. We perform two types of experiments: verification experiment and identification experiment.

5.1   Verification Experiment

In the verification experiment, we perform the FRGC Experiment 3 and the system's performance is quoted as a true accept rate (TAR) at a given false accept rate (FAR). In the experiment, the gallery images come from the Fall 2003 semester and the probe entries come from the Spring 2004 semester. The result of this experiment is a receiver operating characteristic (ROC) curve.

Generally, nose and forehead regions are supposed to be the most steady regions, and are used for recognition. Here we compare the performance of nose-forehead region with our scheme in Fig.5.

The verification rates at 0.001 FAR are 94.0% and 95.0%, respectively. We can see that our scheme performs better. The results demonstrate that regions

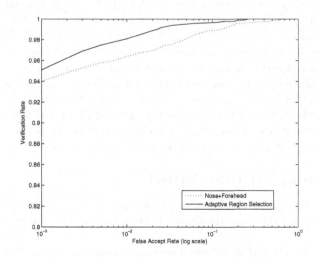

Fig. 5. ROC curves

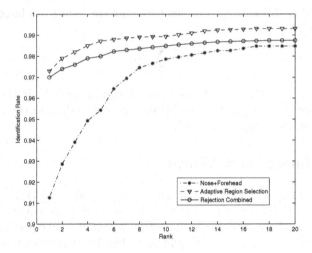

Fig. 6. CMC curves

covering cheeks contain useful information for face recognition, and forehead region will deform in certain expression. The results of our method with rejection classifier are not reported because the experiment is a one-to-one matching experiment, and there is no need to use rejection.

5.2 Identification Experiment

In the experiment, we take the earliest image of every participant and use it as the gallery image for the subject. All subsequent images for each subject are used as probes. The system's performance is quoted as a rank-one recognition rate and the result is a cumulative match characteristic (CMC) curve.

The results of using regions of nose and forehead, regions adaptively selected and regions adaptively selected combined with rejection are presented. The rank one recognition rates are $91.2\%, 97.3\%, 97.0\%$ respectively(See Fig.6). The identification rate with the rejection classifier is slightly reduced by 0.3% compared with the region-based method. The reason for this is that there is a probability that the classifier may also reject the correct identity. It can be avoided by improving the threshold δ_{reject} in rejection process. However, the selection of δ_{reject} should be balanced between the time consumption and recognition rate. The identification rate of our adaptive region selection scheme is 97.3%, which shows that it is important to use cheek region for recognition.

5.3 Comparing with Other Methods

We compare our adaptive region selection scheme with some other 3D face recognition methods on the same database. Their performance comparison is shown in Table 1.

Note that our algorithm outperforms each method presented except for that of Faltemier [7]. Faltemier extracts 28 regions on the face, and matches them

Table 1. The comparison with other methods

	Chang [3]	Mian [4]	Cook [8]	Faltemier [7]	This Paper
FRGC Experiment 3	NA	NA	92.01%	94.8%	95.0%
Rank One Recognition Rate	92.3%	96.2%	94.6%	98.1%	97.3%

respectively, then score-based fusion is performed on the individual region match score. Compared with Faltemier's algorithm, only the regions that are useful for recognition are used in this paper, which will largely shorten the recognition time.

6   Conclusion and Future Work

In this paper, we have proposed a robust 3D face recognition method based on rejection and adaptive region selection. The contributions of this paper are as follows: (1) Facial curve in the nose region which is simple and robust to expressions is used to reject unlikely faces before accurate matching. (2) An adaptive regions selection scheme is proposed. Facial curves in the regions of cheeks and forehead are compared to produce the facial deformation mapping, then regions used for recognition are selected according to the deformation mapping. (3) An automatic face normalization algorithm using the nose tip and PCA is proposed. Experiments have been done on FRGC v2.0 data set. Encouraging results have demonstrated the effectiveness of our method.

Although our method works well on common faces of approximate symmetrical face, it can fail when nose tip is located incorrectly, which causes incorrect PCS. Fortunately, this is a rare case and most scanners can be handled by our algorithm.

Acknowledgments. Thanks to FRGC organizers for providing the face data. This work is sponsored by National Science Foundation of P.R.China(60775025), Program for New Century Excellent Talents in University, Natural Science Foundation of Jiangsu Province(BK2007116).

References

1. Zhao, W., Chenllappa, R., Phillips, P.J., Rosenfeld, A.: Face recognition: A literature survey. ACM. Comput. Surv. 35(4), 399–458 (2003)
2. Bowyer, K.W., Chang, K., Flynn, P.: A survey of approaches and challenges in 3d and multi-modal 3d + 2d face recognition. Comput. Vis. Image. Und. 101(1), 1–15 (2006)
3. Chang, K.I., Bowyer, K.W., Flynn, P.J.: Multiple nose region matching for 3d face recognition under varying facial expression. IEEE T. Pattern. Anal. 28(10), 1695–1700 (2006)

4. Mian, A., Bennamoun, M., Owens, R.: An efficient multimodal 2d-3d hybrid approach to automatic face recognition. IEEE T. Pattern. Anal. 29(11), 1927–1943 (2007)
5. Besl, P.J., Mckay, H.D.: A method for registration of 3-d shapes. IEEE T. Pattern. Anal. 14(2), 239–256 (1992)
6. Wang, Y.M., Pan, G., Wu, Z.H., Wang, Y.G.: Exploring facial expression effects in 3D face recognition using partial ICP. In: Narayanan, P.J., Nayar, S.K., Shum, H.-Y. (eds.) ACCV 2006. LNCS, vol. 3851, pp. 581–590. Springer, Heidelberg (2006)
7. Faltemier, T.C., Bowyer, K.W., Flynn, P.J.: A region ensemble for 3-d face recognition. IEEE Transactions on Information Forensics and Security 3(1), 62–72 (2008)
8. Cook, J., Cox, M., Chandran, V., Sridharan, S.: Robust 3D face recognition from expression categorisation. In: Lee, S.-W., Li, S.Z. (eds.) ICB 2007. LNCS, vol. 4642, pp. 271–280. Springer, Heidelberg (2007)
9. Li, C., Barreto, A.: An integrated 3D face-expression recognition approach. In: 2006 IEEE International Conference on Acoustics, Speech and Signal Precessing, pp. 1–4. IEEE Press, Toulous (2006)
10. Martinez, A.M.: Recognizing imprecisely localized, partially occluded, and expression variant faces from a single sample per class. IEEE T. Pattern. Anal. 24(6), 748–763 (2002)
11. Beumier, C., Acheroy, M.: Automatic 3d face authentication. Image. Vision. Comput. 18(4), 315–321 (2000)
12. Nagamine, T., Uemura, T., Wasuda, I.: 3D facial image analysis for human identification. In: 11th International Conference on Computer Vision and Applications, pp. 324–327. IEEE Press, Hague (1992)
13. Turk, M., Pentland, A.: Face recognition using eigenfaces. In: 1991 IEEE Computer Society Conference on Computer Vision and Pattern Recognition, pp. 586–591. IEEE Press, Maui (1991)
14. Dorai, C., Jain, A.K.: COSMOS-A representation scheme for 3d free-form objects. IEEE T. Pattern. Anal. 19(10), 1115–1130 (1997)
15. Jost, T., Hugli, H.: A multi-resolution ICP with heuristic closest point search for fast and robust 3D registration of range images. In: 4th International Conference on 3-D Digital Imaging and Modeling, pp. 1–7. IEEE Press, Bannf (2003)
16. Phillips, P.J., Flynn, P.J., Scruggs, T., Bowyer, K.W.: Overview of the face recognition grand challenge. In: 2005 IEEE Computer Society Conference on Computer Vision and Pattern Recognition, pp. 947–954. IEEE Press, San Diego (2005)

Face Recognition via AAM and Multi-features Fusion on Riemannian Manifolds

Hongwen Huo and Jufu Feng

Key Laboratory of Machine Perception (Peking University), MOE
Department of Machine Intelligence School of Electronics Engineering and Computer Science,
Peking University, Beijing, 100871, P.R. China
{huohw,fjf}@cis.pku.edu.cn

Abstract. We develop a novel face recognition algorithm which is robust to random position perturbations of key points and does not require face alignment, e.g. resizing, rotating, cropping, etc. In our proposed method, a well trained Active Appearance Model (AAM) is first divided into several regions by special landmarks, and each region is given a label by a template. This model is then fed to new coming facial images to segment the images into irregular regions. In these regions, multi-features fusion matrices are calculated and embedded to related Riemannian manifolds to train classifiers which are combined to construct a final classifier. Our experiment results show its accuracy, efficiency, and robustness on FERET and A-R human face database.

1 Introduction

Face recognition has drawn more and more attention in recent years. This interest is motivated by its broad range of applications in many fields. In almost all existed automatic face recognition systems, face alignment is a necessary step [1] [2] [3] [4] [5]. Without this step, many classical pattern recognition techniques can not have good results in following steps. However, how to align two facial images has been an inherently difficult problem for a long time. In many face alignment methods, eyes are often manually located first and then used as anchor points [1] [5]. Therefore, in many automatic face recognition systems, eye automatic detection is often necessary before classifications. However, this alignment method can not be robust all the time, especially when there are occluding structures (hair, glasses, etc.) over eyes. Some papers use AAM to align two facial images without eye locating, but after aligning step, face deformations are still unavoidable. The target facial images are also translated, rotated, resized and cropped to a certain pattern to continue the recognition approach [1] [3] [5]. Here the target images will be deformed inevitably and therefore some information of the original images will be changed or lost.

In this paper, we show a new face recognition approach in which neither face alignment nor deforming original images are necessary. In our proposed method, a well trained Active Appearance Model (AAM) (Figure 1) with special landmarks will be fed to a new coming facial image to segment the image into some irregular regions [6] [7]. In these regions, raw features (intensity derivatives, edge orientation, texture features, Gabor responses, etc.) are extracted respectively, and combined together by covariance

H. Zha, R.-i. Taniguchi, and S. Maybank (Eds.): ACCV 2009, Part III, LNCS 5996, pp. 591–600, 2010.
© Springer-Verlag Berlin Heidelberg 2010

matrices [8] [9]. Since covariance matrices with different region labels live in different manifolds, we calculate this feature on related Riemannian manifolds formulated by symmetric positive definite matrices (nonsingular covariance matrices, so called tensors in this paper). Finally several classifiers trained on manifolds are combined to give the class label of the new coming facial image.

In traditional face recognition methods, the final recognition rates always badly depend on accurate positions of key points detected. In this paper, because our proposed method depends on region information rather than point information, there are almost no changes in final recognition accuracy while applying random perturbations to positions of key points when these perturbations do not change regions segmented seriously.

The paper is organized as follows. In Section 2, we briefly introduce AAM and covariance matrices of irregular regions for multi-features fusion. In Section 3, we present an introduction to Riemannian geometry and our face recognition algorithm on the tensor space. In Section 4, we describe our experiment results.

2   Multi-features Fusion of Irregular Regions

2.1   Active Appearance Model (AAM)

Active appearance model (AAM) algorithm is an important method for locating deformable objects in many applications. As described by Cootes et al [6], the models were generated by combining a model of shape variation with a model of the appearance variations in a shape-normalized frame. We require a training set of labeled images, where key landmark points are marked on each example object. For instance, to build a face model we require face images marked with points at key positions to outline the main features (Figure 1).

With a full appearance model generated above and a reasonable starting approximation, an efficient scheme for adjusting the model parameters is proposed by Cootes et al. in [6], so that a synthetic sample is generated, which matches the new facial image as closely as possible (Figure 3).

In these appearance models, we mark some special key points first. After the matching approach described above, we segment the facial image into several irregular regions by the specially marked points (Figure 3). This division is obviously beneficial to keep information of the new image, because shapes of most important components of human face (eyes, nose, mouth, etc.) are reserved perfectly in these regions. Until now,

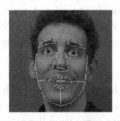

Fig. 1. AAM Model

Fig. 2. AAM Model segmented by special landmarks into irregular regions

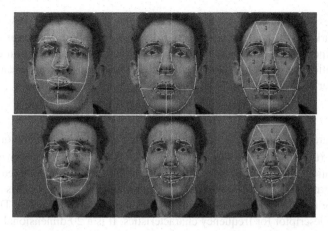

Fig. 3. Examples for AAM Models fed to faces and segmention

there are not any deformations on the new facial image, while deformations just appear on the model and the contours of irregular regions segmented previously on the model.

2.2   Multi-features Matrices of Irregular Regions

Covariance matrix of rectangle region is proposed by Oncel Tuzel et al. as a fast descriptor for object detection [8] [9]. Here we give a new form of this covariance feature on irregular regions and reinterpret it from a new perspective.

Let R be a region with N points. Let F be the $N \times d$ dimensional feature region extracted from R

$$F(R) = [f(x_1, y_1), \ f(x_1, y_2), \ ... \ ], \ (x_i, y_j) \in R \tag{1}$$

where $f(x, y) = [\phi_1(x, y) \ \phi_2(x, y) ... \phi_d(x, y)]^T$, and the function ϕ_i can be any mapping such as intensity, gradients, Gabor responses, etc. Let $\{z_k\}_{k=1...N}$ be the $d-$ dimensional feature points inside F. We represent the irregular region F with $d \times d$ covariance matrix of a the feature points

$$C_F = \frac{1}{N-1} \sum_{k=1}^{N} (z_k - \mu)(z_k - \mu)^T \tag{2}$$

where μ is the mean of points inside F.

The covariance matrix above proposes a natural way of fusing multiple features which might be correlated. The diagonal entries of the covariance matrix represent the variance of each feature extracted and the non-diagonal entries represent the correlations. At the same time, noise corrupting individual samples are largely filtered out with an average filter μ during covariance computation (2).

We use templates covering irregular regions to segment the facial image (Figure 3). These templates are defined just by their vertices, which are specially marked in the appearance models (Figure 2). When models we built match a new face, shapes of the templates change because of the moving of their vertices. Regions with the same template marks in different images are considered as corresponding regions.

In our experiments, raw features we choose for multi- features fusion do not have any information regarding the number of points. This implies a certain scale invariance over irregular regions in different images.

$$F(R) = [V_{Shape} \ V_{Texture} \ V_{Gabor}] \tag{3}$$

where x, y are pixel location, V_{Shape} is a 5 dimensional vector which consists of I_x, I_y, I_{xx}, I_{yy} (the first and second order derivatives of the intensity) and $\arctan \frac{I_y}{I_x}$ (the edge orientation). The second term $V_{Texture}$ is a texture descriptor obtained from Local Binary Pattern (LBP) on 3×3 neighborhood of pixel (x, y) [10] [11]. It is a 10 dimensional vector (nine uniform patterns and one non-uniform pattern) [10]. The last term V_{Gabor} is a descriptor for frequency characteristics. It is a 20 dimensional vector. It is also called a Gabor jet [1] which is generated by a set of Gabor kernels in five scales and four orientations $(0, \pi/4, \pi/2, 3\pi/4)$ at a certain convolution point (x, y). At last, all these feature vectors are normalized to $[0, 1]$.

With the defined mapping ϕ, the input image is mapped to a $d = 35$ dimensional feature image. The multi-features fusion matrix of an irregular region is a 35×35 matrix and due to symmetry only upper triangular part is stored, which has only 630 different values.

3   Face Recognition on Riemannian Manifolds

Since covariance matrices do not lie on Euclidean space, a lot of traditional machine learning techniques are not appropriate to learn the classifiers. The space of d-dimensional nonsingular covariance matrices can be represented as a connected Riemannian manifold. See [12][13][9] for more detailed descriptions. Now we focus of the space Sym_n^+ of positive definite symmetric matrices (tensors) and briefly introduce it in section 3.1.

3.1   Tensor Space

Each point on Riemannian manifolds has a neighborhood which can be mapped homeomorphously to $\mathbb{R}^m$. In the case of tensors, there are some important simplifications. Let $W = UDU^T$ be a diagonalization, where matrix U is orthonormal, and $D = \text{DIAG}(d_i)$ is the diagonal matrix of eigenvalues. We can represent the exponential mapping as

$$\exp(W) = \sum_{k=0}^{+\infty} \frac{W^k}{k!} = U \exp(D)U^T = U \, \text{DIAG}(\exp(d_i)) \, U^T \tag{4}$$

Generally, the exponential map $\exp(W)$ is onto but only one-to-one mapping. But on tensor space, $\exp(W)$ is a one-to-one, onto and continuously differentiable mapping. Therefore, its inverse mapping logarithm is given by

$$\log(\Sigma) = \sum_{k=1}^{+\infty} \frac{(-1)^{k+1}}{k} (\Sigma - I)^k = U \log(D)U^T = U \, \text{DIAG}(\log(d_i)) \, U^T \tag{5}$$

On Sym_n^+, Riemannian metric on the tangent space of each point Σ is given by an inner product. If W_1 and W_2 are two tangent vectors at Σ, Riemannian metric is defined by

$$\langle W_1, W_2 \rangle_{\Sigma} = \langle \Sigma^{-\frac{1}{2}} W_1 \Sigma^{-\frac{1}{2}}, \ \Sigma^{-\frac{1}{2}} W_2 \Sigma^{-\frac{1}{2}} \rangle_{\Sigma} = \mathrm{Tr}\left(\Sigma^{-\frac{1}{2}} W_1 \Sigma^{-1} W_2 \Sigma^{-\frac{1}{2}}\right) \quad (6)$$

From the definition of Riemannian metric (6) and the definition of logarithm mapping (5), the distance between two points on tensor space is defined as

$$\mathrm{dist}\left(\Sigma_1, \Sigma_2\right) = \mathrm{dist}\left(\mathrm{I}, \ \Sigma_1^{-\frac{1}{2}} \Sigma_2 \Sigma_1^{-\frac{1}{2}}\right) = \mathrm{Norm}\left(\Sigma_1^{-\frac{1}{2}} \Sigma_2 \Sigma_1^{-\frac{1}{2}}\right) \quad (7)$$

where $\mathrm{Norm}\left(\Sigma\right)^2 = \|\log\left(\Sigma\right)\|^2 = \sum_{i=1}^{n}\left(\log\left(\sigma_i\right)\right)^2$.

Now an orthogonal coordinate system on the tangent space is defined with the vector operation. For a vector $\overrightarrow{\Sigma\Lambda} \in T_{\Sigma} Sym_n^+$, we define its minimal representation in the orthonormal coordinate system as

$$\mathrm{Vec}_{\Sigma}\left(\overrightarrow{\Sigma\Lambda}\right) = \mathrm{Vec}\left(\log\left(\Sigma^{-\frac{1}{2}} * \Lambda\right)\right) = \mathrm{Vec}\left(\Sigma^{-\frac{1}{2}} \ \overrightarrow{\Sigma\Lambda} \ \Sigma^{-\frac{1}{2}}\right) \quad (8)$$

The mapping Vec_{Σ} realizes an explicit isomorphism between $T_{\Sigma} Sym_n^+$ and $\mathbb{R}^{n(n+1)/2}$ with the canonical metric.

Let $\Sigma_1, \Sigma_2, ..., \Sigma_N$ be the set of points on a Riemannian manifold Sym_n^+, The Karcher mean [14] is a tensor minimizing the sum of squared distances

$$C\left(\Sigma\right) = \arg\min \sum_{i=1}^{N} \mathrm{dist}^2\left(\Sigma, \Sigma_i\right) \quad (9)$$

where dist is defined in (7). In the case of tensor space, the manifold has a non-positive curvature, so that there is one and only one mean value which can be calculated by the Newton gradient descent algorithm, which iterates by computing first order approximations to the mean on the tangent space and usually converges very fast.

3.2   Face Recognition on Tensor Space

On Riemannian manifolds, a simple and straightforward classification approach would be to map the manifold to a higher dimensional Euclidean space which is more flattened. However, this method can not preserve the distances between the points on the manifolds orbicularly [9]. Therefore we should train tensor space classifiers which can reflect the global structure of the manifolds.

Let $\Sigma_1, \Sigma_2, ..., \Sigma_N$ be points on a Riemannian manifold Sym_n^+, we want to find a function $f(\Sigma) : Sym_n^+ \mapsto R$, which divides Sym_n^+ into parts based on the training set of labeled items.

First we define mappings from neighborhoods on Sym_n^+ to connected Euclidean space. Here we use the logarithm maps, $\log_{\Sigma}$, which map the neighborhood of points $\Sigma \in Sym_n^+$ to its tangent spaces T_{Σ}. Because $\log_{\Sigma}$ is a homeomorphism around the neighborhood of the point, the structure of Sym_n^+ is preserved locally [9]. We learn the classifiers on the tangent space which is a vector space. The mean value of the points (9) on Sym_n^+ minimizes the sum of squared distances on Sym_n^+, therefore it is an appropriate approximation.

As shown in section 2.2 and Figure 3, we have segmented faces into several irregular regions by templates. For each region of all training samples, we compute their multi-features fusion matrices respectively, and regard the matrices as points Σ_i on a related Riemannian manifold Sym_n^+. Then the Karcher mean $\bar{\Sigma}_j$ for each region is computed. We map points to the tangent space of $\bar{\Sigma}_j$ and train classifiers on it for each region. Finally, the output of these classifiers (one classifier for one region. We test four base classifiers: KNN, LDA, L-SVM, K-SVM. Please see section 4 for more details) are combined using a fusion methodology to make the final decision.

Many methods on combining multiple classifiers have been proposed. In our paper, four fusion rules are adopted. Two rules are simple: majority voting and sum rule [15]; and two rules are complicated: priori selection method and posteriori selection method [16].

Majority voting. Each classifier $C_k(x)$ assigns a class label to the input face data, $C_k(x) = i$. We represent this event as a binary function,

$$T_k(x \in X_i) = \begin{cases} 1, & C_k(x) = i \\ 0, & otherwise \end{cases} \tag{10}$$

By a majority voting, the final fusion classifier is

$$\beta(x) = \arg_i \max \sum_{k=1}^{K} T_k(x \in X_i) \tag{11}$$

Sum rule. We assume that $C_k(x)$ is the classifier we get from the kth region. According to the sum rule, the final fusion classifier is

$$\beta(x) = \arg_i \max \sum_{k=1}^{K} P(X_i|C_k(x)) \tag{12}$$

where $P(X_i|C_k(x))$ is the probability that x belongs to X_i under the measure of classifier $C_k(x)$.

Priori selection. Instead of simply counting the percentage of training samples in the region that are correctly classified, we can calculate the average of probability outputs from correct classifiers. The probability can be further weighted by the distances between the training faces and the test face. Consider the face $x_j \in X_i$ as one of the k-nearest neighbors of the test face x, the $p(X_i|x_j, C_k)$ provided by the classifier C_k can be regarded as a measure of the classifier accuracy for the test face x based on its neighbor x_j, Suppose we have N training faces in the neighborhood, then the final fusion classifier is [17]

$$\beta(x) = \arg_i \max \frac{\sum_{j=1}^{N} p(X_i|x_j, C_k)W_j}{\sum_{j=1}^{N} W_j} \tag{13}$$

where $W_j = 1/d_j$ is the distance between the test face x, and its neighbor face x_j.

Posteriori selection. If the class assigned by the classifier C_k is known, $C_k(x) = X_i$, then this information can be exploited as well. Suppose we have N training faces in the neighborhood, and let us consider the face $x_j \in X_k$ as one of the k-nearest neighbors of the test face x, then the final fusion classifier is [18]

$$\beta(x) = \arg_i \max \frac{\sum_{x_j \in X_k} p(X_i|x_j, C_k)W_j}{\sum_{j=1}^{N} p(X_i|x_j, C_k)W_j} \tag{14}$$

where $W_j = 1/d_j$ is the distance between the test face x, and its neighbor face x_j.

4 Experiments

We perform the experiments on FERET face database [19] and A-R face database [20]. *fb* of FERET includes 1195 probes with the same lighting and *fc* includes 194 probes with different lighting. Therefore tests on *fc* is more difficult than on *fb*. The AR-face database includes 26 frontal images with different facial expressions, illumination conditions, and occlusions for 126 subjects. Images were recorded in two different sessions 14 days apart. Thirteen images were recorded under controlled circumstances in each session.

<table>
<tr><td colspan="5">**Table 1.** Recognition Rate on *fb* of FERET</td><td colspan="5">**Table 2.** Recognition Rate on *fc* of FERET</td></tr>
<tr><td></td><td>Majority voting</td><td>Sum rule</td><td>Prior</td><td>Posteri</td><td></td><td>Majority voting</td><td>Sum rule</td><td>Prior</td><td>Posteri</td></tr>
<tr><td>KNN</td><td>0.81</td><td>0.79</td><td>0.86</td><td>0.89</td><td>KNN</td><td>0.32</td><td>0.34</td><td>0.41</td><td>0.38</td></tr>
<tr><td>LDA</td><td>0.82</td><td>0.85</td><td>0.91</td><td>0.88</td><td>LDA</td><td>0.32</td><td>0.29</td><td>0.42</td><td>0.47</td></tr>
<tr><td>L-SVM</td><td>0.84</td><td>0.87</td><td>0.92</td><td>0.90</td><td>L-SVM</td><td>0.38</td><td>0.40</td><td>0.49</td><td>0.53</td></tr>
<tr><td>K-SVM</td><td>0.87</td><td>0.90</td><td>0.94</td><td>0.96</td><td>K-SVM</td><td>0.51</td><td>0.54</td><td>0.65</td><td>0.63</td></tr>
</table>

In our first experiment, four kinds of classifiers (KNN, LDA, Linear-SVM and Kernel-SVM) and four kinds of combining methods (section 3.3) have been tested on the tangent space of manifold Sym_n^+. The test results are shown in Tabel 1, Tabel 2 and Tabel 3. From the results shown in tables we can see, K-SVM + Priori Selection and K-SVM + Posteriori Selection have the best combining results. We compare these two combining schemes on Riemannian manifolds with other classical face recognition algorithms which need manual eye locating and face aligning before classification. And the rank curves on *fb*, *fc*, A-R database are plotted in Figure 4, Figure 5 and Figure 6. We can see clearly that the accuracy of our methods are not worse than Fisherface, Eigenface or EBGM algorithms, but our methods do not need manual eye locating, facial images alignment or face deformation before classification while the others need.

In our second experiment, we test the validity of our proposed segmentation method. Here, we compare our segmentation method with methods proposed in [8] [10], which just divide faces to rectangle regions. We test three schemes on *fb* of FERET database (K-SVM + Posteriori Selection): no face alignment + rectangle division; face alignment

Table 3. Recognition Rate on A-R database

	Majority voting	Sum rule	Prior	Posteri
KNN	0.84	0.82	0.87	0.87
LDA	0.82	0.82	0.90	0.91
L-SVM	0.84	0.87	0.87	0.91
K-SVM	0.87	0.92	0.93	0.95

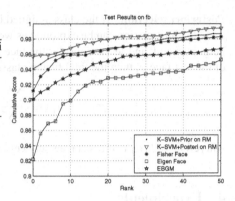

Fig. 4. Test results on *fb* of FERET

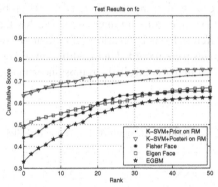

Fig. 5. Test results on *fc* of FERET

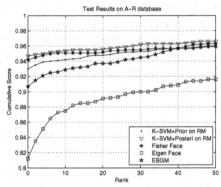

Fig. 6. Test results on A-R database

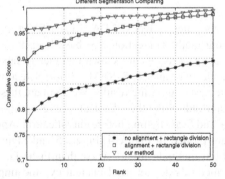

Fig. 7. Different segmentations on *fb* of FERET

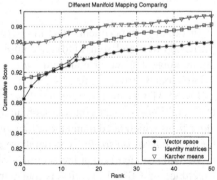

Fig. 8. Different maps on *fb* of FERET

+ rectangle division and our method. The comparing results are shown in Figure 7. Our segmentation scheme is better than the other two.

In our third experiment, we test three different manifolds mapping approaches:

- Our method, which maps the points to the tangent spaces at the Karcher means of points on manifolds.
- The mean calculation is ignored and points are always mapped to the tangent space at the identity matrix.
- We learn classifiers on the vector space. We ignore the geometry of Sym_n^+, and stack the upper triangular part of the covariance matrix into a vector.

These three methods are tested on fb of FERET (K-SVM + Posteriori Selection). The results are shown in figure 8. We can see that the original method outperforms all the other approaches significantly. The second best result is achieved by mapping points to the tangent space at the identity matrix followed by the vector space approaches.

5   Conclusion

We presented a novel face recognition approach which is robust to random position perturbations of key points and does not need manual eye locating, two facial images alignment or face deformation. The templates that we use to divide AAM models into irregular regions preserve original face information well. The multi-features fusion matrices on Riemannian manifolds combine different kinds of features (shape, texture, Gabor, et al) together. On the manifold Sym_n^+, we train classifiers for each region and combine them to a final classifier which is tested on FERET and A-R database, the results show that our method is accurate and robust while facial images alignment is no longer necessary.

Acknowledgements

This work was supported by NSFC (60635030), NKBRPC (2004CB318000).

References

1. Wiskott, L., Fellous, J.M., Kruger, N., von der Malsburg, C.: Face Recognition by Elastic Bunch Graph Matching. IEEE Trans. on Pattern Analysis and Machine Intelligence 19(7), 775–779 (1997)
2. Zhao, W., Chellappa, R., Phillips, P.J., Rosenfeld, A.: Face Recognition:A Literature Survey. ACM Computing Surveys 35(4), 399–458 (2003)
3. Belhumeur, P., Hespanha, J., Kriegman, D.: Eigenfaces vs. Fisherfaces:Recognition Using Class Specific Linear Projection. IEEE Transactions on Pattern Analysis and Machine Intelligence 19(7) (July 1997)
4. Moghaddam, B.: Principal Manifolds and Probabilistic Subspaces for Visual Recognition. IEEE Transactions on Pattern Analysis and Machine Intelligence 24(6) (July 2002)
5. He, X., Yan, S., Hu, Y., Niyogi, P., Zhang, H.: Face Recognition Using Laplacianfaces. IEEE Transactions on Pattern Analysis and Machine Intelligence 27(3) (March 2005)

6. Cootes, T.F., Edwards, G.J., Taylor, C.J.: Active Appearance Models. In: Burkhardt, H., Neumann, B. (eds.) ECCV 1998. LNCS, vol. 1407, pp. 484–498. Springer, Heidelberg (1998)
7. Lanitis, A., Taylor, C.J., Cootes, T.F.: Automatic Interpretation and Coding of Face Images Using Flexible Models. IEEE Transactions on Pattern Analysis and Machine Intelligence 19(7), 743–756 (1997)
8. Tuzel, O., Porikli, F., Meer, P.: Region covariance: A fast descriptor for detection and classification. In: Leonardis, A., Bischof, H., Pinz, A. (eds.) ECCV 2006. LNCS, vol. 3952, pp. 589–600. Springer, Heidelberg (2006)
9. Tuzel, O., Porikli, F., Meer, P.: Human Detection via Classification on Riemannian Manifolds. In: Proc. Computer Vision and Pattern Recognition, USA (June 2007)
10. Ahonen, T., Hadid, A., Pietikainen, M.: Face Recognition with Local Binary Patterns. In: Pajdla, T., Matas, J.G. (eds.) ECCV 2004. LNCS, vol. 3021, pp. 469–481. Springer, Heidelberg (2004)
11. Ojala, T., Pietikainen, M., Maenpaa, T.: Multiresolution Gray-scale and Rotation Invariant Texture Classification with Local Binary Patterns. IEEE Transactions on Pattern Analysis and Machine Intelligence 24, 971–984 (2002)
12. Pennec, X., Fillard, P., Ayache, N.: A Riemannian framework for tensor computing. Intl. J. of Computer Vision 66(1), 41–66 (2006)
13. Boothby, W.M.: An Introduction to Differentiable Manifolds and Riemannian Geometry. Academic Press, London (2002)
14. Karcher, H.: Riemannian center of mass and mollifier smoothing. Commun. Pure Appl. Math. 30, 509–541 (1977)
15. Wang, X., Tang, X.: Using Random Subspace to Combine Multiple Features for Face Recognition. In: IEEE International Conference on Automatic Face and Gesture Recognition (2004)
16. Ko, A.H.-R., Sabourin, R., de Souza Britto Jr., A.: A New Dynamic Ensemble Selection Method for Numeral Recognition. In: Haindl, M., Kittler, J., Roli, F. (eds.) MCS 2007. LNCS, vol. 4472, pp. 431–439. Springer, Heidelberg (2007)
17. Didaci, L., Giacinto, G., Roli, F., Marcialis, G.L.: A study on the performances of dynamic classifier selection based on local accuracy estimation. Pattern Recognition 38(11), 2188–2191 (2005)
18. Giacinto, G., Roli, F.: Methods for Dynamic Classifier Selection. In: International Conference on Image Analysis and Processing (ICIAP 1999), pp. 659–664 (1999)
19. Phillips, P.J., Wechsler, H., Huang, J., Rauss, P.: The FERET database and evaluation procedure for face recognition algorithms. Image and Vision Computing, 295–306 (1998)
20. Martinez, A.M., Benavente, R.: The AR face database. Technical Report 24, CVC Tech. Report

Gender Recognition via Locality Preserving Tensor Analysis on Face Images

Huining Qiu[1,2], Wan-quan Liu[1], and Jian-Huang Lai[2]

[1] Dept. of Computing, Curtin University of Technology
GPO Box U1987, Perth, WA 6845, Australia
w.liu@curtin.edu.au
[2] Dept. of Applied Mathematics, Sun Yat-sen University
510275, Guangzhou, China
qiuhuining@gmail.com, stsljh@mail.sysu.edu.cn

Abstract. In this paper we propose a new tensor based analysis algorithm for face gender recognition, in which we consider the different feature structures of male/female images respectively. Given a gender labeled face dataset, we aim to obtain their meaningful low-dimensional data representation which preserves their intrinsic male/female structures, and this is achieved by combining tensor analysis with a local geometric preserving constraint on the tensor decomposition. In the proposed approach, a similarity graph is built to represent images of the same gender and separate those of different genders. Technically, a 5-mode (w.r.t gender, pose, illumination, expression, pixels) tensor decomposition is used to analyze the packed image matrix, which is constrained on the proposed graph and this graph can preserve as much as possible on the information of gender in the decomposed component data. The objective of gender recognition is formulated as an optimization problem and then solved by an alternating algorithm. Finally, experiments are implemented on several face databases and it is proved that the proposed approach can enhance gender discriminant capability significantly compared to the tensor approach, while has already achieved a comparable recognition performance as a state-of-art algorithm.

1 Introduction

Without much effort human is able to recognize a person's gender quickly from his/her facial appearance, but this is not an easy task for computers. Automatic gender recognition is an important problem in computer vision, and it attracts much attention of researchers from psychology, pattern recognition and computer vision [1,2,3,4]. While some other studies highly concern about divergent aspects of this problem, such as combination of automatic face detection and gender classification [5,4], or comparisons of discriminant information between different facial parts [6]; however in this paper we mainly focus on extracting effective facial features for gender recognition. A typical face gender recognition system can be shown as a diagram in Fig.1.

H. Zha, R.-i. Taniguchi, and S. Maybank (Eds.): ACCV 2009, Part III, LNCS 5996, pp. 601–610, 2010.
© Springer-Verlag Berlin Heidelberg 2010

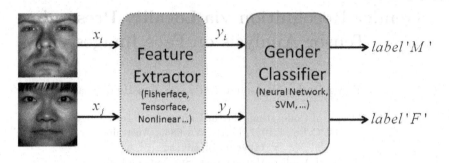

Fig. 1. Diagram of Gender Recognition

Face images are generally of high dimensionality and may not suitable for direct discriminant feature extraction. Dimensionality reduction algorithms are employed both to reduce the computational cost and to extract the most useful features for classification. Earlier gender recognition algorithms take raw facial image as linear input and work on low resolution images (e.g. SEXNET [1]), and the emergence of kernel technique seems a convincing direction both for low computational costs and high performance. For example, Moghaddam and Yang [7] reported that kernel-based SVMs performs better than other gender classifiers, which shows how useful to capture the nonlinear structure of face dataset. In spite of these kernel-related algorithms, many linear dimensionality reduction algorithms are also developed in recent years.

Though linear dimensionality reduction algorithms are simple and computationally fast, they are rarely able to capture nonlinearity of face data. While nonlinear dimensionality reduction algorithms are usually derived from a structural view of the dataset and can capture the intrinsic nonlinear variations of face data, they can hardly provide an explicit mapping from a high dimensional data space X to a low dimensional embedding space Y. Some techniques on developing linear approximation of nonlinear methods, or developing linear methods with nonlinear constraints, have been successfully applied to face recognition, gait recognition [8],[9], etc recently. They are the main motivations for our work in this paper.

The main purpose of this paper is to develop a nonlinear constrained multilinear analysis for gender recognition. Multilinear analysis in face recognition, like Tensorface [10,11], is proved to be useful for capturing variations in face dataset. Tensor modelling of face images basically assumes that a face image is a multilinear function of several variation factors such as person, illumination, viewpoint, expression, pixels etc; however this might not be totally true, and the multilinear approximation can be improved further by imposing nonlinear constraints. The important scheme for this paper is to impose a locality preserving constraint on the decomposed components, which are expected to improve the discriminant capability for gender recognition.

The rest of this paper is organized as follows: in section 2, we briefly review the methods of tensor analysis and graph-based embedding algorithms.

Following that a new algorithm for gender recognition is proposed in section 3, and experimental results are shown in section 4. Finally we conclude the paper in section 5.

2   Tensorface and Graph-Based Embedding

In this section we briefly review the algorithms of Tensorface and Graph-based constrained embedding. These two approaches are then combined to derive the proposed algorithm for gender recognition in this paper. To the best of our knowledge, this is the first time this technique is used for gender recognition.

2.1   Tensor Analysis of Facial Images

Multilinear analysis for face recognition is first introduced by Vasilescu and Terzopoulos [10,11]. In this section we mainly interpret such idea for face gender recognition. Given a face image database $X = \{X_i\}_{i=1}^N$, it is assumed that each face image is a multilinear function of several factors of variations, i.e. gender, pose, illumination, expression, thus the full database is formed by a 5-mode tensor

$$T = Z \times_1 U_g \times_2 U_p \times_3 U_l \times_4 U_s \times_5 U_x \qquad (1)$$

where $\times_k$ denotes the mode-k product, Z is the core tensor which controls interactions among dimensions and U_g, U_p, U_l, U_s, U_x are the corresponding gender, pose, illumination, expression, and pixel variational subspaces, whose dimensionality are denoted as $N_g = 2$, N_p, N_l, N_s, N_x respectively. Thus the face tensor $T \in \mathbb{R}^{2 \times N_p \times N_l \times N_s \times N_x}$. For tensor analysis, High Order SVD (HOSVD) can be performed to find a least square approximation of the face tensor

$$\min_{U_g', U_p', U_l', U_s', U_x'} \left\| Z \times_1 U_g' \times_2 U_p' \times_3 U_l' \times_4 U_s' \times_5 U_x' - T \right\|^2 \qquad (2)$$

where U_g', U_p', U_l', U_s', U_x' in the decomposition is usually truncated to lower dimensionality, and they can be viewed as eigen-components in each gender/pose/illumination/pixel modes respectively. To solve the above optimization problem, (2) is actually a standard numerical problem which can be solved using public computing tools in [12]. Once we obtained the face tensor decomposition from (2), we can project an image x to any one or more subspaces using tensor product. For example the projection to a gender subspace is

$$Y_x = x \times_1 Z \times_2 U_p' \times_3 U_p' \times_4 U_l' \times_5 U_x' \qquad (3)$$

and then we can take the projected features Y_x for subsequent recognition task.

2.2   Graph-Based Constrained Embedding

Yan et al. [8] proposed Graph Embedding as a general framework for nonlinear dimensionality reduction with application in face recognition, we now interpret it for our face gender recognition problem.

Given an image $x_i \in \mathbb{R}^D$ in high dimensional space, we can obtain its low dimensional representation $y_i \in \mathbb{R}^d$ where $d << D$, using some dimensionality reduction methods such as tensor projection in subsection 2.1. Then we have two point set $X \subseteq \mathbb{R}^D$ and $Y \subseteq \mathbb{R}^d$, which should have similar data structure. To describe and impose constraint of the structure, a graph G can be constructed in the original data space to reflect the near or faraway relations between points, and the projected data is required to preserve these relation as much as possible. Such a concept leads to the general objective form of graph embedding:

$$y^* = \min_{y^T By = d} \sum_{i \neq j} \|y_i - y_j\|^2 S_{ij} \tag{4}$$

where S_{ij} is the edge weighting between points x_i and x_j, d is a constant and B is the constraint matrix defined to avoid trivial solutions. Usually, soft edge weighting from heat kernel are adopted for building the graph weighting, that is to define:

$$S_{ij} = \begin{cases} e^{-\frac{\|x_i - x_j\|^2}{t}}, & \text{if } \mathbf{x}_i \text{ are } \mathbf{x}_j \text{ neighbors;} \\ 0, & \text{otherwise.} \end{cases} \tag{5}$$

where t is a diffusion parameter of the heat kernel. And B is usually defined to be a diagonal matrix for scale normalization of

$$B = diag(d_{11}, d_{22}, \ldots, d_{NN}), \quad and \quad d_{ii} = \sum_{j=1}^{N} S_{ij} \tag{6}$$

Of course B can be defined differently in applications but we don't explore this issue further in this paper.

The idea of preserving locality data structure is for general purpose, and can be applied to many dimensionality reduction algorithms. The research in this paper is to combine it with face tensor analysis for gender recognition.

3   Locality Preserving Tensor Analysis

In this section, we present the formulation of locality preserving tensor analysis, and propose a new algorithm to solve it.

3.1   Problem Formulation

As we pointed out in Section 2.2 that graph-based constraint is extensible for dimensionality reduction algorithms, and from Section 2.1 we know that projecting features on tensor eigen-components is also a kind of dimensionality reduction process. Further, we notice that the tensor analysis for gender recognition does not make use of label information at all, so the gender eigen-components can hardly reflect the different distribution of male and female image clusters. In order to design suitable gender recognition algorithm, it is necessary to impose a structure constraint while doing the face tensor decomposition. This can be achieved as we build a similarity graph $G = (X, S)$ from gender labels

$$S_{ij} = \begin{cases} e^{-\frac{\|\mathbf{x}_i - \mathbf{x}_j\|^2}{t}}, & \text{if } \mathbf{x}_i \text{ and } \mathbf{x}_j \text{ are both male or female;} \\ 0, & \text{otherwise.} \end{cases} \tag{7}$$

In this process we require that projections on the gender eigen-components should preserve the similarity relations as much as possible. Mathematically this leads to an optimization problem.

$$y^* = \min_{y^T B y = 1} \sum_{i \neq j} \|y_i - y_j\|^2 S_{ij} \tag{8}$$

where B is the same as (6). By substituting the projected y from (3), the objective function can be rewritten as

$$(Z^*, U_g^*, U_p^*, U_l^*, U_s^*, U_x^*) = \min_{\substack{Z, U_g, U_p, U_l, U_s, U_x \\ y^T B y = 1}} \sum_{i \neq j} \|x_i \times_1 R - x_j \times_1 R\|^2 S_{ij} \tag{9}$$

where R is a 4-mode tensor without gender component, i.e.,

$$R = Z \times_2 U_p \times_3 U_l \times_4 U_s \times_5 U_x \tag{10}$$

and y is the projected gender data columns.

3.2 Computational Algorithm

We now consider how to solve the optimization problem in (9). It is known that there is no closed form solution for general tensor decomposition, and we need to use iterative algorithms to obtain suboptimal solutions. Instead of optimizing six variables $(Z, U_g, U_p, U_l, U_s, U_x)$ simultaneously, we use an alternating scheme which solve them iteratively. This implies that in each iteration we only optimize one variable and regard others as constants. Notice that we can always compute the core tensor by $Z = X \times_1 U_g^T \times_2 U_p^T \times_3 U_l^T \times_4 U_s^T \times_5 U_x^T$, so there are only five variables to optimize. Rename the five variables U_g, U_p, U_l, U_s, U_x to be V_1, V_2, V_3, V_4, V_5, and assume the current optimizing variable is V_k while other variables are fixed, then the objective function can be written as:

$$\sum_{i \neq j} \|x_i \times_1 R - x_j \times_1 R\|^2 S_{ij} \tag{11}$$

$$= Tr \left(V_k^T \left(\sum_i D_{ii} X_i R_{(k)} R_{(k)}^T X_i^T - \sum_{i,j} S_{ij} X_i R_{(k)} R_{(k)}^T X_i^T \right) V_k \right) \quad (12)$$

$$= Tr \left(V_k^T \left(D_k - S_k \right) V_k \right) \quad (13)$$

with a constraint

$$1 = y^T D y = Tr \left(y^T D y \right) = Tr \left(V_k^T D_k V_k \right) \quad (14)$$

where $R_{(k)}$ is the mode-k matrix unfolding of tensor $V_1 \times \cdots \times V_{k-1} \times V_{k+1} \times \cdots \times V_5$ and D_k, S_k are denoted for

$$D_k = \sum_i D_{ii} X_i R_{(k)} R_{(k)}^T X_i^T, \quad S_k = \sum_{i,j} S_{ij} X_i R_{(k)} R_{(k)}^T X_i^T \quad (15)$$

Then the original objective function is equivalent to a trace-ratio minimization problem:

$$\min_{Z, U_g, U_p, U_l, U_s, U_x} \frac{Tr \left(V_k^T \left(D_k - S_k \right) V_k \right)}{Tr \left(V_k^T D_k V_k \right)} \quad (16)$$

Along this direction, the optimized V_k can be computed by solving the following generalized eigenvector problem:

$$\left(D_k - S_k \right) u = \lambda D_k u \quad (17)$$

Then in the next iteration, we alternate to optimize V_{k+1} while fixing all other $V_j, j \neq k + 1$, and repeat the same updating procedure to obtain the eigen solution. Repeat this alternating and iterating procedure until changes of all variables are small enough, and the algorithm can terminate then. Next we present the recognition algorithm.

Finally, we need to point out that the above proposed formulation and computational procedure are dealing with a 5-mode tensor model of face images. Yet it can be easily extended to more or less N-mode tensor models, especially by fixing the expression and/or illumination directions the algorithm can adapt to face images varying mainly gin poses/illuminations.

3.3   Recognition

If a solution of the constrained tensor decomposition is obtained by the above Locality Preserving Constrained Tensor (LPC-Tensor) algorithm as summarized in Table.1, so that we have $X \doteq Z \times_1 U_g \times_2 U_p \times_3 U_l \times_4 U_s \times_5 U_x$, then for any image x we can obtain its projections on each subspace. Then various classifiers can be used for recognition based on the low-dimensional data representations.

Table 1. LPC-Tensor Algorithm for Gender Recognition

Input: given a face image set $X = \{x_i\}_{i=1}^{N}$ with gender labels, with its 5-mode face tensor $T \in \mathbb{R}^{2 \times N_p \times N_l \times N_s \times N_x}$, and the required new dimensions $N_g', N_p', N_l', N_s', N_x'$ for final tensor decomposition, parameter t of heat kernel.

Output: all components of the locality preserving constrained tensor, i.e. Z, U_g, U_p, U_l, U_s, U_x.

Procedure:

0. Initialization: set $U_g = \begin{pmatrix} I_{N_g' \times N_g'} \\ 0_{(2-N_g') \times N_g'} \end{pmatrix}$, $U_p = \begin{pmatrix} I_{N_p' \times N_p'} \\ 0_{(N_p-N_g') \times N_p'} \end{pmatrix}$, $U_l = \begin{pmatrix} I_{N_l' \times N_l'} \\ 0_{(N_l-N_l') \times N_l'} \end{pmatrix}$, $U_s = \begin{pmatrix} I_{N_s' \times N_s'} \\ 0_{(N_s-N_s') \times N_s'} \end{pmatrix}$, $U_p = \begin{pmatrix} I_{N_x' \times N_x'} \\ 0_{(N_x-N_x') \times N_x'} \end{pmatrix}$.

1. Build constraint graph and compute edge weights: for every image $x_i, x_j \in X$, if x_i and x_j share the same gender label then let $S_{ij} = e^{-\frac{\|x_i - x_j\|^2}{t}}$, otherwise let $S_{ij} = 0$.

2. Do iteration:
      for loop $= 1$: max_loops
            let $V_1 = U_g$, $V_2 = U_p$, $V_3 = U_l$, $V_4 = U_s$, $V_5 = U_x$;
            for k $= 1 : 5$
                  update core tensor $Z = X \times_1 V_1^T \times_2 V_2^T \times_3 V_3^T \times_4 V_4^T \times_5 V_5^T$;
                  compute D_k, S_k by (15);
                  solve the eigen-vector problem (17) for V_k;
            end
            if $\| (V_1, V_2, V_3, V_4, V_5) - (U_g, U_p, U_l, U_s, U_x) \| < \epsilon$, break;
      end

3. Output the tensor decomposition components: $Z, U_g = V_1, U_p = V_2, U_l = V_3$, $U_s = V_4, U_x = V_5$.

---

4 Experiments

In this section we use the Extended Yale B and FERET database to evaluate the gender recognition performance of the proposed algorithm (LPC-Tensor), and compare it with several widely used feature extraction methods, i.e. PCA, LDA, LPP, and the original tensor approach. Before starting the experimental process, we first need to set up some common experimental configurations.

4.1 Experimental Configuration

It is known that alignment and normalization are important for good performance of face recognition algorithms. The same rule is also true for face gender recognition. In our experiments, we manually align each face image by its two eyes coordinates and one mouth coordinates. In addition, gray level normalization are also performed for each image.

For recognition, the nearest neighborhood classifier is used for all algorithms. With these configurations, we compare several typical algorithms on the following face databases.

4.2 Results on the Yale B and Extended Yale B Database

The Yale B, plus the Extended Yale B face database [13,14], totally consists of 38 individuals (29 male and 9 female), with 9 varying poses and 64 different illumination conditions. Since no expression variation is provided, the expression component of our algorithm is fixed to one dimension and we just omit it safely. We have made full use of all these images in our experiments. Firstly, all images are cropped and aligned using their two eyes coordinates and one mouth coordinates, then resized into a size of 112x92, followed by a normalization pre-processing of histogram equalization. For each round of test, we randomly divide the poses and illuminations set into two nearly equal parts, and use one part of all selected individuals's images for training, the left part for testing. It can be seen that for every individual we have chosen their images from the same poses and illuminations. This selection is important to ensure the consistency of the image data structures.

We have run the routine for 15 times, in which we record the best recognition rate of all involved algorithms, and finally get their average performance. The final results we obtained are shown in Table.2. From the results we can see that the proposed algorithm has achieved better performance than other feature extraction methods.

Table 2. Gender Recognition Comparisons on the YaleB+Extended Database

Method	Recognition Rate		
	overall	male	female
PCA	71.67	72.47	70.45
LDA	80.67	83.33	79.83
LPP	76.87	77.12	76.33
Raw-Tensor	80.35	82.33	79.48
LPC-Tensor	**87.33**	**87.50**	**86.67**

4.3 Results on the FERET Database

The FERET face database [15] is another challenging database with varying poses and illuminations. It contains 1199 individuals, however each individual might have different number of images. For purpose of forming a consistent face images manifold, we only collect 540 male images and 540 female images from the database, and all of them have three frontal/left/right poses, as well as fixed illumination variations. The routine of training and testing is similar to that we described for the Yale B database.

Results obtained from this experiment obtained by running the routine for 15 times and accumulating to average the recognition rate of all involved algorithms. The final comparison results are shown in Table.3.

The discriminant capability of proposed algorithm outperforms other methods. Also the recognition rates for both male and female of all algorithms are better than those on Yale B database. Though such good performance may relate to our careful selection of face images, we can still conclude in general that the consistent structure of face dataset with more images has important impact for face gender recognition.

Table 3. Gender Recognition Comparisons on the FERET Database

Method	Recognition Rate		
	overall	male	female
PCA	77.56	79.87	75.36
LDA	88.67	89.94	87.84
LPP	82.58	86.78	80.38
Raw-Tensor	90.86	91.26	88.64
LPC-Tensor	**92.45**	**93.37**	**90.28**

5 Conclusions and Future Work

In this paper we proposed a locality preserving constrained tensor decomposition algorithm for gender classification. The algorithm can enhance the performance by preserving the intrinsic structure of face dataset in tensor decomposition. Experimental results show the effectiveness of the algorithm. To improve the computation efficiency, we need make further efforts on seeking faster solutions for optimization problems formulated in this paper. The recent results [16,17] on fast implementation of tensor decomposition will motivate to go forward.

Acknowledgement

This project was supported by a grant supported by National Science Foundation of China with grant No. 60675016, a grant supported by National Science Foundation of Guangdong with grant No. U0835005, and an ARC Linkage Project supported by Australian Research Council.

References

1. Cottrell, G.W., Metcalfe, J.: Empath: face, emotion, and gender recognition using holons. In: NIPS-3: Proceedings of the 1990 conference on Advances in neural information processing systems, vol. 3, pp. 564–571. Morgan Kaufmann Publishers Inc., San Francisco (1990)

2. Bruce, V., Burton, A.M., Hanna, E., Healey, P., Mason, O., Coombes, A., Fright, R., Linney, A.: Sex discrimination: how do we tell the difference between male and female faces? Perception 22, 131–152 (1993)
3. Tamura, S., Kawai, H., Mitsumoto, H.: Male/female identification from 8×6 very low resolution face images by neural network. Pattern Recognition 29(2), 331–335 (1996)
4. Makinen, E., Raisamo, R.: Evaluation of gender classification methods with automatically detected and aligned faces. IEEE Trans. Pattern Anal. Mach. Intell. 30(3), 541–547 (2008)
5. Yang, Z., Li, M., Ai, H.: An experimental study on automatic face gender classification. In: International Conference on Pattern Recognition, vol. 3, pp. 1099–1102 (2006)
6. Kawano, T., Kato, K., Yamamoto, K.: A comparison of the gender differentiation capability between facial parts. In: Proceedings of 17th International Conference on Pattern Recognition (ICPR 2004), Washington, DC, USA, vol. 1, pp. 350–353. IEEE Computer Society, Los Alamitos (2004)
7. Moghaddam, B., Yang, M.H.: Gender classification with support vector machines. In: Proc. of Int'l Conf. on Automatic Face and Gesture Recognition (FG 2000), Grenoble, France, March 2000, pp. 306–311 (2000)
8. Yan, S., Xu, D., Zhang, B., Zhang, H.J., Yang, Q., Lin, S.: Graph embedding and extensions: A general framework for dimensionality reduction. IEEE Transactions on Pattern Analysis and Machine Intelligence 29(1), 40–51 (2007)
9. Xu, D., Yan, S., Tao, D., Lin, S., Zhang, H.J.: Marginal fisher analysis and its variants for human gait recognition and content- based image retrieval. IEEE Transactions on Image Processing 16(11), 2811–2821 (2007)
10. Vasilescu, M.A.O., Terzopoulos, D.: Multilinear analysis of image ensembles: Tensorfaces. In: Heyden, A., Sparr, G., Nielsen, M., Johansen, P. (eds.) ECCV 2002. LNCS, vol. 2350, pp. 447–460. Springer, Heidelberg (2002)
11. Vasilescu, M.A.O., Terzopoulos, D.: Multilinear image analysis for facial recognition. In: ICPR (2), pp. 511–514 (2002)
12. Bader, B.W., Kolda, T.G.: Matlab tensor toolbox version 2.2 (January 2007), http://csmr.ca.sandia.gov/~tgkolda/tensortoolbox/
13. Georghiades, A., Belhumeur, P., Kriegman, D.: From few to many: Illumination cone models for face recognition under variable lighting and pose. IEEE Trans. Pattern Anal. Mach. Intelligence 23(6), 643–660 (2001)
14. Lee, K., Ho, J., Kriegman, D.: Acquiring linear subspaces for face recognition under variable lighting. IEEE Trans. Pattern Anal. Mach. Intelligence 27(5), 684–698 (2005)
15. Phillips, J.P., Moon, H., Rizvi, S.A., Rauss, P.J.: The feret evaluation methodology for face-recognition algorithms. IEEE Transactions on Pattern Analysis and Machine Intelligence 22(10), 1090–1104 (2000)
16. Rana, S., Liu, W., Lazarescu, M., Venkatesh, S.: Recognising faces in unseen modes: A tensor based approach. In: CVPR (2008)
17. Rana, S., Liu, W., Lazarescu, M., Venkatesh, S.: Efficient tensor based face recognition. In: ICPR, pp. 1–4 (2008)

A Chromosome Image Recognition Method Based on Subregions

Toru Abe, Chieko Hamada, and Tetsuo Kinoshita

Tohoku University
2-1-1 Katahira, Aoba-ku, Sendai 980–8577, Japan
{beto@isc,dachiko@ka.riec,kino@isc}.tohoku.ac.jp

Abstract. To make a visual examination of a chromosome image for various chromosome abnormalities, individual chromosome regions have to be determined in a subject image and classified into distinct chromosome types in advance. We propose a subregion based method to improve this process. The proposed method regards each chromosome region as a series of subregions and iterates a search for subregions in the subject image consecutively. In this method, chromosome region classification can be performed simultaneously with its determination for each subregion, and features in the subregions can be integrated effectively for recognizing (determining and classifying) the entire chromosome region.

1 Introduction

A visual examination of a chromosome image for various chromosome abnormalities plays an important role in many clinical practices, including treatment and prevention of genetic disorders, radiation dosimetry, toxicology, etc [1].

Generally, the visual chromosome examination requires the following [2]:

1. staining a set of chromosomes in a cell nucleus and capturing its image,
2. determining individual chromosome regions in the subject image,
3. classifying the determined regions into the 24 distinct chromosome types (1, 2, ..., 22, X, and Y).

With proper staining techniques (e.g. G-banding technique etc.), a characteristic series of light and dark bands appears along the longitudinal axis of a chromosome (Fig. 1 (a)). The band appearance on a chromosome is called a banding pattern, and it is unique to each type of chromosome [3]. For determining and classifying the chromosome regions in an image, many methods have been proposed [4,5,6,7,8,9,10]. In most of them, individual chromosome regions are extracted from the subject image (Fig. 1 (b)), the longitudinal profile of intensity on each region is acquired as its banding pattern, and the extracted regions are classified into the 24 distinct chromosome types according to their banding patterns (Fig. 1 (c)). The classification result is inspected for abnormalities of number, where there are one or more entire chromosomes additional to or missing from the normal complement. The banding pattern on each region

H. Zha, R.-i. Taniguchi, and S. Maybank (Eds.): ACCV 2009, Part III, LNCS 5996, pp. 611–620, 2010.
© Springer-Verlag Berlin Heidelberg 2010

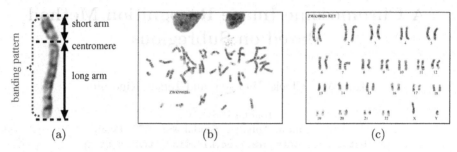

Fig. 1. (a) An example of banding pattern (G-banded chromosome 5), (b) chromosome image, (c) determination and classification results [11]

is visually examined for abnormalities of structure, where part of the bands are lost (deletion), repeated (duplication), shifted (translocation), etc [1].

Most of the existing methods for chromosome region classification require that individual chromosome regions are extracted accurately from the subject image in advance, and they also assume that each extracted region has the appearance of normal bands. However, chromosome regions in an image frequently touch or overlap each other and have some parts difficult to distinguish them from the background, and thus the accurate extraction of individual chromosome regions is hard to achieve [12,13]. Furthermore, aberrant bands occur on the extracted region because of various reasons (e.g., region extraction failures, region overlaps, structural chromosome abnormalities, etc.), and consequently the region appearance often deviates from the normal [4,8].

To overcome these problems, we propose a novel chromosome image recognition method based on subregions. The proposed method regards each chromosome region as a series of subregions and iterates a search for subregions in the subject image consecutively. As a result, chromosome region classification can be performed simultaneously with its determination for each subregion, and features in the subregions can be integrated effectively for recognizing (determining and classifying) the entire chromosome region.

This paper is organized as follows: Section 2 describes procedures in the proposed method; Section 3 explains the detail of the subregion search and chromosome region recognition in the subject image; Section 4 provides experimental results. Some conclusions and perspectives are discussed in Section 5.

2   Procedures in the Proposed Method

The proposed method regards each chromosome region as a series of subregions and iterates a search for subregions in the subject image consecutively. In this method, a reference banding pattern is made by averaging samples for every chromosome type (Fig. 2 (a)). Each reference banding pattern for an entire chromosome region is divided into several parts, and they are used as the templates for recognizing the subregions of a chromosome. In the following, the

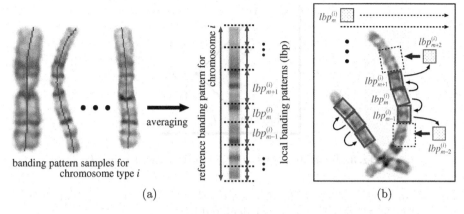

Fig. 2. (a) Reference banding pattern and local banding patterns, (b) consecutive subregion searches

divided parts are referred to as local banding patterns (lbp), and the m th local banding pattern of the chromosome type i is denoted by $lbp_m^{(i)}$.

Firstly, as shown in Fig. 2 (b), the subject image is searched for the subregion corresponding to a template. If the subregion corresponding to $lbp_m^{(i)}$ is detected, secondly, the neighborhood of the detected subregion is searched for the next subregion corresponding to the adjoining $lbp_{m+1}^{(i)}$ (or $lbp_{m-1}^{(i)}$). By iterating the search for corresponding subregions consecutively, with the first detected subregion as the starting point, one subregion after another is tracked. Through this iteration, the entire region of the chromosome is determined in the image, and at the same time the chromosome type i is assigned to the determined region.

By taking the proposed approach, the following advantages are expected in the chromosome image recognition:

- As the consecutive subregion searches, region classification is performed simultaneously with region determination for each subregion, and the results of preceding subregion searches are utilized for the following searches. Accordingly, the achievement of stable region determination can be expected.
- By excluding the results of failed subregion searches, features in the subregions are effectively integrated while reducing aberrant band influence, and region classification is performed according to these integrated features. Consequently, the achievement of accurate region classification can be expected.

3   Subregion Search and Chromosome Region Recognition

3.1   Subregion Search

A subregion search is made by scanning the subject image I_S with a template lbp and seeking for subregions where the mean-squared-error (MSE) to lbp are sufficiently small. The MSE to lbp is computed at every position within a search

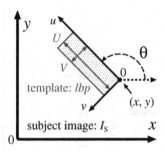

Fig. 3. Template *lbp* set at (x, y) in the subject image I_S

area set in I_S. As shown in Fig. 3, when *lbp* (U in length and V in width) is set at (x, y) in I_S, the MSE $e^2(x, y)$ is calculated by:

$$e^2(x, y) = \frac{1}{UV} \sum_{u=0}^{U-1} \sum_{v=0}^{V-1} (I'_S(x', y') - lbp(u, v))^2, \tag{1}$$

$$I'_S(x', y') = \alpha I_S(x', y') + \beta, \tag{2}$$

$$x' = x + u\cos\theta - v\sin\theta, \tag{3}$$

$$y' = y + u\sin\theta + v\cos\theta, \tag{4}$$

where θ is the rotation angle of *lbp* and it is set so as to minimize $e^2(x, y)$.

Since the dimensions and intensities of chromosome regions vary with every image, the proposed method adjusts the dimensions of *lbps* to those of chromosome regions in I_S and adapts the intensities of I_S to those of *lbps*.

- Suppose that the reference image I_R is used for making *lbps* (i.e., reference banding patterns) and the subject image I_S is searched with these *lbps*. By binarizing I_R on the basis of intensities, the mode w_R of region widths and the sum A_R of region areas are measured in the binarized image. From these measurements, the sum L_R of region lengths can be estimated by $L_R = A_R/w_R$. Similarly, w_S, A_S, L_S are determined in the binarized I_S. To adjust the *lbp* dimensions, the proposed method sets the *lbp* width to w_S and magnifies the *lbp* length by L_S/L_R.
- To adapt the intensities of I_S, for every rotation angle θ, the intensities of pixels overlapped with *lbp* are transformed by (2), where α and β are set to minimize $e^2(x, y)$.

In the proposed method, subregions within the search area for $lbp_m^{(i)}$ are sorted by their MSE in ascending order, and the top N subregions are chosen as the candidates to correspond with $lbp_m^{(i)}$. If the candidate subregions corresponding to $lbp_m^{(i)}$ are chosen, the area should be searched for the subregion corresponding to the following $lbp_{m+1}^{(i)}$ can be determined according to these candidate subregions. As shown in Fig. 4 (a), the proposed method sets a rectangle area $sa_{m+1}^{(i)}$ at each candidate subregion for $lbp_m^{(i)}$, circumscribes a rectangle about all $sa_{m+1}^{(i)}$, and

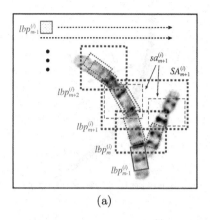

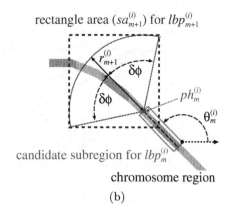

Fig. 4. (a) Search area $SA^{(i)}_{m+1}$ for $lbp^{(i)}_{m+1}$, (b) rectangle area $sa^{(i)}_{m+1}$ set at each preceding candidate subregion

uses this larger rectangle area $SA^{(i)}_{m+1}$ as the search area for $lbp^{(i)}_{m+1}$. As shown in Fig. 4 (b), each rectangle area $sa^{(i)}_{m+1}$ is set as follows:

1. determining the head $ph^{(i)}_m$ of a candidate subregion for $lbp^{(i)}_m$,
2. setting a sector at $ph^{(i)}_m$ with radius $r^{(i)}_{m+1} = \gamma \times U^{(i)}_{m+1}$, direction $\theta^{(i)}_m$, and central angle $2\delta\phi$ (γ and $\delta\phi$ are constants set beforehand),
3. circumscribing a rectangle $sa^{(i)}_{m+1}$ about the sector,

where $U^{(i)}_{m+1}$ is the length of $lbp^{(i)}_{m+1}$ and $\theta^{(i)}_m$ is the rotation angle of $lbp^{(i)}_m$.

By iterating the subregion search and the search area setup (for the starting point, an entire area of the subject image is regarded as the search area), one set of subregions (N at the most) after another is chosen as the candidates to correspond with each lbp.

3.2   Chromosome Region Recognition

Since the proposed method chooses a set of subregions as the candidates to correspond with each lbp, for recognizing an entire chromosome region, it is necessary to select a subregion from every candidate set and determine a combination of the candidate subregions. In the proposed method, for each chromosome region, inadequate subregions are eliminated from the candidate sets, and then the optimum combination of candidate subregions is determined.

Eliminating Inadequate Candidate Subregions. When a candidate subregion has a high MSE value, even if this subregion corresponds to lbp, it is surmised that the aberrations (chromosome region overlaps, chromosome abnormalities, etc.) occur there. In the proposed method, to reduce the aberrant band influence on the chromosome region recognition, subregions whose MSE values are greater than a given threshold T_{MSE} are eliminated from the candidate sets.

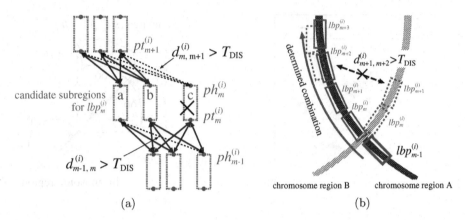

Fig. 5. (a) Eliminating disconnected candidate subregions, (b) determining the optimum combination of candidate subregions

Furthermore, to make up a combination of the candidate subregions into a single continuous region, in the proposed method, disconnected subregions are eliminated from the candidate sets. Let the head and tail of a candidate subregion for $lbp_m^{(i)}$ be $ph_m^{(i)}$ and $pt_m^{(i)}$, respectively. The distance between two adjoining candidate subregions is defined by:

$$d_{m-1,m}^{(i)} = \|ph_{m-1}^{(i)} - pt_m^{(i)}\| \quad \left(\text{or} \quad d_{m,m+1}^{(i)} = \|ph_m^{(i)} - pt_{m+1}^{(i)}\|\right) \quad (5)$$

When the distances $d_{m-1,m}^{(i)}$ from a candidate subregion for $lbp_m^{(i)}$ to all adjoining candidate subregions for $lbp_{m-1}^{(i)}$ are greater than a given threshold T_{DIS}, this candidate subregion for $lbp_m^{(i)}$ is eliminated (if all distances $d_{m,m+1}^{(i)}$ are greater than T_{DIS}, this candidate subregion is also eliminated). For example, in Fig. 5 (a), the candidate subregion 'a' and 'b' for $lbp_m^{(i)}$ have adjoining candidate subregions where the distances are $d_{m-1,m}^{(i)} \leq T_{\text{DIS}}$ or $d_{m,m+1}^{(i)} \leq T_{\text{DIS}}$, on the other hand, 'c' has no adjoining candidate subregions of $d_{m-1,m}^{(i)} \leq T_{\text{DIS}}$, even though it has adjoining candidate subregions of $d_{m,m+1}^{(i)} \leq T_{\text{DIS}}$. Consequently, 'a' and 'b' are kept in the candidate set, while 'c' is eliminated from the candidate set.

Determining Optimum Combination. For recognizing an entire chromosome region, the proposed method selects a subregion from the set of candidates for every lbp and determines a combination of the candidate subregions. To determine the optimum combination, candidate subregions are selected so as to minimize the overall MSE in the combination of the selected subregions on the condition that the distance d between two adjoining candidate subregions is not greater than T_{DIS} (Fig. 5 (b)).

Through this process, the entire region of a chromosome is determined as a combination of subregions in the subject image, and at the same time a chromosome type is assigned to the determined region.

4 Experiments

We implemented a prototype system based on the proposed method, and conducted chromosome image recognition experiments.

4.1 Chromosome Images

The experiments were carried out on the chromosome images that are opened to public by the website at the Wisconsin State Laboratory of Hygiene and ZooWeb [11]. Thirty-one chromosome images were used in the experiments (each image was 768×576 pixels in size). Fig. 6 shows examples of an original chromosome image and its binarized image. These images were divided into two sets: one (15 images) was used as subject images I_S, and the other (16 images) was used as reference images I_R employed for making templates (lbp).

Reference banding patterns for chromosome 1, 2, ..., 5 were made from I_R. As shown in Fig. 7, each reference banding pattern was divided into several lbp, and a single lbp (marked with '*') was selected to search for the starting point subregion of each chromosome type. In the experiments, these procedures were carried out manually.

4.2 Experimental Results

In the experiments, the number of chosen candidate subregions was set to $N = 3$, the parameters for a sector were set to $\gamma = 2, \delta\phi = 90°$ (described in Sect. 3.1), the threshold of MSE was set to $T_{MSE} = 5000$, and the threshold of distance was set to $T_{DIS} = 15$pixels (described in Sect. 3.2).

Fig. 8 shows an example of chromosome image recognition result. Every I_S was searched for subregions with a starting point lbp. The subregions were sorted by their MSE in ascending order, and the top 30 subregions were chosen as the starting points. From these subregions, chromosome region recognition was started individually, and the combinations of subregions were determined. The determined combinations for each chromosome type (1, 2, ..., 5) in every I_S were sorted by their overall MSE in ascending order. In Fig. 8 (a), correct regions

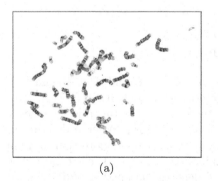
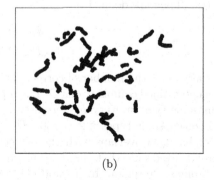

(a)   (b)

Fig. 6. Examples of an original chromosome image (a) and its binarized image (b)

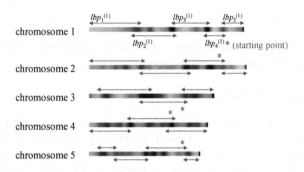

Fig. 7. Temples *lbp* used in the experiments

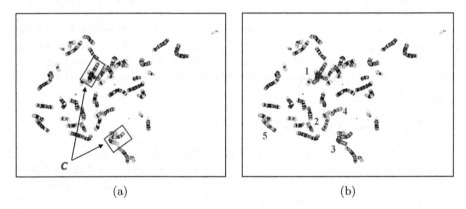

(a)   (b)

Fig. 8. (a) Examples of correct chromosome regions (chromosome 1), (b) examples of determined combinations

(chromosome 1) were marked with 'C', and in Fig. 8 (b), determined combinations (top 5) were shown with their orders (the correct regions were recognized in the first and third).

To evaluate the chromosome recognition results, recall R and precision P were used. They are defined by:

$$R = |C \cap D|/|C|, \qquad (6)$$
$$P = |C \cap D|/|D|, \qquad (7)$$

where $|C|$ is the number of correct chromosome regions C and $|D|$ is the number of determined combinations D. The top k determined combinations for each chromosome type in every I_S were used as D (therefore, $|C| = 15$ subject images × 5 chromosome types × 2 = 150, $|D| = 15 \times 5 \times k = 75k$). When a determined combination overlaps with the correct chromosome region (more than 60% in area), we decide that the determined combination corresponds correctly to the chromosome region. In (6) and (7), $|C \cap D|$ denotes the number of determined combinations which correspond correctly to the chromosome regions.

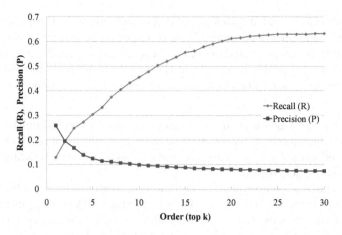

Fig. 9. Average recall R and precision P with different top k combinations

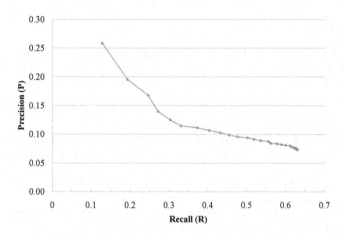

Fig. 10. Relation between average R and P by varying k

The average R and P for 5 chromosome types and 15 subject images were computed by varying k. Fig. 9 shows the average R and P with different k, and Fig. 10 shows the relation between the average R and P by varying k. Currently, fundamental functions in the proposed method were implemented naively, therefore the recognition accuracies were low (e.g., $R = 0.6$ and $P = 0.09$ at $k = 20$). However, by improving the subregion search method and developing an effective *lbp* selection method, the increase in accuracy can be expected.

5   Conclusions

In this paper, we have proposed a subregion based method for recognizing chromosome images. The proposed method regards each chromosome region as a series of subregions and iterates a search for subregions in the subject image consecutively. The proposed method can be expected to achieve stable chromosome region determination and accurate chromosome region classification.

However, several problems remain in the proposed method. To achieve effective chromosome image recognition, we plan to improve and expand the proposed method:

- To increase the accuracy and efficiency of chromosome recognition, we will improve the subregion search method itself and develop a method of determining effective *lbps* (i.e., effective parts in each reference banding pattern) for the subregion search.
- To recognize a complement of chromosome regions in the subject image effectively, we will consider a method of utilizing previous recognition results on some chromosome types for recognizing the other chromosome types, and we need to develop a method for selecting correct chromosome regions from recognition results (i.e., determined combinations of subregions).

References

1. Gersen, S.L., Keagle, M.B. (eds.): The principles of clinical cytogenetics, 2nd edn. Humana Press (2004)
2. Graham, J., Piper, J.: Automatic karyotype analysis. Meth. Mol. Biol. 29, 141–185 (1994)
3. Harnden, D.G., Klinger, H.P. (eds.): ISCN1985: An international system for human cytogenetic nomenclature. S. Karger AG (1985)
4. Groen, F.C.A., Kate, T.K., Smeulders, A.W.M., Young, I.T.: Human chromosome classification based on local band descriptors. Pattern Recognit. Lett. 9(3), 211–222 (1989)
5. Carothers, A., Piper, J.: Computer-aided classification of human chromosomes: a review. Statistics Computing 4(3), 161–171 (1994)
6. Ritter, G., Pesch, C.: Polariy-free automatic classification of chromosomes. Computational Statistics Data Analysis 35, 351–372 (2001)
7. Wu, Q., Liu, Z., Chen, T., Xiong, Z., Castleman, K.R.: Subspace-based prototyping and classification of chromosome images. IEEE Trans. Pattern Anal. Machine Intell. 14(9), 1277–1287 (2005)
8. Moradi, M., Setarehdan, S.K.: New features for automatic classification of human chromosomes: A feasibility study. Pattern Recognit. Lett. 27(1), 19–28 (2006)
9. Kao, J., Chuang, J., Wang, T.: Chromosome classification based on the band profile similarity along approximate medial axis. Pattern Recognit. 41(1), 77–89 (2008)
10. Legrand, B., Chang, C., Ong, S., Neo, S.Y., Palanisamy, N.: Chromosome classification using dynamic time warping. Pattern Recognit. Lett. 29(3), 215–222 (2008)
11. ZooWeb: Karyotypes home page,
    http://worms.zoology.wisc.edu/zooweb/Phelps/karyotype.html
12. Charters, G.C., Graham, J.: Trainable grey-level models for disentangling overlapping chromosomes. Pattern Recognit. 32(8), 1335–1349 (1999)
13. Schwartzkopf, W., Bovik, A., Evans, B.: Maximum-likelihood techniques for joint segmentation-classification of multispectral chromosome images. IEEE Trans. Med. Imag. 24(12), 1593–1610 (2005)

Co-occurrence Random Forests for Object Localization and Classification

Yu-Wu Chu and Tyng-Luh Liu

Institute of Information Science, Academia Sinica, Taipei 115, Taiwan
{ywchu,liutyng}@iis.sinica.edu.tw

Abstract. Learning techniques based on random forests have been lately proposed for constructing discriminant codebooks for image classification and object localization. However, such methods do not generalize well to dealing with weakly labeled data. To extend their applicability, we consider incorporating co-occurrence information among image features into learning random forests. The resulting classifiers can detect common patterns among objects of the same category, and avoid being trapped by large background patterns that may sporadically appear in the images. Our experimental results demonstrate that the proposed approach can effectively handle weakly labeled data and meanwhile derive a more discriminant codebook for image classification.

1 Introduction

Recent research efforts on object classification and localization have supported that, especially for the latter, the bounding box or shape mask information is useful for accomplishing the related tasks. However, while providing such information for a large dataset is laborious, it has been noticed that the background clutter within a bounding box encompassing a target object can be distracting and cause misclassifications. The situation becomes even worse when the provided data are only weakly labeled. That is, an image is marked as positive (without any bounding box information) for some object class if it does contain such an object of interest. Otherwise, it is treated as a negative one. To alleviate this unfavorable effect, exploring the co-occurrence evidence has been proposed, e.g., in [1] and shown to be a feasible approach. In this work, we propose a novel implementation of *random forests* that effectively incorporates the co-occurrence information to perform proper splits and yield a discriminant codebook for both object classification and localization.

1.1 Related Work

A number of object localization schemes rely on that the target location in each of the training data is annotated with a bounding box [2], [3], [4]. The procedure is typically performed in the following three steps. First, interest points are detected within object areas of all images. Second, for each object category, a codebook is generated by partitioning the feature space into several regions.

H. Zha, R.-i. Taniguchi, and S. Maybank (Eds.): ACCV 2009, Part III, LNCS 5996, pp. 621–632, 2010.

(a)   (b)   (c)

Fig. 1. (a) Original image. (b) The probability map produced by RF. (c) The probability map produced by our method. Observe that the co-occurrence information can help random forests to prefer common patterns, such as car doors, wheels, to specific patterns, such as road textures in the images.

The features in the same region yield a visual word, and the collection of them forms a codebook. This leads to a bag-of-visual-words representation. Third, object models are learned with a chosen classification algorithm, e.g., SVM. With the scores evaluated by the object models, localization can be done by scanning a given testing image to obtain the best one which indicates the possible object location, or by labeling each pixel with the one that its object model achieves the highest score. However, the above-mentioned techniques are often time-consuming during the test stage, and also do not generalize well to handle the weakly labeled data. On the other hand, techniques based on *multiple instance learning* for exploiting the weakly labeled data have been proposed to learn the object models [5], [6], [7], but most of them focus on image classification rather than object localization.

Bosch et al. [1] consider the co-occurrence information to find regions of interest (ROIs), and report that the knowledge of ROIs can improve image classification accuracy. Yet in [8], [9] the authors have integrated the co-occurrence information with existing classification schemes to address object recognition. Nevertheless, these techniques are all computationally expensive.

Owing to its efficiency, classification with random forests has been used in tackling various computer vision problems, such as codebook generation [10], image classification [1], and image segmentation [11]. In particular, Shotton et al. [11] apply random forests to learning a discriminant codebook. While the resulting codebook could achieve accuracy improvements for both image classification and segmentation, its quality may suffer from noisy labeling.

1.2 Our Approach

Our method exploits the efficiency of random forests and the co-occurrence information between images to alleviate the effects of noisy labels. The key idea is to uncover common patterns among most of the images rather than specific patterns in a few images, as illustrated in Fig. 1. As a result, we expect to derive a codebook that is discriminant for both image classification and object localization on weakly labeled formulations.

2 Random Forests (RF)

In this section, we give a brief review of random forests. A random forest is an ensemble of decision trees with randomness. Each decision tree is constructed by recursively splitting each internal node into left and right nodes until the stop criterion is met, e.g., there are too few examples in the node, all data in the node have the same class label c, or the desired depth L is reached. At each internal node n, a split function f partitions the training data set S_n into two subsets S_l and S_r:

$$S_l = \{\mathbf{v} \in S_n | f(\mathbf{v}) \le 0\}, \tag{1}$$
$$S_r = S_n \backslash S_l. \tag{2}$$

When growing the tree, we choose a split function at each node n to maximize the score function that measures the degree of separation of the training data. Following [12], the score function S is defined as the *normalized information gain*:

$$S(n, f) = \frac{2I_{C,f}(n)}{H_C(n) + H_f(n)}, \tag{3}$$

where $H_C(n)$ is the class *entropy* of node n, $H_f(n)$ is the split entropy of node n, and $I_{C,f}(n)$ is the *mutual information* between the class distribution and the given split function f of node n. They are defined respectively as follows:

$$H_C(n) = - \sum_c p(c|n) \log p(c|n), \tag{4}$$

$$H_f(n) = - \sum_{p \in \{l,r\}} p(S_p|n) \log p(S_p|n), \tag{5}$$

$$I_{C,f}(n) = \sum_c \sum_{p \in \{l,r\}} p(c, S_p|n) \log \frac{p(c, S_p|n)}{p(c|n)p(S_p|n)}. \tag{6}$$

Moreover, the randomness of random forests can be drawn from two aspects: training data, and split functions. First, each decision tree is grown with different subset of the training samples. Second, the split function at each internal node is generated randomly to divide the data into two subsets, and the best one of them is chosen according to the score function in (3).

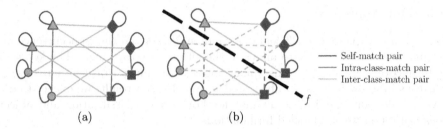

—— Self-match pair
—— Intra-class-match pair
······ Inter-class-match pair

(a)   (b)

Fig. 2. Each pattern represents a feature in an image. The patterns with the same shape belong to the same image, and the patterns with the same color belong to the same class. Therefore, there are four images, eight features, and two classes in this figure. We assume these features are in the same node n. Each pair of features connected by the line represents a CoFP. (a) There are three types of CoFPs illustrated with different line colors. (b) A split function f separates the features in the node n into two disjoint sets, S_l and S_r. It also divides the CoFPs into three disjoint sets: the set of pairs of features connected by the dotted lines $S_{\hat{c}}$, the set of pairs of features connected by the solid lines in bottom left plane $S_{\hat{l}}$, and the set of pairs of features connected by the solid lines in top right plane $S_{\hat{r}}$.

After a random forest is learned, the class probability distribution of leaf node n in a tree is denoted as $p(c|n)$, which is estimated by the posterior distribution over the training data falling into leaf node n. The final classification result of a test sample x is obtained by averaging the class distribution over the leaf nodes reached in all trees:

$$p(c|N_x) = \frac{1}{T} \sum_{t=1}^{T} p(c|n_t), \tag{7}$$

where n_t is the leaf node in tree t reached by sample x and N_x is the set of all such leaf nodes in the given random forest.

3   Co-occurrence Random Forests (CoRF)

In our formulation, image X_i is represented by a set of features, which can be the detected interest points, or randomly sampled patches with variant scales and positions. The conventional random forests treat all features in all the training images as training samples. Therefore, they would discover specific patterns from particular images, but not common patterns among most of images which the latter is what we want. This is mostly due to the lack of correlated information between features. It is thus reasonable to expect that taking account of the co-occurrence information would guide the random forest algorithm to discover proper patterns. In what follows we will describe how to incorporate the co-occurrence information into the random forest algorithm.

3.1   Co-occurrence Feature Pairs

There is a match function $g_{i,j} : (A, B) \rightarrow m$, which presents a mapping between two sets of features, where $A \in X_i$, $B \in X_j$, and $m = 1$ if (A, B) is matched, otherwise $m = 0$. In other words, the mapping indicates co-occurrence relations between two sets, X_i and X_j. The match function g is qualified by a cost function $\mathcal{C}$, for example, the sum of the distances between match pairs. Assume the function g^* is the minimum cost. We define a feature pair $(A, B) \in \{(C, D) | g_{i,j}^*(C, D) = 1, C \in X_i, D \in X_j\}$ as a co-occurrence feature pair (CoFP). A CoFP (A, B) is the best mapping between two sets according to the cost function $\mathcal{C}$. In this paper, we assume that CoFPs of two sets of features are one-to-one mapping. A feature on one set maps at most one feature on another set, and the number of match pairs is as many as possible.

As illustrated in Fig. 2a, each CoFP can be divided into three groups: self-match pairs, intra-class-match pairs, and inter-class-match pairs. A self-match pair is a CoFP from the same image. In other words, the interest point matches to itself. An intra-class-match pair is a CoFP from two different images which are labeled as the same class. An inter-class-match pair is a CoFP from two different images which are labeled as different classes. Therefore, CoFPs are labeled as following. If a CoFP comes from images in the same class c, i.e. a self-match pair or an intra-class-match pair, it is labeled as class c. Otherwise, it is labeled as ϕ, which denotes a mismatch pair, i.e. an inter-class-match pair. The information, i.e the CoFPs and their labels, is applied to any classification model to determine the CoFP belongs to the specific class c or the background clutter ϕ.

However, the cost function is affected by the selection of the distance function between features which would affect CoFPs directly. The Euclidean distance is a good choice, but it might suffer from the curse of dimensionality [13]. Besides, finding the optimal function g^* is time-consuming, while the feature dimension and/or the number of features in each image are large. We instead incorporate learning the distance function into the classification model.

3.2 Implicit Co-occurrence Feature Pairs

As aforementioned, searching the optimal match function g^* is time-consuming. Therefore, we utilize tree structures to reduce search space and make this problem easier. We assume that a similarity or decision tree has been built. In the tree, if features fall into the same node, we could say they are similar to each other. In other words, each pair of features in the node is a candidate of the CoFPs. Besides, it is easy to prove that the candidates in the node are the subset of the candidates in its parent node. Because we assume that two sets of features are one-to-one mapping, the candidates of the CoFPs can be removed if they are the candidates in its descendant nodes. As a result, the CoFPs are discovered by the bottom-up strategy. In addition, the number of CoFPs in the node $\hat{n}$ is computed efficiently by the following equation

$$|S_{\hat{n}}| = \sum_{i,j} \min(|S_n \cap X_i|, |S_n \cap X_j|), \tag{8}$$

where $|\cdot|$ is the number of elements in the set, S_n is the set of the features in the node n, X_i is the set of the features in the image i, and $S_{\hat{n}}$ is the set of the CoFPs in the node $\hat{n}$. Note that elements in the node n are features, and elements in the node $\hat{n}$ are CoFPs which are generated from the set S_n. In the next subsection, we exploit the number of CoFPs, to guide the random forest algorithm to discover the proper patterns. Because, we do not search for the exactly match pairs, this mapping is called implicit co-occurrence feature pairs (iCoFPs). iCoFPs have the same properties as CoFPs except the exact mapping.

3.3   Learning Co-occurrent Random Forests

In random forests, we divide the set of features at each node into two disjoint sets according to the split function f which is defined as

$$f(\mathbf{v}) = \mathbf{v}(i) + b, \tag{9}$$

where $\mathbf{v} \in \mathbb{R}^d$ is a feature vector, $i \in \{1, \cdots, d\}$ is a dimension index, and b is a bias. f also separates the iCoFP set $S_{\hat{n}}$ at node $\hat{n}$ into three disjoint subsets $S_{\hat{l}}$, $S_{\hat{r}}$, and $S_{\hat{c}}$ implicitly, as illustrated in Fig. 2b. Note that $S_{\hat{c}}$ is the residual set of $S_{\hat{n}}$, i.e. the mismatch pair set in the sublevel of $S_{\hat{n}}$, or precisely $S_{\hat{c}} = S_{\hat{n}} \backslash (S_{\hat{l}} \cup S_{\hat{r}})$. In other words, it can not be split anymore. As a result, the co-occurrence information, i.e. iCoFPs, can be incorporated into the random forest algorithm, and we call this algorithm the co-occurrence random forest algorithm. iCoFPs and their labels which are defined in the previous subsection are treat as the input data of the random forest algorithm. The split function which divides the features into two parts are the same as (9). As aforesaid, the separation on the features implies divide the iCoFPs into three parts. So, the score function which measures the degree of separation of the iCoFPs in the node $\hat{n}$ is defined as

$$S(\hat{n}, f) = \frac{2I_{\hat{C}, f}(\hat{n})}{H_{\hat{C}}(\hat{n}) + H_f(\hat{n})}, \tag{10}$$

where

$$H_{\hat{C}}(\hat{n}) = - \sum_{c \in \{1, \cdots, C, \phi\}} p(c|\hat{n}) \log p(c|\hat{n}), \tag{11}$$

$$H_f(\hat{n}) = - \sum_{\hat{p} \in \{\hat{l}, \hat{r}, \hat{c}\}} p(S_{\hat{p}}|\hat{n}) \log p(S_{\hat{p}}|\hat{n}), \tag{12}$$

$$I_{\hat{C}, f}(\hat{n}) = \sum_{c \in \{1, \cdots, C, \phi\}} \sum_{\hat{p} \in \{\hat{l}, \hat{r}, \hat{c}\}} p(c, S_{\hat{p}}|\hat{n}) \log \frac{p(c, S_{\hat{p}}|\hat{n})}{p(c|n) p(S_{\hat{p}}|\hat{n})}. \tag{13}$$

The joint probability of the class c and the split $S_{\hat{p}}$, the class probability, and the split data probability in (11), (12), and (13) are given respectively by

$$p(c, S_{\hat{p}}|\hat{n}) = \frac{1}{Z} w_{\hat{p}} |\{(\mathbf{v}_1, \mathbf{v}_2)|(\mathbf{v}_1, \mathbf{v}_2) \in c, (\mathbf{v}_1, \mathbf{v}_2) \in S_{\hat{p}}, (\mathbf{v}_1, \mathbf{v}_2) \in S_{\hat{n}}\}|, \tag{14}$$

$$Z = \sum_{c \in \{1, \cdots, C, \phi\}} \sum_{\hat{p} \in \{\hat{l}, \hat{r}, \hat{c}\}} p(c, S_{\hat{p}}|\hat{n}), \tag{15}$$

$$p(c|\hat{n}) = \sum_{\hat{p} \in \{\hat{l}, \hat{r}, \hat{c}\}} p(c, S_{\hat{p}}|\hat{n}), \tag{16}$$

$$p(S_{\hat{p}}|\hat{n}) = \sum_{c \in \{1, \cdots, C, \phi\}} p(c, S_{\hat{p}}|\hat{n}), \tag{17}$$

where $|\cdot|$ is the number of elements in the set which can be computed efficiently by the equation (8), and $w_{\hat{p}}$ is the weight associated with the node $\hat{p}$. $w_{\hat{p}}$ is proportional to the inverse of the diameter of the node. In our experiments, we set $w_{\hat{p}}$ as $w_{\hat{l}} = w_{\hat{r}} = 2w_{\hat{c}}$. Note that if we only consider self-match pairs, our method is equivalent to the traditional random forests. After a co-occurrence random forest is learned, the final classification result of a test sample x can be computed using (7). In the next two sections, we describe how to apply the CoRF to solve object localization and image classification problems.

4   Object Localization

For object localization, we use the voting approach to generate the final probability map. The probability of each patch x in test image I is calculated by equation (7). Then, the probability of each pixel i is figured out by

$$p(c|i, I) = \frac{1}{N} \sum_{\{j | i \in \mathcal{R}_{x_j}\}} p(c|N_{x_j}), \tag{18}$$

where x_j is a patch in the test image, $\mathcal{R}_{x_j}$ represents the region that is covered by the patch x_j, and N is the number of patches that cover the pixel i. Therefore, we could get the probability map.

5   Image Classification

For image classification, we consider support vector machines (SVMs) as the classifier with the linear kernel [10] or the pyramid match kernel [11], [14] to measure the similarity between two images. Each node in the random forests denotes a visual word, and each image is represented by the histogram of hierarchical visual words. Note that, for the linear kernel, we only use the leaf nodes as the visual words without utilizing the hierarchical structure of the trees.

The pyramid match kernel [14] is defined as

$$\tilde{K}(X_i, X_j) = \frac{K(X_i, X_j)}{\sqrt{K(X_i, X_i)K(X_j, X_j)}}, \tag{19}$$

where

$$K(X_i, X_j) = \sum_{l=1}^{L} w_l N_l \tag{20}$$

$$= w_1 \mathcal{I}(H_1(X_i), H_1(X_j))$$

$$+ \sum_{l=2}^{L} (w_l - w_{l-1}) \mathcal{I}(H_l(X_i), H_l(X_j)), \tag{21}$$

$$N_l = \mathcal{I}(H_l(X_i), H_l(X_j)) - \mathcal{I}(H_{l+1}(X_i), H_{l+1}(X_j)) \tag{22}$$

$$\mathcal{I}(H_l(X_i), H_l(X_j)) = \sum_{b=1}^{B} \min(H_{l,b}(X_i), H_{l,b}(X_j)), \tag{23}$$

L is the depth of the tree, w_l is the weight at the level l, N_l is the newly match at the level l, and $H_{l,b}(X)$ is the bth bin of histogram representation of the feature set X at the level l. Each tree t forms one pyramid match kernel $\tilde{K}_t$. The final kernel over all trees is obtained by $\tilde{K} = \frac{1}{T} \sum_t \tilde{K}_t$. In [11], the weight w_l is set as $\frac{1}{2^{L-l}}$ which is proportional to the depth of the node. In contrast, we set the weight $w_{l,b}$ as the following steps. Initially, the diameter of the leaf node has a unit length, and the diameter of the internal node is the sum of its children's diameter. After computing the diameters of all nodes, the weight of the node is set to the inverse of its diameter and the sum of all weights in the tree is normalized to one. Because the built trees are usually imbalance, and the leaf node has more discriminant power than the internal node. In our setting, the weight at each level is not the same, and each bin has its weight which is proportional to the inverse of its diameter. In addition, we could improve the pyramid match kernel by weighting the histogram intersection with $p(c|b)$, the class prior given the visual word b. The histogram intersection in (23) is modified as follows

$$\mathcal{I}(H_l(X_i), H_l(X_j)) = \sum_{b=1}^{B} p(c|b) \min(H_{l,b}(X_i), H_{l,b}(X_j)). \tag{24}$$

The class prior can help mask the interest area in the image, and filter out the irrelevance samples.

6   Experiments

In this section, we evaluate our method on the Graz-02 dataset, which contains three categories with large variations in locations, scales, lighting conditions, and viewpoints. We test each class versus background class individually. Various visual descriptors could be used, such as SIFT [15], geometric blur [16], color descriptor [10], [11], and so on. In our experiments, the best one is class dependent.

In all experiments, we use the following setting, which is similar to [10]. In each image, 8,000 features are randomly extracted with variant scales and positions. We choose the color wavelet descriptor as our feature descriptor. Among all features extracted from all training images, we randomly select 20,000 features to train each tree with 50 tests for each split. Five trees are learned, and each of them contains about 1,000 leaf nodes.

Table 1. Pixel labeling results on Graz-02 (The pixel precision-recall EER)

Bike	RF	CoRF	RF.GT	CoRF.GT	[17].GT	[4].GT
L=8	53.9	56.7	60.0	58.9		
L=11	54.6	57.1	60.7	59.1	61.8	66.4
L=14	54.7	57.1	61.0	59.0		
Car	RF	CoRF	RF.GT	CoRF.GT	[17].GT	[4].GT
L=8	44.0	44.8	52.4	54.9		
L=11	42.8	46.4	52.8	56.0	53.8	54.7
L=14	40.1	46.2	51.3	56.8		
Person	RF	CoRF	RF.GT	CoRF.GT	[17].GT	[4].GT
L=8	30.5	35.1	39.4	39.1		
L=11	32.6	34.5	38.8	40.4	44.1	51.4
L=14	33.0	34.4	38.2	40.8		

6.1   Object Localization

For object localization, train/test split is the same as the one in [4], [17]. For each category, the first 150 odd numbered images are used for training, and the first 150 even numbered images are used for testing. The performance is measured as the pixel level classification rate at equal error rate, which is the point that the recall meets the precision. The results are shown in Table 1. The number in the leftest column indicates the maximum tree depth L. The suffix GT means that the method is trained with ground truth shape masks. In the most of the cases, our method outperforms the traditional random forests. In Fig. 3, we observe that the co-occurrence information guides the random forest algorithm to select more meaningful features, and alleviates the effect of weakly labeled data. Moreover, the pixel level probability map which is produced by our method is more compact than the conventional manner. However, there is still a large gap of the accuracy between working with ground truth data and weakly labeled data for object localization. More clues should be exploited, e.g. spatial configuration [18], to reduce the gap.

6.2   Image Classification

For image classification, we use the same train/test split as the one in [10]. For each category, the first 150 even numbered images are used for training, and the first 150 odd numbered images are used for testing. The performance is measured as the image classification rate at equal error rate, which is the point that the false positive rate meets the false negative rate. We perform the image classification with different kernels: the linear kernel (LK), the intersection kernel (IK), and the pyramid match kernel (PMK). The intersection kernel is similar to the pyramid match kernel. The difference between them is that the intersection kernel only uses the leaf nodes as the codebook. The suffix p represents that the histogram intersection is weighted by the class prior $p(c|n)$. The PMK1 uses the weight in equation (20) that is suggested by Shotton et el. [11], and the

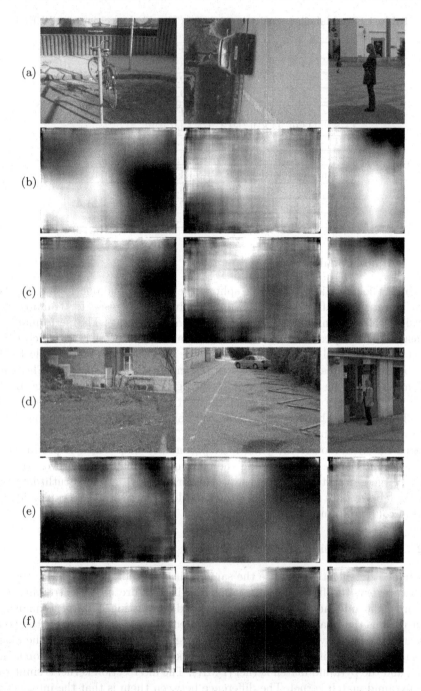

Fig. 3. Part of results on Graz-02. (a) and (d) are the original images. (b) and (e) are the probability map produced by RF. (c) and (f) are the probability map produced by our approach.

Table 2. Image classification results on Graz-02 (EER)

Bike	LK	IK	IK.p	PMK1	PMK1.p	PMK2	PMK2.p
RF	83.3	82.7	83.2	80.8	81.3	82.2	82.7
CoRF	85.2	82.7	83.0	79.2	82.3	82.8	83.2
Moosmann et el. [10]	84.4	-	-	-	-	-	-
Car	LK	IK	IK.p	PMK1	PMK1.p	PMK2	PMK2.p
RF	80.8	80.8	81.6	78.1	78.8	80.8	81.6
CoRF	80.1	82.8	83.6	79.7	81.2	82.7	83.5
Moosmann et el. [10]	79.9	-	-	-	-	-	-
Person	LK	IK	IK.p	PMK1	PMK1.p	PMK2	PMK2.p
RF	88.5	87.0	87.2	86.0	86.7	87.2	87.3
CoRF	86.5	87.5	88.0	85.8	87.5	87.0	88.2
Moosmann et el. [10]	-	-	-	-	-	-	-

PMK2 uses the weight we suggest in section 5. The results are shown in Table 2. Some conclusions could be derived from this table. In all cases, the class prior improves the results as in [11]. This also verifies the result mentioned in [19]. The results of PMK2 are similar to the results of IK and both of them are better than the results of PMK1. In other words, the leaf node has more discriminant power than the internal node. In most of the cases, our method is better than the conventional random forests. Again, the co-occurrence information could guide the random forest algorithm to discover the proper patterns.

7   Conclusions and Future Work

We have proposed a learning technique to exploit the co-occurrence information when image data are only weakly labeled. As demonstrated, by more effectively identifying common patters among images of the same class, CoRF can learn a more discriminant codebook, and locate the object position more accurately. Consequently, our method can accomplish better accuracies in both object localization and image classification. However, there is still a significant gap of the accuracy between working with ground truth data and weakly labeled data for object localization than that for image classification [10], [11]. To bridge this gap would be the main focus of our future work.

Acknowledgments. The work is supported in part by NSC grants 95-2221-E-001-031-MY3 and 97-2221-E-001-019-MY3.

References

1. Bosch, A., Zisserman, A., Munoz, X.: Image classification using random forests and ferns. In: ICCV (2007)
2. Lampert, C.H., Blaschko, M.B., Hofmann, T.: Beyond sliding windows: Object localization by efficient subwindow search. In: CVPR (2008)

3. Blaschko, M.B., Lampert, C.H.: Learning to localize objects with structured output regression. In: Forsyth, D., Torr, P., Zisserman, A. (eds.) ECCV 2008, Part I. LNCS, vol. 5302, pp. 2–15. Springer, Heidelberg (2008)
4. Fulkerson, B., Vedaldi, A., Soatto, S.: Localizing objects with smart dictionaries. In: Forsyth, D., Torr, P., Zisserman, A. (eds.) ECCV 2008, Part I. LNCS, vol. 5302, pp. 179–192. Springer, Heidelberg (2008)
5. Chen, Y., Bi, J., Wang, J.Z.: Miles: Multiple-instance learning via embedded instance selection. PAMI (2006)
6. Qi, G.J., Hua, X.S., Rui, Y., Mei, T., Tang, J., Zhang, H.J.: Concurrent multiple instance learning for image categorization. In: CVPR (2007)
7. Yang, L., Jin, R., Sukthankar, R., Jurie, F.: Unifying discriminative visual codebook generation with classifier training for object category recognition. In: CVPR (2008)
8. Bar-Hillel, A., Hertz, T., Weinshall, D.: Object class recognition by boosting a part-based model. In: CVPR (2005)
9. Sahbi, H., Audibert, J.Y., Rabarisoa, J., Keriven, R.: Context-dependent kernel design for object matching and recognition. In: CVPR (2008)
10. Moosmann, F., Triggs, B., Jurie, F.: Randomized clustering forests for building fast and discriminative visual vocabularies. In: NIPS (2006)
11. Shotton, J., Johnson, M., Cipolla, R.: Semantic texton forests for image categorization and segmentation. In: CVPR (2008)
12. Geurts, P., Ernst, D., Wehenkel, L.: Extremely randomized trees. Machine Learning (2006)
13. Grauman, K., Darrell, T.: Approximate correspondences in high dimensions. In: NIPS (2006)
14. Grauman, K., Darrell, T.: The pyramid match kernel: discriminative classification with sets of image features. In: ICCV (2005)
15. Lowe, D.: Distinctive image features from scale-invariant keypoints. IJCV (2003)
16. Berg, A.C., Berg, T.L., Malik, J.: Shape matching and object recognition using low distortion correspondences. In: CVPR (2005)
17. Marszatek, M., Schmid, C.: Accurate object localization with shape masks. In: CVPR (2007)
18. Lazebnik, S., Schmid, C., Ponce, J.: Beyond bags of features: Spatial pyramid matching for recognizing natural scene categories. In: CVPR (2006)
19. Uijlings, J., Smeulders, A., Scha, R.: What is the spatial extent of an object? In: CVPR (2009)

Solving Multilabel MRFs Using Incremental α-Expansion on the GPUs

Vibhav Vineet and P.J. Narayanan

Center for Visual Information Technology
International Institute of Information Technology
Hyderabad, India
{vibhavvineet@research.,pjn@}iiit.ac.in

Abstract. Many vision problems map to the minimization of an energy function over a discrete MRF. Fast performance is needed if the energy minimization is one step in a control loop. In this paper, we present the incremental α-expansion algorithm for high-performance multilabel MRF optimization on the GPU. Our algorithm utilizes the grid structure of the MRFs for good parallelism on the GPU. We improve the basic push-relabel implementation of graph cuts using the atomic operations of the GPU and by processing blocks stochastically. We also reuse the flow using reparametrization of the graph from cycle to cycle and iteration to iteration for fast performance. We show results on various vision problems on standard datasets. Our approach takes 950 milliseconds on the GPU for stereo correspondence on Tsukuba image with 16 labels compared to 5.4 seconds on the CPU.

1 Introduction

Low-level vision problems like stereo correspondence, restoration, segmentation, etc., are usually modeled as a label assignment problem. A label from a given set is assigned to each pixel or block in an image. These problems are often modeled in a Markov random-field (MRF) framework. Geman and Geman [17] formulated the maximum a-posteriori (MAP) estimation of the MRF as an energy minimization problem. Minimization of these energy functions is computationally expensive. Several algorithms have been proposed to improve the computational performance [9,4,1,2]. However, real time performance on regular images is still a challenge on the traditional hardware. Several vision applications like robot navigation, surveillance, etc., require the processing to be completed at close to video frame-rates.

Solving computationally expensive problems on parallel architectures is another way to improve the efficiency. However, not all algorithms are easily scalable to parallel hardware models. The contemporary graphics processing units (GPUs) are emerging as popular high performance platforms because of their huge processing power at reasonable costs. The Compute Unified Device Architecture (CUDA) [19] from Nvidia provides a general-purpose parallel programming interface to the modern GPUs. The emerging standard of OpenCL also

H. Zha, R.-i. Taniguchi, and S. Maybank (Eds.): ACCV 2009, Part III, LNCS 5996, pp. 633–643, 2010.
© Springer-Verlag Berlin Heidelberg 2010

promises to provide portable interfaces to the GPUs and other parallel processing hardware. The grid structure of the MRFs arising in vision problems makes the GPU an ideal platform for energy minimization problems. However, synchronization and memory bandwidth are bottlenecks for implementing them on the GPUs.

In this paper, we explore MRF optimization on the GPU. In particular, we propose a method to efficiently use the GPU and their atomic capability for high performance. We present the incremental α-expansion algorithm for multilabel MRFs. Our method retains the grid structure of the graph, common to low-level vision problems. We also propose a method to map dynamic energy minimization algorithms [4] to the GPU architecture. We recycle and reuse the flow from the previous MRF instances. A novel framework is also proposed based on the observation that the most of the variables in the MRF get the final labels quickly. Reuse of the flow from one cycle to the next as well as from one iteration to the next in the first cycle, and shifting the graph constructions to the parallel GPU hardware are the innovative ideas that produce high performance. We achieve a speedup of 5-6 times on different multi-labeling problems on standard datasets.

We tested our algorithm on different problems such as stereo correspondence, image restoration, and photomontage. Stereo correspondence results are shown on Tsukuba, Venus and Teddy images. Image restoration results are shown on Penguin and House images and photomontage on Panorama and Family images. All the datasets are taken from the Middlebury MRF page [14]. The energy functions used are the same as used by them. Our approach takes 950 milliseconds on the GPU for stereo correspondence on Tsukuba image with 16 labels compared to 5.4 seconds on the CPU.

1.1   Literature Review

Some of the key algorithms which are used to minimize energy functions defined over MRF include α-expansion and $\alpha\beta$-swap [3], max-product loopy belief propagation [20] and tree-reweighted message passing [12]. α-expansion involves constructing a graph over which maxflow/mincut algorithms are applied repeatedly. The Ford-Fulkerson's algorithm [21] to solve maxflow/mincut problem is popular and several fast implementations are available today [3,10]. Push-relabel method [7] is more parallelizable and was implemented on the Connection Machines by Goldberg et al. [5].

Recently efforts have been made to solve the optimization algorithms on the parallel architecture. Push-relabel algorithms have been implemented on the GPU recently [13,8]. They demonstrate solution of bilabel problems on the GPU. Liang et al. [15] designed a new parallel hardware to solve belief propagation algorithm efficiently. Delong and Boykov [18] gave a scalable graph-cut algorithm for N-D grids which attains non-linear speedup with respect to the number of processors on commodity multi-core platforms. Schmidt et al. [23] present an efficient graph cuts algorithm for planar graphs motivated by the work of Borradaile and Klein [22].

2   MRF Energy Minimization on the GPUs

Many vision problems are naturally formulated as energy minimization problems. These discontinuity preserving functions have two terms, data term and smoothness term. The general form of the function is:

$$E(f) = \sum D_p(f_p) + \sum V_{p,q}(f_p, f_q)$$

where $D_p(f_p)$, the data term, measures the cost of assigning a label $f_p \in L$ to pixel $p \in P$ and $V_{(p,q)}(f_p, f_q)$, the smoothness term, measures the cost of assigning the labels f_p and f_q to the adjacent pixels p and q.

The MRF is modeled as a graph with a grid structure with fixed connectivity. We use the α-expansion algorithm to minimize the energy, which is posed as a series of two-label graph cuts. We use a flagged graph cuts using the push-relabel algorithm for these. We also reuse the flows to initialize the current MRF instance from the previous iterations and cycles. Two basic steps of updation and reparameterization are also parallelized on the GPUs.

2.1 α-Expansion Algorithm

The α-expansion [3] is a popular move-making energy minimization algorithm (Algorithm 1). Steps 2 to 4 form a cycle and the step 3 is an iteration within a cycle. The algorithm starts from an intial labelling and makes a series of moves, which involve label change of the random variables, until there is no decrease in the energy. After each iteration of α-expansion, the random variable in the MRF retains either its current label or takes a new label α. One cycle of α-expansion algorithm involves iterating over all the labels.

Given a current labelling f, there are exponential number of moves possible in Step 3. Graph cuts algorithm efficiently computes next configuration f' in polynomial time. It involves constructing a graph based on the current labeling and the label α. Vertices with label α do not take part in the iteration but all others attempt to relabel themselves with α. There are two ways to construct the graph involved. Kolmogorov et al. [10] construct the graph without any auxiliary vertices, while Boykov et al. [3] introduce auxiliary vertices. The α-expansion method involves constructing graph in each iteration. This is

---

Algorithm 1. α-EXPANSION

1: Intialize the MRF with an arbitrary labelling f.
2: **for** each label $\alpha \in L$ **do**
3:    Find $f' =$ arg min $E(f')$ among f' within one α-expansion of f, current labelling
4: **end for**
5: **if** $E(f') < E(f)$ **then**
6:    goto step 2
7: **end if**
8: return f

---

a time consuming step. It takes 1.2 seconds on the Tsukuba image for stereo correspondence problem with 16 labels on the CPU.

2.2   Flagged Graph Cuts on the GPU

The push-relabel algorithm finds the maximum flow in a directed graph. Each vertex u in the graph has two quantities associated with it: height value $h(u)$ and excess flow $e(u)$. The algorithm involves two basic operations: *Push* and *Relabel*. It has been implemented on the ealier version of CUDA, with and without the atomic capability [13,8]. We extend prior work to handle α-expansion [13].

Push Operation: The push operation can be applied at a vertex u if $e(u) > 0$ and its height $h(u)$ is equal to $h(v) + 1$ for at least one neighbor $v \in G^r$, the residual graph. Algorithm 2 explains the implementation of the push operation on the GPU.

Algorithm 2. KERNEL2_PUSH

Input: A residual graph, $G^r(V, E)$.
1: Load height $h(u)$ from the global memory to the shared memory of the block.
2: Synchronize the threads of the block to ensure the completion of load.
3: **if** u is in the current graph **then**
4:     Push excess flow to eligible neighbors atomically without violating constraints.
5:     Update edge-weights of (u, v) and (v, u) atomically in the residual graph G^r.
6:     Update excess flows $e(u)$ and $e(v)$ atomically in the residual graph G^r.
7: **end if**

Relabel Operation: Local relabel operation is applied at a vertex u if it has positive excess flow but no push is possible to any neighbor due to height mismatch. The height of u is in-creased in the relabeling step by setting it to one more than the minimum height of its neighboring nodes in the residual graph G^r. Algorithm 3 explaines the implementation of local relabel performed on GPUs.

Algorithm 3. KERNEL3_RELABEL

Input: A residual graph, $G^r(V, E)$.
1: Load height $h(u)$ from the global memory to the shared memory of the block.
2: Synchronize the threads of the block to ensure the completion of load.
3: **if** u is in the current graph **then**
4:     Update the activity bit of each vertex in the residual graph G^r.
5:     Compute the minimum height of the neighbors of u in the residual graph G^r.
6:     Write the new height to the global memory $h(u)$.
7: **end if**

Push-relabel algorithm finds the maxflow/mincut on an edge-capacitated graph. Graph construction is central to any energy minimization method based on the

Table 1. Comparison of running times(in milliseconds) for one graph cut on GTX 280 with that of Boykov on the CPU on different images

Image	Graph Cuts		Graph Construction		Total		
	GPU	CPU [11]	GPU	CPU [11]	GPU	CPU [11]	
Flower	37	188	0.15	60	37.15	248	
Sponge	44	142	0.15	61	44.15	203	
Person	61	140	0.15	60	61.15	201	

graph cuts. Our graph-construction exploits the grid-structures of the MRFs defined over images. We adapt the graph construction of Kolmogorov *et al.* [10], which maintains the grid structure. α-expansion repeatedly finds the mincut based on the current graph, the current labelling of the pixels, and the label α. Thus the structure of the graph changes for each iteration using α. We use a flagged graph-cuts method, which helps in retaining the grid structure of the graph. We keep a flag bit with each vertex in the graph, which is set if the vertex is part of the current graph. Each vertex participates in the computationonly only if the flag is set (Step 3 of Algorithm 2 and 3). This way, we maitain the grid structure and restrict the overall computation. The graph is constructed based on the energy functions which can change over iterations for some problems. To reduce the overall computation time, the evaluation of the energy functions and the graph construction are performed on the GPU. Our energy function and graph construction are same as in [14]. Table 1 compares the times for bilabel segmentation on some standard datasets on the GPU and the CPU.

2.3   Stochastic Cut

Most of the pixels get their final label after a few iterations on different datasets. This relates to the fact that the MRF constitutes both simple and difficult variables [16]. The simple variables settle and get their final label within few iterations of the graph cuts algorithm. Only few vertices exchange flows with their neighbours later. Processing vertices which are unlikely to exchange any flow with their neighbours results in inefficient utilization of the resources.

We determine blocks of vertices that are active at different stages of the graph cuts algorithm. An active block has at-least one pixel that has exchanged flow in the previous step. The activity is determined based on the change in the edge-weights and is marked for each block. Based on the active bit, the kernel executes the other parts of the algorithm. Figure 1(a) shows the number of active blocks as the computation progresses. This behaviour of the MRF is data dependent. In the case of the Tsukuba image for stereo correspondence problem, we see that the number of active blocks decreases significantly within a few iterations of the graph cuts. However, in the case of the Penguin image for restoration problem, the number of active blocks remains almost same throughout the computation. We delay the processing of a block based on its activity bit by a fixed amount. A block is processed in every iteration if it is active, otherwise the block is processed only after 10 iterations. This delaying has no effect on the final convergence as

Algorithm 4. KERNEL4_STOCHASTIC

Input: A residual graph, $G^r(V, E)$.
1: Check the active bit of the block.
2: Perform Flagged Graph Cuts every iteration on all the above blocks and every 10th iteration on the inactive blocks.

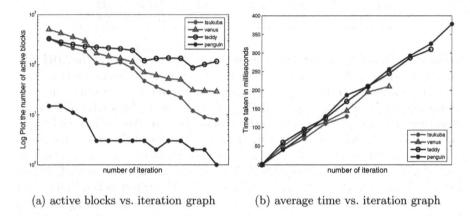

(a) active blocks vs. iteration graph   (b) average time vs. iteration graph

Fig. 1. (a) Number of active blocks vs. iteration number and (b) average time vs. iteration number on different datasets

Goldberg *et al.* [7] proves that the convergence of the push-relabel algorithm is independent of the order of processing of the push and relabel operation for each vertex. However, to maintain the preflow condition at all time, we can apply the above approach only to the push operation. Algorithm 4 explains the working of the push-relabel algorithm with stochastic cuts on the GPUs. Figure 1(b) shows the time taken by each iteration averaged over all cycles.

2.4   Increamental α-Expansion on the GPU

Energy minimization algorithms try to reach the global minima of the energy functions. They will converge faster if initialized close to optimum point. Initialization can have a huge impact on the computation time. Reusing the flow has been the method to initialize better. Kohli and Torr [4] describe a reparameterization of the graph to initialize it for later frames in dynamic graph cuts. Komodakis *et al.* [2] extends this concept to multilabeling problems. Alahari *et al.* [1] give a simpler model for the same using dynamic α-expansion.

   We adapt these methods to get an incremental α-expansion algorithm. We make three modifications to speed the overall process.

 – First, we adapt the re-parameterization given by Kohli and Torr to the push-relabel algorithm. The final graph of the push-relabel method and the final residual graph of the Ford-Fulkersons method are the same. We can

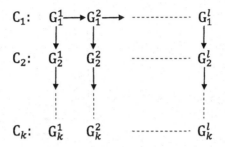

Fig. 2. Incremental α-expansion. Arrows indicate reparameterization based on the differences in graph constructed. G_i^j is the graph for iteration j of cycle i.

Algorithm 5. KERNEL5_INCREMENTAL

Input: A residual graph, $G^r(V, E)$.
1: Initialize the graph
2: for the first cycle:
3:     Construct graph G_1^1 for $\alpha = 1$, save in `prev`
4:     Perform 1-expansion for label 1 using flagged graph cuts
5:     Save final excess flow graph in `eflow`
6: **for** labels l from 2 to L **do**
7:     Construct graph G_1^l for current label l
8:     Reparametrize `eflow` based on difference with `prev`
9:     Perform l-expansion for label l using flagged graph cuts
10:     Save final excess flow graph in `eflow`
11: **end for**
12: for latex cycles i, iterations j
13:     Construct graph G_i^j
14:     Reparameterize based on G_i^j and $G_{(i-1)}^j$
15:     Perform l-expansion for label l using flagged graph cuts

---

apply similar reparametrization steps to the leftover flow for the push-relabel algorithm. The graph is updated using reparameterization from one step to another instead of being constructed from scratch.

– Second, we adapt the cycle-to-cycle relation used by Komodakis et al. and Alahari et al. to α-expansion. For this, we store the graph at the start of each iteration for future use. The final excess flows at the end of each iteration of a cycle is also stored for use with the same iteration of the next cycle. The edge weights for an iteration in the next cycle are compared with the stored edge weights from the previous cycle. Reparametrization is applied to the stored excess flow from the previous iteration, based on their difference. The reparametrized graph is used for the graph cuts in Step 3 of Algorithm 1, leading to faster convergence. Cycle-to-cycle reuse of flow typically results in a speed up of 3 to 4 times in practice.

– Third innovation is the incremental step for the later iterations of first cycle, which has no stored value for reparametrization. Nodes with label i do not

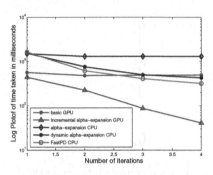

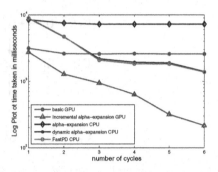

(a) Stereo: Tsukuba Image with 16 labels

(b) Stereo: Teddy Image with 60 labels

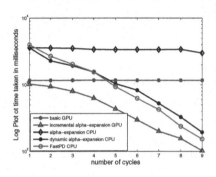

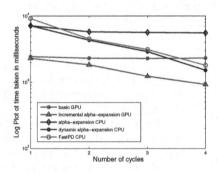

(c) Restoration: Penguin Image with 256 labels

(d) Photomontage: Panorama Image with 7 labels

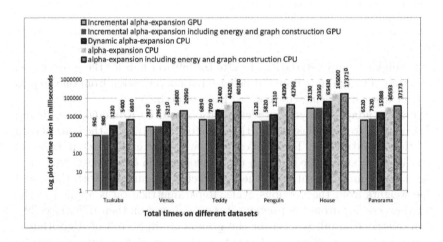

(e) Total times on different datasets

Fig. 3. Timings on different datasets from Middlebury MRF page [14]. (a)-(d) include only α-expansion timings.

take part in the iteration i of each cycle; all other nodes do. The graph remains nearly the same from iteration i to iteration $(i + 1)$, with a few nodes with label $(i + 1)$ dropping out and those with label i coming in. We reparametrize the final excess flows from iteration i using the difference between the graphs at the start of iterations i and $(i + 1)$ for the first cycle. In our experience, the iteration-to-iteration reuse of flow for the first cycle reduces the running time of the first cycle by 10-20%.

Figure 2 and Algorithm 5 explain our approach for the incremental α-expansion. The incremental α-expansion algorithm needs to store L graphs G^j, $1 \leq j \leq L$, one for each iteration. It also stores L excess flows at the end of each iteration of a cycle. The first cycle needs one additional graph to be stored.

3   Experimental Results

We conducted experiments on a single Nvidia GTX 280 graphics adapter with 1024MB memory on-board (30 multiprocessors, 240 steam processors) connected to an Quad Core Intel processor (Q6600 @ 2:4GHz) with 4GB RAM running Fedora Core 9. We tested our algorithm on different standard problems such as stereo correspondence, image restoration, and photomontage on various images. Stereo correspondence results are shown on Tsukuba, Venus and Teddy images. Image restoration results are shown on Penguin image and photomontage on the Panorama image. All the datasets are taken from the Middlebury MRF page [14]. The energy functions used are the same as used by them.

Figures 3(a), 3(b) shows the results of our approach on Tsukuba, Teddy images respectively for stereo correspondence. The results of restoration problem on Penguin image is shown in Figure 3(c) and of photomontage problem on Panorama image in Figure 3(d). Timings are shown on Middlebury code on the CPU, Fast-PD and dynamic α-expansion on the CPU, our basic implementation without flow reuse, and the complete incremental α-expansion. Our incremental α-expansion on the GPUs is 5-8 times faster than the α-expansion on the CPU using Middlebury code [14]. Impact of flow-reuse can also be seen from the graphs in Figure 2.4. Stereo correspondence on Tsukuba image with 16 labels takes 772 milliseconds on the GPU compared to 5.4 seconds on the CPU. Dynamic α-expansion [1] and Fast-PD [2] takes 3.23 seconds for the same. Figure 3(e) compares the total times for convergence for different levels of optimization discussed above on various datasets. Recently, Liang *et al.* [15] proposed belief propagation based optimization algorithm on the GPU to solve the energy minimization problems, which achieved 4 times speedup compared to the sequential algorithms. Our proposed algorithm achieves better performance than them.

4   Conclusion

In this paper, we presented the incremental α-expansion algorithm for high-performance multilabel MRF optimization on GPU. We efficiently utilize the resources available on the current GPUs. We are able to get a speedup of 5-8 times on standard datasets on various problems. Our system brings a near-real time processing of MRF to the reach of most users as the GPUs are now very popular.

References

1. Alahari, K., Kohli, P., Torr, P.H.: Reduce, Reuse & Recycle: Efficiently Solving Multi-Label MRFs. In: CVPR (2), pp. 16–29 (2008)
2. Komodakis, N., Tziritas, G., Paragios, N.: Fast, Approximately Optimal Solutions for Single and Dynamic MRFs. In: CVPR (2), pp. 1–8 (2007)
3. Boykov, Y., Veksler, O., Zabih, R.: Fast approximate energy minimization via graph cuts. TPAMI 23(11), 1222–1239 (2001)
4. Kohli, P., Torr, P.H.S.: Dynamic graph cuts for efficient inference in markov random fields. TPAMI 29(12), 2079–2088 (2007)
5. Alizadeh, F., Goldberg, A.: Implementing the push-relabel method for the maximum flow problem on a connection machine. Technical Report STAN-CS-92-1410, Stanford University (1992)
6. Anderson, R.J., Setubal, J.C.: On the parallel implementation of goldberg's maximum flow algorithm. In: SPAA, pp. 168–177 (1992)
7. Goldberg, A.V., Tarjan, R.E.: A new approach to the maximum-flow problem. J. ACM 35(4), 921–940 (1988)
8. Hussein, M., Varshney, A., Davis, L.: On implementing graph cuts on cuda. In: First Workshop on General Purpose Processing on Graphics Processing Units, October 2007, Northeastern University (2007)
9. Juan, O., Boykov, Y.: Active graph cuts. In: CVPR (1), pp. 1023–1029 (2006)
10. Kolmogorov, V., Zabih, R.: What energy functions can be minimized via graph cuts? TPAMI 26(2), 147–159 (2004)
11. Szeliski, R., Zabih, R., Scharstein, D., Veksler, O., Kolmogorov, V., Agarwala, A., Tappen, M.F., Rother, C.: A comparative study of energy minimization methods for markov random fields. In: Leonardis, A., Bischof, H., Pinz, A. (eds.) ECCV 2006. LNCS, vol. 3952, pp. 16–29. Springer, Heidelberg (2006)
12. Kolmogorov, V.: Convergent Tree-Reweighted Message Passing for Energy Minimization. TPAMI, 1568–1583 (2006)
13. Vineet, V., Narayanan, P.J.: CUDA cuts: Fast graph cuts on the GPU. In: IEEE CVPR workshop on Visual Computer Vision on GPUs, pp. 1–8 (2008)
14. Middlebury MRF Page (2009), http://vision.middlebury.edu/MRF/
15. Liang, C., Cheng, C., Lai, Y., Chen, L., Chen, H.: Hardware-Efficient Belief Propagation. In: CVPR (2009)
16. Kovtun, I.: Partial Optimal Labeling Search for a NP-Hard Subclass of (max, +) Problems. In: DAGM-Symposium (2003)
17. Geman, S., Geman, D.: Stochastic relaxation, Gibbs distributions and the Bayesian restoration of image. TPAMI (1984)
18. Delong, A., Boykov, Y.: A Scalable graph-cut algorithm for N-D grids. In: CVPR (2009)
19. Corporation, N.: CUDA: Compute unified device architecture programming guide. Technical report, Nvidia (2007)

20. Freeman, W.T., Pasztor, E.C.: Learning Low-Level Vision. In: IEEE International Conference on Computer Vision (1999)
21. Ford, L.R., Fulkerson, D.R.: Flows in Networks. Princeton University Press, Princeton (1962)
22. Borradaile, G., Klein, P.N.: An $O(n \log n)$ algorithm for maximum st-flow in a directed planar graph. In: Proceedings of 17th ACM-SIAM Symposium on Discrete Algorithms (2006)
23. Schmidt, F.R., Töppe, E., Cremers, D.: Efficient Planar Graph Cuts with Applications in Computer Vision. In: CVPR (2009)

Non-rigid Shape Matching Using Geometry and Photometry

Nicolas Thorstensen and Renaud Keriven

Universite Paris-Est, Ecole des Ponts ParisTech, IMAGINE
{thorstensen,keriven}@imagine.enpc.fr
http://imagine.enpc.fr

Abstract. In this paper, we tackle the problem of finding correspondences between three-dimensional reconstructions of a deformable surface at different time steps. We suppose that (i) the mechanical underlying model imposes time-constant geodesic distances between points on
the surface; and that (ii) images of the real surface are available. This is
for instance the case in spatio-temporal shape from videos (e.g. multi-
view stereo, visual hulls, etc.) when the surface is supposed approxima-
tively unstretchable. These assumptions allow to exploit both geometry
and photometry. In particular we propose an energy based formulation
of the problem, extending the work of Bronstein *et al.* [1]. On the one
hand, we show that photometry (i) improves accuracy in case of locally
elastic deformations or noisy surfaces and (ii) allows to still find the right
solution when [1] fails because of ambiguities (e.g. symmetries). On the
other hand, using geometry makes it possible to match shapes that have
undergone large motion, which is not possible with usual photometric
methods. Numerical experiments prove the efficiency of our method on
synthetic and real data.

1   Introduction

Most of the objects observed in the real world are non-rigid. This makes them
particularly important for computer vision. What makes non-rigid shapes challenging is that their associated deformations exhibit a potentially infinite number
of degrees of freedom. As a consequence they are hard to analyze. One typical
example is the three-dimensional (3D) reconstruction of a person in a multiple
cameras environment. More generally, matching 3D-reconstructed shapes have
numerous applications, among which are reconstruction-based animation, motion analysis, shape recognition, physical phenomena analysis, etc.

A subject observed at different times usually results in meshes in different
poses. In such a situation, image-based matching algorithms [2,3] tend to fail, as
the motion in between the two poses is too large. Assuming the object surface is
approximately unstretchable, Bronstein *et al.* [1] designed a matching framework
where geodesic distances between automatically chosen key points are preserved.
Yet, such a criterion fails in case of ambiguities like symmetries. It also yields
inaccuracy when the unstretchability hypothesis is violated.

H. Zha, R.-i. Taniguchi, and S. Maybank (Eds.): ACCV 2009, Part III, LNCS 5996, pp. 644–654, 2010.

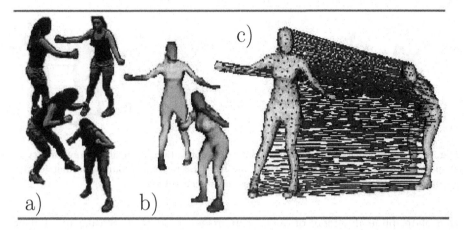

Fig. 1. a) Multiple views of a person in two different poses; b) Mesh based representation of the reconstructed object and heat map of the geodesic distance to the lower left foot; c) Correspondence result after optimization

1.1 Our Contributions

Therefore we propose to take the best of both worlds and design an extension of the work of [1] by adding a photometric term to their energy. We obtain a robust multi-resolution 3D surface mapping procedure that combines photometric and geometric information(c.f. Figure 1). We experiment it for non-rigid surface correspondence between two surfaces observed a different time steps in a multiple cameras environment and demonstrate its superiority.

The paper is organized as follows. Section 2 reviews previous work for non-rigid shape matching. Section 3 states the problem formulation and Section 4 explores the algorithmic implementation. Finally, numerical experiments on real data are reported in Section 5 and Section 6 concludes.

2 Related Work

The correspondence problem is one of the fundamental challenges in computer vision. Might it be in the context of optical flow, calibration or surface registration. For rigid surface and point cloud registration, Iterative Closest Point (ICP) and its variants [4] are the standard algorithms. Operating on a purely geometric level, they rely on approximated differential quantities, e.g. curvature, or more robust surface descriptors [5]. Recently, several algorithms also address the problem of non rigid surface registration. They can be mainly divided into two categories: geometric and photometric. Whereas geometric methods assume the geometry known, photometric methods estimate structure and motion.

2.1 Geometric Methods

A non-rigid counterpart to ICP was introduced in [6]. Further in [7], the authors propose a non rigid registration method by piecewise rigid registration and local

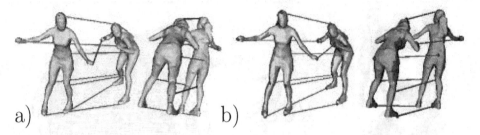

Fig. 2. a) Initialization using solely geometric information is sensible to symmetry in shapes. b) Color coded labeling of the meshes (see text) and our photometric plus geometric initialization, where ambiguities have been solved.

thin plate spline alignment of range scan images. Elad *et al.* [8] take an intrinsic point of view of the matching problem. By isometrically embedding two surfaces into a common Euclidean space the problem is reduced to the simpler of rigid matching between surfaces. Following this idea, Bronstein *et al.* [9] take it one step further and solve the correspondence problem by embedding the surface directly into another. The major drawback of this approach is the difficulty to handle ambiguities like shape symmetries. As the method solely relies on the distance function of the surface, the algorithm tends to wrongly match pairs of symmetric points (see Figure 2).

2.2   Photometric Methods

On the photometric side, non rigid registration is commonly known under the name of scene flow. Vedula *et al.* [2] were the first to introduce the concept of scene flow which is the 3D extension of 2D optical flow. It is the simultaneous reconstruction of structure and motion between time frames. Further work on scene flow was undertaken by other teams [10,11,3]. As pointed out by Starck *et al.* [12], such approaches are limited to small displacements.

2.3   Where Geometry Meets Photometry

Lastly, one can take advantages of both approaches. Several recent papers address this problem. In [13], Starck *et al.* provide a method to register shapes from silhouette. The method embeds the two surfaces into a common spherical domain. Using the analytic expression of geodesic distances on the sphere allows to minimize the geometric distance between correspondences and distance between the associated color feature. This work is the most related to ours in the sense that they perform an isometric mapping into a common metric space and use geodesic distances as regularization for the appearance minimization. In order to be robust with respect to topological changes, hey then developed a matching algorithm based on a Markov random field optimization [12]. A much more heuristic approach is used by Ahmed *et al.* [14]. A set of SIFT features is computed which are then used for initialization of a refinement model. Lastly, the work of Varanasi et al. [15] makes also use of SIFT. The 3D position of the interest points are used to compute a sparse estimate of the motion field. By applying a diffusion operator on the sparse motion field, they recover a dense motion field.

Most of the algorithms presented so far rely on heuristics to put two temporal meshes into correspondence. In this work we want to consider a more rigorous model and propose a variational refinement method using ideas from variational stereo [16] and geometric embedding methods [8,9]. In this way, we recover temporal correspondences between meshes at different resolution and independently of the combinatorial configuration. Further, our method can handle local elastic deformations such that the correspondence is consistent with the observed images.

3   Variational Matching

Let S^1 and S^2 be the two surfaces to match. Each of them is observed by a certain number of cameras. Although not required, we simplify notations and suppose that the number and positions of the cameras are constant, so that both surfaces are observed by n cameras defined by their respective projections $\Pi_1, \ldots \Pi_n$. We denote by I_i^k the ith image of surface k.

Following [9], we use a Lagrangian point of view where a set of m correspondences are constrained to move on the surface such that they minimize a given energy. We denote (P_i^1, P_i^2) such a correspondence where $P_i^k \in S^k$ and $\Theta = \{(P_i^1, P_i^2), 1 \leq i \leq m\}$ the set of all correspondences. m is a fixed integer that can be estimated during initialization (see Section 4.2). Our energy is a function of parameter Θ that writes:

$$E_{tot}(\Theta) = \alpha E_{geom}(\Theta) + \beta E_{photo}(\Theta) \tag{1}$$

The first term E_{geom} is the geometric part, taken from the work of Bronstein et al. [1] while E_{photo} is our photometric attachment. As usual, α and β are positive constants that control the relative weights among these terms. Minimizing energy (1) with respect to Θ will position the correspondences on the mesh such that their projections in the images minimize a photometric dissimilarity measure while geodesic distances on the surfaces are respected.

3.1   Geometry

Bronstein et al. [9] propose to embed near-isometric surfaces one into another by minimizing the following energy:

$$E_{geom}(\Theta) = \sum_{i>j} (d_{S^1}(P_i^1, P_j^1) - d_{S^2}(P_i^2, P_j^2))^2. \tag{2}$$

where d_{S^k} is the geodesic distance on surface S^k. Again, this energy suffers mainly from two weaknesses: (i) symmetries yield ambiguities and (ii) if the object undergoes locally elastic deformations between shape S^1 and shape S^2, geodesic distances are not exactly preserved. Note that this is also the case when the surface are 3D reconstructions, since they are unavoidably noisy.

3.2   Photometry

For our image matching term E_{photo}, we chose the normalized cross-correlation to measure similarity between corresponding points. Its simplicity, robustness in the presence of varying lighting conditions and differentiability make it a common choice in variational methods. Each surface point is generally seen from several cameras and one might be tempted to correlate multiple pairs of images. However, in our experiments, the number of cameras is relatively small. Thus, using information from only one pair of camera for each surface point reveals to be enough.

As a first step, for each surface S^k, we associate to each point $M \in S^k$ an optimal image $I^k_{l^k(M)}$. Choice of labels l^k might be guided by different criteria. Here, we compute partitions of the surfaces following [17]. This method assigns smoothly each point to a label corresponding to the camera from which it is best viewed. Using graph-cut optimization, the labeling is obtained by minimizing a weighted sum of two terms which realizes a good trade off between resolution and color continuity, while respecting occlusions (c.f. Figure 2b).

Let $l^k(i)$ be a short notation for $l^k(P^k_i)$, our photometric energy then writes:

$$E_{photo}(\Theta) = \sum_{i=1}^{m} g[NCC(I^1_{l^1(i)} \circ \Pi_{l^1(i)}, I^2_{l^2(i)} \circ \Pi_{l^2(i)})(P^1_i, P^2_i)] \qquad (3)$$

where g is a positive decreasing function and $NCC(f^1, f^2)(M^1, M^2)$ denote the normalized cross-correlation of functions f^1 and f^2 between two related neighborhoods of points M^1 and M^2.

Following the stereovision work of Keriven et al. [16], we approximate locally the surfaces by their tangent planes at points M^k. In their case, only one surface is considered and M_1 and M_2 are the same point, with the same tangent plane, thus the same neighborhood. Their correlation boils down to correlating image regions related by a homography. In our case, we suppose that the tangent plane to S^1 at point M^1 and the tangent plane to S^2 at M^2 are related by a given two-dimensional isometry $\mathcal{I}_{M^1,M^2}$ sending M^1 to M^2. Under this assumption, neighborhoods on the respective tangent planes are related and the correlation $NCC(f^1, f^2)(M^1, M^2)$ is correctly defined. Moreover, it (and its derivatives) remains easy to compute since corresponding image regions are still related by a homography.

Introducing the isometry $\mathcal{I}_{M^1,M^2}$ are each point pair (M^1, M^2) might be thought as problematic since one would require to match the surfaces to know it, yielding a chicken and egg problem. Practically, this is not the case. As usual, we will minimize the energy by mean of a gradient descent starting from a coarse initialization (see Section 4). This approximate solution reveals to be sufficient to obtain a robust $\mathcal{I}_{M^1,M^2}$. We proceed the following way: (i) each correspondence point P^k_i defines a geodesic distance map $d_{S^k}(P^k_i,.)$ on S^k; (ii) the gradients of these distance maps at a given point M^k defines local directions that should correspond from one surface to the other if M^1 corresponds to M^2; (iii) as a consequence, the best[1] isometry from the tangent plane at M^1 to the one at M^2 that sends both M^1 to M^2, and the distance gradients directions at M^1 to the ones at M^2, is a good estimate of $\mathcal{I}_{M^1,M^2}$. Please note that computing distance maps is no extra cost since it is part of E_{geom}. Note also that the isometries $\mathcal{I}$ are actually needed only for the pairs (P_i^1, P_i^2) and that they will be refined during the gradient descent iterations as the pairs moves.

4 Optimization

4.1 Discretization

We suppose that the surfaces are both discretized as collections of triangles. Following [9], points P_i^k are taken as barycenters of triangle vertices. Θ consists in a choice of triangles and corresponding barycentric coordinates. The geodesic distances between all vertices of the mesh are computed using the Fast Marching algorithm for triangular surfaces [18,19]. Geodesic distance is then interpolated like in [9] (note that the problem is not only to interpolate the distance at some barycenter, but also the distance to some barycenter).

For the photometric part of the energy, discretization is not a particular issue: the labeling method [17] is designed for triangle meshes, and we use a standard normal interpolation method to estimate the tangent planes.

Minimizing the energy with respect to both the P_i^1's and the P_i^2's is obviously not well posed. Although different cases might happen, in our experiments we have no further constraint on the choice of the points to be matched. Thus, we fix points P_i^1 to their initial position (see Section 4.2) and minimize the energy with respect to the positions of points P_i^2.

As written above, we use a classical gradient descent. Properly minimizing it is not trivial because the problem is non-convex. In order to cope with local minima, we apply a multi resolution strategy, considering the problem at several scales. Once a solution is found at a coarse scale, it is used to initialize the problem at a finer scale. Our problem has two scalable dimensions. The first one is the number of correspondences and the second is the scale of the images. This leads to a two step multi resolution scheme. Starting with a small number of correspondences, we iteratively increase the number of points by interpolating the solution from the coarser level to the next finer level. This scheme is adapted from [20]. Then, at each level, we perform a gradient descent in a multi scale manner using a Gaussian pyramid of the images.

4.2 Initialization

We first have to initialize the correspondences. Copying [20], we take advantage of the geodesic distance maps and use the farthest point sampling (FPS) strategy [21] to get geometry-based feature points on the surfaces. For near isometric

---

[1] In the least squares sense.

surfaces we can expect the sampling to be almost identically distributed on both surfaces S^1 and S^2 [9]. Taking photometry into account to avoid geometric ambiguities, we then reject points that have an autocorrelation score below a given threshold, thus corresponding to non textured regions. As in [20], points are then associated using branch and bound optimization [22], yielding m initial pairs. Here, to the initial geodesic distance based criterion, we add a photometric one in order to get rid of geometric ambiguities. Because no correlation is possible (at this stage, tangent planes cannot yet be related by isometries), we use SIFT descriptor based similarity, being thus invariant to scale and orientation. The results of the initialization of the correspondences can be viewed in Figure 2. Note how geometric ambiguities are solved.

4.3 Gradient Descent

Optimization is performed at all scales until convergence is reached, i.e. norm of the gradient is below a given threshold. The expressions of the gradients of the geometric and the photometric parts of our energy can be found in [20] and [16] respectively. Remember that Θ consists in these coordinate but also in the choice of the triangles to which the barycenters are related. As in [9], the gradients are computed for a fixed such choice. However, when a point P_i^k gets out of its related triangle, we force it to stop at the reached edge and assign it to the triangle at the "other side" of this edge. Doing this way, points travel gently from one triangle to another if needed.

5 Results

In order to validate the proposed method, we run several experiments on real and synthetic data. First, we test it on a synthetic dataset. In a second experiment, we validate our algorithm on real images.

5.1 Validation

Our first experiment focuses on the validation of our energy by testing the algorithm on a synthetic dataset (8 cameras) and comparing to the result of [9]. This experiment aims at justifying the photometric part of the energy. The parameter α is set to 1.0 whereas β equals 8.0. We take 12 pairs of correspondences and a 3 level Gaussian pyramid. The advantages of our initialization having already be demonstrated on Figure 2, we rather launch the original method proposed by Bronstein et al. [9] with our initialization. The red dots in the left image of Figure 3a are some of the P_i^1 projected on the front image of S^1. The red dots in the right image of Figure 3a are the projections of the corresponding P_i^2 obtained after running the optimization of [9]. The green dots correspond to the result obtained with our combined photometric-geometric optimization. One can clearly see, the green dots are consistent with the initial sampling in the left image although the zone around the knee and shoulder exhibit elastic

Fig. 3. a) On the left, the front image of the first mesh, red dots being the projections of some key points. On the right, the front image of the second mesh, showing the reprojections of the corresponding points, in red obtained with the method in [9] (initialized with our method), in green obtained with our method. b) Shows the same correspondences directly on the meshes with the same color code. The inaccuracies of [9], here due to local elastic deformations, are corrected by our photometric + geometric criterion.

deformation. Whereas the red dots in the right image ignore the image signal and are pushed away by the local elastic deformations. Figure 3b shows the same points on the meshes.

5.2 Real Data

In order to see how our method performs, we run several experiments on image data courtesy of J. Starck[2] [23], again with 8 cameras. In this experiment the number of correspondences is 150 and the number of image levels is set to 3. α and β are set to 0.9 and 1.5 respectively. The results are depicted in Figure 4. Notice how the method of [9] fails to solve the matching problem. Local elastic deformations are observed in both cases (Figure 4a and 4c) and wrong matches occur because of symmetry. Nevertheless, our method can handle the symmetries and local elastic deformations as can be noticed the around the hair and the back in Figure 4b and in the zones located on the skirt and the hair in Figure 4d.

---

[2] http://personal.ee.surrey.ac.uk/Personal/J.Starck/

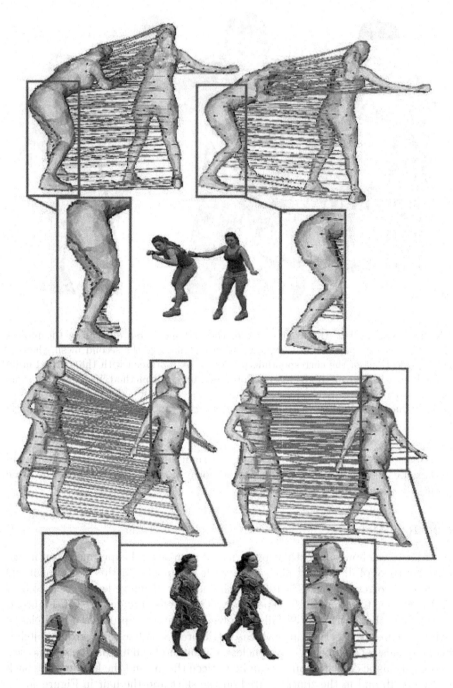

Fig. 4. Results on a real-worl dataset[23]. a) and c) show the results obtained using the method in [9]. b) and d) are obtained using our method.

6   Conclusion

We have described a variational framework for the correspondence problem of non-rigid surfaces coming from multi-view reconstruction or from any setup that provides images of the scene. By using photometric and geometric information, our method improves the one by Bronstein *et al.* [9] and allows to cope with elastic stretches and symmetries of the shape. Like in the initial work, and contrary to usual photometric methods, we are not limited to small deformations. Numerical experiments show the success of our method. Our future work includes extending our framework to surfaces with varying topology. A first step in this direction could be the use of more robust embedding such as the one proposed in [24]. Another improvement is the use of second order information in the gradient descent in order to perform Newton steps. Finally, we notice that regularization is important in low-textured image regions. Therefore we currently investigate the effect of automatically setting the control weights as proposed in [25] in another context.

Acknowledgement. We would like to thank A.M. and M.M. Bronstein for their kind help and for providing their code.

References

1. Bronstein, A., Bronstein, M., Kimmel, R.: Generalized multidimensional scaling: a framework for isometry-invariant partial surface matching. Proc. National Academy of Sciences (PNAS) 103(5), 1168–1172 (2006)
2. Vedula, S., Baker, S., Rander, P., Collins, R., Kanade, T.: Three-dimensional scene flow (2005)
3. Pons, J.P., Keriven, R., Faugeras, O.: Multi-view stereo reconstruction and scene flow estimation with a global image-based matching score. The International Journal of Computer Vision 72(2), 179–193 (2007)
4. Gelfand, N., Mitra, N.J., Guibas, L.J., Pottmann, H.: Robust global registration. In: Desbrun, M., Pottmann, H. (eds.) Eurographics Association, pp. 197–206 (2005) ISBN 3-905673-24-X
5. Belongie, S., Malik, J., Puzicha, J.: Shape matching and object recognition using shape contexts. IEEE Transactions on Pattern Analysis and Machine Intelligence 24, 509–522 (2002)
6. Amberg, B., Romdhani, S., Vetter, T.: Optimal step nonrigid icp algorithms for surface registration. In: IEEE Conference on Computer Vision and Pattern Recognition, CVPR (2007)
7. Brown, B., Rusinkiewicz, S.: Global non-rigid alignment of 3-D scans. ACM Transactions on Graphics (Proc. SIGGRAPH) 26(3) (August 2007)
8. Elad, A., Kimmel, R.: On bending invariant signatures for surfaces. In: IEEE Trans. on Pattern Analysis and Machine Intell. LNCS, vol. 25, pp. 1285–1295. Springer, Heidelberg (2003)
9. Bronstein, A., Bronstein, M., Kimmel, R.: Efficient computation of isometry-invariant distances between surfaces. SIAM J. Sci. Comput. 28 (2006)

10. Furukawa, Y., Ponce, J.: Dense 3d motion capture from synchronized video streams. In: IEEE International Conference on Computer Vision and Pattern Recognition (CVPR). IEEE, Los Alamitos (2008)
11. Huguet, F., Devernay, F.: A variational method for scene flow estimation from stereo sequences. In: ICCV, pp. 1–7 (2007)
12. Starck, J., Hilton, A.: Correspondence labelling for wide-timeframe free-form surface matching. In: IEEE International Conference on Computer Vision, ICCV (2007)
13. Starck, J., Hilton, A.: Spherical matching for temporal correspondence of non-rigid surfaces. In: ICCV, pp. 1387–1394 (2005)
14. Ahmed, N., Theobalt, C., Roessl, C., Thrun, S., Seidel: Dense correspondence finding for parametrization-free animation reconstruction from video. In: IEEE International Conference on Computer Vision and Pattern Recognition (CVPR). IEEE, Los Alamitos (2008)
15. Varanasi, K., Zaharescu, A., Boyer, E., Horaud, R.: Temporal surface tracking using mesh evolution. In: Forsyth, D., Torr, P., Zisserman, A. (eds.) ECCV 2008, Part II. LNCS, vol. 5303, pp. 30–43. Springer, Heidelberg (2008)
16. Keriven, R., Faugeras, O.: Complete dense stereovision using level set methods. In: Burkhardt, H.-J., Neumann, B. (eds.) ECCV 1998. LNCS, vol. 1406, p. 379. Springer, Heidelberg (1998)
17. Allène, C., Pons, J.P., Keriven, R.: Seamless image-based texture atlases using multi-band blending. In: 19th International Conference on Pattern Recognition, Tampa, US (December 2008)
18. Sethian, J.A.: Fast marching methods. SIAM Review 41, 199–235 (1999)
19. Kimmel, R., Sethian, J.: Computing geodesic paths on manifolds (1998)
20. Bronstein, M., Bronstein, A., Kimmel, R.: Efficient computation of isometry-invariant distances between surfaces. Techn. Report CIS-2006-02, Dept. of Computer Science, Technion, Israel (2006)
21. Moenning, C., Dodgson, N.A.: Fast marching farthest point sampling. In: Euro-Graphics (September 2003)
22. Dasgupta, S., Papadimitriou, C., Vazirani, U.: Algorithms. McGrawHill, New York (2007)
23. Starck, J., Hilton, A.: Surface capture for performance based animation. IEEE Computer Graphics and Applications 27(3), 21–31 (2007)
24. Bronstein, A., Bronstein, M., Kimmel, R., Mahmoudi, M., Sapiro, G.: A gromov-hausdorff framework with diffusion geometry for topologically-robust non-rigid shape matching. International Journal of Computer Vision (IJCV) (submitted)
25. Vu, H., Keriven, R., Labatut, P., Pons, J.: Towards high-resolution large-scale multi-view stereo. In: Conference on Computer Vision and Pattern Recognition (CVPR) (June 2009)

Beyond Pairwise Shape Similarity Analysis

Peter Kontschieder, Michael Donoser, and Horst Bischof*

Institute for Computer Graphics and Vision, Graz University of Technology
{kontschieder,donoser,bischof}@icg.tugraz.at

Abstract. This paper considers two major applications of shape matching algorithms: (a) query-by-example, i.e. retrieving the most similar
shapes from a database and (b) finding clusters of shapes, each represented by a single prototype. Our approach goes beyond pairwise shape
similarity analysis by considering the underlying structure of the shape
manifold, which is estimated from the shape similarity scores between
all the shapes within a database. We propose a modified mutual kNN
graph as the underlying representation and demonstrate its performance
for the task of shape retrieval. We further describe an efficient, unsupervised clustering method which uses the modified mutual kNN graph
for initialization. Experimental evaluation proves the applicability of our
method, e.g. by achieving the highest ever reported retrieval score of
93.40% on the well known MPEG-7 database.

1 Introduction

Shape is a key feature for computer vision applications. For example, contour-
based object recognition methods [1,2,3] have recently shown to outperform appearance based methods, because shape is a strong feature for recognition as
psychophysical studies [4] have shown. Object contours are invariant to extreme
illumination conditions and large variations in texture or color and for some
categories shape is more generic than appearance. Automated comparison and
grouping of shapes is very often the basis in the areas of human detection [5] or
action recognition [6].

The key part in all these applications is a robust and efficient shape matching
method, which allows quantifying the similarity between two input shapes. The
calculated similarity scores are the basis for different tasks, like retrieving most
similar shapes, identifying clusters within databases or finding exemplary shape
prototypes. These tasks are complicated by the fact that similarities of shapes do
not lie in a metric space, e.g. are asymmetric or violate the triangle inequality.
Therefore Euclidean analysis is not sufficient for handling shape similarities.
State-of-the-art shape matching performs pairwise analysis and ignores the fact
that distances between all other shapes contain important information about
the shape manifold. Therefore, recently some effort was put on post-processing
the obtained similarity scores by analyzing the estimated similarities between

---

* The authors gratefully acknowledge financial support from Research Studios Austria
  Project μSTRUCSCOP under project number 818651.

H. Zha, R.-i. Taniguchi, and S. Maybank (Eds.): ACCV 2009, Part III, LNCS 5996, pp. 655–666, 2010.

all given shapes to increase the discriminability between different shape groups as e. g. in [7,8].

In this paper we focus on the analysis of given shape similarity scores. Hence, we assume that we have a shape matching method which is invariant with respect to geometric transformations like translation, rotation and scale and is also robust against noise and outliers. We have chosen the method of Ling and Jacobs [9] which achieves state-of-the-art results on reference datasets. Our underlying idea is to process shape similarities beyond the pairwise formulation based on analyzing the emerging shape manifold and its geodesics. We show that it is possible to significantly improve results for two important shape matching applications: (a) query-by-example, i. e. the retrieval of most similar shapes and (b) the automated clustering of silhouettes. Although different outputs are desired for both applications we show that we can use the same underlying representation for both tasks.

The simplest shape retrieval approach is to compare the query shape to all other shapes within a database and to sort the similarities by increasing dissimilarity score. Such an approach ignores the fact that also distances to all other shapes contain important information about the overall shape manifold. Therefore, we propose a method that allows to improve retrieval results by analyzing the underlying structure of the shape manifold. We capture the manifold structure of the data by defining a neighborhood for each data point in terms of a modified version of a mutual k-nearest neighbor graph which yields improved performance on all analyzed databases.

Shape clustering identifies similar groups of shapes and corresponding cluster prototypes as e. g. presented in [10,11]. We propose a novel efficient clustering approach and show that it is possible to use the same data-structure as in the retrieval task, i. e. the modified mutual k-nearest neighbor graph, to obtain state-of-the-art clustering results.

Section 2 of this paper describes the proposed combined normalization and graph-based analysis scheme for given affinity matrices to improve shape retrieval. In Section 3 we present our novel, unsupervised clustering algorithm which benefits from the previous sub-manifold analysis through initially stable label assignment. Finally Section 4 provides an exhaustive evaluation of the shape retrieval and clustering results for reference databases.

2   Shape Retrieval by Modified Mutual kNN Graph

Given a set of N shapes, a shape matching algorithm e. g. [12,9,13] can be applied to obtain a $N \times N$ distance matrix A to describe the pairwise relations between all shapes in terms of a dissimilarity measure. Such descriptions are typically asymmetric, violate the triangle inequality and are therefore non-metric. Ideally the dissimilarities are low between intra-class shapes and high for extra-class objects. Unfortunately, shape matching methods do not show this ideal behavior, that is why we introduce a post-processing step that deploys *matrix normalization* and subsequent *analysis* on the original distance matrices.

The provided distance matrix allows comparing shapes beyond a pairwise formulation, based on the emerging shape manifold and its geodesics. This was e.g. considered in [7,14], where the authors aim on finding element-wise normalization parameters σ_{ij} which generates a $N \times N$ affinity matrix W from a distance matrix A by

$$w_{ij} = \exp\left(-\frac{a_{ij}^2}{\sigma_{ij}^2}\right) . \tag{1}$$

The proper choice of σ_{ij} allows to pull intra-class objects together ($\sigma_{ij} \gg a_{ij}$) and push extra-class objects apart ($\sigma_{ij} \ll a_{ij}$). We normalize by using *local scaling* which was proposed by Zelnik-Manor and Perona in [14]. They define

$$\sigma_{ij} = \sigma_i \sigma_j \quad \text{with} \quad \sigma_i = a_{iK(i)} , \tag{2}$$

where $K(i)$ is the index of the Kth nearest neighbor of object i. The normalization scheme enforces embedding of sub-manifolds which represent separable clusters for all objects within the regions defined by σ_{ij}. Analysis of such regions is typically performed using graph based methods which aim on capturing the underlying local structure. Connected regions in such graphs are exploited to reflect the interdependence between objects, i.e. by finding shorter paths between matching objects than between non-matching objects.

The set of neighborhood graphs is shortly described in the following: Let each shape be represented by a vertex $v \in V$ in the graph $G(V, E)$. The edge weights $e(v_i, v_j)$ between vertices (v_i, v_j) are determined by the non-negative normalized affinity matrix distances w_{ij}, where $w_{ij} = 0$ means that there is no connection between vertices (v_i, v_j). The amount of connections between the vertices can be regularized with respect to the chosen neighborhood graph:

- The ε-neighborhood graph $G_\varepsilon(W, \varepsilon)$ connects all vertices (v_i, v_j) if $w_{ij} \le \varepsilon$
- The (symmetric) k nearest neighbor graph $G_k(W, k)$ connects all vertices (v_i, v_j) if $v_i \in k\text{NN}(v_j)$ or $v_j \in k\text{NN}(v_i)$
- The mutual k nearest neighbor graph $G_m(W, k)$ connects all vertices (v_i, v_j) if $v_i \in k\text{NN}(v_j)$ and $v_j \in k\text{NN}(v_i)$

$k\text{NN}(v_j)$ denotes the set of k nearest neighbors of vertex v_j. The use of ε-neighborhood graphs requires w_{ij} on same scales which means that the object points in the underlying regions have to form non-elongated, tight clusters. In contrast, k nearest neighbor graphs are able to connect regions on different scales, since only the absolute neighborhood ranking is of interest. k nearest neighbor and ε-neighborhood graphs are widely used for analyses while mutual k nearest neighbor graphs are mostly ignored despite their interesting properties.

The mutual kNN graph does not allow mixing differently scaled regions and may thus be considered as a hybrid form of ε-neighborhood and k nearest neighbor graphs since it is able to cluster regions with both, high or low density. As the normalization step is trying to enforce an establishment of tight and densely settled sub-manifolds, the mutual neighborhood constraint (which requires that two connected objects belong to each others k neighborhood) intuitively seems to be supportive for the analysis step. The major limitation of the mutual k nearest neighbor graph lies in its inherent inability to generate single clusters from mixed density regions, especially if there are isolated regions or single isolated objects within a cluster. In order not to relinquish on the mutual neighborhood constraint but enclose such objects or regions, we introduce a *non-symmetric mutual neighborhood criterion* that allows edge construction in a modified mutual k nearest neighbor graph $G_{mm}(N, k)$ between v_i and v_j if

$$v_j \in kNN(v_i) \quad \text{and} \quad v_i \in ckNN(v_j) , \tag{3}$$

where $c \geq 1$. The asymmetry coefficient c allows to control the range of neighborhood incorporation during the mutual k nearest neighbor graph construction. Considering extremal values for $\{c = 1, c = \infty\}$, this parameter allows tuning between symmetric mutual and standard kNN graph behaviour.

In addition to the modification in the graph construction, we exploit possible asymmetries of the input affinity matrix W. We exchange edge weights $e(v_i, v_j)$ with the smaller distance of w_{ij} and w_{ji} according to

$$e(v_i, v_j) = \min(w_{ij}, w_{ji}) \quad \text{where} \quad e(v_i, v_j) > 0 \tag{4}$$

which leads to an undirected graph, i. e. a symmetric affinity matrix W.

For a certain query shape, shape retrieval is performed by exploiting the graph structure in terms of connectivity and path lengths. Thus, the order of the retrieved shapes is determined by the path lengths of connected objects in the graph.

3   Shape Clustering and Prototype Identification

Shape clustering finds groups of similar shapes. Since we focus on analyzing affinity matrices, any pairwise clustering algorithm can be considered for this step. Instead of applying one of the standard approaches we propose a novel, unsupervised clustering method which is based on the modified mutual kNN graph G_{mm} presented in Section 2. We use the same underlying data structure for retrieval and clustering. As it is shown in Section 4, our method outperforms the recently proposed affinity propagation [15] algorithm, which is considered as state of the art for non-metric clustering.

Our method is inspired by the graph-based segmentation framework of Felzenszwalb and Huttenlocher [16] but significantly differs due to a different merging criterion and beneficial initialization derived from the modified mutual kNN graph. In addition, our method intrinsically provides representative prototypes for each cluster. The algorithm consists of two subsequent steps: First, we identify a set of stable initial labels derived from the vertex degrees of potential cluster prototypes. Second, an agglomerative clustering approach iteratively refines the initial labeling effort until certain cluster merging conditions are not fulfilled anymore.

3.1   Label Initialization

The initialization of our clustering method uses the proposed modified mutual kNN graph $G_{mm}(V, E)$. The aim of label initialization is to find an initial partition of the graph by assigning a unique label $l(v_i)$ to all its nodes in such a way that (structurally) coherent and connected nodes receive identical labels. To identify the initial cluster prototypes we first determine the degree d of a vertex v_i by the cardinality of its neighborhood $M(v_i) = \{v_j | e(v_i, v_j) \in E\}$ according to

$$d(v_i) = |M(v_i)| . \tag{5}$$

We define a set of triples $D = (\{v_1, d_1, M_1\}, \ldots, \{v_N, d_N, M_N\})$ which stores the degree and the set of neighbors for all nodes. Let $\tilde{D}$ be the sorted triples from D with respect to d in a non-decreasing order. The degree (and thus the position) of a vertex in $\tilde{D}$ can be associated with its 'popularity' to be connected to within the graph (remember that $d_i \leq (c \cdot k)$ and hence $|E| \leq c \cdot kV$). Vertices with high degrees are considered to be more stable and thus more appropriate as cluster prototypes than those with lower degrees. Label initialization is an iterative process which starts with assignment of labels from lowest to highest degree nodes according to

$$l(M_i) = v_i \quad \text{with} \quad \{v_i, d_i, M_i\} \in \tilde{D}, \ \forall \ i = 1 \ldots N \tag{6}$$

and delivers a set of initial labels $L_I = (l_1, \ldots, l_q), q \leq N$. Since objects are likely to be found in each others neighboring sets multiple times, the labels may also be overwritten multiple times during the initialization process. In a subsequent step we check that every initially assigned label in L_I is also its own label $l(v_i) = v_i$.

In such a way, the provided labeling defines an initial partition of the input graph $G_{mm}(V, E)$, which we refer to as clusters $C = \{C_1, \ldots, C_q\}$. The assigned labels simultaneously identify the sets of cluster members $M_1, \ldots, M_q$, along with the cluster prototypes

$$v_{C_i} = l(v_i) . \tag{7}$$

Please note that our subsequent clustering algorithm is generic and can be initialized with different strategies.

3.2   Clustering

The main idea of our clustering method is to iteratively merge the clusters $C = \{C_1, \ldots, C_q\}$ provided by the initialization described in Section 3.1. In each step, we evaluate a criterion comparing intra to inter-cluster distances which decides whether two currently considered clusters should be merged or not.

The clustering algorithm is based on the evaluation of four different distance measures: the intra-cluster distance $Intra(C_i)$, the intra-cluster path length $PIntra(v_{C_i}, C_i)$, the inter-cluster distance $Inter(C_i, C_j)$ and the inter-class upper bound distance $Inter_{bnd}(C_i, C_j)$. While the first two analyze intra cluster distances and therefore compactness of single clusters, the latter two describe the dissimilarity between two given clusters.

The intra-cluster distance $Intra(C_i)$ is defined as

$$Intra(C_i) = \max_{e \in C_i} w(e), \tag{8}$$

which is the maximum edge weight $w(e)$ between all cluster nodes associated to the cluster C_i.

The intra-cluster path length $PIntra(v_{C_i}, C_i)$ is defined as the sum of shortest paths between the cluster prototype v_{C_i} and all associated intra-cluster elements M by

$$PIntra(v_{C_i}, C_i) = \sum_{m=1}^{|M|} u(v_{C_i}, M_m), \tag{9}$$

where $u(v_i, v_j)$ denotes the shortest path between two nodes of the graph, which can be calculated by e. g. using Johnson's or Dijkstra's algorithm. The intra-cluster path length quantifies how suitable a node v_i is to be a cluster prototype.

In contrast to using the minimal distances between clusters as proposed in [13], we define the inter-class distance $Inter(C_i, C_j)$ between two clusters as the shortest path between the corresponding cluster prototype as

$$Inter(C_i, C_j) = u(v_{C_i}, v_{C_j}), \tag{10}$$

where for cluster pairs (C_i, C_j) with non-existing paths $u(v_{C_i}, v_{C_j})$ we set $Inter(C_i, C_j) = \infty$.

Finally, we define a cluster-pair specific upper bound for the inter-cluster distances $Inter_{bnd}(C_i, C_j)$ which regulates the compatibility of two clusters to be merged as

$$Inter_{bnd}(C_i, C_j) = \min \left(Intra(C_i) + T\tau(C_i), \ Intra(C_j) + T\tau(C_j) \right). \tag{11}$$

$\tau(C_i)$ is the normalized intra-cluster path length defined as

$$\tau(C_i) = \frac{PIntra(v_{C_i}, C_i)}{|C_i|} \tag{12}$$

and is a self-scaling tolerance value, which together with the parameter T influences the overall granularity of the clustering results.

Our clustering algorithm is described in detail in Algorithm 1. We expect the initially derived clusters $C = \{C_1, \ldots, C_q\}$ (found by label initialization) with higher cardinality to be better suited as prototypes than those with lower cardinality. Let $\widetilde{C} = \{\widetilde{C}_1, \ldots, \widetilde{C}_q\}$ with $|\widetilde{C}_1| \leq |\widetilde{C}_2| \leq, \ldots, \leq |\widetilde{C}_q|$ denote the initially obtained clusters, sorted with respect to their cardinality in non-decreasing way. The merging process now iteratively considers cluster pairs for merging, analyzing the criterion

$$Inter(\widetilde{C}_i, C_j) \leq Inter_{bnd}(\widetilde{C}_i, C_j), \tag{13}$$

where for C_j all other clusters are iteratively considered.

The merging process simply assigns the joined set of members $M_i \cup M_j$ to the prototype with the smaller intra-cluster path length, updates the prototype label and deletes the deprecated cluster from C. Please note that as it is described in Algorithm 1, clusters containing only a single node are separately handled. The merging process is either halted by graph-topological issues (when only isolated or connected components are left) or by insuperable inter-cluster dissimilarities.

Algorithm 1: Clustering

Input: 1. Modified mutual kNN graph $G_{mm}(V, E)$ with $|V| = N$ vertices. The number of edge connections in the graph has an upper boundary of $|E| \leq ckN$. 2. Initial partition $C = \{C_1, \ldots, C_q\}, q \leq N$ of $G_{mm}(V, E)$, together with associated prototypes v_{C_i} as defined in Section 3.1.

Output: Resulting clusters $C_R = \{C_1, \ldots, C_r\}, r \leq q$ together with their labels $L_R = (l_1, \ldots, l_r)$, simultaneously denoting the respective cluster prototypes.

1. Determine shortest paths U between all initial cluster prototypes v_{C_i} and V.
2. Store cluster members $M = \{M_1, \ldots M_q\}$ for all clusters $C = \{C_1, \ldots C_q\}$ together with current internal distances $Intra(C_i)$.
3. Sort C with respect to its cardinality in non-decreasing order in $\widetilde{C}$.
4. Iterate sub-steps (a)...(c) through $\widetilde{C}$ until no further merging is possible.
   (a) **If** $|\widetilde{C_i}| = 1$: Find smallest relative change for $\dfrac{PIntra(v_{C_j}, [C_j])}{PIntra(v_{C_j}, [\widetilde{C_i} \cup C_j])}, \forall \, \widetilde{C_i} \neq C_j$ and mark for merge.
   (b) **Else: If** $\left(Inter(\widetilde{C_i}, C_j) \leq Inter_{bnd}(\widetilde{C_i}, C_j) \right), \forall \, \widetilde{C_i} \neq C_j$, Mark $\widetilde{C_i}$ and C_j for merge.
   (c) **Merge:** If marked clusters are found: Determine new prototype $v_C \leftarrow \arg\min_{v \in \{v_{\widetilde{C_i}}, v_{C_j}\}} PIntra(v, [\widetilde{C_i} \cup C_j])$, update member list and $Intra(C)$. Remove deprecated cluster from $\widetilde{C}$.
5. Return final clustering result C_R with labels L_R.

4   Experimental Results

We evaluate the proposed methods for the tasks of shape retrieval (Section 4.1) and clustering (Section 4.2) on the well-known KIMIA99 and MPEG-7 databases. The KIMIA99 database consists of 99 shapes which can be grouped into 9 classes, each consisting of 11 objects [17]. The MPEG-7 CE-Shape-1 database is widely used for testing the performance of shape description and matching algorithms [9,13]. It consists of 1400 silhouette images which are grouped into 70 classes with 20 objects per class.

In all experiments we use the shape matching method IDSC+DP (inner distance shape context with dynamic programming matching) proposed by Ling and Jacobs in [9] to build the input dissimilarity matrices. This algorithm can be considered as state of the art, i.e. it is one of the top ranking algorithms on MPEG-7.

4.1   Shape Retrieval Experiments

For evaluating the shape retrieval performance we apply the proposed normalization and analysis scheme described in Section 2 on the similarity matrices of KIMIA99 and MPEG-7. In all experiments we set $K = 8$ for the local scaling normalization and use $k = 6$ nearest neighbors with asymmetry coefficient $c = 2$.

Table 1 shows the results for KIMIA99. Scores are calculated as the sum of correctly retrieved shapes from all classes within the first 10 objects. Therefore the best resulting score for each of them is 99. We show the best shape matching results achieved without post-processing and in addition the results of Yang et al. [7] who presented improvements which analogously to ours are set on top of existing shape similarity matrices. They worked on the same shape similarity matrix provided by IDSC-DP which allows a fair and direct comparison. As can be seen, our approach is the first to achieve a perfect retrieval score of 100% and boosts the results of the non-processed similarity matrix by approximately 3%.

Table 1. Perfect retrieval results for KIMIA99 database with proposed method. We compare to results of state-of-the-art approaches (taken from [7]).

Algorithm	1st	2nd	3rd	4th	5th	6th	7th	8th	9th	10th	Score [%]
Shock Edit [17]	99	99	99	98	98	97	96	95	93	82	96.57
IDSC+DP [9]	99	99	99	98	98	97	97	98	94	79	96.77
Shape Tree [13]	99	99	99	99	99	99	99	97	93	86	97.88
Graph Transduction [7]	99	99	99	99	99	99	99	99	97	99	99.79
Our method	99	99	99	99	99	99	99	99	99	99	**100.00**

The retrieval rate for the MPEG-7 database is measured by the so-called bullseye score which counts all matching objects within the 40 most similar candidates. Since each class consists of 20 objects, the retrieved score is normalized with the highest possible number of hits (20×1400). The results confirm the proposed normalization and analysis scheme by delivering the highest ever reported retrieval score of 93.40%, boosting the non-processed results by 8%. Table 2 lists a comparison with state-of-the-art approaches. Our post-processing scheme clearly outperforms the recently proposed method of Yang et al. in [7] in terms of retrieval score and execution time with a speed-up of more than 2000. We use their publicly available MATLAB-implementation for comparison. We also implemented our method in MATLAB and the computation time was evaluated for both approaches using a single-core standard desktop PC with 2.3GHz.

In Figure 1 we show some selected shape retrieval results from the MPEG-7 database. We show the query shape (in red) and its first 19 retrieval results without and with application of our proposed method.

Table 2. Highest ever reported bulls eye score for MPEG-7 database with proposed method. We compare to results of state-of-the-art approaches (taken from [7,8]).

| Algorithm | Shape description & matching | | | | Post-proc. | | |
	CSS [18]	IDSC + DP [9]	Hier. Procr. [12]	Shape Tree [13]	Graph Transd. [7]	Densified Spaces [8]	**Our method**
Score [%]	75.44	85.40	86.35	87.70	91.00	93.32	**93.40**
Time [s]	-	-	-	-	6444	-	**3.2**

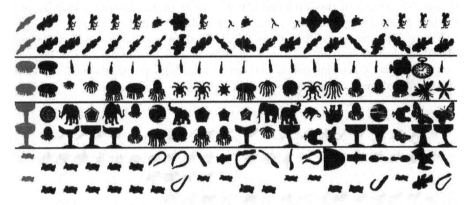

Fig. 1. Comparison of retrieval results before (odd rows) and after improving affinity matrix (even rows) on samples from MPEG-7 database. The first column shows the query shapes (in red) followed by their best 19 matching objects.

To evaluate the influence of different parameter settings on the retrieval scores we show parameter dependent retrieval scores for the MPEG-7 database in Table 3. As can be seen the results are quite stable when using parameters in the range of $5 \leq k \leq 8$ and $2 \leq c \leq 4$. Furthermore Table 3 clearly shows that the introduction of our asymmetry criterion c for the construction of the modified mutual kNN graph performs substantially better than a standard symmetric mutual nearest neighbor graph ($c = 1$).

Table 3. Retrieval scores in % for MPEG-7 database with previous local scaling normalization ($K = 8$) as a function of the modified mutual kNN graph construction parameters c (asymmetry criterion) and k (number of nearest neighbors)

c vs. k	4	5	6	7	8
1	65.61	80.49	88.88	90.28	92.03
2	89.64	92.66	**93.40**	93.36	92.99
3	90.99	93.19	93.01	92.95	92.73
4	91.40	93.02	92.95	92.75	92.52

4.2   Shape Clustering Experiments

For evaluating clustering performance we applied our method presented in Section 3 again on the KIMIA99 and the MPEG-7 databases. We compare our results with the MATLAB implementation of affinity propagation [15]. Affinity propagation is considered as state of the art in the area of non-metric clustering. It iteratively maximizes the total similarity between data points and their exemplars through message passing. It works in an unsupervised manner and the desired granularity of the clustering result can be controlled via a so-called *preference* parameter. For standard parameterization, affinity propagation suggests to use the median of the input affinity matrix as preference parameter. In our method we set the granularity parameter $T = 1$, see Equation (11).

Figure 2 compares results for the KIMIA99 database. Each row denotes one identified cluster, starting with its respective cluster prototype. As can be seen we get a perfect clustering result, in contrast to affinity propagation which is not able to merge some of the clusters.

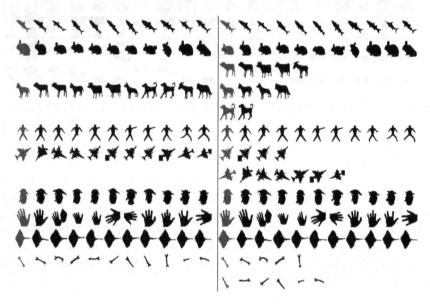

Fig. 2. Clustering results on KIMIA99 database with standard parameterization, where each row represents one identified cluster with its associated prototype in the first column (red). Left: Perfect results of our proposed algorithm. Right: Affinity propagation identifies 13 clusters.

Figure 3 compares the algorithms on the MPEG-7 database. Figure 3(a) shows the execution time as a function of the number of input shapes with default parameterization. It is clearly demonstrated that our approach outperforms affinity propagation in terms of execution time. In Figure 3(b) we show the achieved clustering quality results with respect to the number of detected clusters for the

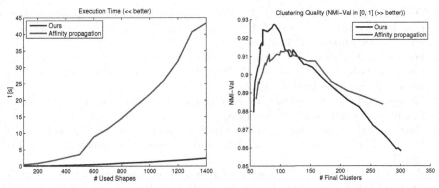

(a) Execution time as a function of the number of input shapes on MPEG-7 database.

(b) Comparison of clustering quality quantified by NMI-value vs. number of detected clusters, controlled by granularity parameters. (The higher the better.)

Fig. 3. Comparisons between affinity propagation and our clustering method on MPEG-7 database

whole 1400×1400 MPEG-7 database. We changed the granularity parameters (T in our approach and the *preference* vector for affinity propagation) to deliver different numbers of cluster. We used the normalized mutual information (NMI) to quantify the final clustering quality [19]. As can be seen, we get a substantially better NMI-value (the higher, the better), close to the true number of clusters (70).

5   Conclusion

In this work we have presented a novel shape retrieval and clustering method that, applied on top of any existing shape matching algorithm, allows to significantly improve results in shape retrieval and clustering. We take a step beyond the conventional, pairwise shape comparison by investigating the emerging shape-manifolds through efficient normalization and a novel, graph-based analysis. Experiments demonstrated the applicability of out method concerning execution time, retrieval rates and clustering performance, e. g. by achieving the highest ever reported retrieval scores on the well-known MPEG-7 and KIMIA99 databases. Since our approach is generic and can be applied to any similarity matrix, we plan to further evaluate our method on standard machine learning databases.

References

1. Shotton, J., Blake, A., Cipolla, R.: Multiscale categorical object recognition using contour fragments. IEEE Trans. on Pattern Analysis and Machine Intelligence 30(7), 1270–1281 (2008)

2. Opelt, A., Pinz, A., Zisserman, A.: A boundary-fragment-model for object detection. In: Leonardis, A., Bischof, H., Pinz, A. (eds.) ECCV 2006. LNCS, vol. 3952, pp. 575–588. Springer, Heidelberg (2006)
3. Ferrari, V., Tuytelaars, T., Gool, L.V.: Object detection by contour segment networks. In: Leonardis, A., Bischof, H., Pinz, A. (eds.) ECCV 2006. LNCS, vol. 3953, pp. 14–28. Springer, Heidelberg (2006)
4. Biederman, I., Ju, G.: Surface vs. edge-based determinants of visual recognition. Cognitive Psychology 20, 38–64 (1988)
5. Gavrila, D.M.: A Bayesian, exemplar-based approach to hierarchical shape matching. IEEE Trans. on Pattern Analysis and Machine Intelligence 29, 1408–1421 (2007)
6. Weinland, D., Boyer, E.: Action recognition using exemplar-based embedding. In: Proc. IEEE Conf. on Computer Vision and Pattern Recognition (CVPR), pp. 1–7 (2008)
7. Yang, X., Bai, X., Latecki, L.J., Tu, Z.: Improving shape retrieval by learning graph transduction. In: Forsyth, D., Torr, P., Zisserman, A. (eds.) ECCV 2008, Part IV. LNCS, vol. 5305, pp. 788–801. Springer, Heidelberg (2008)
8. Yang, X., Koknar-Tezel, S., Latecki, L.: Locally constrained diffusion process on locally densified distance spaces with applications to shape retrieval. In: Proc. IEEE Conf. on Computer Vision and Pattern Recognition, CVPR (2009)
9. Ling, H., Jacobs, D.: Shape classification using the inner-distance. IEEE Trans. on Pattern Analysis and Machine Intelligence 29(2), 286–299 (2007)
10. Schmidt, F.R., Farin, D., Cremers, D.: Fast matching of planar shapes in sub-cubic runtime. In: Proc. IEEE Intern. Conf. on Computer Vision, ICCV (2007)
11. Yankov, D., Keogh, E.: Manifold clustering of shapes. In: Proc. Intern. Conf. on Data Mining (ICDM), pp. 1167–1171 (2006)
12. McNeill, G., Vijayakumar, S.: Hierarchical procrustes matching for shape retrieval. In: Proc. IEEE Conf. on Computer Vision and Pattern Recognition (CVPR), vol. 1, pp. 885–894 (2006)
13. Felzenszwalb, P.F., Schwartz, J.D.: Hierarchical matching of deformable shapes. In: Proc. IEEE Conf. on Computer Vision and Pattern Recognition, CVPR (2007)
14. Zelnik-Manor, L., Perona, P.: Self-tuning spectral clustering. In: Advances in Neural Information Processing Systems (NIPS), pp. 1601–1608. MIT Press, Cambridge (2004)
15. Frey, B.J., Dueck, D.: Clustering by passing messages between data points. Science 315, 972–976 (2007)
16. Felzenszwalb, P.F., Huttenlocher, D.P.: Efficient graph-based image segmentation. Intern. Journal of Computer Vision 59(2), 167–181 (2004)
17. Sebastian, T., Klein, P., Kimia, B.: Recognition of shapes by editing their shock graphs. IEEE Trans. on Pattern Analysis and Machine Intelligence 26(5), 550–571 (2004)
18. Mokhtarian, F., Abbasi, S., Kittler, J.: Efficient and robust retrieval by shape content through curvature scale space. In: Proc. of International Workshop on Image Databases and Multimedia Search, pp. 35–42 (1996)
19. Strehl, A., Ghosh, J.: Cluster ensembles – a knowledge reuse framework for combining multiple partitions. The Journal of Machine Learning Research 3, 583–617 (2003)

Globally Optimal Spatio-temporal Reconstruction from Cluttered Videos

Ehsan Aganj[1], Jean-Philippe Pons[2], and Renaud Keriven[1]

[1] IMAGINE, École des Ponts ParisTech 6 Av Blaise Pascal - Cité Descartes,
Marne-la-Vallée, France
[2] CSTB, 290 route des Lucioles, BP 209, 06904 Sophia-Antipolis, Cedex, France

Abstract. We propose a method for multi-view reconstruction from videos adapted to dynamic cluttered scenes under uncontrolled imaging conditions. Taking visibility into account and being based on a global optimization of a true spatio-temporal energy, it offers several desirable properties: no need for silhouettes, robustness to noise, independent from any initialization, no heuristic force, reduced flickering results, etc. Results on real-world data proves the potential of what is, to our knowledge, the only globally optimal spatio-temporal multi-view reconstruction method.

1 Introduction

In recent years, several methods for automatic generation of complete spatio-temporal models of dynamic scenes from multiple videos have been proposed [1,2,3,4,5,6,7,8,9,10,11,12,13,14,15]. In particular, the most recent ones have proven effective for full-body marker-less motion capture. Many of these techniques rely on the visual hull concept[16], among which [1,3,15]. Computationally efficient, they suffer from several limitations: they provide an approximate reconstruction; this one has to be a closed surface; and, above all, silhouettes have to be segmented in the videos, practically limiting the method to controlled condition capture with a known background. This latest limitation may be lifted when prior knowledge about the geometry is available: free-form deformation of a template body model [2,11,15], Laplacian deformation of a laser scan of the initial pose [4,5], etc. Yet, these methods are unable to recover genuine geometric details such as facial expressions and clothing folds and wrinkles. An exception might be the method proposed by Furukawa et al. [6]. Yielding visually impressive results, this method does not rely on global optimization and handles the occlusion problem via heuristics.

1.1 Our Approach

In this paper, we propose a method for multi-view reconstruction from videos adapted to dynamic cluttered scenes under uncontrolled imaging conditions. Taking visibility into account and being based on a global optimization of a true spatio-temporal energy, it offers several desirable properties.

H. Zha, R.-i. Taniguchi, and S. Maybank (Eds.): ACCV 2009, Part III, LNCS 5996, pp. 667–678, 2010.
© Springer-Verlag Berlin Heidelberg 2010

Starting from work by Labatut et al. [17], our method might be seen as its spatio-temporal extension. It is based on modeling an evolving three-dimensional surface as a four-dimensional surface [1,18,7]. More precisely, we first generate a quasi-dense 3D point cloud of the scene at each time step and merge the result into a 4D point cloud. This process is conducted in a lenient manner, thus possibly retaining many false matches. Then, we build an adaptive decomposition of the 3D+time space by computing the 4D Delaunay triangulation of this cloud. Finally, we label the Delaunay pentatopes as empty or occupied thus generating a 4D surface. Graph-cut based, this assignment is globally optimal and compatible with the visibility in input images. Optionally but not necessarily, the 3D surfaces corresponding to each time step might be obtained considering 3D slices.

1.2   Contributions

Our method has several significant advantages. First, it is not based on visual hulls:

- The videos do not have to be taken under controlled conditions. The background might be cluttered.
- It can handle closed as well as open scenes. For example, it can simultaneously recover the walls and (potentially moving!) furnitures of an indoor scene and a complete reconstruction of subjects seen from all sides in the input images.

Second, it is based on a global optimum:

- It is robust and does not depend on some initialization.
- It exploits visibility information to guide the position of the surface. As a result, it avoids the minimum cut solution from being an empty surface. Hence it exonerates from the usual techniques proposed so far to solve this problem (ballooning term, silhouette information, photo-flux, etc.). Moreover, this visibility information is not enforced as a hard constraint but integrated in the very optimization framework, hence yielding robustness to outliers.

Finally, and mainly, compared to the independent frame-by-frame computations of [17], it profits from the 4D representation:

- Regularization is handled both in space and time, yielding more robustness to noise both in geometry and in visibility reasoning.
- Points extracted at one given time step transfer information to the surrounding time steps. As a result, more details are obtained at each time step.
- Flicking artifacts in synthesized views are reduced, as consecutive 3D slices have similar geometry and connectivity by construction.
- The temporally continuous representation, which is defined at any time, optionally enables interpolation of objects shape between consecutive frames.

The output of our method might be use for different purposes: as a 4D compact representation; as a list of consecutive 3D meshes; as an initialization for variational spatio-temporal stereovision methods [7].

The remainder of this paper is organized as follows. Section 2 gives some background on the different techniques needed in our approach. In Section 3, we describe in detail the different steps of our algorithm. Section 4 discusses numerical experiments that demonstrate the potential of our approach for reconstructing cluttered scenes from real-world data.

2   Background

2.1   Delaunay Triangulation

Most of the following definitions are taken from [19]. We also refer the interested reader to some computational geometry textbooks [20,21]. In the sequel, we call k-*simplex* the convex hull of $k + 1$ affinely independent points. For example, a 0-simplex is a point, a 1-simplex is a line segment, a 2-simplex is a triangle and a 3-simplex is a tetrahedron. In this paper, we will also consider 4-simplices: they are known as *pentachorons* or *pentatopes*. Let $E = \{p_1, \ldots, p_n\}$ be set of points in $\mathbb{R}^d$. The *Voronoi region*, or *Voronoi cell*, denoted by $V(p_i)$, associated to a point p_i is the region of space that is closer from p_i than from all other points in E: $V(p_i) = \{p \in \mathbb{R}^d \ : \ \forall j, \ \|p - p_i\| \le \|p - p_j\|\}$.

The *Voronoi diagram* of E, denoted by Vor(E), is the partition of space induced by the Voronoi cells $V(p_i)$. See Figure 1*(a)* for a two-dimensional example of a Voronoi diagram.

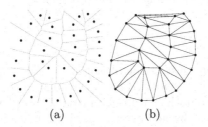

(a)   (b)

Fig. 1. *(a)* Voronoi diagram of a set of points in the plane. *(b)* Its dual Delaunay triangulation.

The *Delaunay triangulation* Del(E) of E is defined as the geometric dual of the Voronoi diagram: there is an edge between two points p_i and p_j in the Delaunay triangulation if and only if their Voronoi cells $V(p_i)$ and $V(p_j)$ have a non-empty intersection. It yields a *triangulation* of E, that is to say a partition of the convex hull of E into d-dimensional simplices (i.e. into triangles in 2D, into tetrahedra in 3D, into pentatopes in 4D and so on). See Figure 1*(b)* for a two-dimensional example of a Delaunay triangulation. The fundamental property of the Delaunay triangulation is called the *empty circle* (resp. *empty sphere* in 3D, resp. *empty hypersphere* in higher dimensions) property: in 2D (resp. in 3D, resp. in 4D), a triangle (resp. tetrahedron, resp. pentatope) belongs to the Delaunay triangulation if and only if its circumcircle (resp. circumsphere, resp. circumscribed hypersphere) does not contain any other points of E in its interior.

2.2 Energy Minimization by Graph Cuts

Given a finite directed graph $\mathcal{G} = (\mathcal{V}, \mathcal{E})$ with nodes $\mathcal{V}$ and edges $\mathcal{E}$ with non-negative weights (capacities), and two special vertices, the source s and the sink t, an s-t-cut $\mathcal{C} = (\mathcal{S}, \mathcal{T})$ is a partition of $\mathcal{V}$ into two disjoint sets $\mathcal{S}$ and $\mathcal{T}$ such that $s \in \mathcal{S}$ and $t \in \mathcal{T}$. The cost of the cut is the sum of the capacity of all the edges going from $\mathcal{S}$ to $\mathcal{T} : c(\mathcal{S}, \mathcal{T}) = \sum_{(p,q) \in \mathcal{S} \times \mathcal{T} | p \to q \in \mathcal{E}} w_{pq}$. The minimum s-t-cut problem consists in finding a cut $\mathcal{C}$ with the smallest cost: the Ford-Fulkerson theorem [22] states that this problem is equivalent to computing the maximum flow from the source s to the sink t and many classical algorithms exist to efficiently solve this problem. Such a cut can be viewed as a binary labeling of the nodes: by building an appropriate graph, many segmentation problems in computer vision can be solved very efficiently [23]. More generally, global minimization of a whole class of energy is achievable by graph cuts [24].

Kirsanov and Gortler [25] first proposed to use graph cuts on complexes to globally optimize surface functionals and also developed the idea of using random sparse complexes for their flexibility over regular subdivisions: this differs from the graphs commonly used in computer vision, which are often regular grids in the input images or in the bounding volume of the scene. Our approach similarly relies on a sparse complex-based graph: this graph however directly derives from an adaptive space decomposition efficiently provided by the Delaunay triangulation. Moreover the specifies of our graph construction are quite different and tailored to the multi-view reconstruction problem.

3 Method

Our spatio-temporal reconstruction algorithm consists in four steps: (i) a quasi-dense 3D point cloud is generated for each frame, each point memorizing the two or more images from which it has been triangulated. An spatio-temporal 4D point cloud is obtained by adding time as the fourth dimension to all the 3D points; (ii) the Delaunay triangulation of the 4D point cloud is computed; (iii) the Delaunay pentatopes (full-dimensional simplices in $\mathbb{R}^4$) are labeled inside or outside the spatio-temporal object minimizing some energy, a 4D oriented surface is then extracted as the set of 4D tetrahedra lying between inside and outside pentatopes; (iv) the 3D surface at a given time is obtained by intersecting this 4D hyper-surface with a temporal plane.

3.1 4D Point Cloud Generation, 4D Delaunay Triangulation

Given multiple video sequences of a dynamic scene, we first make a dense 3D point cloud for each time instant. Let I_k^t, $k \in \{1, \cdots, n\}$, $t \in [0, T]$ denote the input video sequence. For each image we extract interest points $x_{k,i}^t$ of several types (in practice Harris points and DOGs) without any scale information and with thresholds such that their number is high enough. For each image pair in a time instant t, $(I_k^t, I_{k'}^t)$ whose visual fields intersect, for all $(x_{k,i}^t, x_{k',j}^t)$ of the same type verifying the epipolar constraint up to a certain error (due to point extraction but also to calibration), we triangulate the corresponding 3D point $X_{kk',ij}^t$. Let H be the homography from I_k^t to $I_{k'}^t$ induced by the plane at $X_{kk',ij}^t$ normal to the optical ray of $x_{k,i}^t$, we evalute the normalized cross correlation (NCC) between a given neighborhood of $x_{k,i}^t$ and its image by H around $x_{k',j}^t$. Then for each $x_{k,i}^t$, we keep the m best point $x_{k',j}^t$ according to NCC, only if their NCC is higher than a given threshold, and add the corresponding $X_{kk',ij}^t$ to the point cloud at time instant t (in practice $m = 1$ or 2). The final 3D point cloud is then obtained by merging close 3D points, so that a point of the cloud comes from possibly more than two images.

Now we construct a "global" spatio-temporal point cloud by regarding time as a fourth dimension, and treating it similarly to the three spatial dimensions. At first sight, this is questionable since space is not homogenous to time regarding physical units. We obtain physical homogeneity of our 4D space by considering a scaling factor v between space and time dimensions. This scaling factor is homogeneous to a speed, and can be interpreted as a reference displacement per time unit. The global point cloud is obtained by taking a 4D point $(X_i^t, vt) \in \mathbb{R}^4$ for the point X_i^t generated from the input images in time t. At the end, we compute the 4D Delaunay triangulation of the spatio-temporal cloud storing in each vertex the list of the views and keypoints from which it has been generated.

3.2   4D Hyper-surface Extraction

In this step we compute a four-dimensional representation of the dynamic scene by extracting a 4D mesh from the Delaunay triangulation of the point cloud. This is done by labeling Delaunay pentatopes as inside or outside of the spatio-temporal scene. The final oriented hypersurface is then extracted as the set of facets between inside and outside pentatopes. The exact nature of these "facets" deserves clarification: they are tetrahedra with 4D coordinates, so they are indeed *simplicial* pieces of a hypersurface in $\mathbb{R}^4$. Now we make a graph of neighbor pentatopes which we will use to find the optimal label assignment. For that, we take Delaunay pentatopes as vertices and we add edges between every two pentatopes which are neighbor via a two or three dimensional face. In addition, we add a link between each vertex of the graph and the sink and the source. A globally optimal label assignment is then efficiently found by applying the graph cuts optimization method on this graph.

In the sequel, we note S the surface to be reconstructed. As discussed above, S is a union of 4D Delaunay facets. In order to find an optimal solution satisfying both spatial and temporal constraints, we minimize an energy composed of two terms, one dealing with visibility, and the other dealing with spatial and temporal smoothness,

$$\mathrm{E}(S) = \mathrm{E}_{\mathrm{vis}}(S) + \mathrm{E}_{\mathrm{smooth}}(S) \tag{1}$$

In the rest of this section, we give the exact definition of these two terms and we describe how they can be implemented in the graph cuts framework.

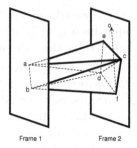

Fig. 2. The tetrahedra *acde* and *bcdf* have a one-dimensional intersection (the segment *cd*), but they should be connected in the graph (refer to text for details)

Visibility term. The visibility term that we propose for a spatio-temporal scene is a careful extension of the static case proposed in [17]. The idea of their work is that if a point belongs to the final surface then it should be visible in the views from which it has been triangulated. This yields to the penalization of all the facets intersecting the ray between the point and the cameras from which it has been generated. In the dynamic case the same argument holds. A point which belongs to the final hypersurface should be visible in all its generating views. Consequently, all 4D pentatopes which intersect a 4D ray emanating from the point to the camera center of one of its generating views should be labeled as outside, and the pentatope behind the point should be labeled as inside. We remark that the spatio-temporal center of a camera at a given frame is its 3D center positioned in the temporal plane of that frame. Similarly to the static case, in order to make an energy which can be minimized via graph cuts, we take the number of intersections of a ray with the oriented hypersurface as the visibility term. At this point, there are several important remarks to be made.

First, the visibility of a point at a given frame is defined only in the temporal plane corresponding to that frame. Therefore, the rays between the point and its generating views lie completely in the temporal plane which passes through that point.

Second, a 4D facet of the Delaunay triangulation passes generally through several consecutive frames. As a consequence, each intersection of a ray with a facet is considered as a penalizing "vote" for the facet. The final vote is then computed as the sum of all votes coming from different frames intersecting the facet. This is an important property since it makes a global visibility vote on every 4D facet taking in account the temporal coherence.

Third, contrarily to the static case presented in [17] where edges of the graph are only "full dimensional facets" (3D triangles) between Delaunay simplices, in the dynamic case, in addition to these facets we add an edge between every two pentatopes which are not neighbors via a full-dimensional facet (4D) but via a 3D facet. Figure 2 shows an example of this situation. For simplicity reasons we consider a lower dimensional scene: points are on 2D planes, time is the third dimension and the spatio-temporal object is extracted from the 3D Delaunay triangulation of the point cloud. Points *a* and *b* are on frame 1, and points *c,d,e*

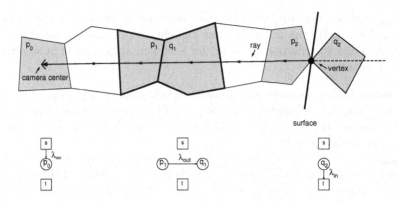

Fig. 3. Top: A 3D slice of the 4D triangulation. A ray emanating from a vertex to a camera center intersects 3D cells. Bottom: The corresponding visibility-related energy term that penalizes the number of intersections with the ray and the edge weights of the crossed pentatope in the graph.

and f are on frame 2. Point o is the center of a camera from which f has been generated. The tetrahedra $acde$ and $bcdf$ have a one-dimensional intersection (the segment cd), but they should be connected in the graph since the ray fo intersects cd and therefore a penalization term should be added between them. It is important to note that despite the 3D intersection of the ray with the face acd, no penalization term should be added between the tetrahedra $abcd$ and $bcdf$. That is because $abcd$ does not appear in the static representation of the scene on frame 2.

The intersections of the ray with the triangulation can be computed in the four-dimensional space handling carefully the situation discussed above. However, as a ray always lies completely in a temporal plane, we propose to find these intersections more easily by intersecting the 3D ray with the 3D intersection of the triangulation with the temporal plane. Obviously only the pentatopes which make a full-dimensional (4D) temporal intersection should appear in the temporal slice. In this case, a 3D facet intersected by a ray will correspond to an edge of the graph, and the unnecessary intersections discussed in the example above will be omitted by definition.

We should remark that the 3D intersection of a 4D Delaunay triangulation with a plane is a polyhedron which contains generally cells with more than four vertices. Figure 3 shows the 3D object and a ray intersecting the cells. The vertices p_0, p_1, q_1, p_2 and q_2 shown in Figure 3(bottom) are the vertices of the graph which correspond to the pentatopes whose temporal intersections make the cells p_0, p_1, q_1, p_2 and q_2 shown in Figure 3(top) respectively. Different visibility terms are added. The cell containing the camera should be labeled as outside: a term λ_∞ is added to the edge from source to p_0. A 3D facet crossed by the ray from inside to outside should be penalized: a term λ_{out} is added to the edge from p_1 to q_1. The cell behind the origin of the ray should be labeled as inside: a term λ_{in} is added to the edge from q_2 to the sink. The positive weights

λ_{in}, λ_{out} and λ_∞ take into account the confidence in the reconstructed vertex yielding the ray. By summing up these visibility terms over all the frames, we make a complex distribution of "vote" for each pentatope taking in account the time coherence.

Spatio-temporal smoothness. In order to take in account both spatial smoothness and temporal continuity, we propose to minimize the area of the 4D surface in $\mathbb{R}^4$. This yields to the sum of volumes over all the 4D tetrahedra between inside and outside pentatopes,

$\mathrm{E}_{\text{smooth}}(S) = A(S) = \int_S \mathrm{d}S = \sum_{T \in S} A(T)$ where S is the 4D surface to be reconstructed, T is a 4D tetrahedra, and $A(T)$ is the volume of the tetrahedra T in $\mathbb{R}^4$. Minimizing this term encourages smoothness in time and in space. As in the static case, this is trivially minimized in the graph cuts framework: for each pair of pentatopes (sharing a tetrahedra T) represented by vertices p and q in our graph, a term $w = A(T)$ is added the edge $p \rightarrow q$ and to its opposite edge $q \rightarrow p$.

3.3   3D Surface Extraction

The output 4D mesh cannot be used directly for rendering. Fortunately, the 3D scene at a given time instant is easily obtained by intersecting this 4D mesh with a temporal plane. This task can be performed very efficiently, even in real-time on GPUs (Graphics Processor Units), since it reduces to a *marching tetrahedra* algorithm [26] on the tetrahedra of the 4D mesh, with the temporal coordinate of vertices used as the scalar field for isocontouring. It produces one triangle or one quad per boundary tetrahedron intersected by the selected temporal plane.

4   Experimental Results

We have implemented our method using *CGAL* (Computational Geometry Algorithms Library, homepage: www.cgal.org) [27]. CGAL defines most data structure and algorithms needed in our method. For the computation of 4D Delaunay triangulation we have used the Quickhull algorithm library (QHull) [28] (homepage: www.qhull.org).

Fig. 4. Some images of the "Trousers" dataset

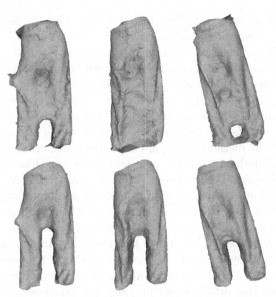

Fig. 5. A comparison between our method and the method of [17] applied independly in each frame. Top: 3D meshes obtained by the method of [17]. Bottom: corresponding 3D slices of the 4D representation obtained by our method.

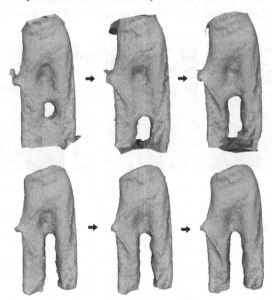

Fig. 6. The first three consecutive frames of the Trousers dataset reconstructed by (Top): the method of [17] (Bottom): our method. The frame-by-frame reconstruction of the method [17] makes no temporal continuity. In contrast, our method reconstructs correctly the trouser, avoids flicking artifacts and provides a much more continuous motion.

In our first experiment, we have tested our method on the first 60 frames of the "Trousers" sequence which is courtesy of R. White, K. Crane and D.A. Forsyth [29]. The sequence is acquired by 8 cameras at a 640×480 resolution. Figure 4 shows some images of this dataset. Despite their highly textured images, it is in fact a quite challenging dataset because of the very fast and complex motion of cloth and folds and severe self occlusion in various parts of the video. Regarding to an approximate size of the object we have chosen a spatio-temporal scaling factor $v = 30$ (space unit/frame). Figure 5 shows a comparison between our method and the method of [17] applied independly in each frame. We have compared the 3D meshes output by their method for some frames of the sequence with the corresponding 3D slices of our 4D spatio-temporal scene. A total number of 793769 points have been generated for the initial point cloud. To provide a fair comparison, we have used the same point clouds in both methods.

We observe that the method of [17] fails to separate correctly the two trouser legs when there is not enough distance between them. In addition, as shown in figure 6, their frame-by-frame reconstruction makes no temporal continuity. In contrast, relying on a global optimization, our method reconstructs correctly the trouser, avoids flicking artifacts and provides a much more continuous motion. This perfectly illustrates the capability of our approach to take advantage of temporal coherence in order to obtain more detailed and more continuous result. Please see supplemental material for a video illustrating better the result of our method. The computational times of our method and the method of [17] for this

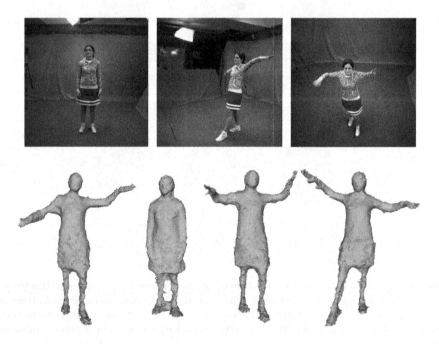

Fig. 7. Top: Some images of the "Dancer" dataset. Bottom: Some 3D slices extracted from the 4D representation of the "Danser" dataset, obtained by our method.

experiment are 210 and 112 minutes respectively on a standard workstation. However, the most expensive part of our method is the computation of the 4D Delaunay triangulation. Fortunately, this can be strongly reduced using an optimized 4D Delaunay code.

In a second experiment, we have tested our method on the first 40 frames of the "Dancer" dataset which was made available to us by the 4Dviews company (http://4dviews.com). It is acquired by 14 calibrated and synchronized video cameras. Figure 7(top) shows some images of this dataset. The result shows that despite the lowly textured parts of the images, our method makes a correct 4D representation of the dancer. Figure 7(bottom) shows some 3D slices extracted from the 4D object.

Finally, we should remark that in order to have better visualization and to make better comparisons we have smoothed the results of our experiments. However, the output of our method might be used as a 4D compact representation, as a list of consecutive 3D meshes or as an initialization for variational spatio-temporal stereovision methods.

5   Discussion and Conclusion

We have presented a new method for multi-view reconstruction from videos adapted to dynamic cluttered scenes under uncontrolled imaging conditions. The main idea of our method is to regard time as the fourth dimension, and to extract a hyper-surface from the 4D Delaunay triangulation of the input points as the spatio-temporal representation of the scene. This is done by labeling Delaunay pentatopes as empty or occupied. A globally optimal assignment is efficiently found using graph cuts. We have validated our method on real video sequences. Our results prove the potential of what is, to our knowledge, the only globally optimal spatio-temporal multiview reconstruction method.

References

1. Aganj, E., Pons, J.P., Ségonne, F., Keriven, R.: Spatio-temporal shape from silhouette using four-dimensional Delaunay meshing. In: ICCV (2007)
2. Ahmed, N., de Aguiar, E., Theobalt, C., Magnor, M., Seidel, H.P.: Automatic generation of personalized human avatars from multi-view video. In: Proc. VRST 2005, pp. 257–260 (2005)
3. Ahmed, N., Theobalt, C., Rössl, C., Thrun, S., Seidel, H.P.: Dense correspondence finding for parametrization-free animation reconstruction from video. In: CVPR (2008)
4. de Aguiar, E., Stoll, C., Theobalt, C., Ahmed, N., Seidel, H.P., Thrun, S.: Performance capture from sparse multi-view video. In: ACM SIGGRAPH (2008)
5. de Aguiar, E., Theobalt, C., Stoll, C., Seidel, H.P.: Marker-less deformable mesh tracking for human shape and motion capture. In: CVPR (2007)
6. Furukawa, Y., Ponce, J.: Dense 3D motion capture from synchronized video streams. In: IEEE Conference on Computer Vision and Pattern Recognition (2008)

7. Goldlücke, B., Magnor, M.: Space-time isosurface evolution for temporally coherent 3D reconstruction. In: CVPR, vol. 1, pp. 350–355 (2004)
8. Neumann, J., Aloimonos, Y.: Spatio-temporal stereo using multi-resolution subdivision surfaces. IJCV 47(1-3), 181–193 (2002)
9. Pons, J.-P., Keriven, R., Faugeras, O.: Multi-view stereo reconstruction and scene flow estimation with a global image-based matching score. IJCV 72(2), 179–193 (2007)
10. Starck, J., Hilton, A.: Surface capture for performance based animation. IEEE Computer Graphics and Applications 27(3), 21–31 (2007)
11. Theobalt, C., Ahmed, N., Lensch, H., Magnor, M., Seidel, H.P.: Seeing people in different light-joint shape, motion, and reflectance capture. TVCG 13(4), 663–674 (2007)
12. Varanasi, K., Zaharescu, A., Boyer, E., Horaud, R.P.: Temporal surface tracking using mesh evolution. In: Forsyth, D., Torr, P., Zisserman, A. (eds.) ECCV 2008, Part II. LNCS, vol. 5303, pp. 30–43. Springer, Heidelberg (2008)
13. Vedula, S., Baker, S., Kanade, T.: Image-based spatio-temporal modeling and view interpolation of dynamic events. ACM TOG 24(2), 240–261 (2005)
14. Vedula, S., Baker, S., Seitz, S., Kanade, T.: Shape and motion carving in 6D. In: CVPR (2000)
15. Vlasic, D., Baran, I., Matusik, W., Popović, J.: Articulated mesh animation from multi-view silhouettes. ACM Transactions on Graphics 27(3) (2008)
16. Laurentini, A.: The visual hull concept for silhouette-based image understanding. IEEE Trans. Pattern Anal. Mach. Intell. 16(2), 150–162 (1994)
17. Labatut, P., Pons, J.P., Keriven, R.: Efficient multi-view reconstruction of large-scale scenes using interest points, delaunay triangulation and graph cuts. In: ICCV (2007)
18. Cheung, G.K.M., Baker, S., Kanade, T.: Shape-from-silhouette across time part i: Theory and algorithms. IJCV 62(3), 221–247 (2004)
19. Boissonnat, J.D., Oudot, S.: Provably good sampling and meshing of surfaces. Graphical Models 67, 405–451 (2005)
20. Boissonnat, J.D., Yvinec, M.: Algorithmic Geometry. Cambridge University Press, Cambridge (1998)
21. de Berg, M., van Kreveld, M., Overmars, M., Schwarzkopf, O.: Computational Geometry, Algorithms and Applications. Springer, Heidelberg (1997)
22. Ford, L.R., Fulkerson, D.R.: Flows in Networks. Princeton University Press, Princeton (1962)
23. Greig, D.M., Porteous, B.T., Seheult, A.H.: Exact maximum a posteriori estimation for binary images
24. Kolmogorov, V., Zabih, R.: What energy functions can be minimizedvia graph cuts? IEEE Trans. Pattern Anal. Mach. Intell. 26(2), 147–159 (2004)
25. Kirsanov, D., Gortler, S.J.: A discrete global minimization algorithm for continuous variational problems. Harvard computer science technical report: Tr-14-04. Technical report, Cambridge, MA (07/2004) (2004)
26. Guéziec, A., Hummel, R.: Exploiting triangulated surface extraction using tetrahedral decomposition. TVCG 1(4), 328–342 (1995)
27. Boissonnat, J.D., Devillers, O., Teillaud, M., Yvinec, M.: Triangulations in CGAL. In: Annual Symposium on Computational Geometry, pp. 11–18 (2000)
28. Barber, C.B., Dobkin, D.P., Huhdanpaa, H.: The quickhull algorithm for convex hulls. ACM Transactions on Mathematical Software 22, 469–483 (1996)
29. White, R., Crane, K., Forsyth, D.: Capturing and animating occluded cloth. In: SIGGRAPH (2007)

Author Index